Language Acquisition

Language Acquisition

Core Readings

edited by
Paul Bloom

The MIT Press
Cambridge, Massachusetts

Third printing, 2000

First MIT Press edition, 1994
© 1993 Harvester Wheatsheaf

Printed and bound in the United States of America.

Library of Congress Cataloging-in-Publication Data

Language acquisition : core readings / edited by Paul Bloom.
    p.   cm.
  Includes bibliographical references (p.).
  ISBN 0-262-02372-5.—ISBN 0-262-52187-3 (pbk.)
  1. Language acquisition. I. Bloom, Paul. 1963–
P118.L2536   1994
401'.93—dc20   93-27417
                                                        CIP

Contents

v

Acknowledgments

The editor and publisher acknowledge with thanks permission granted to reproduce in this volume the following material previously published elsewhere. Every effort has been made to trace copyright holders, but if any have been inadvertently overlooked the publisher will be pleased to make the necessary arrangement at the first opportunity.

Overview

Bloom, P. "Language development," in *Handbook of Psycholinguistics*, 1993, copyright © 1993 Academic Press Inc., reprinted by permission of Academic Press and the author.

Part 1: The onset of language development

Fernald, A. "Human maternal vocalizations to infants as biologically relevant signals: An evolutionary perspective," in Barkow *et al.*, *The Adapted Mind: Evolutionary psychology and the generation of culture*, 1992, copyright © 1992 Oxford University Press, reprinted by permission of Oxford University Press.

Part 2: Word learning

Part 3: Syntax and semantics

Cromer, R. "Language growth with experience without feedback," in *Journal of Psycholinguistic Research*, 16, 3, 1987, copyright © 1987 Plenum Publishing Corporation, reprinted by permission of Plenum Publishing Corporation.

Part 4: Morphology

Rumelhart, D. E. and McClelland, J. L. "On learning the past tenses of English verbs," in *Parallel Distributed Processing*, Volume 2, 1986, copyright © 1986 The MIT Press, reprinted by permission of The MIT Press.

Pinker, S. "Rules of language," in *Science*, 253, 530–5, 2 August 1991, copyright © 1991 the American Association for the Advancement of Science, reprinted by permission of the A.A.A.S. and the author.

Gordon, P. "Level-ordering in lexical development," in *Cognition*, 21, 1985, copyright © 1985 Elsevier Science Publishers B.V., reprinted by permission of Elsevier Science Publishers and the author.

Part 5: Acquisition in special circumstances

Goldin-Meadow, S. and Mylander, C. "Beyond the input given: The child's role in the acquisition of language," in *Language*, 66, 2, 1990, copyright © 1990 the Linguistic Society of America, reprinted by permission of the Linguistic Society of America and the authors.

Newport, E. L. "Maturational constraints on language learning," in *Cognitive Science*, 14, 1990, copyright © 1990 Elissa L. Newport, reprinted by permission of the author.

Part 6: Alternative perspectives

Karmiloff-Smith, A. "Innate constraints and developmental change," copyright © 1993 Annette Karmiloff-Smith, adapted from Carey, S. and Gelman, R., eds, *The Epigenesis of Mind: Essays on biology and cognition*, 1991, adapted by permission of Lawrence Erlbaum Associates.

Marler, P. "The instinct to learn," in Carey, S. and Gelman, R., eds, *The Epigenesis of Mind: Essays on biology and cognition*, 1991, copyright © 1991 Lawrence Erlbaum Associates, reprinted by permission of Lawrence Erlbaum Associates and the author.

Preface:
Language acquisitions

Paul Bloom

Language acquisition is one of the most important domains within the sciences of the mind, but it does not constitute a coherent field of study. Each aspect of language has unique properties, and it is unlikely that a single theory could capture the entire learning process. The psychological mechanisms that allow children to acquire the meanings of words, for instance, are almost certainly distinct from those that underlie their capacity to form and understand questions, or to establish narrative structure in story-telling. As such, there is no single process that one could call "language acquisition"; instead, we are left with the task of explaining different *acquisitions* (of word meaning, syntactic structure, morphological rules, and so on), and exploring the relationships that hold between them, if any.

Why study these acquisitions? One motivation is an interest in the learning process itself. Even assuming that children innately possess a substantial base of linguistic knowledge, there exists considerable variation across languages. A child acquiring English, for instance, has to figure out what "dog" means, what the past tense of "go" is, and how to order nouns and adjectives. These are the acquisitions that any adequate theory must account for, and explaining how all normal children come to possess such knowledge on the basis of limited input poses puzzles of extraordinary intellectual depth.

But there are other reasons for studying language acquisition. Scholars from Aristotle to Wittgenstein have used the process of a child acquiring her first language as a way to explore broader questions about the nature of grammar, thought, and meaning. Philosophers turn to the logical problem of lexical acquisition when debating the nature of word meaning, linguists use the study of language acquisition to explore the nature of universal grammar, and psychologists have analyzed everything from infant babbling to over-generalization of the past-tense morpheme when contrasting theories of learning and mental representation.

The eighteen articles collected below reflect both motivations—a concern with language acquisition for its own sake, and a desire to use theory and evidence from this domain to enlighten us on other, broader issues.

With the exception of the final section, the order of the papers roughly recapitulates the developmental process, starting with the infant's early sensitivity to linguistic input, followed by word learning, syntactic and semantic development, use and misuse of grammatical morphology, and ending with the adult's not-very-successful attempt to acquire a first or second language. The authors apply several different research methodologies, including experimental manipulation, analysis of spontaneous speech samples, and computer modeling, and the theoretical perspectives they adopt are similarly diverse, ranging from linguistic theory to evolutionary biology.

The collection begins with an introduction to the field of language acquisition; this outlines the sequence of normal language development, discusses the nature of the input that children receive, and then reviews four learning problems—the acquisition of word meaning, determining the syntactic categorization of new words, determining whether subjects are optional or obligatory, and recovering from errors of verb morphology and semantics. This review provides a useful, though not essential, background for the other articles in this collection.

In the section devoted to the onset of language acquisition, Fernald adopts the perspective of evolutionary theory in her discussion of maternal vocalizations to infants. She argues that adults have evolved to use a certain style of speech that infants resonate to—what Darwin has called "the sweet music of the species"—and that this facilitates both social development and language acquisition. Petitto provides an interesting counterpoint to this, presenting evidence that the infant's sensitivity to language applies equally to speech and sign, and that in the course of lexical and syntactic development the linguistic use of sign can be dissociated from non-linguistic gesturing. It is an intriguing question how to reconcile these two positions; in particular, are infants really sensitive to properties of *speech*, or do they instead respond to abstract linguistic properties that appear across all modalities?

The section on word learning begins with Baldwin's finding that an infant's hypothesis about the meaning of a novel word is based in part on what the speaker is attending to when she uses this word. This suggests that non-verbal "social" cues (e.g., what the speaker is looking at) play a role even at the earliest stages of lexical development. Focusing on slightly older children, Markman outlines a contemporary perspective on the logic of word learning (attributed to Quine) and reviews some compelling evidence for the existence of certain constraints on children's inferences about word meaning; these include the "whole-object assumption" and the "taxonomic assumption," which work together to bias children to construe novel labels as referring to kinds of whole objects, as well as the "mutual exclusivity assumption," which leads children to expect that words do not have overlapping extensions.

In contrast, Gleitman argues that the problem of word learning cannot be solved solely through the sorts of constraints and biases proposed by Markman, Baldwin, and others. At least for verbs, Gleitman maintains that children must exploit innate mappings from syntactic structure to semantic structure—a process that she calls "syntactic bootstrapping." Studies with 1- and 2-year-olds support the claim that children possess these mappings and can apply them in the course of word learning. Finally, Huttenlocher and Smiley report a detailed study of the speech of ten children in the single-word period, concluding that there is no substantial difference in the nature of these early words and those lexical items possessed by older children and adults.

A central concern in the study of language acquisition is children's understanding of syntax–semantics mappings and the role that this plays in grammatical development. The first three papers within the syntax and semantics section provide different perspectives on this issue. Clark and Carpenter examine errors in the early use of the passive construction, and suggest that these are the result of children extending the cognitive category SOURCE in ways that are inappropriate for adults. Gropen, Pinker, Hollander, and Goldberg describe a set of studies addressing the acquisition of verbs like "pour" and "fill"; the results support their semantically-based theory of how children acquire the argument structure of novel verbs. Bowerman focuses on domains, such as the structure of prepositions, where different languages describe the world (or our conception of the world) in different ways. Contrary to the proposal that there exist universal mappings that guide grammatical development (as in the theories advanced by Clark and Carpenter, and Gropen *et al.*), children appear to show no biases when acquiring these domains, and thus very dissimilar systems—such as prepositions in English vs. prepositions in Korean—are acquired with equal ease. This supports Bowerman's proposal that children's understanding of syntax–semantics mappings is the *result* of early language development—not the basis for it. Reconciling Bowerman's results with the other findings that do show strong influences of semantics on syntactic development is a goal of any descriptively adequate theory of language acquisition.

The other papers in this section focus on formal syntax. Crain outlines a theory of the nature of universal grammar and its role in language development, reviewing recent experimental findings and relating them to debates over the role of parameter setting and maturation in the course of grammatical development. Cromer discusses children's developing understanding of complex sentences such as "The wolf is fun to bite" and "The wolf is glad to bite," providing us with an interesting case-study of syntactic development that occurs solely through experience, without feedback. (In addition, this is probably the only acquisition paper ever written that mentions Princess Diana.)

Rumelhart and McClelland's paper on morphology has been highly influential within linguistics and psychology. It presents an associationist theory of the acquisition of past-tense morphology and tests this model through a connectionist computational model, which does not explicitly represent any symbols or rules. Pinker argues against this, suggesting that although there may be an associationist component to morphological knowledge, evidence from children and adults shows that there also exist mentally represented rules that underlie the productive use of morphology. Gordon reports an experiment showing an understanding of "level-ordering" constraints on morphological processes in young children. He argues that this precocious knowledge (and the lack of evidence for such constraints in the input that children receive) supports a strongly nativist theory of this aspect of morphological knowledge.

In the section on acquisition in special circumstances, Goldin-Meadow and Mylander review the development of children deprived of linguistic input and discuss the structural properties of the communication systems that they create. Newport deals with a related issue, exploring how people at different ages come to acquire first and second languages. She finds strong critical period effects in the development of syntax and morphology, and proposes a novel explanation of this phenomenon, one that does not appeal to the maturation of a distinct language capacity.

In the final section, Karmiloff-Smith presents several experimental case-studies of developmental discontinuities and argues that they support the theory that although certain aspects of language and cognition are initially modular, the sharp dichotomy between modules and central systems disappears through the course of development.

The final paper by Marler brings the collection full circle; he returns to the biological perspective adopted by Fernald, and uses song development in birds as a way to clarify conceptual issues concerning language acquisition in human children.

Overview:
Controversies in language acquisition

Paul Bloom

Introduction

The question of how children acquire natural language has long occupied center stage within the sciences of the mind. In antiquity, philosophers such as Aristotle and Plato studied the case of a child learning a new word as a way to gain insights into both human psychology and the nature of word meaning. Word learning has been explored by more contemporary philosophers such as Quine and Fodor, who have used the logical structure of the acquisition problem to defend positions ranging from radical behaviorism to mad-dog nativism. Within linguistics, it has been argued that the main theoretical goal of this discipline should be to explain how children can come to possess knowledge of language through limited and impoverished experience (i.e., "Plato's problem"; see Chomsky, 1986).

As for cognitive psychology, every theoretical perspective has had the burden of explaining language acquisition. It could be argued that behaviorism's well-known failure in that domain (Brown and Hanlon, 1970; Chomsky, 1959) is why operant conditioning has been widely rejected as a theory of human learning. More recently, language development has served as the battle-ground for alternative perspectives such as connectionism and modularity.

As Pinker (1989a) notes, this focus on language acquisition should not be very surprising: Just as the emergence of natural language within the human species may be the most important aspect of our evolution, the acquisition of language is likely to be the most impressive intellectual accomplishment of individual humans. In fact, even if someone was uninterested in humans per se, they might still benefit from the study of children's acquisition of language—as children appear to be the only things (either living or non-living) capable of performing this task. As such, computer scientists interested in language might study children for much the same reason that Leonardo da Vinci, who was interested in building a flying machine, chose to study birds.

There are radically different perspectives about the nature of the acquisition process. For some scholars, knowledge of language is presumed to be the product of general learning capacities, and is acquired in much the same way that children learn how to ride a bicycle or to play chess (e.g., Anderson, 1983; Inhelder and Piaget, 1964). But one prominent alternative is that the human capacity for language is the product of a mental organ or faculty (Chomsky, 1980; Fodor, 1983), and thus there is no "learning" of language, just the growth of this faculty under certain environmental conditions, akin to the growth of arms or of the visual system.

All theorists agree, however, that there do exist differences between natural languages. In English, the name for dog is "dog," in French, it is "chien"; in English, adjectives precede nouns, in French, they follow them, and so on. Although these differences might well be superficial from a theoretical point of view, we need to explain how children come to speak the particular language that they are exposed to. In other words, we need a theory of language acquisition.

This chapter reviews a small subset of topics within the study of language acquisition, with special focus on areas where there has been both recent progress and continuing debate. The following section begins with a brief overview of the course of language development and the nature of adult input. "The acquisition of word meaning" turns to the problem of how children learn the meanings of words and "The emergence of syntax" concerns how they learn the syntactic categories to which these words belong. The following two sections focus on more specific issues in syntactic, semantic, and morphological development: "Parameter setting" reviews a particular theory within the principles-and-parameters framework, and "Cognitive architecture and recovery from error" discusses how children might recover from morphological and semantic overgeneralizations. The final section concludes.

A brief overview

The course of language development

Language acquisition begins at birth, if not in the womb. Children who are only a few days old can discriminate their own language from another, presumably through sensitivity to language-specific properties of prosody (Mehler *et al.*,

1988). Habituation studies show that infants start off being able to distinguish all phonemic contrasts made in natural language, but this ability fades over time and by about twelve months of age a child is capable only of distinguishing the speech sounds of the language to which she is exposed (see Gerken (1993) for a review).

By about seven to ten months, children begin reduplicative babbling, producing sequences such as "bababab" or "dadadada." At this age, deaf children will also start to babble—with their hands, producing sequences of sign-language syllables that are fundamentally identical to the syllabic units found in vocal babbling (Petitto and Marentette, 1991). In general, there appear to be no significant differences between the acquisition of spoken and signed languages (Newport and Meier, 1985; Petitto, 1988; Petitto and Marentette, 1991), suggesting that the human capacity for language is geared to acquire abstract linguistic structure, and not specifically to acquire speech.

Children produce their first words—excluding "mama" and "dada"—by about ten or eleven months (Nelson, 1973), and understand some words several months prior to this (e.g., Huttenlocher and Smiley, 1987). The most common class of words in children's early lexicons are names, either for specific individuals ("Mama"), objects ("car"), or substances ("water"); such words appear early for children of all languages and cultures (Gentner, 1982). Other early words include action verbs ("give"), adjectives ("big"), and certain hard-to-categorize expressions such as "hi" and "no!". Children's first words tend to refer to salient objects and actions in the child's environment; more abstract expressions, such as mental-state verbs, occur later.

By about eighteen months, there is a "word spurt" or "naming explosion" in which there is a rapid increase in children's acquisition and use of words. At about the same time, children start to combine words into two-word phrases, such as "more cookie" and "big toy." There is a strong correlation between the emergence of phrases and the onset of the word spurt (Bates, Bretherton, and Snyder, 1988; Nelson, 1973), supporting the view that there is some interdependence between word learning and syntactic development (see "Syntactic cues to word meaning" below).

The utterances that children produce at this stage are often called "telegraphic speech" (Brown and Bellugi, 1964), because they are very short, and because function words and morphemes (such as "the," "and," "of," and "-ed") are absent, giving children's sentences the minimalist flavor of telegrams or classified ads.

Even at this initial stage of grammatical competence, however, children command certain properties of the adult language. For one thing, word-order errors are very rare (e.g., L. Bloom, 1970; P. Bloom, 1990b; Braine, 1963, 1976; Brown, 1973; Pinker, 1984). In fact, knowledge of word order appears to exist even prior to the onset of telegraphic speech. In one study, seventeen-month-olds were exposed to two videos, one where Big Bird was tickling Cookie Monster and the other where Cookie Monster was tickling Big Bird. They tended to look to the appropriate video when they heard "Big Bird is tickling Cookie Monster" vs. "Cookie Monster is tickling Big Bird," indicating a sensitivity to the semantic contrast between the sentences, something which would be impossible without some understanding of English word order (Hirsh-Pasek, Golinkoff *et al.*, 1985). Children's obsession with word order extends even to languages where grammatical relations are encoded through case-markers. When acquiring such "free word order" languages, some children have been observed initially to use word order to express grammatical relations, and not utilize the word-order freedom that an adult speaker would use (e.g., Newport and Meier, 1985 on ASL; see Pinker, 1984 for a review).

Two other properties of telegraphic speech are the frequent omission of subjects and other constituents (see "Parameter setting" below) and the absence of closed-class morphology (i.e., "function words" such as determiners, prepositions, prefixes, and suffixes). When closed-class morphemes do appear in child language, they emerge in a relatively fixed order; some morphemes, such as the present progressive ("-ing," as in "walking"), show up earlier than others, such as the third-person regular ("-s," as in "walks") (Brown, 1973; de Villiers and de Villiers, 1973). Factors such as semantic complexity and phonological salience each partially determine the order of emergence of these morphemes, with frequency in adult speech less relevant (see de Villiers and and de Villiers, 1985 for review). This suggests that these morphemes are absent in the first stages of word combinations because (i) they tend to be unstressed and hard for the child to perceive (and possibly to produce) and (ii) children find it difficult to produce long strings of words and thus omit closed-class morphemes in their speech because they add little of essence to the meaning of sentences (e.g., P. Bloom, 1990a; Brown, 1973; de Villiers and de Villiers, 1985; Gerken, 1987; Gleitman and Wanner, 1982).[1]

Sometime before the age of about $2\frac{1}{2}$, the two-word stage ends. Children's utterances gradually increase in average length over a period of years, and function words become increasingly frequent in the contexts where they are grammatically required. More advanced syntactic devices begin to appear, such as yes–no questions ("Is there food over there?"), relative clauses ("The cookie that I ate"), and "control"-structures ("I asked him to leave"). Late-occurring errors include morphological overregularization (e.g., "goed" instead of "went," "mans" instead of "men"), and usages of words in inappropriate semantic contexts (e.g., "I giggled the baby," instead of "I made the baby giggle") (see "Cognitive architecture and recovery from error" below). Children's vocabulary increases steadily after the word spurt; one often-cited estimate is that children acquire about nine new words a day from the age of eighteen months to six years (Carey, 1978).

Finally, just as with the development of stereo vision in primates or the acquisition of song by birds (Marler, 1991), there is a critical period in language development for humans. If exposed to a language prior to the age of 7, children are capable of becoming totally fluent, but after this age, the prognosis becomes gradually worse. Studies of Chinese and Korean immigrants to the United States found that those who arrived after the age of 7 never became totally competent in English, regardless of how long they were exposed to it (Johnson and Newport, 1989); a similar result has been found with people acquiring ASL as a first language (Newport, 1991).

As one would expect, there is no consensus about what all of the above findings actually mean for a theory of language development. Some investigators see them as reflecting the growth of a genetically-encoded language faculty. Alternatively, one might view children as learning language through use of more general cognitive and social capacities, and thus stages of development correspond to the sorts of intermediate levels of competence that one would find in the acquisition of any complex intellectual domain. A third view is that children acquire the grammar of their language at a very early age, and the "patterns of development" reflect the maturation of peripheral processing mechanisms and the development of non-linguistic social and cognitive capacities. The extent to which these different perspectives are correct can be resolved only by looking at certain specific domains in detail.

Input to language development

Just as children may be specifically equipped to acquire language, adults seem to be inclined to make this task easier for them. Fernald (1992) reviews evidence suggesting that there exist universals in how human adults communicate with their offspring. Such communication tends to be slow high-pitched speech with smooth, exaggerated intonation contours. While sometimes dubbed "motherese" (Newport, Gleitman, and Gleitman, 1977), this mode of communication tends to be used by both males and females when interacting with infants. Darwin (1877; cited by H. Gleitman, 1991) called it "the sweet music of the species" and infants resonate to it, preferring to listen to motherese than to the normal style of adult-to-adult speech (Fernald, 1985).

There may be several reasons why the inclination to use motherese has evolved. One speculation is that it helps establish a social bond between the caretaker and the offspring; across different languages and cultures, there appear to be universal speech patterns used to express praise, soothing, and disapproval—and infants respond to these prosodic and pitch differences in the appropriate manner (Fernald, 1992). But some of the benefits of motherese may be specifically linguistic. Grammatical phrase boundaries are often marked by changes in prosodic structure such as a pause or a change in pitch (Cooper and Paccia-Cooper, 1980), and thus exaggerated intonation might give infants clues as to how to parse adult utterances, which could help them to acquire the syntactic structure of their language, (e.g., Gleitman and Wanner, 1982; Morgan, 1986). Supporting this, seven- to ten-month-olds prefer to listen to motherese where pauses (signaling the end of a sentence or phrase) coincide with a fall in pitch, suggesting that they expect a correspondence between the different prosodic cues to syntactic structure (Hirsh-Pasek, Kemler-Nelson *et al.*, 1987).

Parental input appears to be optimal in other ways. Mothers' speech to children is virtually perfect from a grammatical standpoint (Newport, Gleitman, and Gleitman, 1977), providing children with a reliable source of "positive evidence" (tokens of grammatical sentences) in the course of grammatical development. Some scholars have speculated that children also receive "negative evidence"—information as to which sentences are ungrammatical (Gold, 1967). Of course, adults do not explicitly announce to children that such-and-so is not a grammatical utterance. But they might react in some consistent way to children's ungrammatical sentences (by showing disapproval, for instance, or by responding with a non-sequitur). If there are robust and universal correlations between children's ungrammatical sentences and adult behavior, and if children are sensitive to these correlations, then negative evidence might play some role in language development, particularly with regard to how children recover from error.

The first test of this hypothesis was carried out by Brown and Hanlon (1970), who found no correlation between the grammaticality of children's utterances and parental approval or disapproval. Nor was there a correlation between children's grammaticality and whether or not the parent responded with a non-sequitur. As one might expect, parents are interested (and respond to) the content of what their children say, not to the structural properties of their sentences.

Several recent studies further explore this issue, and have found that some parents respond differentially to children's errors; for instance, some repeat their children's ungrammatical sentences more often than they repeat grammatical sentences (Bohanon and Stanowicz, 1988; Demetras, Post, and Snow, 1986; Hirsh-Pasek, Treiman, and Schneiderman, 1984; Penner, 1987). As Grimshaw and Pinker (1989) point out, however, these effects are weak, apply only with younger children, and—most important of all—occur in only some of the parent–child dyads studied. But all children acquire language, and there is no evidence that those children with laissez-faire parents are fated to become linguistically retarded.

Note also that the sort of extensive parental–child interaction characteristic of middle-class Western families may be the exception around the world; in other cultures, children acquire language in radically different contexts (e.g., Heath, 1983).[2] For these reasons, there is a growing consensus that negative evidence cannot play an essential role in the acquisition process (for discussion, see Bohanon, MacWhinney, and Snow, 1990; Gordon, 1990; Grimshaw and Pinker, 1989; Marcus, in press; Morgan and Travis, 1989).

This is not to say, however, that children could learn language solely by hearing a string of sentences, without any supporting context. Following Macnamara (1972), most theories of language development assume that children have some access not only to tokens of the language but to some non-linguistic encoding of the context. The need for some mapping between children's linguistic structure and their cognitive construal of the world is most obvious for theories of word learning, but may also apply for the acquisition of syntax (e.g., P. Bloom, 1990b, 1993a; Macnamara, 1972, 1982, 1986; Pinker, 1979, 1984; Wexler and Culicover, 1980).

The acquisition of word meaning

Perhaps the deepest mystery in the study of language acquisition is how children come to learn the meanings of words. Although there is considerable theoretical and empirical work on this topic, we have little understanding of how the process takes place. This might have to do with the nature of this problem; while syntax and phonology can be argued to be "closed" or "modular" systems, the same cannot be true of word meaning. An adequate theory of how children learn the meanings of words such as "dogs" and "giving" requires some account of what it is to possess the corresponding concepts of DOGS and GIVING—which might in turn involve nothing less than a full-blown theory of human cognition (for different perspectives, see Carey, 1988; Jackendoff, 1986; Keil, 1989; Lakoff, 1987).

As a starting point, many investigators have construed the process of word learning as hypothesis formation and testing. The adult uses a new word, the child notes the context in which the word is used, and formulates a hypothesis concerning the concept to which the word corresponds. Further instances where the word is used cause the child to strengthen, modify, or reject this initial hypothesis.

While this conception is implicit within much of psychology, philosophy, and linguistics, details differ: Depending on one's theory of the child's conceptual resources, the initial hypothesis may be a single innate primitive concept (Fodor, 1981), or it can be some combination of innate primitive concepts, either as a set of necessary or sufficient conditions (e.g., Bruner, Olver, and Greenfield, 1966; Inhelder and Piaget, 1964), or as a prototype or family-resemblance structure (e.g., Rosch, 1973). Under some accounts, this initial hypothesis undergoes continued revision and modification (Bruner, Olver, and Greenfield, 1966); alternatively, a single exposure might serve to trigger the requisite innate concept (Fodor, 1981; see also Carey, 1978, 1982 on "fast mapping").

Quine (1960) and Goodman (1983) discuss conceptual puzzles that arise from this perspective. From a logical standpoint, there is an infinity of possible hypotheses that are consistent with any exposure or set of exposures to a new word. Consider an adult pointing to Fido and saying to a child, "Look at the dog." Imagine that somehow the child is capable of determining what in the environment the word is intended to describe and that the relevant word is "dog," not "look," "at," or "the." There are countless possible meanings of this novel word. It could refer to the basic-level kind (dogs), a subordinate kind (poodle), a superordinate kind (animal), to the individual (Fido), to the color of the entity being pointed to (brown), to its shape (oblong), its size (large), a part of the entity (tail), and so on. There are also "crazy" hypotheses that are consistent with the word–scene pairing; the word "dog" could refer to the category including dogs and ex-Presidents, or to dogs until the year 2000 and then cats.

More generally, the crazy-hypothesis problem (or "the new riddle of induction"; Goodman, 1983) is that there is an infinity of inductive generalizations that are consistent with any finite set of instances. One solution is that there is an innate ordering on the hypotheses children make (Fodor, 1981). Children have evolved, for instance, to guess DOGS when exposed to a word that describes a dog, and this concept is ranked slightly ahead of the concept BROWN and far ahead of the concept DOGS UNTIL THE YEAR 2000 AND THEN CATS. More generally, it has been argued that the logic of the word-learning problem requires that children possess special constraints on word meaning; these preclude certain classes of hypotheses from being considered in the first place, and lead children to favor some hypotheses over others. In the following section, some proposed constraints are discussed and supporting evidence reviewed. "Problems with constraints" discusses some criticisms of these constraints, and "Syntactic cues to word meaning" addresses the possible role of syntax in word learning.

Constraints on word meaning

One proposed constraint is called the "whole object assumption," which is that "a novel label is likely to refer to the whole object and not to its parts, substance, or other properties" (Markman, 1990: 59). In several experiments, investigators have found that children ranging in age from 2 to 5 will initially categorize a word referring to a novel object as a name for that object, and not as referring to a part of the object, a property of the object, or the stuff of which the object is made (e.g., Baldwin, 1989; Macnamara, 1982; Markman and Hutchinson, 1984; Markman and Wachtel, 1988; Soja, Carey, and Spelke, 1991; Taylor and Gelman, 1988).

Related to this is a second constraint, which is that "labels refer to objects of the same kind rather than to objects that are thematically related" (Markman, 1990: 59). Thematically related entities include those that fall into "spatial, causal, temporal, or other relations," such as a dog and its bone, a dog and the tree that it is under, a dog and the person who is petting it, and so on. One important aspect of this proposal is that it is intended to be special to word learning. In a task that does not involve language, children are highly sensitive to thematic relations (for instance, they will put a dog and a bone together when asked to sort objects into different piles) (Markman, 1981). Markman's hypothesis is that this "taxonomic assumption" forces children to override this bias and attend to taxonomies (such as the kind DOG) when faced with the task of inferring the meaning of a new word.

Markman and Hutchinson (1984) present a set of studies that directly test this hypothesis. In one experiment, 2- and 3-year-olds were randomly assigned to one of two conditions. In the "no-word condition," they were shown a target picture (e.g., a dog) along with two other pictures, one of the same category (e.g., another dog), the other that was thematically related (e.g., a bone), and told, "See this? Can you find another one?" In the "novel-word condition," children were shown the same pictures and told, "See this dax. Can you find another dax?" Markman and Hutchinson found that children in the no-word condition tended to choose the thematic associate (the bone) while children in the novel-word condition tended to choose the object that belongs to the same category as the target (the other dog). This suggests that the taxonomic assumption is special to word learning. Similar findings emerge from the work of Hutchinson (1984), and Backscheider and Markman (1990), who studied eighteen- to twenty-four-month olds.

These constraints are posited to explain the acquisition of words that refer to kinds of whole objects (e.g., "dog"), but the majority of lexical items acquired by children are not of this nature. Even 2-year-olds possess words that refer to specific individuals ("Fred"), substances ("water"), parts ("nose"), properties ("red"), actions ("give"), and so on. This motivates further constraints that determine how words can relate to one another within the lexicon; these can lead children to override the whole object and taxonomic constraints.

One such proposal is the "mutual exclusivity" assumption (Markman and Wachtel, 1988), which is that each object can have only one label. This assumption does not hold for adults, as pairs of words such as "dog" and "pet" or "dog" and "Fido" are not mutually exclusive. But it could be argued that children are biased to assume that words have mutually exclusive reference and give up this assumption only when there is clear evidence to the contrary. The fact that children appear to have some difficulty with class-inclusion relations (where categories exist at different levels of abstraction, such as "dog" and "animal") has been taken as evidence that children are reluctant to abandon this assumption.

Further evidence from Markman and Wachtel (1988) illustrates the role that this assumption can play in language development. When children are given a novel word describing a novel object, they will interpret the word as referring to that object (following the taxonomic and whole object constraints), but when given a novel word describing an object for which they already have a name, they will move to other, less favored hypotheses, such as construing the novel word as a name for a part of the object or a name for the substance of which the object is composed. In a pior study by Golinkoff *et al.* (1985), children were shown two objects, one familiar and the other unfamiliar (for instance, a cup and a pair of tongs). When told (e.g.,) "Point to the fendle", they would tend to point to the unfamiliar object, suggesting that they assumed that "fendle" could not mean "cup," a result predicted by mutual exclusivity.

An alternative to mutual exclusivity is what Clark (1987) has called the "principle of contrast." Following Bolinger (1977), she argues that there are no synonymous forms in natural language. In particular, every word differs in meaning from every other word, though in some cases (e.g., "couch" and "sofa," "cup" and "mug") the difference is very subtle. If children possess the principle of contrast, this could lead them to structure their lexicon so as to avoid interpreting new words as synonymous with existing forms.

Note that the principle of contrast is much weaker than mutual exclusivity. While it predicts that a child will construe a new word as having a different *meaning* than a word that the child already possesses, the two words are free to overlap in reference. In particular, it is consistent with the principle of contrast that a child might construe a new word as having a dialectical or register difference from one that she already knows, or assume that it refers to a subordinate or superordinate. Thus the principle of contrast cannot, in itself, capture the findings of Golinkoff *et al.* (1985) and Markman and Wachtel (1988). I will return to this principle in "Cognitive architecture and recovery from error," as a proposed explanation for how children recover from certain sorts of morphological and semantic errors.

While constraints such as mutual exclusivity and the principle of contrast might explain why children sometimes abandon the taxonomic and whole-object assumptions, they do not explain how children actually acquire names for parts, substances, or abstract entities, let alone how they learn the meanings of verbs, prepositions, determiners, and so on. But since the very same problems that occur for the acquisition of words like "dog" and "cup" also apply for words such as "water," "giving" and "on," any theory of acquisition must address these words as well (P. Bloom, in press; Nelson, 1988).

One possibility is that the sorts of inferences children make will vary according to the ontological category of the entity to which a word refers. Soja, Carey, and Spelke (1991: 182–3) posit that the following two procedures apply in the process of word learning.

> *Procedure 1*
> Step 1: Test to see if the speaker could be talking about a solid object; if yes,
> Step 2: Conclude that the word refers to individual whole objects of the same type as the referent.

> *Procedure 2*
> Step 1: Test to see if the speaker could be talking about a non-solid substance; if yes,
> Step 2: Conclude that the word refers to portions of substance of the same type as the referent.

Procedure 1 operates as a restricted version of the whole object and taxonomic assumptions, while Procedure 2 can account for the acquisition of substance names. One could also posit an additional Procedure 3 that tests whether the speaker is talking about an animate entity with its own distinctive characteristics and, if it does, causes the child to conclude that the word refers to that particular individual; such a procedure might account for the precocious acquisition of proper names (P. Bloom, 1990b).

Problems with constraints

Some scholars, most notably Nelson (1988, 1990), have argued that the constraint approach is fundamentally misguided. One criticism was mentioned above; the same problems that arise for the acquisition of a word like "dog" also arise for words like "run" and "nap," and most of the constraints currently proposed apply only to object names. The extensions proposed by Soja, Carey, and Spelke (1991) partially deal with this problem, but they assume that children are somehow capable of determining what the speaker is talking about in the first place.

A second objection focuses on the claim that these constraints are present prior to word learning, perhaps as part of a special language acquisition device. Many investigators have suggested that children go through a stage (lasting for six to twelve months) where they use words in ways that violate proposed constraints. One-year-olds have been observed to apply words only in highly restricted contexts (e.g., Barrett, 1986; Lucariello and Nelson, 1986); for instance, only using "car" when watching cars move on the street from a certain location (L. Bloom, 1973). Children might also use words in "complexive" ways; for instance, a child might use the word "clock" to refer to clocks, to dials and timers, to bracelets, to objects that make buzzing noises, and so on, suggesting that the word refers not to a kind of object, but to "an associative complex of features" (Rescorla, 1980). Only when these usages largely disappear does the naming explosion begin. Nelson (1988) suggests that this is the point when the child "seems to have achieved the realization that words name categories of objects and events," which implies that the constraints are the *result* of early lexical development. If this were true, then they clearly cannot serve as an explanation for how children acquire their first words.

Finally, Nelson notes that the results found by Markman and other researchers suggest more of a bias than a constraint. Children do not always choose the taxonomic choice in Markman and Hutchinson's (1984) novel-word task, for instance, but instead show only a statistical trend to do so. Along the same lines, Gathercole (1987, 1989) presents a host of counter-examples to the proposals of Clark and Markman from both the experimental literature and naturalistic observations (but see Clark, 1988, 1990). This suggests that children possess more of a bias than an absolute constraint, which once again is said to undermine the notion that the constraints are genetically hard-wired, and exist prior to word learning.

All of these points have spawned considerable debate (Behrend, 1990; P. Bloom, in press; Kuczaj, 1990; Markman, 1989, 1990; Nelson, 1988, 1990) and some general points can be made. The argument that children must establish which entity the adult is describing in order to figure out which constraints to apply seems fundamentally correct. But it does not necessarily suggest a crucial flaw with the constraint framework, just a gap, and the issue is being pursued by scholars within this perspective (e.g., Baldwin, 1991, Macnamara, 1982, 1986). One framework for a solution involves exploring children's capacity to infer the intentions of adults, a project which links the problem of word learning to questions about children's innate "theory of mind"—their initial understanding of the beliefs and desires of others (e.g., Wellman, 1990).

The claim that there is a stage in which children do not understand words in the same way as adults is a matter of some debate. Some analyses suggest that children actually obey constraints on word meaning at the onset of lexical development (e.g., Backscheider and Markman, 1990; Huttenlocher and Smiley, 1987; Macnamara, 1982; Petitto, in press). But even if there are discontinuities, they might reflect neural maturation (as Nelson herself notes). If one accepts the possibility that constraints on word meaning are genetically encoded, then there is no reason to expect them to emerge at twelve months rather than eighteen months. It is possible, then, that an early stage of non-adult-like word use is the result of children's attempt to acquire words before the appropriate neural constraints have kicked in; the fact that the naming explosion tends to occur at the same time as the onset of productive syntax may support this speculation (see also Gleitman, 1981).

Finally, there are many replies that the constraint theorist could offer to Nelson's observation concerning the seemingly probabilistic nature of the constraints and the known counter-examples in the literature. It is possible that "constraint" is a misnomer and that children actually possess "biases" to favor certain hypotheses over others. But this does not substantively change the theory; after all, biases can also be innate—consider, for instance, newborn infants' preference to track human faces (Johnson *et al.*, 1991). Alternatively, children might possess absolute constraints, but given their well-known performance deficits and their problems coping with experimental situations, this knowledge may not be adequately reflected in their behavior.

Nelson's own position is that constraints on word meaning do not exist. She rejects the sort of hypothesis formation and testing model sketched out at the beginning of this section, arguing that "children, like adults, do not seek certainty of reference, but only communicability." She adopts a Wittgensteinian (1953) alternative that conceptualizes understanding of language as the capacity to participate in a language-game. As such, the development of language is better viewed as a social convergence process, where the adult and child work together to attain communicative success (Nelson, 1985; Vygotsky, 1962).

Nelson supports her perspective by citing several studies suggesting that mothers tailor their naming practices to the age and capacities of the child (e.g., Mervis, 1984), but these studies are not by themselves problematic for the notion of innate constraints. A constraint theorist might argue that regardless of how some mothers might aid children in the process of word learning, children are still faced with a logical infinity of candidate hypotheses—and psychologists have to develop a theory of the sorts of mental mechanisms that allow children to infer the correct hypothesis from the linguistic and non-linguistic context that they are exposed to, i.e., a theory of constraints. In other words, it is unclear how Nelson's alternative makes the induction problem discussed by Quine and Goodman go away. Note also that the most radical version of a Wittgensteinian account, one that attempts to describe the child's capacity in purely behavioral terms, without any appeal to mental processes or representations, is almost certainly not feasible as a theory of language learning (e.g., Chomsky, 1959; Macnamara, 1982).

Nevertheless, Nelson's own account is thoroughly mentalistic and could be viewed as staking out a middle ground between Plato and Wittgenstein. It is similar in certain regards to the "naive theory" proposals of Carey (1986, 1988) and Keil (1989), who suggest that children possess structured theories of certain conceptual domains (e.g., biology). New words are acquired as theoretical terms, characterized not in terms of combinations of features (i.e., definitions or prototypes) but through their interaction with other aspects of a larger conceptual structure. It has been argued that this alternative can explain developmental transitions in children's knowledge of terms such as "animal" and "alive" (Carey, 1986).

It is unclear at this point whether these perspectives can provide a plausible explanation of how children acquire simple basic-level expressions such as "cup" and "dog." But the mere existence of such approaches suggests that there may be worthwhile alternatives to the straightforward "hypothesis-testing" theory of the acquisition and representation of word meaning. Theories that involve grammatical cues to meaning, discussed below, also illustrate further directions in the study of how children acquire words.

Syntactic cues to word meaning

In an important paper written over thirty-five years ago, Brown (1957) suggested that young children might "use the part-of-speech membership of a new word as a first clue to its meaning." To test this, he showed preschoolers a picture of a strange action done to a novel substance with a novel object. One group of children was told: "Do you know what it means to sib? In this picture, you can see sibbing" (verb syntax); another group was told: "Do you know what a sib is? In this picture, you can see a sib" (count noun syntax); and the third group was told: "Have you seen any sib? In this picture, you can see sib" (mass noun syntax). Then the children were shown three pictures, one that depicted the identical action, another that depicted the identical object, and a third that depicted the identical substance. They were asked to "show me another picture of sibbing" (or "another picture of a sib" or "another picture of sib"). Brown found that children were sensitive to the syntax when inferring the meaning of the new word; they tended to construe the verb as referring to the action, the count noun as referring to the object, and the mass noun as referring to the substance.

Children's capacity to use syntax to infer meaning, a process sometimes called "syntactic bootstrapping" (Gleitman, 1990), has been documented in several domains. Katz, Baker, and Macnamara (1974) found that even some seventeen-month-olds were capable of attending the difference between count noun syntax ("This is a sib") and noun—phrase syntax ("This is sib") when determining whether a novel word was a name for a kind of object or a proper name (see also Gelman and Taylor, 1984). When 3-year-olds acquire new words, nouns focus the child on basic-level kinds, while adjectives draw children's attention towards properties (Gelman and Markman, 1985; Taylor and Gelman, 1988; Waxman, 1990).

Brown's (1957) initial work on the count—mass contrast has been extended to younger children; 2- and 3-year-olds will tend to construe a novel count noun as referring to a kind of individual (such as a bounded physical object) and a novel mass noun as referring to a kind of non-individuated entity (P. Bloom, in press a, in press b; Landau, Jones, and Smith, 1988; Soja, 1992). This sensitivity extends even to words that refer to non-material entities; 3-year-olds will construe a plural count noun that describes a series of sounds as referring to the individual sounds, and a mass noun describing the same series as referring to the undifferentiated noise (P. Bloom, in press a).

The developmental relationship between these syntax—semantics mappings and the constraints on word learning discussed above is unclear. One possibility is that the shift to specific grammatical categories might arise through the course of development, as a fine-tuning of more general constraints on word meaning (Landau, Jones, and Smith, 1988; Markman, 1989). For instance, children might start off with the assumption that *labels* refer to whole objects of the same kind (Markman and Hutchinson, 1984), and only later restrict this inference to the syntactic category of *count nouns*—and also alter the notion of "whole object" to include entities such as parts, collections, and non-material entities, all which are nameable by count nouns. Alternatively, constraints on word meaning in the sense discussed by Markman might not exist as psychological mechanisms. The syntax—semantics mappings could be innate, and there might never be a stage of development where children possess constraints on meaning that apply to all words in general (P. Bloom, in press a; Macnamara, 1986).

In any case, shifting the focus from "labels" to specific parts of speech allows for an explanation of how children might acquire a broad class of words. When exposed to count noun syntax (e.g., "This is a sib"), they will be constrained to interpret the word as referring to a kind of individual, such as "dog" or "cup"; when exposed to mass noun syntax (e.g., "This is some sib"), they will interpret the word as having non-individuated reference, as with the words "water" and "sand"; and when exposed to noun phrase (NP) syntax (e.g., "This is sib"), they will interpret the word as referring to a particular individual, as with "Fred" and "Mary." Given that an understanding of these mappings exists very early in language development (e.g., Katz, Baker, and Macnamara, 1974; Soja, 1992), they could play an important role in the acquisition of the meanings of nominals.

A distinct line of research concerns the acquisition of verbs, where there are intricate connections between syntactic structure and semantic or conceptual representations (Gleitman, 1990; Jackendoff, 1990; Pinker, 1989b; Talmy, 1985). Gleitman and her colleagues have carried out several studies suggesting that young children are capable of exploiting mappings from syntax to semantics in the course of verb acquisition (e.g., Hirsh-Pasek, Gleitman, et al., 1988; Landau and Gleitman, 1985; Naigles, 1990; see Gleitman, 1990 for a review).

In one study, twenty-seven-month-olds were shown two videos, one of a pair of puppets each performing the same action, the other of one puppet causing another to perform an action. Then the children heard an unknown verb in either the intransitive form ("Big Bird is gorping with Cookie Monster") or the transitive form ("Big Bird is gorping Cookie Monster"). When given the intransitive form, children tended to look more at the scene where each puppet performed an action; when given the transitive form, children tended to look more at the scene where one puppet performed an action on another (Hirsh-Pasek, Gleitman *et al.*, 1988).

In another study, Naigles (1990) showed twenty-four-month-olds a video of a rabbit pushing a duck up and down, with both the duck and the rabbit making circles with one arm. As they watched the video, they were presented with a novel verb in either the intransitive form ("The rabbit and the duck are gorping") or the transitive form ("The rabbit is gorping the duck"). Then they were shown two videos, one that had the rabbit and the duck making arm circles (but without any pushing), the other that had the rabbit pushing the duck (but without making arm circles), and told "Where's gorping now? Find gorping!" When the children had been given the verb in the intransitive form, they tended to look more at the video that had the animals making arm circles; when given a verb in the transitive form, they tended to look more at a video that had one animal pushing the other. These studies suggest that children are sensitive to the syntactic contrast between intransitive and transitive syntax when inferring how many participants are involved in the act that the verb describes.

Criticisms could be raised about the scope of these results. For one thing, it is unclear whether children are actually using the grammatical information to infer aspects of verb meaning and store them in the lexicon, as opposed to merely using grammatical context to draw short-term inferences (Gathercole,

1986). For another, the syntax–semantics correspondences discussed by Gleitman and others may not be universal; if not, then they could not apply at the initial stages of word learning (Pinker, in press).

Finally, it should be stressed that these syntax-based approaches do not constitute a complete theory of word learning. At best, syntax can provide a clue to the broad semantic category that the novel word belongs to—whether it refers to a kind of individual (count noun), a property (adjective), an activity with one entity acting upon another (transitive verb), and so on. But it cannot tell the child the *precise* meaning of the word, whether it corresponds to "cup" vs. "dog" (both count nouns), to "good" vs. "bad" (both adjectives), or "punch" vs. "kick" (both transitive verbs) (P. Bloom, in press a; Pinker, in press). Nevertheless, if very young children can use syntax to determine the general semantic category of a novel word, this source of information can significantly narrow down the possible meanings that it could have.

The emergence of syntax

The hypothesis that young children can learn aspects of word meaning through a sensitivity to grammatical structure assumes that they are able to parse adult utterances into categories such as "noun" and "verb." More generally, linguistic theory explains adult understanding of language in terms of rules and principles that map over such syntactic categories. In English, for instance, adjectives precede nouns within the noun phrase; "the big dog" is acceptable, "the dog big" is not. To acquire English, children must not only learn the order of adjectives and nouns (which is not universal), they must categorize words such as "dog" and "idea" as nouns, and words such as "big" and "unpleasant" as adjectives.

Once children have acquired some of the rules of English and have categorized some words, this task of categorizing new words becomes relatively straightforward. For instance, given that we know that "the" is a determiner, and "dog" is a noun, we can infer upon hearing "I saw the gorp dog" that "gorp" is probably an adjective (see Pinker, 1984 for an explicit algorithm of this process). But how do children *initially* determine the syntactic categories of novel words? Without some means of doing so, they cannot acquire and use properties of syntax.

Proposals can be distinguished in terms of how they characterize children's telegraphic speech. One class of theories—dubbed "discontinuous"—views children as gradually converging on grammatical competence through revision and extension of non-grammatical representations. Thus they assume that children's early word combinations are not governed by adult-like grammatical rules and principles (e.g., Bowerman, 1973, 1976; Braine, 1963, 1976; Macnamara, 1982; Maratsos, 1982, 1983; Schlesinger, 1971, 1988). Other accounts—dubbed "continuous"—propose that children possess knowledge of grammatical categories from the very onset of linguistic development. Such theories assume that the early word combinations of telegraphic speech are the result of rules and principles that order syntactic categories (L. Bloom, 1970; P. Bloom, 1990b; Brown and Bellugi, 1964; Menyuk, 1969; Miller and Ervin, 1964; Pinker, 1984; Valian, 1986).

Discontinuous theories

One sort of discontinuous theory is that children initially categorize parts of speech according to their "distributional properties," such as what words they go before, what words they go after, and their absolute position within an utterance. As a result of this analysis, children cluster words and phrases into categories that gradually come to correspond to "noun" and "verb," "count noun" and "mass noun" (Karmiloff-Smith, 1979; Levy, 1988; Maratsos and Chalkley, 1981). Under the strongest version of this hypothesis, semantic properties of words—what they mean—are irrelevant.

This solution was known as a "discovery procedure" by linguists in the 1940s, and is motivated by the widely perceived failure to find semantic correlates to syntactic categories. It is false, for instance, that all count nouns are names for objects (e.g., "problem") or that all verbs name actions (e.g., "seem"). Further, some analyses of children's spontaneous speech suggest distributional categories; Braine (1963) characterized children's first word combinations in terms of a "pivot grammar," analyzing two-word utterances as combinations of a small class of high-frequency words (pivots) that appear in fixed positions with a larger class of low-frequency words (open-class words) that appear in different positions. Such an analysis is both non-semantic and non-syntactic, it is "distributional" in the strongest sense. Finally, evidence that children might use prosody to carve up sentences into grammatical relevant units (Hirsh-Pasek, Kemler-Nelson *et al.*, 1987) introduces another source of evidence that a non-semantic procedure could use.

Nevertheless, without some semantic information to limit the space of alternatives, a purely distributional analysis is unlikely to succeed (see Pinker, 1987 for a critical discussion). The number of correlations through which an unconstrained analysis would have to sift is enormous. For instance, in his analysis of the grammatical contrast between count nouns and mass nouns, Gordon (1982) has calculated that the child who tried to distinguish these two parts of speech through purely distributional differences would have to consider over eight billion possible contexts in order to converge on the distinction—and yet children command count/mass syntax by about the age of $2\frac{1}{2}$ (P. Bloom, in press a, in press b; Gordon, 1982, 1985, 1988; Soja, 1992).

More generally, the pivot grammar analysis does not appear to describe the early word combinations of all children (Bowerman, 1973; Braine, 1976) and there is evidence that even 2-year-olds possess productive grammars, with categorization errors virtually non-existent (P. Bloom, 1990b; Brown, 1973; Maratsos, 1982; Pinker, 1984; Valian, 1986). When one also takes into account the very precocious understanding of syntax–semantics mappings (see "Syntactic cues to word meaning" above), it seems that semantic information is likely to play some role in the assignment of new words to syntactic categories.

One motivation for distributional theories is that children can rapidly acquire semantically arbitrary distinctions, such as the gender contrast in a language like French (Karmiloff-Smith, 1979; Levy, 1988). Such a finding is important, but the mere fact that children can acquire these distinctions does not necessarily entail that they do so through the sort of distributional procedure discussed by Maratsos and Chalkley (1981). An alternative is that children might (for example) acquire gender contrasts within nouns and adjectives because they are disposed to search for these sorts of markings—not because they are analyzing all possible relations among words within adult utterances. Moreover, they might be able to acquire these sorts of semantically arbitrary regularities only after they have used some other procedure to infer which words are nouns and which are adjectives in the first place—in other words, this sort of categorization may be based on syntax, not on a distributional analysis.

In general, it is crucial to distinguish the capacity to syntactically categorize words based on their distributional properties from the capacity to draw inferences over syntactic structure. As noted above, someone who hears "I saw a glubble" can infer that "glubble" is a noun— because, in English, "a" is a determiner and nouns follow determiners. But this sort of inference is based on an understanding of syntactic structure, which is precisely the knowledge that a learning procedure is supposed to yield. To put it another way, inference over syntactic structure provides a useful way grammatically to categorize new words, but it is not available to young children, who have not yet acquired the relevant syntactic knowledge. Inferences based on properties of words such as being the first word in a sentence, following the word "cat" etc. *are* available to very young children, but they are of dubious use in the course of language development, for the reasons noted above.[3]

A different discontinuous theory is that children start with rules ordering conceptual categories such as "object word" and "action word." At a later point in development these categories somehow get transformed into the appropriate syntactic ones. Schlesinger (1981: 230), for instance, suggests that "... the child's earliest semantic categories are narrowly circumscribed and ... he extends them gradually into the broader categories of the adult grammar through semantic assimilation." This analysis is motivated by "semantic" descriptions of children's telegraphic speech, where they possess rules that order these sorts of semantic categories, not categories such as noun and verb (Bowerman, 1973; Braine, 1976; Macnamara, 1982; Schlesinger, 1971, 1988).

One problem is that the idea of "semantic assimilation," that of a category becoming more abstract as a result of experience, is quite vague, and without some theory of how "object word" becomes "noun" such a theory runs the risk of begging the major theoretical question. Furthermore, although child language does have a semantically transparent flavor, with (for instance) a high proportion of nouns naming objects, and a high proportion of verbs naming actions, even the youngest of children do use at least some nouns that do not describe objects, and some verbs that do not describe actions. Similarly, as Maratsos (1982) has argued, children do not make the errors that one would expect if they were limited to the sorts of semantic categories posited by Schlesinger and Macnamara. For instance, nouns that seemingly name events (e.g., nap) are not miscategorized as verbs, even by very young children.

Continuous theories

An alternative perspective is that children possess grammatical knowledge from the onset of language development, as part of an innate language faculty. As such, the problem for children is to hook up innate grammatical categories to the words that they are learning, and thus to "bootstrap" (Pinker, 1984) their way into the grammar of natural language. From this standpoint, the puzzle runs deep: nouns, for instance, do not sound the same across all languages, and do not always appear in the same position within sentences. One class of theories of how children syntactically categorize their first words involves universal mappings from cognition to syntax; children use these mappings (perhaps with the aid of prosodic or distributional information) to categorize their first words; principles of grammar can facilitate the categorization of further words and phrases.

One specific proposal has been dubbed "semantic bootstrapping" (Grimshaw, 1981; Pinker, 1984, 1987); this is the hypothesis that children exploit one-way mappings from cognition to syntax (e.g., all names of objects are count nouns). These mappings are part of a special language-acquisition device, not grammatical knowledge per se, and do not apply in the other direction (e.g., all count nouns are not names of objects). Thus children might learn that "dog" describes a solid object and infer that "dog" is a count noun. Once they have acquired the determiner "a," they could learn from phrases such as "a dog" that count nouns follow "a," and they could infer from a phrase such as "a problem" that "problem" is a count noun. In this way, these early categorizations, acquired through semantic bootstrapping, could allow children to acquire further count nouns for which the bootstrapping procedure does not apply.

An alternative proposal is that the syntax–semantics mappings that children use are actually part of knowledge of language, and apply in both directions throughout the course of language development. For instance, adults and children are argued to possess mappings from the grammatical category "count noun" to the semantic category "kind of individual," where "individual" is defined in a sufficiently abstract way so as to include abstract entities such as "problem" and bounded periods of time such as "day" (see Bach, 1986; P Bloom, in press a, in press b; Jackendoff, 1991; Langacker, 1987). This hypothesis gains support from experimental analyses of adult and children's acquisition of new words (P. Bloom, in press b) and is consistent with both the capacity to infer syntactic structure from word meaning (semantic bootstrapping) and word meaning from syntactic structure (syntactic cues to word meaning).

Unlike syntactic cues to word meaning, however, there is little direct support for the claim that mappings from semantics to syntax (however described) enable children to syntactically categorize new words. This is largely because of methodological limitations; while there are many techniques (e.g., preferential looking) that can explore how children younger than 2 construe the meaning of a new word, it is as yet impossible to test how these children categorize the syntactic category to which a word belongs. As such, all of the evidence for semantic cues to syntactic structure for children's early words is based on analyses of spontaneous speech data. In particular, these semantic approaches are supported by the strong isomorphism between syntax and semantics in telegraphic speech (Pinker, 1984). For instance, although some of children's count nouns do not refer to objects and some of their verbs do not refer to actions (thus showing that their categories are syntactic, not conceptual), their proportions of object count nouns and action verbs are higher than for adults, which is consistent with the view that children exploit semantic cues to categorize these first words.

The strongest argument for this sort of mapping theory is that, unlike the other alternatives discussed above, it offers an explicit account of how children can acquire syntactic structure. It is based on universals of language that are plausible (e.g., object names are categorized as nouns) and appears to offer an explicit and workable procedure which could allow children successfully to categorize at least some words. It remains to be seen whether more direct empirical confirmation will be found, or whether some sort of explicit alternative approach will emerge.

One final concern is the apparent contradiction between the claim that children use syntax to acquire word meaning and the claim that they use the meanings of words to acquire syntax. For instance, it has been argued both that children use their knowledge that the word "dog" refers to a kind of object to infer that "dog" is a count noun, and that they are using their knowledge that "dog" is a count noun to infer that "dog" refers to a kind of object. Clearly both of these proposals cannot be right, at least not for the same words.

From a logical standpoint, there are two possibilities: The first is that children use some sort of non-semantic procedure to determine the syntactic structure of sentences, and then use this syntactic information to initially acquire the meanings of some words (as proposed by Gleitman, 1990); the second is that children use some sort of non-syntactic procedure to determine the meanings of words and then use this semantic information to determine the syntactic categories to which the words belong (as proposed by Pinker, 1984). Each possibility rests on a non-trivial assumption regarding the process of language development; the first assumes that it is possible to learn the syntactic category of a word without knowing what it means; the second assumes that it is possible to learn the meaning of a word without knowing its syntactic category.

There are no conclusive arguments in favor of either view, but certain considerations favor the second hypothesis, that children first learn the meanings of some words, determine their syntactic categorization, and only then use syntactic structure to infer the meanings of further words. For one thing, children appear to acquire the meanings of words prior to learning syntax (Meier and Newport, 1990). For another, as argued above, there does not as yet appear to be any alternative to semantics as a cue to syntactic structure; for instance, distributional evidence is probably not sufficient.

This suggests a hybrid view, in which children apply non-syntactic procedures (e.g., the whole object and taxonomic constraints; Markman, 1990) to acquire the meanings of a small subset of words and use either semantic bootstrapping (Grimshaw, 1981; Pinker, 1984) or more general syntax–semantics mappings (P. Bloom, in press b) to determine the grammatical categories to which these words belong. Once children develop some command of syntactic structure, syntactic information could facilitate the acquisition of the meanings of other words, and might play an essential role in the acquisition of some aspects of verb semantics (Gleitman, 1990).

Parameter setting: The case of null subjects

One recent approach to the study of syntactic development is the "principles and parameters" theory (e.g. Chomsky, 1986; Hyams, 1986; Manzini and Wexler, 1987; Roeper and Williams, 1987). Its premise is that grammatical differences across languages are the result of limited variation on universal principles; this variation is captured in terms of "parameters" which are set by children through simple positive evidence. Acquiring the grammar of a language, then, is the process of determining the correct values for these linguistically-defined parameters.

This differs from more orthodox theories of language development in that it assumes that the grammatical structure of natural language is almost entirely genetically encoded; the sole role of input is to select among the different alternatives that are biologically available. Thus the role of input for a parameter-setting theory is to "trigger" an innately encoded grammar; it does not serve as the basis for induction or analysis.

The most worked-out case of parametric change in language development concerns the optionality of overt subjects. For some languages, such as English and French, tensed sentences must have overt subjects, as in "I go to the movies." For others, such as Italian and Spanish, null subjects are possible, as in "vado al cinema" (literally, "go to the movies"). Part of language acquisition involves a child's determining whether subjects are obligatory or optional in the language to which she is exposed.

This contrast is posited to result from different settings of a grammatical parameter; one effect of this difference is whether the language has the option of a phonologically empty subject or topic in a tensed sentence (Chomsky, 1981; Huang, 1984; Hyams, 1986; Rizzi, 1982). Although acquisition theorists standardly refer to this as the "null subject parameter," it should be stressed that under most accounts the optionality of subjects is just one property of this parameter. For instance, it is sometimes maintained that the same setting that allows for the optionality of subjects also determines whether a language will have expletive subjects, which are subject NPs that have no meaningful content, such as "it" in "it is raining" (Hyams, 1986). As such, the parameter could just as well have been dubbed "the overt expletive parameter" (Kim, in press).

Since the publication of Hyams (1986), the null subject parameter has been the focus of considerable study. One reason for this has to do with Hyams's proposal that the initial setting of this parameter is for subjects to be optional (as in Italian, but not English) and that children acquiring English go through a long period where they have not yet set their parameter to the appropriate setting. This proposal is discussed in the section below. More generally, studying how children acquire this property of grammar allows us critically to examine the predictions that parameter theories make about developmental change and the role of triggering data; some implications and extensions are reviewed in "Null subjects and the logic of parameter setting" below.

Explanations for subject omission in child English

One of the main characteristics of telegraphic speech is the occasional omission of words and phrases. In particular, it has long been noted that children acquiring English frequently produce sentences with missing subjects, such as "hug Mommy," "play bed," "writing book," and "see running" (from Bowerman, 1973).

One class of explanations for these utterances posits that children know that subjects in English are obligatory, but omit them due to performance factors. Put differently, although they might sometimes say "play bed" instead of "I play in bed," they would agree that this sentence is ungrammatical. (Unfortunately, 2-year-olds are too young to make this sort of explicit judgment.) Candidate theories of the nature of the processing deficit have focused on children's difficulty in constructing long strings of morphemes (e.g., L. Bloom, 1970, 1991; P. Bloom, 1990a, 1993; Pinker, 1984) as well as their difficulty in producing certain phonological strings (Gerken, 1991).

Putting aside the question of subject omission, most scholars agree with Chomsky (1964) that children suffer from performance factors, more so than adults, and that these factors cause them occasionally to omit constituents. Two-year-olds not only omit subjects, they also omit objects, verbs, determiners, prepositions, and so on (e.g., L. Bloom, 1970; Bowerman, 1973; Braine, 1974, 1976; Feldman, Goldin-Meadow, and Gleitman, 1978; Pinker, 1984). There have been competence explanations proposed for some of these omissions, such as deletion rules in children's grammars or phrase-structure rules with optional categories, but there is little doubt that at least some omissions occur for non-grammatical reasons (see Pinker, 1984 for discussion). For one thing, children will also omit elements when asked to imitate adult sentences (Brown and Fraser, 1963; Ervin, 1964; Gerken, 1991). For another, one needs to explain the general fact that young children's utterances are so short—it is hard to imagine some aspect of children's grammar that would restrict them to sentences that are an average of two words long.

Given the existence of performance limitations in child language, many scholars have argued that these can explain children's subjectless sentences. A similar explanation for older children's difficulty with certain properties of grammar have been extended by Crain (1991) and Grimshaw and Rosen (1990).

The alternative is that children possess a grammar that is in some sense different from that of adult English speakers. Under one theory, this grammatical account was of a grammar such as Italian ("pro-drop"; see Hyams, 1986); more recently, it has been proposed that these children possess a Chinese-like grammar ("topic-drop"; see Hyams and Wexler, 1993). As a result of either processing limitations or neural maturation of grammatical capacities, children go through a long period where they are insensitive to triggering data that would lead them to switch their null subject parameter to the English-like setting. There are a range of different theories as to the precise nature of the trigger and the reason why children are initially insensitive to it (Hyams, 1986, 1989; Hyams and Wexler, 1993; Lebeaux, 1987; Lillo-Martin, 1987; Pierce, 1987).

One argument in support of this parametric hypothesis is that subjects are omitted more frequently than objects (Hyams, 1986). In one analysis of three 2-year-olds (first studied by Brown, 1973 and stored on the CHILDES computer database; MacWhinney and Snow, 1985), subject NPs were omitted on average 55 percent of the time, while obligatory objects were omitted only an average of 9 percent of the time (P. Bloom, 1990a). This supports the claim that although some omissions (about 10 percent, say) are the result of processing problems, the preponderance of subject omissions is due to the fact that these children are encoding a null subject grammar.

There are other subject/object differences, however, that suggest an alternative explanation. The same study found that overt subjects are more likely to be pronouns than overt objects and that, among non-pronoun overt subjects and objects, subjects tend to be significantly shorter. While greater subject omission might be due to grammatical factors, the other two phenomena suggest that there is a subject/object asymmetry that is independent of grammar, which perhaps results from factors having to do with pragmatics and processing load, both of which might lead to greater deletion of subjects than objects (P. Bloom, 1990a, 1993; Pinker, 1984).

Another explanation for the subject/object difference emerges from the research of Gerken (1991). Using an imitation task, she found that children are far more likely to omit subjects than objects (as expected by the null subject account), but that they are also more likely to omit *articles* from subject NPs than from object NPs and the identical pattern occurs in children's spontaneous speech. The omission of articles cannot be due to the mis-setting of a parameter, and supports Gerken's claim that processing difficulties which specifically apply to metrical structure are the cause of subjectless sentences in child English.

A different argument advanced in support of the null subject theory is that at the point at which children stop omitting subjects, there are a multitude of other transitions in their grammars. The optionality of overt subjects is just one (quite salient) deductive consequence of the null subject parameter; others concern linguistic properties such as the presence or absence of expletives, morals (words like "must" and "will"), certain sorts of questions, and so on. These other effects can provide "triggers" that lead the child exposed to English to realize that her language actually has obligatory subjects. In particular, once children learn that English has expletives and modals, they should reset the parameter and stop omitting subjects (Hyams, 1986).

Hyams (1986) reviews data from different sources and suggests that is exactly what occurs: At the same point that children acquire expletives and modals, they stop omitting subjects. This conclusion, however, was based on published observations from a variety of sources; until recently there has been no careful statistical analysis of the relationship between subject omission and other aspects of child language. In the first large-scale analysis of this, Valian (1991) studied the speech of twenty-one children acquiring English and five children acquiring Italian, analyzing the frequency of omitted subjects and how it relates to factors such as the onset of expletive use, the onset of modal use, and inflectional morphology—all which have been argued to serve as triggers for the end of the null subject period. She also looked at performance factors, such as MLU (the mean length of the children's utterances), the number of different types of verbs and direct objects that children used, and the average length of the verb phrase (VP).

Valian found that even prior to the age of 2, Italian children were omitting subjects almost twice as often as the English children (see also Bates, 1976). There was no correlation between the proportion of omitted subjects and the grammatical factors at which Valian looked, but there were significant correlations between subject omissions and non-grammatical factors, such as age, MLU, and VP-length (see L. Bloom, 1991 for a review of similar findings). This suggests that children who are exposed to Italian possess null subject grammars at an early age (and thus omit subjects very frequently). Children acquiring English know that subjects are obligatory but omit them due to processing factors; as their capacity to form long strings of words improves, the rate of omission decreases.

In sum, there is considerable evidence that even very young children acquiring English understand that subjects are obligatory. They omit far fewer subjects than children acquiring a language such as Italian, these omissions appear to be the result of performance considerations, and the gradual decline in subject omission is correlated with non-grammatical factors such as age. This is consistent with the proposal that the initial setting of the null subject parameter is that subjects are obligatory (as in English) and only when hearing sentences without subjects (as in Italian), will the child switch her parameter (P. Bloom, 1990b, 1993; Rizzi, 1982).

Nevertheless, the issue is hardly closed. The theory of null subjects is in flux and it is conceivable that there exists some grammatical milestone (not explored by Valian) that coincides with a decrease in subject omission in children acquiring English. Further, there are puzzles that arise when one considers precisely how parameters can be set; these are discussed below.

Null subjects and the logic of parameter setting

The null subject parameter serves to illustrate the role of subset relations in language development (Berwick, 1982, 1985; Manzini and Wexler, 1987). The "subset principle"—which applies to all facets of language development, not just parameter setting—can be summarized as follows: When there are grammatical options that produce languages that fall into subset–superset relations, the learner should always choose the grammar that generates the smaller language. For instance, if the only effect of the null subject parameter is the possible optionality of subjects, then the English setting would produce a proper subset of the Italian setting. Every sentence that one could produce with the English setting (e.g., "I go to the movies") one could also produce with the Italian setting, but there are sentences that one could produce with the Italian setting and not with the English setting (e.g., "go to the movies"). In other words, a language which allows only overt subjects is a subset of a language with both overt subjects and null subjects.

To take another example from Pinker (1984, 1989a), a language which has "fixed word order" (only subject–verb–object, for instance) is a subset of a language with "free word order" (all orders of subject, verb, and object). The subset principle states that the initial hypothesis of the child should be that the target language has fixed word order, and this hypothesis should be abandoned only upon exposure to positive evidence. This is consistent with the data on children's acquisition of word order across different languages (see "The course of language development" above).

What is the motivation for this principle? Assume that children obey the subset principle and choose the smaller language. If this is the language spoken by adults, no further grammatical development is needed; if not, then simple positive evidence suffices to cause grammatical change. For instance, if children start with an obligatory subject language, being exposed to a single sentence with a missing subject could cause them to shift their parameter to the larger (Italian-like) setting. Consider the consequences, however, if children violate the subset principle and start with the larger language. If a child's grammar allows both "I go to the movies" and "go to the movies," and the adult language allows only for the first type of sentence, what could cause the child to switch her grammar?

If negative evidence existed, then parental feedback could lead children to "retract" their overgeneralizations and move to the smaller grammar, but in the absence of such evidence (see "Input to language development" above), there is no obvious way for a child who has an overly large grammar to move to a smaller one. This motivates the subset principle.

In the case of the null subject parameter, then, the subset principle predicts that the child's initial hypothesis is that subjects are obligatory, as in English, and only through positive evidence will she move to the larger grammar where subjects are optional, as in Italian (e.g., P. Bloom, 1990a). However, Hyams's (1986) alternative, that children start off with the optional subject setting of the parameter, also does not violate the subset principle, since, under her analysis, the two settings of the parameter do not fall into a subset relationship. Instead, "null subject" languages and "non-null subject" languages overlap, so that each has properties that the other lacks. Italian, for instance, has sentences such as "go to the movies" which do not appear in languages like English, while English has sentences such as "It is raining" (with expletive "it") that do not appear in languages such as Italian. Thus, with regard to the null subject parameter, English and Italian do not fall into a subset–superset relation; rather, they overlap, and the subset principle thus makes no prediction as to which should be the default setting.

It might be argued that there is something unrealistic about applying this principle to the actual course of development. Consider again the hypothetical child who starts with an optional subject grammar and assume, contrary to Hyams (1986), that such a grammar is a proper subset of an obligatory subject language such as English. A child with English-speaking parents might never be corrected (or get any special feedback) when she produces a sentence without a subject. But one could argue that a child would have to be quite dense to go for years without ever noticing that her parents are never omitting subjects. This cannot serve as *proof* that her parents are not speaking an Italian-like language—after all, Italian speakers could choose not to omit subjects—but it does serve as evidence. The notion that the non-appearance of a form over time could lead a child to conclude that this form is not grammatical in the target language has been dubbed "indirect negative evidence" (Chomsky, 1981). Note that this sort of evidence is more consistent with a "hypothesis-testing model" of grammatical change (e.g., Valian, 1990) than with a parameter-setting model, as it involves frequency-based induction, not triggering.

Valian (1990) raises some problems with the proposal that all children start off with obligatory subject grammars and only upon hearing sentences without subjects shift to an optional subject grammar. She notes that there are plenty of subjectless sentences in adult English; examples include imperatives ("Put that down!"), responses (Person A: "What are you doing?"; Person B: "Thinking"), some questions ("Want lunch now?"), and other cases that are not as easily classifiable ("Seems like rain", "Wouldn't be prudent"). The existence of these sentences requires some theory of how children come to possess these subtle conditions on subject omission in a non-null subject language; how they acquire rules of ellipsis, for instance, and how they distinguish imperatives from non-imperatives. More to the point, somehow they have to filter out all of these sentences when determining the parametric status of adult language. If children are not capable of realizing that "Want lunch now?" is an exceptional case, this should cause them mistakenly to reset the null subject parameter and assume that English allows for optional subjects in all tensed clauses.

Valian's own solution is to abandon a triggering analysis and instead adopt a hypothesis-testing model, where children try out both parameter settings and determine which better captures the patterns in the target language. One alternative, however, is that the child has sufficient knowledge of the pragmatic circumstances under which subjects can be omitted in an obligatory subject language to filter out utterances such as "Want lunch now?" (Kim, in press).

A related hypothesis is that children focus on embedded clauses only when setting parameters (Roeper, 1973; Roeper and Weissenborn, 1990). In the case of the null subject parameter this would largely solve the problem posed by Valian; in a language such as English, embedded sentences do not allow for deletions. One cannot say "I asked if want lunch now," even though "Want lunch now?" is marginally acceptable. Similarly "Seems like rain" is somewhat acceptable, and so is "I think that it seems like rain"—but not "I think seems like rain," where the subject is omitted from the embedded clause. This proposal allows us to extend the proposal made by Rizzi (1982) and P. Bloom (1990a) as follows: The initial setting of the parameter is that subjects are obligatory, and only when exposed to embedded clauses without subjects (as in Italian, but not in English) will children switch to a null subject grammar.

Other questions arise: Can children possess both settings of a parameter at the same time (Valian, 1990)? What is the role of parameter-setting in second language acquisition (Flynn, 1987)? Is parameter-setting consistent with gradual changes in children's knowledge (P. Bloom, 1993)? Subject omission in child language is a useful domain in which to explore the relationship between the idealizations of the grammatical theory of parameters and the actual process of language development.

Cognitive architecture and recovery from error: The case of verbs

There are domains of language development (such as the acquisition of word order) where children are virtually error-free. These are frustrating from the standpoint of acquisition research; after all, we study children because they have not completed the acquisition process—to the extent that child language is perfect, one might just as well run experiments on adults. Errors, on the other hand, offer important insights. They might illustrate false or intermediate knowledge of the adult language and thus inform us about the manner in which children infer properties of language on the basis of the input they receive. In the case of subjectless sentences in the acquisition of English (discussed in the section above), errors such as "writing book" prompted hypotheses as to the nature of parametric change and the roles of competence and performance in the course of grammatical development.

For any systematic error, three descriptive questions arise: Why do children make this error, what is the time-course of this error, and what makes them stop? While these questions have been addressed in the domains of word meaning and syntactic competence, they have received the most attention with regard to the overregularization of verbs. The sections below focus on the past-tense morpheme, as this has been at the center of these debates, and briefly consider similar issues that arise in the study of verb semantics.

The phenomenon of overregularization

Most verbs in English form the past tense by adding the suffix "-ed," as in walk–walked, pass–passed, dance–danced, turn–turned, and so on. These are called "regular" verbs, and contrast with the approximately 180 "irregular" verbs where the past tense relates to the stem in some other way. Some irregular past-tense forms differ entirely from their stems (go–went), others are identical (hit–hit), and others involve different sorts of vowel or consonant changes while preserving most of the phonological structure of the stem (eat–ate, grow–grew, feel–felt) (see Bybee and Slobin, 1982). Adults know the past-tense forms of these irregular verbs (e.g., "went" is the past tense of "go"), and also know that the regular "-ed" suffix *cannot* apply to these verbs (e.g., "goed" is not an acceptable past tense of "go").

The regular rule is productive; adults can use it to create past-tense forms that they have never heard before. Upon hearing a new present-tense verb such as "kermit," an adult can use it in the past-tense form, saying "I kermitted the file to my computer yesterday." Berko (1958) found evidence for the same sort of productivity with young children. If she showed them a picture of a man doing an activity and told them: "Here is a man who likes to rick. Yesterday he did the same thing. Yesterday he ...," children will obediently say "ricked." This finding refutes the naive claim that children acquiring language are limited to imitating the forms that they hear. In this task (and many others, see Marcus *et al.*, 1992 for a review), children are quite capable of using a word to which they had never been exposed before.

Evidence for this productivity also appears in children's spontaneous speech (Ervin, 1964). Children will say things such as "I goed to the store" or "He breaked the glass." The standard characterization of the time-course of such errors is as a U-shaped curve, where the "U" is plotted as the percentage of correct performance over time. The left tail of the "U" is the earliest stage of morphological production, in which the child is performing perfectly, using both regulars ("walked") and irregulars ("broke") correctly. This is followed by a long period of overgeneralization (the sagging middle of the "U") where children overregularize, producing forms such as "goed" and "breaked." Finally, children stop overregularizing and return to adult-like competence (the right tail of the "U").

One explanation for the initial two stages of the process is as follows: Children first acquire all of the past-tense forms through rote memory; they record that the past tense of "walk" is "walked" and the past tense of "break" is "broke." At this early stage there is no psychological difference between the two classes of past-tense verbs, neither is "regular" or "irregular." The onset of the second stage is when children determine that there is a productive rule at work (add the suffix "-ed" to form the past tense). Children start to overapply this rule, producing forms such as "breaked" and "goed."

But what causes children to stop overregularizing and return to adult performance? One logical possibility is negative evidence—perhaps children receive some sort of punishment or feedback whenever they produce such forms and use this feedback to expunge these overregularizations from their lexicons. But negative evidence does not appear to exist (see "Input to language development" above), and in particular, no investigator has found that children get differential feedback for their usage of verb morphology (Marcus, in press).

The second logical possibility is that children and adults are "conservative"; unless they hear an adult use a form, they will reject it as ungrammatical. But this is demonstrably false. As the Berko (1958) study shows, children (and adults) are willing to use past-tense forms that they have never heard before. Furthermore, if children are conservative, why do they overgeneralize in the first place?

Perhaps the most promising source of explanation has to do with some sort of "blocking" or "elsewhere" condition (Aronoff, 1976; Kiparsky, 1982; Pinker, 1984). Such a condition prohibits the application of a rule that would produce an item that already exists in the lexicon.[4] Thus the past-tense form "goed" is blocked by "went," and the plural form "mans" is blocked by "men." The same sort of blocking can apply to the output of semantic rules; "gooder" sounds worse than "nicer" because "gooder" is blocked by the pre-existing lexical form "better," while nothing blocks "nicer." Clark (1987) argues that this can be derived from the principles of contrast and conventionality (see "Constraints on word meaning" above), but see Marcus *et al.* (1992) for a critical discussion of this.

Assuming that children possess such a principle, the solution may go as follows (e.g., Pinker, 1984): Children start off acquiring all past-terms forms by rote, then induce the "-ed" rule. Overapplication of this rule leads to overregularization. But as irregular forms such as "broke" and "went" are reintroduced into the lexicon, they block the application of the past-tense rule and the child stops overregularizing.

There are problems with this analysis, however (Gathercole, 1987; Marcus *et al.*, 1992). First, why would a child overregularize in the first place? Given that she initially has the word "went" encoded as the past-tense of "go," one would expect blocking or contrast to keep her from using "goed"—but it does not. Second, the blocking theory predicts that there should be no period where the child uses both "goed" and "went" at the same time. But this is false; irregular past tenses and overregularizations co-exist for years in children's lexicons (e.g., Cazden, 1968).

One defense of the blocking theory is that children might not know that "broke" is the past-tense form of "break." Thus children's productive use of "breaked" as a past tense of "break" would not violate contrast or blocking. Only once children come to realize that the adult form "broke" is synonymous with their rule-generated form "breaked" will they expunge "breaked" from their lexicon—and this process might take years (Clark, 1988, 1990).

This discussion of overregularization is based on certain premises—children possess a rule, they go through a stage where they believe that certain irregulars have "-ed" past tenses, and they need to recover from these errors. The theories discussed below challenge these assumptions and suggest radically different explanations for children's errors.

Alternative conceptualizations

Since the earliest discussion of overregularization, the competence involved has been described as an implicit rule—add "-ed" to form the past tense—and children's errors are assumed to result from overapplication of this rule. One might think that this is the only type of explanation possible. But parallel distributed processing (PDP) or connectionist models provide an alternative to this sort of theory.

Under one connectionist analysis, the capacity to determine the past-tense form of a verb stem is acquired through an associative network which can extract statistical regularities from the environment. Rumelhart and McClelland (1986) provide an explicit computer model that succeeds in capturing certain core properties of children's behavior—without positing any internalized rules, or any distinction between regular verbs and irregular verbs. The model works by being "trained" on correspondences between the phonological patterns of verb stems and phonological patterns of the past-tense forms; these are represented by activation patterns of pools of units which are linked up in parallel to other units. After training is complete, the network will produce a string of output patterns corresponding to "walked" when presented with the input "walk" and patterns corresponding to "went" when presented with the input "go." Further, the development of the model appears to capture the U-shaped curve; early in learning, the model performs correctly, then it overregularizes, then it returns to correct behavior. Rumelhart and McClelland (1986: 267) conclude: "We have shown that a reasonable account of the acquisition of past tense can be provided without recourse to the notion of a 'rule' as anything more than a *description* of the language."

This model has been the subject of considerable critical discussion, most notably from Pinker and Prince (1988, 1991). Two criticisms are worth noting. First, Pinker and Prince argue that treating the morphological alteration as a mapping from different phonological forms is psychologically incorrect. They argue that a past-tense rule applies to the verb stem (which is stored in the lexicon) and not to the sound of the verb. For instance, "ring" and "wring" have the same sound, but they are different stems and thus have different past tense forms: "rang" and "wrung." Similarly, the past tense form of "go" is "went" but if one coins a new stem with the same sound but derived from a name—for instance, a verb "Go" which means to play the Japanese game of "Go" against someone—it does not inherit the irregular morphology of its homophonic form. One would say "He Go-ed six opponents during last week's competition," not "He went six opponents during the competition." In general, verbs derived from other parts of speech are subject to the regular rule, regardless of their sound or meaning.

Pinker and Prince argue that the past-tense rule is a universal default, and applies to any form not lexically marked as having an irregular past tense. They further suggest that to capture this property of language in a PDP network would require explicitly wiring up such a model to encode rules; in other words, it would have to implement a symbolic system (for discussion, see also Lachner and Bever, 1988; MacWhinney and Leinbach, 1991; Marcus *et al.*, 1992; Pinker, 1991).

A second criticism is that the Rumelhart and McClelland model succeeds in capturing the U-shaped curve only through unrealistic assumptions about the input. In particular, Rumelhart and McClelland started by first feeding their model a much higher proportion of irregular verbs than regular verbs and then following this with a set of verbs where the proportion of irregular verbs was much smaller. The motivation for this training procedure is that irregulars tend to be high frequency and thus one might expect them to be learned first by children. In an analysis of child speech, however, Pinker and Prince (1988) found that the ratio of irregular to regular verbs does not change at the period when children start to overregularize. Therefore the connectionist model would not adequately predict the outcome of the actual conditions of language development. More generally, Pinker and Prince argue that the onset of overregularization is not predicted by any properties of the input, but instead corresponds to the point at which children learn the regular rule of English (see also Marcus *et al.*, 1992).

The import of these criticisms is a matter of some debate; some scholars have argued that the problems are special to the particular model advanced by Rumelhart and McClelland but that other implementations can cope with them (e.g., MacWhinney and Leinbach, 1991; Plunkett and Marchman, 1991); others suggest that the problems are endemic to all models that lack a rule-based component (e.g., Lachner and Bever, 1988; Pinker and Prince, 1988, 1991).

Some recent results from Marcus *et al.* (1992) support a rule-based theory of children's overgeneralizations. Despite a long-standing interest in over-generalization by acquisition theorists, some basic facts were unknown. In particular, Marcus *et al.* noted that there existed only crude estimates of how frequently children overregularize. Using the CHILDES database (MacWhinney and Snow, 1985), they analyzed the spontaneous speech of eighty-three children. Their main result was that overgeneralization errors were strikingly rare—the median rate of error was an error rate of 2.5 percent. They *do* find a U-shaped curve, however: Children go through an extended period of correct usage before their first error, then errors start to occur, and later decrease in adulthood.

The low rate of errors supports the following account (see also MacWhinney, 1978): Regular past tenses are produced by a rule, whereas irregulars are stored in associative memory. When children and adults have an irregular form stored in memory, blocking stops the regular rule from applying, and thus forms such as "goed" and "runned" are unacceptable. Children overregularize because their memory trace for past-tense forms is not strong enough to guarantee perfect retrieval, and when a child fails to retrieve an irregular such as "went," the regular rule is applied, producing "goed." This is supported by the fact that the more often parents use a given irregular verb—and thus the stronger the memory encoding by the child—the less likely a child is to overregularize this verb.

Under this view, overgeneralizations are speech errors, no different in kind from those occasionally made by adults. The only developmental transition that must be explained is how children acquire the "-ed" rule in the first place; Marcus *et al.* (1992) present some hypotheses, but there is as yet no definitive account.

The controversy over the cause of these errors will continue; the question of whether or not a past-tense "rule" exists relates to the more general debate over the potential of PDP modeling as a theory of human cognition. But the existence of large-scale analyses of past-tense errors and the use of computational models to test specific hypotheses have considerably sharpened this controversy. Unlike problems such as the acquisition of word meanings or the nature of parametric change, it might not be unreasonable to expect this very specific issue—why do children overregularize and why do they stop?—to be resolved within some of our lifetimes.

Overregularization of semantic alternations

Not all of the research into overgeneralization concerns morphological phenomena such as past-tense marking. One of the most extensively studied areas in linguistics and language acquisition focuses on the different syntactic contexts in which verbs can appear. The examples below show the alternation between active and passive, the dative alternation, and the causative alternation; for a comprehensive review, see Pinker (1989b).

> *Passive*
> Joan likes Mary/
> Mary is liked by Joan
> Joan stole the money/
> The money was stolen by Joan
>
> *Dative*
> Fred sent a package to Igor/
> Fred sent Igor a package
> Fred told a story to Igor/
> Fred told Igor a story
>
> *Causative*
> The glass broke/
> Bill broke the glass
> The baby burped/
> Bill burped the baby

One intriguing property of these alternations is that not all verbs can participate in them. The examples below are cases where the alternation does not hold.

> *Passive*
> Joan weighs 100 pounds/
> *100 pounds is weighed by Joan
>
> *Dative*
> Fred reported the story to the newspaper/
> *Fred reported the newspaper the story
>
> *Causative*
> The baby cried/
> *Bill cried the baby

These exceptions pose a puzzle for theories of language acquisition, one first noted by Baker (1979). Consider the following three claims. First, children are *productive*. For instance, even if they never heard "burped" in the causative form, they could say "Bill burped the baby." Second, children receive *no negative evidence*. Thus if they produce a sentence such as "Bill cried the baby," there exists no external input that could inform them of their error. Third, the exceptions are *arbitrary*. There is no reason why "burp" can appear in the causative form but "cry" cannot, or why "told" can appear in the dative form, while "reported" cannot.

At least one of these three claims must be false; if they were all true, there would be no way for children (or adults) to come to understand that sentences such as "Bill cried the baby" or "100 pounds was weighed by Joan" are ungrammatical. By virtue of being productive, children will produce such utterances, there would be no feedback informing them that these sentences are ill-formed (no negative evidence), and there would be no way for them to infer that these verbs should not appear in these contexts (arbitrariness). Given that we do reject sentences such as those above, this suggests that one of the three claims must be false.

Negative evidence does not exist, and since children do appear to be productive (see below), the only alternative is to reject the arbitrariness claim. Thus the reason why we accept some verbs in these alternations and reject others is because we possess criteria as to which verbs can appear in which syntactic context, and can apply these criteria in a productive manner.

More generally, it is argued that the conditions on verb usage reflect the way the components of grammar interact with each other and with conceptual structure. For instance, the causative alternation is often argued to require "direct causation," and the reason why "burp" can participate in this alternation and "cried" cannot is that we construe burping a baby as being direct and causing a baby to cry as indirect. This condition on causative usage is itself derived from more basic syntax–semantics mappings, sometimes called "linking rules." Pinker (1989b) provides an extensive theory of the nature of linking rules and how they can resolve Baker's paradox; see Bowerman (1990) for a critical discussion, and Gropen *et al.* (1991) for a reply.

How do we know children can productively use verbs in different syntactic contexts? One source of evidence is experimental; when taught novel verbs, young children are capable of productively using them in different syntactic contexts. For instance, in one study, children were shown a pig doing a headstand and told "The pig is pilking." They were then shown a bear causing a tiger to do a headstand and asked "What's the bear doing?" Children would often say "Pilking the tiger," showing that they are capable of productively using novel verbs in the causative form. Similar studies have been done for other verb alterations, such as the passive and the dative. For all of these, children are not only capable of productivity; they also appear to have some understanding of the semantic restrictions on which verbs can and cannot appear in these contexts (see Gropen *et al.*, 1989; Gropen *et al.*, 1991; Pinker, Lebeaux, and Frost, 1987; see Pinker, 1989b for a review).

Furthermore, just as with past-tense morphology, children appear to overgeneralize the semantic alternations. Bowerman (1982) gives examples of causatives produced by her daughters from the ages of 2 to 10 that are unacceptable for adults; these include:

> You sad me [= make me sad]
> Mommy, can you stay this open? [= make it stay]
> I'm singing him [= making him sing]
> Who deaded my kitty cat? [= made dead]
> This one always sweaties me [= makes me sweat]
> Don't giggle me [= make me giggle]

The existence of these errors is further evidence for productivity, but it also motivates a theory of why children overextend these semantic rules and what causes them to stop.

As with morphology, blocking or contrast is likely to play some role. For instance, it is likely that the reason why "dead" cannot be causativized for adults is that the existing English verb "kill" blocks the alternation. The child who asked "Who deaded my kitty cat?" might either not know the verb "killed" or could be failing to retrieve it from memory.

But this cannot be the whole explanation. There is no existing English verb that means "make giggle," yet "Don't giggle me" is still unacceptable for adults. Thus the theories advanced by Clark (1987) and Marcus *et al.* (1992) cannot apply. Why then would children produce such an utterance? It could be that they have not yet completely acquired the relevant semantic restrictions on the use of the causative (Bowerman, 1982; Mazurkewich and White, 1984). Alternatively, such errors might be due to children's different understanding of the pragmatic conditions under which one could violate or stretch the semantic rules (Pinker, 1989b). Given that these types of errors occur late in development, the discovery of what makes them go away could enlighten us as to the very final steps of grammatical development.

Conclusion

The review above constitutes just a small sample of current research in language acquisition. Other areas include (to choose almost at random) the role of spatial cognition in the acquisition of nouns and prepositions (e.g., Landau and Jackendoff, in press), children's understanding of conditions on pronoun interpretation (e g., Grimshaw and Rosen, 1990), and the infant's capacity to attend to the relevant object or situation in the course of acquiring a new word (e.g., Baldwin, 1991)—not to mention all of the research concerning the acquisition of phonology or the development of pragmatic knowledge and discourse skills.

These areas are sufficiently diverse that few scholars are optimistic about the prospects of coming up with "a theory of language acquisition." The type of theory required for how children come to understand language-specific properties of wh-questions is likely to be quite different from the appropriate theory of how they learn the meaning of "cup," and both will differ from an account of how children come to obey turn-taking conventions in conversation.

These different domains of study do share some important properties, however, and these can explain why the study of language acquisition has intrigued scholars from so many fields. For one thing, the acquisition of complex linguistic structure on the basis of impoverished input poses puzzles of a theoretical depth rarely found in psychology, but at the same time these puzzles admit of direct empirical tests of the sort not usually applicable in linguistics and philosophy. More important, despite the often painfully specific character of acquisition problems (how do children learn that "goed" is not the past tense of "go"? how do they learn that "garments" is a count noun, but "clothing" is a mass noun?) there is the intuition that the study of these problems will provide insights into issues that concern all cognitive scientists: the nature of language and meaning, the mechanisms of developmental change, and the architecture of the mind.

Acknowledgments

I thank Andrew Barss, Felice Bedford, Laura Conway, Morton Ann Gernsbacher, Gary Marcus, Steven Pinker, Nancy Soja, and Karen Wynn for very helpful comments on an earlier version of this paper.

Notes to "Overview"

1. One recent theory explains the lack of closed-class morphemes in telegraphic speech as the result of young children's inability to represent these morphemes as part of their linguistic repertoire (e.g., Guilfoyle and Noonan, 1989; Radford, 1990a, 1990b). It is proposed that children start off with grammars that encode only open-class categories (nouns, verbs, adjectives) and then, perhaps through neural maturation, the capacity to have a full-fledged grammar emerges. One problem with this proposal is that this property of early child language is not universal. In languages where closed-class morphemes are stressed and syllabic, closed-class morphemes appear in children's speech prior to the age of 2, at the point when children acquiring English are barely combining nouns and verbs (see Aksu-Koc and Slobin, 1985 on Turkish; and Pye, 1983 on Quiché Mayan). In addition, children acquiring English comprehend closed-class morphemes long before they are capable of producing them (e.g., Gerken, 1987), which undermines any grammatical theory of the "telegraphic" nature of children's early utterances.

2. One particularly interesting set of studies has focused on children who have created their own gestural communication system ("home-sign") in the absence of exposure to a target language (see Goldin-Meadow and Mylander, 1990 for a review). To the extent that these systems possess the same syntactic and semantic properties of natural language, these studies suggest that, in the limit, input may actually be unnecessary for language development. Studies of "creolization," which is the process through which a rudimentary communication system (a pidgin) gets transformed into a full-blown language (a creole), are also relevant in this regard (see Bickerton, 1984).

3. I am grateful to Steven Pinker for discussion of this issue.

4. Why does blocking exist at all? One could imagine an alternative system where the presence of a rule precludes the use of a rote form, instead of vice versa. Thus "went" would be unacceptable because of the existence of "goed" and there would be no irregulars at all.

One possibility (discussed in Pinker and Bloom, 1990) is that blocking has a functional explanation. For virtually any system with productive rules, there will be cases where it is unclear which rule to apply or how to apply it. For instance, many languages encode words that denote kinds of individuals as being count nouns (e.g., "a dog"), and words that denote kinds of portions as mass nouns (e.g., "much water"); and this rule can be productively applied by children and adults (P. Bloom, in press b). But there are indeterminate cases, such as peas, where it is cognitively unclear whether to encode it as a kind of individual or a kind of portion. As a result, the categorization of such cases within a given language is arbitrary; in some languages, "pea" is a count noun; in others, it is a mass noun. Children must be equipped so that these arbitrary choices override their own biases in how to apply productive rules; even if a child acquiring English finds it more sensible to view "pea" as denoting a kind of portion (and would, in the absence of input, encode it as a mass noun), she must acquire it as a count noun, because this is how it is encoded in English, and she must speak the same language as the rest of the community. The clearest case of the need for arbitrary convention to override individual preference is in the case of names. There is no *logical* reason to describe dogs as "dogs" and not as "cats," but given that this is how everyone else does it, children must be predisposed to acquire this arbitrary sound and to prefer it over their own inventions.

In general, some bias to favor rote-over-rule might evolve in any domain where there are (i) rules that generate novel forms; (ii) instances where it is unclear how to apply these rules, and (iii) the requirement of social conformity (i.e., everyone within a community must use the same form). If so, one might expect to find mechanisms similar to blocking in other cognitive structures that satisfy these criteria.

References to "Overview"

Aksu-Koc, A. A. and Slobin, D. I. (1985). "The acquisition of Turkish." in D. I. Slobin (ed.), *The Crosslinguistic Study of Language Acquisition, Volume 1: The data.* Hillsdale, NJ: Erlbaum.

Anderson, J. R. (1983). *The Architecture of Cognition.* Cambridge, MA: Harvard University Press.

Aronoff, M. (1976). *Word Formation in Generative Grammar.* Cambridge, MA: MIT Press.

Bach, E. (1986). "The algebra of events." *Linguistics and Philosophy,* **9**, 5–16.

Backscheider, A. and Markman, E. M. (1990). "Young children's use of taxonomic assumptions to constrain word meanings." Unpublished manuscript, Stanford University.

Baker, C. L. (1979). "Syntactic theory and the projection problem." *Linguistic Inquiry,* **10**, 533–81.

Baldwin, D. A. (1989). "Priorities in children's expectations about object label reference: Form over color." *Child Development,* **60**, 1291–306.

Baldwin, D. A. (1991). "Infant contributions to the achievement of joint reference." *Child Development,* **62**, 875–90.

Barrett, M. D. (1986). "Early semantic representations and early word-usage." In S. A. Kuczaj II and M. D. Barrett (eds), *The Development of Word Meaning: Progress in cognitive development research.* New York: Springer-Verlag.

Bates, E. (1976). *Language and Context.* New York: Academic Press.

Bates, E., Bretherton, I., and Snyder, L. (1988). *From First Words to Grammar: Individual differences and dissociable mechanisms.* Cambridge: Cambridge University Press.

Behrend, D. A. (1990). "Constraints and development: A reply to Nelson (1988)." *Cognitive Development*, **5**, 313–30.

Berko, J. (1958). "The child's learning of English morphology." *Word*, **14**, 150–77.

Berwick, R. C. (1982). *Locality Principles and the Acquisition of Syntactic Knowledge.* Doctoral dissertation. MIT.

Berwick, R. C. (1985). *The Acquisition of Syntactic Knowledge.* Cambridge, MA: MIT Press.

Bickerton, D. (1984). "The language bioprogram hypothesis." *Behavioral and Brain Sciences*, **7**, 173–212.

Bloom, L. (1970). *Language Development: Form and function in emerging grammars.* Cambridge, MA: MIT Press.

Bloom, L. (1973). *One Word at a Time: The use of single word utterances before syntax.* The Hague: Mouton.

Bloom, L. (1991). *Language Development from Two to Three.* Cambridge: Cambridge University Press.

Bloom, P. (1990a). "Subjectless sentences in child language." *Linguistic Inquiry*, **21**, 491–504.

Bloom, P. (1990b). "Syntactic distinctions in child language." *Journal of Child Language*, **17**, 343–55.

Bloom, P. (1993). "Grammatical continuity in language development: The case of subjectless sentences." *Linguistic Inquiry*.

Bloom, P. (in press a). "Possible names: The role of syntax–semantics mappings in the acquisition of nominals," *Lingua*.

Bloom, P. (in press b). "Semantic competence as an explanation for some transitions in language development." In Y. Levy (ed), *Other Children, Other Languages: Theoretical issues in language development.* Hillsdale, NJ: Erlbaum.

Bohanon, J. N., MacWhinney, B., and Snow, C. (1990). "No negative evidence revisited: Beyond learnability or who has to prove what to whom." *Developmental Psychology*, **26**, 221–6.

Bohanon, J. N. and Stanowicz, L. (1988). "The issue of negative evidence: Adult responses to children's language errors." *Developmental Psychology*, **24**, 684–9.

Bolinger, D. (1977). *Meaning and Form.* London: Longman.

Bowerman, M. (1973). *Early Syntactic Development.* Cambridge: Cambridge University Press.

Bowerman, M. (1976). "Semantic factors in the acquisition of rules for word use and sentence construction." In D. M. Morehead and A. E. Morehead (eds), *Normal and Deficient Child Language.* Baltimore, MD: University Park Press.

Bowerman, M. (1982). "Starting to talk worse: Clues to language acquisition from children's late speech errors." In S. Strauss (ed.), *U-Shaped Behavioral Growth.* New York: Academic Press.

Bowerman, M. (1990). "Mapping thematic roles onto syntactic functions: Are children helped by innate 'linking rules'?" *Journal of Linguistics*, **28**, 1253–89.

Braine, M. D. S. (1963). "On learning the grammatical order of words." *Psychological Review*, **70**, 323–48.

Braine, M. D. S. (1974). "Length constraints, reduction rules, and holophrastic phrases in children's word combinations." *Journal of Verbal Learning and Verbal Behavior*, **13**, 448–56.

Braine, M. D. S. (1976). "Children's first word combinations." *Monographs of the Society for Research in Child Development*, **41**.

Brown, R. (1957). "Linguistic determinism and the part of speech." *Journal of Abnormal and Social Psychology*, **55**, 1–5.

Brown, R. (1973). *A First Language: The early stages.* Cambridge, MA: Harvard University Press.

Brown, R. and Bellugi, U. (1964). "Three processes in the child's acquisition of syntax." In E. H. Lenneberg (ed.), *New Directions in the Study of Language.* Cambridge, MA: MIT Press.

Brown, R. and Fraser, C. (1963). "The acquisition of syntax." In C.N. Cofer and B. Musgrave (eds), *Verbal Behavior and Learning: Problems and processes.* New York: McGraw-Hill.

Brown, R. and Hanlon, C. (1970). "Derivational complexity and order of acquisition in child speech." In J. R. Hayes (ed.), *Cognition and the Development of Language.* New York: Wiley.

Bruner, J. S., Olver, R., and Greenfield, P. M. (eds) (1966). *Studies in Cognitive Growth.* New York: Wiley.

Bybee, J. L. and Slobin, D. I. (1982). "Rules and schemes in the development and use of the English tense." *Language*, **58**, 265–89.

Carey, S. (1978). "The child as word learner." In M. Halle, J. Bresnan, and A. Miller (eds), *Linguistic Theory and Psychological Reality* (pp. 264–93). Cambridge, MA: MIT Press.

Carey, S. (1982). "Semantic development: The state of the art." In E. Wanner and L. R. Gleitman (eds), *Language Acquisition: The state of the art*. New York: Cambridge University Press.

Carey, S. (1986). *Conceptual Change in Childhood*. Cambridge, MA: MIT Press.

Carey, S. (1988). "Conceptual differences between children and adults." *Mind and Language*, **3**, 167–81.

Cazden, C. B. (1968). "The acquisition of noun and verb inflections." *Child Development*, **39**, 433–48.

Chomsky, N. (1959). "A review of B. F. Skinner's Verbal Behavior." *Language*, **35**, 26–58.

Chomsky, N. (1964). "Formal discussion." In U. Bellugi and R. Brown (eds), "The acquisition of language." *Monographs of the Society for Research in Child Development*, **29**, 35–9.

Chomsky, N. (1980). *Rules and Representations*. New York: Columbia University Press.

Chomsky, N. (1981). *Lectures on Government and Binding*. Dordrecht: Foris.

Chomsky, N. (1986). *Knowledge of Language: Its nature, origin, and use*. New York: Praeger.

Clark, E. V. (1987). "The principle of contrast: A constraint on language acquisition." In B. MacWhinney (ed.), *Mechanisms of Language Acquisition*. Hillsdale, NJ: Erlbaum.

Clark, E. V. (1988). "On the logic of contrast." *Journal of Child Language*, **15**, 317–35.

Clark, E. V. (1990). "On the pragmatics of contrast." *Journal of Child Language*, **17**, 417–32.

Cooper, W. E. and Paccia-Cooper, J. (1980). *Syntax and Speech*. Cambridge, MA: Harvard University Press.

Crain, S. (1991). "Language acquisition in the absence of experience." *Behavioral and Brain Sciences*, **14**, 597–650.

Darwin, C. H. (1877). "A biographical sketch of a young child." *Kosmos*, **1**, 367–76.

Demetras, M. J., Post, K. N. and Snow, C. E. (1986). "Feedback to first language learning: The role of repetitions and clarification questions." *Journal of Child Language*, **13**, 275–92.

de Villiers, J. G. and de Villiers, P. A. (1973). "A cross-sectional study of the acquisition of grammatical morphemes in child speech." *Journal of Psycholinguistic Research*, **2**, 267–78.

de Villiers, J. G. and de Villiers, P. A. (1985). "The acquisition of English." In D. I. Slobin (ed.), *The Crosslinguistic Study of Language Acquisition, Volume 1: The data*. Hillsdale, NJ: Erlbaum.

Ervin, S. (1964). "Imitation and structural change in children's language." In E. H. Lenneberg (ed.), *New Directions in the Study of Language*. Cambridge, MA: MIT Press.

Feldman, H., Goldin-Meadow, S., and Gleitman, L. R. (1978). "Beyond Herodotus: The creation of language by linguistically deprived deaf children." In E. Lenneberg (ed.), *New Directions in the Study of Language*. Cambridge, MA: MIT Press.

Fernald, A. (1985). "Four-month-old infants prefer to listen to motherese." *Infant Behavior and Development*, **8**, 181–95.

Fernald, A. (1992). "Human maternal vocalizations to infants as biologically relevant signals: An evolutionary perspective." In J. J. Barkow, L. Cosmides, and J. Tooby (eds), *The Adapted Mind: Evolutionary psychology and the generation of culture*. Oxford: Oxford University Press.

Flynn, S. (1987). *A Parameter Setting Model of L2 Acquisition*. Dordrecht: Reidel.

Fodor, J. A. (1981). "The present status of the innateness controversy." In J. A. Fodor (ed.), *Representations*. Cambridge, MA: MIT Press.

Fodor, J. A. (1983). *Modularity of Mind*. Cambridge, MA: MIT Press.

Gathercole, V. C. (1986). "Evaluating competing theories with child language data: The case of the count–mass distinction." *Linguistics and Philosophy*, **6**, 151–90.

Gathercole, V. C. (1987). "The contrastive hypothesis for the acquisition of word meaning: A reconsideration of the theory." *Journal of Child Language*, **14**, 493–531.

Gathercole, V. C. (1989). "Contrast: A semantic constraint?" *Journal of Child Language*, **16**, 685–702.

Gelman, S. A. and Markman, E. M. (1985). "Implicit contrast in adjectives vs. nouns: Implications for word-learning in preschoolers." *Journal of Child Language*, **12**, 125–43.

Gelman, S. A. and Taylor, M. (1984). "How two-year-old children interpret proper and common names for unfamiliar objects." *Child Development*, **55**, 1535–40.

Gentner, D. (1982). "Why nouns are learned before verbs: Linguistic relativity versus natural partitioning." In S. A. Kuczaj II (ed.), *Language Development, Vol II: Language, thought, and culture*. Hillsdale, NJ: Erlbaum.

Gerken, L. A. (1987). "Telegraphic speech does not imply telegraphic listening." *Papers and Reports on Child Language Development*, **26**, 48–55.

Gerken, L. A. (1991). "The metrical basis for children's subjectless sentences." *Journal of Memory and Language*, **30**, 1–21.

Gerken, L. A. (1993). "Child phonology." In M. A. Gernsbacher (ed.), *Handbook of Psycholinguistics*. San Diego, CA: Academic Press;

Gleitman, H. (1991). *Psychology*. New York: Norton.

Gleitman, L. R. (1981). "Maturation determinants of language growth." *Cognition*, **10**, 103–14.

Gleitman, L. R. (1990). "The structural sources of word meaning." *Language Acquisition*, **1**, 3–55.

Gleitman, L. R. and Wanner, E. (1982). "Language acquisition: The state of the state of art." In E. Wanner and L. Gleitman (eds), *Language Acquisition: The state of the art*. Cambridge: Cambridge University Press.

Gold, E. M. (1967). "Language identification in the limit." *Information and Control*, **10**, 447–74.

Goldin-Meadow, S. and Mylander, C. (1990). "Beyond the input given: The child's role in the acquisition of language," *Language*, **66**, 323–55.

Golinkoff, R. M., Hirsh-Pasek, K., Lavallee, A., and Baduini, C. (1985). "What's in a word? The young child's predisposition to use lexical contrast." Paper presented at the Boston University Conference on Language Development, Boston, MA.

Goodman, N. (1983). *Fact, Fiction, and Forecast*. Cambridge, MA: Harvard University Press.

Gordon, P. (1982). *The Acquisition of Syntactic Categories: The case of the count/mass distinction*. Doctoral dissertation, MIT.

Gordon, P. (1985). "Evaluating the semantic categories hypothesis: The case of the count/mass distinction." *Cognition*, **20**, 209–42.

Gordon, P. (1988). "Count/mass category acquisition: Distributional distinctions in children's speech." *Journal of Child Language*, **15**, 109–28.

Gordon, P. (1990). "Learnability and feedback: A commentary on Bohanon and Stanowicz." *Developmental Psychology*, **26**, 217–20.

Grimshaw, J. (1981). "Form, function, and the language acquisition device." In C. L. Baker and J. McCarthy (eds), *The Logical Problem of Language Acquisition*. Cambridge, MA: MIT Press.

Grimshaw, J. and Pinker, S. (1989). "Positive and negative evidence in language acquisition." *Behavioral and Brain Sciences*, **12**, 341.

Grimshaw, J. and Rosen, S. T. (1990). "Knowledge and obedience: The developmental status of the binding theory." *Linguistic Inquiry*, **21**, 187–222.

Gropen, J., Pinker, S., Hollander, M., and Goldberg, R. (1991). "Affectedness and direct objects: The role of lexical semantics in the acquisition of verb argument structure." *Cognition*, **41**, 153–95.

Gropen, J., Pinker, S., Hollander, M., Goldberg, R., and Wilson, R. (1989). "The learnability and acquisition of the dative alternation in English." *Language*, **65**, 203–57.

Guilfoyle, E. and Noonan, M. (1989). "Functional categories and language acquisition." Unpublished manuscript, McGill University, Montreal

Heath, S. B. (1983). *Ways with Words*. Cambridge: Cambridge University Press.

Hirsh-Pasek, K., Gleitman, H., Gleitman, L. R., Golinkoff, R., and Naigles, L. (1988). "Syntactic bootstrapping: Evidence from comprehension." Paper presented at the Boston University Conference on Language Development, Boston, MA.

Hirsh-Pasek, K., Golinkoff, R., Fletcher, A., DeGaspe Beaubien, F., and Cauley, K. (1985). "In the beginning: One word speakers comprehend word order." Paper presented at Boston University Conference on Language Development, Boston.

Hirsh-Pasek, K., Kemler-Nelson, D. G., Jusczyk, P. K., Wright, K., and Druss, B. (1987). "Clauses are perceptual units for prelinguistic infants." *Cognition*, **26**, 269–86.

Hirsh-Pasek, K., Treiman, R., and Schneiderman, M. (1984). "Brown and Hanlon revisited: Mother's sensitivity to ungrammatical forms." *Journal of Child Language*, **11**, 81–8.

Huang, J. (1984). "On the distribution and reference of empty pronouns." *Linguistic Inquiry*, **15**, 531–47.

Hutchinson, J. E. (1984). *Constraints on Children's Implicit Hypotheses About Word Meanings*. Unpublished doctoral dissertation, Stanford University.

Huttenlocher, J. and Smiley, P. (1987). "Early word meanings: The case of object names". *Cognitive Psychology*, **19**, 63–89.

Hyams, N. (1986). *Language Acquisition and the Theory of Parameters*. Dordrecht: Reidel.

Hyams, N. (1989). "The null subject parameter in language acquisition." In O. Jaeggli and K. Safir (eds), *The Null Subject Parameter*. Dordrecht: Reidel.

Hyams, N. and Wexler, K. (1993). "On the grammatical basis of null subjects in child language," *Linguistic Inquiry*.

Inhelder, B. and Piaget, J. (1964). *The Early Growth of Logic in the Child*. New York: Norton.

Jackendoff, R. (1986). *Semantics and Cognition*. Cambridge, MA: MIT Press.

Jackendoff, R. (1990). *Semantic Structures*. Cambridge, MA: MIT Press.

Jackendoff, R. (1991). "Parts and boundaries." *Cognition*, **41**, 9–45.

Johnson, J. S. and Newport, E. L. (1989). "Critical period effects in second language learning: The influence of maturational state on the acquisition of English as a second language." *Cognitive Psychology*, **21**, 60–99.

Johnson, M. H., Dziurawiec, S., Ellis, H., and Morton, J. (1991). "Newborns' preferential tracking of face-like stimuli and its subsequent decline." *Cognition*, **40**, 1–19.

Karmiloff-Smith, A. (1979). *A Functional Approach to Language Acquisition*. New York: Cambridge University Press.

Katz, N., Baker, E., and Macnamara, J. (1974). "What's in a name? A study of how children learn common and proper names." *Child Development*, **45**, 469–73.

Keil, F. C. (1989). *Concepts, Kinds, and Cognitive Development*. Cambridge, MA: MIT Press.

Kim, J. J. (in press). "Null subjects: Comments on Valian (1990)." *Cognition*.

Kiparsky, P. (1982). *Explanation in Phonology*. Dordrecht: Foris.

Kuczaj, S. (1990). "Constraining constraint theories." *Cognitive Development*, **5**, 341–4.

Lachner, J. and Bever, T. (1988). "The relation between linguistic structure and associationist theories of language learning: A constructive critique of some connectionist learning models." *Cognition*, **28**, 195–247.

Lakoff, G. (1987). *Women, Fire, and Dangerous Things: What categories reveal about the mind*. Chicago: Chicago University Press.

Landau, B. and Gleitman, L. R. (1985). *Language and Experience*. Cambridge, MA: Harvard University Press.

Landau, B. and Jackendoff, R. (in press). "'What' and 'where' in spatial language and spatial cognition." *Behavioral and Brain Sciences*.

Landau, B., Jones, S., and Smith L. B. (1988). "The importance of shape in early lexical learning." *Cognitive Development*, **3**, 299–321.

Langacker, R. W. (1987). "Nouns and verbs." *Language*, **63**, 53–94.

Lebeaux, D. (1987). "Comments on Hyams." In T. Roeper and E. Williams (eds), *Parameter-setting*. Dordrecht: Reidel.

Levy, Y. (1988). "On the early learning of grammatical systems: Evidence from studies of the acquisition of gender and countability." *Journal of Child Language*, **15**, 179–86.

Lillo-Martin, D. (1987). "Parameters in the acquisition of American Sign Language." Paper presented at the Boston University Conference on Language Development, Boston, MA.

Lucariello, J. and Nelson, K. (1986). "Content effects on lexical specificity in maternal and child discourse." *Journal of Child Language*, **13**, 507–22.

Macnamara, J. (1972). "The cognitive basis of language learning in children." *Psychological Review*, **779**, 1–13.

Macnamara, J. (1982). *Names for Things: A study of human learning*. Cambridge, MA: MIT Press.

Macnamara, J. (1986). *A Border Dispute: The place of logic in psychology*. Cambridge, MA: MIT Press.

MacWhinney, B. (1978). "The acquisition of morphophonology." *Monographs of the Society for Research in Child Development*, **43**.

MacWhinney, B. and Leinbach, J. (1991). "Implementations are not conceptualizations: Revising the verb learning model." *Cognition*, **40**, 121–57.

MacWhinney, B. and Snow, C. E. (1985). "The Child Language Data Exchange System." *Journal of Child Language*, **12**, 271–96.

Manzini, R. and Wexler, K. (1987)."Parameters, binding theory, and learnability." *Linguistic Inquiry*, **18**, 413–44.

Maratsos, M. P. (1982). "The child's construction of grammatical categories." In E. Wanner and L. R. Gleitman (eds), *Language Acquisition: The state of the art*. Cambridge: Cambridge University Press.

Maratsos, M. P. (1983). "Some current issues in the study of the acquisition of grammar." In P. Mussen (ed.), *Carmichael's Handbook of Child Psychology*, J. H. Flavell and E. M. Markman (eds), *Volume III: Cognitive Development*. New York: John Wiley & Sons.

Maratsos, M. P. and Chalkley, M. (1981). "The internal language of children's syntax: The ontogenesis and representation of syntactic categories." In K. Nelson (ed.), *Children's Language*, Vol. 2. New York: Gardner Press.

Marcus, G. F. (in press). "Negative evidence in language acquisition." *Cognition*.

Marcus, G. F., Pinker, S., Ullman, M., Hollander, M., Rosen, T. J., and Xu, F. (1992). "Overgeneralization in language acquisition." *Monographs of the Society for Research in Child Development.*

Markman, E. M. (1981). "Two different principles of conceptual organization." In M. E. Lamb and A. L. Brown (eds), *Advances in Developmental Psychology*. Hillsdale, NJ: Erlbaum.

Markman, E. M. (1989). *Categorization and Naming in Children: Problems of induction*. Cambridge, MA: MIT Press.

Markman, E. M. (1990). "Constraints children place on word meanings." *Cognitive Science*, **14**, 57–77.

Markman, E. M. and Hutchinson, J. E. (1984). "Children's sensitivity to constraints in word meaning: Taxonomic versus thematic relations." *Cognitive Psychology*, **16**, 1–27.

Markman, E. M. and Wachtel, G. F. (1988). "Children's use of mutual exclusivity to constrain the meaning of words." *Cognitive Psychology*, **20**, 121–57.

Marler, P. (1991). "The instinct to learn." In S. Carey and R. Gelman (eds), *The Epigenesis of Mind: Essays on biology and cognition*. Hillsdale, NJ: Erlbaum.

Mazurkewich, I. and White, L. (1984). "The acquisition of the dative alternation: Unlearning overgeneralizations." *Cognition*, **16**, 261–83.

Mehler, J., Jusczyk, P. W., Lambertz, G., Halsted, N., Bertoncini, J., and Amiel-Tison, C. (1988). "A precursor of language acquisition in young infants." *Cognition*, **29**, 143–78.

Meier, R. P. and Newport, E. L. (1990). "Out of the hands of babes: On a possible sign advantage in language acquisition." *Language*, **66**, 1–23.

Menyuk, P. (1969). *Sentences Children Use*. Cambridge, MA: MIT Press.

Mervis, C. B. (1984). "Early lexical development: The contributions of mother and child." In C. Sophian (ed.), *Origins of Cognitive Skills*. Hillsdale, NJ: Erlbaum.

Miller, W. R. and Ervin, S. M. (1964). "The development of grammar in child language." In U. Bellugi and R. Brown (eds,), "The acquisition of language." *Monographs of the Society for Research in Child Development*, **29**, 9–39.

Morgan, J. L. (1986). *From Simple Input to Complex Grammar*. Cambridge, MA: MIT Press.

Morgan, J. L. and Travis, L. L. (1989). "Limits on negative information on language learning." *Journal of Child Language*, **16**, 531–52.

Naigles, L. (1990). "Children use syntax to learn verb meanings." *Journal of Child Language*, **17**, 357–74.

Nelson, K. (1973). "Structure and strategy in learning to talk." *Monographs of the Society for Research in Child Development*, **38**.

Nelson, K. (1985). *Making Sense: The acquisition of shared meaning*. New York: Academic.

Nelson, K. (1988). "Constraints on word meaning?" *Cognitive Development*, **3**, 221–46.

Nelson, K. (1990). "Comment on Behrend's 'Constraints and Development.'" *Cognitive Development*, **5**, 331–9.

Newport, E.L. (1991). "Contrasting concepts of the critical period for language." In S. Carey and R. Gelman (eds), *The Epigenesis of Mind: Essays on biology and cognition*. Hillsdale, NJ: Erlbaum.

Newport, E. L., Gleitman, H. R., and Gleitman, L. R. (1977). "Mother I'd rather do it myself: Some effects and non-effects of maternal speech style." In C. E. Snow and C. A. Ferguson (eds), *Talking to Children: Language input and acquisition*. Cambridge: Cambridge University Press.

Newport, E. L. and Meier, R. P. (1985). "The acquisition of American Sign Language." In D. I. Slobin (ed.), *The Crosslinguistic Study of Language Acquisition, Vol. 1: The data*. Hillsdale, NJ: Erlbaum.

Penner, S. (1987). "Parental responses to grammatical and ungrammatical child utterances." *Child Development*, **58**, 376–84.

Petitto, L. A. (1988). "'Language' in the pre-linguistic child." In F. S. Kessel (ed.), *The Development of Language and Language Researchers*. Hillsdale, NJ: Erlbaum.

Petitto, L. A. (in press). "Modularity and constraints in early lexical acquisition: Evidence from children's early language and gesture." *Minnesota Symposium on Child Psychology, Volume 25.*

Petitto, L. A. and Marentette, P. F. (1991). "Babbling in the manual mode: Evidence for the ontogeny of language." *Science*, **251**, 1493–6.

Pierce, A. (1987). "Null subjects in the acquisition of French." Paper presented at the Boston University Conference on Language Development, Boston, MA.

Pinker, S. (1979). "Formal models of language learning." *Cognition*, **7**, 217–83.

Pinker, S. (1984). *Language Learnability and Language Development*. Cambridge, MA: Harvard University Press.

Pinker, S. (1987). "The bootstrapping problem in language acquisition." In B. MacWhinney (ed.), *Mechanisms of Language Acquisition*. Hillsdale, NJ: Erlbaum.

Pinker, S. (1989a). "Language acquisition." In D. N. Osherson and H. Lasnik (eds), *An Invitation to Cognitive Science, Volume 1: Language*. Cambridge, MA: MIT Press.

Pinker, S. (1989b). *Learnability and Cognition*. Cambridge, MA: MIT Press.

Pinker, S. (1991). "Rules of language." *Science*, **253**, 530–5.

Pinker, S. (in press). "How could a child use verb syntax to learn verb semantics?" *Lingua*.

Pinker, S. and Bloom, P. (1990). "Natural language and natural selection." *Behavioral and Brain Sciences*, **13**, 707–84.

Pinker, S., Lebeaux, D. S., and Frost, L. A. (1987). "Productivity and constraints in the acquisition of the passive." *Cognition*, **26**, 195–267.

Pinker, S. and Prince, A. (1988). "On language and connectionism: Analysis of a Parallel Distributed model of language acquisition." *Cognition*, **28**, 73–193.

Pinker, S. and Prince, A. (1991). "Regular and irregular morphology and the psychological status of rules of grammar." *Proceedings of the 17th Annual Meeting of the Berkeley Linguistics Society*. Berkeley, CA: Berkeley Linguistics Society.

Plunkett, K. and Marchman, V. (1991). "U-shaped learning and frequency effects in a multi-layered perceptron: Implications for child language acquisition." *Cognition*, **38**, 43–102.

Pye, C. (1983). "Mayan telegraphese: Intonational determinants of inflectional development in Quiche Mayan." *Language*, **59**, 583–604.

Quine, W. V. O. (1960). *Word and Object*. Cambridge, MA: MIT Press.

Radford, A. (1990a). "The syntax of nominal arguments in early child English." *Language Acquisition*, **3**, 195–223.

Radford, A. (1990b). *Syntactic Theory and the Acquisition of English Syntax: The nature of early child grammars of English*. Oxford: Basil Blackwell.

Rescorla, L. (1980). "Overextension in early language development." *Journal of Child Language*, **7**, 321–35.

Rizzi, L. (1982). *Issues in Italian Syntax*. Dordrecht: Foris.

Roeper, T. (1973). "Connecting children's language and linguistic theory." In T. Moore (ed.), *Cognitive Development and the Acquisition of Language*. New York: Academic Press.

Roeper, T. and Weissenborn, J. (1990). "How to make parameters work: Comments on Valian." In I. Frazier and J. de Villiers (eds), *Language Processing and Language Acquisition*. Dordrecht: Kluwer.

Roeper, T. and Williams, E. (eds) (1987). *Parameter-setting*. Dordrecht: Reidel.

Rosch, E. (1973). "Natural categories." *Cognitive Psychology*, **4**, 328–50.

Rumelhart, D. E. and McClelland, J. L. (1986). "On learning the past tenses of English verbs." In J. L. McClelland and D. E. Rumelhart (eds), *Parallel Distributed Processing: Explorations in the microstructure of cognition, Volume 2: Psychological and biological models*. Cambridge, MA: MIT Press.

Schlesinger, I. M. (1971). "Production of utterances and language acquisition." In D. I. Slobin (ed.), *The Ontogenesis of Grammar*. New York: Academic Press.

Schlesinger, I. M. (1981). "Semantic Assimilation in the Acquisition of Relational Categories." In W. Deutsch (ed.), *The Child's Construction of Language*. New York: Academic Press.

Schlesinger, I. M. (1988). "The origin of relational categories." In Y. Levy, I. M. Schlesinger, and M. D. S. Braine (eds), *Categories and Processes in Language Acquisition*. Hillsdale, NJ: Erlbaum.

Soja, N. N. (1992). "Inferences about the meanings of nouns: The relationship between perception and syntax." *Cognitive Development*, **7**, 29–45.

Soja, N. N., Carey S., and Spelke, E. S. (1991). "Ontological categories guide young children's inductions of word meaning: Object terms and substance terms." *Cognition*, **38**, 179–211.

Talmy, L. (1985). "Lexicalization patterns: Semantic structure in lexical forms." In T. Shopen (ed.), *Language Typology and Syntactic Description. Vol. 3: Grammatical categories and the lexicon*. New York: Cambridge University Press.

Taylor, M. and Gelman, S. (1988). "Adjectives and nouns: Children's strategies for learning new words." *Child Development*, **59**, 411–19.

Valian, V. (1986). "Syntactic categories in the speech of young children." *Developmental Psychology*, **22**, 562–79.

Valian, V. (1990). "Null subjects: A problem for parameter-setting models of language acquisition." *Cognition*, **35**, 105–22.

Valian, V. (1991). "Syntactic subjects in the early speech of American and Italian children." *Cognition*, **40**, 21–81.

Vygotsky, L. (1962). *Thought and Language.* Cambridge, MA: MIT Press.

Waxman, S. (1990). "Linguistic biases and the establishment of conceptual hierarchies: Evidence from preschool children." *Cognitive Development*, **5**, 123–50.

Waxman, S. and Gelman, R. (1986). "Preschoolers' use of superordinate relations in classifications and language." *Cognitive Development*, **1**, 139–56.

Wellman, H. M. (1990). *The Child's Theory of Mind.* Cambridge, MA: MIT Press.

Wexler, K. and Culicover, P. (1980). *Formal Principles of Language Acquisition.* Cambridge, MA: MIT Press.

Wittgenstein, L. (1953). *Philosophical Investigations.* Oxford: Blackwell.

PART 1

The Onset of Language Development

Human Maternal Vocalizations to Infants as Biologically Relevant Signals:
An evolutionary perspective

Anne Fernald

When talking to infants, human mothers use vocal patterns that are unusual by the standards of normal conversation. Mothers, as well as fathers and adults who are not parents, speak consistently more slowly and with higher pitch when interacting with infants, in smooth, exaggerated intonation contours quite unlike the choppy and rapid-fire speech patterns used when addressing adults. To praise an infant, mothers typically use wide-range pitch contours with a rise-fall pattern. To elicit an infant's attention, they also use wide-range contours, but often ending with rising pitch. When soothing an infant, mothers tend to use long, smooth, falling pitch contours, in marked contrast to the short, sharp intonation patterns used in warning or disapproval. This use of exaggerated and stereotyped vocal patterns in mothers' speech to infants has been observed in numerous European, Asian, and African cultures and appears to be a universal human parental behavior.

Why do mothers make such sounds to infants? With other widespread human maternal behaviors such as nursing hungry infants and rocking distressed infants, the question "Why?' yields satisfying answers on both the proximal and ultimate levels specified by Tinbergen (1963). Nursing and rocking are understandable in terms of proximal physiological mechanisms functioning to provide nourishment and to regulate infant arousal, as well as in terms of species-typical parental strategies contributing to the survival and fitness of the offspring. Although hypotheses about the evolutionary history of particular human behaviors can always be disputed, the plausibility of ultimate explanations for such maternal actions as nursing and rocking is strengthened by compelling evidence for phylogenetic continuity. All mammals nurse their young, and almost all nonhuman primates carry their young, providing tactile and vestibular input known to have important short- and long-term regulatory effects on primate infant behavior. But ape and monkey mothers do not communicate vocally with their infants in ways that bear obvious resemblance to the melodic infant-directed speech of human mothers. Is there evidence that infant-directed speech, like nursing and rocking, is a human maternal behavior that has evolved to serve specific functions?

In this paper, I argue that the characteristic vocal melodies of human mothers' speech to infants are biologically relevant signals that have been shaped by natural selection. In the first section, I discuss the current debate about the status of human language as an evolved mechanism, as a way of examining criteria for when it is appropriate to invoke natural selection as a causal explanation for the evolution of human behavior. In particular, I examine the anti-adaptationist argument that language is an "exaptation" and therefore not a product of selection, as well as the argument that adaptive features must be designed for optimal efficiency. In the next two sections, the characteristics of mothers' speech to infants are described in some detail, along with research on the communicative functions of intonation in infant-directed speech. In the final sections, I examine infant-directed speech in the context of ethological research on vocal communication and maternal behavior in nonhuman primates, in order to identify selection pressures relevant to understanding the adaptive functions of human maternal speech.

The current debate on human language and natural selection

The question of whether language is a product of natural selection is a subject of lively current debate among philosophers and psycholinguists armed with arguments and counter-arguments from evolutionary biology. Given that we have no fossil record to document the origins and subsequent evolution of the language faculty, or any other complex behavioral capability, this question is likely never to be resolved.[1] However, the current debate has served to sharpen the focus on a number of issues fundamental to an understanding of human behavior within an evolutionary framework. This debate will be discussed in some detail here, since it is relevant to a central question in this paper. What kinds of evidence are needed to support the claim that a given human behavior reflects the influence of Darwinian natural selection? This lengthy preamble is necessary to set the stage for the subsequent discussion of the adaptive functions of human maternal speech.

Although officially banned by the Parisian Société de Linguistique in 1888, speculations on the origins of language became no less abundant or diverse as a result of this decree. In 1971, Hewes published a bibliography containing 2,600 titles of scholarly works on the topic, to which he had added another 2,500 references two years later (Hewes, 1973). Although controversy about the origins of language indeed goes back a long way, the current debate has been prompted by recent reformulations of neo-Darwinian theory within the field of biology. In two widely cited papers, Lewontin (1978) and Gould and Lewontin (1979) object to naive and inappropriate uses of the "adaptationist paradigm," which attempt to account for all characteristics of living organisms as optimal solutions to adaptive problems. Lewontin's (1979) objections, in particular, focus on the excesses of sociobiological theorizing in recent years. While sounding a valuable and timely warning about the dangers of superficial applications of evolutionary principles to the study of human behavior, these critiques of "naive adaptationism" have had an unfortunate backlash effect, contributing to widespread skepticism about the legitimacy of adaptationist reasoning at any level in relation to language and other human behavior.

Central to the anti-adaptationist argument are recent discussions by Gould and his colleagues about the role of adaptation in the emergence of evolutionary novelty. By drawing a comparison with the "spandrels" of St. Marcos, the triangular spaces formed by the intersection of arches supporting the dome of the cathedral, Gould and Lewontin (1979) make the point that apparently functional design elements can result entirely from architectural constraints. The art historian who concluded that these spandrels were the starting point, rather than a by-product, of the design would have made a serious mistake. By analogy, the conclusion that all biological forms have evolved as functional adaptations to local conditions also fails to take the nature of architectural constraints into account. In a later paper, such structural by-products are called "exaptations," defined as "characters, evolved for other usages (or for no function at all), and later 'coopted' for their current role" (Gould and Vrba, 1982: 6). As an example, Gould and Vrba cite Darwin's reference to unfused sutures in the skulls of young mammals, often viewed as an adaptation for facilitating passage of the neo-natal skull through the birth canal. As Darwin points out, however, young birds and reptiles, which emerge from shells rather than through birth canals, also have cranial sutures, suggesting that this structure "has arisen from the laws of growth, and has been taken advantage of in the parturition of the higher animals" (Darwin, 1859). Although these unfused sutures may be vitally necessary in mammalian parturition, they are regarded as exaptations rather than adaptations, since they are not explicitly designed by natural selection to serve their present function.

The claim that language is an exaptation, a side effect of the evolution of other cognitive faculties in humans, is a central point of contention in the current debate on the evolutionary status of language. Chomsky (e.g., 1972) and Piattelli-Palmarini (1989) argue that language emerged as a qualitatively new capacity in humans and may have arisen from non-adaptationist mechanisms. Such processes, which can act as alternatives to direct selection for the establishment of particular characteristics, include genetic drift, allometry, and pleiotropic gene action (Gould and Lewontin, 1979). The fact that the design of language is in many respects arbitrary and "nonoptimal" should count as further evidence for its nonadaptive origins, according to Piattelli-Palmarini. Objecting to the claim that language is an exaptation rather than an adaptation, Pinker and Bloom (1990) argue that grammar is an exquisitely complex, task-specific mechanism, not unlike other complex behavioral capabilities such as stereopsis and echolocation, which have clearly been shaped by natural selection. Two of the many interesting arguments offered by Pinker and Bloom in favor of viewing human language as a product of natural selection are particularly relevant to the concerns of this paper: first, that exaptations do not represent true alternatives to natural selection, but are in fact consistent with neo-Darwinian theory; and second, that the arbitrariness of language should not be interpreted as evidence against an adaptationist explanation.

Exaptations are not inconsistent with natural selection

Gould and Vrba (1982) introduced the term *exaptation* in order to clarify confusion surrounding the concept of adaptation. Some evolutionary biologists designate a feature as adaptive only if it was built by natural selection to perform its current function (e.g., Williams, 1966), while others prefer a broader definition that includes any feature currently enhancing fitness, regardless of its origin (e.g., Bock, 1980). Gould and Vrba object to this broad definition of adaptiveness, on the grounds that it conflates current utility with historical genesis and neglects features that are now useful but that may have evolved originally to serve other functions. The concept of exaptation was intended to fill this gap in the terminology of evolutionary biology and to highlight the neglected role of nonadaptive aspects of form in constraining evolution. By Gould and Vrba's definition, exaptations include new roles performed by old features, as in the mammalian cranial sutures noted by Darwin, as well as features that have become specialized to perform roles very different from the ones for which they originally evolved. As an example of this latter case, feathers were initially selected for insulation and not for flight. Legs in terrestrial animals are also exaptations rather than adaptations, since they evolved from lobed fins, which were used for swimming rather than for walking.

Gould and Vrba (1982) are careful to point out that the concept of exaptation is not anti-selectionist. On the contrary, they argue that their main theme is "cooptability for fitness," the process by which exaptations originate as nonadaptations, or as adaptations for another function, and then are refined by subsequent selection to perform a new role. While the limbs of salamanders, elephants, and humans indeed all arose from primordial fins, selective pressures, in the context of architectural constraints, have operated over millennia to adapt them further for efficiency in their current roles. Similarly, in the case of mammalian cranial sutures, a feature that evolved originally to accommodate skull growth in birds and reptiles became an exaptation for parturition in mammals. However, the design features of these sutures in mammalian skulls have presumably undergone complementary adaptation with features of the mammalian pelvic cavity, since otherwise parturition would be impossible. Since the evolution of all complex structures is fundamentally constrained by the characteristics of previously existing structures, as with fins and legs, the concept of exaptation does not represent a radical departure from the orthodox Darwinian account of adaptation. It could even be argued that all adaptations are in some sense exaptations, since the current functions of adaptive features inevitably differ to some extent from those of their Pliocene precursors.

Given the essential compatibility of the exaptation concept with traditional thinking about natural selection, it is surprising that it has been billed as central to a "new theory of evolution" by Piattelli-Palmarini (1989) and others. This allegedly new and better theory assumes "that full-blown evolutionary novelty can also suddenly arise, so to speak, for no reason, because novelty caused by sheer proximity between genes is not governed by function and it, therefore, eludes strict adaptationism" (Piattelli-Palmarini, 1989: 8). Pinker and Bloom argue that this account reflects a misunderstanding of biological principles. While novelty can indeed arise from nonadaptive features, it is utterly improbable that full-blown functional complexity will arise *de novo*, given that the design of complex biological structures necessarily derives from stepwise incremental modification of previously existing structures (e.g., Dawkins, 1986). The precursors to complex biological structures may emerge as exaptations, but it is only through subsequent natural selection that these structures achieve the complexity to perform their highly specialized roles.

Thus, even if the origin of linguistic competence in hominids lies in faculties initially serving other social and cognitive functions, human language has undoubtedly undergone subsequent adaptation for its specialized functions. Mammals may owe their legs to fins designed for swimming, not for walking, but the transitional evolutionary status of terrestrial fins as an exaptation obviously did not exempt mammalian limbs from the further influence of natural selection. This is an important point that has been lost in the anti-adaptationist arguments about language and selection. The earliest linguistic competence may indeed have been an exaptation, but one that was eventually "coopted for fitness," in Gould and Vrba's words. As such, we can acknowledge both its possible exaptive origins and its refinement by natural selection for its current specialized function. Piattelli-Palmarini recognizes that exaptations may "later on, happen to acquire some adaptive value," such that "selection for" takes place "on top of" a previous feature that emerged through nonadaptive processes (1989: 11). And yet he later emphatically asserts that "adaptive constraints have no role to play in a scientific approach to language and thought" (1989: 20), as if the acknowledgment of exaptive origins entails rejection of any role for natural selection in the subsequent evolution of language.

It is as important to avoid "naive exaptationism" as it is to guard against superficial adaptationist stories. To identify a feature as an exaptation does not mean that feature "is not the product of natural selection"—only that it did not always serve its present function. Indeed, most human behaviors serving biological functions that enhance fitness should probably be regarded as exaptations, modified through natural selection for subsequent specialization. The manual dexterity enabling specialized human hand movements now used in food gathering, eating, caretaking, tool use, and communication derives from the ability of prosimian ancestors to grasp branches. Human emotional expressions evolved from ritualized facial and vocal displays in other ancestral species, displays derived from behaviors that originally had no signaling function (Tinbergen, 1952). The use of stereotypical vocal patterns in human mothers' speech to infants is also undoubtedly an exaptation, with evolutionary origins in ancestral nonhuman primate vocalizations used for very different purposes. The claim that such human behaviors are exaptations rather than adaptations is a claim about origins, which does not require rejection of an adaptationist explanation for the current fit between these behaviors and the biological functions they serve.

Arbitrariness and nonoptimality are not incompatible with natural selection

A second issue addressed in Pinker and Bloom's (1990) critique of anti-adaptationist accounts of the evolution of language is whether evidence for arbitrariness in the design of natural languages should be interpreted as evidence against the formative role of natural selection. Piattelli-Palmarini argues that "adaptive constraints are typically insufficient to discriminate between real cases and an infinity of alternative, incompatible mechanisms and traits which, although abstractly compatible with the survival of a given species, are demonstrably absent" (1989: 19). Implicit here is the view that adaptationist arguments all rest on the Panglossian assumption of the best-of-all-possible worlds, i.e., that adaptations necessarily represent optimal solutions. As Pinker and Bloom point out, however, the idea that nature aspires to perfection was never taken seriously by modern evolutionary theorists. One reason is that trade-offs of utility among conflicting adaptive goals are inevitable and ubiquitous, because optimization for one function often compromises optimization for other concurrent functions. The gorgeous but unwieldy tail of the peacock is an obvious example. A second reason, discussed at length by Dawkins (1986), is that since evolution can exploit only existing variability and build only on existing structures, adaptations are fundamentally constrained by what is available. Thus Piattelli-Palmarini's argument that the absence of optimal design features constitutes evidence against natural selection in the evolution of language reflects a misconstrual of the adaptationist position.

The classic example of design optimization in nature is the vertebrate eye. Many evolutionary theorists have echoed Darwin in observing how elegantly the eye exemplifies adaptive engineering in the service of a well-specified function. Although several different types of eye have evolved among invertebrate species, a single basic type of image-forming eye prevails among vertebrates. The features of this basic design reflect constraints arising directly from the physical properties of light, such as the optics of lenses necessary to bend light rays in order to focus an image on the retina. Other design features reflect constraints imposed by particular environments during the course of evolution. For example, since the vertebrate eye initially evolved in water, it is sensitive only to a narrow band of wavelengths of electromagnetic radiation, the "spectrum of visible light," which is transmitted through water without significant attenuation (R. D. Fernald, 1988). Although all vertebrate eyes share this basic feature, they also differ impressively in structural details across species, reflecting the selective pressures of ecological conditions peculiar to the habitat and way of life of particular species. Nocturnal birds such as owls have retinas consisting largely of rods, sensitive to very low light levels, while birds requiring high acuity in bright sunlight, such as eagles and hawks, have retinas comprised primarily of cones. Such exquisite adaptations to specific ecological conditions, all relatively minor variations on the basic design scheme, make it clear why Darwin felt the eye to be an organ "of extreme perfection and complication," and why the eye is so often cited as a compelling example of the shaping and refinement of biological mechanisms through natural selection.

In the case of the vertebrate eye, the fact that many of the selective forces that have guided evolution are unchanging physical properties of the world accounts for the cross-species convergence on common design features that are clearly functional (see Shepard, 1992). Such "nonarbitrary" features are characteristic of all vertebrate sensory systems, as well as other biological systems strongly constrained by the physical nature of the environment. However Piattelli-Palmarini's (1989) suggestion that nonarbitrary design is the hallmark of *all* adaptive complexity misses an important distinction. While some adaptations enable animals to cope with relatively invariant aspects of the physical world, others have evolved to enable animals to interact successfully in the rapidly shifting social world. Just as in the case of sensory systems, adaptations for social interaction occur in response to environmental pressures. The critical difference is that in the evolution of social behavior, the "environment" includes not only the immutable laws of physics but also the more malleable behavior of conspecifics.

To the extent that the evolution of social behaviors is constrained by the perceptual predispositions and behavioral response tendencies of conspecifics, which are also subject to evolutionary change, the design features of social adaptations are intrinsically more "arbitrary" than those of the visual system.

In runaway sexual selection, for example, the aesthetic preferences of females act as a strong selective pressure for otherwise useless male adornments, such as extravagant tail plumage. Males also capitalize on preexisting female sensory biases, as in frog species in which female preferences for male calls can be predicted from properties of the female auditory system (Ryan *et al.*, 1990). In both cases, male characteristics have been shaped in an "arbitrary" fashion, in the sense that females could conceivably have developed different visual preferences or auditory tuning curves, resulting in different selective pressures and outcomes. Of course, the evolution of such male characteristics is not entirely negotiable, since the laws of physics must still be respected if otherwise arbitrary visual and vocal signals are to be effectively transmitted and received. The important point to be made here is that evolved mechanisms that provide an interface between an organism and the physical world are fundamentally more constrained than are mechanisms that evolve to coordinate interactions among conspecifics, as in communication systems. A communication system must be *shared* by conspecifics in order to function effectively, although adaptations for communication could be designed in diverse ways while still satisfying this basic requirement.

To summarize so far, the current debate on the evolution of human language (Piattelli-Palmarini. 1989; Pinker and Bloom, 1990) has focused attention on the more general question of when it is appropriate to invoke natural selection as a causal explanation for human behavior. Skepticism about the legitimacy of adaptationist reasoning has been fueled by the misleading claim that characteristics that qualify as exaptations rather than as adaptations are exempt from the process of natural selection. The argument made here is that the origin of a human behavior as an exaptation does not preclude the influence of natural selection in the subsequent refinement of that behavior for its current specialized function. A second misguided assumption in the anti-adaptationist position is that the presence of arbitrary design features provides evidence against evolution by natural selection. However, because social behaviors in general, and communicative behaviors in particular, evolve in response to relatively variable physiological and behavioral characteristics of conspecifics, they are free to be arbitrary in some respects, as long as they are shared by group members. Human maternal speech to infants will provide an example of an exaptation that emerged from vocal behaviors originally serving other functions in our primate ancestors and that has design features shaped by natural selection in the course of hominid evolution.

The prosodic characteristics of mothers' speech to infants

This section will focus on the acoustic characteristics of prosody in speech to infants in English and other languages. If the vocal modifications of infant-directed speech indeed serve important biological functions in early human development, as will be argued in subsequent sections, then the prosodic characteristics of caretakers' speech should exhibit similar features across diverse cultures. The cross-cultural universality of prosodic modifications in infant-directed vocalizations is crucial evidence for the claim that this special form of speech is a species-specific caretaking behavior.

Cross-language research on the prosody of infant-directed speech

Although research on parental speech to children focused initially on the simplified linguistic features typical of early language input (e.g., Snow and Ferguson, 1977), in the last decade there has been increasing interest in prosodic as well as linguistic features of child-directed speech. The use of high pitch and exaggerated intonation in speech to children had been widely observed by anthropologists and linguists in such diverse languages as Latvian (Ruke-Dravina, 1976), Japanese (Chew, 1969), Comanche (Ferguson, 1964), and Sinhala (Meegaskumbura, 1980). However, Garnica's (1977) spectrographic analysis of English speech to children provided the first systematic acoustic evidence for the reported prosodic modifications in mothers' speech. Garnica documented the higher mean fundamental frequency (F_0) and wider F_0 range in speech to 2-year-old children than in speech to adults, as well as the more frequent use of rising F_0 contours. In an acoustic analysis of German mothers' speech, Fernald and Simon (1984) found that even with newborns, mothers use higher mean F_0, wider F_0 excursions, longer pauses, shorter utterances, and more highly stereotyped F_0 contours than in speech to adults, as shown in Figure 1.1.1. Although the use of exaggerated F_0 contours and repetitiveness is a prominent feature of mothers' speech to infants throughout the first year of life, Stern, Spieker, Barnett, and MacKain (1983) found these prosodic features to be more pronounced in speech to four-month-old infants than in speech to younger or older infants.

The prosodic modifications most consistently observed in studies of American English (Garnica, 1977; Jacobson *et al.*, 1983; Stern *et al.*, 1983) and German (Fernald and Simon, 1984; Papousek, Papousek, and Haekel, 1987) include higher mean pitch, higher pitch maxima and minima, greater pitch variability, shorter vocalizations, and longer pauses. In a recent cross-language comparison of parental speech in French, Italian, Japanese, German, and British and American English, Fernald *et al.* (1989) found comparable prosodic modifications in speech to twelve-month-old infants across these six language groups. Furthermore, fathers as well as mothers altered their intonation when addressing infants in these languages, as shown in Figure 1.1.2. Similar prosodic features have also been reported in two studies of mothers' speech to

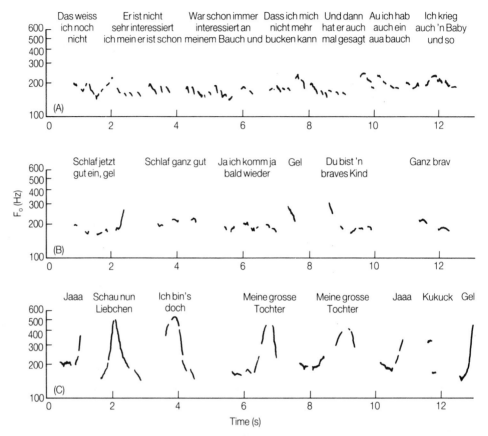

Figure 1.1.1 *Pitch contours from one subject in three conditions*: (a) *speech to adults (AD speech)*; (b) *speech addressed to absent infant (Simulated ID speech), and* (c) *speech to newborn infant, held in mother's arms (ID speech). Ordinate shows fundamental frequency (F₀) in hertz, plotted logarithmically. From "Expanded Intonation Contours in Mothers' Speech to Newborns" by A. Fernald and T. Simon, 1984,* Developmental Psychology, 20, *with permission of the American Psychological Association.*

infants in Mandarin Chinese (Grieser and Kuhl, 1988; Papousek, 1987). In the first systematic acoustic study of maternal speech in a nonindustrialized cultural group, Eisen and Fernald (in preparation) have found that Xhosa-speaking mothers in South Africa also use higher mean F_0 and exaggerated F_0 contours when interacting with infants.

While acoustic analyses of parental speech in different languages have revealed global prosodic modifications that are similar across cultures, there is also evidence for cultural variability. In both Japanese (Fernald *et al.*, 1989) and Mandarin Chinese (Papousek, 1987), mothers seem to show less expansion of pitch range compared with American and European samples, although the

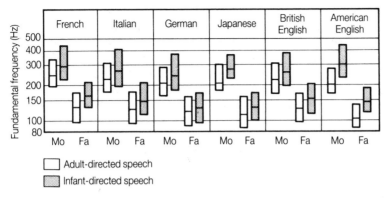

Figure 1.1.2 *Cross-language comparison of fundamental frequency (F$_0$) characteristics of mothers' (Mo) and fathers' (Fa) speech to adult and infants. For each bar, the bottom line represents the mean F$_0$ minimum, the top line represents the mean F$_0$ maximum, and the intersecting line represents the mean F$_0$ per utterance. The extent of the bar corresponds to the F$_0$ range. From A. Fernald, T. Taeschner, J. Dunn, M. Papousek, B. Boysson-Bardies, and I. Fukui, 1989,* Journal of Child Language, 16, *with permission of Cambridge University Press.*

differences are small and the findings inconsistent (see Grieser and Kuhl, 1988). Of the cultures studied so far, American middle-class parents show the most extreme prosodic modifications, differing significantly from other language groups in the magnitude of intonational exaggeration in infant-directed speech (Fernald *et al.*, 1989). These findings may reflect culture-specific "display rules" governing the public expression of emotion. While in middle-class American culture, emotional expressiveness is not only tolerated but expected, in Asian cultures exaggerated facial and vocal displays are considered less acceptable (Ekman, 1972). In any event, the variations across cultures in the prosody of speech to children reported to date are relatively minor, and the few reports of cultures in which no special infant-directed speech register is used (e.g., Ratner and Pye, 1984) are difficult to interpret (see Fernald *et al.*, 1989). The common pattern of results emerging from comparative research on parental speech is one of impressive consistency across cultures in the use of exaggerated intonation in speech to infants.

Relations between prosodic form and communicative function in mothers' speech

In addition to descriptive studies that focus on the global features of parental prosody, a few studies have begun to investigate the fine structure of infant-directed intonation in relation to particular contexts of interaction. The question of interest in this research is whether specific prosodic forms in mothers' speech are regularly associated with specific communicative intentions. In particular, do mothers use context-specific intonation patterns when involved in routine caretaking activities such as soothing or comforting, eliciting attention, expressing praise or approval, or prohibiting the infant? When soothing a distressed infant, for example, mothers are more likely to use low pitch and falling pitch contours than to use high, rising contours (Fernald, Kermanschachi and Lees, 1984; Papousek, Papousek, and Bornstein, 1985). When the mother's goal is to engage attention and elicit a response, however, rising pitch contours are more commonly used (Ferrier, 1985; Ryan, 1978). Bell-shaped pitch contours occur most frequently when the mother is attempting to maintain the infant's attention (Stern, Spieker and MacKain, 1982). These results, all based on observations of American middle-class mothers, suggest that maternal prosody is modulated in accordance with the infant's affective state and that mothers use intonation differentially to regulate infant arousal and attention.

Are these relations between prosodic form and communicative function universal across languages? Preliminary observations suggest that certain associations of relatively stereotyped intonation patterns with particular communicative intentions share striking similarities across cultures (Fernald, 1992). For example, Approval vocalizations in English, German, French, and Italian are typically high in mean F_0 and wide in F_0 range, with a prominent rise-fall F_0 contour, as shown in Figure 1.1.3. In contrast, Prohibition vocalizations in these languages are typically low in mean F_0 and narrow in F_0 range, as well as shorter, more intense, and more abrupt in onset. Comfort vocalizations, while similar to Prohibitions in low mean F_0 and narrow F_0 range, are longer, less intense, and softer in onset than Prohibitions. In musical terms, Comfort vocalizations have a smooth "legato" quality, in marked contrast to the sharp "staccato" quality of Prohibitions. It is important to note, however, that these stereotyped prosodic patterns are characterized not only by F_0 characteristics such as contour shape, as shown in Figure 1.1.3, but also by differences in amplitude envelope and spectral composition. Thus an adequate characterization of prosodic contour types will involve developing a taxonomy based on complex functions of graded changes along these multiple acoustic dimensions, research that is currently in progress. In the meantime, these initial observations suggest that across a variety of languages, common communicative intentions are associated with particular prosodic forms in maternal speech to preverbal infants.

What would account for this correspondence between characteristic patterns of prosodic features and specific motivational states? One explanation could be that these context-specific maternal vocalizations are essentially expressions of vocal affect, which are similar in form across cultures just as facial expressions are universal across cultures (Ekman, 1972). In research on universal features of vocal expressions, there is general agreement that adult listeners are fairly accurate in recognizing emotions from vocal cues, although there is less

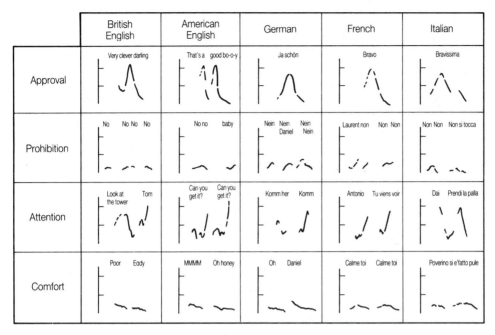

Figure 1.1.3 *Examples of pitch contours from Approval, Prohibition, Attention, and Comfort vocalizations in British, American, German, French, and Italian mothers' speech to twelve-month-old infants.*

consensus about which acoustic correlates differentiate among vocal expressions of different emotions (Scherer, 1986). However several studies indicate that increases in mean F_0 and F_0 range, are typical of vocal expressions of enjoyment and happiness, while decreases in mean F_0 and F_0 range, especially when accompanied by harsh voice quality, characterize expressions of irritation and anger. Scherer (1985, 1986) has proposed that these acoustic patterns are shaped by physiological and motor responses related to the underlying emotional state. Cosmides (1983) has stressed that consistent acoustic configurations in emotional expressions also yield important information about the speaker's intentions and motivations. A correspondence between particular vocal features and motivational states may even be general across different bird and mammal species. The biologist Morton (1977) found that high tonal sounds in animal repertoires are associated with fear, appeasement, or friendly approach, while low, harsh sounds are associated with threat. One interesting result consistent with such hypotheses is Tartter's (1980) finding that smiling while talking alters the shape of the human vocal tract, resulting in higher mean F_0. Whatever the underlying mechanisms influencing sound production, mothers' infant-directed approval vocalizations are high in mean F_0 and wide in F_0 range, prosodic features typical of happy vocal expressions, while prohibition vocalizations have prosodic features typical of angry expressions.

Although universal production constraints on vocal affect expressions undoubtedly do influence the sound patterns of maternal speech, the context-specific vocalizations illustrated in Figure 1.1.3 are not simply expressions indexing the mother's emotional or motivational state. While infant-directed praise vocalizations are positive in tone, and prohibitions are negative in tone, these vocalizations also have a strong *pragmatic* character. When the mother praises the infant, she uses her voice not only to express her own positive feelings, but also to reward and encourage the child. And whether or not the mother feels anger when producing a prohibition, she uses a sound well designed to interrupt and inhibit the child's behavior. Thus the exaggerated prosody of mothers' speech is used instrumentally to influence the child's behavior, as well as expressively, revealing information about the mother's feelings and motivational state. In this respect, the use of prosody in human maternal speech is similar to the use of vocal signals by some nonhuman primates, a proposal to be explored in later sections.

The descriptive findings on speech to human infants reviewed so far provide a foundation for the argument that the exaggerated prosodic patterns of infant-directed speech serve important developmental functions. The cross-linguistic data suggest that maternal vocalizations have common acoustic features that are potentially highly salient as auditory stimuli for the infant and that mothers tend to use specific prosodic patterns in particular contexts of interaction. However, such descriptive findings can provide only indirect support for claims about the communicative functions of prosody in early development. The next section will consider two additional kinds of relevant evidence, integrating research findings on the capabilities and predispositions of human infants with results from experimental studies directly testing hypotheses about the influence of maternal prosody on infant perception and behavior.

Communicative functions of intonation in infant-directed speech

Why do adults engage in such unusual vocal behavior, speaking in *glissandi* sometimes exceeding two octaves in pitch range, in the presence of a young infant? Early investigations of the influence of mothers' speech on infant development focused exclusively on syntactic and semantic features of language input in relation to children's language production (see Snow, 1977). This research was motivated by the hypothesis that the primary function of the special infant-directed speech style is to teach language to a linguistic novice. However, the fact that mothers quite consistently simplify their speech and use exaggerated intonation even when interacting with newborns, long before language learning is a central developmental issue, suggests that the modifications in infant-directed speech serve prelinguistic functions as well.

A model of multiple developmental functions of intonation in speech to infants over the first year of life is presented in Figure 1.1.4. According to this model, the characteristic prosodic patterns of mothers' speech serve initially to elicit infant attention, to modulate arousal and affect, and to communicate affective meaning. Only gradually, toward the end of the first year, does the prosody of mothers' speech begin to serve specifically linguistic functions, facilitating speech processing and comprehension. With its emphasis on the prelinguistic regulatory functions of intonation in mother–infant interaction, this model proposes biological predispositions rather than linguistic or cultural conventions as primary determinants of the use and effectiveness of exaggerated intonation in speech to infants. This model of the multiple developmental functions of infant-directed intonation will serve to organize support for the argument that human maternal speech is an adaptive mechanism. The claim that this special vocal behavior has been selected for in evolution requires

input driven

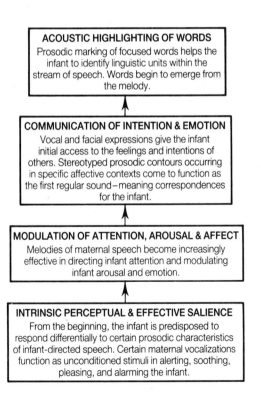

Figure 1.1.4 *Developmental functions of prosody in speech to infants.*

evidence on the proximal level that human maternal vocalizations have design features that are particularly advantageous in establishing communication with the young infant. This section will review the growing number of research findings demonstrating that the exaggerated melodies of mothers' speech are highly salient to young infants, influencing infant attention, arousal, emotion, and language comprehension.

The perceptual and affective salience of intonation in infant-directed speech

At birth, and probably even before birth, infants are attentive to prosodic cues in speech. Very young infants are able to make discriminations based on several prosodic parameters, including frequency (Wormith, Pankhurst, and Moffitt, 1975), intensity (Steinschneider, Lipton and Richmond, 1966), duration (Miller and Byrne, 1983), rise-time (Kearsley, 1973), and temporal pattern (Clarkson and Berg, 1983; Demany, McKenzie and Vurpillot, 1977). Newborns show a preference for their own mother's voice over another woman's voice (DeCasper and Fifer, 1980), an effect that is presumably due to prenatal familiarization. The recent finding that newborns can discriminate between speech samples spoken in their mother's native language and in an unfamiliar language, even when the stimuli are low-pass filtered (Mehler *et al.*, 1990), provides further evidence for the prenatal development of sensitivity to prosodic information in vocal signals.

The idea that the melodic intonation of mothers' speech is a prepotent stimulus for the human infant, effective at birth, was proposed half a century ago by Lewis (1936/1951). Lewis argued that "the voice at the outset is not a neutral stimulus; it possesses an affective character for the child—in other words, it evokes a response" (1936/1951: 52). This immediately compelling quality of maternal speech, because of its salient perceptual features and affective tone, underlies the most basic of the developmental functions of prosody shown in Figure 1.1.4. The claim that maternal intonation functions initially at this level assumes not only that prosodic features are discriminable by young infants, but also that they are qualitatively different in their effects on the infant. Several studies document such differential effects of prosodically varied auditory signals on infant behavior. For example, moderately intense sounds elicit cardiac deceleration, an orienting response, while signals higher in intensity elicit acceleration, a defensive reaction (Berg, 1975). Similarly, signals with a gradual rise-time in intensity elicit eye opening and orienting, while a more abrupt rise-time leads to eye closing and withdrawal (Kearsley, 1973).

In this sense, the characteristic infant-directed Prohibition vocalizations described earlier, high in intensity with an abrupt rise-time, function initially as *unconditioned* stimuli. That is, they elicit a defensive response from the infant that is directly attributable to acoustic rather than to linguistic features. Comfort sounds provide another example of maternal vocalizations that elicit unconditioned responses from young infants. Studies of acoustic signals most effective in soothing distressed infants have identified three types of sounds that reduce crying. First, low-frequency sounds are more effective than high-frequency sounds (Bench, 1969). Second, continuous sounds are more soothing than intermittent signals (Birns *et al.*, 1965). Third, white noise is particularly effective in soothing a crying infant (Watterson and Riccillo, 1983). When mothers use their voice to calm a distressed infant, they frequently incorporate all three of these acoustic features. Comfort vocalizations are typically low in pitch and continuous rather than intermittent. Mothers also intersperse these vocalizations with "shhh" sounds, which are similar to white noise (Fernald, Kermanschachi, and Lees, 1984). Thus, in both Comfort and Prohibition vocalizations addressed to infants, mothers quite intuitively exploit infants' innate predisposition to respond differentially to particular acoustic qualities of sounds.

Maternal intonation and infant attention

At the second level of the model shown in Figure 1.1.4, the prosody of mothers' speech functions with increasing effectiveness to engage infant attention and to modulate arousal and emotion. Over the first six months of life, the infant's visual capabilities and motor coordination improve dramatically (e.g., Aslin, 1987). By the age of three to four months, infants can recognize individual faces and orient to voices much more quickly and reliably than before. The appearance of the social smile, which is initially elicited most effectively by high-pitched voices (Wolff, 1963), is another landmark development around the age of two months. All of these new skills contribute to infants' growing ability to respond selectively and appropriately to the intonation of the mother's voice over the first few months.

The argument I am making here is not just that infants are responsive in general to prosody before they are responsive to linguistic structure in speech, but that the exaggerated intonation patterns of mothers' speech are *particularly* effective in eliciting attention and affect in very young infants. Supporting evidence comes from a number of auditory preference studies in which infants could listen either to typical adult-directed (AD) speech or to infant-directed (ID) speech (e.g., Friedlander, 1968). In a listening preference study with four-month-old infants, subjects were operantly conditioned to make a head turn to one side or the other in order to be rewarded with a short recorded segment of ID or AD speech, spoken by one of several unfamiliar women (Fernald, 1985). Infants made significantly more head turns to the side on which ID speech was available as a reinforcer. What was it about ID speech that was more appealing to infants? Since natural vocalizations were used as stimuli in this study, it was impossible to evaluate the role of any particular linguistic or acoustic feature in eliciting the infant preference. Although it could have been some prosodic characteristic of ID speech that was especially attractive to infants, it was also possible that the words themselves were more familiar in the ID speech samples.

To investigate the hypothesis that it was the prosody rather than the words of ID speech that elicited the infant listening preference, it was necessary to eliminate the lexical content of the natural speech stimuli and to isolate the three major acoustic features of intonation: fundamental frequency, amplitude, and duration. In three follow-up studies, we presented infants with synthesized signals derived from the F_0, amplitude, and temporal characteristics of the original natural speech stimuli (Fernald and Kuhl, 1987). Thus each of these experiments focused on a particular prosodic variable in the absence of phonetic variation. Our goal was to determine whether four-month-old infants, when given the choice between listening to auditory signals derived from the prosodic characteristics of either AD or ID speech, would show a listening preference for particular prosodic features of ID speech. We found a strong infant preference for the F_0 patterns of ID speech, but no preference for either the amplitude or duration patterns of ID speech. The results suggest that the F_0 characteristics of mothers' speech are highly salient and rewarding to infants and may account for the listening preference for natural ID speech found in the original Fernald (1985) study.

One interpretation of these findings is that infants are innately predisposed to pay attention to the acoustic characteristics of ID speech. However, the finding that the pitch contours of ID speech are sufficient to elicit the infant listening preference does not preclude an interpretation based on learning. By four months of age, infants have had a lifetime of experience with ID speech in association with many gratifying forms of caretaking and social interaction. It could be that four-month-old infants attend more to the pitch contours of ID speech because these melodies have become positively associated with nurturance. The recent findings of Cooper and Aslin (1990), however, suggest that early postnatal experience could not account entirely for the infant listening preference. Using a visual-fixation-based auditory preference procedure, Cooper and Aslin found that both newborns and one-month-old infants preferred ID over AD speech. Although there was a difference in the absolute magnitude of the ID speech preference between the two ages, there was no significant difference in the relative magnitude of the effect, suggesting that the listening preference was as strong in newborns as it was at one month of age. These findings indicate that the preference for the exaggerated prosody of ID speech is already present at birth and does not develop gradually with postnatal experience.

Research on this early listening preference has been extended in several interesting directions by Werker and McLeod (1989). Infants at four and eight months of age were shown video recordings of both male and female adults reciting identical scripts in ID and AD speech. Werker and McLeod included measures of both attentional preference and affective responsiveness in the two speech conditions. They found that infants at both ages attended longer to ID speech than to AD speech when spoken by either a male or a female. Furthermore, infants responded with significantly more positive affect to male and female ID speech than to AD speech. By demonstrating that the infant listening preference for ID speech extends to male voices, the results of this study suggest that the relatively high mean F_0 of the female voice is not the critical parameter in eliciting infant attention. Instead, it is probably the exaggerated F_0 modulation, within either the male or female F_0 range, that is the most engaging feature of ID speech.

The power of ID speech to engage infant attention has also been shown using a psychophysiological measure, in addition to the behavioral preference measures just described. In a study of infant cardiac orienting, we presented twenty-four four-month-old infants with vocalic sounds differing in pitch range. The stimuli consisted of repetitions of the monosyllable /a/, spoken with either the narrow F_0 range typical of AD speech or the wide F_0 range typical of ID speech, but identical in amplitude characteristics and duration. We found that infants showed reliably greater heart rate deceleration when listening to the wide-range pitch contours (Fernald and Clarkson, in preparation). These results provide convergent psychophysiological evidence of the differential attentional responsiveness of young infants to the exaggerated prosodic contours of ID speech.

Maternal intonation and infant emotion

The melodies of mothers' speech not only captivate attention, but also engage the infant emotionally. In *The First Relationship: Infant and mother*, Daniel Stern (1977) describes an interchange between a mother and her three-month-old son, halfway through a feeding session:

> His eyes locked on to hers, and together they held motionless for an instant. The infant did not return to sucking and his mother held frozen her slight expression of anticipation. This silent and almost motionless instant continued to hang until the mother suddenly shattered it by saying "Hey!" and simultaneously opening her eyes wider, raising her eyebrows further and throwing her head up and toward the infant. Almost simultaneously, the baby's eyes widened. His head tilted up and, as his smile broadened, the nipple fell out of his mouth. Now she said, "Well hello! ... heelló ... heeellóooo!", so that her pitch rose and the "hellos" became longer and more stressed on each successive repetition. With each phrase the baby expressed more pleasure, and his body resonated almost like a balloon being pumped up, filling a little more with each breath. (p. 3)

Anyone who has interacted intensively with a young infant knows the shared pleasure of such moments, and the power of the voice to modulate and sustain that pleasure. Such observations echo those of early investigators of mother–infant interaction who reported that young infants respond differentially to positive and negative affect in the voice (Bühler and Hetzer, 1928; Lewis, 1936/1951) and smile earlier to voices than to faces (Wolff, 1963). It is therefore surprising that recent research on infants' perception of emotional signals has focused almost exclusively on the face. In fact, the ability to recognize emotional facial expressions appears to develop rather slowly over the first year. Numerous studies of infants' discrimination and categorization of facial displays indicate that it is not until seven months of age that infants reliably recognize happy and angry facial expressions (see Nelson, 1987, for a review). Moreover, two recent studies of infants' perception of facial-plus-vocal displays (Caron, Caron, and Maclean, 1988; Werker and McLeod, 1989) suggest that in the first half year of life infants are more responsive to the voice than to the face.

In a recent series of experiments in our laboratory, we investigated infants' responsiveness to positive and negative vocalizations in unfamiliar languages as well as in English. This research was designed to address four questions: (a) Do young infants respond differentially to positive and negative affective expressions in the voice, at an age when they are not yet showing selective responsiveness to positive and negative affect in the face? (b) Do infants respond appropriately to vocal expressions differing in affective tone? (c) Are infants more responsive to affective vocalizations in ID speech than in AD speech? (d) Are infants responsive to affective vocalizations spoken in languages with which they are completely unfamiliar?

In an auditory preference procedure, infants were presented with Approval and Prohibition vocalizations, typical of those used by mothers when praising or scolding an infant. The subjects in these studies were five-month-old infants from monolingual English-speaking families. Each infant heard Approval and Prohibition vocalizations spoken in ID speech in German, Italian, or Japanese. English Approvals and Prohibitions were presented in both ID speech and AD speech. When listening to English, infants responded with differential and appropriate affect to these positive and negative vocal expressions in ID speech only. That is, they showed more positive affect to Approvals and more negative affect to Prohibitions in ID speech but not in AD speech. When listening to ID speech in German and Italian, infants also responded with differential and appropriate affect. In Japanese, however, infants listened with neutral affect to Approvals as well as to Prohibitions.

Why should American infants respond affectively to infant-directed Approval and Prohibition vocalizations in two unfamiliar European languages as well as in English, but not in Japanese? Although Japanese mothers elevate their pitch when speaking to infants, the pitch range used by Japanese mothers in ID speech is narrower than that used by European mothers (Fernald *et al.*, 1989). Japanese vocalizations may be more difficult for infants to distinguish. In fact, Japanese vocal expressions of emotion are difficult for European adults to interpret (Shimoda, Argyle, and Riccibitti, 1978), perhaps for the same reason.

If research on the auditory preferences of Japanese infants reveals that infants familiar with Japanese respond with appropriate affect to Approvals and Prohibitions in their language, this finding would suggest the early influence of cultural differences in mother–infant interaction. Perhaps five-month-old American infants are already accustomed to the wider pitch modulations and dynamic range characteristic of affective vocalizations in cultures encouraging emotional expressiveness, so that German and Italian are more "familiar" to them in terms of prosodic characteristics than is Japanese. Research in progress on the prosodic characteristics of Japanese mothers' speech and on the responsiveness of Japanese infants to Approval and Prohibition vocalizations in different languages will enable us to explore further these intriguing questions.

Four major findings emerge from these studies on infants' responsiveness to affective vocal expressions. First, at the age of five months, when infants are not yet showing consistent selective responsiveness to positive and negative facial expressions, infants do respond differentially to positive and negative vocal expressions, suggesting that the voice is more powerful than the face as a social signal in early infancy. Second, infants respond with appropriate affect to positive and negative vocal expressions, smiling more to Approvals than to Prohibitions. Third, infants are more responsive to affective vocalizations in ID speech than in AD speech, suggesting that the exaggerated prosodic characteristics of maternal vocalizations to infants increase their salience as vocal signals. And finally, young infants are responsive to affective vocalizations spoken with infant-directed prosody even in languages that they have never heard before, providing evidence for the functional equivalence of such ID vocalizations across cultures. These findings indicate that the melodies of mothers' speech are compelling auditory stimuli, which are particularly effective in eliciting emotion in preverbal infants.

The finding that American infants differentiate maternal vocalizations in some but not all languages suggests that cultural differences in the nature and extent of emotional expressiveness may also have an early influence on infants' responsiveness to vocal signals. A process of early cultural "calibration" might account for these cross-language differences. According to this explanation, infants in all cultures are initially responsive to the same vocal cues, in that they find smooth, wide-range pitch contours of moderate loudness to be pleasing, while they find low, narrow pitch contours that are short, staccato, and loud to be more aversive. However, cultural differences in display rules governing emotional expression may determine the levels and range of emotional intensity to which the infant is routinely exposed and which the infant comes to expect in social interaction with adults.

Maternal intonation and the communication of intention

At the third level of the model shown in Figure 1.1.4, infants gain access to the feelings and intentions of others through the intonation of infant-directed speech. That is, infants begin to learn to interpret the emotional states of others and to make predictions about the future actions of others, using information available in vocal and facial expressions. It is important to note that this third level of processing of vocal signals is quite different from the selective responsiveness of young infants to affective vocalizations described in the preceding section. When the five-month-old infant smiles to an Approval or startles to a Prohibition, the prosody of the mother's voice influences the infant directly. The infant's differential responses in no way presuppose an ability to decode the emotions expressed by the mother. Rather, the infant listens with pleasure to pleasant sounds and with displeasure to unpleasant sounds, without necessarily understanding anything about the affective states motivating the production of these vocalizations. Such maternal vocalizations are potent signals not because they inform the infant about the mother's emotional state, but because they directly induce emotion in the infant. Of course, since pleasant-sounding praise vocalizations are often accompanied by smiles and other indexes of positive affect, while negative vocalizations co-occur with other signs of negative affect, infants have ample opportunity to learn about the contexts of occurrence of particular vocal forms, reinforcing their positive and negative associations. The important distinction to be made here is that initially these characteristic vocal patterns influence the infant by virtue of their intrinsic acoustic features, strengthened through frequent association with other forms of affective input, although they are not yet appreciated as "cues" to the emotional state of the speaker.

Evidence that infants in the second half-year of life are developing the ability to read the emotional signals of others through facial and vocal expressions comes primarily from research on "social referencing." Klinnert, Campos, Sorce, Emde, and Svejda (1983) review several studies showing that infants around the age of eight months seek out and appropriately interpret emotional signals from adults, especially in situations of uncertainty for the infant. For example, when an eight-month-old infant is undecided as to whether to cross the visual cliff or to approach an ambiguous toy, the infant will look to the mother. If the mother responds with exaggerated facial and vocal signs of happiness, the infant will typically proceed; however, if the mother responds with exaggerated expressions of fear, the infant will withdraw. Unfortunately, the relative potency of facial and vocal cues in this situation has not been adequately investigated. Although the mother's facial expressions appear to be sufficient to regulate the infant's behavior, it is not yet known whether vocal cues are also sufficient (Klinnert *et al.*, 1983).

Another question that has yet to be addressed is whether infants in the social referencing paradigm are responsive only to highly exaggerated emotional displays. Given the finding described earlier that younger infants respond affectively to ID speech but not to AD speech, it seems likely that the exaggerated vocal and facial expressions typically used by mothers interacting with infants would provide especially salient information about the mother's emotional state. A recent study with adult subjects provides indirect support for the hypothesis that information about emotion and communicative intent is conveyed with special clarity through the exaggerated intonation of ID speech (Fernald, 1989). Subjects listening to content-filtered ID and AD speech samples were asked to identify the communicative intent of the speaker, using only prosodic information. We found that listeners were able to use intonation to identify the speaker's intent with significantly higher accuracy in speech addressed to infants. This finding suggests that the prosodic patterns of ID speech are more distinctive and more informative than those of AD speech and may provide the preverbal infant with reliable cues to the affective state and intentions of the speaker.

Could infants potentially make use of such prosodic contours to gain access to the communicative intent of the speaker? Research on infants' perception of melodies provides indirect evidence for the salience of pitch patterns in the preverbal period. By six months, infants can extract the melodic contour in a tonal sequence even when the sequence is transposed into a different frequency range (Trehub, Thorpe, and Morrongiello, 1987). Infants appear to encode information about contour as opposed to absolute frequencies, since they perceive transposed melodies as similar or equivalent. This holistic mode of auditory processing, in which the relational features of a tonal sequence are retained, could enable infants to encode the prominent melodic patterns of infant-directed speech and recognize these characteristic melodies across variations in speaker, segmental content, and pitch range.

Maternal intonation and early language development

At the fourth level of the model shown in Figure 1.1.4, the prosodic patterns of ID speech increasingly serve linguistic functions. While the infant perceives prosodic contours holistically in the earlier preverbal period, words gradually begin to emerge from the melody toward the end of the first year. As the child develops the ability to use language to extract meaning from the mother's vocalizations, the prosody of maternal speech helps to draw the infant's attention to particular linguistic units within the continuous stream of speech. In a study of mothers' use of prosodic emphasis to mark focused words in speech to infants and adults, we found that prosodic cues in ID speech were not only more emphatic than those in AD speech, but also more consistent and more highly correlated (Fernald and Mazzie, 1991). When highlighting focused words, mothers used a distinctive prosodic strategy in speech to their infants. Focused words occurred most often on exaggerated pitch peaks in the final position in phrases in ID speech, while in AD speech the acoustic correlates of lexical stress were much more variable.

Does the use of exaggerated prosody actually help the infant to recognize focused words in continuous speech? In a recent study of the influence of intonation patterns on early lexical comprehension, we found that infants in the early stages of language acquisition are better able to recognize familiar words in ID speech than in AD speech (Fernald and McRoberts, 1991). In this study fifteen-month-old infants were tested in an auditory-visual matching procedure. On each trial, infants were presented with pairs of colored slides of familiar objects, accompanied by a recorded vocalization drawing their attention to one of the two objects (e.g., "Look at the *ball*! See the *ball*?"). The vocal stimuli were presented with the target word stressed in either ID or AD intonation. The index of comprehension in this procedure was whether infants looked longer at the picture matching the target word. We found that when target words were presented in ID speech, infants recognized the target words more reliably than in AD speech. Follow-up studies suggest, however, that by eighteen months infants have acquired the ability to identify familiar words equally well in AD speech and ID speech, although exaggerated intonation may still be important in acquiring new words at this age. These findings suggest that, at least in English, the acoustic highlighting of new words in mothers' speech may facilitate language comprehension in infants just beginning to learn language. Whether the dramatic pitch peaks of ID speech actually enhance the intelligibility of focused words or serve primarily as an attention-focusing device is a question still to be addressed.

To summarize so far, the exaggerated melodies of mothers' speech to infants serve many different functions in early development, prior to the acquisition of language. The distinctive prosodic patterns of maternal speech are prepotent signals for the infant at birth and are effective in the early months in eliciting and maintaining attention and in modulating arousal. Prior to the time when the mother's speech sounds can influence her child's behavior symbolically through their referential power, her intonation affects the child directly. When her intention is to arouse and delight the infant, she uses smooth, wide-range pitch contours, often with rising intonation; when her goal is to soothe, she rocks the infant and speaks with low, falling pitch. And just as the vestibular rhythms of rocking have a direct calming effect on the child (e.g., Byrne and Horowitz, 1981), the acoustic features of the mother's soothing melodies also function directly to decrease arousal and calm the infant. Thus in the first year of the infant's life, the communicative force of the mother's vocalizations derive not from their arbitrary meanings in a linguistic code, but more from their immediate musical power to arouse and alert, to calm, and to delight. Although the exaggerated pitch patterns of maternal vocalizations may eventually help the child in the second year to identify linguistic units in speech, the human voice becomes meaningful to the infant through maternal intonation much earlier in development. Through this distinctive form of vocal communication the infant begins to experience emotional communion with others, months before communion through symbols is possible.

Constraints on the evolution of vocal communication systems

In making the argument that human maternal speech is an adaptive mechanism, it is necessary to demonstrate not only that this special form of vocal communication serves critical biological functions in early development, but also that this behavior meets other criteria for invoking a selectionist account. One question of interest is whether this human vocal behavior shares common design features with vocal behaviors in other species where natural selection has more obviously played a formative role in shaping vocal signals to serve particular functions. This section will present research findings from the ethological literature on vocal communication in nonhuman animals, focusing on studies that attempt to elucidate the functional significance of particular vocal adaptations. Three questions will be addressed: First, how do constraints on perceptual and production mechanisms, as well as characteristics of the environment, influence the evolution of vocal repertoires? Second, what selective pressures appear to favor the evolution of graded versus discrete vocal signals? And finally, how do ritualized vocal signals function to enhance signal detectability? The ethological research reviewed in the context of these three questions will suggest which forms of evidence are most relevant in evaluating the claim that the special form of infant-directed speech used by human mothers is a caretaking behavior that has also been influenced by natural selection.

In discussing the functional significance of courtship calls in certain animals, Darwin (1872) described them as "sweet to the ears of the species," referring to the special power of such species-specific signals to please and entice a potential mate. Darwin's daring speculation that communicative signals in animals are as susceptible to the influence of natural selection as are morphological features is now widely accepted. However, in the absence of a fossil record of such ephemeral phenomena as vocal sounds—see Note 1—the evidence for adaptation in signal systems consists primarily of correlational findings relating acoustic and functional characteristics of species-specific vocalizations to other characteristics and conditions of the species that are likely to have exerted selective pressure on vocal forms. While necessarily indirect, such converging ethological evidence has become increasingly sophisticated in recent years, leading convincingly to the conclusion that the vocal repertoires of closely related species have been shaped differentially by evolution. Small variations in vocal forms between species are correlated with subtle differences in species-specific perceptual sensitivities, social organization, and habitat characteristics.

Perceptual and production constraints on the evolution of vocal signals

The primary function of animal sounds in social species is communication. With very few exceptions (e.g., in the production of echolocation sounds by bats), the specialized sound-producing organs found across the animal kingdom have evolved to send signals to other animals (Krebs and Dawkins, 1984). The idea that the acoustic signals typical of a species are "well designed" to be detected and recognized by conspecifics is widely accepted in the ethological literature. In some cases, the responsiveness of young animals to acoustic signals emerges without social experience. Swamp sparrows reared in isolation, for example, respond with greater cardiac orienting to the swamp sparrow call than to the call of a related species, on first exposure to these sounds (Dooling and Searcy, 1980). In other avian species, prenatal exposure to the mother's call (Gottlieb, 1980) and brief postnatal experience with conspecific vocalizations (Marler, 1984) are instrumental in the development of selective responsiveness to species-specific signals. However, even when the emergence of auditory selectivity in animals requires some learning and is not, so to speak, "hardwired," genetic mechanisms are implicated (see Gould and Marler, 1987). Such selective responsiveness to particular animal sounds of high biological relevance reflects the influence of natural selection according to Marler, Zoloth, and Dooling (1981):

> As a recurrent finding in ethological studies, developing young animals manifest responsiveness to particular environmental stimuli. These especially salient stimuli are associated with events that are fraught with special biological significance for all species members, such as predator detection or sexual communication. The selectivity of such innate responsiveness is sometimes so narrow that it is hard to imagine peripheral structures that could explain the specificity of responsiveness, especially when mediated by receptor systems known to be responsive to broader ranges of stimuli. To the extent that environmental events with special significance in the life of an organism are predictable over transgenerational time, adaptive species-specific genetic control over stimulus responsiveness becomes feasible. (p. 167)

Physiological and perceptual characteristics involved in sound production and reception are one source of evolutionary pressure shaping the form of vocal communication in a species. In some cases, the evolution of species-specific vocal signals seems to have been constrained primarily by the perceptual limitations of the conspecific recipient, as in the frog mating calls mentioned earlier. By comparing the auditory tuning curves in two closely related species of tree frog, Ryan *et al.* (1990) found that the auditory sensitivity of the female was the driving force in the evolution of the male mating call in one of these species. In this species, sound production in the male has been adapted to fit the preexisting perceptual bias of the female. Thus the effectiveness of species-specific vocalizations crucial to success in reproduction depends on the match between male production capabilities and female perceptual thresholds. It is important to note, however, that while the acoustic characteristics of such signals are highly constrained, given the particular physiological characteristics of the female of the species, they are also "arbitrary" in the sense that other mating signals would have evolved if, by chance, the tuning curves of the female tree frog had happened to be slightly different.

One very general constraint on the acoustic structure of vocal productions is the body size of the animal producing the signal. The frequency of phonation tends to be lower in larger animals simply because of the physics of sound production. The vocal signals of elephants and mice differ in spectral characteristics in part because resonant frequencies are directly related to the size of the animal's vocal cavities and sound producing organs. Similarly, the vocalizations of large male baboons have more energy present at lower frequencies than the vocalizations of smaller males or female baboons. Reviewing a large number of studies of avian and mammalian vocalizations, Morton (1977) observed the association mentioned earlier between acoustic structure and motivational state. Harsh, low-frequency sounds commonly signal threat or hostility, while higher-frequency, more tonal sounds signal fear, appeasement, or friendly approach. Morton explained this structural convergence in terms of a "motivation-structural rule." Because they give the impression of larger body size, harsh, lower-frequency vocalizations have been selected for across species as signals in hostile interactions, according to Morton, just as piloerection has evolved as a visual signal that increases apparent size. Conversely, the higher-frequency, tonal vocalizations used by many animals in fearful or friendly motivational states are effective in eliciting approach and support because they resemble the vocalizations of smaller, nonthreatening animals. The linguist Ohala (1984) has extended Morton's reasoning to include intonation patterns in human speech, observing that falling F_0 contours are commonly associated with assertive meanings, while rising F_0 contours are associated with nonassertive or conciliatory meanings. Such examples of apparent "sound symbolism" in human and nonhuman animal vocal signals reflect selection for acoustic features related to characteristics of both production mechanisms and complementary perceptual response biases.

Environmental constraints on the evolution of vocal signals

While there are numerous examples in the ethological literature in which physiological, perceptual, and cognitive characteristics of conspecifics, as well as predators, have apparently shaped the evolution of biologically significant vocal signals, the acoustic ecology of the natural habitat also plays a formative role. Marler (1965) was among the first to propose that ecological factors as well as perceptual constraints may have exerted selective pressures on the structure of acoustic communication. For example, alarm calls across a number of avian species consist of narrow-band, high-pitched calls, which appear to have two important advantages. Because of their particular acoustic structure, such alarm calls propagate widely and are very difficult for a predator to localize (Green and Marler, 1979).

Research on monkeys inhabiting East African rain forests has explored further the interaction of vocal signal characteristics and features of the environment in the evolution of communication systems. Obviously, a vocalization signaling a biologically important event can be effective only if it can be heard by the appropriate recipient. According to Brown (1989), several factors determine the audibility of vocal signals in the rain forest, including signal characteristics that facilitate transmission, signal degradation resulting from attenuation in the rain forest environment, and the intensity and spectral composition of environmental background noise, which can mask this signal. In an elegant series of field and laboratory studies, P. M. Waser, Brown, and colleagues have shown how the acoustic structure of vocal signals in various primate species has been adapted for optimal sound transmission in the particular habitat in which these signals have evolved. In a study of four species of African monkey, Waser and Waser (1977) found that the frequency spectrum of distance calls is optimal for efficient transmission through the forest canopy. Moreover, these monkeys vary their position when calling so as to maximize the audible range of their signals throughout the day, in accordance with daily fluctuations in temperature gradients.

By analyzing the attenuation properties of the rain forest habitat, Waser and Brown (1986) discovered a "sound window" ideal for the propagation of frequencies near 200 Hz. Relating these features of the habitat acoustics to the characteristics of vocalizations used by two species of monkeys indigenous to this habitat, Waser and Brown found that three of the seven species-specific calls studied make use of the optimal sound window for long-distance propagation. For the four remaining calls, the loss in audible distance resulting from the use of a dominant frequency outside the sound window appeared to be compensated for by a 10 dB increase in sound intensity at the signal source. Waser and Brown (1986) also analyzed the characteristic background noise in the rain forest, generated by birds, insects, and other species, as well as by weather, discovering a quiet zone in the ambient noise between 500–800 Hz. Here too they found an orderly relation between the habitat acoustics and the design features of indigenous monkey calls. Short-range calls appear to be constrained to some extent by the spectrum of background noise in the rain forest, while long-range calls are governed more by attenuation properties of the habitat.

In discussing these provocative findings, Brown (1989) emphasizes that the form of species-specific vocal signals is often a compromise reflecting selection for a number of different acoustic attributes. For example, the most effective frequency for signal transmission through the moist, leafy atmosphere of the rain forest may not be optimal for obscuring the location of the animal emitting the call. This selection for multiple functional attributes of the vocal signal frequently results in a form that does not reflect an optimal specification for any particular isolated attribute. Such complex interactions in the process of adaptation over evolutionary time can make it exceeding difficult to disentangle and identify with confidence the forces at work in selection. However, by combining acoustic and functional analysis of vocal signals with both perceptual studies of auditory sensitivity and acoustic analysis of habitat characteristics, the ethological research described here provides valuable convergent evidence on the intricate fit between species-specific vocalizations and the biological functions they serve.

Graded and discrete vocalizations in primate communication

The extent of signal variability within the repertoires of different primate species is a feature of vocal communication systems that appears to be correlated not only with environmental conditions but also with type of social organization. The signal systems of lower primate species consist almost exclusively of discrete categories of vocalizations with nonoverlapping acoustic features. Among higher primates, in contrast, graded signals are more common. Graded signals exhibit considerable acoustic variability within a vocalization category and often overlap in acoustic attributes to some extent with vocalizations in other categories. While their potential ambiguity can pose problems for signal interpretation, graded signals are much more powerful than discrete signals in conveying subtle information about mood and intention.

Marler (1965, 1976) has suggested that the functional significance of discrete versus graded signal systems is related to the social structure and ecological conditions typical of different primate species. In strongly territorial groups, where a substantial portion of the vocal repertoire is dedicated to intergroup signaling, discrete repertoires are most common. The need to use loud, far-ranging calls in communication between groups may have favored the evolution of unambiguous, nonoverlapping signal categories. Discretely organized vocal repertoires are also favored when acoustic signals are not accompanied by complementary information from other sensory modalities, as is the case in long-distance calling by territorial males living in dense forests. Nonterritorial primates, in contrast, are more likely to develop graded vocalizations. Marler (1976) speculates that graded signals have been selected for in primate species that rely heavily on close-range signals within the group. Signals that function in close-range communication are less vulnerable to attenuation and distortion than are long-range calls and thus may be less constrained in the direction of discreteness and invariance. Moreover, the graded vocal signals common in close-range communication within the group can be richly supplemented by redundant visual information, including facial expressions and postural displays. Since animals interacting within the group can often see as well as hear each other, the visual signals accompanying vocalizations may help in decoding the subtleties and ambiguities of graded signals.

It is just these subtleties and potential ambiguities, however, that give graded vocal signals their enormous communicative power. Continuously varying calls can convey nuances of mood and motivation through slight shifts in pitch, intensity, spectrum, or tempo impossible with more stereotyped signals. Graded signals seem particularly appropriate to the intricate communicative acts and subtle negotiations that are so common in the complex social groups of the higher primates. For example, de Waal (1982) describes the gradual escalation in intimidation vocalizations and displays during a competition for power in a captive chimpanzee colony:

> Several times a day Nikkie would be seen sitting somewhere on his own, his hair on end, hooting. His hoot gradually swelled until it ended in a loud screech. Then he would dart across the enclosure and thump heavily on the ground or against one of the metal doors. ... To begin with, his intimidation displays did not seem to be directed at anyone in particular, but later on they took place more and more frequently in Yeroen's vicinity. Finally he started hooting directly at Yeroen. He would sit opposite him and swing large pieces of wood in the air. (p. 121)

De Waal (1982) describes several other encounters among these chimpanzees in which the hoots of the attacking animal and the screams of the victim incite agitation and aggression, as well as supportive behavior, among other members of the troop. These episodes illustrate the potential of such continuously varying vocalizations not only to index gradual shifts in the motivational state of the vocalizing animal, but also to induce emotional changes in the listener.

Marler's (1965, 1976) speculation that human speech is much more likely to have evolved from a richly graded vocal system than from a repertoire of discrete signals is interesting in this context. Human speech is indeed a continuously varying acoustic signal, but one on which our perceptual mechanisms frequently superimpose discrete categories, as in the categorical perception of certain consonants. In its prosodic structure, however, human speech has fully retained this gradient dimension. The power of prosody in human communication to convey subtle changes in the speaker's emotions and intentions and also to engage and persuade the listener can be seen as a direct legacy from the graded vocal systems of the higher nonhuman primates.

Ritualized vocalizations: Signal function and signal detectability

A widely accepted principle of the evolution of communication systems is that social signals evolve originally from other behaviors with no signaling function. That is, signals are usually exaptations, or "derived activities" (Tinbergen, 1952), which evolve from nonsignal behaviors through the process of ritualization. Ethologists disagree, however, on how best to characterize the nature and function of communication among nonhuman animals. The idea that a central function of vocalizations is to *persuade* the listener departs from the more prevalent view of communication, which emphasizes the sending and receiving of information (e.g., Smith, 1977). In the first of two articles challenging this traditional focus on the efficiency of information reception by the receiver of a signal, Dawkins and Krebs (1978) argue that natural selection will favor signals that benefit the sender rather than the receiver. According to this more "cynical" view of the evolution of communication, animals use signals primarily in order to manipulate the behavior of other animals, rather than to convey useful information. This instrumental function of nonhuman animal signals is comparable to human advertising slogans, which are designed to persuade rather than to inform, according to Dawkins and Krebs. Thus "the evolutionary ritualisation of derived activities can be better understood in terms of selection for effective manipulation than in terms of selection for effective information transfer" (Dawkins and Krebs, 1978: 385).

In a later article on the adaptive functions of social signals, Krebs and Dawkins (1984) expand their previous narrow focus on manipulation in the context of exploitative communication. They argue that ritualized signals are the product of the coevolution of what they call the "manipulator" and the "mind-reader" roles. The manipulator uses signals to influence the behavior of others, usually to its own advantage, while the mind-reader uses signals to predict the future actions of others. As animals become sensitive to subtle cues allowing them to predict other animals' behavior, this increased sensitivity is favored by natural selection. Yet it is this same sensitivity that enables one animal to manipulate another. A dog baring its teeth can be the "victim" of mind reading by other animals, but can also manipulate other animals into retreating by baring its teeth with no intention of attacking. Thus mind reading and manipulation coevolve, according to Krebs and Dawkins, and communicative signals are shaped by this process of coevolution.

A second intriguing argument made by Krebs and Dawkins (1984) is that fundamentally different kinds of signals evolve depending on whether communication is cooperative or noncooperative. In exploitative situations both between and within species, the reactor benefits in general from resisting the persuasion of the manipulator, resulting in one form of arms-race coevolution. For example, skilled "salesmanship" in the use of prominent courtship displays by the males of a species may be complemented by heightened "sales-resistance" on the part of females, since females cannot afford to respond indiscriminately to sexual overtures. The features most commonly associated with signals designed for persuading unwilling victims, according to Krebs and Dawkins, are just those features most effective in advertising: bright packaging, exaggeration, rhythmic repetition, and high redundancy. In cooperative situations, however, where the reactor benefits from being influenced by the manipulator, a different kind of signal typically evolves. When signals are cooperative, as in affiliative interactions within kinship groups, evolution favors "cost-minimizing conspiratorial whispers," rather than conspicuous, repetitive signals (Krebs and Dawkins, 1984: 391).

Regardless of whether communication is cooperative or noncooperative, effective signals must incorporate design features that ensure detectability. Krebs and Dawkins (1984) cite Wiley's (1983) interpretation of the evolution of ritualized signals in terms of signal detection theory. Wiley proposes four features that increase the reliability of signal detection in noisy environments:

1. *Redundancy*, resulting from predictable relationships among the different components of a familiar signal, facilitates accurate identification of the signal even if only part of it is heard. Repeating parts of a signal, or the entire signal, is a simple form of redundancy used to enhance detectability.
2. *Conspicuousness* by exaggeration of acoustic features enhances the signal-to-noise ratio by increasing the contrast between the signal and the irrelevant background stimulation.
3. *Small repertoires* of signals reduce the listener's uncertainty and enhance performance in signal detection tasks. With fewer and more distinctive categories in which potential signals can be classified, the opportunity for identification errors is minimized.
4. *Alerting components* at the beginning of a signal increase detectability and recognition by letting the listener know when to expect the message component of the signal.

These four adaptations for efficient communication all benefit a signaler by counteracting noise in communication. Noise can result from irrelevant background sounds, as well as from signal distortion or attenuation in the external environment, as illustrated in the research on habitat acoustics described earlier (Brown, 1989). However, noise in its technical sense can also result from characteristics of the receiver, such as the high threshold or cautiousness typical of "sales-resistant" females (Wiley, 1983). Krebs and Dawkins conclude that signal evolution will always reflect a compromise between detectability considerations and the economics of signal production. Increasing signal salience can incur additional costs, such as extra energy expenditure and enhanced risk of predation. Thus the use of such costly ritualized signals evolves only when the stakes are sufficiently high, as with signals used to attract a mate or to defend resources. In the use of cooperative signals, which are designed to influence willing reactors, selection can favor less extravagant signals, as long as they meet the criteria for detectability.

To summarize this section, ethological research suggests that many different kinds of selective pressure can influence the design of species-specific vocalizations, including physiological constraints on signal production and perception, environmental features affecting sound propagation, communicative functions of vocal signaling both within and between social groups, and engineering features ensuring signal detectability by both willing and unwilling listeners. Recent theoretical formulations of the interrelated social and ecological constraints on signal evolution (Dawkins and Krebs, 1978; Krebs and Dawkins, 1984) emphasize that animals use vocalizations for persuasion. In the complex social systems of the higher primates, where communication is focused increasingly on intricate interactions within the group, persuasive vocal signaling becomes more prevalent and more powerful through the use of graded vocalizations. Through intonation, humans also make use of graded signals, which are highly effective in interpersonal communication and which share common features with vocalizations of nonhuman primates and other species.

The argument for design in human maternal speech

What kinds of evidence are needed to support the inference that the special form of speech used by human mothers with infants has evolved as a species-specific parenting behavior? It is important, although hardly sufficient, that this infant-directed speech form is widespread across human cultures and is beneficial to parents and infants in their early interactions. Two more demanding criteria need to be addressed in invoking a selectionist argument. First, it has to be shown that this maternal vocal behavior is particularly well engineered for effective communication with preverbal infants, and not just for communication in general. And second, it has to be shown how the use of infant-directed speech by human mothers could have been selected for as a parenting behavior contributing to reproductive success.

Design features of infant-directed prosody

The human infant is a noisy system, in various senses of the word, and the exaggerated prosody of infant-directed speech is exquisitely designed to boost the signal relative to the noise. The principal noise that the mother's voice must overcome is not, and never was, the attenuation characteristics of the rain forest or savannah, since mother–infant communication in higher primates takes place at very close range. Rather, the noise that interferes most with signal reception is intrinsic to the young infant, resulting from the perceptual, attentional, and cognitive limitations associated with immaturity. For example, human infants like adults are more sensitive to sounds at 500 Hz than at 200 Hz, which means that a 500-Hz signal will sound louder than a 200-Hz signal when both are presented at the same intensity. However, because young infants have higher auditory thresholds than adults (Schneider, Trehub, and Bull, 1979), sounds need to be more intense for infants in order to be detected. By elevating the fundamental frequency of the voice when addressing an infant, mothers effectively compensate for this sensory limitation by moving into a pitch range in which infants are relatively more sensitive, thus increasing the perceived loudness of the signal.

The exaggerated pitch continuity of mothers' vocalizations may also provide a processing advantage for the immature auditory system of the human infant, simplifying the initially demanding task of tracking the voice of a single speaker. Even for adults, the prosodic contours of speech enable the listener to attend selectively to one voice among many (Nooteboom, Brokx, and DeRooij, 1976), although adults can use linguistic as well as acoustic structure in accomplishing this task. Infants, in contrast, have no knowledge of linguistic structure and must at first rely entirely on the prosodic coherence of the speech stream in selectively attending to a particular voice. In these and many other ways, the characteristic prosodic features of maternal speech provide the immature listener with acoustic signals that are high in perceptual salience and relatively easy to process (see Fernald, 1984). Just as the calls of birds and mammals are finely tuned to the perceptual limitations of conspecifics and ingeniously engineered to transcend the noise of the environment, the exaggerted vocalizations of human mothers' speech are well designed to accommodate the perceptual predispositions of infants and to overcome the noise in the system due to infants' initial processing limitations.

It is intriguing that the features that selection favors in enhancing signal detectability, according to Wiley (1983)—conspicuousness, redundancy, small repertoires, and alerting components—are all robustly characteristic of infant-directed vocalizations in human speech and decidedly uncharacteristic of adult-directed speech. The *conspicuousness* or perceptual prominence of ID vocalizations results from the elevation of pitch and expansion of pitch range typical of maternal speech across languages, as well as from the use of short vocalizations clearly separated by substantial pauses (Fernald *et al.*, 1989). *Redundancy* in signaling is also strikingly prevalent in speech to infants. Stern *et al.* (1983) report that mothers repeat over 50 per cent of their phrases when interacting with two-month-old infants. Prosodic repetition is common too (Fernald and Simon, 1984), often with slight melodic variations, which keep these repetitive runs interesting as well as highly predictable for the infant (Stern, 1977). The use of *small vocal repertoires*, the third feature described by Wiley, is reflected in mothers' tendency to use relatively stereotyped prosodic contours in specific interactional contexts, as shown in Figure 1.1.3. Moreover, the first words learned by infants generally include "uh-oh," "bye-bye," "peek-a-boo," and other social routines marked by distinctive and highly stereotyped prosody. Finally, the use of *alerting components*, another common feature in ritualized nonhuman animal calls, is also typical of human mothers' speech. In mother–infant play with objects, American mothers frequently call the infant's name or say "Look!" or "What's that?" using elevated pitch in order to engage the infant's attention before labeling the object. Popular mother–infant games like peek-a-boo have alerting components built into the vocal routines accompanying the action (Fernald and O'Neill, in press).

These same signal-enhancing features are described by Krebs and Dawkins (1984) as "advertising" strategies especially effective in persuading unwilling reactors. Bright packaging, rhythmic repetition, exaggeration, and high redundancy also characterize the ritualized vocalizations of human mothers to their infants. In this case, however, communication is cooperative and the reactor is willing. This apparent exception to Krebs and Dawkins's claim that such conspicuous and costly vocalizations will emerge primarily in the service of noncooperative communication is actually quite consistent with their reasoning: Ritualized vocalizations are selected for when they function in biologically significant activities in noisy environments or with "cautious reactors." In mother–infant communication, the reactor is immature rather than cautious, and the noise is attributable to perceptual limitations of the infant rather than to features of the habitat. But this developmental noise is formidable, however temporary, and specially designed vocalizations are needed to ensure signal detection and recognition by an inexperienced listener.

In accord with the idea that manipulation or persuasion is a central function of animal vocalizations, the signal-enhancing features of mothers' speech also seem well designed for persuading the infant listener. As she soothes, alerts, or praises, the mother is directly influencing the infant's state and level of arousal through her voice. This instrumental function of maternal speech, described earlier in relation to the first two levels of the model shown in Figure 1.1.4, is indeed manipulative, as the mother intuitively and skillfully uses the music of her voice to elicit attention, modulate arousal, and induce emotion in the preverbal infant. The primitive communicative force of maternal speech in this context is close to that of the graded vocalizations used by nonhuman primates, which achieve their impact by affecting the motivational state of the listener. The analogies drawn by Krebs and Dawkins (1984) between ritualized animal signals and both advertising and musical sounds are equally apt in relation to human maternal vocalizations, which also function more immediately to modulate emotion and motivation than to transmit information.

A final argument for the special design features of infant-directed speech has to do with the neurological immaturity of the human infant's auditory system at birth. Until the auditory cortex matures, the young infant relies more on subcortical auditory structures (Whitaker, 1976), which are better suited for the holistic analysis of acoustic signals than for the high-resolution temporal analysis ultimately required for processing speech sounds. For both human and nonhuman primates, subcortical pathways are involved in the recognition of graded acoustic signals and in the production and reception of affective messages (Lamendella, 1977). Marler (1976) has observed that the retention of continuous auditory processing mechanisms for graded signals in music and in the intonation of speech is considered to be a primitive trait in humans. However, the development of limbic and hypothalamic pathways for processing continuously varying affective signals was probably a major evolutionary advance for our nonhuman primate ancestors, enabling much subtler and more differentiated forms of cooperative social communication. It is interesting to note that the earliest vocal communication between the human mother and her infant is emotional in nature and is mediated by intonation, a graded acoustic signal, which the infant can perceive using phylogenetically older and simpler auditory processing mechanisms than those that will eventually develop to process the linguistic units in speech.

Adaptive functions of mothers' speech to infants

Behaviors that are adaptations must have contributed differentially to reproductive fitness in the evolutionary past. Given their crucial biological role in enhancing reproductive success, species-typical parenting behaviors are often seen as prototypical examples of behavioral adaptations. However, parenting behaviors differ dramatically across species in the domain and time-frame of their influence on the young. Some parental behaviors are adaptations for the immediate survival of the young during infancy, an obvious prerequisite for reproductive success, while others have been selected for because of their long-term contribution to the future fitness of the offspring. In arguing for the precision and efficiency of design features in human maternal speech to infants. I have focused on the adaptive functions of this parenting behavior during the infancy period. However, I would also like to argue, somewhat more speculatively, that the use of prosodically modified vocalizations in early mother–infant communication may have had adaptive advantages extending beyond the infancy period over the course of hominid evolution.

Primate parenting behaviors are among the most complex in the animal world. For most reptiles to reproduce successfully, they must survive the first year of life and mate appropriately. Mammals, in contrast, need to survive and mate, and then to nurture and protect their offspring until maturity. Across the primate order, the evolution of an increasingly long period of relative helplessness and dependency in the young has placed extensive demands on parental skills and commitment. From the point of view of basic behavioral equipment, newborn monkeys, apes, and humans are fundamentally similar. They all show reflexive rooting, sucking, and grasping responses, and they all cry when distressed and are comforted when held (Mason, 1968). But differences among primate species in the strength and persistence of these primitive infantile responses are striking. A newborn rhesus monkey placed on its back will right itself immediately, unless given something to cling to. A newborn chimpanzee in the same situation will wave its arms about irregularly, unable to right itself, until it is several weeks old. The human infant will not develop the ability to turn over until around the age of three months and will not be capable of locomotion until the age of eight months.

> Viewed as a collection of responses preadapted to nursing and maintaining contact with the mother, the behavior of the chimp never displays the same

reflex-like efficiency as that of the monkey. Indeed, if evolution had not brought about complementary changes in the behavior of the chimp mother that permitted her to compensate for the behavioral deficiencies of her infant, its chances of survival would be slim. (Mason, 1968)

As Mason suggests, the lengthening of the period of immaturity among higher primate species has coevolved with specialized parenting skills designed to compensate for the increased helplessness of the young. Of course, the complementary evolution of parental behaviors appropriate to the characteristics and needs of the young is evident in every species in which brood care is typical. What is remarkable about parenting behaviors in higher primates is their flexibility in accommodating the continually changing needs of the young throughout a relatively long period of dependency. An experiment by Rumbaugh (1965) demonstrated the extent to which primates will modify their behavior in unusual ways in order to accommodate the needs of the young. When the arms of an infant squirrel monkeys were taped so that it was unable to cling, the mother responded with bipedal carrying and cradling of the infant, both highly atypical behaviors under normal circumstances. Berkson (1974) and Rosenblum and Youngstein (1974) report numerous other examples from field studies in which monkey mothers resourcefully compensate for infant disabilities in ways that are appropriate to the developmental status of the infant. In this respect, primates differ dramatically from reptiles, where parenting behaviors are minimal or nonexistent, as well as from most other mammals, where parenting skills are critical only during a brief period and consist of a relatively fixed and limited repertoire of behaviors.

The evolution of this primate capacity for flexible accommodation to the needs and limitations of the infant is epitomized in human parental behavior. Human mothers nurse and carry their infants, as do other primates, but with an incomparably greater diversity of means to the common biological ends, including using bottles to feed and prams to carry the infant. Human mothers' use of a special infant-directed speech style is also an accommodation to the immaturity of the infant, compensating for early perceptual, attentional, and cognitive limitations, and changing gradually as the infant develops. This species-specific parental vocal behavior is not characterized by a fixed repertoire of discrete signals, but rather by the flexible use of graded prosodic variations to influence the state and behavior of the infant and to optimize communication with an immature and inexperienced listener. Moreover, mothers of deaf infants are quite capable of translating the lively dynamic rhythms of infant-directed speech into the visual modality. What is common in mothers' interactions with both deaf and hearing infants is the use of a highly salient display that engages the infant both perceptually and affectively and that is contingent on the infant's emotional and behavioral responses. In its biological utility, its compensatory functions, and its flexibility of use, human maternal speech is similar to many other primate parenting behaviors that have evolved through natural selection.

The adaptive functions served by parental behaviors specialized for feeding, soothing, carrying, and communicating with young infants are fairly obvious in that these infant-directed behaviors enhance the likelihood of survival early in life. What is not as obvious is that such caretaking behaviors can have long-term regulatory effects on the infant's physiology and behavior extending far beyond the period of infancy. Hofer's (1981, 1987) extensive research with infant rats has revealed enduring negative effects on the infant's thermoregulation, motor behavior, and behavioral reactivity resulting from early separation from the mother. These findings suggest that under normal circumstances, the regulatory effects of maternal behavior "are exerted over long periods of time through repeated episodes of stimulation delivered by the mother to the infant during their ongoing social relationship" (Hofer, 1981: 93). Studies with both rats and monkeys indicate that the premature removal of these powerful regulatory influences can result in a kind of physiological withdrawal (Hofer, 1987). Hofer concludes that such biological processes hidden within the rhythmic stimulation of early human mother–infant interaction may help to explain both the formation of attachments and the intense painfulness of loss in adulthood as well as in infancy.

Hofer's (1987) ideas about the long-term regulatory functions of early mother–infant interaction suggest a psychobiological basis for the relation between maternal responsiveness and infant socioemotional development that is central to attachment theory (Ainsworth, 1973). In Bowlby's (1969) original formulation of attachment theory, he proposed that mother–infant attachment had evolved primarily as an adaptation designed to protect the infant from predators. More recent research proposes that the quality of attachment in infancy is related to social competence in childhood, as well as to the quality of emotional relationships and parenting skills in adulthood (Main, Kaplan, and Cassidy, 1985). From this broader perspective, early mother–infant attachment has adaptive consequences extending well beyond the period of infancy. It is important to remember that the prolonged period of immaturity evolved in primates not only because it takes time to grow a large and complex brain, but also because it takes time to acquire the intricate social skills prerequisite for successful reproduction in these species. In primates, reproductive success depends not only on parenting behaviors that ensure infant survival, but also on parenting behaviors that enable the infant to become a competent member of the social group and ultimately to function effectively as a parent as well. From quite different perspectives, both Hofer's (1987) psychobiological research and research on infant attachment (e.g., Main, Kaplan, and Cassidy, 1985) suggest that human maternal behaviors in the period of evolution could have had both immediate consequences for infant survival and early development and long-term consequences related to socioemotional development later in life.

Are these conjectures reasonable, given that we have no evidence for the contribution of particular parenting behaviors to reproductive success in the era of hominid evolution? And in particular, how could the use of melodic vocalizations in mothers' interactions with infants have enhanced fitness in our hominid ancestors? Assuming, with Hofer (1987), that rhythmic tactile and vestibular stimulation has a powerful regulatory influence on all mammalian infants, rhythmic maternal vocalizations may have become a potent form of auditory stimulation for infants in a species in which speech was evolving as a primary means of communication. Mothers' use of exaggerated, highly salient vocal patterns would have been effective then, as they are now, in engaging and maintaining infants' attention and in modulating arousal and affect. And through the melodies of the mother's voice, infants could gain early access to her feelings and intentions. This experience of emotional communion through repeated episodes of rhythmic vocal stimulation may have led to what Stern (1985) calls "affect attunement" between mother and infant, giving the infant crucial early experience in mind reading and establishing the basis for effective interpersonal communication with other conspecifics. Could such early experience have provided a reproductive advantage to the offspring of mothers more skillful in establishing communication with their infants? If sensitive and responsive maternal care in infancy enhanced the ability of offspring to read accurately the social signals of conspecifics and to function more effectively in later interpersonal relationships, the offspring of more competent mothers may ultimately have been more successful in attracting desirable mates and in parenting their own infants. To the extent that early emotional experience contributed to the development of social competence, and social competence contributed to success in reproduction and parenting, maternal behaviors effective in establishing emotional communication in infancy could have had long-term as well as short-term consequences related to fitness.

Given our reliance on linguistic symbols to decode meanings in speech, it is perhaps difficult for us to appreciate just how important it is to be able to communicate through emotional signals. The predisposition to be moved by as well as to interpret the emotions of others and the ability to discern the intentions and motivations of others through expressions of the voice and face are remarkable evolutionary advances in communicative potential among the higher primates. Human mothers intuitively and skillfully use melodic vocalizations to soothe, to arouse, to warn and to delight their infants, and to share and communicate emotion. While the acquisition of language will eventually give the child an access to other minds that is immeasurably more powerful and intricate than that of other primates, human symbolic communication builds on our primate legacy, a foundation of affective communication established in the preverbal period.

Note to 1.1

1. Although fossil evidence can help one make inferences about adaptation, it is not, of course,

criterial. This is because the fossil record can preserve both adaptations and nonadaptive aspects of the phenotype. The ultimate criterion for demonstrating adaptation is good design for accomplishing a function that would have promoted reproduction in ancestral environments.

References to 1.1

Ainsworth, M. D. S. (1973). "The development of infant–mother attachment." In B. M. Caldwell and H. N. Ricciuiti (eds), *Review of Child Development Research* (Vol. 3). Chicago, IL: University of Chicago Press, 1–94.
Aslin, R. N. (1987). "Visual and auditory development in infancy." In J. D. Osofsky (ed.), *Handbook of Infant Development* (2nd edn). New York: John Wiley & Sons.
Bench, J. (1969). "Some effects of audio-frequency stimulation on the crying baby." *The Journal of Auditory Research*, 9, 122–8.
Berg, W. K. (1975). "Cardiac components of defense responses in infants." *Psychophysiology*, 12, 224.
Berkson, G. (1974). "Social responses of animals to infants with defects." In M. Lewis and L. A. Rosenblum (eds), *The Effect of the Infant on Its Caretaker*. New York: John Wiley & Sons.
Birns, B., Blank, M., Bridger, W., and Escalona, S. (1965). "Behavioral inhibition in neonates produced by auditory stimuli." *Child Development*, 36, 639–45.
Bock, W. J. (1980). "The definition and recognition of biological adaptation." *American Zoology*, 20, 217–27.
Bowlby, J. (1969). *Attachment*. Middlesex, England: Penguin Books.
Brown, C. W. (1989). "The acoustic ecology of East African primates and the perception of vocal signals by grey-cheeked Mangabeys and blue monkeys." In R. J. Dooling and S. H. Hulse (eds), *The Comparative Psychology of Audition*. Hillsdale, NJ: Erlbaum.
Bühler, C. and Hetzer, H. (1928). "Das erste Verständnis für Ausdruck im ersten Lebensjahr." *Zeitschrift für Psychologie*, 107, 50–61.
Byrne, J. M. and Horowitz, F. D. (1981). "Rocking as a soothing intervention: The influence of direction and type of movement." *Infant Behavior and Development*, 4, 207–18.
Caron, A. J., Caron, R. F., and Maclean, D. J. (1988). "Infant discrimination of naturalistic emotional expressions: The role of face and voice." *Child Development*, 59, 604–16.
Chew, J. J. (1969). "The structure of Japanese baby talk." *Association of Teachers of Japanese*, 6, 4–17.
Chomsky, N. (1972). *Language and Mind*. New York: Harcourt, Brace, & World.
Clarkson, M. G. and Berg, W. K. (1983). "Cardiac orienting and vowel discrimination in newborns: Crucial stimulus parameters." *Child Development*, 54, 162–71.
Cooper, R. P. and Aslin, R. N. (1990). "Preference for infant-directed speech in the first month after birth." *Child Development*, 61, 1584–95.
Cosmides, L. (1983). "Invariances in the acoustic expression of emotion during speech." *Journal of Experimental Psychology*, 9, 864–81.
Darwin, C. (1859). *On the Origin of Species*. London: J. Murray.
Darwin, C. (1872/1956). *The Expression of Emotions in Man and Animals*. Chicago: University of Chicago Press.
Dawkins, R. (1986). *The Blind Watchmaker: Why the evidence of evolution reveals a universe without design*. New York: Norton.
Dawkins, R. and Krebs, J. R. (1978). "Animal signals: Information or manipulation?" In J. R. Krebs and N. B. Davies (eds), *Behavioural Ecology: An evolutionary approach*. Sunderland, MA: Sinauer Associates, 282–309.
DeCasper, A. J. and Fifer, W. P. (1980). *Science*, 208, 1174–6.
Demany, I., McKenzie, B., and Vurpillot, E. (1977). "Rhythm perception in early infancy." *Nature*, 266, 718–19.
de Waal. F. (1982). *Chimpanzee Politics: Power and sex among apes*. Baltimore, MD: The Johns Hopkins University Press.
Dooling, R. and Searcy, M. (1980). "Early perceptual selectivity in the swamp sparrow." *Developmental Psychobiology*, 13, 499–506.

Eisen, J. M. and Fernald, A. (in preparation). *Prosodic Modifications in the Infant-directed Speech of Rural Xhosa-speaking Mothers.*

Ekman, P. (1972). "Universals and cultural differences in facial expressions of emotion." In J. Cole (ed.), *Nebraska Symposium on Motivation.* Lincoln: University of Nebraska Press, 207–83.

Ferguson, C. A. (1964). "Baby talk in six languages." *American Anthropologist,* **66**, 103–14.

Fernald, A. (1984). "The perceptual and affective salience of mothers' speech to infants." In L. Feagans, C. Garvey, and R. Golinkoff (eds), *The Origins and Growth of Communication.* Norwood, N.J.: Ablex.

Fernald, A. (1985). "Four-month-old infants prefer to listen to motherese." *Infant Behavior and Development,* **8**, 181–95.

Fernald, A. (1989). "Intonation and communicative intent: Is the melody the message?" *Child Development,* **60**, 1497–510.

Fernald, A. (1992). "Meaningful melodies in mothers' speech to infants." In H. Papousek, U. Jurgens, and M. Papousek (eds), *Nonverbal Vocal Communication: Comparative and developmental approaches.* Cambridge: Cambridge University Press.

Fernald, A. and Clarkson, M. (in preparation). *Infant Cardiac Orienting to Infant-directed Vocalizations.*

Fernald, A., Kermanschachi, N., and Lees, D. (April 1984). *The Rhythms and Sounds of Soothing: Maternal vestibular, tactile, and auditory stimulation and infant state.* Paper presented at the International Conference on Infant Studies, New York.

Fernald, A. and Kuhl, P. K. (1987). "Acoustic determinants of infant preference for motherese speech." *Infant Behavior and Development,* **10**, 279–93.

Fernald, A. and McRoberts, G. (April 1991). *Prosody and Early Lexical Comprehension.* Paper presented at the meeting of the Society for Research on Child Development, Seattle.

Fernald, A. and Mazzie, C. (1991). "Prosody and focus in speech to infants and adults." *Developmental Psychology,* **27**, 209–21.

Fernald, A. and O'Neill, D. K. (in press). "Peekaboo across cultures: How mothers and infants play with voices, faces, and expectations." In K. McDonald and A. D. Pelligrini (eds), *Play and Culture.* Buffalo, NY: SUNY Press.

Fernald, A. and Simon, T. (1984). "Expanded intonation contours in mothers' speech to newborns." *Developmental Psychology,* **20**, 104–13.

Fernald, A., Taeschner, T., Dunn, J., Papousek, M., Boysson-Bardies, B., and Fukui, I. (1989). "A cross-language study of prosodic modifications in mothers' and fathers' speech to preverbal infants." *Journal of Child Language,* **16**, 477–501.

Fernald, R. D. (1988). "Aquatic adaptations in fish eyes." In J. Atema, R. R. Fay, A. N. Popper, and W. N. Tavolga (eds), *Sensory Biology of Aquatic Animals,* New York: Springer-Verlag, 435–66.

Ferrier, L. J. (1985). "Intonation in discourse: Talk between 12-month-olds and their mothers." In K. Nelson (ed.), *Children's Language* (Vol. 5). Hillsdale, NJ: Erlbaum, 35–60.

Friedlander, B. Z. (1968). "The effect of speaker identity, voice inflection, vocabulary, and message redundancy on infants' selection of vocal reinforcement." *Journal of Experimental Child Psychology,* **6**, 443–59.

Garnica, O. (1977). "Some prosodic and paralinguistic features of speech to young children." In C. E. Snow and C. A. Ferguson (eds), *Talking to Children: Language input and acquisition.* Cambridge, MA: Cambridge University Press, 63–88.

Gottlieb, G. (1980). "Development of species identification in ducklings: VI. Specific embryonic experience required to maintain species-typical perception in Peking ducklings." *Journal of Comparative and Physiological Psychology,* **94**, 499–587.

Gould, J. L. and Marler, P. (1987). "Learning by instinct." *Scientific American,* **255**, 74–85.

Gould, S. J. and Lewontin, R. C. (1979). "The spandrels of San Marco and the Panglossian program: A critique of the adaptationist programme." *Proceedings of the Royal Society of London,* **205**, 281–8.

Gould, S. J. and Vrba, E. S. (1982). "Exaptation—a missing term in the science of form." *Paleobiology,* **8**, 4–15.

Green, S. and Marler, P. (1979). "The analysis of animal communication." In P. Marler and J. G. Vandenbergh (eds), *Handbook of Behavioral Neurobiology: III. Social behavior and communication.* New York: Plenum Press, 73–158.

Grieser, D. I. and Kuhl, P. K. (1988). "Maternal speech to infants in a tonal language: Support for universal prosodic features in motherese." *Developmental Psychology,* **24**, 14–20.

Hewes, G. W. (1973). "Primate communication and the gestural origin of language." *Current Anthropology.* **14**, 5–24.

Hofer, M. A. (1981). "Parental contributions to the development of their offspring." In D. J. Gubernick and P. H. Klopfer (eds), *Parental Care in Mammals.* New York: Plenum Press, 77–115.

Hofer, M. A. (1987). "Early social relationships: A psychobiologist's view." *Child Development,* **58**, 633–47.

Jacobson, J. L., Boersma, D. C., Fields, R. B., and Olson, K. L. (1983). "Paralinguistic features of adult speech to infants and small children." *Child Development,* **54**, 436–42.

Kearsley, R. B. (1973). "The newborn's response to auditory stimulation: A demonstration of orienting and defensive behavior." *Child Development,* **44**, 582–90.

Klinnert, M., Campos, J. J., Sorce, J. F., Emde, R. N., and Svejda, M. (1983). "Emotions as behavior regulators: Social referencing in infancy." In R. Plutchik and H. Kellerman (eds), *Emotion in Early Development Vol. 2: The emotion.* New York: Academic Press, 57–86.

Krebs, J. R. and Dawkins, R. (1984). "Animal signals: Mind-reading and manipulation." In J. R. Krebs and N. B. Davies (eds), *Behavioral Ecology: An evolutionary approach.* Oxford: Blackwell Scientific Publications, 380–402.

Lamendella, J. T. (1977). "The limbic system in human communication." In H. Whitaker and H. Whitaker (eds), *Studies in Neurolinguistics* (Vol. 3). New York: Academic Press, 157–222.

Lewis, M. M. (1936/1951). *Infant Speech: A study of the beginnings of language.* London: Routledge & Kegan Paul.

Lewontin, R. (1978). "Adaptation." *Scientific American,* **239**, 157–69.

Main, M., Kaplan, N., and Cassidy, J. (1985). "Security in infancy, childhood, and adulthood: A move to the level of representation." In I. Bretherton and E. Waters (eds), *Growing Points of Attachment Theory and Research.* (Monographs of the Society for Research in Child Development, Vol. 50 [1–2]). Chicago, IL: University of Chicago Press, 66–104.

Marler, P. (1965). "Communication in monkeys and apes." In I. DeVore (ed.), *Primate Behavior: Field studies of monkeys and apes.* New York: Holt, Rinehart & Winston, 544–84.

Marler, P. (1976). "Social organization, communication and graded signals: The chimpanzee and the gorilla." In P. P. G. Bateson and R. A. Hinde (eds), *Growing Points in Ethology.* Cambridge: Cambridge University Press.

Marler, P. (1984). "Song learning: Innate species differences in the learning process." In P. Marler and H. S. Terrace (eds), *The Biology of Learning.* Berlin: Dahlem Konferenzen, 289–309.

Marler, P., Zoloth, S., and Dooling, R. (1981). "Innate programs for perceptual development: An ethological view." In G. Gollin (ed.), *Developmental Plasticity: Behavioral and biological aspects of variations in development.* New York: Academic Press, 135–72.

Mason, W. A. (1968). "Early social deprivation in the nonhuman primates: Implications for human behavior." In D. C. Glass (ed.), *Environmental Influence, Biology and Behavior Series.* New York: Rockefeller University Press.

Meegaskumbura, P. B. (1980). "Tondol: Sinhala baby talk." *Word,* **31**, 287–309.

Mehler, J., Jusczyk, P., Lambertz, G., Halsted, N., Bertoncini, J., and Amiel-Tison, C. (1990). "A precursor of language acquisition in young infants." *Cognition,* **29**, 143–78.

Miller, C. L. and Byrne, J. M. (1983). "Psychophysiological and behavioral response to auditory stimuli in the newborn." *Infant Behavior and Development,* **6**, 369–89.

Morton, E. S. (1977). "On the occurrence and significance of motivation-structural rules in some bird and mammal sounds." *American Naturalist,* **111**, 855–69.

Nelson, C. A. (1983). "The recognition of facial espressions in the first two years of life: Mechanisms of development." *Child Development,* **58**, 889–909.

Nooteboom, S. G., Brokx, J. P. L., and DeRooij, J. J. (1976). "Contributions of prosody to speech perception." *IPO Annual Progress Report,* **5**, 34–54.

Ohala, J. J. (1984). "An ethological perspective on common cross-language utilization of F_0 of voice." *Phonetica,* **41**, 1–16.

Papousek, H. (April 1987). *Models and Messages in the Melodies of Maternal Speech in Tonal and Non-tonal Languages.* Paper presented at the meeting of the Society for Research in Child Development, Baltimore, MD.

Papousek, M., Papousek, H., and Bornstein, M. H. (1985). "The naturalistic vocal environment of young infants: On the significance of homogeneity and variability in parental speech." In T. Field and N. Fox (eds), *Social Perception in Infants.* Norwood, NJ: Ablex, 269–97.

Papousek, M., Papousek, H., and Haekel, M. (1987). "Didactic adjustments in fathers' and mothers' speech to their three-month-old infants." *Journal of Psycholinguistic Research*, **16**, 491–516.

Piattelli-Palmarini, M. (1989). "Evolution, selection, and cognition: From 'learning' to parameter setting in biology and the study of language." *Cognition*, **31**, 1–44.

Pinker, S. and Bloom, P. (1990). "Natural language and natural selection." *Behavioral and Brain Sciences*, **13**, 713–33.

Ratner, N. B. and Pye, C. (1984). "Higher pitch in BT is not universal: Acoustic evidence from Quiche Mayan." *Journal of Child Language*, **2**, 515–22.

Rosenblum, L. A. and Youngstein, K. P. (1974). "Developmental changes in compensatory dyadic response in mother and infant monkeys." In M. Lewis and L. A. Rosenblum (eds), *The Effect of the Infant on Its Caretaker*. New York: John Wiley & Sons, 211–26.

Ruke-Dravina, V. (1976). "Gibt es Universalien in der Ammensprache?" *Salzburger Beiträge zur Linguistik*, **2**, 3–16.

Rumbaugh, D. M. (1965). "Maternal care in relation to infant behavior in the squirrel monkey." *Psychological Reports*, 171–6.

Ryan, M. (1978). "Contour in context." In R. Campbell and P. Smith (eds), *Recent Advances in the Psychology of Language*. New York: Plenum Press, 237–51.

Ryan, M. J., Fox, J. H., Wilczynski, W., and Rand, A. S. (1990). "Sexual selection for sensory exploitation in the frog Physalaemus pustulosus." *Nature*, **343**, 66–7.

Scherer, K. R. (1985). "Vocal affect signaling: A comparative approach." *Advances in the Study of Behavior*, **15**, 189–244.

Scherer, K. R. (1986). "Vocal affect expression: A review and a model for future research." *Psychological Bulletin*, **99**, 143–65.

Schneider, B. A., Trehub, S. E., and Bull, D. (1979). "The development of basic auditory process in infants." *Canadian Journal of Psychology*, **33**, 306–19.

Shepard, R. N. (1992). "The perceptual organization of colors: An adaptation to regularities of the terrestrial world?" In J. H. Barkow, L. Cosmides, and J. Tooby (eds), *The Adapted Mind: Evolutionary psychology and the generation of culture*. Oxford: Oxford University Press.

Shimoda, K., Argyle, M., and Riccibitti, P. (1978). "The intercultural recognition of emotional expressions by three national racial groups: English, Italian and Japanese." *European Journal of Social Psychology*, **8**, 169–79.

Smith, W. J. (1977). *The Behavior of Communicating: An ethological approach*. Cambridge, MA: Harvard University Press.

Snow, C. E. (1977). "The development of conversation between mothers and babies." *Journal of Child Language*, **4**, 1–22.

Snow, C. E. and Ferguson, C. E. (1977). *Talking to Children: Language input and acquisition*. Cambridge, MA: Cambridge University Press.

Steinschneider, A., Lipton, E. L., and Richmond, J. B. (1966). "Auditory sensitivity in the infant: Effect of intensity on cardiac and motor responsivity." *Child Development*, **37**, 233–52.

Stern, D. N. (1977). *The First Relationship: Infant and mother*. Cambridge: Harvard University Press.

Stern, D. N. (1985). *The Interpersonal World of the Infant*. New York: Basic Books.

Stern, D. N., Spieker, S., Barnett, R. K., and MacKain, K. (1983). "The prosody of maternal speech: Infant age and context related changes." *Journal of Child Language*, **10**, 1–15.

Stern, D. N., Spieker, S., and MacKain, K. (1982). "Intonation contours as signals in maternal speech to prelinguistic infants." *Developmental Psychology*, **18**, 727–35.

Tartter, V. C. (1980). "Happy talk: Perceptual and acoustic effects of smiling on speech." *Perception and Psychophysics*, **27**, 24–7.

Tinbergen, N. (1952). "'Derived' activities: Their causation, biological significance, origin and emancipation during evolution." *Quarterly Review of Biology*, **17**, 1–32.

Tinbergen, N. (1963). "On aims and methods of ethology." *Zeitschrift für Tierpsychologie*, **20**, 410–29.

Trehub, S. E., Thorpe, L. A., and Morrongiello, B. A. (1987). "Organizational processes in infants' perception of auditory patterns." *Child Development*, **58**, 741–9.

Waser, P. M. and Brown C. H. (1986). "Habitat acoustics and primate communication." *American Journal of Primatology*, **10**, 135–54.

Waser, P. M. and Waser, M. S. (1977). "Experimental studies of primate vocalisations: Specializations for long-distance propagation." *Zeitschrift für Tierpsychologie*, **43**, 239–63.

Watterson, T. and Riccillo, S. C. (1983). "Vocal suppression as a neonatal response to auditory stimuli." *Journal of Auditory Research*, **23**, 205–14.

Werker, J. F. and McLeod, P. J. (1989). "Infant preference for both male and female infant-directed talk: A developmental study of attentional and affective responsiveness." *Canadian Journal of Psychology*, **43**, 230–46.

Whitaker, H. A. (1976). "Neurobiology of language." In E. C. Carterette and M. P. Friedman (eds), *Handbook of Perception* (Vol. 7). New York: Academic Press, 121–44.

Wiley, R. H. (1983). "The evolution of communication: Information and manipulation." In T. R. Halliday and P. J. B. Slater (eds), *Communication*. Oxford: Blackwell Scientific Publications, 156–215.

Williams, G. C. (1966). *Adaptation and Natural Selection: A critique of some current evolutionary thought*. Princeton, NJ: Princeton University Press.

Wolff, P. H. (1963). "Observations on the early development of smiling." In B. M. Foss (ed.), *Determinants of Infant Behavior, II*. London: Methuen, 113–34.

Wormith, S. J., Pankhurst, D., and Moffitt, A. R. (1975). "Frequency discrimination by young infants." *Child Development*, **46**, 272–5.

– 1.2

Modularity and Constraints in Early Lexical Acquisition:
Evidence from children's early language and gesture

Laura Ann Petitto

The ontogeny of language and gesture

Only one explanation of human language ontogeny fully accounts for over a decade of findings in my laboratory concerning signing and speaking children's use of early lexical and gestural forms: Humans are born with a predisposition to discover particular sized units with particular distributional patterns in the input, guided by innately specified structural constraints (e.g., Jusczyk, 1986; Petitto, 1984, 1985a, 1985b, 1987; Pinker, 1984; Pinker and Bloom, 1990). At birth, this nascent structure-seeking mechanism is sensitive to the patterned organization of natural language phonology common to all world languages (e.g., Fernald *et al.*, 1989), be they spoken or signed (e.g., rhythmic, temporal, and hierarchical organization) and is particularly sensitive to structures in the input that correspond to the size and distributional patterns of the syllable in spoken and signed languages (e.g., Mehler and Fox, 1985; Petitto and Marentette, 1991a). Irrespective of whether an infant is exposed to spoken or signed languages, this nascent structure-seeking mechanism is capable of utilizing whichever channel (or modality) is receiving the structured input—and it will do so without any modification, loss, or delay to the timing, sequence, and maturational course associated with reaching all linguistic milestones in language acquisition (e.g., Petitto, 1984, 1985a, 1985b, 1986, 1987, 1988; Petitto and Marentette, 1990, 1991b), providing systematic language exposure begins very early (preferably at birth). For example, deaf children acquiring signed languages from birth and hearing children acquiring spoken languages from birth achieve all linguistic milestones on an identical time course (e.g., Petitto, 1984, 1985a, 1985b, 1986, 1987, 1988).[1] Even more surprising, "bilingual" hearing children in deaf or deaf and hearing homes, who are exposed to both a signed and spoken language from birth, achieve all linguistic milestones in both modalities at the same time (e.g., vocal and manual babbling, first words and first signs, first grammatical combinations of words and signs, respectively, and beyond), and on the same maturational time-course as other monolingual hearing and deaf children (Petitto and Marentette, 1990, 1991b); indeed, their general pattern of language acquisition follows those reported in the literature for hearing children in bilingual homes acquiring two spoken languages (e.g., Genesee, 1987). One would expect that if speech were more suited to the human brain's maturational needs in ontogeny, this very group of children would attempt to glean every morsel of speech that they could get from their environment—perhaps even turning away from the signed input—favoring instead the speech input. But this is not what happens. Signed and spoken languages are acquired effortlessly by these children, and all of the children, including the deaf children of deaf parents, acquire signed languages in the same way, at the same time, exhibiting the same linguistic, semantic, and conceptual complexity (stage for stage) as hearing children acquiring spoken languages (see also Petitto and Charron, 1987).

Such findings compel the conclusion that all infants initially attend to and seek to discover very particular aspects of language structure at birth, irrespective of the modality of the input. Indeed, linguistically structured input—and not modality—is the critical factor required to trigger human language acquisition. This early template or structure-seeking mechanism constitutes the initial contents (or, "representation") of the nascent human language capacity at birth, which matures throughout development. At birth, it is initially blind to modality; it is "amodal" (i.e., it is capable of seeking specific structures in multiple modalities). When specific structures in the input correspond with those in the infant's nascent template, a tacit decomposition of the elements of the match begins. The product of such decompositions can then serve both as the units over which infants discover the permissible segments and combinatorial rules of their target language, and as the basis from which systematic motor production programs of early language units are derived: Hence, witness the existence of vocal and manual babbling. Each completed analysis permits the child to extract larger and larger components of language structure from the input, thereby propelling very early linguistic development from one period to the next. Again, this entire process is not special to speech. Importantly, the infant's structure-seeking mechanism permits him or her to begin the language acquisition process through very early tacit analysis of particular structures in the input—especially the general prosodic and sublexical phonological structures of language—well in advance of the infant having to know either the meanings or the grammar of the target language.

It follows from my arguments that the means by which the language capacity can be expressed *in ontogeny* need not be restricted (a priori) to exactly two modalities, spoken and signed. For obvious reasons, any productive system of language must be (a) perceivable, (b) producible by the human body, and (c) potentially segmentable (a restricted set of segments must be capable of multiple combinatorial possibilities). In principle, properties of the human body that satisfy these constraints could serve as language articulators (i.e., a means for expressing the contents of the language capacity). Although the oral-aural (speech) and manual-visual (sign) modalities are clearly best suited for language transmission and reception in ontogeny, it is possible that—under certain extraordinary circumstances—other units (perhaps the lower limbs in combination with facial markers) could serve as a vehicle by which the contents of the language capacity can be expressed. Note, however, that motor production systems alone do not constitute knowledge of language, as one essential feature of language is its underlying structure, and the structure of language is not wholly derived from the organization of any given motor production system—be it the hands, face, or mouth—although, clearly, a given modality does exert some influence on language structure. This fact is immediately apparent when considering the structure of signed and spoken languages: Both signed and spoken languages are produced with radically different articulators (both are subserved by different neurological motor substrates in the brain), yet both exhibit identical levels of language structure (e.g., phonological, morphological, syntactic, semantic, discourse). Moreover, both signed and spoken languages are acquired in highly similar ways, with babbling serving as one particularly revealing example: The *common* syllabic organization observed both in the vocal babbling of hearing infants and in the manual babbling of deaf (and hearing) infants exposed to signed languages, despite radical modality differences, could only be the product of a *common* brain-based structure-seeking mechanism (e.g., Petitto and Marantette, 1991a).

The claim, then, is that humans are born with a nascent structure-seeking mechanism, blind to modality, which initially attends to and seeks to discover particular units with particular distributional patterns in the input, corresponding in size and organization to the phonetic and syllabic units common to all languages (spoken or signed). The saliency of particular types of patterns over others in the input is entirely commensurate with what we know about other brain-based biological systems, such as the visual system. For example, the specialization of particular cells to particular patterns of visual stimuli (e.g., form, size, and orientation) is a well-known system of this sort (Hubel and Wiesel, 1959). However, the nascent human language capacity can seek particular linguistic patterns in multiple modalities (e.g., the pursuit of particular patterns is neither restricted to visual nor to speech stimuli). Implicit in this theory is the claim that the infant's tacit structure-seeking analyses are the product of innately specified mechanisms that respond to specific patterns unique to world languages (i.e., units possessing phonetic and syllabic size and organization, as well as the phonological and prosodic markers specified earlier), and not to general perceptual, or general cognitive dimensions. In this way, they are domain-specific pattern analyzing mechanisms. Particularly dramatic support for this claim comes from the study discussed here in which young deaf infants consistently differentiate between signs (identical to words) and gestures throughout development, even though signs and gestures reside in the same modality, and even though some signs and gestures share formation and referential properties. The infants' failure to confuse signs and gestures suggests that gestures must violate the structural requirements of the nascent structure-seeking mechanism and that a structure-seeking mechanism exists, sorting through the input and searching for a particular structure and no other. Thus, as is shown here, *aspects* of human language acquisition must be driven by language-specific knowledge—knowledge that is not wholly derived from infants' general cognitive capacities (see also Petitto, 1984, 1985a, 1985b, 1987, 1988).

A clear implication here is that, in ontogeny, humans can acquire language in either the spoken or signed modalities, be they hearing or deaf. Once the child is exposed to structured linguistic information in one modality (e.g., the verbal modality in hearing children), the alternative, "unused" modality (e.g., the gestural–visual modality in hearing children), can then serve secondary signaling and augmenting functions. However, signaling and augmenting functions are "piggybacked" onto the child's emerging linguistic and conceptual capacities and not vice versa.

Like other biological phenomena, mastery of a target competence—in this case, a target language—depends on the organism's ability to receive and maintain a steady sample of input despite a constantly varying environment (e.g., Mayr, 1982; Shatz, 1985). Young infants' early gestures (e.g., pointing) provide them with a mechanism by which they can attract a caretaker's attention, who then responds with a communicative exchange that invariably contains linguistic content. Indeed, it is widely known that young children's gestures elicit rich linguistic input from caretakers, especially names for things (e.g., Shatz, 1985). This use of gesturing constitutes a "mechanism of self-control" (e.g., Shatz, 1985; see also Petitto, 1985b, 1988). That is, early gestures ensure that the young infant receives and maintains ample linguistic input. This input constitutes the "data" over which the child tacitly performs his or her language structure-seeking analyses that will ultimately yield "knowledge of language" (e.g., Chomsky, 1975; Gleitman and Wanner, 1982; Petitto, 1987, 1988; Pinker, 1979, 1984).

Children's later gestures (e.g., twelve–twenty-four months) serve an important augmentative function. They are used to augment (through emphasis) the child's failed communicative interactions, which, at first, typically involved only their primary linguistic system. As is shown in this chapter, support for this claim comes from a variety of observations, including: (a) Symbolic gestures (empty-handed gestures that "stand for" or "represent"

(margin annotation:) input driven

referents) in hearing and deaf children occur only *after* children are able to first comprehend and/or produce the corresponding primary linguistic form (i.e., the word or sign, respectively). The reverse ordering was never observed. (b) Young children (from around eleven months old and beyond) produce even their *earliest* lexical forms in constrained ways that correspond to different word/sign types (object names, property words, event words, etc.; Carey, 1982; Huttenlocher and Smiley, 1987; Keil, 1989; Markman, 1989; Petitto, 1988; Quine, 1969). However, their use of symbolic gestures within this same time-period was used both within and across word/sign type boundaries; this revealing finding suggests that the knowledge underlying gesture and language is distinct, and provides key insights into the nature and type of linguistic and conceptual constraints underlying children's early lexicon. (c) Children use their symbolic gestures largely to augment their primary linguistic system (be it spoken or signed), often when a communicative interaction between adult and child fails and almost always to request objects rather than to identify or name them.

To review, once systematic input is received in a primary channel, the alternative channel can then assume global signaling and augmenting roles, drawing from and driven by the contents of the blossoming linguistic capacity. However, without systematic input, the "unused" channel—again, the gestural–visual modality in the case of hearing children—remains an unsystematic signaling device, which then takes on very different, but none-theless useful, language-eliciting and language-augmenting functions. The distinction between primary linguistic systems and gestures is so powerful in ontogeny that the language–gesture distinction is maintained even in infants acquiring signed languages. Indeed, the child exposed to signed languages carves out this distinction even though the input channel contains both language and gesture in a single gestural–visual modality, and even though language and gesture in signed languages can be tantalizingly close in their formational and referential properties. That the language–gesture distinction is observed even in extremely young infants acquiring signed languages provides additional support for the claim that the human infant is predisposed to discover particular linguistic structures in the input, guided by innately specified structural constraints that have unique (domain-specific) representation and that can be mapped onto multiple production channels at birth—as signed language studies have clearly demonstrated that the newborn's specifically linguistic structural analyses of the input is not specific to the speech modality. Importantly, hearing children's very ability to produce gestures reflects their residual capacity to receive and produce language in the gestural–visual modality, should they have been exposed to it.

Thus, comparative analyses of gesture and language provide a clear window into the biological foundations of human language. Later, I focus on one type of gesture in language acquisition, the symbolic gesture, because the perceived similarities between this particular type of gesture and children's first words have been used to support extremely powerful theories of mind (e.g., Acredolo and Goodwyn, 1985, 1988; Bates, Benigni, *et al.*, 1979; Bates, Bretherton, *et al.*, 1983; Goodwyn and Acredolo, 1991; Lock, 1978; Piaget, 1962; Shore, O'Connell, and Bates, 1984; Werner and Kaplan, 1963). Although a clear prediction of the theory that I have just outlined is that children's early lexical and gestural use will be similar on some dimensions, it clearly predicts that critical *differences* should also exist between them. Similarities will occur because augmentative gestural signaling is parasitic on the child's emerging linguistic and conceptual capacities. Differences will occur because aspects of language (e.g., the infant's structure-seeking capacity) constitute domain-specific knowledge.

However, current research on children's gestures has focused nearly exclusively on the similarities between gestures and language rather than on the differences between them. Indeed, many researchers compare young children's gestures and early lexicon, stressing the similarities between the two, and then conclude that gestural communication and language are fundamentally continuous because of these similarities. Aside from the fact that language is often defined in simplistic ways in the service of such comparisons (e.g., language exclusively in terms of its "communicative function"), the basic problem with this approach is that it makes the hypothesis that gestures are positively related to human language wholly *unfalsifiable*. What is the metric for counting similarities? How many must there be in order to conclude that the young child's gestures resemble the use of language in an interesting way (e.g., see Seidenberg and Petitto, 1987)?

That similarities exist between children's symbolic gestures and first words is not denied in this chapter; children's symbolic gestures and early lexicon do share referential and communicative properties. Nevertheless, I show here that despite these similarities, key differences exist that shed new light on the unique constraints that underlie human language acquisition in particular, as compared with other general cognitive and communicative capacities to symbolize. In the course of doing so, I hope to provide insights into the nature of gestures, the constraints that underlie early lexical knowledge, and, most importantly, the types of knowledge underlying human language acquisition.

Types of gestures in human development

All humans gesture. An intriguing feature of human development is that infants also produce gestures well before the onset of their first words. Many children continue to gesture while producing their early words and beyond. Summarized here are the variety of gestural types common to most children.

Beginning around nine months and continuing throughout the first three years, infants use indexical gestures ("pointing gestures") in a wide variety of contexts, performing various communicative functions, such as requesting and denoting. By thirteen months, however, children display a fascinating ability to produce a variety of non-indexical gestures and other manual actions with and without objects in hand. For example, if presented with an empty cup, most children will bring it to their lips and produce drinking-like motions ("actions with objects"). Or, when desiring to be held, many children will raise their arms above their heads to be picked up; likewise, when desiring an object, many children will produce the classic "beg gesture," whereby they hold out their hand, often opening and closing it ("empty-handed instrumental gestures"). Further, children also produce a variety of culturally established gestures (e.g., waving "hello" and "bye-bye"; "yes" and "no" head nods) and routinized gestures in games (e.g., "itsy-bitsy spider") that are found in many societies ("social gestures"). Later, around fifteen months, children produce empty-handed gestures for things and events in the world ("symbolic gestures"). For example, if presented with a closed jar, some children will spontaneously produce an empty-handed "twist" gesture.

The main distinction drawn among the various types of gestures involves the extent to which gestural types *symbolize* referents (e.g., object, person, place; what is referred to) and events in the world, rather than simply refer to them. Minimally, a gesture is a manual form that refers to or picks out a referent or event in the world. Gestures, however, can also be used to symbolize ("stand for" or "represent") a given referent or event. Although the pointing gesture can refer to (or pick out) referents and events, it typically does not symbolize them. Indeed, a single pointing form can refer to a potentially infinite class of referents. Further, there is a literal, physical identity between the form of "actions with objects" and what one does with a given object once in hand ("brushing" actions with brushes is what one does with a brush to realize its function). Similarly, the form of instrumental gestures appears to be part of the action associated with a given referent or event. For example, the form of the "beg" or "give me" gesture appears to be tied to the actual behavior used in the act of receiving (or taking), rather than a schematic representation of it (the child enacts rather than depicts). In contrast, the form of symbolic gestures involves some degree of representation. The child could, but does not, actually twist open a jar when producing the "twist" gesture. Symbolic gestures preserve partial information about actions that are associated with objects (e.g., twisting hand motions when opening jars), but they are not the enactment of the designated activity (e.g., children do not literally open a jar). In this sense, then, it has been argued that, for example, a form such as the "twist" gesture is a schematic representation for jars because they can be said both to refer to (pick out) and represent (symbolize) the referents (e.g., Bates, Benigni, *et al.*, 1979; Bates, Bretherton, *et al.*, 1983; Werner and Kaplan, 1963).

Attributions of lexical status to children's gestures: When are gestures said to be linguistic?

Little controversy exists over children's indexical gestures, social gestures, and other clearly nonlinguistic activities (e.g., scratching, reaching, grabbing). Most researchers studying the gestures of hearing children set aside these three types, as they are typically not judged to have lexical (linguistic) status. An analysis of instrumental gestures was provided earlier and in Petitto (1988). However, "actions with objects" and "symbolic gestures" remain the subjects of controversy, with the linguistic status of symbolic gestures constituting the most lively debate of all. Indeed, symbolic gestures and their referential and representational (symbolic) status have been directly compared to the referential and representational status of children's first words, with identical linguistic status (grammatical and semantic) attributed to both (e.g., Acredolo and Goodwyn, 1985, 1988, 1990; Bates, Benigni, *et al.*, 1979; Bates, Bretherton, *et al.*, 1983; Goodwyn and Acredolo, 1991; Lock, 1978; Piaget, 1962; Shore *et al.*, 1984; Werner and Kaplan, 1963). Consequently, the existence of symbolic gestures has been regarded as providing critical insights into the knowledge that underlies the human language acquisition process.

Actions with objects in hand

Initially, some researchers made very strong claims about children's "actions with objects." Indeed, previous researchers referred to this type of manual activity as "gestures with objects," and they explicitly claimed that the thirteen-month-old's manual activities with objects did not constitute *pre*linguistic acts at all. Rather, they were said to be the gestural equivalents of linguistic names for things and were considered to be a kind of "noun or object name" (Bates, Bretherton, *et al.*, 1983). It was claimed that when a child produces an action with an object in hand (e.g., drinking motions with a cup), the use of this hand activity is *functionally identical* to the child's early use of words (e.g., saying *drink* upon noticing a cup). Similarly, the word "cup" is used with cups and not other objects. In the same way that a child uses the word "cup" to pick out a referent as being a member of a known class or kind, it was argued that the child's use of the *action* for cup is also showing that this gestural act is true of the objects that belong to the class or kind "cup." The presumption here is that children will not produce *function violations*. That is, children will not "drink" with, for example, a hammer, because this manual act is not "true" of the class or kind within which hammer resides.

I have argued elsewhere that the claims made here are most probably false (Petitto, 1985a, 1985b; see especially 1988). First, close examination of children's entire range and use of actions with objects (ages nine through twenty months) reveals that they are not used in a way that is functionally identical to children's use of early words. Children (thirteen months and beyond) will produce methodical and repetitive sequences of actions with objects in hand with no apparent communicative function or intent. That is, they do not use "actions with objects" communicatively, whereas they do so freely with their corresponding first words occurring within the same time-period. For example, children will produce the action for cup without any apparent communicative intent (eye gaze fixed at object rather than adult), but will use the word "cup" in rich and varied ways to identify cups, to comment upon liquid being added to a cup, to be given a cup, and so forth (with eye gaze to adult, and/or from object to adult or vice versa). Second, children (thirteen to eighteen months) routinely begin by making function violations when producing actions with objects, suggesting that object functions must be learned, and are learned over time. Although thirteen-month-old children would pick up a spoon, place it in an empty cup, and "stir," they were equally likely to pick up other objects that shared certain critical physical dimensions with spoons and "stir" with them as well (e.g., hammer, mirror); importantly, children produced correctly many of the words for objects *prior* to producing the correct functions (or actions) associated with the same objects (Petitto, 1988). Thus, it appears that children's "actions with objects" in hand are not used identically to linguistic names or "nouns." Rather, they appear to be complex actions associated with objects, an observation originally made by Piaget (1962).

Symbolic gestures

Children's empty-handed symbolic gestures are by far the most interesting type of gesture, and they are the focus of this chapter. Because there appears to be general correspondences between this type of gesture and children's early lexicon, they have recently received much attention. In general, some children produce symbolic gestures within the same time-period when they exhibit a period of rapid vocabulary growth (fifteen to eighteen months, or eighteen to twenty-four months). Both symbolic gestures and words are used communicatively and intentionally; both are used referentially; both appear to have some representational component; both appear to be used in functionally correct ways. Thus, researchers have claimed that children's early *symbolic gestures* and early *words* are deeply equivalent; symbolic gestures are said to have lexical status, albeit in the gestural mode. Moreover, they are said to be parallel expressions of reference. Indeed, the single persistent assertion common to many current studies is that symbolic gestures and words have equal symbolic status, that is, gestures *mean* the same thing as words (e.g., Acredolo and Goodwyn, 1985, 1988, 1990; Bates, Benigni, *et al.*, 1979; Bates, Bretherton, *et al.*, 1983; Goodwyn and Acredolo, 1991; Lock, 1978; Piaget, 1962; Shore *et al.*, 1984; Werner and Kaplan, 1963).

Consequences for theories of mind

The previous interpretation of children's symbolic gestures and words has been used to support a very powerful theory of mind. Because both gesture and word are said to have equal symbolic status, it has been argued that the representation of language in the brain is routed in general cognitive capacities (cognitive–general model). Indeed, correspondences between early symbolic gestures and first words have been regarded as " . . . providing support for the hypothesis that strides in cognitive abilities such as memory, categorization, and symbolization underlie [the first symbolic gesture and first word] milestone in both modalities" (Goodwyn and Acredolo, 1991: 2). Although the identical data would also support the equally plausible hypothesis that similarities between gestures and words are driven by a specifically linguistic capacity, this possibility is not considered. Instead, the interpretation here has been used to challenge a major alternative theory of language representation in child development, one in which language is considered to be a distinct mental capacity, reflecting domain-specific knowledge that is not wholly derived from general cognitive capacities (domain-specific model). In this latter view, distinct representational structures underlie language but no other communicative capacity such as gesturing; we know this view as a "modular" model of the brain.

Thus, we have a situation in child development where very strong claims are being made about the brain-based knowledge that underlies human language acquisition, which, in turn, rely entirely on the claim that children's gestures and language are used in symbolically and functionally equivalent ways.

Existing evidence

None of the brain-based claims that gestures and words have equal symbolic status is based on *data samples* and/or *data analyses* that would support the claims (e.g., Acredolo and Goodwyn, 1985, 1988, 1990; Bates, Benigni, *et al.*, 1979; Bates, Bretherton, *et al.*, 1983; Goodwyn and Acredolo, 1991; Lock, 1978; Piaget, 1962; Shore *et al.*, 1984; Werner and Kaplan, 1963). For example, although Goodwyn and Acredolo (1991) employ very commendable criteria for what constitutes a symbolic gesture or word, the basic data sample of the children's *gestures* were collected from audiotaped telephone interviews containing mothers' *verbal* reports. That is, the gestures produced by the children were never actually seen or analysed by the experimenters; this is true for the children's words as well. The data in this and related studies include:

1. lists of symbolic gestures and their English glosses, as well as their grammatical categories (e.g., common noun, proper noun);
2. the age at which the mother said that her child first produced symbolic gestures (as compared with first words); and
3. the manner in which the mother said the symbolic gestures were used (spontaneous, imitative, elicited) and acquired (directly taught by a parent, spontaneous imitation/parental actions, etc.) as compared with words.

In summary, use of mothers' reports—which involve a mother's attributions of meaning to her child's forms and are typically based on her memory of its use—makes it difficult to interpret these researchers' potentially important claims.

Mothers' reports cannot be used as primary data in child language, either for words (e.g., Huttenlocher and Smiley, 1987) or gestures (e.g., Petitto, 1985a, 1985b, 1988). As Brown and Hanlon (1970) noted, parents pay far more attention to the meaning of their children's utterances rather than to the syntactic form. The identical phenomenon exists when parents evaluate their children's gestures (Petitto, 1985a, 1985b, 1988). Parents do not interpret children's gestures based on how they were used in the past, or whether there are consistent correlations between particular gestural forms and their referents. For example, in studies of parental attributions in my laboratory (e.g., Petitto, 1988), one parent, in the same taping session, attributed a *single meaning* to her child's gesture, even though the child used *multiple gestural forms*, in the identical context, at different times. Conversely, a *single gestural form* was interpreted as having *multiple meanings* at different times throughout the session; these findings are representative of the other mothers in our studies. In the same study, a deaf researcher was asked to transcribe a videotape of a *hearing* boy aged ten and eleven months (see Petitto, 1988, for details). Based on the child's natural repertoire of gestures (e.g., reaching, grasping, banging, pointing gestures, and other motoric hand movements), she reported nearly 100 "sign" utterances, including complex sign combinations. Thus, parents and researchers alike freely attribute a variety of complex desires, intentions, and knowledge to children's gestures, based on their interpretation of what they think the child means, rather than on the actual gestural form used to convey it.

In order to assess claims about the symbolic status of gestures, the appropriate data need to be gathered. That is, children's actual gestures must be studied, rather than the researcher's English glosses of mothers' reports of their children's gestures. Once the data are gathered, the following types of analyses can be conducted: (a) identification of the gestural forms, relative frequency, and distribution of all forms both within and across children over time; (b) the range of referents over which the forms are applied (and vice versa); and (c) a comparison of the forms/range of referents for both gestures and words, and all other analyses detailed here.

Predications and objectives

If symbolic gestures *mean* the same thing as words, it would follow that they are used in ways highly similar to children's use of early words, particularly their words for objects. Construed as a testable hypothesis about the language acquisition process, the prediction is that there will be consistent word and gesture use with regard to the same or highly similar range of objects in the world.

Studying the question in the context of signed languages offers a unique window into the knowledge that underlies human language acquisition. In signed languages, both gesture and language reside in a single modality, the gestural–visual modality. Thus, the existence of signed languages provides a "natural experiment" regarding the two conflicting models of the brain. For hearing children, gestures and words are produced using different modalities (gestural and vocal), which may clue them into any different referential properties of early gestures and words, should they exist. This is not the case with children acquiring signed languages. If children's gestures and early lexical items have equal symbolic status (mean the same thing), we might expect to see especially close correspondences between them in children acquiring signed languages. If, however, distinct knowledge structures underlie children's gestural and lexical use, then their use should differ. Indeed, when I first began this research, one question intrigued me most: Will the young signing children show *any* evidence of differentiating gestures from signs given that both are in the same modality?

In the remaining portion of this chapter, I focus largely on what I have learned about young hearing and deaf children's symbolic gestures. I provide the first analyses of the form of children's symbolic gestures, especially with regard to the range of referents over which the form(s) are applied. I also provide the first comparisons between the range of referents for symbolic gestures and the range of referents for early words in hearing children and early signs in deaf children. This makes it possible to determine whether symbolic gestures and early language have equal symbolic status.

Subjects

To examine the questions asked earlier, I summarize the findings from one group of six children whose results are representative of all of the other children studied in my laboratory. The six subjects included three hearing children of hearing parents acquiring spoken languages (languages: two French, one English), and three profoundly deaf children of deaf parents acquiring signed languages (languages: two Langue des Signes Québécoise, LSQ, one American Sign Language, ASL),[2] ages eight through twenty months.[3]

Methods

Procedures

Monthly videotapes of each child and a parent were collected (see Petitto and Kampen, in preparation, for a full report on the procedures and analyses used in this study). After an initial warm-up period in which the child played with toys, four controlled elicitation tasks were administered to assess the child's production and comprehension of words and/or signs and gestures, including common gestures and those produced by the children themselves. Every videotaping session also contained a period with (a) the parent and child in free play and (b) the child alone in free play. Further, monthly reports of the child's lexical and gestural activity were collected from the parent using the Bates and Fenson assessment battery ("MacArthur Communicative Development Inventory: Infants and Toddlers"), and detailed experimenter reports were also made at the end of each taping session. Videotaped sessions served as the primary data in this study and parental and experimenter reports were used only to ensure that our samples were representative of the child's behavior at any given age.

Data transcription

Detailed transcriptions of the entire content of each videotape were made by two independent observers and entered into a computer database. Transcriptions were entirely theory-neutral. In this transcription system, the precise physical form of the child's every manual activity is coded with diacritics that represent the internal and external features of the hand(s), such as its handshape, movement, and location in space; head, face, and body movements are also coded (see also Petitto, 1988; Petitto and Marentette, 1991a). Then, the precise manner of use is coded for each manual activity, including whether the form

1. was produced in a spontaneous, imitative, or elicited manner;
2. was used with or without objects in hand;
3. was used "referentially" (used in relation to a referent in the world; if so, the precise referent was specified);
4. was used "communicatively" (produced with clear communicative intent; e.g., involved eye gaze with an adult);
5. had "conventional meaning" (manual activity with established cultural meaning that was not the standard sign in either ASL or LSQ);[4] or
6. was a standard word or sign (or "lexical form"; more on this later).

Information about the apparent function of the manual form for the child as well as detailed information about the context were also coded. Finally, mothers' manual activity was also coded. Mothers' reactions to the child's manual activity (mothers' apparent interpretation), and the child's reaction to the mother's manual activity were also coded. Children's verbal productions were coded in a similar manner, except that extremely detailed phonetic transcriptions were not made for each form; in particular, an unidentifiable vocalization would be coded as a "voc" and then the other information would be subsequently coded.

Unique features of transcription system

Use of this transcription system permitted frequency and distributional analyses of all of the types of children's manual and verbal activities over time, and across thousands of contexts, in a way that has simply never before been provided in the literature. Moreover, it permitted within and across child comparisons of manual and verbal activities in a manner that has also never been provided before. Importantly, this transcription system permitted the following crucial analysis necessary to make attributions of meaning to children's forms: For every manual and verbal form, it was possible to identify the precise range of referents to which it was produced in relation. Conversely, for every referent, the exact manual and verbal form(s) that were used with it were also wholly identifiable.

Data analyses

The overall behavioral patterns and their frequencies and distributions were identified within and across children over time, for example (a) empty-handed activity; (b) manual activity with objects in hand; (c) head, face, and body movements; and (d) lexical forms (including ill-articulated and proto-forms; see Petitto and Kampen, in preparation, for details). Children's use of empty-handed activity was compared with their use of manual activity with objects in hand, and children's use of empty-handed activity was compared with their use of lexical forms. Of particular interest was the nature of the relationship between a given form and its referent—in other words, we were interested in a form's meaning as well as the range of meanings that children expressed through their use of gestures and lexical forms.

The set of "symbolic gestures" and the set of "lexical forms"

Similar criteria were used to determine whether a manual or verbal form was to be considered a candidate for inclusion in the set of "symbolic gestures" or the set of "lexical forms," respectively. Both manual and verbal forms minimally had to "refer." Operationally, this meant that a form had to be used in relation to a referent (e.g., eye gaze includes gaze to a target referent, and/or related referents if none existed in the world). There were also the following form requirements:

1. As was noted in the introduction, the form of symbolic gestures contains a representational component; thus, to be considered a candidate for inclusion in the set of symbolic gestures, in addition to referring, a manual form also had to contain a representational component; that is, the child may not have actually produced the manual form by physically manipulating a target referent.

2. To be considered a candidate as a "lexical form," a further requirement was that verbal or manual forms had to be produced according to the standard— or approximation to standard-articulary constraints of the adult word or sign (respectively); importantly, the child did not have to produce the exact adult form (ill-formed and ill-articulated forms, baby words and signs, and proto words and signs were accepted), and the child did not have to demonstrate adult usage (adult meaning).

These criteria both capture the critical features used to identify children's symbolic gestures and words in the literature and, at the same time, they are overinclusive relative to them. For example, a form did not have to be produced spontaneously in order to be considered a candidate for inclusion in the set of "symbolic gestures" or set of "lexical forms"; the analyses of possible symbolic gestures was also expanded to include forms produced nonmanually (i.e., on the face, head, and body). This procedure was adopted to "stack the deck against our hypothesis," that is, to find as many candidates for our analyses as possible, should they exist.

Attribution of meaning: Do symbolic gestures and lexical forms have equal symbolic status?

The identical criteria were used to evaluate the symbolic status of the forms just discussed. In order to determine whether children's set of "symbolic gestures" and set of "lexical forms" had equal symbolic status (i.e., the *same meaning*), it was necessary to determine the child's grasp of the meaning of lexical and symbolic gestural forms.

The study of word meaning has a long, thorny history, and at least three critical distinctions must be made when studying it: (a) What is the meaning of a word? (b) What is an individual's grasp of the meaning of a word? and (c) How can researchers determine an individual's (a child's) meaning of a word?[5] In Petitto (1985a, 1985b, 1988), I attempt to answer these questions. I discuss cognitive notions of reference and argue that the meaning of, for example, a common noun, is the range of referents over which it could potentially refer (be applied). Like others, I argue that an individual's word meanings have both intensional and extensional referential properties, and that an individual's word meanings are conceptually constrained across kinds or types of words (e.g., kinds of objects, kinds of events, kinds of possessions, kinds of locations). I further argue that a revealing way to determine the child's grasp of the meaning of a word is to examine the range of referents over which a given word is applied. Here, I use similar analyses to examine the meaning of children's lexical and symbolic gestural forms.

In this study, meaning is determined by observing the relationship between a child's form (be it lexical or symbolic gestural) and the entire range of referents over which the form applied. Once this is done, the meanings of all of a given child's lexical forms and all of her symbolic gestural forms are compared, within the child and across children. Note that the more general problems associated with extensional (associationist, and/or behaviorist) theories of word meaning are not at issue here, nor do they detract from the value of using this particular method as an operational measure of children's competence (e.g., see Petitto, 1985a, 1985b, 1988; see also Huttenlocher and Smiley, 1987, for an excellent discussion of the controversy over determining word meanings in child language, and the database that is required in order to make attributions of meaning to children's lexical forms).[6] Once the sets of symbolic gestures and lexical forms were identified, the following analyses were used to assess their meaning: (a) was a given form used systematically? (i.e., was it used in a stable manner across multiple contexts?); (b) was a given form used in relation to a preferent, was this use systematic, was this use restricted to a particular referent or was it applied over a range of referents?; (c) if a form was applied over a "range of referents," did it constitute a restricted or unrestricted class? Whether a form was used in communicatively and semantically varied ways was also evaluated.

Children's symbolic gestures and lexical forms could—or could not—have been used in the ways detailed here. To be clear, these analyses were seeking to determine any shared pattern of use between the two sets, should they exist, and it was unbiased as to whether a given form was a standard lexical form in the adult language, a gesture, or otherwise.

Reliability

Reliability was assessed for both data transcription and data analysis procedures by two independent coders, with an overall reliability of 89.7 percent (see Petitto and Kampen, in preparation).

Results

A select sample of the analyses conducted on the present data are provided here (see Petitto and Kampen, in preparation, for a full report). There were 4,841 protocols collected from the six children over the course of twelve months. As is standard in the literature, 145 (2.99 percent) of the manual forms were excluded from further analysis because they either occurred one time only ($n = 39$) or they were culturally established social gestures and/or routinized gestures in games ($n = 106$); note, however, that symbolic gestures occurring one time only were not excluded from analysis. Manual forms occurred alone ($n = 2,986$) and in combination with other forms ($n = 1,133$); combinations were comprised mostly of points plus manual actions, or combinations of manual actions, as there were virtually no empty-handed, non-indexical gesture plus gesture combinations in the entire corpora. Most all of the children's manual activity with objects and empty-handed activity were produced spontaneously, which was also true of most of their tokens of lexical forms ($n = 577$).

Here, I first provide an overview of the types and frequency and distribution of the gestures produced alone by the children; this information should provide a basis to interpret the findings regarding symbolic gestures, per se. Then, I provide an overview of how children used symbolic gestures as compared to their early lexicon. One striking finding of this study involved the constrained ways in which children used even their earliest lexical forms; the significance of this finding relative to children's use of symbolic gestures is discussed in the final pages of this chapter.

Gestural types, frequency, and distribution

Types

Six types of manual activity were observed:

1. *motoric hand activity* (e.g., banging, scratching; beginning (b.) around nine months (mths) and peaking (p.) fifteen–eighteen (mths);
2. *pointing* (e.g., to objects, locations, b. seven–nine mths, p. eighteen–twenty-four);
3. *social gestures* (e.g., waving "hello," "bye-bye," "yes-no" head nods; b. twelve mths and beyond) and other highly routinized manual forms common in parent–child games (e.g., patty-cake);
4. *actions with objects in hand* (e.g., brushing with a brush; b. twelve mths and beyond);
5. *instrumental gestures* (e.g., raising arms to be picked up; b. twelve mths, p. fifteen–eighteen mths);
6. *symbolic gestures* (e.g., empty-handed downward movements at side of head while gazing at a comb; b. fourteen–eighteen mths—save one form that appeared at twelve months in one child—p. eighteen–twenty-four mths).

The aforementioned represents the types and approximate developmental sequence of children's manual activities. These findings are entirely commensurate with other data reported in the literature (e.g., Bates, Benigni, *et al.*, 1979; Bates, Bretherton, *et al.*, 1983; Zinober and Martlew, 1985)—although researchers typically do not provide type and frequency data as well as distributional analyses of types over time, especially with regard to children's entire range of manual productions over time (studies by Goldin-Meadow, e.g., Goldin-Meadow and Morford, 1985, constitute the only exception to my knowledge).

Frequency and distribution of types

The types of manual activity produced by the hearing and deaf children, as well as their relative frequency of occurrence, are shown in Figure 1.2.1. What is most

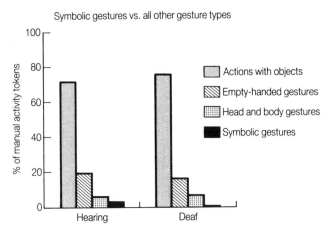

Figure 1.2.1   *Types and relative frequency of manual activity in the hearing and deaf children.*

striking about Figure 1.2.1 is that both the types and the frequencies of gestures are highly similar across the two groups of children.

Figure 1.2.2 shows the relative frequency and distribution of gesture types over time for all of the children. Several important points to note are:

1. Actions with objects were by far the most frequent type found in all six children (*n* = 44 types, 1,888 tokens). The 1,888 tokens were used mostly in noncommunicative ways, consisting largely of actions associated with

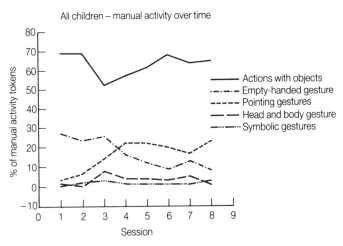

Figure 1.2.2   *Distribution and relative frequency of manual activity by type for all children over time.*

playing with specific objects (e.g., hammering a peg, brushing hair with a hairbrush; 68 percent), followed next by nonrelevant motoric actions with objects (e.g., banging, swatting; 29 percent); the relatively few instances of communicative use involved some token of demonstrative "showing" (e.g., child offers object to an adult; 1 percent), and "requests" (e.g., child holds up one object, such as a toy coin, to obtain a similar one in adult's hand; 2 percent).

2. Empty-handed activity ($n = 12$ types: 485 tokens) included instrumental gestures ($n = 3$ types), which were used almost exclusively to request referents, and empty-handed manual activity produced in play ($n = 9$ types; e.g., stroking, patting, pressing); this "empty-handed activity" type of manual activity was significantly less frequent as compared with actions with objects, and they were even less frequent than pointing ($n = 509$). Head and body gestures occurred less frequently than most of the other types ($n = 7$ types, 104 tokens), but not less than symbolic gestures.

3. Symbolic gestures were the least frequent type to occur of all ($n = 6$ types, forty-eight tokens). Thus, across all children, there were only forty-eight tokens of symbolic gestures out of 4,507 tokens, or 1.1 percent.

Although infrequent, symbolic gestures were nonetheless produced with apparent communicative intent, they appeared to be appropriate to the context, they were referential and contained a representational component. Are *these* forms fundamentally similar to the way children used their first words?

Use of symbolic gestures as compared to use of the early lexicon

The hearing and deaf children spontaneously used symbolic gestures in similar contexts (only in the presence of a referent) and with a similar communicative function (to request). Both groups of children extracted similar salient perceptual features from referents that were then produced in gestural form. For example, hearing and deaf children's symbolic gestures for a toy telephone all involved the feature of bringing the telephone receiver to the ear, although the specific forms of this (and other) symbolic gestures varied within and across children. Some symbolic gestures were used first by the child and some were used by parents and then subsequently used by the child. In either case, parents tended to produce the symbolic gesture themselves.

The hearing and deaf children produced their early lexicon on the same time-course; deaf children do not acquire first signs earlier than hearing children acquire first words (see Note 1). Indeed, deaf and hearing children achieved all early (lexical) and later (grammatical) linguistic milestones on a similar time-course and sequence (see also Petitto and Marentette, 1990, 1991b). Furthermore, the children used their early lexicon with similar communicative functions (e.g., to name objects). Finally, the semantic and grammatical content of both groups of children's lexicon was strikingly similar (see also Petitto and Charron, 1987).

Thus, there were similarities between hearing and deaf children's use of symbolic gestures, and there were similarities between hearing and deaf children's lexical use. However, there were important differences between both groups of children's (a) use of symbolic gestures versus their (b) use of the lexicon that are described below.

Frequency of symbolic gestures versus words/signs

The children's symbolic gestures occurred infrequently relative to their words and signs. There were only forty-eight tokens of symbolic gestures (see Table 1.2.1) as compared with 577 tokens of lexical items (see Table 1.2.2). Three of the six types of symbolic gestures were used by all six children, and the three remaining types were used by one hearing child only; indeed, as is shown in Table 1.2.1, one hearing child (H2) produced all six types and the most tokens, revealing that there are individual differences in children's propensity to produce symbolic gestures.

Distribution of symbolic gestures versus words/signs

Symbolic gestures enter the children's behavioral repertoire relatively late, around fourteen–fifteen months (save one form produced by one child that her mother used, i.e., smacking lips for cookies) and their frequency and distribution remains atypically constant over time. Conversely, children's vocabulary production begins around twelve months and continues a dramatic

Table 1.2.1 *Number of types/tokens of symbolic gestures produced by the deaf and hearing children*

	Deaf			Hearing		
	D1	D2	D3	H1	H2	H3
Types	2	2	1	1	6	2
Tokens	7	4	4	2	17	14

Table 1.2.2 *Number of types/tokens of lexical items produced by the deaf and hearing children*

	Deaf			Hearing		
	D1	D2	D3	H1	H2	H3
Types	22	8	12	11	57	2
Tokens	207	24	52	25	267	2

rise throughout the entire period when symbolic gestures maintain a constant pattern of infrequent use. Thus, although children's early lexical use climbs and increases in frequency, their use of symbolic gestures does not increase and remains infrequent. Symbolic gestures are indeed a nonrobust phenomenon in child development.

Lack of increased complexity over time

Unlike children's early lexical development, symbolic gestures exhibit a flat mean length of utterance (MLU; Brown, 1973). That is, there was no increase in the internal complexity of symbolic gestures—either formationally or referentially—over time, even though the complexity of children's words and signs increased steadily over time.

Although it is true that, unlike words and signs, children typically do not get systematic gestural models, parents do produce their children's symbolic gestures (as well as pointing, instrumental gestures, and actions with objects). Thus, it remains a puzzle why children would not use symbolic gestures more if they had equal symbolic status with lexical forms.

Inconsistent forms

An example of a symbolic gesture is as follows. One symbolic gesture—the "phone" symbolic gesture—was used in relation to a toy telephone and was produced by four of the six children (two deaf, two hearing). It was produced in relation to the same toy telephone but its form varied both within a child and across children: (a) a clenched fist at the side of the head, (b) a flat hand at side of head, (c) two flat hands at side of head. Interestingly, the form was typically accompanied by opening/closing mouth movements plus vocalizations, even in the deaf children who, clearly, could not hear, and whose parents used TTYs (a form of teletype machine). Note that variation of form was common for all of the forty-eight tokens of symbolic gestures reported here. However, we simply did not find a similar degree of variation in the form of children's early words across instances of use and/or contexts.

Restricted communicative and discourse functions

Symbolic gestures were used by the children largely in "request" contexts ($n = 36/48$; 75 percent); for example, to get something from someone. Only three tokens (6.25 percent) of symbolic gestures were used to "comment upon" (or name) a referent, and eight tokens (16.67 percent) were produced as responses to questions (e.g., "what do you do with this?"). Conversely, the children's lexical items were used largely to "comment upon" or name referents.

Interestingly, children would spontaneously produce symbolic gestures in discourse contexts where use of their primary linguistic channel had somehow failed—either because they were misunderstood by an adult or because they did not have the corresponding word in systematic production (recall that comprehension–production asymmetries exist in early acquisition; e.g., Golinkoff and Hirsh-Pasek, 1987). That is, symbolic gestures were used in ways that *augmented* their primary linguistic channel.

Context dependent

All of the children's symbolic gestures were exceedingly context dependent and this did not change over time. That is, gestures (symbolic or otherwise) were used only when the object referred to was physically present. The referent was nearly always an object (as opposed to a person, location, attribute, etc.), and their forms always reflected some salient physical action associated with the referent. Although some early words/signs in our corpora were initially context dependent, their frequencies were greater than symbolic gestures, the forms were consistent, they were used with a broad communicative scope (they did not exhibit a restricted communicative function), and they ceased to be context dependent over time.

Order of occurrence

Symbolic gestures appeared only *after* the child was able to *comprehend* and/or produce the meaning of the word or sign to which the gesture corresponded. Said another way, words and signs were comprehended *prior* to the onset of such symbolic gestures. No child produced a symbolic gesture unless he or she first had the corresponding word in comprehension, and/or production, suggesting that children's use of symbolic gestures is dependent on their knowledge of language rather than the reverse.

Kind boundaries

To understand the meaning of the manual and verbal forms for the child, each form was examined in relation to the range of referents over which it was applied (form–referent pairings). Similarly, each referent was examined in relation to the range of forms that were used with it (referent–form pairings; see section on "attribution of meaning" above). The analysis revealed that the form–referent (and referent–form) pairings observed with the children's lexical forms were different from those observed with symbolic gestures.

When the hearing and deaf children produced a lexical form, the range of referents over which it was applied formed particular word (sign) types or kinds, that is, type of object names, type of action/event words, type of property words, and so forth. For example, four of the six children produced the lexical form "open" (two deaf, two hearing). When "open" was produced by these children, it was used to refer specifically to the *action or event* involved in opening a variety of things (e.g., jars, refrigerator doors, boxes). Importantly, the lexical item "open" was not also used as the *name* for the object being opened; for example, "open" was not used as *the name* for jars—it was not used as the word or sign for glass containers with lids. "Open" was not used as a type of object name, nor was it used *to name* specific objects that are kept in jars (e.g., cookies; "open" was not used as the name for sweet round objects that are eaten). That is, "open" was never used both as a type of action/event word and as a type of object name. Instead, "open" and other action/event words (e.g., "give") were produced with proper extensions unique to the type "action and event words." This finding was true of all of the children's lexical forms, across all word/sign types. Each child's use of each lexical form was constrained along particular word/sign types from its first use and across many contexts over time.

Indeed, with few exceptions (3/577 tokens; 0.5 percent), the children used their lexical forms in ways that did *not* cross the boundaries of different word/sign types (see Petitto and Kampen, in preparation, for details). Although the meaning of a given lexical item may have been under- or overextended relative to its meaning in the adult language, it was not used in ways that violated the boundaries of its type. This finding corroborates those reported in a study of lexical use and meaning by Huttenlocher and Smiley (1987) in slightly older hearing children (range eleven–thirty months). However, the present study provides the first evidence that children's earliest lexical items are constrained along kind boundaries even when acquiring signed languages.

Unlike words or signs, when children produced a symbolic gesture, the range of referents over which it was applied did not always form particular types or kinds of object names, event words, property words and so on. It was common for a child to use a particular symbolic gesture in relation to, for example, a known type of related object in one context and, in another context, to use the same symbolic gesture in relation to objects from a different type. Variable use of the same or similarly formed symbolic gesture was common in the children.[7] For example, four of the children (two deaf, two hearing) produced a curved index finger pointed toward the far back of the mouth ("point-in-mouth"), and one hearing boy produced this form twelve times; his use of this gesture aptly captures the children's use of their symbolic gestures. He produced the form (a) upon noticing the experimenter playing a toy flute, (b) when requesting a raisin, (c) when requesting a grape that was inside of a tightly closed jar after failing repeatedly to open it, and so on. Thus, the child produced one form with at least three different referents: flute, raisin, and grapes (we assume for the moment that the jar itself was not the referent in the third case mentioned). One interpretation of this symbolic gesture is that the child has used the form "point-in-mouth" in relation to object types, with the raisins and grapes constituting the object type "things one eats" (*form–object type*). In this view, the child's use of the form in relation to the flute would be a problem, because the flute, although an object, is clearly a different type of object from "things one eats." A second interpretation is that the child has used the form "point-in-mouth" in relation to action/event types (*form–action/event type*). In other words, the child's symbolic gesture could have been functioning in a verb-like manner. Here, too, the child's intended action/event type is not obvious. The form "point-in-mouth" may be conveying the action/event "eat" regarding the raisin and grapes, but the flute is still a problem. Thus, a problem for either of the two interpretations is that the child produced a form that has crossed type boundaries, and this did not occur with the children's lexical items.

Although it is always possible to argue that the "point-in-mouth" gesture is being used to convey a more general action/event type (e.g., "put in mouth"), the possible attributions are potentially infinite. For example, the second and third cases could also be further attributed to meaning "hungry," as in "I'm hungry" ("I want that raisin/grape"). Although this is, in principle, true of attributing meaning to children's single words (e.g., Bloom, 1973), children do help narrow the possibilities through their use of actual lexical forms. In fact, a more parsimonious explanation of the "point-in-mouth" symbolic gesture—and other symbolic gestures—is that the children are producing stylized context-bound actions associated with referents (whose form implicitly contains other information such as the referent's location), and that these forms are not functioning as symbols that "stand for" (or represent) the referents.

Especially dramatic differences between language and gesture are uncovered when both types of information occur in the same modality. Two of the deaf children (age twenty months) produced the symbolic gesture "twist" in relation to jars at the same time that they produced the fully articulated adult sign OPEN.[8] Whereas OPEN was used exclusively to convey the action of opening (e.g., boxes, jars, drawers), the symbolic gesture "twist" was used in relation to the following range of referents: jar (the object itself), the specific objects in jars (e.g., cookies, raisins), to open (to get the jar opened), to close (to get the jar closed). Interestingly, the gesture was used only after the children's use of the lexical item OPEN had failed to get a response from an adult. That is, the "twist" gesture was used exclusively as an apparent last resort, to emphasize and augment primary linguistic information.

It could be argued that symbolic gestures violate Markman's mutual exclusivity principle (ME) (e.g., Markman, 1989).[9] Briefly, the ME principle postulates that young children assume that each object category has one category term: "A single object cannot be both a cow and a bird or a dog" (p. 187) (see also Gleitman and Wanner, 1982; Slobin, 1985). In the present study, recall that all symbolic gestures are produced only after the child first has the corresponding lexical form in comprehension and/or production. For example, the children who produced the symbolic gesture for the toy telephone first produced the lexical item "telephone." Because a single object appears to have at least two category terms—the gesture connoting the object (in some contexts) and the lexical sign—this situation may constitute an apparent violation of the ME principle, thereby revealing yet another way that early language and gesture differ.

To review, there were important differences between children's use of lexical items, be they words or signs, and their use of gestures. Children's use of lexical items was consistently constrained along word/sign type boundaries, whereas their use of gestures was variable. Even when the lexical item and the gesture were in the same modality, the lexical item did not cross type boundaries, but the gestures often did.

No gesture + gesture combinations

There were no combinations of symbolic gestures, even during the period when hearing and deaf children were producing two-word and two-sign combinations (respectively). That is, there were no symbolic gesture + symbolic gesture combinations, even though there were word + word combinations in the hearing children and sign + sign combinations in the deaf children.

Summary

Hearing and deaf children's use of symbolic gestures was similar. Hearing and deaf children's use of the early lexicon was also similar. However, the hearing and deaf children's use of symbolic gestures versus their use of the lexicon differed. Several factors differentiated children's use of symbolic gestures as compared to their use of words and signs. They were as follows:

1. The frequency of symbolic gestures was low (they constitute a nonrobust phenomenon in child development).
2. The distribution of symbolic gestures remained uncommonly steady over time.
3. The forms and referential complexity of symbolic gestures did not increase over time ("flat MLU").
4. The forms of symbolic gestures were inconsistent.
5. Symbolic gestures were used with restricted communicative function (largely requests).
6. Symbolic gestures were far more context dependent than the children's words or signs.
7. Symbolic gestures were produced only after children first had the corresponding word or sign in comprehension and/or production and were often used to augment a failed communicative exchange involving their primary linguistic system.
8. Symbolic gestures were used in ways that crossed the boundaries of word/sign types in some contexts and did not do so in other contexts; however, children's use of words and signs was consistently used in ways that followed the boundaries of word/sign types.
9. There were no symbolic gesture + symbolic gesture combinations, even though children were combining their lexical items.

Discussion and conclusion

On the nature of gestures

All manual activity termed *gestures* in the literature are not the same, and they occur with vastly different frequencies. Most of the manual activity that children produce are really actions—not gestures—with objects in hand, and the next frequent class to occur, empty-handed gestures, are used with grossly restricted forms and communicative functions. Symbolic gestures are the least frequent type of gestures to occur in spontaneous development, and they occur late relative to children's first words or signs. Once children begin to use symbolic gesture, its power is meager as compared to that of the word or sign.

That all children produce actions with objects in hand most frequently indicates that this information plays some role in the representation of objects as well as the corresponding words that symbolize them, particularly regarding the *functions of objects* (what one does with an object; what it is used for). However, it cannot be said that the functions of objects and the situational contexts within which they occur make up the contents of children's early lexical representations (e.g., Bowerman, 1980; Nelson, 1974; Snyder, Bates, and Bretherton, 1981). Indeed, the representation of human language involves much more than its communicative function, even in very young children. As is indicated in the present study, as well as other related studies (e.g., Petitto and Marentette, 1991a), specifically linguistic structural information regarding *language form*, and other *conceptual constraints* (e.g., constraints on word/sign types) also appear to be part of the young child's lexical representations.

As was indicated in the introduction, gestures serve a useful role in ontogeny. Early gestures (e.g., pointing) appear to be a primitive signaling device, on the same ontogenetic continuum with crying. They elicit language and attention. Gestures elicit language rich in referential information; they elicit names for things (e.g., Shatz, 1985). Also in the introduction is the observation that later symbolic gestures appear to serve a secondary role in language ontogeny—one that augments the child's primary linguistic system. Symbolic gestures appear to be parasitic on language rather than the reverse (e.g., see also Goldin-Meadow and Morford, 1989; McNeill, 1985); recall that words and signs occur first in comprehension and/or production in language ontogeny before the child produces a symbolic gesture.

Recent claims regarding the equal symbolic status of children's gestures are wholly unsupported by the present data (e.g., Acredolo and Goodwyn, 1985, 1988, 1990; Goodwyn and Acredolo, 1991). For example, Acredolo and Goodwyn (1985, 1990) provide a case-study of the first author's daughter, Kate Acredolo. The child was reported to have forty symbolic gestures possessing the same symbolic status as words. In addition, they reported that Kate produced these symbolic gestures *prior* to age nineteen months, that is, before her vocabulary spurt. Although these reports are interesting, the authors do not provide crucial information required to evaluate their claims. First, the authors do not report the relative frequency and distribution of the child's other gestures as compared with her symbolic gestures, thereby rendering the impression that her production of forty symbolic gestures was more robust than it may have been. As was seen in the present study, once the relative frequency and distribution of symbolic gestures was compared to the full range of gestures produced by a child, we find that symbolic gestures are a nonrobust phenomenon in child development. Second, and most importantly, approximately 95 percent of the child's types of symbolic gestures were either directly taught to the child or "encouraged" (e.g., "Once Kate's interest in such gestures were noticed, the adults around her began to encourage the development of new gestures by pairing discrete actions with objects and conditions," Acredolo and Goodwyn, 1990: 18).

Given that symbolic gestures were directly taught or encouraged, it is of little surprise that the child in the study, as well as those in other studies (e.g., Goodwyn and Acredolo, 1991), produced symbolic gestures in a manner resembling early words and, at times, earlier than their words. Indeed, what I believe these researchers are picking up is an *artifact* of the fact that humans can learn either a signed or spoken language with no loss or delay in the timing and sequencing of language milestones.[10] When taught specific symbolic gestures (especially those used by the parents themselves), the child is merely learning lexical, or quasi-lexical, items in another modality—and, in the case of hearing children, a modality that could have been used for acquiring signed languages.

A final puzzle is this: Given that adults both teach and use symbolic gestures, why do we not see *more* symbolic gesturing in children? Why are there not greater similarities of use between children's early symbolic gestures and early words? In understanding the answer to these questions, the essential features of early language representation are laid bare. Gestural input to children lacks critical regularities in structure, both sublexically and syntactically. The forms of parents' symbolic gestures vary, and parents do not produce combinations of symbolic gestures. In other words, gestures are not formed from a restricted set of combinatorial units and are not hierarchically organized; indeed, they lack phonology, prosody, and syntax. Gestures do bear meaning and communicative information. However, proposals in child language that offer either the semantic or the communicative functions of language as being the exclusive explanatory mechanism that drives very early language acquisition are not supported by the present research. As seen here, meaning and/or communicative function alone, although important, are simply not adequate to support the use of a gesture as a form that possesses equal status with the word or sign.

The basic units of language structure that infants need in the input are not present in symbolic gestural input. Specifically, sublexical, phonetic, and syllabic organization as well as other phonotactic information (prosodic cues that bind segments into phrasal, clausal, and lexical bundles) are absent. The innate predisposition to discover these particular linguistic structures in the input is so strong that the child does not systematize symbolic gestural input, even though it shares similarities of reference and meaning with words. Without syllabic and phonotactic information, infants cannot set up the nascent representations of *language form* that I would argue are part of the very early representation of language, and are required before children can progress to adult linguistic competence. Like words and signs, children use symbolic gestures meaningfully. Unlike words and signs, the internal formational and referential complexity of symbolic gestures does not increase over time, demonstrating both the strengths and the limits of a referential system without structured input.

Constraints on early lexical knowledge

Looking across individual meanings of words and signs, as compared to symbolic gestures, certain commonalities characterize the words and signs, but not the gestures. Children did not use particular words or signs across the bounds of different word/sign types (e.g., object names, property words, event words; e.g., Huttenlocher and Smiley, 1987), but did so with gestures. These results indicate that children's first lexical use is constrained along the bounds of word/sign types—even in signed languages (for other discussions of constraints on early lexical acquisition see Carey, 1982; Gelman and Coley, 1992; Keil, 1989; Macnamara, 1982; Markman, 1989; Quine, 1969; Waxman, Shipley, and Shepperson, 1992).

Knowledge underlying language acquisition

There are similarities between symbolic gestures and language in human development. However, critical differences exist between them that have not received much attention in previous research on this topic. The child's clear differentiation between language and gesture in ontogeny suggests that distinct forms of knowledge govern their use. Indeed, young deaf infants' differentiation of language and gesture—even though both reside in the same modality—provides dramatic support for this analysis.

My claim, then, is that aspects of the structural and conceptual underpinnings of children's knowledge and use of language are fundamentally distinct from their knowledge and use of gesture. Knowledge of language is not wholly derived from a general cognitive capacity to symbolize. Instead, the findings from this and related studies compel us to conclude that domain-specific knowledge is involved in the human language acquisition process. Specifically linguistic and conceptual constraints are at work from birth to help the child discover particular structures in the input and not others.

Acknowledgments

I am especially grateful to Kevin N. Dunbar for discussing the issues in this chapter with me and for his insightful comments on earlier drafts of the chapter. I also thank Marta Meana, Paul Bloom, and Susan Goldin-Meadow for comments on an earlier version of this work. This research was supported by Natural Sciences Engineering Research Council of Canada, McGill IBM Cooperative Project, and McDonnell-Pew Center Grant in Cognitive Neuroscience.

Notes to 1.2

1. One group of researchers has claimed that first signs are acquired earlier than first words (e.g., Bonvillian, Orlansky, and Novack, 1983). However, see Pettito (1988) for a critique of why these claims are unfounded. See also Bellugi and Klima (1982), Meier (1991), Newport and Meier (1985), and Pettito and Marentette (1990, 1991b) for a review of the early lexical and later grammatical milestones in sign language acquisition; these studies demonstrate that signed and spoken languages are acquired in surprisingly similar ways and on a similar time-course, despite the modality differences.
2. ASL and LSQ are two entirely distinct, natural signed languages. Further, neither language is the signed counterpart of the spoken majority language (e.g., English or French, respectively). Each signed language has its own grammar (linguistic units and rules for combining them).
3. Videotaping and data analyses for all but two of the hearing children were conducted until the children were over 4 years old. However, ages eight through twenty months capture the relevant period under question in the literature (the transition from prelinguistic to linguistic expression). See Petitto and Kampen (in preparation) for additional details.
4. For example, the common form used to convey "quiet" (index finger to pursed lips while producing a "shhh" sound) is used by deaf and hearing children and adults to indicate "quiet," but the sign QUIET in ASL (and in LSQ) is produced with a different handshape and movement.
5. I thank Paul Bloom for pointing out the need to make this particular distinction explicit.
6. Huttenlocher and Smiley (1987) stated that "Indeed, the data from mother reports are not highly concordant with independent observational data [refs]. Regular observations of a sufficient number of utterances, using a standard method of recording context, are essential in getting a proper data base" (p. 67). Though arrived at independently (e.g., Petitto, 1984, 1985a, 1985b, 1987, 1988), similar methods are used in the present study.
7. Even though the children's forms of symbolic gestures were variable, there was no evidence that each variation of a form was a different symbolic gesture (e.g., similar to a different word or sign) in their repertoire of forms.
8. The "twist" gesture was also produced by the three hearing children.
9. I thank Sandeep Prasada for first pointing this out to me.
10. See especially Petitto and Marentette's (1990, 1991b) study of hearing children in bilingual signing and speaking homes who acquire both signed and spoken language milestones on the same maturational time-course.

References to 1.2

Acredolo, L. P. and Goodwyn, S. W. (1985). "Symbolic gesturing in language development: A case study." *Human Development*, **28**, 40–9.

Acredolo, L. P. and Goodwyn, S. W. (1988). "Symbolic gesturing in normal infants." *Child Development*, 59, 450–66.

Acredolo, L. P. and Goodwyn, S. W. (1990). "Sign language in babies: The significance of symbolic gesturing for understanding language development." *Annals of Child Development*, 7, 1–42.

Bates, E., Benigni, L. F., Bretherton, I., Camaioni, L., and Volterra, V. (1979). *The Emergence of Symbols: Cognition and communication in infancy.* New York: Academic Press.

Bates, E., Bretherton, I., Shore, C., and McNew, S. (1983). "Names, gestures and objects: Symbolization in infancy and aphasia." In K. Nelson (ed.), *Children's Language* (Vol. 4). Hillsdale, NJ: Lawrence Erlbaum Associates.

Bellugi, U. and Klima, E. (1982). "The acquisition of three morphological systems in American Sign Language." *Papers and Reports on Child Language Development*, 21, Stanford, CA: Stanford University, 1–35.

Bloom, L. (1973). *One Word at a Time.* The Hague: Mouton.

Bonvillian, J. D., Orlansky, M. D., and Novack, L. L. (1983). "Developmental milestones: Sign language acquisition and motor development." *Child Development*, 54, 1435–45.

Bowerman, M. (1980). "The structure and origin of semantic categories in the language-learning child." In M. L. Foster and S. Brandes (eds), *Symbol as Sense.* New York: Academic Press.

Brown, R. (1973). *A First Language: The early stages.* Cambridge, MA: Harvard University Press.

Brown, R. and Hanlon, C. (1970). "Derivational complexity and order of acquisition in child speech." In J. R. Hayes (ed.), *Cognition and the Development of Language.* New York: Wiley.

Carey, S. (1982). "Semantic development: The state of the art." In E. Wanner and L. Gleitman (eds), *Language Acquisition: The state of the art.* Cambridge: Cambridge University Press, 347–89.

Chomsky, N. (1975). *The Logical Structure of Linguistic Theory.* New York: Plenum Press.

Fernald, A., Taeschner, T., Dunn, I., Papousek, M., de Boysson-Bardies, B., and Fukui, I. (1989). "A cross-language study of prosodic modifications in mothers' and fathers' speech to preverbal infants." *Journal of Child Language*, 16, 477–501.

Gelman, S. and Coley, J. (1992). "Language and categorization: The acquisition of natural kind terms." In S. A. Gelman and J. P. Byrnes (eds), *Perspectives on Language and Thought: Interrelations in development.* Cambridge: Cambridge University Press.

Genesee, F. (1987). *Learning Through Two Languages.* Cambridge, MA: Newbury House.

Gleitman, L. and Wanner, E. (1982). "Language acquisition: The state of the state of the art." In E. Wanner and L. Gleitman (eds), *Language Acquisition: The state of the art.* Cambridge: Cambridge University Press, 3–48.

Goldin-Meadow, S. and Morford, M. (1985). "Gesture in early language: Studies of deaf and hearing children." *Merrill-Palmer Quarterly*, 31, 145–76.

Goldin-Meadow, S. and Morford, M. (1989). "Gesture in early child language." In V. Volterra and J. Erting (eds), *From Gesture to Language in Hearing and Deaf Children.* Berlin: Springer-Verlag, 249–62.

Golinkoff, R. M. and Hirsh-Pasek, K. (1987, October). *A New Picture of Language Development: Evidence from comprehension.* Paper presented at the 12th Annual Boston University Conference on Language Development. Boston, MA.

Goodwyn, S. W. and Acredolo, L. P. (1991, April). *Symbolic Gesture Versus Word: Is there a modality advantage for onset of symbol use?* Paper presented at the Biennial Meeting of the Society for Research in Child Development, Seattle, WA.

Hubel, D. H. and Wiesel, T. N. (1959). "Receptive fields of single neurons in the cat's visual cortex." *Journal of Physiology*, 148, 547–91.

Huttenlocher, I. and Smiley, P. (1987). "Early word meanings: The case of object names." *Cognitive Psychology*, 19, 63–89.

Jusczyk, P. W. (1986). "A review of speech perception research." In K. Boff, L. Kaufman, and J. Thomas (eds), *Handbook of Perception and Human Performance* (Vol. 2). New York: Wiley.

Keil, F. (1989). *Concepts, Kinds, and Cognitive Development.* Cambridge: MIT Press.

Lock, A. (ed.) (1978). *Action, Gesture, and Symbol.* New York: Academic Press.

McNeill, D. (1985). "So you think gestures are nonverbal?" *Psychological Review*, 92, 350–71.

Macnamara, J. (1982). *Names for Things.* Cambridge, MA: MIT Press/Bradford Books.

Markman, E. (1989). *Categorization and Naming in Children: Problems of induction.* Cambridge: MIT Press/Bradford Books.

Mayr, E. (1982). *The Growth of Biological Thought.* Cambridge, MA: Harvard University Press.

Mehler, J. and Fox, R. (eds) (1985). *Neonate Cognition*. Hillsdale, NJ: Lawrence Erlbaum Associates.

Meier, R. (1991). "Language acquisition by deaf children." *American Scientist*, **79**, 60–70.

Nelson, K. (1974). "Concept, word and sentence: Interrelations in acquisition and development." *Psychological Review*, **81**, 267–85.

Newport, E. and Meier, R. (1985). "The acquisition of American Sign Language." In D. Slobin (ed.), *The Crosslinguistic Study of Language Acquisition* (Vol. 1). Hillsdale, NJ: Lawrence Erlbaum Associates, 881–938.

Petitto, L. A. (1984). *From Gesture to Symbol: The relationship between form and meaning in the acquisition of personal pronouns in American Sign Language*. Unpublished doctoral dissertation, Harvard University, Boston, MA.

Petitto, L A. (1985a, October). *On the Use of Pre-linguistic Gestures in Hearing and Deaf Children*. Paper presented at the 10th Annual Boston University Conference on Language Development. Boston, MA.

Petitto, L. A. (1985b). *"Language" in the Pre-linguistic Child* (Tech. Rep. No. 4). Montreal: McGill University, Department of Psychology.

Petitto, L. A. (1986). *From Gesture to Symbol: The relationship between form and meaning in the acquisition of personal pronouns in American Sign Language*. Bloomington, Indiana: Indiana University Linguistics Club Press, 1–105.

Petitto, L. A. (1987). "On the autonomy of language and gesture: Evidence from the acquisition of personal pronouns in American Sign Language." *Cognition*, **27**(1), 1–52.

Petitto, L. A. (1988). "'Language' in the pre-linguistic child." In F. Kessel (ed.), *Development of Language and Language Researchers: Essays in honor of Roger Brown*. Hillsdale, NJ: Lawrence Erlbaum Associates, 187–221.

Petitto, L. A. and Charron, F. (1987). *Semantic Categories in the Acquisition of Langue des Signes Québécoise (LSQ) and American Sign Language (ASL): A comparison of signing children's first signs with speaking children's first words* (Tech. Rep. No. 7). Montreal: McGill University, Department of Psychology.

Petitto, L. A. and Kampen, D. (in preparation). *The Ontogeny of Language and Gesture: Are early symbolic gestures names for things?*

Petitto, L. A. and Marentette, P. F. (1990, October). *The Timing of Linguistic Milestones in Sign Language Acquisition: Are first signs acquired earlier than first words?* Paper presented at the 15th Annual Boston University Conference on Language Development, Boston, MA.

Petitto, L. A. and Marentette, P. F. (1991a). "Babbling in the manual mode: Evidence for the ontogeny of language." *Science*, **251**, 1493–6.

Petitto, L. A. and Marentette, P. F. (1991b, April). "The timing of linguistic milestones in sign and spoken language acquisition." In L. Petitto (chair), *Are the Linguistic Milestones in Signed and Spoken Language Acquisition Similar or Different?* Symposium conducted at the Biennial Meeting of the Society for Research in Child Development, Seattle, WA.

Piaget, J. (1962). *Play, Dreams and Imitation*. New York: Norton.

Pinker, S. (1979). "Formal models of language learning." *Cognition*, **7**, 217–83.

Pinker, S. (1984). *Language Learnability and Language Development*. Cambridge, MA: Harvard University Press.

Pinker, S. and Bloom, P. (1990). "Natural language and natural selection." *Behavioral and Brain Science*, **13**, 707–78.

Quine, W V. (1969). *Ontological Relativity and Other Essays*. New York: Cambridge University Press.

Seidenberg, M. S. and Petitto, L. A. (1987). "Communication, symbolic communication, and language in child and chimpanzee: Comment on Savage-Rumbaugh, McDonald, Sevcik, Hopkins, and Rupert (1986)." *Journal of Experimental Psychology, General*, **116**(3), 279–87.

Shatz, M. (1985). "An evolutionary perspective on plasticity in language development." *Merrill-Palmer Quarterly*, **31**, 211.

Shore, C., O'Connell, B., and Bates, E. (1984). "First sentences in language and symbolic play." *Developmental Psychology*, **20**(5), 872–80.

Slobin, D. (1985). "Crosslinguistic evidence for the language-making capacity." In D. Slobin (ed.), *The Crosslinguistic Study of Language Acquisition, Vol. 2: Theoretical issues*. Hillsdale, NJ: Lawrence Erlbaum Associates, 1157–256.

Snyder, L., Bates, E., and Bretherton, I. (1981). "Content and context in early lexical development." *Journal of Child Language*, **8**, 565–81.

Waxman, S., Shipley, E., and Shepperson, B. (1992). "Establishing new subcategories: The role of category labels and existing knowledge." *Child Development* **62**, 127–38.

Werner, H. and Kaplan, B. (1963). *Symbol Formation*. New York: Wiley.

Zinober, B. and Martlew, M. (1985). "The development of communicative gestures." In M. D. Barrett (ed.), *Children's Single-word Speech*. New York: Wiley.

PART 2

Word Learning

Infant Contributions to the Achievement of Joint Reference

Dare A. Baldwin

Word learning depends critically on the achievement of joint reference. To learn a new word, one must, on at least one occasion, link that word with the very object, scene, or event to which a proficient speaker of the language is referring. Achieving joint reference is a complex undertaking, even in what would seem to be the simplest case, the case of object labels. The world is littered with objects, so when a new label is heard, how does one know *which* object to connect with that label? And how does one know that the object label should be linked with the object per se, as opposed to its color, shape, size, movement patterns, etc.? Originally posed by philosophers such as Quine (1960) and Wittgenstein (1953), the latter question has recently received considerable attention from researchers (see, for example, Baldwin, 1989; Markman, 1989, 1992; Merriman and Bowman, 1989). However, it is the former aspect of the joint reference problem—in particular, the question of how an *infant* word-learner identifies the correct object upon hearing a new label—that is the focus of the present research.

Some time ago, Bruner and his colleagues (e.g., Bruner, 1978; Churcher and Scaife, 1981; Scaife and Bruner, 1975) pointed out the important role that joint *attention* undoubtedly plays in facilitating joint reference for infant word-learners. Their point was that joint reference occurs quite naturally if adult and infant happen to be focused on the same thing at the time of the adult's utterance (see also Quine, 1973). Joint attention at the time of labeling is easily achieved if adults do much of the work; that is, if adults are careful to label objects at a time when infants are already focused on them. It turns out that parents, or at least Western, middle-class parents, are reasonably accommodating in this respect. By the time infants are about nine months old, mothers frequently follow infants' line of regard or pointing gesture and label the object on which infants' attention is focused (e.g., Collis, 1977; Leung and Rheingold, 1981; Masur, 1982; Murphy, 1978). Harris, Jones, and Grant (1983) found that a full 70 percent of mothers' utterances referred to the object already occupying the focus of six- to ten-month-olds' attention.

Such adult vigilance appears to play an important role in infants' label-learning success. Harris *et al.* (1986) demonstrated that mothers of infants learning language at a normal rate made more references to objects that were at the current focus of infants' attention than did mothers of slower language-learners. Similarly, Tomasello and his colleagues (e.g., Tomasello, Mannle, and Kruger, 1986; Tomasello and Todd, 1983) found that infants had larger vocabularies the more time they typically spent in joint attentional focus with their mothers. Further, maternal directiveness (i.e., failing to follow in on infants' attentional focus when labeling) was negatively related to the proportion of object labels in infants' productive vocabularies. In a lexical training study (Tomasello and Farrar, 1986), infants were more likely to learn to comprehend a new label if that label was presented at a time when infants were already focused on its referent, as opposed to when the label was presented in an attempt to redirect their attentional focus (i.e., when an adult held up a toy and uttered its label at a time when infants were not focused on any particular object). Thus word learning is most likely to take place when cooperative labeling on parents' part reduces the effort that infants themselves must direct toward joint reference.

However, these same studies also indicate that parents are not always able to follow in on infants' focus of attention at the time of labeling. In some cases, infants are actually focused on an incorrect referent at the time that a label is uttered. Instances of such "discrepant labeling" are far from uncommon: They have been observed across a number of studies (e.g., Harris *et al.*, 1986; Harris, Jones, and Grant, 1983; Tomasello and Farrar, 1986; Tomasello and Mannle, 1985). In Collis's (1977) study, mothers' labels failed to correspond with the object infants were looking at about 50 percent of the time, and this occurred for roughly 30 percent of mothers' labels in the Harris, Jones, and Grant (1983) study. The phenomenon of discrepant labeling raises interesting questions concerning the social processes governing joint reference. In cases of discrepant labeling, adult and infant are attending to different objects at the time the label is uttered: Joint attention is violated. Is joint reference also necessarily violated, and if so, what are the implications for word learning? These questions cannot be answered until we know the extent to which infants themselves actively contribute to the achievement of joint reference.

It is possible that, when discrepant labeling occurs, infants tend to link the label with whichever object is currently occupying their focus, thus leading them to establish an incorrect word–object mapping. This is the scenario we would expect if associative principles are the sole mechanisms that govern word learning. In the case of discrepant labeling, temporal contiguity, for instance, pulls for infants to link the label with the object of their own focus.

On the other hand, infants may possess skills that allow them to avoid mapping errors when faced with discrepant labeling. Adults tend to offer explicit cues concerning the referent of a label that they utter. For example, parents typically look at or point to the object they are labeling (e.g., Messer, 1978), even in cases of discrepant labeling (when infants happened to be focused on a different object). If infants notice these nonverbal cues at some point, and if they also realize that the cues are informative about the reference of the label being uttered, then infants themselves may be capable of actively salvaging joint reference when discrepant labeling occurs. The speaker's nonverbal cues would alert infants to the discrepancy of focus, enabling them to block a mapping error. And perhaps infants can go further than just avoiding an incorrect mapping under conditions of discrepant labeling. By checking and following the speaker's cues to the correct object after hearing the label, infants may even discover the correct referent as well. That is, infants may be able to use the speaker's cues correctly to interpret the label's reference, despite the violation of joint attention at the time of labeling.

If infants possess such a "cue-sensitive" understanding—an appreciation of the linguistic relevance of speakers' nonverbal cues—then the burden adults carry for infants' word-learning success is to some degree alleviated. Infants need not make mapping errors when adults fail to achieve follow-in labeling, as long as adults provide salient and unambiguous cues as to the correct referent.

All in all, an early understanding that nonverbal cues are relevant to word reference would smooth the course of word learning by preventing mapping errors. Infants of about eighteen months and older have been observed to learn new object labels based on only one or two exposures to that label (e.g., Nelson and Bonvillian, 1973). With label learning proceeding at such a rapid pace, the ability to use others' nonverbal cues to clarify word reference would be crucial for avoiding a proliferation of mapping errors. Moreover, the cue-sensitive understanding could help to speed the course of word learning in another way as well; this ability would provide infants with more opportunities for learning the connection between labels and their referents. They could conceivably pick up on word–object mappings under conditions of discrepant labeling (roughly 50 percent of instances in Collis's data) as well as under follow-in conditions.

Current evidence indicates that associative principles such as temporal contiguity play a role in early word learning. For instance, a word is more likely to be learned the smaller the gap in time between presentation of the word and its referent (e.g., Whitehurst, 1979; Whitehurst, Kedesdy, and White, 1982). Temporal contiguity is generally a good guide to identifying the correct referent of an adult's utterance, given that, on many occasions, adults do follow-in labeling. Temporal contiguity is misleading only when discrepant labeling occurs. What is in question, then, is whether infants favor nonverbal cues over temporal contiguity specifically when faced with discrepant labeling.

At present, there is no empirical evidence to clarify whether infants appreciate the linguistic significance of a speaker's nonverbal cues. While infants as young as nine–twelve months can follow nonverbal cues such as pointing and line-of-regard (e.g., Butterworth and Cochran, 1980; Butterworth and Grover, 1988; Churcher and Scaife, 1981; Grover, 1982; Lempers, 1976; Leung and Rheingold, 1981; Murphy and Messer, 1977; Scaife and Bruner, 1975), it has yet to be determined whether infants understand that nonverbal cues can and should be used to help in determining the reference of a novel label.

As described earlier, recent research points to a learning advantage for follow-in labeling over labeling that occurs during an attempt to redirect infants' attentional focus (e.g., Tomasello and Farrar, 1986). If infants' word-learning difficulties in the absence of follow-in labeling were clearly the result of mapping errors, then these results could already be taken as evidence *against* the cue-sensitive understanding under present discussion. However, these difficulties may have occurred simply because the demands of switching attentional focus reduced infants' ability to learn the labels. Because these studies did not specifically diagnose the incidence of mapping *errors*, they do not speak to the question of present interest.

The following study was designed to yield evidence concerning the likelihood of mapping errors when joint attention is violated at the time of labeling. In a discrepant labeling condition, the experimenter uttered a new label precisely at a time when infants were focused on an incorrect referent. If infants lack an understanding of the linguistic significance of nonverbal cues, temporal contiguity should lead them to make mapping errors in this situation. That is, when subsequently tested for comprehension of a new label, infants should select the object upon which they were themselves focused at the time they heard the new label. On the other hand, if infants are sensitive to nonverbal cues as relevant to word-reference, they could avoid making mapping errors in the discrepant labeling condition. Thus they might fail to link the label with either object, or they might link the label with its correct referent, despite the fact that they were looking at a different object at the time the new label was actually uttered.

Each infant also participated in a follow-in labeling condition, in which the experimenter labeled the object upon which infants were already focused. In the follow-in case, joint reference can be achieved solely through the auspices of temporal contiguity, hence word learning should proceed without error. Thus the follow-in labeling condition was designed to provide a baseline level of word learning in the laboratory situation.

In the present study, several types of nonverbal cues were available to infants. One cue was line of visual regard: The experimenter looked at the object upon which infants themselves were focused during follow-in labeling, and during discrepant labeling, the experimenter looked at a different object. At least two other cues were also available: Voice direction and body posture. The experimenter's body and utterances were oriented toward infants during follow-in labeling, while her body and voice were oriented down and away from infants during discrepant labeling. This study does not clarify the particular cue, or set of cues, that infants might consult for word-learning purposes.

The study also included a control to determine whether infants in the two labeling situations indeed established word–object mappings. It is possible that the adult's nonverbal cues might increase infants' interest in the object of the adult's focus, leading them to prefer that toy on the comprehension tests, without any word mapping having occurred at all. To test this alternative explanation, half of the infants were asked preference-control questions (e.g., "Where is your favorite one?") after follow-in labeling or discrepant labeling, rather than comprehension questions. Infants' selections in response to such questions should simply reflect their toy preferences. If infants were to display a different pattern of selections for the preference-control questions than for the comprehension questions, then comprehension performance could not be merely a function of their preference for one toy over the other.

An additional feature of the present study was an assessment of infants' comprehension of well-known, familiar labels, such as *dog*, *bottle*, and *ball*. Infants' ability to select the correct object when asked about familiar labels provides another kind of baseline estimate; it is informative about the highest level of comprehension performance that could reasonably be expected with the comprehension measure utilized in the study.

Method

Subjects

Ninety-four infants between sixteen and nineteen months participated in the study. The data from thirty of the infants were omitted,[1] leaving sixty-four infants from two equal-sized age groups: sixteen- to seventeen-month-olds ($M = 16.4$ months) and eighteen- to nineteen-month-olds ($M = 18.4$ months). All infants were full-term at birth, developing normally, and came from monolingual, native English-speaking families. Boys and girls were represented equally in the two age groups.

According to parental report using an adapted version of the Bates (1979) early-language questionnaire, infants in both age groups generally possessed productive vocabularies in excess of fifty words. As expected, the older infants possessed somewhat larger vocabularies, both receptive and productive, than the younger infants. The sixteen- to seventeen-month-olds already understood an average of 180 words (range: 67 to 332; object labels 64 percent of total), and they were already producing an average of sixty-one words (range: 5 to 176;

object labels 67 percent of total). The eighteen- to nineteen-month-olds understood an average of 225 words (range: 82 to 359; object labels 62 percent of total), and they produced ninety-two words on average (range: 2 to 308; object labels 69 percent of total). Infants' vocabulary size did not predict their comprehension performance in the experimental situation on any measure, either for novel or familiar labels.

Materials

Stimuli

Each infant saw five pairs of toys, three familiar and two novel. Parents were interviewed by phone to select the familiar toys for each infant. All infants saw the same two pairs of novel toys: One pair included a green, oblong, extendable periscope and a disc encircled by yellow, rubber suction-cups, and the other pair was comprised of a set of multi-colored, wooden cubes strung together by elastic and a blue, cylindrical, collapsible telescope. Criteria for selection of the novel toys were that a) toys be novel, attractive, balanced in salience within a pair, and manipulable for infants between sixteen and nineteen months of age, and b) the two toys in a pair be visually distinct from one another.

Novel labels

Two novel labels were used in the study: *Peri* and *toma*. These word forms were selected according to: a) novelty for infants, b) distinctiveness from one another and from the familiar labels used in the study, and c) ease of pronunciation for infants. Novel labels (which obey the rules of English phonology) were used instead of standard English labels to allow counterbalanced assignment of the labels to the four different novel toys.

Equipment

A video camera equipped with a stop-watch function and a video cassette recorder equipped with frame-by-frame viewing capability were used to record the infants' and experimenter's behavior during the experimental session. The time-stamped video record provided continuous information about the temporal flow of events.

Phone questionnaire concerning familiar labels

Prior to the laboratory visit, parents were interviewed about infants' familiarity with eighteen object labels: *airplane, rabbit, bird, cat, doll, ball, sock, duck, car, shoe, spoon, flower, bottle, dog, banana, boat, cup,* and *keys*. Only labels that parents were certain children understood were used in the experimental session.

Design

The study included two conditions: Follow-in labeling and discrepant labeling. The two conditions each included two phases: a) a training phase, in which a new label was introduced to infants under controlled conditions, and b) a test phase, in which infants were either asked comprehension questions regarding the newly trained novel label (e.g., "Where is the *peri*?"), or preference-control questions regarding the novel toys involved in the preceding training (e.g., "Where is your favorite one?"). The training phases of the follow-in labeling and discrepant labeling conditions differed in certain essential ways. First, the experimenter's nonverbal cues differed in the follow-in labeling versus discrepant labeling conditions. In the follow-in labeling condition, the experimenter uttered the novel label while looking at the toy which the infant was already examining, the "visible" toy. In contrast, the experimenter looked down into a bucket containing a second toy, the "bucket" toy, while labeling in the discrepant labeling condition. An additional difference between the follow-in and discrepant labeling conditions concerns how the experimenter coordinated labeling with the infant's focus on the visible toy. In the follow-in labeling condition, the experimenter glanced at the infant between labeling utterances to check when the infant was focusing on the visible toy. However, in the discrepant labeling condition, the experimenter avoided looking at the infant. Instead, she intermittently glanced at a side-view mirror which displayed the infant's activities to ascertain when the infant was focused on the visible toy. This procedure was chosen to minimize confusion that infants might experience regarding the experimenter's focus of attention. If the experimenter were to look at infants intermittently during discrepant labeling, infants might become confused as to whether discrepant or follow-in labeling was occurring.

Each infant participated in both follow-in labeling and discrepant labeling conditions with one trial of each condition. However, half of the infants answered comprehension questions after follow-in and discrepant labeling, while the other half answered preference-control questions after follow-in and discrepant labeling. The order in which infants experienced follow-in labeling versus discrepant labeling was balanced with respect to age group and question type (i.e., comprehension vs. preference-control). Assignment of toy pairs, target toy (i.e., the labeled toy), and labels was also counterbalanced with respect to age group, question type, and the direction of the experimenter's focus (i.e., follow-in labeling vs. discrepant labeling). During the test questions for any given infant, the target toys appeared equally often in the right- vs. left-hand position. Assignment of the familiar toys was also roughly counter-balanced with respect to age group, experimenter's focus, and question type (precise counterbalancing could not be achieved because infants differed in terms of which six labels they previously comprehended). Comprehension questions about the familiar labels were intermixed with questions about the novel labels in both comprehension and preference-control test phases. This intermixing occurred in a fixed order for all subjects.

Procedure

After a short warm-up period with two familiar toys, the infant was placed in an infant seat at a table, with the parent seated nearby, and the experimenter seated across the table from the infant. Parents filled out the language questionnaire during the session in order to keep parent–infant interaction to a minimum. The first activity of the experimental procedure was a brief familiarization with the comprehension test format using the familiar toys that were available during warm-up: The infant was asked one or two comprehension questions concerning one of the familiar items (e.g., "Where is the *ball*? Can you find the *ball*?") and the experimenter clapped and cheered when the infant touched or picked up the correct toy. The familiarization procedure was the same for all infants, regardless of whether they were asked comprehension questions or preference-control questions.

Discrepant labeling condition: Training

The experimenter produced a colored, plastic bucket (rattling it until the infant looked at it), opened the bucket, removed the two novel toys, and placed them side by side on the table. She then placed one of the novel toys back inside the bucket, making certain that the infant watched her do this. Returning to the still-visible toy, she demonstrated what it could do, and then handed it over for the infant to explore. Then the experimenter grasped the bucket in both hands, while keeping it upright so that the infant was unable to see what was inside. She waited until the infant was looking at the visible toy (using the side-view mirror to make this judgment), looked down into the bucket, uttered a novel label (e.g., "It's a *toma*"), and maintained her gaze toward the bucket for four seconds. The labeling procedure was then repeated three more times; each time the labeling was initiated when infants were looking at the visible toy. Thus infants were exposed to the label a total of four times during the training, and each and every exposure occurred when they were examining the visible toy. The experimenter continued to hold the bucket throughout the training. After the experimenter uttered the fourth label, she waited four seconds, then rattled the bucket until the infant looked at it, whereupon she angled the bucket so the infant could see the toy inside. She then removed the toy from the bucket, demonstrated what it could do, and offered it to the infant. Both toys were left available to infants for up to thirty seconds. Thereafter, the experimenter removed the toys, and the test phase began.

Follow-in labeling condition: Training

The training procedure for the follow-in labeling condition was identical to that of the discrepant labeling condition, except that the experimenter gazed in the direction of the visible toy at the time of uttering the novel label, and the mirror, though present, was not used by the experimenter. As in the discrepant labeling condition, the experimenter was careful to produce the novel label only when infants were already focused on the visible toy. The experimenter held the bucket throughout follow-in labeling just as she did throughout discrepant labeling.

Test phase

The test phase examined the consistency with which infants selected a particular toy in response to questioning by the experimenter. The test phase included either comprehension or preference-control questions concerning the novel toys as well as comprehension questions about a familiar label. A given infant answered the same type of question in both follow-in and discrepant labeling conditions.

When asked questions about novel toys, infants were shown the two novel toys from the immediately preceding training phase. When asked about a familiar label, infants were shown two familiar toys. The same two novel toys appeared for each and every novel label question, and the same two familiar toys appeared for each and every familiar label question. An array of only two toys was decided upon to reduce the information-processing load on infants, and the same two toys were used for each question to help reduce the influence of novelty and familiarity effects on infants' toy selections.

Comprehension questions

For infants who were asked comprehension questions during the test phase, the experimenter began by placing the two novel toys on a tray. She offered the tray to the infant while encouraging the infant to select one of the toys (e.g., "There's a *peri* here. Can you point to the *peri*? Point to the *peri*."). The experimenter was careful to look only at the infant's face during questioning to avoid biasing the infant's selection via nonverbal cues. When the infant made a selection, the experimenter said "Did you find it?" in a neutral tone, regardless of which toy was chosen. If infants showed the toy they selected to the parent seated nearby, the parent likewise responded in a neutral manner (e.g., the parent said "Oh" or "That's nice" in a neutral tone regardless of which toy infants selected) based on prior instruction from the experimenter. The experimenter then retrieved the toys and began the next question trial. Infants were asked eight comprehension questions in all for each condition, four concerning the newly trained novel label and four concerning a familiar label. If infants failed to respond to a question twice in a row, the experimenter moved to the next question trial. If infants became disturbed or failed to answer six questions in succession, the comprehension testing was discontinued.

Containers of different kinds (e.g., a tray, a basket, and a pouch) were used to present the toys to infants during questioning. This variety helped maintain infants' interest. For the same reason, questions were asked in several different ways (e.g., "Point to the *peri*" vs. "Where is the *peri*?"). The use of these different questions and containers occurred in a prearranged order that was held constant for all test phases.

Preference-control questions

Preference-control questions involved asking infants to select one of the two toys without any mention of the novel label (e.g., "Point to the one you like" or "Where's your favorite one?"). The experimenter asked infants a total of four preference-control questions and four familiar label comprehension questions for each condition. Containers and questions varied in the same fixed order as in comprehension questioning.

Coding and reliability

Test phase coding

Infants' responses to comprehension or preference-control questions were coded in terms of a) which of the two toys infants selected first in response to the question, and, in some cases, b) which of the two toys infants used in responding to the experimenter's request (e.g., "Show Mommy the *peri*"). Coders were blind to the training conditions of the novel labels, and hence did not know which toy was the correct referent of a given label. The test phases of eight randomly selected infants were coded independently by two coders. They demonstrated 92 percent agreement in their judgments of which toy infants selected first and which toy infants used to perform a requested action.

Looks during training coding

Coders judged a) whether infants were looking at the visible toy at the time of the experimenter's labeling utterance, b) when infants looked to the experimenter and/or the bucket, and c) whether these looks occurred in response to hearing labels. Coders' view of the experimenter was screened, thus coders were blind to condition (i.e., follow-in vs. discrepant labeling). Based on the follow-in and discrepant training phases experienced by seven randomly selected infants, two coders demonstrated 91 percent agreement.

Differential labeling coding

To verify that the experimenter maintained equivalent enthusiasm during follow-in as opposed to discrepant labeling, coders judged, on a seven-point scale, the overall level of enthusiasm with which the experimenter produced the label. During this coding the video monitor was screened; thus coders were blind to whether follow-in versus discrepant labeling was occurring. The training phases of all sixty-four infants were coded.

Feedback coding

To examine whether feedback from the experimenter might have biased infants' toy selections, one coder judged whether the experimenter seemed pleased or displeased on hearing the experimenter's "Did you find it?" feedback. The coder was blind as to which toy the infant had actually selected prior to the experimenter's utterance. Feedback judgments were made for eight randomly-selected infants who answered comprehension questions (in both the follow-in and discrepant labeling conditions). Comparisons between the coder's enthusiasm judgments and infants' actual selections revealed no relationship between feedback and infants' pattern of selections: The experimenter was rated as enthusiastic on only 50.4 percent of instances in which infants had just made a correct selection (i.e., the visible toy after follow-in labeling or the bucket toy after discrepant labeling). Thus infants were just as likely to receive somewhat unenthusiastic feedback to a correct choice as to receive somewhat enthusiastic feedback. Moreover, the experimenter's feedback was judged to be enthusiastic on 54.7 percent of cases when infants had made an *incorrect* selection. Clearly, the experimenter's feedback was not biased in favor of correct performance on infants' part.

Results

Looks during training

The training phase lasted approximately thirty seconds, with no significant differences in length of the training phase for follow-in vs. discrepant labeling (follow-in labeling $M = 31.62$ seconds [$SD = 7.12$] and discrepant labeling $M = 34.39$ seconds [$SD = 10.20$]). During the training phase, infants were looking at the visible toy at the time the experimenter uttered the novel label, regardless of whether follow-in versus discrepant labeling occurred. However, infants quite often looked away from the toy at other points during the training phase. Of particular interest is the extent to which infants looked toward the experimenter and/or the bucket after hearing a label (or both in immediate sequence in response to labeling, to be called "responsive sequential looking"). Such monitoring behavior may provide information about the degree to which infants were sensitized to the experimenter's nonverbal cues. Table 2.1.1 displays a summary of infants' pattern of looks with respect to the three looking measures.

Overall, infants demonstrated a sizable amount of monitoring in both experimental conditions; for example, in both follow-in and discrepant training phases virtually all infants (sixty-two out of sixty-four) looked at least once toward the experimenter in response to labeling. A 2 (age) X 2 (question type: comprehension vs. preference-control) X 2 (experimenter's focus: follow-in vs. discrepant) mixed-design MANOVA including all three looking measures revealed a main effect of experimenter's focus, $F (3. 58) = 13.44$, $p < .00005$, but no effects of age or question type, and no significant interactions. The main effect of experimenter's focus was due to a higher level of monitoring during discrepant labeling than during follow-in labeling, as is apparent from Table 2.1.1. Subsequent univariate tests revealed that the main effect of experimenter's focus held up for the looks-to-experimenter [$F(1, 60) = 5.08$, $p < .05$] and responsive sequential looks [$F(1, 60) = 35.03$, $p < .0005$] measures, but not for the looks-to-bucket measure.

The looks-during-training results are noteworthy on two counts. First, the absence of a main effect or interactions involving question type helps to verify the equivalence of the training phases for infants who were asked comprehension questions and those who were asked preference-control questions. More importantly, the greater incidence of monitoring during discrepant labeling suggests that infants were sensitized to the discrepancy between their own and the speaker's focus, and sought to identify the target of the speaker's focus. However, the comprehension data presented next are needed to clarify whether infants *used* what they noticed about the speaker's focus to help them in determining the reference of the novel label.

Novel toy selections

Selection of the visible toy

If infants fail to understand the significance of the speaker's focus for the reference of the novel label, when tested for comprehension they should select

Table 2.1.1   *Mean number of looks during training*

	Follow-in	Discrepant
Looks to experimenter	4.02 (1.90)	4.86 (2.53)
Looks to bucket	1.97 (2.00)	2.28 (1.96)
Responsive sequential looks	0.23 (0.53)	0.95 (0.90)

Note: Standard deviations in parentheses.

the visible toy regardless of whether the label was introduced during follow-in or discrepant labeling. In contrast, infants who are sensitive to the linguistic relevance of the speaker's focus should select the visible toy less often when it is introduced during discrepant relative to follow-in labeling. Also in question is whether infants' selections differ when asked comprehension questions versus preference-control questions. Thus of particular interest in the comprehension results is the possibility of an interaction between the direction of the experimenter's focus (i.e., follow-in vs. discrepant labeling) and the type of question infants were asked (i.e., comprehension vs. preference-control questions). Infants' toy selections were analyzed by means of a 2 (age) X 2 (question type) X 2 (experimenter's focus) mixed-design ANOVA.[2] Because infants varied in the number of questions they answered, their performance was analyzed in terms of the proportion of questions for which they selected the visible toy out of the total number of questions answered.[3] The ANOVA revealed a main effect of question type, $F(1, 60) = 5.22$, $p < .05$. As may be seen in Table 2.1.2, this main effect was due to infants who were asked comprehension questions selecting the visible toy more frequently than infants who were asked preference-control questions.

The ANOVA also revealed a main effect due to experimenter's focus, $F(1, 60) = 5.65$, $p < .05$, reflecting a greater selection of the visible toy after follow-in labeling than after discrepant labeling. Finally, the ANOVA yielded a significant question type by experimenter's focus interaction, $F(1, 60) = 5.27, p < .05$. No other effects were significant.

An analysis of simple effects (Keppel, 1982) conducted to determine the locus of the interaction revealed that infants who were asked comprehension questions selected the visible toy more frequently in the follow-in labeling condition than in the discrepant labeling condition, $F(1, 60) = 10.92$, $p < .01$. This finding is consistent with the prediction that infants appreciate the linguistic relevance of the speaker's nonverbal cues.

Table 2.1.2   *Mean percent selection of the visible toy*

| | Comprehension Questions | |
	Follow-in	*Discrepant*
16- to 17-month-olds	65 (26)	53 (36)
18- to 19-month-olds	72 (30)	34 (25)
Both age groups	69 (28)	44 (32)
	Preference-Control Questions	
	Follow-in	*Discrepant*
16- to 17-month-olds	48 (31)	46 (30)
18- to 19-month-olds	42 (23)	42 (28)
Both age groups	45 (27)	44 (29)

Note: Standard deviations in parentheses.

The simple-effects analysis further revealed that the experimenter's focus during label training did not significantly affect infants' tendency to select the visible toy in response to the preference-control questions. That is, when asked a question such as "Where is your favorite one?", infants were equally likely to select the visible toy after discrepant labeling and after follow-in labeling. Thus the impact of the experimenter's focus on infants' response to *comprehension* questions can more clearly be interpreted as reflecting knowledge of word–object mappings.

In addition, the simple-effects analysis provided specific evidence concerning whether word mappings were established. For follow-in labeling, infants selected the visible toy significantly more often when asked comprehension questions than when asked preference-control questions, $F(1, 60) = 12.02$, $p < .01$. Thus, in the follow-in labeling condition, infants who were asked comprehension questions chose the visible toy more often than they would have by preference alone, again suggesting that the comprehension questions indeed tapped word learning.

However, performance on comprehension questions and preference-control questions did not differ for the discrepant labeling condition. This was true both when the results were collapsed across age, and when each age group was considered individually. This analysis thus fails to clarify whether word mappings per se were established during discrepant labeling.

Tests against chance performance

Also in question is whether infants selected the correct toy more often than would be expected if they were merely making random selections. Recall that the correct toy would be the visible toy in the follow-in labeling condition, and the bucket toy in the discrepant labeling condition. In the follow-in labeling condition, infants who were asked comprehension questions selected the visible toy more often than would be expected by chance, $t(30) = 3.82$, $p < .001$, while infants who were asked preference-control questions did not differ significantly from chance in their pattern of selection. The same pattern of results emerged when the two age groups were considered separately, with $t(14) = 2.34$, $p < .05$ for younger infants, and $t(14) = 2.99$, $p < .01$ for older infants, respectively, who were asked comprehension questions. Thus infants as young as sixteen to seventeen months were able to map the novel labels to the correct objects when labels were introduced during follow-in labeling.

In the discrepant labeling condition, by contrast, infants performed at a level consistent with random responding regardless of whether they were asked comprehension or preference-control questions. However, it is worth noting that when the two age groups were considered separately, older infants selected the bucket toy (the correct toy) more often than would be expected by chance when asked comprehension questions following discrepant labeling, $t(14) = 2.56$, $p < .05$ (they did not differ from chance when asked preference-control questions). Younger infants performed at levels not significantly different from chance for both comprehension and preference-control questions in the discrepant labeling condition.

Up to this point, then, three main findings have emerged. First, infants were able to link a new label with its appropriate referent in the follow-in labeling condition. Second, infants did *not* fall prey to mapping errors when discrepant labeling occurred: They did not link the novel label to the visible toy. In fact, older infants were significantly *less* likely than would be expected by chance to display mapping errors. However, younger infants did not systematically link labels with *any* object when faced with discrepant labeling. Apparently younger infants were able to inhibit a mapping when discrepant labeling occurred, yet they were unable actively to infer the correct mapping. Finally, older infants' greater-than-chance selection of the bucket toy after discrepant labeling suggests that they may have been able to go beyond inhibiting errors actively to infer the correct referent of the label. However, given the absence of differences between comprehension and preference-control questions, it remains somewhat inconclusive at this point in the analysis whether older infants indeed established word mappings in the case of discrepant labeling.

Criterion-based results

Infants' selection patterns across both labeling conditions were also examined. If infants actively consult the speaker's nonverbal cues, they should systematically select both a) the visible toy after follow-in labeling *and* b) the bucket toy after discrepant labeling. On the other hand, if infants fail to recognize the significance of such cues, they should systematically select the *visible* toy after both follow-in and discrepant labeling. For these analyses, a criterion of at least three out of four same-toy selections (for a given condition) was used because it was relatively rare for infants to select the same novel object on all four questions. Table 2.1.3 displays the criterion-based results in contingency-table format.

Of the twenty-three infants who answered all four comprehension questions in both labeling conditions, eleven fit the pattern predicted by the cue-sensitive understanding (i.e., visible toy after follow-in labeling and bucket toy after discrepant labeling). This frequency is both well above chance (Binomial test $p < .00005$) and significantly greater than that obtained for preference-control questions [$X^2(1) = 7.74$, $p < .01$]. In contrast, only three of the twenty-three infants who were asked comprehension questions displayed the pattern to be expected if infants failed to consult nonverbal cues (i.e., selection of the visible toy after both follow-in and discrepant labeling), which does not differ from the 2.25 predicted by chance nor, by Fisher's exact test, from the frequency observed among infants who were asked preference-control questions.

In sum, like the previous findings, the criterion-based results point to an early sensitivity to the linguistic significance of the speaker's nonverbal cues: A

Table 2.1.3 *Number of infants who met the three or four out of four selection criterion*

Comprehension questions

		Discrepant labeling		
		3 or 4	2	0 or 1
	3 or 4	3 (2.25)	2 (2.70)	11 (2.25)
Follow-in labeling	2	3 (2.70)	0 (3.23)	1 (2.70)
	0 or 1	1 (2.25)	2 (2.70)	0 (2.25)

Preference-control questions

		Discrepant labeling		
		3 or 4	2	0 or 1
	3 or 4	1 (2.05)	2 (2.46)	2 (2.05)
Follow-in labeling	2	2 (2.46)	0 (2.95)	2 (2.46)
	0 or 1	3 (2.05)	4 (2.46)	5 (2.05)

Note: Only infants who answered all four test questions included. Chance frequencies in parentheses.

significant number of infants linked the label with the correct toy across both follow-in labeling *and* discrepant labeling. These findings indicate that some infants were able to go beyond the avoidance of mapping errors during discrepant labeling; they used the speaker's nonverbal cues in an active way as a guide to the correct interpretation of the novel label.

Comprehension of familiar labels

Infants' responses to comprehension questions about familiar labels were examined to provide baseline information about the sensitivity of the comprehension measure. Comprehension performance for the novel versus familiar labels can be compared directly if we consider only those infants who were asked comprehension questions about both novel and familiar labels.

As shown in Table 2.1.4, infants' overall comprehension performance was better for familiar labels ($M = 72$ percent, $SD = 24$) than novel labels ($M = 63$ percent, $SD = 30$), but the familiar versus novel label difference was significant only in the discrepant labeling condition, paired $t(31) = 2.21$, $p < .05$. As is clear from Table 2.1.4, this difference in the discrepant labeling condition was primarily due to differences between novel versus familiar label performance in younger infants. In general, then, infants performed nearly as well on the comprehension questions regarding novel labels that they had heard only four times as they did on questions regarding labels that they had known for some time, with the exception that younger infants tended to respond more accurately to familiar labels when novel labels were introduced under conditions of discrepant labeling.

Table 2.1.4 *Mean percent correct for infants who were asked comprehension questions about both novel and familiar labels*

	16- to 17-month-olds	
	Follow-in	*Discrepant*
Familiar labels	78 (23)	60 (29)
Novel labels	65 (26)	47 (36)
	18- to 19-month-olds	
	Follow-in	*Discrepant*
Familiar labels	79 (22)	73 (19)
Novel labels	72 (30)	66 (25)

Note: Standard deviations in parentheses.

Ruling out alternative explanations

The results considered thus far suggest that infants of sixteen to nineteen months are sensitive to the speaker's nonverbal cues as a source of information about the reference of novel object labels. However, there are several plausible alternative explanations that must be ruled out before this conclusion can be accepted. First, decreased selection of the visible toy following discrepant labeling may have occurred simply because during discrepant labeling infants became a) distracted, and/or b) irritated by the experimenter's inattentive and relatively directive behavior. If distracted, infants may have spent less time examining the visible toy during discrepant labeling than during follow-in labeling, and therefore may have been less able to map the novel label to the visible toy. If irritated, infants may have been less responsive to comprehension questions, and hence less likely to display a mapping of the novel label to the visible toy. A direct measure of distraction was available in the data—the time infants spent examining the visible toy during the training phase of follow-in versus discrepant labeling. Infants' irritation could be diagnosed by their performance on familiar label comprehension questions that followed discrepant labeling. If irritated, infants should also have been uncooperative in answering questions about familiar labels, and hence have displayed poorer familiar label comprehension performance after discrepant as opposed to follow-in labeling (note in Table 2.1.4 that younger infants indeed displayed a decrement in familiar label comprehension performance after discrepant labeling relative to follow-in labeling).

Another possibility is that infants avoided selecting the visible toy after discrepant relative to follow-in labeling as a result of differences in the way the experimenter presented the labels during these training phases. Perhaps the experimenter produced the label less enthusiastically during discrepant training than during follow-in training. As described earlier, such differential labeling on the experimenter's part was measured by having blind observers code the enthusiasm with which the experimenter produced the novel labels in the two types of training phases.

The validity of these alternative explanations was tested by entering the three measures, each tied to a separate alternative, as covariates in a 2 (age) X 2 (question type) X 2 (experimenter's focus) ANCOVA with the dependent variable being the proportion of time infants selected the visible toy. This analysis revealed the same pattern of effects as the original analysis: No significant age differences, a significant main effect of question type, $F(1, 57) = 5.41$, $p < .05$, a significant main effect of experimenter's focus, $F(1, 57) = 4.21$, $p < .05$, and a significant question type X experimenter's focus interaction, $F(1, 57) = 5.61$, $p < .05$. An analysis of simple effects verified that this interaction followed the same pattern as originally observed. In sum, this analysis demonstrates that the measures associated with the proposed alternatives do not, by themselves, account for the effects obtained.

Discussion

The present investigation attempted to clarify infants' contribution to the achievement of joint reference; specifically, whether infants can actively make use of a speaker's nonverbal cues for interpreting novel object labels. If so, infants could identify the referent of new label, even when the label refers to a different object than the one upon which infants themselves are focused. This cue-sensitive understanding could play a crucial role in helping infants to avoid many mapping errors because a) it is not uncommon for adults to label a different object than the one occupying infants' focus (e.g., Collis, 1977; Harris, Jones, and Grant, 1983), and b) word learning proceeds very quickly when infants reach sixteen–nineteen months; words can be learned based on only one or two exposures.

The findings provided clear support for an early appreciation of the linguistic significance of the speaker's nonverbal cues. Infants did not tend to make mapping errors when they were introduced to novel labels under discrepant labeling conditions. Rather, they tended to select the visible toy when it was the correct referent (i.e., when introduced during follow-in labeling), but not when it was an incorrect referent (i.e., when presented during discrepant labeling). This is a striking result. During discrepant labeling, not only were infants looking at an incorrect referent at the time they heard the novel label, but the incorrect referent was in fact the only novel object in sight. Infants would seem to have been under considerable pressure to establish an incorrect mapping. Yet they did not.

Although infants used the speaker's focus to guide their interpretation of novel labels, they did not use the speaker's focus to guide their object preferences, based on their responses to preference-control questions. It is clear, therefore, that the comprehension results indeed reflect word learning. Infants' reduced tendency to select the visible toy in response to comprehension questions following discrepant labeling could not have been the result of demand characteristics introduced by the training circumstances, or such a pattern would have emerged for the preference-control questions as well as for the comprehension questions.

All in all, infants' performance indicates that they possess at least one word-learning strategy that goes beyond simple associative processes such as temporal contiguity. Namely, infants spontaneously use the speaker's nonverbal cues to guide the word–object associations that they form. This is not to say that infants can deal with the discrepant labeling situation effortlessly. Rather, it seems to be easier for infants to learn labels under conditions of follow-in labeling than discrepant labeling, just as others have demonstrated (e.g., Harris, Jones, and Grant, 1983; Tomasello and Farrar, 1986). What is significant is that infants possess abilities which buffer them from making errors during discrepant labeling.

Avoiding errors versus inferring correct mappings

There is some question as to whether infants were able to do more than merely inhibit mappings (and hence avoid errors) when discrepant labeling occurred. The criterion-based results indicated that at least some of the infants successfully used the speaker's cues to establish a mapping with the bucket toy during discrepant labeling. Similarly, eighteen- to nineteen-month-olds selected the bucket toy in response to comprehension questions more often than would be expected by chance following discrepant labeling (although not significantly more often than infants who were asked preference-control questions).

Why did many infants experience difficulty in establishing correct mappings during discrepant labeling? One possibility to consider is that these infants were entirely insensitive to the linguistic implications of the discrepancy between their own and the speaker's focus. However, if this were so, the criterion-based results should have displayed some incidence of mapping errors, which they did not. A second possibility is that infants' appreciation of the discrepancy in focus led them to block a mapping, but they were not yet able to use the speaker's cues in an active way to seek out the correct referent. Finally, perhaps most infants *were* capable of using the speaker's cues in an active way to infer the correct mapping, but many were unable to display this ability due to intervening obstacles. Several such obstacles were present in this study. For example, the correct referent was actually hidden from view throughout the period of labeling. Thus infants could not simply solve the mapping problem by immediately glancing over to the object at which the experimenter was looking. Infants would need to be able mentally to represent the object in the bucket, and link the label to this representation during the training phase, or else they would need to inhibit a mapping between the label and the visible toy, while retaining the label in memory until the bucket toy was revealed. Perhaps if these additional obstacles to mapping were removed, many more infants would reveal an ability to infer the correct mapping from the adult's nonverbal cues when discrepant labeling occurs.

Infants' sensitivity to nonverbal cues during training

Infants' pattern of looks during the training phase was also indicative of the cue-sensitive understanding. When the experimenter produced a label, infants looked more frequently toward the experimenter and showed more glances between the experimenter and the bucket during discrepant than follow-in labeling. These findings suggest that infants noted the discrepancy between their own and the experimenter's focus, leading them to check the experimenter's focus more frequently and to attempt to pinpoint the target of the experimenter's focus. Infants' tendency to check the experimenter's face during discrepant labeling suggests that line-of-regard is an important cue to infants. Again, however, line-of-regard was not the only cue available to infants concerning the speaker's focus in this situation, and such redundancy of cues is probably typical of most everyday interactions. Thus, even when infants do not glance up at a speaker's face, they may nevertheless be aware of a discrepancy in focus.

The looks-during-training results also help to rule out a low-level interpretation for the comprehension results. Given that the experimenter seldom looked in infants' direction during discrepant labeling, infants might have lost interest in the experimenter, leading them to ignore the experimenter's utterance, and hence, for this relatively low-level reason, to inhibit a mapping between the label and the visible toy. However, the fact that infants showed an *increased* tendency to look toward the experimenter (and between the experimenter and the bucket) during discrepant labeling suggests that they did not ignore the experimenter, but rather were specifically seeking information concerning the experimenter's focus.

Nature and source of infants' cue-sensitive understanding

The ability infants displayed in the present study can be interpreted in both a "frugal" and a "profligate" light, to use Premack's (1988) terms. A frugal interpretation is that infants possess only a low-level understanding of both nonverbal cues and the way that nonverbal cues relate to correct mappings.

Infants may follow nonverbal cues because they have learned that these cues predict interesting visual experiences; they may use nonverbal cues as a guide to word reference because they have come to realize that nonverbal cues and labels tend to be directed toward the same object. In particular, infants may appreciate the relation between nonverbal cues and word reference, without understanding why this relation exists. Though superficial, this ability would nevertheless be an effective aid to word learning by enabling infants to avoid mapping errors when discrepant labeling occurs. How might such a superficial understanding of nonverbal cues be acquired? Perhaps when infants have learned to comprehend labels, they notice that, when an adult speaker utters those labels, he or she tends to look or gesture toward the labels' referents.

In contrast, the profligate interpretation views infants as possessing a tacit understanding of *why* nonverbal cues should be consulted when establishing word–object mappings. Perhaps infants implicitly understand that both labels and nonverbal cues reflect what a speaker is thinking about. When infants hear a label they do not know, they interpret this label in light of the available nonverbal cues, because they understand that nonverbal cues and labels converge on the same thing, the speaker's mental focus. Put another way, infants may understand that when uttering a label, a speaker intends to refer to a particular object, while also understanding that nonverbal cues are a good source of information about the target of that intent. Thus the profligate view attributes to infants some elementary understanding of mental phenomena such as "intent" and "focus of attention," as well as an understanding that both nonverbal cues and labeling utterances bear some relation to these mental phenomena.

The profligate explanation for infants' tendency to use nonverbal cues to guide word mappings is of course both speculative and controversial (see Baldwin, 1988; Shatz, 1983; and Smiley, 1987). Nevertheless, a number of researchers have argued recently that infants of about this age are sensitized to others' focus of attention and understand that nonverbal cues signal focus of attention (e.g., Baldwin, 1988; Baron-Cohen, 1989; Bretherton, 1988; Bretherton, McNew, and Beeghly-Smith, 1981; Trevarthen, 1980). There are also some hints that infants are increasingly interested in maintaining joint attentional focus with adults at this time. Bakeman and Adamson (1984) have shown, for instance, that infants begin to spend substantial amounts of their free play time in active coordinated attention with their mothers from the age of about fifteen to eighteen months (e.g., joining with another individual in focusing on a set of objects, both by playing with those objects and looking back and forth between the individual and the objects of focus). Thus it seems possible that infants understand something about the "jointness" of coordinated attention at an early age, and are interested in achieving and maintaining it. The findings of the present research, on a rich interpretation, suggest that infants of sixteen to nineteen months not only appreciate the "jointness" of coordinated attention, but also recognize that language, and in particular, word reference, trades on this intersubjectivity.

Supposing for a moment that the profligate interpretation is correct, we should question how infants could achieve such insight into language and human behavior as early as sixteen to nineteen months of age. Some researchers have argued that such understanding is innately given. For example, Bruner (1983) writes, " ... the 'intent to refer' is unlearned and ... so too is the recognition of that intent in others ... Logically, there would be no conceivable way for two human beings to achieve shared reference were there no initial disposition for it" (p. 122) (see also Leslie and Happe, 1989). Macnamara (1982, 1990) specifically argues that infants are innately supplied with an ability to recognize the intent to refer in another person's *utterance*. Perhaps, however, infants could acquire an understanding that labels and nonverbal cues converge on a speaker's intent to refer with only the nonverbal cues side of this triangle innately specified. According to this scenario, infants recognize from early on that nonverbal cues reflect some information about other people's intentions and focus of attention, while not yet understanding that language similarly manifests such mental phenomena. Infants might then build up such an understanding about language through observing the way that nonverbal cues are correlated with language use. There would seem to be ample opportunity for such observation given the rich array of cues that adults tend to supply when talking to young children (e.g., Collis, 1977; Messer, 1978, 1983; Murphy and Messer, 1977; Ninio and Bruner, 1978).

Conclusion

The findings presented here reveal that infants of only sixteen to nineteen months appreciate that speakers supply nonverbal cues which are relevant to the interpretation of novel object labels. At this early age, then, infants are already capable of carrying some of the burden of social coordination that is necessary for the achievement of joint reference. This enables them to establish word–world correspondences with only a modicum of error. Thus these findings help to illuminate the rapid trajectory that is characteristic of early semantic development.

Acknowledgments

This research was supported in part by a US Department of Education Jacob Javitts Memorial Fellowship, a Stanford University Special Dissertation Grant, and NIH Grant 20382 to Ellen M. Markman. The paper is based on a dissertation submitted in partial fulfillment of the requirements for the Ph.D. at Stanford University. A portion of the results was presented at the biennial meeting of the

International Society for Infant Studies in Montreal, Canada, April 1990. Many thanks to the parents and infants who volunteered their participation; to Kathy Jo Bruni, Susan Gussie, Jeff Hagan, Laura Holderness, Jennifer Jauquet, Margie Morse, and Parmjit Sohi for their help with video-tape coding; to Judith Wasow for her administrative efficiency; and to Eve Clark, Anne Fernald, John Flavell, Jim Greeno, Ellen Markman, and Lou Moses for their advice about the research and their comments concerning earlier drafts of this paper.

Notes to 2.1

1. Infants were omitted due to excessive fussiness or fatigue (eleven infants), experimenter error (five infants), parental overinvolvement (one infant), and/or when the design criteria of the study were not satisfied (thirteen infants). The latter basis for omission included a) when infants happened to look away from the toy they were holding at the time the experimenter uttered the novel label during the training phase (six infants); b) when infants spontaneously produced a label for a toy that was intended to be novel (two infants); and c) when infants provided fewer than two interpretable responses for a given item on the comprehension or preference-control questions (five infants). The omitted infants did not differ from the infants included in the experimental sample on any of the parental report measures of vocabulary development.
2. Preliminary analyses revealed no effects or interactions involving either gender or order of condition (i.e., follow-in labeling first vs. follow-in labeling second). For simplicity of presentation, all analyses are presented without these variables.
3. Based on Winer's (1971) recommendation, proportions in all analyses were submitted to the arcsin transformation ($X_{ijk} = 2$ arcsin $\sqrt{X_{ijk}}$), with values close to zero or unity corrected in the following way:

$$X'_{ijk} = 2 \text{ arcsin } \sqrt{X_{ijk} \pm [1/(2n)]}.$$

However, for case of comprehension, the mean scores (and standard deviations) reported throughout the article are those for the *untransformed* proportions (expressed as percentages).

References to 2.1

Bakeman, R. and Adamson, L. B. (1984). "Coordinating attention to people and objects in mother–infant and peer–infant interaction." *Child Development*, **55**, 1278–89.

Baldwin, D. A. (1988). *Linguistic Advances During the Single-word Period: Using language for mental impact*. Paper presented at the 5th Australian Developmental Conference, Sydney, Australia.

Baldwin, D. A. (1989). "Priorities in children's expectations about object label reference: Form over color." *Child Development*, **60**, 1291–306.

Baron-Cohen, S. (1989). "Perceptual role taking and protodeclarative pointing in autism." *British Journal of Developmental Psychology*, **7**, 113–27.

Bates, E. (1979). *The Emergence of Symbols: Cognition and communication in infancy*. New York: Academic Press.

Bretherton, I. (1988). "How to do things with one word: The ontogenesis of intentional message making in infancy." In M. D. Smith and J. L. Locke (eds), *The Emergent Lexicon: The child's development of a linguistic vocabulary*. New York: Academic Press, 225–57.

Bretherton, I., McNew, S., and Beeghly-Smith, M. (1981). "Early person knowledge as expressed in gestural and verbal communications: When do infants acquire a 'theory of mind'?" In M. E. Lamb and L. R. Sherrod (eds), *Infant Social Cognition*. Hillsdale, NJ: Erlbaum, 333–74.

Bruner, J. (1978). "From communication to language: A psychological perspective." In I. Markova (ed.), *The Social Context of Language.* NY: Wiley, 255–87.

Bruner, J. (1983). *Child's Talk.* New York: W. W. Norton & Co.

Butterworth, G. E. and Cochran, E. (1980). "Towards a mechanism of joint visual attention in human infancy." *International Journal of Behavioural Development,* 3, 253–72.

Butterworth, G. and Grover, L. (1988). "The origins of referential communication in human infancy." In L. Weiskrantz (ed.), *Thought without Language.* Oxford: Clarendon Press, 5–24.

Churcher, J. and Scaife, M. (1981). "How infants see the point." In G. Butterworth and P. Light (eds), *Social Cognition: Studies of the development of understanding.* Chicago, IL: University of Chicago Press, 110–36.

Collis, G. M. (1977). "Visual co-orientation and maternal speech." In H. R. Schaffer (ed.), *Studies in Mother–Infant Interaction.* London: Academic Press, 355–75.

Grover, L. (1982). *The Comprehension and Production of the Pointing Gesture in Human Infancy.* Paper presented to the 40th Annual Convention of the International Council of Psychologists, Southampton.

Harris, M., Jones, D., Brookes, S., and Grant, J. (1986). "Relations between the non-verbal context of maternal speech and rate of language development." *British Journal of Developmental Psychology,* 4, 261–8.

Harris, M., Jones, D., and Grant, J. (1983). "The nonverbal context of mothers' speech to infants." *First Language,* 4, 21–30.

Keppel, G. (1982). *Design and Analysis: A researcher's handbook (2nd edition).* Englewood Cliffs, NJ: Prentice-Hall, Inc.

Lempers, J. D. (1976). *Production of Pointing, Comprehension of Pointing, and Understanding of Looking Behavior in Young Children.* Unpublished doctoral dissertation, Stanford University.

Leslie, A. M. and Happe, F. (1989). "Autism and ostensive communication: The relevance of metarepresentation." *Development and Psychopathology,* 1, 205–12.

Leung, E. H. and Rheingold, H. L. (1981). "Development of pointing as a social gesture." *Developmental Psychology,* 17, 215–20.

Macnamara, J. (1982). *Names for Things: A study of human learning.* Cambridge, MA: MIT Press.

Macnamara. J. (1990). "Children as common sense psychologists." *Canadian Journal of Psychology,* 43, 426–9.

Markman, E. M. (1989). *Categorization and Naming in Children: Problems of induction.* Cambridge, MA: MIT Press.

Markman, E. M. (1992). "The whole object, taxonomic, and mutual exclusivity assumptions as initial constraints on word meanings." In J. P. Byrnes and S. A. Gelman (eds), *Perspectives on Language and Cognition: Interrelations in development.* Cambridge: Cambridge University Press.

Masur, E. F. (1982). "Mothers' responses to infants' object-related gestures: Influences on lexical development." *Journal of Child Language,* 9, 23–30.

Merriman, W. E. and Bowman, L. L. (1989). "The mutual exclusivity bias in children's word learning." *Monographs of the Society for Research in Child Development* (Serial No. 20, Vol. 54).

Messer, D. J. (1978). "The integration of mothers' referential speech with joint play." *Child Development,* 49, 781–7.

Messer, D. J. (1983). "The redundancy between adult speech and nonverbal interaction: A contribution to acquisition?" In R. M. Golinkoff (ed.), *The Transition from Prelinguistic to Linguistic Communication.* Hillsdale, NJ: Lawrence Erlbaum, 147–59.

Murphy, C. M. (1978). "Pointing in the context of a shared activity." *Child Development,* 49, 371–80.

Murphy, C. M. and Messer, D. J. (1977). "Mothers, infants, and pointing: A study of gesture." In H. R. Schaffer (ed.), *Studies in Mother–Infant Interaction.* NY: Academic Press, 325–54.

Nelson, K. E. and Bonvillian, J. (1973). "Concepts and words in the two-year-old: Acquisition of concept names under controlled conditions. *Cognition,* 2, 435–50.

Ninio, A. and Bruner, J. (1978). "The achievement and antecedents of labeling." *Journal of Child Language,* 5, 1–15.

Premack, D. (1988). "'Does the chimpanzee have a theory of mind?': Revisited." In R. W. Byrne and A. Whiten (eds), *Machiavellian Intelligence.* Oxford: Clarendon Press, 160–79.

Quine, W. V. O. (1960). *Word and Object.* Cambridge, MA: MIT Press.

Quine, W. V. (1973). *The Roots of Reference.* La Salle, IL: Open Court.

Scaife, M. and Bruner, J. (1975). "The capacity for joint visual attention in the infant." *Nature,* 253, 265–6.

Shatz, M. (1983). "Communication." In J. Flavell and E. Markman (eds), *Cognitive Development*, P. Mussen (gen ed.), *Handbook of Child Psychology* (4th edition). NY: Wiley, 841–89.

Smiley, P. A. (1987). *The Development of the Concept of Person: The young child's view of the other in action and interaction*. Unpublished doctoral dissertation, University of Chicago.

Tomasello, M. and Farrar, M. J. (1986). "Joint attention and early language." *Child Development*, **57**, 1454–63.

Tomasello, M. and Mannle, S. (1985). "Pragmatic of sibling speech to one-year-olds." *Child Development*, **56**, 911–17.

Tomasello, M., Mannle, S., and Kruger, A. (1986). "The linguistic environment of one to two year old twins." *Developmental Psychology*, **22**, 169–76.

Tomasello, M. and Todd, J. (1983). "Joint attention and lexical acquisition style." *First Language*, **4**, 197–212.

Trevarthen, C. (1980). "The foundations of intersubjectivity: Development of interpersonal and cooperative understanding in infancy." In D. Olson (ed.), *The Social Foundations of Language and Thought: Essays in honor of J. S. Bruner*. NY: Norton, 316–42.

Whitehurst, G. J. (1979). "Meaning and semantics." In G. J. Whitehurst and B. J. Zimmerman (eds), *The Functions of Language and Cognition*. New York: Academic Press, 115–39.

Whitehurst, G. J., Kedesdy, J., and White, T. G. (1982). "A functional analysis of meaning." In S. A. Kuczaj II (ed.), *Language Development. Volume I: Syntax and semantics*. Hillsdale, NJ: Lawrence Erlbaum, 397–427.

Winer, B. J. (1971). *Statistical Principles in Experimental Design*. New York: McGraw-Hill.

Wittgenstein, L. (1953). *Philosophical Investigations*. New York: Macmillan.

Constraints Children Place on Word Meanings

Ellen M. Markman

Children acquire the vocabulary of natural languages at remarkable speed. In a carefully documented study of an individual child's vocabulary acquisition, Dromi (1987) reports a point at which her child began acquiring new vocabulary at the rate of forty-five words a week. This fits with calculations reported by Carey (1978): by age six children have learned 9,000–14,000 words which works out roughly to nine new words a day from about eighteen months on. It is still largely a mystery as to how children acquire language at this astonishing rate.

A traditional explanation for how children form categories and acquire category terms was to assume a kind of general, all-purpose, inductive mechanism. Inhelder and Piaget (1964) and Bruner, Olver, and Greenfield (1966) implicitly held some form of this model. This view about how categories are acquired contains many implicit assumptions about the nature of categories, about the way in which they are learned, and about how children's abilities to categorize change with development (for a discussion of these issues, see Markman, 1989). For example, these theories assume that concept learning begins by the learner encountering a positive exemplar of the category. From that exemplar the learner formulates a tentative hypothesis about what the criteria might be that define the category. This hypothesis must then be evaluated against subsequent information. New instances that are consistent with the hypothesis support it, while inconsistent information requires that it be revised. But reformulating hypotheses in the face of negative evidence is not a trivial problem and children up until the age of 6 or 7 have been shown to have great difficulty in dealing with all but the simplest kinds of hypotheses. In sum, even 6-year-olds have trouble solving these kinds of inductive problems, yet 2-year-olds are very successfully solving the inductive problems involved in acquiring new terms. These young children must, therefore, acquire terms in ways that do not require sophisticated, logical-deductive, hypothesis testing (Markman, 1987; 1989; Markman and Hutchinson, 1984; Markman and Wachtel, 1988).

Another related problem with the traditional view of concept learning is that it does not face the fundamental problem of induction pointed out by Quine (1960), namely, that for any set of data there will be an infinite number of logically possible hypotheses that are consistent with it. The data are never sufficient logically to eliminate all competing hypotheses. How is it, then, that humans so frequently converge on the same hypotheses? To take a concrete example, suppose a child hears someone label a dog as *dog*. The child could think that the label refers to a specific individual (e.g., Rover), or to one of its parts (e.g., tail), or to its substance, size, shape, color, position in space, and so on. Given that it is not possible for anyone, let alone a young child, to rule out every logically possible hypothesis, how is it that children succeed in figuring out the correct meanings of terms?

The answer is that humans are constrained to consider only some kinds of hypotheses or at least to give them priority over others. This may be especially true for children first trying to learn the concepts that their language encodes. The way children succeed in acquiring these terms so rapidly is that they are limited in the kinds of hypotheses they consider. Children do not always have to reject hypotheses on the basis of negative evidence. They can implicitly reject them by being biased against them in the first place. In this paper, I summarize some of the evidence for specific constraints on hypothesis that young children may use.

The whole object and taxonomic assumptions

When an adult points to an object and labels it, the novel term could refer to the object, but it could also refer to a part of the object, or its substance, or color, or weight, and so on. One way children initially constrain the meaning of terms is to honor the *whole object assumption* and thereby assume that a novel label is likely to refer to the whole object and not to its parts, substance or other properties (Carey, 1978; Mervis, 1987).

Once children decide a term refers to the whole object, they still need to decide how to extend it to other objects. Markman and Hutchinson (1984) proposed that children honor the *taxonomic assumption* in extending objects' labels to other objects. This assumption states that labels refer to objects of the same kind rather than to objects that are thematically related. To see why this constraint is needed it is helpful to consider what young children confront when someone teaches them a word via ostensive definition, that is, when someone points to an object and labels it. Some variant of ostensive definition makes up a large part of the way very young children acquire new words because they do not yet know enough language for one to define a new term for them or contrast with other terms, and so on. Again, suppose someone points to a dog and calls it a dog. *Dog* could be a proper name, or it could mean *furry*, or *brown*, or any of a huge number of other properties. Moreover, dog could also refer to "the dog and his bone," or "Mommy petting the dog" or "the dog under a tree." In other words, objects are often found in spatial, causal, temporal or other relations with other objects, so what prevents the child from thinking that the label refers to the objects that are related? These last examples of thematic relations pose a particular problem because children are very interested in such relations and often find them more salient than categorical or taxonomic relations.

On a number of tasks designed to assess children's ability to categorize objects, younger children have been found to prefer to organize objects according to thematic relations (cf. Gelman and Baillargeon, 1983; Markman and Callanan, 1983, for reviews). For example, on sorting tasks 6- and 7-year-olds often sort objects on the basis of their taxonomic category such as vehicles, buildings, animals, and people. In contrast, younger children often sort objects in groups that represent causal, temporal, spatial or other relations among the objects. These relations emphasize events rather than taxonomic similarity. For example, children might put a boy and a dog together because the boy is taking the dog for a walk. This interest in thematic relations has been found in object sorting, oddity tasks, and studies of memory and word association (see Markman, 1981). From these studies, we can conclude that children are often more interested in the thematic relations among objects than among taxonomic relations, or that thematic relations can sometimes be easier for children to notice than taxonomic ones. Even though children may find thematic relations more salient, single nouns rarely encode thematic relations. For example, English does not have a single word for thematically related objects such as a boy and his dog, or a spider and its web, or a baby and its bottle. In fact, in a recent linguistic attempt to define the notion "word," Di Sciullo and Williams (1987) suggest that one way to distinguish words from phrases is that "words are generic in meaning in a way that phrases are not." They suggest that this generic quality of words may result from the fact that words do not have tense markings while phrases do. To take their example, "compare the word *robber* and the phrase *man who is robbing the bank*. One cannot say *John is a bank robber* to mean 'John is robbing a bank at this very moment.' *Robber* seems to denote a permanent property, whereas *is robbing a bank* is completely timely." The taxonomic constraint might be one consequence of words being generic in Di Sciullo and Williams's sense.

To return to Quine's problem of induction, on the one hand children readily learn labels for object categories, concrete nouns such as *ball* or *dog*. On the other hand, children often notice thematic relations between objects. How is it that children readily learn labels for categories of objects if they are attending to these relations between objects instead? Hutchinson and I (Markman and Hutchinson, 1984) proposed that the solution is that children expect labels to refer to objects of the same kind or same taxonomic category. This assumption would allow them to rule out many potential meanings of a novel term, in particular, many thematic meanings. Even though children consider thematic relations good ways of organizing objects themselves, they do not consider thematic relations as possible meanings for words. Thus, when children believe that they are learning a new *word*, they shift their attention from thematic to categorical organization.

To narrow the hypotheses down to object categories still, of course, leaves open the question of to which of the numerous possible categories the label refers. Objects can be categorized in many different ways and at many different levels, for example, basic, subordinate, or superordinate levels within a hierarchy. Which category children map the label onto is itself an interesting question, one that has been addressed by Markman (1989), Mervis (1987) and Waxman (1992).

The studies of Markman and Hutchinson tested both the taxonomic assumption and the whole object assumption: Children should interpret novel labels as labels for objects of the same type rather than objects that are thematically related. To test this, we conducted a series of studies, each of which compared how children would organize objects when they were not provided with an object label versus when the objects were given a novel label.

One set of studies was conducted with 4- and 5-year-olds to test the hypothesis that hearing a new word will lead them to look for taxonomic relations rather than thematic relations at roughly the superordinate level of categorization. Children were assigned to one of two conditions. In one of the conditions, children were asked to find a picture that was the same as the target. The other condition was the same except that a nonsense syllable was used to label the target picture. In both conditions, children were first shown the target picture. They were then shown two other pictures and had to select one of them as being the same as the target. One of the choice pictures was related in a thematic way to the target, for example, as milk is to cow. The other choice picture was a member of the same superordinate category as the target, for example, as pig is to cow. Examples of the materials used are shown in Table 2.2.1.

On each trial in the *No Word Condition*, the experimenter, using a hand puppet, said, "I'm going to show you something. Then I want you to think carefully and find another one." The experimenter then placed the target picture face up on the table directly in front of the child, and said, "See this?" She placed the two choice pictures to the left and right of the target, then said, "Can you find another one?"

Everything about the procedure for the *Novel Word Condition* was identical to that of the No Word Condition, except that the target picture was now labeled

Table 2.2.1   *Triads used in Markman and Hutchinson's study*

Standard object	Taxonomic choice	Thematic choice
Cow	Pig	Milk
Ring	Necklace	Hand
Door	Window	Key
Crib	Adult bed	Baby
Bee	Ant	Flower
Hanger	Hook	Dress
Cup	Glass	Kettle
Car	Bicycle	Car tire
Sprinkler	Watering can	Grass
Paintbrush	Crayons	Easel
Train	Bus	Tracks
Dog	Cat	Bone

with a novel word. Children were told that the puppet could talk in puppet talk, and that they were to listen carefully to what he said. The instructions now included an unfamiliar label for the target: "I'm going to show you a dax. Then I want you to think carefully and find another dax." "See this dax. Can you find another dax?"

We predicted that children in the Novel Word Condition, because they were given a label, should choose the taxonomically related choice picture more often than children in the No Word Condition. As is typical for children this age, when no word was present they did not often make categorical choices. When children in the No Word Condition had to select between another member of the same superordinate category and a thematically related object, they chose the categorical relation only 25 percent of the time. As predicted, the presence of a new word caused children to seek taxonomic relations. When the target picture was labeled with an unfamiliar word, children were much more likely than children hearing no label to select categorically. They now chose the other category member 65 percent of the time.

The proposal is that children focused on categorical relationships because of the sheer presence of the word, and not because of any particular knowledge about the meaning of the word. One possible alternative explanation is that children translated the novel puppet words into known words which already refer to objects of the same kind. The next study was designed to provide evidence that children use abstract knowledge about words rather than specific known meanings to facilitate taxonomic responding (see Markman and Hutchinson, 1984 for other arguments against this alternative hypothesis). In this study, pictures of artificial objects were used instead of real objects. Children are not likely to translate unfamiliar names for these pictures into known words, because they do not know real word names for them. If the presence of an unfamiliar word still causes children to shift from thematic to taxonomic responding when the materials are also unfamiliar, then this would rule out translation as an explanation for the effect.

Four- and 5-year-old children participated in the study. The design and procedure for this study are essentially the same as that of the previous study. The main difference is that the experimenter first taught children the taxonomic and thematic relations for the artificial objects before asking them to select the picture that was like the target.

Before children saw the target picture and the two choices, they were shown two training pictures that illustrated how the target picture related to each of the choice pictures. One picture showed the target object and the taxonomic choice, side by side. For these pairs, children were told a common function that the two objects shared. An example taxonomic training picture is shown in Figure 2.2.1.

For this example, the experimenter said, "This swims in the water" (pointing to the left-hand object). "This swims in the water" (pointing to the right-hand object).

A second training picture showed the target and the thematic choice in an interactive relationship. The experimenter told the children how the two objects

Figure 2.2.1   *A taxonomically related pair of objects from Markman and Hutchinson (1984).*

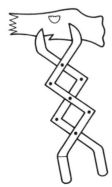

Figure 2.2.2   *A thematically related pair of objects from Markman and Hutchinson (1984).*

interacted. The thematic training picture for the set just given is shown in Figure 2.2.2. For this example, the experimenter said, "This catches this" (pointing to the objects to which she was referring as she said the sentence).

A second example taxonomic training picture is shown in Figure 2.2.3. For this example, the experimenter said, "This pokes holes in things" (pointing to the left-hand object). "This pokes holes in things" (pointing to the right-hand object). The thematic training picture for the same set is shown in Figure 2.2.4. For this picture, the spoken information was "You keep this in here."

After children saw the two training pictures in a set, the pictures were removed from the table. The remainder of the procedure was identical to that of the previous study. In the No Word Condition, the experimenter said, "I'm going to show you something. Then I want you to think carefully, and find another one." The experimenter then placed the target picture face up on the table directly in front of the child, and said, "See this?" She placed the two choice pictures to the left and right of the target, and then said, "Can you find another one?"

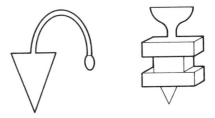

Figure 2.2.3   *A taxonomically related pair of objects from Markman and Hutchinson (1984).*

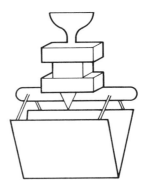

Figure 2.2.4   *A thematically related pair of objects from Markman and Hutchinson (1984).*

As before, everything in the Novel Word Condition was the same except that a novel word was used to label the target picture. After children saw the training pictures, the experimenter said, "I'm going to show you a dax. Then I want you to think carefully, and find another dax. See this dax? Can you say dax? Can you find another dax?" A different unfamiliar word was used for each set.

The results for the choices were parallel to those of the previous studies. As usual, when children in the No Word Condition had to select between another member of the same superordinate category and a thematically related object, they often chose the thematic relation. They selected the other category member a mean of only 37 percent of the time. When the target picture was labeled with an unfamiliar word children were more likely to select categorically. They now chose the other category member a mean of 63 percent of the time. Children hearing a novel word were significantly more likely to select an object from the same category than children not hearing a label. Thus, children place an abstract constraint on what single nouns might mean. Children limit count nouns to refer mainly to objects of the same kind rather than allowing them to refer to objects that are united by thematic relations.

In addition to the work reported here, several other findings support this conclusion. Even children as young as 2 and 3 years place constraints on what unfamiliar words might mean. When presented with two basic level objects, such as two different kinds of dogs, and a third object that was thematically related, such as dog food, very young children showed some tendency to select a dog and dog food. If, however, one of the dogs was labeled with an unfamiliar term, children were now more likely to select two dogs (Markman and Hutchinson, 1984).

Hutchinson (1984) replicated the Markman and Hutchinson (1984) findings using a procedure whereby children were taught a novel word for the target objects as before, but when asked for others, they were free to select none, one, or two additional objects, one of which was related taxonomically to the target and one of which was related thematically. With the exception of the 3-year-old boys, Hutchinson replicated the Markman and Hutchinson (1984) results with this procedure. That is, children spontaneously extended a term to label taxonomically related objects, even when they were free not to.

Waxman and Gelman (1986) have found that a label will induce 3-year-olds to classify taxonomically at the superordinate level, at least for superordinate categories for which the children do have a label. Moreover, they found that a novel label, actually a Japanese term, helped children organize objects taxonomically in a free classification task, where children were to sort pictures of objects into groups.

Waxman and Gelman (1986) compared the effectiveness of hearing a novel label with other means of highlighting the salience of categories. In some cases, children were shown typical instances of the category and told to think about them as a group. In other cases, children were given the common English superordinate term for the categories. Four-year-olds benefited from all of these manipulations. Three-year-olds, however, were helped by the use of labels, but not by seeing typical instances. Moreover, 3-year-olds did just as well when Japanese labels were provided for these familiar superordinate categories as when the known English labels were provided.

Other studies using different kinds of competing hypotheses (e.g., color or substance) have also found evidence for the whole object assumption (Baldwin, 1989; Landau, Smith, and Jones, 1988; Soja, Carey, and Spelke, 1985).

In order for the taxonomic assumption to play a role in early language acquisition, it needs to be available to children younger than 2 and 3 years old. Although children's early language use suggests they honor the whole object and taxonomic assumptions (Huttenlocher and Smiley, 1987), one recent experimental study of very young children's usage of these assumptions was inconclusive (Bauer and Mandler, 1989). Bauer and Mandler (1989) set out to determine whether the labeling effect would hold up for even younger children. In a series of studies, they looked at at sixteen thirty-one-month-old children's tendency to sort thematically and whether labeling would increase the children's tendency to sort taxonomically. Unexpectedly, even the youngest children were sorting taxonomically from the start. That is, even with no labels children were sorting taxonomically around 75 percent of the time. Labeling did not increase this already high level of performance. Bauer and Mandler (1989) have thus convincingly demonstrated that quite young children are capable of sorting taxonomically. However, because of the already high rate of sorting taxonomically, they were unable to test whether children of this age adhere to the taxonomic assumption. That is, it is still important to know whether in those cases where children do show a thematic preference, whether hearing a label causes them to shift to taxonomic sorting. This question was addressed by Backscheider and Markman (1990).

One reason why Bauer and Mandler (1989) achieved such a high rate of taxonomic responding in their young children is that they used a reinforcement procedure whereby they briefly pretrained children to select taxonomically and where this selective reinforcement of taxonomic choices was maintained throughout the testing procedure. This selective reinforcement clearly mattered because, in a control study, Bauer and Mandler achieved an equally high rate of thematic responding by selectively reinforcing thematic rather than taxonomic choices. Since they demonstrated that selective reinforcement is a powerful way to influence children's responses, Bachscheider and I eliminated selective reinforcement from our procedure. Our results replicated the original Markman and Hutchinson (1984) findings, even with eighteen- to twenty-four-month-olds. In the absence of labels, very young children selected taxonomically only 32 percent of the time. That is, they showed the thematic bias seen in older children. In marked contrast, when an object was given a novel label children interpreted the novel label as referring to objects of the same taxonomic category 77 percent of the time. Thus, the taxonomic assumption is used by children by eighteen months of age.

To summarize, there are now a number of studies using several different methodologies which together demonstrate that children from eighteen months on honor the taxonomic assumption. We do not yet know whether younger babies honor the constraint (Nelson, 1988). However, if the taxonomic constraint is already in place by eighteen months, that suggests that it could play a fundamental role in acquiring word meanings even early on in language learning. In particular, it is at roughly eighteen months of age that children undergo the vocabulary spurt where they become capable of acquiring words at very fast rates (Bloom, Lifter, and Broughton, 1985; Corrigan, 1983; Dromi, 1987; Halliday, 1975; McShane, 1979; Nelson, 1973). This very fast form of learning must be a highly constrained form of learning. To speculate, then, the emergence of the whole object and taxonomic constraints may be what accounts for the very young child's sudden ability to acquire words rapidly.

The mutual exclusivity assumption

The whole object assumption leads children to treat novel terms as labels for whole objects—not for parts or substances of objects or for other properties. But children must of course learn terms that refer to parts, substances and other properties. The *mutual exclusivity* assumption, to be discussed next, helps children override the whole object assumption, thereby enabling them to acquire terms other than object labels.

In addition to the whole object and taxonomic assumptions, then, children constrain word meanings by assuming at first that words are mutually exclusive —that each object will have one and only one label. In order for categories to be informative about objects, they will tend to be mutually exclusive, especially at the basic level of categorization. A single object cannot both be a chair and a dresser or a chair and a table. A single object cannot both be a cow and a bird or a cow and a dog. Obviously, however, there are many exceptions: Categories overlap, as in "dog" and "pet," and they are included in one another as in "poodle" and "dog." So mutual exclusivity is not an infallible assumption to make. On the other hand, it is a reasonable one and, as I hope to show, by assuming that terms are mutually exclusive, children make progress in acquiring new words, even if it is at the cost of making some mistakes along the way.

In fact, one piece of evidence in favor of the hypothesis that children assume words will be mutually exclusive is that it helps explain some errors children make. It helps explain, for example, why children find class inclusion difficult (because it violates mutual exclusivity) and why the part–whole relation of collections is simpler (because it maintains mutual exclusivity) (Markman, 1987, 1989).

While honoring the mutual exclusivity assumption, children will nevertheless violate mutual exclusivity under some circumstances. To acquire class-inclusion relations, for example, children must override their initial tendency to assume terms are mutually exclusive. With enough evidence to the contrary, or enough information about the referent of a term, children will allow multiple labels for the same object. The mutual exclusivity bias guides children's initial hypotheses about a word's meaning and without evidence to the contrary, children will maintain this hypothesis. But mutual exclusivity can be overriden. Thus, violations of mutual exclusivity in children's lexicons are not necessarily evidence against this principle. Gathercole (1987), Merriman and Bowman (1989), and Nelson (1988) have all pointed out cases in which mutual exclusivity is clearly violated and a complete theory of how these constraints guide children's word learning must account for the counter-examples and violations to the principle. As a working hypothesis, children are presumed to be biased to assume at first that terms are mutually exclusive, but will relinquish that assumption when confronted with clear evidence to the contrary (see Markman, 1992; Merriman and Bowman, 1989).

Mutual exclusivity is related to several other principles that have been postulated to account for language acquisition, including Slobin's (1973) principle of one-to-one mapping and Pinker's (1984) Uniqueness Principle (see Markman and Wachtel, 1988 for a discussion). A third principle, Clark's (1983, 1987) Principle of Lexical Contrast, is most closely related to mutual exclusivity. Clark argues, following Bolinger (1977), that every word in a dictionary contrasts with every other word and that to acquire words children must assume that word meanings are contrastive. Mutual exclusivity is one kind of contrast, but many terms that contrast in meaning are not mutually exclusive. Terms at different levels of a class-inclusion hierarchy, such as *dog* and *animal*, contrast in meaning in Clark's sense, since obviously the meaning of *animal* is different from that of *dog*. Yet, these terms violate mutual exclusivity. Mutual exclusivity is a more specific and stronger constraint than the principle of contrast. Some of the evidence that Clark (1987) cites for the principle of contrast, however, is also evidence in support of mutual exclusivity.

One problem with the evidence that Clark (1983, 1987) cites in favor of mutual exclusivity is that it comes almost entirely from production data. There may be many reasons why beginning language-learners would be limited in the amount they can produce which would prevent them from expending valuable resources on redundant information. This limitation on production could be for very different reasons than a constraint on the lexicon. A lexical constraint should be apparent in comprehension as well as in production. In fact, Markman and Wachtel (1988) argued that the best evidence for mutual exclusivity would be from comprehension data not from production. They designed six experimental studies of children's comprehension of terms to investigate whether children honor mutual exclusivity. I will summarize these next.

The simplest situation where the principle of mutual exclusivity could be applied is where two objects are presented, one of which already has a known label and one of which does not. If a new label is then mentioned, the child should:

1. on the whole object assumption, look for an object as a first hypothesis about the meaning of the label;
2. on the mutual exclusivity assumption, reject the already labeled object;
3. therefore, assume the other object is being referred to by the novel label.

This was tested in Study 1 of Markman and Wachtel (1988) as well as by Golinkoff *et al.* (1985) and Hutchinson (1986). All three of these studies found that in this simple situation where one could map an unfamiliar word to an unfamiliar object, 3-year-old children use the principle of mutual exclusivity in figuring out the meaning of a new word. Note also that in this situation the child can simultaneously satisfy the taxonomic and mutual exclusivity assumptions. The next study from Markman and Wachtel (1988) examined what happens when this simple mapping strategy is no longer possible, and the taxonomic assumption and mutual exclusivity may conflict.

Suppose a novel word is used to describe a single object. According to the taxonomic and whole object assumptions, a child should first hypothesize that the new word refers to the object as an exemplar of a category of similar objects, and not to the object's part, substance, and so on. Suppose, however, that the object described by the novel term is an object for which the child already has a label. In this case, in order to adhere to the principle of mutual exclusivity, the child would have to reject the novel term as a label for the object, but then may not have any clear alternative as a possible meaning for the term. That is, since there is no other object around to label, the simple novel label–novel object strategy cannot be used. Under these circumstances, there are several different strategies available. Children could decide to abandon mutual exclusivity in these cases and interpret the novel term as a second label for the object. Another possibility is that they could reject the term as a label for the object without coming up with an alternative meaning. Rejecting one meaning for the term, however, leaves the child with a term that is not yet attached to any referent. This in itself may motivate children to try to find some meaning for the novel term. The mutual exclusivity principle does not speak to how children select among the potential meanings, but children might analyze the object for some interesting part or property and interpret the novel term as applying to it. Such an analysis is considerably more difficult than the simple novel label–novel object matching strategy, and there may be many candidate meanings for the term. The remaining studies examine whether children can use mutual exclusivity, in this more difficult situation, to learn part and substance terms.

Study 2 of Markman and Wachtel (1988) addressed whether children can use mutual exclusivity to reject a novel term as a label for an already labeled object, and whether that would motivate them to search for another salient aspect of the object to label. In this study, we attempted to teach children labels for objects with prominent parts. Children heard a novel noun attributed to either a familiar or an unfamiliar object. The term could thus refer to either the object itself or to a salient part of the object.

Three- and 4-year olds heard either familiar or unfamiliar objects labeled with a novel term and were then tested to see whether they thought the term referred to the object as a whole or to a salient part of the object. The set of familiar and unfamiliar objects along with their relevant parts is presented in Table 2.2.2.

Children were assigned to one of two conditions, the Familiar Condition where the object had a known label, or the Unfamiliar Condition where children did not know a label for the object. In both conditions children were taught a label applied to an object with a noticeable part. The labels used were in fact adult labels for the part. In neither condition did children already know a label for the part being taught. For example, children in the Familiar object condition were taught "boom" as the part of a (familiar) fire truck and "dorsal fin" as the part of a (familiar) fish. Children in the Unfamiliar condition were taught "finial" as the part of an (unfamiliar) pagoda, and "trachea" as a part of an (unfamiliar) lung. The prediction is that children will interpret the label as referring to the object itself for unfamiliar objects, but to a part for familiar objects.

As predicted, children interpreted a novel term quite differently depending on whether the object was familiar or not. Children gave a mean of only 20 percent part responses in the Unfamiliar Condition, compared to a mean of 57 percent part responses in the Familiar Condition. Thus, as expected by the mutual exclusivity hypothesis, children hearing a novel term in the presence of an object with a known label were less likely to think the novel term referred to the whole object than were children who heard the term in the presence of an object with no known label.

In Study 2 of Markman and Wachtel (1988), the parts and wholes about which children were questioned in the experimental items differed for the Familiar and Unfamiliar conditions. Study 3 was designed to equate the items in the two conditions. Only unfamiliar objects were used in this study but some of the children were provided with labels for the objects before the experimental labels were taught. In this way, the identical item could be unfamiliar

Table 2.2.2 *Experimental items for Study 2 of Markman and Wachtel (1988)*

	Condition		
	Familiar	Unfamiliar	
Object	Novel label for part	Object	Novel label for part
Fish	Dorsal fin	*Current detector	Detector
Fire truck	Boom	Pipe tool	Damper
Hammer	Claw	*Ritual implement	Crescent
Camera	Focusing grip	*Pagoda	Finial
Telephone	Receiver	Microscope	Platform
Race car	Air foil	*Lung	Trachea

*These items were used in Study 3 as well.

for some children and "familiar" or at least previously labeled for other children.

There were two conditions in the study, the Familiarization condition and the Unfamiliar Condition. The labeling procedure and method of asking children whether the object referred to the part or the whole were virtually identical to that used in Study 2. The main difference is that in the Familiarization condition, children were first taught a label for the object. To do this children were shown a picture of the object, for example the lung, told what it was called, for example, "This is a lung," and given a short description of the function of the object, for example, "We all have two lungs in our chest and use them to breathe." They were given this familiarization with the experimental objects before they were then run in the standard procedure.

In both conditions children were asked about the unfamiliar objects that had been used in Study 2. As before, the experimenter told the children what they were about to see, for example, "Here is a finial," and then presented the picture of the object. She then asked, "Which one is the finial, this whole thing [the experimenter circled the object with her index finger] or just this part [the experimenter pointed to the part]?"

The results from Study 3 replicated those of Study 2. As predicted, children interpreted a novel term quite differently in the two conditions. Children who heard the term (e.g., *trachea*) in the presence of an unfamiliar object (e.g., lung) more often interpreted the term as referring to the object (the lung) and not its part. They gave a mean of 32 percent part responses. In contrast, children in the Familiarization condition interpreted the novel labels as referring to parts of the object. For example, children who had just heard the picture of a lung labeled "lung" interpreted "trachea" as referring to the part (the trachea) and not the object (lung). They gave a mean of 85 percent part responses.

In summary, Study 3 again provides evidence for the mutual exclusivity hypothesis. When a novel term is used in the presence of an object that already has a label, children tend to reject another label for the object, and, in this case, assume the term refers to a part of the object instead. This was true in this study, even though the label for the (previously unfamiliar) object was provided only a few moments before another novel label was taught.

In Study 1 of Markman and Wachtel (1988), children could use a simple strategy of mapping an unfamiliar label to an unfamiliar object to preserve mutual exclusivity. Because there was only one object referred to in Studies 2 and 3, this simple strategy was precluded. Children still adhered to mutual exclusivity in this case, and used it to learn terms for salient parts of objects. However, parts of objects are themselves objects or at least object-like. Thus, learning parts of objects may be as close to the simple mapping strategy as one can get using a single object. The next three studies from Markman and Wachtel (1988) examined whether mutual exclusivity is used by children when the experimenter refers to an object made of a salient substance, using an adjective or mass noun. There are two ways in which this situation differs from that of the studies on learning labels for parts. First, instead of depicting objects with salient parts, we selected objects with a metallic substance we thought would be salient and that young children have not yet labeled. Second, in these studies the object was referred to by an adjective or a mass noun—"See this? It's pewter." This is not the typical way, in English, of designating objects. It therefore provides a strong test of the taxonomic assumption. When an unfamiliar object is labeled, the bias to look for object labels may be strong enough to override grammatical form class information. So even when an adjective or mass noun is used to describe an object, children may interpret it as the label for the object. A commonly heard anecdote, for example, is that young children think that *hot* is the label for stoves because parents refer to stoves by the term *hot* before they label them as "stoves," for example, "Don't touch that, it's hot."

These two issues, then, are examined in Study 4. First, following the taxonomic assumption, will children interpret even a novel adjective as a label for an unfamiliar object? Second, following the mutual exclusivity assumption, will children reject a novel term as a label for a familiar object made from a salient substance?

In Study 4, 3- and 4-year-olds heard a puppet refer to an object as pewter. Half of the children heard the term attributed to a familiar object—a metal cup. Half of the children heard the term attributed to an unfamiliar object—a pair of metal tongs. To introduce the novel term "pewter," a puppet showed the child the object (either the metal cup or the metal tongs) and said: "See this? It is pewter."

If the tendency to expect an object label is strong enough to override form class cues, then children hearing "pewter" ascribed to the metal tongs should interpret "pewter" as the label for tongs. They should then agree that a different pair of tongs, made from a different substance and of a different color—a pair of wooden tongs—is also pewter. In contrast, when children hear "pewter" ascribed to a familiar object, if they try to adhere to the mutual exclusivity principle, then they should reject "pewter" as the label for the cup. They should, then, deny that a cup made from a different substance and of a different color—a ceramic cup—is pewter. The main prediction, then, is that when the children see an object that is similar in kind to the original object but that is of a different substance, they should agree that it is "pewter" when the object referred to is unfamiliar (the metal tongs) but deny that it is pewter when the object is familiar (the metal cup). Thus children should agree that a pair of wooden tongs is pewter but deny that a ceramic cup is pewter.

This prediction from the mutual exclusivity hypothesis was confirmed. Of the twelve children who were taught that a metal cup was pewter and then asked if a ceramic cup was pewter, only one child thought it was. The other eleven children denied that it was pewter. Thus, even in this more difficult situation, children adhered to the mutual exclusivity principle, denying that a new term could be a label for an object even when it might not be clear to what else the term refers. In contrast, of the twelve children who were taught that metal tongs were pewter, seven of the twelve thought that wooden tongs were also pewter.

Another question addressed by this study is whether children would interpret even a novel adjective or substance term as a label for an unfamiliar object. The results indicate that at least to some extent 3-year-olds are willing to override form class clues in order to interpret the term as a novel label. That is, about half of the children considered "pewter" to be the label for tongs and agreed that wooden tongs were pewter.

Study 5 from Markman and Wachtel (1988) was a modified replication of Study 4 that used a within-subject design. Each child heard one novel substance term applied to a familiar object and a different novel substance term applied to an unfamiliar object. The two substance terms were "chrome" and "rattan." The findings from this study replicated those of Study 4. First, the bias to assume that a novel term refers to a novel object was again strong enough to override discrepancies in grammatical form class. Seventy-five percent of the children who heard the terms "chrome" or "rattan" attributed to novel objects treated the terms as labels for the objects. Second, children were less likely to think that the novel terms were labels for the objects when they already knew a label for the object. Only 40 percent of the children who heard "rattan" and "chrome" attributed to familiar objects treated the terms as labels for the objects; 60 percent rejected the terms as labels.

In Studies 4 and 5, 3- and 4-year-old children treated a novel term as a label for a novel object, but tended to reject the term as a label for a familiar object. Although we know that children are rejecting the novel term as a term for a familiar object, we do not know whether they have in fact accepted the term as a substance term. Study 6 attempted to get at children's hypotheses about the meanings of the terms more directly by giving children a forced-choice between object labels and substance labels.

In this study, we labeled an object using a novel term, for example, "See this (a metal cup)? It's chrome," as in the previous studies. Children were then shown a similar object but of a different substance (e.g., a ceramic cup). They were also shown a chunk of the substance itself—for example, an unformed piece of chrome. They were then asked "Which is chrome? This thing here or this stuff here?" This procedure is similar to that used by Soja, Carey, and Spelke (1985) in their investigation of children's acquisition of count nouns and mass nouns. The question for the present study is whether children will interpret a term as a substance term in the presence of an object as long as the object has a known label. In other words, will mutual exclusivity help children override their bias for object labels to interpret a novel term as a substance term?

As in Studies 4 and 5, children heard a familiar object (a hat) or an unfamiliar object (an odd-shaped container) labeled as rattan. They also heard a familiar object (a cup) or an unfamiliar object (tongs) labeled as chrome. The experimental test for whether children interpreted the term as a label for the object or the substance was to give children a choice between a similar object of a different substance and the substance itself. To illustrate, for the familiar rattan condition, children were shown the rattan hat and told "See this? It's rattan." They were then shown a plastic hat and a piece of rattan and asked: "Which one is rattan, this stuff here [pointing to the piece of rattan] or this thing here [pointing to the hat]?"

The predictions were that when children heard a novel term applied to a novel object, they should have chosen the object as the referent of the term, but when they heard the term applied to a familiar object, they should have chosen the substance as the referent of the term. This prediction was supported. The mean number of object responses was .57 out of 1 for the unfamiliar condition compared to only .13 out of 1 for the familiar condition. Thus, in support of the mutual exclusivity hypothesis, when children heard a novel term applied to a familiar object, they rejected the term as a label for the object and interpreted it as a substance term instead.

In sum, these studies provided evidence that children do, in fact, assume that words tend to be mutually exclusive. The first study, along with Golinkoff *et al.* (1985) and Hutchinson (1986), demonstrated that when a novel object label is heard, children assume that it refers to a novel object rather than to an object whose label is already known. To use mutual exclusivity in this situation, children can adopt a simple strategy of mapping the novel label onto the novel object (see Merriman and Bowman, 1989 and Gathercole 1987, for other interpretations). The remaining studies explored whether children adhere to the principle of mutual exclusivity when this simple strategy can no longer be used.

If a novel label is applied to an object for which children already have a label, then they should, by mutual exclusivity, reject the new term as an object label. If that object, however, is the only one around, then children cannot interpret the term as a label for a different object. Instead they must analyze the same object for some property or attribute to label. Studies 2–6 provided evidence that 3- and 4-year-olds try to maintain mutual exclusivity of terms even in this more difficult situation. Children interpreted a novel label as referring to the object itself when the object did not yet have a label. In contrast, as predicted, they interpreted the label as referring to part or substance of the object when the label for the object was already known.

Conclusions

Together, the studies reported here show how constraints such as the taxonomic and whole object assumptions and the assumption of mutual exclusivity can guide children's initial hypotheses about what words can mean, thereby helping to solve the problem of induction that word meaning poses. Young children possess the knowledge that single nouns are more likely to refer to objects of the same kind than to objects associated by their participation in a common event or theme. This knowledge helps explain how children acquire new words. By constraining the meaning of a term to categorical relations, children are able to rule out a huge number of other potential meanings for any given term. In particular, relational and thematic meanings would be eliminated from consideration by the constraint that nouns refer to object categories. By limiting the number and kind of hypotheses that children need to consider, this constraint simplifies the problem of language learning.

The whole object assumption leads children to expect terms to refer to objects—not to their parts or substances or other properties. The disadvantage of this constraint is obvious—languages are filled with terms that refer to parts and substances and other properties of objects. Mutual exclusivity can help remedy this limitation of the whole object assumption. First, it provides children with grounds for rejecting a class of hypotheses about a term's meaning. Namely, the new term should not be another object label. Second, it motivates children to acquire terms other than object labels. Having rejected one meaning of a term, children would be left with a word for which they have not yet figured out a meaning. This should then motivate them to find a potential meaning for the novel term, leading them to analyze the object for some other property to label. In this way, the mutual exclusivity assumption motivates children to learn terms for attributes, substances and parts of objects.

Thus, this function of mutual exclusivity helps overcome a major limitation of the whole object assumption which leads children to look for only object labels. Although the whole object assumption provides a critical first hypothesis about word meanings, children must eventually be able to learn terms for properties of objects and not just terms for objects alone. These two principles complement each other. The taxonomic and whole object assumptions clearly have priority when the object being labeled has no previously known label, since mutual exclusivity is not relevant in those cases. When one object has a known label and another has no known label, then both mutual exclusivity and the whole object assumptions can be met. The whole object and mutual exclusivity assumptions compete when a child hears a term applied to an object for which they already know a label. Here mutual exclusivity can motivate children to learn terms other than object labels.

One can envision how the mutual exclusivity principle can be used successively to constrain the meanings of terms. Suppose a child already has words for apple and for red and now someone refers to the apple as "round." Now, by mutual exclusivity, the child can eliminate apple and red as the meaning of "round" and try to analyze the object for some other property to label. There are still many unanswered questions as to how this analysis would proceed. But at least we can conclude that as each successive word is learned it further constrains the meanings of the yet-to-be-learned words, thereby helping children figure out their meaning.

In sum, children are helped in early language acquisition by the whole object, taxonomic, and mutual exclusivity assumptions. These biases guide children's initial hypotheses and eliminate numerous hypotheses from consideration and thereby help them solve the inductive problem posed by word learning.

Acknowledgments

This paper is based on a talk given in the symposium *Structural Constraints on Cognitive Development*, Psychonomics, 1986 and borrows heavily from Markman (1992). This work was supported in part by NIH Grant HD 20382. I would like to thank Rochel Gelman, Douglas Medin, Steven Pinker, and Elizabeth Spelke for their thoughtful comments on this manuscript.

References to 2.2

Backscheider, A. and Markman. E. M. (1990). *Young Children's Use of Taxonomic Assumption to Constrain Word Meaning*. Unpublished manuscript. Stanford University, Stanford, CA.

Baldwin, D. A. (1989). "Priorities in children's expectations about object label reference: Form over color." *Child Development*, **60**, 1291–306.

Bauer, P. J. and Mandler, J. M. (1989). "Taxonomies and triads: Conceptual organization in one- to two-year-olds." *Cognitive Psychology*, **21**, 156–84.

Bloom, L., Lifter, K., and Broughton, J. (1985). "The convergence of early cognition and language in the second year of life: Problems in conceptualization and measurement." In M. Barrett (ed.), *Children's Single-word Speech*. New York: Wiley, 149–80.

Bolinger, D. (1977). *Meaning and Form*. London: Longman.

Bruner, J., Olver, R., and Greenfield, P. (eds) (1966). *Studies in Cognitive Growth*. New York: Wiley.

Carey, S. (1978). "The child as word learner." In M. Halle, J. Bresnan, and A. Miller (eds), *Linguistic Theory and Psychological Reality*. Cambridge, MA: MIT Press, 264–93.

Clark, E. V. (1983). "Meanings and concepts." In J. H. Flavell and E. M. Markman (eds), *Handbook of Child Psychology (Vol. 3): Cognitive development*. New York: Wiley. (P. H. Mussen [general ed.]), 787–840.

Clark, E. V. (1987). "The principle of contrast: A constraint on language acquisition." In B. MacWhinney (ed.), *The 20th Annual Carnegie Symposium on Cognition*. Hillsdale NJ: Erlbaum.

Corrigan, R. (1983). "The development of representational skills." In K. W. Fischer (ed.), *Levels and Transitions in Children's Development*. San Francisco: Jossey-Bass.

Di Sciullo, A. and Williams, E. (1987). *On the Definition of Word*. Cambridge, MA: MIT Press.

Dromi, E. (1987). *Early Lexical Development*. Cambridge, MA: Cambridge University Press.

Gathercole, V. C. (1987). "The contrastive hypothesis for the acquisition of word meaning. A reconsideration of the theory." *Journal of Child Language*, **14**, 493–531.

Gelman, R. and Baillargeon, R. (1983). "A review of some Piagetian concepts." In J. H. Flavell and E. M. Markman (eds), *Handbook of Child Psychology (Vol. 3)*. New York: Wiley (P. H. Mussen [general ed.]).

Golinkoff, R. M., Hirsh-Pasek, K., Lavallee, A., and Baduini, C. (1985). *What's in a Word?: The young child's predisposition to use lexical contrast*. Paper presented at the Boston University Conference on Child Language, Boston, MA.

Halliday, M. A. K. (1975). "Learning how to mean." In E. H. Lenneberg, and E. Lenneberg (eds), *Foundations of Language Development: A multidisciplinary approach* (Vol. I). New York: Academic, 239–65.

Hutchinson, J. E. (1984). *Constraints on Children's Implicit Hypotheses about Word Meanings*. Unpublished doctoral dissertation, Stanford University, Stanford, CA.

Hutchinson, J. E. (1986, April 4–6). *Children's Sensitivity to the Contrastive Use of Object Category Terms.* Paper presented at Stanford 1986 Child Language Research Forum. Stanford University, Stanford, CA.

Huttenlocher, J. and Smiley, P. (1987). "Early word meanings: The case for object names." *Cognitive Psychology*, **19**, 63–89.

Inhelder, B. and Piaget, J. (1964). *The Early Growth of Logic in the Child.* New York: Norton.

Landau, K. B., Smith, L. B., and Jones, S. S. (1988). "The importance of shape in early lexical learning." *Cognitive Development*, **3**, 299–321.

McShane, J. (1979). "The development of naming." *Linguistics*, **17**, 879–905.

Markman, E. M. (1981). "Two different principles of conceptual organization." In M. E. Lamb and A. L. Brown (eds), *Advances in Developmental Psychology*, Hillsdale, NJ: Erlbaum.

Markman, E. M. (1987). "How children constrain the possible meanings of words." In U. Neisser (ed.), *Concepts and Conceptual Development: Ecological and intellectual factors in categorization.* Cambridge, Cambridge University Press.

Markman, E. M. (1989). *Categorization and Naming in Children: Problems of induction.* Cambridge, MA: MIT Press, Bradford Books.

Markman, E. M. (1992). "The whole object, taxonomic, and mutual exclusivity assumptions as initial constraints on word meanings." In J. P. Byrnes and S. A. Gelman (eds), *Perspectives on Language and Cognition: Interrelations in development.* Cambridge: Cambridge University Press.

Markman, E. M. and Callanan, M. A. (1983). "An analysis of hierarchical classification." In R. Sternberg (ed.), *Advances in the Psychology of Human Intelligence* (Vol. 2). Hillsdale, NJ: Erlbaum.

Markman, E. M. and Hutchinson, J. E. (1984). "Children's sensitivity to constraints on word meaning: Taxonomic vs. thematic relations." *Cognitive Psychology*, **16**, 1–27.

Markman, E. M. and Wachtel, G. F. (1988). "Children's use of mutual exclusivity to constrain the meanings of words." *Cognitive Psychology*, **20**, 121–57.

Merriman, W. E. and Bowman, L. L. (1989). "The mutual exclusivity bias in children's word learning." *Monographs of the Society for Research in Child Development*, Serial No. 220.

Mervis, C. B. (1987). "Child-basic object categories and early lexical development." In U. Neisser (ed.), *Concepts and Conceptual Development: Ecological and intellectual factors in categorization.* Cambridge: Cambridge University Press, 201–33.

Nelson, K. (1973). "Structure and strategy in learning to talk." *Monographs of the Society for Research in Child Development*, **38** (Serial No. 149).

Nelson, K. (1988). "Constraints on word learning?" *Cognitive Development*, **3**, 221–46.

Pinker, S. (1984). *Language Learnability and Language Development.* Cambridge, MA: Harvard University Press.

Quine, W. V. O. (1960). *Word and Object.* Cambridge, MA: MIT Press.

Slobin, D. I. (1973). "Cognitive prerequisites for the development of grammar." In C. A. Ferguson and D. I. Slobin (eds), *Studies of Child Language Development.* New York: Springer-Verlag, 45–54.

Soja, N., Carey, S., and Spelke, E. (1985, April). *Constraints on Word Learning.* Paper presented at the 1985 Biennial Convention of the Society for Research in Child Development, Toronto, Canada.

Waxman, S. A. (1992). "Early convergences between linguistic and conceptual organization." In J. P. Byrnes and S. A. Gelman (eds), *Perspectives on Language and Cognition: Interrelations in development.* Cambridge: Cambridge University Press.

Waxman, S. A. and Gelman, R. (1986). "Preschoolers' use of superordinate relations in classification and language." *Cognitive Development*, **1**, 139–56.

The Structural Sources of Verb Meanings

Lila Gleitman

> If we will observe how children learn languages, we will find that, to make them understand what the names of simple ideas or substances stand for, people ordinarily show them the thing whereof they would have them have the idea; and then repeat to them the name that stands for it, as "white," "sweet," "milk," "sugar," "cat," "dog."
>
> (John Locke, 1690/1964, Book 3.IX.9)

Is vocabulary acquisition as straightforward as Locke supposes? Three hundred years after publication of *An Essay Concerning Human Understanding*, Locke's is still the dominant position on this topic for the very good reason that common sense insists that he was right: Word meanings are learned by noticing the real-world contingencies for their use. For instance, it seems obvious to the point of banality that the verb pronounced /run/ is selected as the item that means "run" because this is the verb that occurs most reliably in the presence of running events.

Or is it? Who has ever looked to see? One trouble with questions whose answers are self-evident is that investigators rarely collect the evidence to see if they pan out in practice.

It is not my purpose in the present discussion to try to defeat the obviously correct idea that a crucial source of evidence for learning word meanings is observation of the environmental conditions for their use. I believe, however, that what is correct about such a position is by no means obvious, and therefore deserves serious study rather than acceptance as a background fact in our field.

I shall largely limit the discussion to the topic of acquiring verb meanings for two reasons: First, because the underpinnings of verb and noun learning are likely to differ significantly; and second, because it is in the former domain that I and my colleagues have some experimental evidence to offer in support of the position I want to adopt. Even within this subtopic, to begin at all I will have to make critical assumptions about some heady issues that deserve study in their own right. Particularly, I will not ask where the concepts that verbs encode come from in the first place, for example, how the child comes to conceive of such notions as "run" (or "think" or "chase"). I want to look at the learner at a stage when he or she can entertain such ideas, however this stage was arrived at.[1] Second, I reserve for later discussion the question of how the child determines which word in the heard sentence is the verb—that it is the phonological object /run/, not /horse/ or /marathoner/—that is to be mapped onto the action concept.

The question that remains seems a very small one: How does the learner decide *which particular phonological object* corresponds to *which particular verb concept*, just Locke's topic. But I shall try to convince you that this question is harder than it looks. For one thing, matching the meanings to their sounds is the one part of acquisition that cannot have any very direct innate support. This is because the concept "run" is not paired with the sound /run/ in Greek or Urdu, so the relation must be learned by raw exposure to a specific language. Moreover, it is not clear at all that the required pairings are available to learners from their ambient experience of words and the world.

In the first half of this article, I set out some of the factors that pose challenges to the idea that children can induce the word meanings from their contexts in the sense that Locke and his descendants in developmental psycholinguistics seem to have in mind. In this discussion, I will allude repeatedly to the work and theorizing of Steve Pinker, because he seems to me to be the most serious and acute modern interpreter of ideas akin to Locke's in relevant regards.[2] Then, in response to these challenges to the theory of learning by observation, I will sketch a revised position laid out by Landau and Gleitman (1985), illustrating it with some recent experimental evidence from our laboratory. The idea here is that children deduce the verb meanings in a procedure that is sensitive to their syntactic privileges of occurrence. They *must* do so, because either (a) there is *not enough* information in the whole world to learn the meaning of even simple verbs, or (b) there is *too much* information in the world to learn the meanings of these verbs.

Part I: Some difficulties of learning by observation

At peril of caricaturing Locke—but who doesn't?—I select him as one who argued for a rather direct relation between knowledge and the experience of the senses. He frequently used the case of individuals born without sight as a testing ground for such a position. According to Locke, both sighted and blind people ought to be able to learn the meanings of such words as *statue* and *feel* and *sweet*, but the blind ought to be unable to acquire *picture* and *see* and *red*, for the concepts that these words express are primitive (i.e., not derivable from other concepts) or derivable from primitives that are available only to the eye.

Barbara Landau and I were directly inspired by Locke to study the acquisition of vision-related terms by blind babies (Landau and Gleitman, 1985). As our studies evolved, we realized that exactly the same conceptual issues about learning arise for sighted vocabulary-learners as for blind ones, so I will move on to discussion of such normally endowed children. The blind population, which I discuss first, is perhaps special only as the biographical point of origin of our own thinking but will serve to dramatize some issues that seem less startling in the ordinary case. These have to do with how resistant the word-learning function is to the evidence of the senses.

Locke's idea: Differences in experience should yield differences in the meanings acquired

Landau and I were astonished to discover how much alike were the representations of vision-related terms by blind and sighted children at age 3, despite what would appear to be radical differences in their observational opportunities. For instance, all these babies showed by their comprehension performances that they took *look* and *see* as terms of perception, distinct from such contact terms as *touch*. As an example of this, a blind child told to "Touch but don't look at . . . " a table would merely bang or tap it. But if told "Now you can look at it," she explored all its surfaces systematically with her hands. Moreover, she understood *look* to be the active (or exploratory) and *see* the stative (or achievement) term in this pair. Just as surprising, blind children as well as sighted children understood that *green* was an attribute predicable only of physical objects (they asserted that ideas could not in principle be green while cows might be, for all they knew). Thus the first principle that a theory of observational learning must be subtle enough to capture is that the same semantic generalizations can be acquired in relative indifference to differing environmental experience, if the notion *experience* is cast in sensory-perceptual terms.

Word-to-world pairings and the blind child's semantic conjectures

While we found the surprising result that blind children shared much knowledge about vision-related terms with their sighted peers, we also achieved the unsurprising result that there were some differences in how these two populations understood these terms to refer to their own perceptions: Blind children think that *look* and *see* describe their own *haptic* perceptions, but sighted children think these same words describe their own *visual* perceptions. Thus blindfolded sighted children of 3 years turn their faces skyward if told to "Look up!" but a blind child of the same age holds her head immobile and searches the space above with her hands in response to the same command (see Figures 2.3.1 and 2.3.2).[3]

This outcome is of just the sort that is subject to seemingly obvious explanations involving the extralinguistic contexts of use: The difference in interpretation for blind and sighted seems to be directly attributable to differences in environmental contingencies for the words' use. Specifically, we reasoned (as does everyone to whom one presents this set of facts): A blind child's caretaker will use the terms *look* and *see* intending the child to perceive in whatever ways her sensorium makes available. And since the blind child's way of discovering the nature of objects is by exploring them manually, the caretaker will surely use *look* and *see* to this child only when an object is near enough to explore manually. That is, the caretaker should say "Look at this boot" to her blind baby only if a boot is nearby, ready to be explored manually. The contexts of use for these words thus should include—among many other properties—conversationally pertinent objects that are near at hand. Had the caretaker instead rattled a boot noisily by the child's ear whenever she

Figure 2.3.1 *A sighted blindfolded child's response to the command "Look up!" (Reproduced from Landau and Gleitman, 1985: 58, with permission of the artist, Robert Thacker.)*

Figure 2.3.2   *A blind child's response to the command "Look up!" (Reproduced from Landau and Gleitman, 1985: 56, with permission of the artist, Robert Thacker.)*

said "Look at this boot," the learner would have surmised that *look* meant "listen."

So here we have a straightforward prediction from the environment of use to the formation of a semantic conjecture: By hypothesis, the blind learner decides that *look* involves *haptic* exploration because it is that verb which is used most reliably in contexts in which haptic exploration is possible and pertinent to the adult/child discourse. Landau and I decided to test that prediction to see if it was as true as it was obvious.

To do so we examined videotapes of a mother and her blind child recorded in the period *before* the child uttered any vision-related words or indeed any verbs at all (that is to say, during the learning period for these words). There were 1,640 utterances in the sample. We selected for situational analysis all verbs (excluding *be*) that occurred ten or more times in this corpus; the number of utterances including these common verbs was 248. We then coded all uses of these verbs according to whether they occurred when an object pertinent to the conversation (a) was NEAR enough to the child for her to explore it manually, i.e., within arm's reach, (b) was FARther away than that, or (c) when there was NO such pertinent OBJECT. Each of these three situational categories was further subdivided into cases where the "pertinent object" was specifically mentioned in the verb-containing sentence ("+Linguistic Context" in Table 2.3.1, e.g., a boot was in the child's hand when the mother said "Look at this boot") and cases where the pertinent object was not specifically mentioned but might have been inferred from the larger discourse properties ("–Linguistic Context,"

Table 2.3.1 *Spatial analysis of the mother's use of verbs to the blind child*

	In hand or near		Far		No object		
Verb	+Ling. Object	−Ling. Object	+Ling. Object	−Ling. Object	+Ling. Object	−Ling. Object	Total Cases[a]
Perceptual							
Look	.50	.22	.00	.08	.14	.06	34
See	.33	.06	.44	.11	.00	.06	18
Watch	.56	.00	.44	.00	.00	.00	17
Nonperceptual							
Come	.00	.05	.00	.32	.00	.63	19
Get	.45	.05	.20	.05	.00	.25	27
Give	.97	.00	.03	.00	.00	.00	21
Go	.00	.52	.10	.14	.00	.24	20
Have	.53	.00	.33	.14	.00	.00	11
Hold	1.00	.00	.00	.00	.00	.00	10
Play	.50	.20	.00	.00	.30	.00	10
Put	.97	.00	.00	.00	.03	.00	61

The header row "Proportion used in contexts" spans the six proportion columns.

Note: Reproduced from Landau and Gleitman, 1985: 214, with permission of the publisher, Harvard University Press.

[a]These total to $N = 248$, the number of utterances containing common verbs (those occurring ten or more times in the corpus). The remaining rarer verbs (occurring fewer than ten times) and 183 instances of *be* were excluded from the analysis.

e.g., a boot in the child's hand when the mother said "See?" or "Look at this!"). The results, so coded, are shown in Table 2.3.1.[4]

We hypothesized that *look* and *see* would be among the verbs used most reliably in the NEAR condition accounting for why the child had assigned them the meanings "explore/apprehend *haptically*" (while other verbs would be used less often in this condition and so would not be assigned this property of meaning). But inspection of Table 2.3.1 shows that this hypothesis fails to account for the child's haptic interpretation of *look* and *see*. *Put* and *give* and *hold* are the verbs used most reliably (over 95 percent of the time) under the NEAR condition, while *look* (72 percent, collapsing across the "+ and − Linguistic Object" cases) and especially *see* (39 percent) are not as reliably associated with this environmental condition.

What has gone wrong? Could it really be that the presence of pertinent objects near to hand had nothing to do with the blind child's interpretation of *look* and *see* as haptic? As I will show in Part II of this article, this conjecture about the experiential basis for this aspect of the words' meaning really does succeed, though not when used as in Table 2.3.1: In a procedure that maps isolated word forms against their extralinguistic contexts.

Reserving further discussion for later, it is worth noting here only that the nearbyness analysis of Table 2.3.1 cannot be written off as of some environmental property that is hopelessly irrelevant to the child's interpretation of events. For as it stands, this analysis extracts and explains important distinctions among verbs of physical motion that are in other respects semantically close, such as *give* versus *get*. The child is apparently told, sensibly enough, to *give* what she has in hand (this verb is used in the NEAR condition 97 percent of the time) but to *get* what she does not have (the relevant NEAR percentage for this verb is 50 percent).

Latitude of the hypothesis space

If Table 2.3.1 mirrors the sole analysis that children perform in aid of learning the modality (hand or eye) implicated by *look* and *see*, they will clearly fail. As the blind child did learn, there must be something insufficient or wrong about this analysis. Of course this does not demonstrate that contexts of use cannot account for this aspect of verb learning, or any other; rather, we might conclude that the idea of real-world context, to succeed, must be a good deal more subtle than we (and many others) originally supposed. That is, the response to the findings shown in Table 2.3.1 is usually, and perhaps should be:

> Oh, but the contextual analysis you imposed was so *feeble*. showing that it failed is only showing the failure of Landau and Gleitman's imagination. The child surely imposes a richer analysis on the situation than that, and the only analysis relevant to the hypotheses under test is the one that the child herself imposes.

Fair enough. We limited the child to observing some perceptually salient features of the situation, features that the infancy literature tells us are available even to babies. This is because our aim was to see how far some small and independently documented set of observational primitives could get the learner in extracting simple meaning features for assignment to the verbs. These were that the world is populated with objects that endure over time (Spelke, 1982), and that move relative to each other (Lasky and Gogol, 1978) and with respect to the positions of the child's own body (Acredolo and Evans, 1980; Field, 1976). These assumptions put the child in a position to conceive of the situation as one of objects—in this case, objects whose noun names are known to the child— moving (as described by the verb) between sources and goals. For example, for *give* the object moves from NEAR as action begins to FAR when it ends, and in *get* the object goes from FAR to NEAR.

It can hardly be denied, in light of the infancy evidence, that youngsters do represent situations in terms of the positions and motions of pertinent objects. What is surely false, however, is that such categories are exhaustive among the child's extralinguistic analyses. Infants come richly prepared with means for picking up information about what is going on in their environment—looking, listening, feeling, tasting, and smelling; in fact these different sensory routes appear to be precoordinated for obtaining information about the world (Spelke, 1979). To take a few central examples, infants perceive the world as furnished with objects that are unitary, bounded, and persist over time and space (Gibson and Spelke, 1983; Spelke, 1985), and that cannot occupy two places at one time (Baillargeon, Spelke, and Wasserman, 1985). They distinguish among the varying properties of objects, for example, their rigidity or elasticity (Gibson and Walker, 1984), their colors (Bornstein, 1975), their movement or nonmovement (Ball and Vurpillot, 1976), their positions and motions relative to the child observer (Field, 1976), their animacy (Golinkoff, *et al.*, 1984), causal roles (Leslie, 1982), and even their numerosity (Starkey, Spelke, and Gelman, 1983). If you think there is something that infants cannot or will not notice, look in the next issue of *Developmental Psychology* and you will probably discover that someone proved they can.

Now that I have acknowledged something of the richness of infant perception, why not let the learner recruit this considerable armamentarium for the sake of acquiring a verb vocabulary? Why not assume that the child encodes the situation not only in the restricted terms that yield Table 2.3.1, but in myriad other ways? For instance, over the discourse as a whole, probably the mother has different aims in mind when she tells the child to "look at" some object than when she tells her to "hold" or "give" it. The child could code the observed world for these perceived aims and enter these properties as aspects of the words' meanings. But also the mother may be angry or distant or lying down or eating lunch and the object in motion may be furry or alive or large or slimy or hot, and the child may code for these properties of the situation as well, entering them, too, as facets of the words' meanings.

The problems implicit in such an expansion of the representational vocabulary should be familiar from the literature on syntax acquisition: The trouble is that an observer who notices *everything* can learn *nothing*, for there is no end of categories known and constructable to describe a situation.[5] Indeed, not only learnability theorists but all syntacticians in the generative tradition appeal to the desirability of narrowing the hypothesis space lest the child be so overwhelmed with representational options and data-manipulative capacity as to be lost in thought forever. At least, learning of syntax could not be as rapid and uniform as it appears to be unless children were subject to highly restrictive principles of Universal Grammar, which rein in their hypotheses. As one famous example, learners are said to assume that all syntactic generalizations are structure-dependent rather than serial-order dependent (Chomsky, 1975; Crain and Fodor, in press). In fact, Universal Grammar is claimed to be as constrained as it is owing to the child's requirement that this be so (Wexler and Culicover, 1980).

I put it to you: Are these observations about the difficulties of learning when the hypothesis space is vast no less true of word learning than of syntax? In the domain of vocabulary acquisition as much as that of syntax acquisition, there is remarkable efficiency and systematicity of learning across individuals (and, as the blind children show, across learning environments): The rapidity and accuracy of vocabulary acquisition are jewels in the crown of rationalistically oriented developmental psycholinguistics (see particularly Carey, 1978). So just as in the case of syntax, we have initial grounds for claiming that a limit on the hypothesis space must be a critical source of sameness in the learning function. Bolstering the same view, languages seem to be as alike in their elementary vocabularies as they are in their syntactic devices (Talmy, 1975, 1985). But surprisingly enough, all the telling arguments invoked for syntax to restrict the interpretation of the input—that is, constraints on representations—that are to explain these samenesses in form, content, and learning functions are thrown out the window in most theorizing about the lexicon. *There* it is usually maintained that the child considers many complex, varying, cross-cutting, subtle conjectures about the scenes and events in view so as to arrive at the right answers, comparing and contrasting possibilities across many events, properties, discourse settings, and so forth. In other words, testing and manipulating an exceedingly broad and free-ranging hypothesis space.

In the domain of verb learning, a very few investigators have been responsive to the issues here. Pinker (1987), in a direct and useful discussion of the requirement to limit the space of observables that a learner will consider in matching the event to the unknown verb, wrote as follows:

> Verbs' definitions are organized around a surprisingly small number of elements: "The Main Event," that is, a state or motion; the path, direction, or location of an object, either literal spatial location or some analogue of it in a nonspatial semantic field; causation; manner; a restricted set of the properties of a theme or actor; temporal distribution (aspect and phase); purpose; coreferentiality of participants in an event; truth value (polarity and factivity); and a handful of others. (p. 54)

It is an open question whether Pinker's proposed list is narrow enough to meet the requirement for a realistic set of primitives upon which a verb-learning procedure can operate. Are purposes, truth values, causes, not to speak of "analogues of spatial location in nonspatial semantic fields" really primitives that inhere in the observations themselves? It seems highly unlikely that any choice of *perceptual* constraints will be restrictive enough to delimit the analyses a child performs in reaction to each word-to-world pair. Of course I am not suggesting that there are not principles of perception that are restrictive and highly structured (God forbid!). But they are likely not restrictive enough to account for vocabulary acquisition. How could they be? Perception has to be rich enough to keep the babies from falling off cliffs and mistaking distant tigers for nearby pussycats lest they all disappear from the face of the earth before learning the verb meanings. The very richness of perception guarantees multiple interpretive possibilities at many levels of abstraction for single scenes; but the problem for word learning is to select from among these options the single interpretation that is to map onto a particular lexical item.

Jerry Fodor has suggested to me, maybe seriously, that the problems of alternate encodings of the same scene go away because the caretaker and child are in cahoots, and they are mind-readers. They are so attuned in discourse, being creatures of exactly the same sort, that the child zaps onto exactly the characteristics of the situation that the mother, just then, has in mind to express; and by the same token, the mother more or less unfailingly understands the intents of the child (see Bruner, 1974/1975, for a story about how the attentional conspiracy is to be set up by mother and child).

However, recent evidence leaves room for extreme pessimism concerning these telepathic capabilities in learner and tutor. Golinkoff (1986) examined communicative episodes between mothers and their eleven–eighteen-month-old children and found that, even in the later period, instances of immediate comprehension of the child's desires by the mothers constitute only about half the episodes. For the rest, the mother either initially misunderstands the child's desire or ignores his signals altogether. To be sure, the final outcome of these failed communications is rarely child or mother tantrum; usually they just give up and change the subject. Thus while affability is normally maintained, in practice communication with linguistic novices very often fails. This appears to dispose of the mind-reading solution. It seems that the multiply interpretable world poses a real problem for the language learner and teacher.

Multiply interpretable events

The richness of perception is not the only, or even the major, problem faced by a hypothetical learner who tries to acquire verb meanings from observation. A more difficult problem is that even the homeliest and simplest verbs, though they refer to events perceivable, encode also the unobservable present interests, purposes, beliefs, and perspectives of the speaker. I turn now to this class of problems.

Consider the learning of simple motion verbs, such as *push* or *move*. In a satisfying proportion of the times that caretakers say something like "George pushes the truck," George can be observed to be pushing the truck. But unless George is a hopeless incompetent, every time he pushes the truck, the truck will move. So a verb used by the caretaker to describe this event may represent one of these ideas ("push") or the other ("move").

Moreover, every real event of the pushy sort necessarily includes, in addition to the thrust and goal, various values of trajectory, rate, and so forth, so that such ideas as "slide," "clank," "roll," "crawl," "speed," and so on, are also relevant interpretations of a new verb then uttered. What is left open by the observation is whether that verb represents any or all of these manner differences: No, in the case of *push*, but yes in the case of *roll* or *speed*.

Note that the manner elements just mentioned do fall within the range encoded by verbs in many languages (Talmy, 1985) and are on the narrowed list of perceptual properties suggested by Pinker (1987). I leave aside various other interpretations often called less salient, that is, I ignore more general consideration of the "stimulus-free" character of language use (see Chomsky, 1959), especially the countless fanciful interpretations of this event that could be drawn by worried philosophers. Ignoring these, there are always many highly salient, linguistically sanctioned, interpretations of a single action scene. How is the child to decide which of these interpretations is truly encoded by the particular verb uttered in the presence of such a scene?

It is possible that these ambiguities are eliminated by looking at a verb's uses *across* situations. There will eventually be some instance of moving called /push/ in which the truck is moving rapidly, eliminating "crawl"as a conjecture about the meaning of this item, and so on. By a process of cross-comparison and elimination, it has been proposed that each verb may eventually be distinguishable. In Pinker's (1987) words:

> the child could learn verb meanings by (a) sampling on each occasion in which a verb is used, a subset of the features ... [the features are those mentioned in my earlier quotation of Pinker], (b) adding to the tentative definition for the verb its current value for that feature, and (c) permanently discarding any feature value that is contradicted by a current situation. (p. 54)

I discuss this general idea at some length in a later section of this article. But notice now that, as stated, the position is surely too strong. Even if mothers always and only refer in their speech to the here-and-now in the presence of a young child, it cannot be guaranteed, *pace* Fodor, that child and adult are always attentionally focused in the same way. After all, sometimes the mother is speaking of one thing ("Eat your peas, dear!") while the child is attending to something else altogether (say, the hungry dog under the table). So the learner had better not "discard permanently" any feature that contradicts the current situation *as the child is conceiving it*.

In fact, positive imperatives pose one of the most devastating challenges to any scheme that works by constructing word-to-world pairings, for the mother will utter "Eat your peas!" if and only if the child is not then eating the peas. Thus a whole class of constructions is reserved for saying things that mismatch the current situation.

It follows that the child's confirmation metric for a verb meaning cannot be so stringent as to exclude an interpretation "permanently" if it should mismatch even a very few scenes. The necessarily probabilistic nature of such a procedure complicates its operation to an unknown degree. Even more important, the burden of hypothesis testing for cross-situational analysis becomes ominous as the comparison set (of verbs, properties, scenes, and discourse analyses) required to make it go through enlarges.[6]

Paired verbs that describe single events

Difficult problems can be solved. Impossible ones are harder. Consider such verb pairs as *flee* and *chase, buy* and *sell, win* and *beat, give* and *receive,* and so on. Such pairs are common in the design of verb lexicons. The members of each pair allude to a single kind of event: Whenever the hounds are chasing the fox, the fox is fleeing from the hounds. If some hounds are racing, even with evil intentions, toward a brave fox who holds its ground, they cannot be said to be chasing him. The hounds are chasing only if the fox is fleeing. If the child selects a verb from the stream of speech accompanying such a scene, how then is she to decide whether it means "chase" or "flee"?

Such examples are thrusts to the heart of the observational learning hypothesis. As Pinker (1987) acknowledges,

> Basically, we need to show that the child is capable of entertaining as a hypothesis any possible verb meaning, and that he or she is capable of eliminating any incorrect hypothesis as a result of observing how the verb is used across situations. (p. 54)

But if *chase* and *flee* (and a host of similar pairs) are relevantly used in just the same situations, it follows that it *cannot* be shown that the child is capable of eliminating the incorrect hypotheses by cross-situational observation.

I think the problem is that words do not describe events *simpliciter.* If that is all words did, we would not have to talk. We could just point to what is happening, grunting all the while. But instead, or in addition, the verbs seem to describe specific perspectives taken on those events by the speaker, perspectives that are not "in the events" in any direct way. How far are we to give the learner leave to divine the intents of his or her elders as to these perspectives? Are they talking of hounds acting with respect to foxes, or of foxes with respect to hounds? Speaking more generally, since verbs represent not only events but the intents, beliefs, and perspectives of the speakers on those events, the meanings of the verbs cannot be extracted solely by observing the events.

The subset problem

A related problem has to do with the level of specificity with which the speaker, by the words chosen, refers to the world. Consider the homely little objects in the world, the pencils, the ducks, the spoons. All these objects are supplied with more than one name in a language, for example, *animal, duck, Donald Duck.* I expect that the adult speaker has little difficulty in selecting the level of specificity he or she wants to convey and so can choose the correct lexical item to utter in each case. And indeed the learner may be richly pre-equipped perceptually and conceptually so as to be able to interpret scenes at these various levels of abstraction and to construct conceptual taxonomies (Keil, 1979). But, as usual, this very latitude adds lo the mystery of vocabulary acquisition, for how is the child to know the level encoded by the as yet unknown word? The scene is always the same if the child conjectures the more inclusive interpretation (that is, if the first conjecture is "animal" rather than "duck"). For every time there is an observation that satisfies the conditions (whatever these are) for the appropriate use of *duck*, the conditions for the appropriate use of *animal* have been satisfied as well.

Analogous cases exist in the realm of verb meanings. To return to the instance dramatized by the blind learners, *perceive, see, look, eye* (in the sense of "set eyes on"), *orient*, pose the same subset problem. There is no seeing without looking, looking without eyeing, eyeing without orienting, and so on. All this suggests that not only blind children, but sighted children as well, should have (essentially the same) difficulties in learning the meanings of *look* and *see*, because the distinction between the two words is not an observable property of the situations in which they are used. Yet, as I discussed earlier, it is just these unobservable properties that the blind and sighted 3-year-olds held in common.

Gold (1967) addressed a problem that seems related to this one. He showed formally that learners who had to choose between two languages, one of which was a subset of the other, could receive no positive evidence that they had chosen wrong if they happened to conjecture the superset (larger) language. This is because the sentences they would hear, all drawn from the subset, are all members of the superset as well. It has therefore been proposed that learners always hypothesize the smaller (subset) language; they initially select the most restrictive value of a parameter on which languages vary (Berwick, 1982; Wexler and Manzini, 1987).

But the facts about the lexicon do not allow us to suppose that the child has a solution so simple as choosing the least inclusive possibility; that is, to choose that interpretation which subsumes the smaller set of real-world referents (all the ducks rather than all the animals, or a limited aspect of perception rather than all of it). In the end, learners acquire words at all such levels of specificity. Moreover, neither the most inclusive nor the least inclusive possibilities seem to be the initial conjectures of learners; rather, some middle level of interpretation is the one initially selected, that is, *duck* and *look* (as opposed to *animal/mallard* and *examine/glimpse*) seem to be the real first choices.[7]

In sum, words that stand in a subset relation pose another serious problem for an unaided observation-based learning procedure. This is because the child who first conjectures a more inclusive interpretation can receive no positive evidence from word-to-world mappings that can dissuade him. And the idea that the child always begins with the least inclusive interpretation consistent with the data is falsified by the empirical facts.

Some plausible approaches to solution of this class of problems have been suggested in the literature, particularly with reference to the problem of learning noun meanings. To my knowledge, all of them invoke the idea mentioned earlier—that there is some middling level of abstraction (the "basic" level; Rosch *et al.*, 1976) in terms of which the child naturally parses the perceptual world. Assuming that we can make good on this initial assumption, one further postulate can help an observational learning theory go through. This is that there are no synonyms in the monomorphemic vocabulary of a language (Clark, 1988; Markman and Hutchinson, 1984). In that case, the child may step up or down within a cognitively ordered set of concepts at levels of abstraction higher and lower than the basic one in the cases where a new word is used to describe an entity for which the child already has a known name (for discussion, see Carey, 1985; Jones, Landau, and Smith, 1986; Waxman and Gelman, 1986).

However, it is premature to be too optimistic about this sort of proposal, for it is not at all clear that the notion of "basic categories" can ever be brought to ground. This is because the set of elementary categories underlying the monomorphemic vocabulary may be so large that the constraints from this quarter could be quite insignificant in explaining how the child learns which word encodes which concept. The psycholinguistic literature to date cannot even account for the intuition that, while *grape* and *pea* are basic terms (with the superordinates *fruit* and *vegetable*), *bird* and *tree* seem to be basic (rather than the superordinates of *lark* and *elm*). Notice that if the idea of a basic conceptual level must allude to overall familiarity to repair such problems, it loses all explanatory force for answering to vocabulary acquisition issues. Note also that the descriptive problems for the idea of a basic level grow materially worse when more formal (e.g., *female* or *integer*) or functional (e.g., *equal* or *meet*) terms are considered (for discussion, see Armstrong, Gleitman, and Gleitman, 1983; Fodor, 1981).

More relevant to my present purposes, this class of solutions begins to invoke evidence that is not in the world of observation but rather resides in the design of language itself; in the present case, the child's assumption about the lexicon is that for all practical purposes it excludes synonyms. As I shall argue presently, quite sophisticated presuppositions about the structure of language appear to be necessary to account for the acquisition of vocabulary.

Semantic properties that are closed to observation

The verbs that most seriously challenge the observational learning hypothesis still remain to be discussed: These are the ones that do not refer to the observable world at all.

Locke noted that the meanings of many words involve properties that are not observable, but he did not consider this fact to be fatal to his overall position because his view, most likely warranted, was that those who used such abstract words did not know what they were talking about half the time anyhow. Nevertheless, a key problem for observational learning is that many words are related to the real world only in the most obscure and invisible ways, if at all. Try, for example, to learn the meaning of the word *think* by titrating discourse situations into those in which thinking is going on, somewhere when you hear /think/ versus those in which no thinking is happening. Remember that there is not always brow furrowing or a Rodin statue around to help. Keep in mind also that you are going to have to distinguish as well among *think, guess, wonder, know, hope, suppose,* and *understand,* not to speak of—a few months or years later—*conjecture, figure, comprehend, discover, perceive,* and so forth. Many developmental psycholinguists rule such instances out of school on the grounds that these are not words that children know very well at 2 and 3 years old, but this will not do. After all, we also want to understand the children who manage to survive to become the 4- and 5-year-olds.

I do not really think this topic needs much more belaboring. If the child is to learn the meanings from perceptual discriminanda in the real world, the primitive vocabulary of infant perception has to be pretty narrow to bring the number and variety of data storing and manipulative procedures under control. But no such narrow vocabulary of perception could possibly select the thinkingness properties from events. I conclude that an *unaided* observation-based verb-learning theory is untenable because it could not acquire *think.*

The fitful fit of word to world

Earlier in this discussion, I claimed that a realistic observation-based procedure must operate in terms of probabilistic rather than absolute word-to-world matches, at least because child and caretaker cannot be assumed to be attending to the same aspects of the same scene on every occasion when some verb is uttered. Thus the wise child would not permanently give up on a conjectured verb meaning in the presence of a very small proportion of mismatches to the world. I now ask how serious this objection may be for the viability of such theories. In what proportion of cases, really, do the verbs uttered match up with the scenes in view?

The relation between word and world is probabilistic

There has been almost no systematic work on this topic. The idea that word-to-world contingencies *must* be strong and stable is entrenched in three hundred years of empiricist speculation, and to a large extent this fixed belief has been a barrier to empirical inquiry. Table 2.3.1 in fact describes one of the rare studies in which anyone has attempted to see just how the words line up with their contexts of use. And that analysis, as we have seen, yielded quite puzzling results.

A recent study by Beckwith, Tinker, and Bloom (1989) achieves findings at least as problematic as our own. They are working with a very large maternal corpus of utterances to children in the age range of thirteen–twenty-three months, with a view to understanding the acquisition of verb argument structure. This sample includes about 8,000 verb-containing utterances. The assumption is that only when noun referents in these utterances were present (in the scene in view) would they be of any use to the child learner in acquiring the argument structures. Some 3,000 of the verb-containing utterances failed to meet this criterion and therefore were discarded. To take two specific examples: There were 566 sentences containing the verb *put*, in fifty-five cases (10 percent), the sentence did not refer to the here-and-now. There were eighty sentences with the verb *open*, of which thirty (37.5 percent) were not about the here-and-now. Thus, if these data are at all representative, a child who learns verb meanings by asking about their relations to ongoing scenes must be quite tolerant of counter-examples.

In fact, the prospects for observational learning may be materially worse than emerges in the analysis just described, for this tells us only that 67.5 percent of the time when /open/ is uttered, opening is happening—a somewhat ominous but not necessarily devastating proportion of fit of word to scene. But one must also ask the question in the opposing direction: What is the likelihood, given that an event of opening is in view and has captured the child's attention, that /open/ (rather than some other verb) will be uttered? Can one doubt that this relationship will turn out to be muddy in the extreme? For an ideal case, suppose the door to Alfred's house squeaks loudly, so his attention is invariably captured by the noise as it opens, and hence he invariably looks up and attends whenever it opens. When, every evening, Mother opens the door upon returning from work, what does he hear? I would venture that he rarely hears her say "Hello, Alfred, I am opening the door!" but very often hears "Hello, Alfred, whatcha been doing all day?" (and just as often hears Father say "Shut the door, it's freezing in here!"). In short, any scheme for learning from observation must have some machinery for dealing with the fact that caretaker speech is not a running commentary on scenes and events in view.

Beckwith, Tinker, and Bloom's analysis does presuppose significant further machinery: As mentioned earlier, it summarily discards those utterances that do not refer to the ongoing event. But this is defensible only if it can be shown that the learner who does not know the word meaning, like the analyst who does, has some means for excluding these instances. After all, if the child truly believes that utterances refer to the here-and-now, he or she will simply form the wrong sound/meaning pairings when the adult speaks of things nonpresent.

For instance, if the child hears "Let's get some duck for dinner tomorrow" while throwing a ball, she might assume that /get/ means "throw" and that /duck/ means "ball." This problem seems especially acute for the mother–child discourse Beckwith, Tinker, and Bloom are studying, for the children are very young—on some theories, unable to understand the full sentences and thus really at the mercy of word-to-world pairings.

As no plausible theory is available for reducing the database—in advance of learning—to one which reliably maps verb use onto scenes and events observed, the best guess is that the child acquiring meanings solely from word-to-world pairings must adopt an extremely liberal stance, accepting a meaning in the presence of a low proportion of situational "hits" and tolerating a large proportion of "misses."

Counterexamples and the fitful fit

Such considerations bring me back to one crucial further point. I earlier asserted that cross-situational analysis as proposed by Pinker (1987) is insufficient to save the observation-based learning story, owing to examples such as *chase/flee*, *buy/sell*, and so on, whose real-world contingencies do not differ. But Pinker has pointed out to me that the claim of situational identity for such pairs is somewhat overdrawn, for one can think of some suitably arcane circumstances in which only one member of the pair applies—that is, situations in which one would utter *beat* but not *win*, and so forth. Here are two of Pinker's examples: It is possible for me to *flee the city*, without it being implied that the *city is chasing me*. And it is at least somewhat more natural to say *I bought a Coke from the machine* than to say that *The machine sold me a Coke*. These examples defeat an absolute claim that there are no situations at all in which the meanings of such words can be disambiguated.

But these counter-examples must be evaluated in light of the child's confirmation metric for word-to-world relations, which I have tried to show must be tolerant of a significant proportion of mismatches.

For instance: Suppose Alfred has conjectured, based on some hundreds of uses of /flee/ in the presence of foxes/hounds, dogs/cats, mothers/errant children, and so on, that /flee/ means "chase." (Why not? All the contexts up to now fit "chase" as well as they fit "flee," and Alfred is among the 50 percent of children who guessed wrong). Now he hears "The boy took to his heels and fled the stable," with no bulls visibly in pursuit. What effect should this new data point have? Given Alfred's vexed interactions with /open/, and his consequently liberal evaluation criterion for word-to-world matches (67 percent hits must be good enough), this rare mismatch should have no effect at all on the prior conjecture. That is to say, overwhelmingly often when fleeing is around, chasing is around. No child who learned /open/ from its sometime relation to the world of scenes and events could be deflected by the vanishingly rare dissociation of chasing and fleeing events. As I next argue, a much more appealing procedure for dissociating the two verb meanings is by realizing that the subject noun phrase of /flee/ must represent the one who runs away and that the subject of /chase/ must be the entity in pursuit.

Summary

I mentioned a number of problems for a theory that (solely or even primarily) performs a word-to-world mapping to solve the vocabulary-learning task. These are that:

1. Such a theory fails to account for the fact that children whose exposure conditions are radically different (the blind and the sighted) acquire much the same representations even of vision-related words.
2. Plausible, narrowly drawn candidates for event representation seem to be inadequate in accounting for the learning in certain apparently easy cases—such as expecting that words whose interpretation requires manual contact be uttered when one is in manual contact with something pertinent.
3. Broadening the hypothesis space so as to allow learners to distinguish among the many verb meanings may impose unrealistic storage, manipulation, and induction demands on the mere babes who must do the learning.

In addition, observational learning seems to fail in principle to the extent that:

4. Many verbs are identical in all respects except the perspectives that they adopt toward events (*chase, flee*) or
5. the level of specificity at which they describe a single event (*see, look, orient*) or
6. do not refer to events and states that are observable at all (*think, know*).

Part II: New approaches for vocabulary acquisition

Since children learn verb meanings despite the apparently formidable problems of culling them from exposure to extralinguistic contexts, Landau and I conjectured (1985) that they have another source of information. This additional information derives from the linguistic (syntactic) contexts in which words occur in speech. Children's sophisticated perceptual and conceptual capacities yield a good many possibilities for interpreting any scene, but the syntax acts as a kind of mental zoom lens for fixing on just the interpretation, among these possible ones, that the speaker is expressing. To make use of this information source in acquiring the verb vocabulary, the learner must perform a sentence-to-world mapping rather than a word-to-world mapping.

To explain this position, I return first to the problem Landau and I faced in understanding the blind child's semantic achievements.

How the blind child might have learned the visual terms

Recall that the analysis of Table 2.3.1 was an attempt to explain only the most straightforward, perceptually transparent aspect of a blind learner's acquisition of *look* and *see*; namely, that if these verbs had to do with *haptic* perception, there must have been pertinent objects close to her hands when her mother said those words. Yet even this simple idea seemed to be falsified by our analysis. To find out why, our first step was to return to the data of Table 2.3.1 to see where and when the NEARNESS criterion had failed for so many uses of *look* and *see*. We found that the sentences that fit neatly with the object-nearby criterion were very simple ones: If the mother had said something like "Look at this boot!" or "See? This is a pumpkin," invariably the boot or pumpkin were NEAR, within the child's reach. But if the mother had said, "Let's see if Granny's home!" (while dialing the phone), "Look what you're doing!" (as the child spilled juice), "You look like a kangaroo in those overalls" (which had a pouch), or "Let's go see Poppy" (as they entered a car), the pertinent object was likely to be FAR or there was NO such pertinent OBJECT intended. Clearly, many of the sentences that tripped up our simple story were queer ones indeed. The mother did not seem in most of these cases to mean "examine or apprehend" either haptically or visually, but rather "determine," "watch out" or "resemble." Or else, as in the final example, a motion auxiliary (*go*) in the sentence transparently took off the NEARbyness requirement.

There are two ways to go now: One can claim that the NEARbyness environmental clue to the haptic interpretation was just a snare and delusion— but that is ridiculous. It just *has* to be right that this aspect of the environment was part of what licensed the child's haptic interpretation. The other choice is to find some nonquestion-begging way through which the child could have gotten rid of the sentences that otherwise would threaten the experiential conjecture. (The question-begging way, of course, is to say that the mother did not mean "haptically explore" in the offending sentences.)

How can this be done? A potentially useful clue is that not only the meaning but the syntax too of these offending sentences is special, different from the syntax of sentences in which the child was *really* being told to explore and perceive nearby objects. This syntactic distinction may be available to the learner.

A syntactic partitioning of the verbs commonly used by the mother of the blind baby (based on the same corpus analyzed in Table 2.3.1) according to the subcategorization frames in which each verb appeared in the maternal corpus is shown in Table 2.3.2. The verbs of Table 2.3.1 appear as the columns in this

Table 2.3.2 *Subcategorization frames for the common verbs*

	Perception Verbs		Transfer verbs				Other			
	look	see	give	put	get	hold	play	have	go	come
Look/see only										
V!	8									
V?		1								
V!, S	10									
V?, S		3								
V how S	2^a									
V S		5						1^b		
V like NP	5									
come V NP		3								
Exclude look/see										
V NP PP$_{loc}$			5	31	2					
V NP D$_{loc}$ PP						1^c				
V NP D$_{loc}$				28	2	6				
V D$_{loc}$ NP				1						
V NP NP			16		2					
V NP where S				1^d						
V PP							7^e			
Overlap look/see										
V PP$_{loc}$	3				5				2	2
V D$_{loc}$	2								10	13
V ϕ	2	3							8	4
V NP		3			13	3	3	14		
V AP	2					3				
Totals	34	18	21	61	27	10	10	15	20	19

Note: Adapted from Landau and Gleitman, 1985: 112, with permission of the publisher, Harvard University Press.

[a] E.g., "Look how I'm doing it." [b] "Let's have Barbara babysit" (causative) [c] "Hold the N up to me." [d] "Put it where it belongs." [e] *Play* with the reciprocal preposition *with*, for example, "You're not gonna play with the triangle, so forget it!"

table and the syntactic environments appear as the rows; the numbers in each cell are the number of instances of a verb in some particular syntactic environment. (Specifically, the rows of this table represent subcategorization frames, the sister nodes to the verb under the verb-phrase node.) Notice first that some of the typical syntactic environments for *look* and *see* are quite different from those for the other verbs in the set.

Moreover, we can—with only a little fudging—divide the environments of the vision-related verbs so as to pull apart those environments in which the NEARbyness contextual cue holds and those in which it does not. That analysis is shown in Table 2.3.3. Essentially, the top rows of Table 2.3.3 show the maternal uses of *look* and *see* in their canonical subcategorization frames (e.g.,

Table 2.3.3 *Spatial/syntactic analysis of* look *and* see

	NEAR	FAR	NO OBJECT	"NEAR PROPORTION"
Canonical sentence frames and deictic uses				
Look at NP	3	0	0	
Look D	2	0	0	1.00
Look!	8	0	0	
Look!, This is NP	10	0	0	
See NP	1	2	0	
See?	1	0	0	.72
See? This is NP	3	0	0	
Motion auxiliary				
Come see NP	0	3	0	.00
Other environments				
Look AP	0	1	1	
Look like NP	0	0	5	.18
Look how S	0	2	0	
Look ϕ	2	0	0	
See S	2	3	0	
See ϕ	0	2	1	.25
Total (all environments)				
Look	25	3	6	.73
See	7	10	1	.39

Note: Reproduced from Landau and Gleitman, 1985: 115, with permission of the publisher, Harvard University Press.

"Look at/see the frog," "Look up/down") and the deictic interjective uses that are the most frequent in that corpus (e.g., "Look!, That's a frog!" and "See?, That's a frog!"). When these syntactic types only are considered, the NEAR proportion of *look* rises (to 100 percent, from 72 percent in Table 2.3.1) and so does the NEAR proportion of *see* (to 72 percent from 39 percent). Thus if the learner can and does perform these analyses, the first result is that NEARbyness of the pertinent object becomes a much more reliable real-world clue than previously. But notice that the hypothesis now is that children perform a sentence-to-world mapping rather than the word-to-world mapping shown in Table 2.3.1: The children's interpretation of *extralinguistic* events has been significantly modulated by their attention to *linguistic* events, namely the subcategorization frames.

Landau and I made yet another, and much stronger, claim based on the kinds of outcomes shown in Table 2.3.2. This was that the range of subcategorization frames has considerable potential for partitioning the verb set semantically, and that language-learners have the capacity and inclination to recruit this information source to redress the insufficiencies of observation. This examination of structure as a basis for deducing the meaning is the procedure we have called *syntactic bootstrapping*.[8] This hypothetical procedure stands in contrast to a view that emphasizes observation as the main initial source of evidence for verb-meaning acquisition (*semantic bootstrapping*), devised by Grimshaw (1981) and considerably elaborated by Pinker (1984, 1987).[9] I turn now to a comparison of these two approaches.

The bootstrapping proposals compared

The two bootstrapping proposals are much alike in what they claim about correspondences between syntax and semantics, and they are also alike in proposing that the child makes significant use of these correspondences. First I sketch, very informally, the kinds of syntactic/semantic relationships that are crucially invoked in both proposals.

Syntactic/semantic linking rules

To an interesting degree, the structures in which verbs appear are projections from their meanings. To take a simple example, the different number of noun phrases required by the verbs *laugh*, *smack*, and *put* in the sentences

1. Arnold laughs.
2. Arnold smacks Gloria.
3. Gloria puts Arnold in his place.

is clearly no accident but rather is semantically determined—by how many participant entities, locations, and so forth, the predicate implicates. Similarly, the structural positions of these noun phrases relative to the verb also carry semantic information. Thus, much more often than not, the subject noun phrase will represent the experiencer or causal agent (*Arnold* in sentence 1 and *Gloria* in sentence 3), and paths and goals will appear in prepositional phrases (*in his place* in sentence 3). These links of syntactic position and marking to semantic properties, although by no means unexceptional, typify the ways that English represents semantic-relational structure. In short, verbs that are related in meaning share aspects of their clausal syntax. Zwicky (1971) put the idea this way:

> If you invent a verb, say *greem*, which refers to an act of communication by speech and describes the physical characteristics of the act (say a loud, hoarse, quality), then you know that ... it will be possible to greem (i.e., to speak loudly and hoarsely), to greem for someone to get you a glass of water, to greem at your sister about the price of doughnuts, to greem "Ecch" at your enemies, to have your greem frighten the baby, to greem to me that my examples are absurd, and to give a greem when you see the explanation. (p. 232)

Semantic bootstrapping: Using the semantics to predict the syntax

As I mentioned earlier, both the bootstrapping proposals make critical use of these canonical relations between syntax and semantics. In the semantic bootstrapping procedure, the child first fixes the meaning of a verb by observing its real-world contingencies. I have argued at length that this hypothesis about verb-meaning extraction is too strong, for at least some features are unobservable. Yet no one can doubt that, at least sometimes, the context of use is so rich and restrictive as to make a certain conjecture about interpretation overwhelmingly likely.

Once the verb meaning has been extracted from observation, the semantic bootstrapping hypothesis invokes the linking rules (the canonical syntactic/semantic mappings) to explain how the child discovers the structures that are licensed for the use of these verbs, much in the spirit of Zwicky's comments about the invented word *greem*. For instance, if a verb has been discovered to mean "give," then it will appear in three-argument structures such as *John gives the book to Mary*. This is because the logic of "give" implies one who gives, one who is given, and that which is given, and each of these entities requires a noun phrase to express.

Not only is this position plausible. There is much evidence in its favor. Notably, Bowerman (1974, 1982) showed that children will make just such predictions based on their prior fixing of the verb meanings. That evidence came from instances where children's conjectures were evidently too bold or insufficiently differentiated, that is, where they were wrong—but still understandable. For instance, a child in Bowerman's study commanded "Don't eat the baby—she's dirty!" on an occasion when the mother was about to feed the baby (whose diaper needed changing). Presumably, the child had noted, implicitly of course, that an intransitive motion verb (e.g., *sink*, as in *The ship sank*) could be uttered in a transitive structure (e.g., *The captain sank the ship*) to express the causal agent of this motion. If this is true of *sink* (and *open* and *melt*, etc.), why not of *eat*?

To summarize, the semantic bootstrapping procedure as developed by Grimshaw (1981) and Pinker (1984) works something like this: The child is conceived as listening to the words used and then trying to figure out their meanings by observing their situational concomitants, the word-to-world pairing that I have discussed. Quoting Pinker (1984) again:

> If the child deduces the meanings of as yet uncomprehended input sentences from their contexts and from the meanings of their individual words, he or she would have to have learned those word meanings beforehand. This could be accomplished by attending to single words used in isolation, to emphatically stressed single words, or to the single uncomprehended word in a sentence . . . and pairing it with a predicate corresponding to an entity or relation that is singled out ostensively, one

that is salient in the discourse context, or one that appears to be expressed in the speech act for which there is no known word in the sentence expressing it. (p. 30)

According to this proposal, once the meanings have been derived from observation, the child can project the structures from (innate) knowledge of the rules that map semantic structures onto syntactic structures (variously termed *mapping rules, linking rules, projection rules,* or *semantic redundancy rules*). Perhaps so, but I have been arguing that entities and relations cannot in general be singled out ostensively, that "salience" and the question of what is "expressed in the speech act" are not so easily recoverable as this perspective must insist. For such reasons, Landau and I hypothesized an additional procedure, one that looks quite different from this.

Syntactic bootstrapping: Using the syntax to predict the semantics

The syntactic bootstrapping proposal in essence turns semantic bootstrapping on its head. According to this hypothesis, the child who understands the mapping rules for semantics onto syntax can use the observed syntactic structures as evidence for deducing the meanings. The learner observes the real-world situation but also observes the structures in which various words appear in the speech of the caretakers. Such an approach can succeed because, if the syntactic structures are truly correlated with the meanings, the range of structures will be informative for deducing which word goes with which concept. This sentence-to-world mapping will be quite handy if, as I have argued, word-to-world mapping cannot succeed over the full range of meanings that we know are acquired.

The difference between semantic bootstrapping and syntactic bootstrapping, then, is that the former procedure deduces the structures from the word meanings that are antecedently acquired from the observation of events, while the latter procedure deduces the word meanings from the semantically relevant syntactic structures associated with a verb in input utterances. Note that although the hypothesized procedures are distinct, to hold that one of them is implicated in learning is not to deny that the other one is too. Quite the contrary. It is very likely that they operate in a complementary fashion.

Let us take the examples *put, look,* and *see,* which occurred in the corpus provided by the blind child's mother. Verbs that describe externally caused transfer or change of possessor of an object from place to place (or from person to person) fit naturally into sentences with three noun phrases, for example, *John put the ball on the table.* This is just the kind of transparent syntax/semantics relation that every known language seems to embody. It may therefore not be too wild to conjecture that this relationship is part of the original presuppositional structure that children bring into the language-learning task (Jackendoff, 1978, 1983; Pinker, 1984; Talmy, 1975). That is, "putting" logically implies one who puts, a thing put, and a place into which it is put; a noun phrase is assigned to each of the participants in such an event. In contrast, because one cannot move objects from place to place by the perceptual act of looking at them, the occasion for using *look* in such a structure hardly, if ever, arises (*John looked the ball on the table* sounds unnatural).[10] Hence the chances that /put/ means "put" are raised and the chances that /put/ means "look" are lowered by the fact that the former and not the latter verb appears in three noun-phrase constructions in caretaker speech (see Table 2.3.2). Restating this more positively, the component "transfer" is inserted into a verb's semantic entry in case it is observed to occur in three noun-phrase structures. This happens for /put/ but not for /look/ (see Table 2.3.2).

Verbs of perception and cognition are associated with some other constructions, as they should be. For example, if a verb is to mean "see" (perceive, visually or haptically), it should appear with noun-phrase objects as in *John saw a mouse*, for noun phrases are the categories that languages select to describe such entities as mice. But since events as well as entities can be perceived, this verb should and does also appear with sentence complements, for clauses are the categories selected by languages for expressing whole events (e.g., *Let's see if there's cheese in the refrigerator*). The possibility that /see/ means "see" is increased by appearance in this construction, and the likelihood that /put/ means "see" is decreased by the fact that one never hears *Let's put if there's cheese in the refrigerator* (see again Table 2.3.2). That is, the component "perceptual" (or more likely, "mental") is added to the verb's entry when the sentential complement is observed.

Speaking more generally, certain abstract semantic elements such as "cause," "transfer," "symmetry," and "cognition" are carried on clause structures, which are licensed by semantic information in the lexical entries of verbs. So these structures will be chosen for utterance only to the extent that they fit with the semantics of the verb items. It follows that the subcategorization frames, if their semantic values are known, can convey important information to the verb learner. To be sure, the number of such clause structures is quite small compared to the number of possible verb meanings: It is reasonable to assume that only a limited number of highly general semantic categories and functions are exhibited in the organization that yields the subcategorization frame distinctions. But each verb is associated with several of these structures. Each such structure narrows down the choice of interpretations for the verb. Thus these limited parameters of structural variation, operating jointly, can predict the possible meaning of an individual verb quite closely. Landau and Gleitman (1985) showed that the child's situational and syntactic input, as represented in Tables 2.3.1, 2.3.2 and 2.3.3 were sufficient in principle to distinguish among all the verbs commonly used in the maternal sample for the blind child. This general outcome is schematized in Figure 2.3.3.

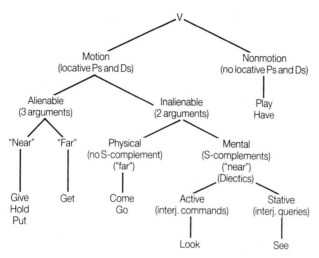

Figure 2.3.3 *A summary of the verb subcategorization and spatial-situational clues to meaning in the maternal corpus (speech to the blind child). (Reproduced from Landau and Gleitman, 1985: 135, with permission of the publisher, Harvard University Press.) For expositional purposes only, the components of the verb meanings (e.g., motion, mental) are organized in a tree diagram here, but it is likely that their real arrangement is as a cross-classification rather than a hierarchy. Postulated conceptual features such as* motion *are shown as the node labels in this tree and are assumed to be discovered through use of the syntactic and situational evidentiary sources listed in parentheses below each such feature.*

   The potential virtues of this syntactically informed verb-learning procedure are considerable:

1. It serves the local purpose of offering a nonmagical explanation for the blind child's acquisition of visual terms, as just described.
2. It points the way toward acquisition of terms when observation fails. This is because, for example, mental verbs such as *think* are unambiguously marked by the syntax (by taking sentence complements) even though their instances cannot be readily observed in the world.
3. It gives the child a way of learning from a very small database. This is because the number of subcategorization frames associated with each verb is small (on the order of ten–twenty), and these are the data requirements for the procedure to work.
4. That database is categorical rather than probabilistic. Though verb uses to the child are usually pertinent to what is going on in the here-and-now, sometimes they are not. For this reason, among the many described earlier, the child learning from observation must store the huge variety of situational contexts in which a word is used so as to evaluate what is "the same" about

all of them. The daunting nature of such a procedure must be kept in mind, as I have tried to emphasize. The problem is that the learner cannot know in advance which scene analysis is relevant to the verb meaning and so must store a multitude of these, awaiting the arrival of sufficient data (sample word-to-world pairs) for performing the cross-situational analysis. In contrast, mothers virtually never speak ungrammatically to their children—that is, use verbs in nonlicensed syntactic environments (Newport, 1977). Thus the child can take one or two instances of a verb in some frame as conclusive evidence that it is licensed in this syntactic environment.

5. What is used in this procedure for learning is part of what must be known by an accomplished speaker. Knowing the subcategorization privileges for each verb is part of what it means to know one's language. In contrast, many of the situational analyses constructed along the way by the semantic bootstrapper will not figure in the final definition of a verb.

In light of all these virtues, it would be nice if this theory turned out to be part of the truth about how the verb vocabulary is acquired. I provide some empirical evidence in its favor later. But first, some presuppositions of the position have to be defended before so apparently abstract a procedure can be considered viable at all. I turn now to such questions. But keep in mind that the approach here does not deny at all that observation of concomitant events is part of the answer to vocabulary acquisition. Rather the idea is to remove part of the burden that a wide-ranging categorization of such events necessarily would impose and to make available a solution in the many cases where observation fails.

Prolegomena to bootstrapping hypotheses

The bootstrapping hypotheses involve a number of presuppositions that require demonstration in their own right, lest all learning questions be begged. In company with all known theories of word learning, they presuppose that the human child, by natural disposition (or learning during the prelinguistic period, see Note 1) is able to conceive of such notions as "running" and "looking" and implicitly understands that words can make reference to such acts and events. Past this background supposition, both semantic and syntactic bootstrapping procedures—but especially the latter—make very strong claims about the child's knowledge *as verb learning begins*. I now go through these claims, mentioning some of the experimental evidence that gives them plausibility.

Are the rules linking semantics and syntax strong and stable enough to support a learning procedure?

If the syntactic structures associated with verbs are uncorrelated with—or hardly correlated with—their meanings, then the child cannot learn much about the meanings by observing the structures. No one doubts the sheer existence of such form/meaning regularities, owing to the results achieved by a generation of linguists, notably Fillmore (1968a, 1968b), Grimshaw (1983), Gruber (1968), Jackendoff (1978, 1983), Levin (1985), McCawley (1968), Vendler (1972), and see the collection of papers in Wilkins (1988). But questions can be raised about the stability, degree, and scope of these relations. That is, how far can a syntactic analysis such as that in Table 2.3.2 succeed in partitioning the lexicon semantically for the learner?

I mention one line of investigation of these questions from our laboratory. Fisher, Gleitman, and Gleitman (1991), following Wexler (1970), reasoned as follows: If similarity in the range of subcategorization frames of verbs is correlated with similarities in their meanings, then subjects asked to partition a set of verbs (a) according to their meanings and (b) according to their licensed structures should partition the verb set in much the same ways. To test this idea, one group of subjects made judgments of meaning similarity for triads of verbs presented to them. Specifically, they chose the semantic outlier in each triad (e.g., shown *eat, drink,* and *sing,* they would probably choose *sing* as the outlier; but shown *eat, drink,* and *quaff,* they might choose *eat*). A semantic space for a set of verbs was derived from these data by tabulating how often two verbs stayed together (i.e., were not chosen as outlier) in the context of all other verbs with which they were compared. Presumably, the more often they stayed together, the more semantically similar they were. A second group of subjects gave judgments of grammaticality for all these same verbs in a large number of subcategorization frames. A syntactic space was derived in terms of the frame overlap among them. The similarity in the syntactic and semantic spaces provided by these two groups was then compared statistically.

The finding was that the frame overlap among the verbs is a very powerful predictor of the semantic partitioning. Verbs that behaved alike syntactically were, to a very interesting degree, the verbs that behaved alike semantically. For example, the semantic grouping of mental verbs (e.g., *think*) was predicted by acceptance of sentence complements, and the semantic grouping of transfer verbs (e.g., *give*) was predicted by acceptance of three noun phrases within the clause. Neatly enough, a semantic subgrouping of verbs of communication (or mental transfer, e.g., *argue, explain*) was predicted by acceptance of both the syntactic environments just mentioned, just as Zwicky proposed (see prior quotation). Thus taken jointly (i.e., in terms of the *range* of frames for a verb), the syntactic selections appear to have considerable semantic resolving power.

The strength of these results is particularly surprising considering the weakness and indirectness of the (triad) procedure used to construct the semantic similarity space and its heavy dependence on the choice of verbs considered. Thus these findings begin to show that a syntactic partitioning of the input can provide important evidence for a learner who is disposed to use such information—as was conjectured for the blind child (see Figure 2.3.3).

The subcategorization frames provide a relatively coarse-grained semantic partitioning of the verb set, quite obviously. Only a limited set of semantic properties are or could be encoded on the verb frames. According to Fisher, Gleitman, and Gleitman (1991), the semantic information in the verb frames is quite principled, limited to properties that (a) affect the argument structure, (b) are domain general (i.e., show up all through the lexicon), and (c) are closed to observation. This coarse partitioning is of considerable significance, however, for solving some of the problems posed in the first section of this article, for instance, deducing that *think* is a mental-state verb, distinguishing between *chase* and *flee*, and so forth, as I try to show later when I discuss our experimental findings. But keep in mind that the *syntax* is not going to give the learner information delicate and specific enough, for example, to distinguish among such semantically close items as *break, tear, shatter,* and *crumble* (Fillmore, 1968b). Luckily, these distinctions are almost surely of the kinds that can be culled from transactions with the world of objects and events.

Are the semantic/syntactic relations the same cross-linguistically?

The first proviso to the semantic usefulness of syntactic analysis for learning purposes is that the semantic/syntactic relations have to be materially the same across languages. Otherwise, depending on the exposure language, different children would have to perform completely different syntactic analyses to derive aspects of the meaning. And that, surely, begs the question at issue.

Recent theorizing in linguistics does support the idea that there are semantic/syntactic linkages that hold across languages. In a recent version of generative grammar (Government/Binding theory; see Chomsky, 1981), some of the relationships are stated as universal principles of language design. One example is the mapping of entities implied by the verb logic one-to-one onto noun-phrase positions in the clause: Every noun phrase in a sentence must receive one and only one thematic role (the *theta criterion*). Moreover, a related principle (the *projection principle*) states that the theta criterion will hold at every level of a derivation; in particular, that argument structure is preserved on the surface clause structures. This is just the organization required by a bootstrapper, semantic or syntactic.

Talmy (1975, 1985) investigated a number of typologically quite different languages and found a variety of striking similarities in how their syntax maps onto the semantics (though to be fair he has found some striking differences too). For those who prefer experimental evidence from linguistically naive subjects, Fisher, Gleitman and Gleitman (1991)—in a very preliminary cross-linguistic foray with their method—showed that the relationship between being a verb of communication and accepting sentence complements and three noun phrases in the clause is as strong and stable in Italian as it is in English.

The two relationships just mentioned (that a noun phrase is assigned to each participant in the event and that verbs encoding the relation between an agent and a proposition accept sentence complements) are not only true cross-linguistically. They have a kind of cognitive transparency that makes them plausible as part of the presuppositional structure children might really bring into the language-learning situation. As Jackendoff (1978) put this point:

> In order to lighten the language-learner's load further, it seems promising to seek a theory of semantics (that is, of conceptualization) in which the projection rules are relatively simple, for then the child can draw relatively straightforward connections between the language he hears and his conception of the world. The methodological assumptions for such a theory would be that syntactic simplicity ideally corresponds to conceptual simplicity; grammatical parallelisms may be clues to perceptual parallelisms; apparent grammatical constraints may reflect conceptual constraints. (p. 203)

From these and related arguments and demonstrations, I think the plausibility of the bootstrapping theories receives at least some initial defense.

Can the learner analyze the sound wave in a way that will support discovery of syntactic structure?

There is a timing difference in the requirements of the semantic and syntactic bootstrapping approaches: For the latter, the learner has to be able to parse the sentences heard in order to derive a syntactic analysis. Moreover, at least some of the mapping rules have to be in place before the verb meanings are known, or else the whole game is over. There is strong evidence supporting both these claims.

Can infants parse?

Once upon a time not so very long ago, it was believed that babies could divide up the sound wave into words but not into phrases. This perspective necessitated complex theories for how learners could derive phrasal categories from the initial wordlike representations (Pinker, 1984). In retrospect, these ideas were somewhat improbable. For one thing, there is evidence that infants are sensitive to such physical properties of the wave form as change in fundamental frequency, silent intervals, and syllabic length, all of which are universal markers of phrase boundaries (Cooper and Paccia-Cooper, 1980; Klatt, 1975; Streeter, 1978; and see Fernald, 1984; Fernald *et al.*, 1989; and Schreiber, 1987, for relevant developmental evidence). As Gleitman and Wanner (1982) pointed out, the physical correlates of word segmentation are far more subtle and less reliable (see Echols and Newport, 1989, for an analysis).[11] More generally, Gleitman and Wanner's reading of the cross-linguistic facts about language learning led them to propose that the infant's analysis of the wave form was as a rudimentary phrase structure tree.

In a similar vein, Morgan and Newport (1981; Morgan, Meier, and Newport, 1987), showed in a series of artificial language-learning experiments that adults could learn phrase structure grammars if provided with phrase-bracketing information but not if provided only with word-level information. This finding led these investigators independently to the same proposal as Gleitman and Wanner's about the child's initial representation of the input wave forms. Hirsh-Pasek *et al.* (1987) and Jusczyk *et al.* (1988) showed that prelinguistic infants listen to maternal speech doctored so as to preserve phrase- and clause-bounding information in preference to speech doctored so as to becloud this information (see Gleitman *et al.*, 1987, for a review of the evidence and its interpretation for a language acquisition theory).

The evidence just cited is not precise enough to give a detailed picture of the infant's phrasal parse. But even so, it is strong enough to support the view that children, even in the prelinguistic period, impose an analysis on the wave form sufficient for partitioning it into phrases. It is incontrovertible that the 2- and 3-year-olds who are the real verb-learners can achieve the analyses of input shown in Table 2.3.2, and which are a requirement for achieving the semantic partitioning of the verb set shown in Figure 2.3.3.

Does the learner know the correspondence rules?

A crucial further requirement for the bootstrapping hypotheses is that the child understands the semantic values of the subcategorization frames. A child who recovers the meaning from observation and who is to deduce the structures therefrom has to know what the semantics of the verb implies about the syntactic structures licensed. And a child who recovers the syntactic structures licensed for verbs from the linguistic contexts in which they are heard has to know what semantic elements are implied by participation in these structures. As Jackendoff emphasized, the burden of learning would certainly be reduced for a child in possession of such information. But do real learners actually have it? There is striking evidence that they do.

Golinkoff *et al.* (1987) developed a very useful paradigm for studying very young children's comprehension. Essentially, they adapted the preferential looking procedure designed by Spelke (1982) for studying infant perception. The setup for the language case is shown in Figure 2.3.4. The child sees different scenes displayed on two video screens, one to the left, one to the right. The scenes are accompanied by some speech stimulus. The mother wears a visor so that she cannot observe the videos and so cannot give hints to her child. Hidden observers are so positioned that they cannot observe the video, but they can observe which way the child is looking and for how long. It turns out that children look sooner and longer at the video that matches the speech input.

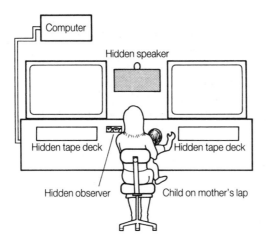

Figure 2.3.4 *Apparatus for the preferential looking experiments. (Reproduced from Naigles, 1990, with permission of* Journal of Child Learning, *published by Cambridge University Press.)*

In a first demonstration relevant to the syntactic bootstrapping hypothesis, Hirsh-Pasek *et al.* (1985) showed that seventeen-month-old children—many of whom had never put two words together in an utterance and knew few if any verbs—understand some facts about the semantic values of English constructions. Two simultaneous videos showed cartoon characters known to the children interacting. For some subjects, the stimulus sentence was *Big Bird is tickling Cookie Monster*. For the others, it was *Cookie Monster is tickling Big Bird*. The children demonstrated by their preferential looking that they knew which sentence described which observed event: They looked longer at the screen showing Big Bird tickling Cookie Monster when they heard the former sentence and at the screen showing Cookie Monster tickling Big Bird when they heard the latter sentence. That is, these children recognize the order of phrases (or something approximating phrases) within the heard sentences and also understand the semantic significance of the ordering for the propositional interpretation of English speech (see Slobin and Bever, 1982, for cross-linguistic evidence on this topic). Note that in this and all other experiments I shall be describing, all the depicted participants are animate, so there is no room for trivializing interpretations such as the strategy of assigning the animate entity to the subject position.

My colleagues and I (Hirsh-Pasek *et al.*, 1988) used this same procedure to investigate one more property of the mapping rules, namely the causative structure for which Bowerman (1974) had found many innovative uses by youngsters: Roughly, intransitive motion verbs (e.g., *Big Bird turns*) can be "transitivized" in English and then will express the causal agent as well (*Cookie Monster turns Big Bird*).

To study this question using the preferential looking method, it is necessary that both entities appear in the stimulus sentence; otherwise the children may use the relatively trivial strategy of looking at the stimulus showing Big Bird if and only if Big Bird is mentioned. Hence, the stimuli used were, for example, *Big Bird is turning Cookie Monster* and *Big Bird is turning with Cookie Monster*. One video showed the two characters turning side by side, and the other video showed one character physically causing the other to turn. In addition to verbs like *turn* that were known to the 2-year-old subjects, unknown ones (by maternal report) were also used. For example, the characters were shown crossing their arms back and forth, or one crossing the arms of the other, along with the stimuli *Big Bird is flexing with Cookie Monster* and *Big Bird is flexing Cookie Monster*. At age twenty-seven months, almost every child tested showed the effect of the structure by looking longest at the syntactically congruent screen.

The conclusions to be drawn are very important ones for the syntactic bootstrapping hypothesis. The paired *actions* are the same, for example, both are of turning in a circle or both are of crossing the arms. What differs is whether a causal agent of that action is also present in that scene. The children seem to know that only the transitive use of the verb can be expressing that cause. More strongly, that causal agent cannot be in an oblique argument position (the *with* phrase). Most strongly of all, they appear to realize that the *with* phrase excludes a transitive reading. This implies that toddlers who are primitive in their own speech are doing an astonishing amount of parsing of the speech of others and are interpreting the structures semantically.

Prior demonstrations of knowledge of mapping rules have generally been with much older children. For instance, Bowerman noted that most spontaneous overgeneralizations of the causative structure ("Don't eat the baby!") are later, in the 3- to 5-year-old period. Pinker and his colleagues have offered many compelling demonstrations of a variety of mapping rules but again mainly with 3- to 5-year-olds (e.g., Pinker, Lebeaux, and Frost, 1987).[12] These findings give general support to the idea that learners recruit the semantic/syntactic correlations somewhere during the course of learning. But the early appearance of these skills is crucial as support for the notion that the child has the mapping rules under control early enough for them to contribute to the acquisition of the verb meanings themselves. As just described, we have documented that twenty-seven-month-olds have these capabilities.

Investigations of syntactic bootstrapping

So far I have tried to show that a number of presuppositions of syntactic bootstrapping are reasonable: The language does exhibit strong and stable syntactic/semantic correlations, and these powerfully predict adult classificatory behavior; infants in the prelinguistic period can and do parse sentences to recover the analyses required for extracting subcategorization frame information; such phrasal information is a requirement for language learning, at least for adults in the artificial language-learning laboratory; children at a very young age and language-learning stage understand the semantic values of at least some syntactic frames.

All of these findings were prolegomena to the syntactic bootstrapping approach. They were adduced because it is critical to determine that the child can come up with the analyses that the position presupposes. But now that I have presented at least some preliminary support that children can meet these prior requirements, the next question is: Do they use syntactic evidence to decide on the meaning of a new word?

Basic findings

The first, and justly famous, work on this topic was done by Roger Brown (1957). He showed 3- to 5-year-olds a picture in which, say, spaghetti-like stuff was being poured into a vessel. This scene was always the same one, but some of the children were asked to show *some blick*, others *a blick*, and still others *blicking*. The children's choices were, respectively, the spaghetti, the vessel, and the action. Evidently, the semantic core of the word classes affects the conjecture about the aspect of the scene in view *that is being labeled linguistically*.

Brown's results, though alluded to respectfully, just sat there for twenty years or so because, in this respect as in many others, Brown was a theorist ahead of his time. Eventually Macnamara took up and advanced these ideas: In his important 1972 paper, he argued forcefully for the place of language structure in language acquisition. Experimentally, Katz, Baker, and Macnamara (1974) showed that children as young as eighteen months used the structure in which new nouns appeared (*a gorp* vs. *Gorp*) to decide whether a new word encoded a class or an individual (i.e., a doll of the gorpish sort or some doll named Gorp). Thus the lexical category assignments of words were shown to carry semantic implications, and these were evidently recruited by learners to deduce the aspect of the world being encoded by the new word.

Naigles (1990), working in my lab and also in the labs of Hirsh-Pasek at Temple University and of Golinkoff at the University of Delaware, extended this kind of demonstration to the case of verb learning (i.e., to the usefulness of syntax for drawing semantic inferences within a single lexical category), thus giving the first direct demonstration of syntactic bootstrapping at work.

Children (mean age twenty-four months) were again put into the preferential looking situation. This time, however, their task was to decide between two utterly disjoint interpretations of a new verb. In the training (learning) period, they saw a single screen and the following mad event: A rabbit is pushing a duck down into a squatting position with his left hand (these were people dressed up as rabbits and ducks so they did have hands). The duck pops up, and the rabbit pushes him down again, and so on. Simultaneously, both rabbit and duck are making big circles in the air with their right arms. Some children heard a voice say *The rabbit is gorping the duck* and other children heard *The rabbit and the duck are gorping* as they watched this scene.

Subsequent to this observation, two new videos appeared on two screens, as shown in Figure 2.3.4. On one screen, the rabbit was pushing the duck down (but with no arm-wheeling). On the other screen, rabbit and duck were wheeling their arms (but with no squatting or forcing to squat). The child then was cued by the voice saying the (syntactically uninformative) sentences *Where's gorping now? Find gorping!* The child's looking time at the screens as a function of her syntactic introducing circumstances was recorded (double-blind as usual, i.e., neither the mother nor the experimenters knew which event was being depicted on the child's left and which was on her right during the test).

Naigles's result was that virtually every infant tested—and there were many, this being a Ph.D. thesis—showed the effect of the syntactic introducing circumstance. Those who heard the transitive sentence apparently concluded that *gorp* means "force-to-squat." Those who heard the intransitive sentence decided that *gorp* means "wheel the arms."[13]

What shall we conclude from this experiment? Clearly the child uses the event context in some way to license conjectures about a verb meaning. But in this case, "The Main Event" is ambiguous not only in principle but in fact. Under these trying circumstances, at least, the learner attends to the information potential of the semantically relevant syntactic evidence. The position I have tried to defend is that the zoom-lens effect of the structural context is critical for vocabulary learning in the real world of multiply interpretable scenes and events.

Notice also what *should not* be concluded from this experiment. Whatever the real power of syntactic bootstrapping when the child is provided with a set of frames for some verb, that full power was not exploited in the present experiment. Only the usefulness of a single syntactic property as disambiguator was tested. Therefore, even if (as I doubt very much) there is enough information in the subcategorization frames of a language to distinguish between "squat" meanings and "wheel" meanings, there certainly is not enough evidence in one or two frames to make this distinction. The verb meanings, insofar as they were acquired at all in this experiment, were learned by inspecting the real-world contingencies, much as Pinker has suggested. But as so often—just about always, if I am right—there was a choice in this situation for how to conceive the scene semantically. How is this choice adjudicated? What Naigles showed was that the syntactic evidence guides the child observer, determining the choice among situationally available options.

A question of scope

So far the experiments I have mentioned have lingered nervously around a few constructions, for example, the lexical causative in English, which is a notorious focus of syntactic extension by adults as well as children. Even if it is accepted that children sometimes do use syntactic evidence to bolster their semantic conjectures, how broad can the scope of such a procedure be? Maybe its role is just to clean up a few little details that are hard to glean from the world—just reverse linking, as Pinker has sometimes put the matter. To investigate the real scope of children's exploitation of the syntactic environment in learning new verb meanings, my colleagues and I have now studied 3- and 4-year-old learners. Let me first suggest why we have now turned to this older population.

The studies I have described so far, performed with children 2 years old and younger, yield evidence that satisfies an explanatory demand of this approach: The bootstrapping procedure has to be able to operate very early in the child's linguistic life, else its role is restricted to a late and ancillary method for refining the observation-based conjectures. But the preferential looking paradigm (which is one of very few that work with toddlers) is too much of a straitjacket to be the only vehicle for investigation of this approach. It is tedious in the extreme to set up (requiring the preparation of movies, etc.), takes hoards of infants to carry out (for some scream or sleep or worse and have to be removed from the premises; and only a few trials can be presented even to the more docile infants). Moreover, it is likely that children's knowledge of the linking rules expands as their language knowledge grows, creating more latitude within which they can learn new meanings from linguistic evidence. (After all, in the end we can do it by looking in the dictionary.)

So now that it has been shown (in Naigles's work) that the use of syntax in verb learning begins very early, certainly by twenty-four months, it is reasonable to refine and expand such findings in studies of older—but still very young—learners. Specifically, Fisher *et al.* (1989) asked whether 3- and 4-year-olds would give us meanings in response to linguistic-situational stimuli upon request. The idea derived from a manipulation attempted by Marantz (1982). He had asked whether children are as quick to learn noncanonical as canonical mappings of semantics onto syntax. He introduced children to novel verbs as they watched a movie. For instance, one movie showed a man pounding on a book with his elbow. Marantz's question was whether children were as quick to learn that *The book is moaking Larry* (the noncanonical mapping) was a way of describing this scene as that *Larry is moaking the book* (the canonical mapping) was a way of describing the scene.

Although the manipulation was an interesting one, unfortunately Marantz never asked the children how they interpreted the scene, so his results are not really relevant to understanding the child's perception of syntactic/semantic correlations. That is, Marantz *presupposed* that a scene viewed has only a single interpretation, an idea I have strenuously opposed throughout this discussion. We now revised this experiment, changing the measure so we could find out about the child's comprehension in these circumstances. In essence, we asked how the nonsense word is interpreted within differing linguistic environments.

As a first step, we showed the *moaking* scene (in which Larry pounds the book with his elbow) to adults. If we said, "This scene can be described as a moaking scene" and then asked them what /moak/ meant, they said "pounding." And if instead we showed them the scene and said, "This is Larry moaking the book," they still asserted that /moak/ means "pound." But when we showed them the scene and said, "This is the book moaking Larry," they answered that /moak/ means "hurt."

This suggests that adults make use of the fact that particular surface syntactic structures are associated with particular semantic values. They seem to bootstrap the meaning from examination of the scene taken together with its syntactic expression, just as the syntactic bootstrapping procedure claims. To be sure, the contextless presentation of /moak/ with this scene irresistibly yields the concept "pound" as its interpretation. So there is much to be said for the idea of *salience* in the interpretation of events (though, to be sure, no one knows *what* exactly). But the important point is that there is a categorical shift in interpretation of the same scene—to a less salient, but still possible, interpretation—in response to its linguistic setting; namely, "pound" if Larry is in the subject position, but "hurt" if the book is in that position.

Fisher *et al.* (1989) now adapted this procedure for children. We took advantage of the idea, popularized by such Penn developmentalists as Waxman, Gelman, Macario, and Massey, that preschoolers will do just about anything to help out a puppet. We introduced a puppet saying, "This puppet sometimes talks puppet-talk so I can't understand him; can you help figure out what he means?" Our sixteen 4-year-old subjects were happy to oblige. They were shown videotaped scenes in which animals were performing certain acts. For example, a rabbit appeared, looked to the left, and then ran rapidly off the screen toward the right. Directly behind the rabbit ran a skunk, also disappearing at the right. So this scene is one that can be interpreted as either one of chasing or of fleeing. Then the child would hear the puppet say either "The rabbit is gorping the skunk" or else "The skunk is gorping the rabbit."

The scenes/structures we investigated were designed to ask whether children are sensitive to a variety of syntactic cues to interpretation. These are shown in Table 2.3.4. The first property investigated was the number of argument positions (Stimuli 1 and 2). For instance, rabbit and elephant are shown eating/feeding and the puppet says either "The rabbit moaks" or "The elephant moaks the rabbit." The second property was canonical structural positions of agent and patient (Stimuli 3 and 4, e.g., *ride/carry*), and the third was the structural positions taken together with prepositional markers of the oblique roles (Stimuli 5 and 6, e.g., *give/take*). Thus we now began to investigate the scope of the structural/semantic linkages to which learners may be sensitive.

The pairs chosen were designed to be revealing of solutions to the problem that I have discussed throughout: Single scenes, multiply interpretable, are shown but accompanied by a novel verb; this verb is introduced to half of the children in one construction and to the other half in another construction.

Table 2.3.4   *Scenarios and their sentential descriptions*

Scenario	Sentence
1. (a) Rabbit eating.	The rabbit moaks.
(b) Elephant feeding rabbit.	The elephant moaks the rabbit.
2. (a) Monkey pushing elephant.	The monkey pumes the elephant.
(b) Elephant falling.	The elephant pumes.
3. (a) Monkey riding elephant.	The monkey gorms the elephant.
(b) Elephant carrying monkey.	The elephant gorms the monkey.
4. (a) Rabbit fleeing skunk.	The rabbit zarps the skunk.
(b) Skunk chasing rabbit.	The skunk zarps the rabbit.
5. (a) Rabbit giving a ball to elephant.	The rabbit ziffs a ball to the elephant.
(b) Elephant taking a ball from rabbit.	The elephant ziffs a ball from the rabbit.
6. (a) Skunk putting blanket on monkey.	The skunk is biffing a blanket on the monkey.
(b) Skunk covering monkey with a blanket.	The skunk is biffing the monkey with a blanket.

Note: All children were exposed to the same six scenes (each scene has two plausible interpretations, called (a) and (b) in the left-hand column). Along with these scenes, half of the children heard (a) stimulus sentences and half heard (b) stimulus sentences (with appropriate counterbalancing across children and stimuli).

The question is whether the introducing syntactic environment enables the observing child to fix on a single meaning for the novel verb.

The outcomes of this experiment were extremely strong. Not every young child responded to each scene/sentence example (sometimes they said something irrelevant or just looked piteously at the experimenter). But when they did respond, their guess was guided heavily by the syntactic frame. For instance, consider the scene in which the rabbit appears to flee, pursued by a skunk. Six (of eight) children who heard the puppet say "The rabbit zarps the skunk" said that /zarp/ means "run away," while only one guessed "chase"; the eighth child did not respond. Symmetrically, all eight who heard "The skunk zarps the rabbit" said that /zarp/ means "chase." Of the eighty-four relevant responses made by these children, seventy-one were congruent with the semantic value implied by the syntactic structure and only thirteen were inconsistent with the structural information, a statistically highly reliable result. Moreover, *for each child, for each scene, and for each syntactic type*, the number of syntactically congruent responses was greater than the noncongruent responses. The level of congruence (about 85 percent) was approximately the same for all three semantic/syntactic relations studied.

One might object that these children were merely paraphrasing verbs that they previously knew to occur in these syntactic environments. That is true, but it does not take away seriously from our interpretation of these findings: Evidently, the children knew that the appropriate meaningful verb had to be one that fitted both with the scene and with the sentence structure heard. This is the reverse of Pinker's claim that the verb meanings must be acquired by extra linguistic observation *in advance of*, and as the basis for, deducing their appropriate syntactic structures. But the results are exactly those expected in the syntactic bootstrapping approach. The syntax guides the choice of interpretive options in ambiguous observational circumstances. As just about all observational circumstances are ambiguous, I believe this is saying a lot about the explanatory value of the learning procedure proposed.

The input

One of several holes in our present evidence has to do with the characteristics of caretaker speech. I have presented a single example corpus (Table 2.3.2) tending to support the idea that caretaker speech is rich enough to yield quite a full range of structures to support a strong variant of the syntactic bootstrapping procedure. And this corpus was for a mother speaking to a blind child, whose word-learning situation may be quite special. We are now analyzing an extensive corpus of mother–child speech in a naturalistic setting (originally collected by Landau and Gleitman) to see whether children characteristically receive the range of structures adequate to support a realistic syntax-based procedure (Lederer, Gleitman, and Gleitman, 1989). So far, the prospects from this larger database look good. Lederer *et al* found that each of the twenty-four verbs most often used by these mothers to their children has a distinctive syntactic distribution. When the usages are pooled across mothers, these distinctions are preserved unmuddied.

The next question is whether the syntactic distributions culled from maternal speech map coherently onto the target semantic space (namely, the semantic space as known by adults). An independent assessment of the *adult* semantic relations among these verbs is required as the evidence. As a first pass, Lederer, Gleitman, and Gleitman (1989) investigated these verbs in the kind of manipulation employed by Fisher, Gleitman, and Gleitman (1991), namely asking adult subjects for judgments of the semantic outlier in all triads of these verbs. The question of interest, of course, concerns the correlation between the semantic similarity space as it emerges from these adult triad judgments and the overlaps and nonoverlaps in the syntactic behavior of the verbs in the maternal corpora (both these similarity spaces are extracted from the data by a cluster analysis). These correlations turn out to be massive and highly reliable, with the maternal subcategorization patterns accounting for about 50 percent of the variance in the adult triad patterns. Considering the roughness of the semantic analysis to which the maternal speech was submitted in this first test, I consider these findings to be the strongest evidence thus far in demonstrating the general feasibility and power of syntactic bootstrapping.

Part III: Conclusions

I began discussion by acknowledging the intuitive power of Locke's view that words are learned by noticing the real-world contingencies for their use. Then I tried to show that such a word-to-world mapping, unaided, was in principle insufficiently constrained to answer the question of how the child matches the verb items with their meanings. The solution that I and my colleagues have offered is that semantically relevant information in the syntactic structures can rescue observational learning from the sundry experiential pitfalls that threaten it. This theory, of course, is the very opposite of intuitive. But when probable solutions fail, less probable ones deserve to be considered. I therefore sketched a rather wide-ranging empirical review that we have undertaken to see whether, after all, children might not be deducing some of the meanings from their knowledge of structural/semantic relations. I believe that the evidence we now have in hand materially strengthens the plausibility of the viewpoint.

Still, the conclusions that can be drawn currently about the generality and pervasiveness of syntactic bootstrapping must be exceedingly tentative, on a variety of grounds. Some of these I have discussed: No one has more than a glimmer of an idea about just how the verb lexicon is organized semantically, and therefore we cannot be very precise about the semantic information potential of the frame specifications. Also, we have at present only the most meager data concerning the orderliness and richness of the child's syntactic input. Facts about cross-linguistic similarities in the syntax/semantics correspondences are even more fragmentary.

Moreover, the position I have tried to defend is that the *range* of frames associated with each verb, operating jointly, narrows the hypothesis space for the verb meaning to such a degree that the faltering and probabilistic observational mapping of words to their meanings can succeed. But the experiments with children that I have reported show only the effects of single frames in the presence of multiply interpretable scenes. These demonstrate the focusing (zoom-lens) power of the syntax for disambiguating aspects of those scenes. But the stronger version of this hypothesis—that the meaning of the verb falls out directly from the range of frame specifications—has yet to receive direct experimental review and confirmation. The accumulating power provided by joint operation of frame/verb relations was inferred for the blind child only by showing that the database provided by the mother was rich and restrictive enough to support such an analysis (see Figure 2.3.3), should the child have been inclined to perform it; Lederer's studies are designed to generalize such a conclusion about the database. In addition, the triad studies with adults (Fisher, Gleitman, and Gleitman, 1991) show that the range of frames associated with verbs is powerfully correlated with a global semantic space that people construct when asked to sort verbs according to their semantic similarity.

Despite these encouraging initial results, what is still required is direct evidence of the semantic resolving power of the complete frame sets associated with particular verbs, for children and adults. Though inquiries on this matter are on our experimental agenda, evidence is not now available, except in the form of parlor games popular in our lab: For intellectuals playing games, at least, and for selected verbs, it is possible to guess which verb an individual has in mind by inspection of a set of frames presented as a sequence of phrasal category labels (under some strong assumptions, i.e., that the frames stand in entailment relations to each other). The appropriate experimental review has yet to be carried out in these terms, so it remains in question just how much of the burden of observational learning can be reduced by the learner's attention to syntactic evidence.

In addition, there are numerous problems with our analyses of input corpora that I have altogether skirted so far. For example, it is not an easy task to decide which structures co-occurring with verbs should actually be considered part of the frame specifications and which are merely adjuncts. To construct Table 2.3.2 (and in Lederer's ongoing work) we had to make some choices, but some of them may be wrong. And if we had these problems in assigning structural descriptions to the mother's utterances, is the learner not similarly beset?[14]

Another problem is the idiomatic verb uses that I mentioned in passing (Note 10, e.g., *John saw his victim out of the room, John looked his enemies in the eye*). It may be significant that these monstrosities are just about totally absent from the maternal corpora we have examined, but absence in fact rather than in principle is a pretty weak reed on which to build so strong a position as the one I have tried to defend.

The largest problem of all is how learners acquire the semantic/syntactic linking rules in the first place. Bowerman's evidence, and all the findings I have just discussed, are understandable only (so far as I can see) by asserting that learners are in possession of such linking rules. But where did they come from? In the present discussion, I have subscribed to a version of Jackendoff's hypothesis that the linking rules are somehow cognitively transparent to the child. But because there is at least *some* cross-linguistic variance in such syntactic/semantic regularities (see Talmy, 1985), I admit that I should be happier to find that they could be derived from some more primitive categories or functions. The problems here cry out for serious investigation.

In light of the various issues just mentioned, one must remain agnostic about both of the bootstrapping proposals, at present. But I hope I have persuaded you that the prospects they open for explanation of the verb-learning feat are enticing enough to make continued investigation seem worthwhile.

It remains to point out that, by their nature, both semantic and syntactic bootstrapping are perilous and errorful procedures, and their explanatory power must be evaluated with this additional proviso in mind. Bowerman's children, drawing syntactic conclusions from meaningful overlap, are sometimes wrong; for instance, one cannot, but children sometimes do, say, "Daddy giggled me."

To take another kind of case, *exit, enter, reach,* and *touch* differ from most verbs describing directed motion through space in not requiring prepositional phrases to express the motion paths (compare *come into the room* but *enter the room*). One outcome of this varying mapping of meaning onto form is errorful learning (the child may say, "I touched on your arm") and its end point, language change (while *exit the stage* was the more common in Shakespeare's time, *exit from the stage* is now on the ascendancy). But syntactic bootstrapping is subject to related kinds of error. For instance, children in the learning period may exchange *push* and *pull,* and *infer* and *imply* have come to be used interchangeably by many adults, perhaps because their syntactic (as well as situational) overlap is misleading. Short of changing the language, how do learners recover from such errors?

The position I have been urging is that children usually succeed in ferreting out the forms and the meanings of the language just because they can play off these two imperfect and insufficient databases (the saliently interpretable events and the syntactically interpreted utterances) against each other to derive the best fit between them. Neither syntactic nor semantic bootstrapping works all the time, nor taken together do they answer all the questions about how children acquire the verb vocabulary and argument structures. But I have tried to show that each of these procedures works very well indeed when it does work, so the wise child should, and probably does, make use of both of them.

Acknowledgments

I thank quite a few colleagues who helped me in the preparation of this article. The first is my husband, Henry Gleitman, who—as always—contributed a large share of the ideas and most of whatever organization and coherence this article contains. Anne Lederer has also been a crucial aid in offering significant ideas, and also helped with a good deal of bureaucratic labor. I had the advantage of discussing the ideas contained herein with Paul Bloom, Noam Chomsky, and Steven Pinker. I also thank several colleagues who read earlier drafts of the article and gave me important comments. These were Adele Abrahamson, Steven Crain, Cynthia Fisher, Roberta Golinkoff, Kathy Hirsh-Pasek, Barbara Landau, Letitia Naigles, Elissa Newport, Thomas Roeper, and Kenneth Wexler. My thanks go as well to Richard Beckwith, who kindly sent me preliminary data and commentary from his work for use in my discussion. The approach described herein was developed in collaboration with a number of colleagues whose work is cited throughout the text. I want also to express appreciation for a University of Pennsylvania Biomedical Research Grant (sponsored by the National Institute of Health under Grant #2-S07-RR-07803-23), which underwrote the more recent experimental work.

Notes to 2.3

1. This is a large simplification of the learning problem for vocabulary, to be sure. It is not likely that learning in this regard is always and only a matter of mapping the words heard onto a preset and immutable set of concepts priorly available to the prelinguistic child. Rather, there is bound to be some degree of interaction between the categories lexicalized in a language and the child's conceptual organization; moreover, that conceptual organization is changing during the period of vocabulary growth, to some degree affecting the nature of lexical entries (for discussion, see Carey, 1985; Pinker, 1989). For present purposes, however, I abstract away from this intriguing class of problems.

2. It is important to be clear about the sense in which many modern theorists seem close to Locke in their position: They believe the ambient environment in which words are heard is used as the primary—perhaps the sole—early basis for forming conjectures about the meanings. But it is just as important to note that Pinker and other recent commentators differ radically from the British Empiricists in almost all other respects. Particularly, Locke held—or is usually read to have held—that the vocabulary in which the description of the environment is couched is sensory. In contrast, modern perspectives often assert that children approach the task of interpreting the world equipped with a very smart perceptual system, as well as sophisticated mental models of the current situation, a belief—desire psychology, a naive physics, more or less correct intuitive theories of semantics and pragmatics, and schemas for possible word meanings. And a couple of generations of inquiry in psychology generally support such an enriched view of the child's mental status as word learning begins. All this sophisticated representational apparatus in obvious ways puts the modern child in a vastly better position to fathom the world than Locke's child. Yet, in some perhaps less obvious ways that I shall be discussing, the increased representational power makes it harder rather than easier to learn the word meanings from observation of their environmental contingencies.

3. A related difference holds for the color words. Sighted children of 4 and 5 years map the color words onto observed hues in the world while blind children ask for help. Perhaps they think the property is stipulative. Asked "Why are the flowers in the woods pink?" one blind child responded, "Because we *name* them pink!" They know these are attributes predictable only of physical objects (they say that an idea cannot be green because "it's only in your head"), but they do not know what the real-world dimension may be. Interestingly, they avoid some choices that their extralinguistic experience appears to make available, for example, that color terms refer to sizes of objects (Landau and Gleitman, 1985, Chapter 8).

4. Notice that we couched the child's representation of the environmental distinction in sensory—perceptual terms (the object is "nearby" or "far away" as the action begins). But the child's representational terminology might instead—or in addition—be "object starts at a nearby/distant *source*." That is, conceptions of these locations as sources and goals of the action rather than physical locations and movements constituting the action might be closer to the child's real representations of the events perceived. Indeed, many others who have coded maternal speech and its context have preferred this latter terminology, which will serve as well in our case, too. The point is that for present purposes the labeling does not matter at all, for the coding imposed will be the same in either case. Note also that the near/far analysis can succeed at all only if the child can determine the discourse addressee. This assumption is plausible because in these transcripts the mother's speech is over 90 percent about the "here-and-now," and in over 90 percent of instances the addressee is the child herself.

5. As so often, Chomsky (1982) set the problem with great clarity:

> The claim we're making about primitive notions is that if data were presented in such a way that these primitives couldn't be applied to it directly, prelinguistically before you have a grammar, then language couldn't be learnt. ... And the more unrealistic it is to think of concepts as having those properties, the more unrealistic it is to regard them as primitives. ... We have to assume that there are some prelinguistic notions which can pick out pieces of the world, say elements of this meaning and this sound. (p. 119)

The analysis of Table 2.3.1 is an attempt to see how far some small set of observational primitives, known experimentally to be available to infants, could get them in extracting a simple meaning feature ("haptic") for assignment to certain verbs.

6. Some ideas for pruning the observational database into a more manageable form for learning have been suggested. Usually these involve ways of filtering out input that is complex by some semantic, structural, or processing criterion (for early attempts, see Newport, Gleitman, and Gleitman, 1977; Shipley, Smith, and Gleitman, 1969). However, the number and nontransparency of the categories that these preanalyses require often seem more troublesome than the problem that they were designed to simplify. Here is an example from Pinker (1984); the task discussed is discovery of exemplars of the (innate) property *subject* from their semantic/pragmatic environmental correlates; the problem addressed is that in many situations those correlates will be absent. I have italicized the linguistic and situational categories in terms of which, according to Pinker, the child is to construct a database suitable for finding the subject exemplars.

> The semantic properties of subject hold only in basic sentences: roughly, those that are *simple, active, affirmative, declarative, pragmatically neutral,* and *minimally presuppositional.* ... The parents ... or the child might filter out nonbasic sentences from the input using various contextual or phonological diagnostics of nonbasicness such as *special intonation, extra marking of the verb, presuppositions set up by the preceding discourse or the context, nonlinguistic signals of the interrogative* or *negative illocutionary force of an utterance,* and *so on.* (p. 47)

7. These results cannot be written off on grounds of the differential frequency of these words in the input corpus, for if the frequencies are changed, the level of categorization does not. For instance, in some houses *Fido* is a more frequent word than *dog*, but in that case the youngest children think that the sound /fido/ means "dog" (Rescorla, 1980).

8. Once Landau and Gleitman embarked on this path, several colleagues (Adele Abrahamson, Paul Bloom, and Henry Gleitman, whom we thank for this observation), asked why we restricted ourselves to subcategorization frames as the source of linguistic evidence recruited by the child, rather than going whole hog for all the kinds of internal evidence potentially available across the sentence. For instance, the child could (and probably does) use selectional restrictions to narrow down the choice of verb meaning, for example, if you know that shrimp have veins, that might help achieve an interpretation of /devein/ in "Devein that shrimp!" (Compare *Devein that pencil!). Our answer was our usual one: For syntactic as well as for semantic categories, our aim was to see how far some extremely restrictive analysis could serve to handle the facts about verb learning. The most plausible choice was the subcategorization frames, which appear to vary with the meaningfully distinct predicates (for a useful discussion, see Wasow, 1985). As children open up to further data sources, they simultaneously increase the complexity of the data manipulations required. Nonetheless, I must agree that the kind of "linguistic inference" (Bloom's term) suggested by these commentators is sure to be part of the final story on vocabulary acquisition.

9. Pinker (1984) actually reserved the term *semantic bootstrapping* for machinery that assigns words to lexical categories. For expository convenience, however, I take the liberty of using this expression to refer to his proposals at their broadest for extracting verb meanings from extralinguistic context.

10. The exceptions are (a) if you believe in psychokinesis such that your looking can move objects, or (b) if the rules of some game make it so that, in effect, an external agent *can* cause an object to move by looking at it, for example, *The shortstop looked the runner back to second base.* Once *look* does mean "cause-to-move-by-perceptually-exploring," it becomes comfortable in this construction. That is, the subcategorization frames, just because they are associated with particular truth values, are a prime linguistic vehicle for the extension of verb meanings and are so used by adults as well as by child learners. Of course, these simple examples vastly underestimate the detail required if these structural properties are to be used for learning purposes. One such problem is that a child must impose the proper parse on the sentence heard, lest *John saw the book on the table* be taken as a counter-example (that is, the analysis is to be of sister nodes under the verb phrase only, and a theory of how the child determines such configurations antecedently is a requirement of the position). Another real difficulty concerns

how children should respond when they run into quirky constructions like *John saw his brother out of the room, John looked his uncle in the eye.*

11. Notoriously, word segmentation in a language like English is so fraught with ambiguity that new pronunciations (e.g., *nother* and *apron* replacing *other* and *napron*) are quite common. Moreover, there are long-lasting segmentation errors by children, for example, one 6-year-old wrote, "The teacher said, Class be smissed!" The phrasal parses suggested by Gleitman and Wanner were rudimentary to the extent that the unstressed elements in the phrases were presumed to be less well analyzed than the stressed elements, and the phrases were unlabeled (but see Joshi and Levy, 1982, for evidence that much of labeling, or its equivalent, can be derived from "skeletal" representations in which there are configurations but no overt labels).

12. But see also Naigles, Gleitman, and Gleitman (in press) for a demonstration that 2-year-olds understand the significance of new motion transitives, even though they may not be brave enough to invent any until they are 3. The children here were asked to act out scenes using a Noah's Ark and its animal inhabitants. For instance, the child might be told to act out "Noah brings the elephant to the ark." But some of the stimuli were more unusual, for example, "Noah comes the elephant to the ark" or "The elephant brings to the ark." The children by their acting-out performances showed that they thought transitive *come* means "bring" and that intransitive *bring* means "come."

13. In the present experiment, the intransitive sentence contained a conjoined nominal (*The duck and the rabbit*) and this might be seen as a defect: Maybe the child knows the difference between a preverbal and a postverbal nominal rather than the difference between a transitive and an intransitive structure. This interpretation is effectively excluded by the version presented earlier (Hirsh-Pasek, Gleitman, *et al.*, 1988) in which the two noun phrases appear in different argument positions, one serially before and one after the verb (*Big Bird is turning with Cookie Monster*). For elegance, however, it certainly would be nice to redo the present experiment with the stimulus type used in the former one.

14. Lederer and Kelly (1989) are now testing whether prosodic distinctions typically disambiguate the readings of sentences in this regard. Pilot laboratory results suggest that native speakers distinguish their pronunciations of ambiguous sentences depending on whether the adjunct or complement reading is intended; native listeners correctly guess which reading was intended about 80 percent of the time. As "motherese" is characterized by exaggerated intonation contours, and infants show strong preference for this style of speech (Fernald *et al.*, 1989), it is likely that children have a physical basis for distinguishing these boundary types.

References to 2.3

Acredolo, L. and Evans, D. (1980). "Developmental changes in the effects of landmarks on infant spatial behavior." *Developmental Psychology*, **16**, 312–18.

Armstong, S., Gleitman, L. R., and Gleitman, H. (1983). "What some concepts might not be." *Cognition*, **13**, 263–308.

Baillargeon, R., Spelke, E., and Wasserman, S. (1985). "Object permanence in 5-month old infants." *Cognition*, **20**, 191–208.

Ball, W. and Vurpillot, E. (1976). "Perception of movement in depth in infancy." *L'Année Psychologique*, **76**, 383–91.

Beckwith, R., Tinker, E., and Bloom, L. (1989, October). *The Acquisition of Non-basic Sentences*. Paper presented at the Boston Child Language Conference, Boston.

Berwick, R. C. (1982). *The Acquisition of Syntactic Knowledge*. Cambridge, MA: MIT Press.

Bornstein, M. H. (1975). "Qualities of color vision in infancy." *Journal of Experimental Child Psychology*, **19**, 401–19.

Bowerman, M. (1974). "Learning the structure of causative verbs: A study in the relationship of cognitive, semantic, and syntactic development." *Proceedings of Research in Child Language Development*, **8**, 142–78.

Bowerman, M. (1982). "Evaluating competing linguistic models with language acquisition data: Implications of developmental errors." *Quaderni di Semantica*, **III**, 5–66.

Brown, R. (1957). "Linguistic determinism and the parts of speech." *Journal of Abnormal and Social Psychology*, **55**, 1–5.

Bruner, J. S. (1974/1975). "From communication to language: A psychological perspective." *Cognition*, **3**, 255–87.

Carey, S. (1978). "The child as word learner." In M. Halle, J. Bresnan, and G. Miller (eds), *Linguistic Theory and Psychological Reality*. Cambridge, MA: MIT Press, 264–93.

Carey, S. (1985). *Conceptual Change in Childhood*. Cambridge, MA: MIT Press, Bradford Books.

Chomsky, N. (1959). "Review of B. F. Skinner, *Verbal Behavior*." *Language*, 35, 26–58.

Chomsky, N. (1975). *Reflections on Language*. New York: Random House.

Chomsky, N. (1981). *Lectures on Government and Binding*. Dordrecht, Holland: Foris.

Chomsky, N. (1982). *Noam Chomsky on the Generative Enterprise: A discussion with R. Hybregts & H. van Riemsdijk*. Dordrecht, Holland: Foris.

Clark, E. V. (1988). "On the logic of contrast." *Journal of Child Language*, **15**, 327–35.

Cooper, W. E. and Paccia-Cooper, J. (1980). *Syntax and Speech*. Cambridge, MA: Harvard University Press.

Crain, S. and Fodor, J. D. (in press). "Competence and performance in child language." In E. Dromi (ed.), *Language and Cognition: A developmental perspective*. Norwood, NJ: Ablex.

Echols, C. H. and Newport, E. L. (1989). *The Role of Stress and Position in Determining First Words*. Unpublished manuscript, University of Rochester, Rochester, NY.

Fernald, A. (1984). "The perceptual and affective salience of mothers' speech to infants." In L. Feagans, C. Garvey, and R. Golinkoff (eds), *The Origins and Growth of Communication*. New Brunswick, NJ: Ablex.

Fernald, A., Taeschner, T., Dunn, J., Papousek, M., Boysson-Bardies, B., and Fukui, I. (1989). "A cross-language study of prosodic modifications in mothers' and fathers' speech to preverbal infants." *Journal of Child Language*, **16** 477–501.

Field, J. (1976). "Relation of young infant's reaching to stimulus distance and solidity." *Child Development*, **50**, 698–704.

Fillmore, C. (1968a). "The case for case." In E. Bach and R. Harms (eds), *Universals of Linguistic Theory*. New York: Holt, Rinehart & Winston, 1–91.

Fillmore, C. (1968b). "Lexical entries for verbs." *Foundations of Langue*, **4**, 373–93.

Fisher, C., Gleitman, H. and Gleitman, L. (1991). "Relationships between verb meanings and their syntactic structures." *Cognitive Psychology*, **23**, 331–92.

Fisher, C., Hall, G., Rakowitz, S., and Gleitman, L. (1989). *Verb-meaning Acquisition is Guided by Syntactic Evidence*. Unpublished manuscript, University of Pennsylvania, Philadelphia.

Fodor, J. A. (1981). "The present status of the innateness controversy." In J. A. Fodor (ed.), *Representations*. Cambridge, MA: MIT Press, 257–316.

Gibson, E. J. and Spelke, E. (1983). "The development of perception." In J. H. Flavell and E. Markman (eds), *Cognitive Development: Vol. III* P. Mussen (ed.), *Handbook of Child Psychology*. New York: Wiley, 1–76.

Gibson, E. J. and Walker, A. S. (1984). "Intermodal perception of substance." *Child Development*, **55**, 453–60.

Gleitman, L., Gleitman, H., Landau, B., and Wanner, E. (1987). "Where learning begins: Initial representations for language learning." In F. Newmeyer (ed.), *The Cambridge Linguistic Survey* (Vol. II). New York: Cambridge University Press, 150–93.

Gleitman, L. and Wanner, E. (1982). "Language acquisition: The state of the state of the art." In E. Wanner and L. Gleitman (eds), *Language Acquisition: The state of the art*. New York: Cambridge University Press, 1–50.

Gold, E. M. (1967). "Language identification in the limit." *Information and Control*, **10**, 447–74.

Golinkoff, R. M. (1986). "'I beg your pardon?': The preverbal negotiation of failed messages." *Journal of Child Language*, **13**, 455–76.

Golinkoff, R. M., Harding, C., Carlson, V., and Sexton, E. (1984). "The child's perception of causal events: The distinction between animate and inanimate objects." *Advances in Infancy Research*, **3**, 145–65.

Golinkoff, R. M., Hirsh-Pasek, P., Cauley, K., and Gordon, L. (1987). "The eyes have it: Lexical and syntactic comprehension in a new paradigm." *Journal of Child Language*, **14**, 23–46.

Grimshaw, J. (1981). "Form, function, and the language acquisition device." In C. L. Baker and J. J. McCarthy (eds), *The Logical Problem of Language Acquisition*. Cambridge, MA: MIT Press, 183–210.

Grimshaw, J. (1983). "Subcategorization and grammatical relations." In A. Zaenen (ed.), *Subjects and Other Subjects*. Bloomington: Indiana University Linguistics Club.

Gruber, J. S. (1968). "Look and see." *Language*, **43**, 937–47.

Hirsh-Pasek, K., Gleitman, H., Gleitman, L. R., Golinkoff, R., and Naigles, L. (1988, October). *Syntactic Bootstrapping: Evidence from comprehension*. Paper presented at Boston Language Conference, Boston.

Hirsh-Pasek, K., Golinkoff, R., Fletcher, A., DeGaspe Beaubien, F., and Cauley, K. (1985, October). *In the Beginning: One word speakers comprehend word order*. Paper presented at Boston Language Conference, Boston.

Hirsh-Pasek, K., Kemler-Nelson, D. G., Jusczyk, P. W., Wright, K., Cassidy, K., Druss, B., and Kennedy, B. (1987). "Clauses are perceptual units for young infants." *Cognition*, **26**, 269–86.

Jackendoff, R. (1978). "Grammar as evidence for conceptual structure." In M. Halle, J. Bresnan, and G. Miller (eds), *Linguistic Theory and Psychological Reality*. Cambridge, MA: MIT Press, 201–28.

Jackendoff, R. (1983). *Semantics and Cognition*. Cambridge, MA: MIT Press.

Jones, S., Landau, B., and Smith, L. (1986, April). *The Importance of Shape in Early Lexical Learning*. Paper presented to the Eastern Psychological Association, New York.

Joshi, A. K. and Levy, L. S. (1982). "Phrase structure trees bear more fruit than you would have thought." *American Journal of Computational Linguistics*, **8**, 1–12.

Jusczyk, P., Hirsh-Pasek, K., Kemler-Nelson, D., Kennedy, L., Woodward, A., and Piwoz, J. (1988). *Perception of Acoustic Correlates of Major Phrasal Units by Young Infants*. Unpublished manuscript, University of Oregon.

Katz, N., Baker, E., and Macnamara, J. (1974). "What's in a name? A study of how children learn common and proper names." *Child Development*, **45**, 469–73.

Keil, F. C. (1979). *Semantic and Conceptual Development*. Cambridge, MA: Harvard University Press.

Klatt, D. H. (1975). "Vowel lengthening is syntactically determined in connected discourse." *Journal of Phonetics*, **3**, 229–40.

Landau, B. and Gleitman, L. (1985). *Language and Experience: Evidence from the blind child*. Cambridge, MA: Harvard University Press.

Lasky, R. E. and Gogol, W. C. (1978). "The perception of relative motion by young infants." *Perception*, **7**, 617–23.

Lederer, A., Gleitman, L., and Gleitman, H. (1989, October). *Input to a Deductive Verb Acquisition Procedure*. Paper presented at the Boston Child Language Conference, Boston.

Lederer, A. and Kelly, M. (1989). *Prosodic Marking of the Adjunct/Complement Distinction*. Unpublished manuscript, University of Pennsylvania, Philadelphia.

Leslie, A. M. (1982). "The perception of causality in infants." *Perception*, **11**, 173–86.

Levin, B. (1985). "Lexical semantics in review: An introduction." In B. Levin (ed.), *Lexical Semantics in Review* (Lexicon Project Working Papers). Cambridge, MA: MIT Center for Cognitive Science.

Locke, J. (1964). *An Essay Concerning Human Understanding*. Cleveland: Meridian Books (original work published 1690).

Macnamara, J. (1972). "Cognitive basis for language learning in infants." *Psychological Review*, **79**, 1–13.

McCawley, J. D. (1968). "The role of semantics in a grammar." In E. Bach and R. Harms (eds), *Universals in Linguistic Theory*. New York: Holt, Rinehart and Winston, 125–70.

Marantz, A. (1982). "On the acquisition of grammatical relations." *Linguistische Berichte*, **80**, 32–69.

Markman, E. and Hutchinson, J. (1984). "Children's sensitivity to constraints on word meaning: Taxonomic vs. thematic relations." *Cognitive Psychology*, **16**, 1–27.

Morgan, J., Meier, R., and Newport, E. L. (1987). "Structural packaging in the input to language learning: Contributions of intonational and morphological marking of phrases to the acquisition of language." *Cognitive Psychology*, **19**, 498–550.

Morgan, J. and Newport, E. L. (1981). "The role of constituent structure in the induction of an artificial language." *Journal of Verbal Learning and Verbal Behavior*, **20**, 67–85.

Naigles, L. G. (1990). "Children use syntax to learn verb meanings." *Journal of Child Language*. **17**, 357–74.

Naigles, L. G., Gleitman, L., and Gleitman, H. (in press). "Children acquire word meaning components from syntactic evidence." In E. Dromi (ed.), *Language and Cognition: A developmental perspective*. Norwood, NJ: Ablex.

Newport, E. L. (1977). "Motherese: The speech of mothers to young children." In N. Castellan,

D. Pisoni, and G. Potts (eds), *Cognitive Theory* (Vol. II). Hillsdale, NJ: Lawrence Erlbaum Associates, Inc.

Newport, E. L., Gleitman, H., and Gleitman, L. (1977). "Mother, I'd rather do it myself: Some effects and noneffects of maternal speech style." In C. E. Snow and C. A. Ferguson (eds), *Talking to Children: Language input and acquisition.* Cambridge: Cambridge University Press, 109–50.

Pinker, S. (1984). *Languge Learnability and Language Development.* Cambridge, MA: Harvard University Press.

Pinker, S. (1987). "Resolving a learnability paradox in the acquisition of the verb lexicon." (Lexicon Project Working Papers 17). Cambridge, MA: MIT Center for Cognitive Science, 1–100.

Pinker, S. (1989). "Review of D. I. Slobin, *The Crosslinguistic Study of Language Acquisition.*" *Journal of Child Language,* **16,** 429–75.

Pinker, S., Lebeaux, D., and Frost, A. (1987). "Productivity and constraints in the acquisition of the passive." *Cognition,* **26,** 185–267.

Rescorla, L. (1980). "Overextension in early language development." *Journal of Child Language,* 7, 321–36.

Rosch, E., Mervis, C. B., Gray, W. D., Johnson, D. M., and Boyes-Braem, P. (1976). "Basic objects in natural categories." *Cognitive Psychology,* 8, 382–439.

Schreiber, P. A. (1987). "Prosody and structure in children's syntactic processing." In H. Horowitz and S. Samuels (eds), *Comprehending Oral and Written Language.* New York: Academic, 243–70.

Shipley, E., Smith, C., and Gleitman, L. R. (1969). "A study in the acquisition of language: Free responses to commands." *Language,* **45,** 322–42.

Slobin, D. I. and Bever, T. G. (1982). "Children use canonical sentence schemas: A crosslinguistic study of word order and inflections." *Cognition,* **12,** 229–65.

Spelke, E. S. (1979). "Perceiving bimodally specified events in infancy." *Developmental Psychology,* **25,** 626–36.

Spelke, E. S. (1982). "Perceptual knowledge of objects in infancy." In J. Mehler, E. Walker, and M. Garrett (eds), *Perspectives on Mental Representations.* Hillsdale, NJ: Lawrence Erlbaum Associates, Inc.

Spelke, E. S. (1985). "Perception of unity, persistence, and identity: Thoughts on infants' conceptions of objects." In J. Mehler and R. Fox (eds), *Neonate Cognition.* Hillsdale, NJ: Lawrence Erlbaum Associates, Inc.

Starkey, P., Spelke, E. S., and Gelman, R. (1983). "Detection of 1–1 correspondences by human infants." *Science,* **210,** 1033–5.

Streeter, L. A. (1978). "Acoustic determinants of phrase boundary perception." *Journal of the Acoustic Society of America,* **64,** 1582–92.

Talmy, L. (1975). "Semantics and syntax of motion." In J. Kimball (ed.), *Syntax and Semantics 4.* New York: Academic, 181–238.

Talmy, L. (1985). "Lexicalization patterns: Semantic structure in lexical forms." In T. Shopen (ed.), *Language Typology and Language Description.* Cambridge, England: Cambridge University Press.

Vendler, Z. (1972). *Res Cogitans.* Ithaca, NY: Cornell University Press.

Wasow, T. (1985). "Postscript." In P. Sells (ed.), *Lectures on Contemporary Syntactic Theories.* Stanford: Center for the Study of Language and Information, 193–206.

Waxman, S. and Gelman, R. (1986). "Preschoolers' use of superordinate relations in classification and language." *Cognitive Development,* 1, 139–56.

Wexler, K. (1970). *Embedding Structures for Semantics.* Unpublished manuscript, University of California, Irvine.

Wexler, K. and Culicover, P. (1980). *Formal Principles of Language Acquisition.* Cambridge, MA: MIT Press.

Wexler, K. and Manzini, R. (1987). "Parameters and learnability in binding theory." In T. Roeper and E. Williams (eds), *Parameter Setting.* Dordrecht: Reidel, 41–76.

Wilkins, W. (ed.) (1988). *Syntax and Semantics. Vol. 21: Thematic relations.* San Diego, CA: Academic.

Zwicky, A. (1971). "In a manner of speaking." *Linguistic Inquiry,* **11,** 223–33.

Early Word Meanings:
The case of object names

Janellen Huttenlocher and Patricia Smiley

Philosophers have proposed that the acquisition of object names is potentially a difficult problem for the word-learner, since the words and ostensive gestures the adult uses to refer to objects could instead refer to parts of those objects, to the material of which the objects are made, etc. (cf. Quine, 1969). Indeed, psychologists have claimed that when young children encounter situations where objects are present, they do *not* initially focus on objectness. Instead, they are said to form groupings that are "complexive," involving various combinations of habitually co-occurring attributes of situations, including the actions and locations of objects, etc. Even the words themselves are said to be, initially, just auditory features of situations where they habitually occur (cf. Piaget, 1962). In short, it has been suggested that young children group their experiences in a fundamentally different way than older children or adults—in terms of co-occurring aspects of situations—and that object names, rather than standing for particular types of objects, are just another type of associate.

These claims about childlike meanings are based on the observation that a word may be used for instances not included in the adult extension (overextension), or for only a subset of such instances (underextension). Consider first overgeneral word use. Two kinds have been noted—uses in the presence of spatiotemporal associates of what is named and uses in the presence of perceptually similar instances. Our focus here is on spatiotemporal associates, since these uses are the empirical basis for the assertion that children create groupings that differ in kind from those of adults. Overgeneral uses based on similarity (cf. Clark, 1973) provide evidence for categories of the same general kinds as those of adults (e.g., an object class broader than dog and narrower than pet), not for fundamentally different kinds of groupings.

Piaget (1962), Vygotsky (1962), and Guillaume (1923/1973) each held that children's overgeneral uses of words to spatiotemporal associates (e.g., "cookie" said to the cookie jar) reflect complexive groupings. More recently, Bowerman (1980) has argued that words are used complexively for instances that share only a few features of a central referent (often the referent initially seen), and that do not necessarily have attributes in common with each other. For example, one child's first use of *moon* is assumed to encode all of the present features, including broad expanse of background, angle of sighting, etc., and subsequent uses to incorporate just one or another of these attributes.

Consider now undergeneral word use. Here also, two kinds have been noted—uses to objects only in particular spatiotemporal or activity contexts, and uses involving similarity-based restrictions (e.g., using *dog* only for collies). Our focus here is the claim that words are applied only in certain restricted spatiotemporal or activity contexts, because these would reflect nonadult groupings (e.g., Bates, Camaioni, and Volterra, 1975; Nelson, 1974, 1983; Snyder, Bates, and Bretherton, 1981). For example, Nelson claims that object words reflect groupings of objects embedded in particular situational contexts, e.g., *ball* as ball-while-rolling or *block* as block-in-exchange-game-with-mommy, not objects of that type in other conditions. Similarity-based restrictions (cf. Anglin, 1977) are not the focus here, since they simply provide evidence for categories of the same general kinds as those of adults.

A set of unexamined assumptions underlies the position that early word use reflects childlike meanings. Some of these assumptions reflect a failure to specify the relation between word use and word meaning (i.e. the word's extension, or the range of instances to which it potentially applies). This relation is problematic in single-word utterances. Utterance function is not explicitly marked in single words as it can be in even two-word utterances (e.g., *want cookie* explicitly marks request; *see cookie* marks indication). However, we show in the present paper that it is possible to distinguish between lexical meaning (i.e., a word's extension) and communicative function for utterances in the single-word period.

The first assumption, made most explicitly by Rescorla (1980), is that usage in the absence of concept instances is evidence of overgeneral meanings (overextension). In other words, those aspects of context which are present during word use are assumed to be concept instances. This argument involves a strong claim about the relation between utterance function and word meaning—namely, that object words only name present objects and events. Yet if children can recall absent objects or acts, single words may be used in the presence of associated aspects of context to make requests or comments. Thus, what is present need not be part of the word's extension, and utterances in the absence of appropriate instances can be interpreted in two very different ways: The child who says "cookie" while reaching toward an opaque cookie jar may have an associative cluster involving cookies, jars, kitchens, and the sound *cookie*. On the other hand, he may have the same notion of *cookie* that adults do and express the likelihood that the jar contains a cookie he wants. A set of criteria for distinguishing between comments and associative clusters is proposed below.

The second assumption is that usage for a restricted range of instances is evidence of undergeneral meanings (underextension). In other words, the range of contexts observed during word use is assumed to exhaust a word's extension. However, such conclusions cannot necessarily be drawn from restricted word use. The likelihood that a sample of spontaneous speech will be restricted in range clearly depends on the size of the sample and the variety of contexts in which that sample is gathered. For example, if the sample includes only uses that are elicited by adult questions, context would be inherently limited. Reported cases of restricted spontaneous word usage tend to be taken from small speech samples and are often produced in response to eliciting questions by adults (e.g., Barrett, 1986; Bloom, 1973).

Finally, this second assumption, that the child's use of a word will exhaust its extension, involves a strong claim about utterance function, namely that words are used for all instances to which they are potentially applicable. Yet, the child's communicative purposes may not apply across the full range of possible contexts. The child who says "cookie" only in the high chair to request cookies may not have a "contextualized" meaning but simply a recurring desire for cookies. If restricted usage were observed, even in a large sample of speech, comprehension tasks which vary contexts (and are independent of communicative purposes) would be important in establishing extensions. However, comprehension tests may not be needed, since there is currently no evidence for contextualized usage in large samples of spontaneous speech across time.

The third assumption, made most explicitly by Bowerman (1980), concerns the aspects of context encoded in early word use. She has argued that, at least for certain object names (e.g., *moon*), the child's initial usage encodes not just the object but also its location, movement, etc. However, one cannot determine from a single instance of naming which aspects of a situation are encoded by a speaker. The context for any single utterance surely includes irrelevant as well as relevant features; that is, when an object word is uttered in the presence of an object, that object is necessarily in some particular location, is or is not involved in an action, etc. The proper way to infer the extension of a word is to examine commonalities across a set of utterances (cf. Edwards, 1978). Even then, of course, there is no principled way to be *certain* of the extension of a word on the basis of its pairing with a particular set of instances. It is always possible to formulate an alternative conceptualization of a given set of instances. In addition, any concept induced could be currently well supported, yet might require revision to accommodate future instances (Goodman, 1955).

In addition to issues concerning the relation between meaning and use, two other unexamined assumptions should be noted. The claim of childlike meanings for object names has been made without considering the full range of types of adult words. Certain adult words encode the actions of a restricted range of objects; e.g., *gallop* encodes a particular movement of a type of object, a horse. Other adult words encode either an object or an act; e.g., *hammer* encodes either the object, or the act of hammering with that object or an alternate suitable object. Still other adult words encode conventional events involving sets of objects, acts and locations; for example, *birthday party* encodes an event that includes songs, cakes with candles, pointed hats, group games, etc. Finally, the adult language includes homonyms, where particular word sounds encode two or more distinct meanings. If any of these types of words appeared in the single-word period, they would be interpreted as having "complexive" meanings, even though they actually mirror adult meaning types.

Further, it has been assumed that if children could form adult concepts, they would acquire the proper adult extensions for words. But even if children acquire only adult concepts, the range of instances they hear paired with a particular word might be more consistent with the formation of a concept other than the one normally encoded with that word. For example, parents may say "apple" mainly when the child is in the high chair in the kitchen, so the child may infer that the context is a defining feature. Parents may say "door" mainly when people are going in or out, and the child may infer that *door* is a word that encodes either object or act, or an act that involves a particular type of object. Griffiths and Atkinson (1978) report that children initially infer this type of extension for *door*. In short, while the acquisition of such concepts might be mistaken for "complexes," for certain words, the acquisition of such meanings might provide evidence *for* rather than *against* the ability to form adult concepts.

Finally, many of the studies which conclude that early word use reflects childlike meanings have collected production data unsystematically. In some cases, the data have consisted of informal observations of only a few utterances of a word (e.g., Guillaume, 1923/1973; Piaget, 1962) rather than systematic samples of all uses of that word for fixed periods of time. In other cases, the data consist of retrospective parent reports of child utterances and context (e.g., Nelson, 1973b; Snyder, Bates, and Bretherton, 1981). In both cases, the relative frequencies of various sorts of usage may be misjudged. Uses in the absence of category instances may be more salient than uses in the presence of instances, and uses in habitual contexts may be more salient than uses in other contexts. Indeed, the data from mother reports are not highly concordant with independent observational data (Bretherton *et al.*, 1983). Regular observations of a sufficient number of utterances, using a standard method of recording context, are essential in getting a proper database.

Even though the unexamined assumptions and methodological problems described above conspire against finding that children possess adultlike object categories, several researchers have noted that most words have proper extensions from the start (Bowerman, 1980; Gruendel, 1977; Macnamara, 1982, Rescorla, 1980). These words presumably meet the strong criterion of consistent use in the presence of the correct range of instances of the same adult word. In addition, Nelson and Bonvillian (1973) studied the acquisition of unfamiliar object names, and found that the majority are learned without extensional errors. Further, Macnamara (1982) reports that his son used object names for classes of objects per se and also honored intercategory distinctions—i.e., he did not use them for properties or actions. Macnamara reports no instances of overgeneral usage; consequently, he does not discuss how such uses could be interpreted, nor does he address the claim that they reflect nonadultlike meanings. Note that some of the same investigators who argue for the existence of complexive meanings find that the majority of words have proper extensions. If a child forms adultlike meanings in some cases and complexive ones in other cases, this would seem to be a problem for the theoretical position that the child's categorization processes are at first immature. Here we systematically gather data on word meanings to determine whether complexive meanings exist in young children, and to evaluate the nature of the young child's ability to categorize objects.

Inferring word meanings from production data

The concern in the present study is with establishing the extensions of children's early object words. As noted above, this involves clarifying the possible relations between a word's extension and its use. The critical case is overgeneral usage (because, to anticipate our results, we find no evidence of undergeneral usage). Utterances in the absence of category instances may involve one of three major types of associative relations between category instances and context. Two of the three kinds of uses, we argue, are not consistent with a complexive meaning interpretation.

Consider first *rare salient associations*; in these cases a word is used in a context which has co-occurred only rarely with an appropriate category instance. For example, we observed a child who saw a cookie in a schoolbag; when he later saw that bag closed he said "cookie." For cases like this, a complexive interpretation is clearly inappropriate; the schoolbag cannot be a meaning feature of *cookie* because it is only a temporary location where cookies are not ordinarily found. Another example involving a repeated but still rare association occurred for most of the subjects in the study. The observer in this study brought a toy bag with a particular set of toys, including a doll, a ball, and a car to the child's home each month. On seeing the bag, children often said one of these object names. These objects—only rarely encountered in this context and not named by adults in this context—were frequently encountered in other contexts. It is thus implausible to argue that this bag is part of the meaning of *baby* or *car*. Because of the temporary nature of the associations, these uses in the absence of category instances are interpretable as comments or requests concerning category instances.

Consider next *habitually associated contexts*. When words are used in contexts habitually associated with concept instances, certain of these uses clearly are not consistent with a complexive interpretation, namely uses in the presence of *asymmetric associates*. Asymmetric associates are aspects of context that typically occur with instances of the category names; however, category instances do *not* typically occur in those situations. In one of our observations, a child said "ball" when he saw his mother's tennis racquet. For this child, as for all the children in our study, balls appeared frequently in a wide variety of contexts. Occasionally, the mother's tennis racquet was present, and when it was, a ball was generally present with it. It is implausible to argue that the racquet is a part of the meaning of *ball* because the omnipresent ball occurs so infrequently with racquets compared to other contexts. Such absent instance uses are interpretable as comments in which the child recalls the object (or other type of category instance) that generally accompanies what he sees.

In constrast, some habitually associated contexts bear a *symmetric relation* to concept instances. These cases do not provide evidence for adult meanings, and are at least consistent with complexive groupings, since they involve aspects of situations that frequently co-occur with category instances and that are named together. For example, shoes are very often on feet when they are seen and named, so if a child says "shoe" when he sees a foot it is unclear whether the utterance is a comment on the absence of the shoe, or whether the utterance encodes one aspect of a complexive meaning where *shoe* means shoe-or-foot.

We are concerned with making inferences about extensions from production data. The extensions of words have also been explored using comprehension tasks, but these have some limitations in comparison to production data. The cases that have been examined using comprehension tasks involve overgeneral uses based on similarity. For example, children who call toy dogs, cats, and teddy bears "dog," can be asked to select the cat from an array of animals. In these tasks, children have been found to select appropriate category instances (e.g., Fremgen and Fay, 1980; Huttenlocher, 1974; Thomson and Chapman, 1977). However, overextensions to spatiotemporal associates would be difficult to test in this way, since the associated contexts are sometimes locations (e.g., rooms) or large stationary objects (e.g., refrigerators) which cannot be placed in arrays of alternatives. Thus, while it is possible to supplement production data with comprehension tasks, reasoned interpretations of production data may be critical in establishing extensions.

Production study

We systematically examined early word use by recording the aspects of context present at the time of every utterance for a group of children during the single-word period (as described under "Method"). The initial step in analyzing the data was to make preliminary tables that displayed the aspects of context present during the uses of each word for each child. This allowed us to determine whether certain aspects of context were constant across uses and which aspects these were. These analyses provided the basis for establishing individual word meanings. Looking across individual meanings, we found that certain commonalities characterized large numbers of words, and that these fell into different types.

The present paper deals with one of these word classes—words used mainly in the presence of particular kinds of small objects. The second major class of words was used for events or states (described in Huttenlocher and Smiley, 1986). There are also other classes of words; e.g., words for persons (Huttenlocher, Smiley, and Prohaska, 1986), and properties (e.g., *dirty*). Children did not use particular words across the bounds of different word types (object names, property words, event words, etc.), with only two possible exceptions in the entire record of utterances. First, one child used a range of sounds (*ba, baba, bay, baboo*) for a range of objects (balls, babies, and bottles), as well as for departures, i.e., to say "bye-bye." The similarity in the initial sounds of these words suggests a phonological difficulty in word production and/or perception, not an isolated case of a meaning complex. By the fourth month of speech (fourteen months of age), this child had developed discriminable sounds for each of the categories. Second, *baby*, which was almost exclusively used for dolls, occurred a few times in relation to tiny objects. This could be an isolated case of a complex, or alternatively, of a homonym which means small in size.

Method

Subjects

The ten subjects were five boys and five girls from middle-class homes in the area around the University of Chicago; parents were college educated. Eight of the children (four boys and four girls) were firstborns. They were seen each month from the time of their first word (at thirteen months for seven of the children) until their MLUs were 2.3 (between twenty-four and thirty months). Some children were visited for a number of months before they used any words.

Procedure

Children were seen for 5h (hours) each month. (They were visited for only 2h if they produced no words or only one word.) When visits were 5h long, production data were gathered for $4\frac{1}{2}$h and the remaining time was used for comprehension tasks. Spontaneous production data were collected during ordinary daily activities at home, in the playground, at the grocery store, etc. In addition, the observer elicited nonverbally object words already in the child's vocabulary. For this purpose, she brought a bag containing a set of small toys each month. These included dolls, balls, stuffed animals, a toy purse, a basket with a lid, etc. The alternate set of objects was used to elicit known words to new exemplars. Some of the objects could also function as containers (the toy bag itself, the purse, the basket); objects for which the child had names were placed in these containers to elicit words to rare, salient associates of objects. For example, the child might be shown a purse and discover a ball inside it; later in the session, the observer would present the empty purse; the child would then have an opportunity to comment on the earlier presence of the ball. Neither of the novel eliciting circumstances (new exemplars and rare, salient associates) was accompanied by verbal prompts.

During the observations, all utterances and nonverbal contexts were transcribed. At the earliest stage, when words were infrequently used, the observer simply wrote down the utterances and contexts. This was feasible since children produced on the average only 3.6 unelicited utterances per hour in the first two months of speech. When speech became frequent, sessions were tape-recorded. Extensive context notes were made, and as much speech as possible was recorded during the sessions. The sessions were later fully transcribed by the observer. Even during the final sessions of the single-word period, most speech and context were recorded as they happened, since production rates were not very high. In the last session, the average production rate for spontaneous utterances across children for the entire period was one utterance per minute. Production rates ranged from one utterance every four minutes to 1.5 utterances per minute. While the most talkative children sometimes produced a sequence of utterances in rapid succession, in these cases the utterances tended to describe the same aspects of context. This made the task of systematically recording context quite manageable. Earlier investigators have noted the tendency for successive utterances to be related to one context (cf. Bloom, 1973).

The contexts of utterances were recorded according to a fixed set of criteria, always including the same aspects of the surrounding situation. The following aspects of context were included: object looked at, its condition (location, movement), its salient features (e.g., color, pattern, wetness, dirtiness); person looked at, his location and state; child's location and state; actions or attempted actions performed by the child; and actions involving another person or an object. In addition, we recorded indicative gestures, eye contact, and behavior having to do with communicative purpose, namely, whether any of the present aspects of context were habitually or recently associated with the named object, person, action, or property, and whether the child used request intonation.

The presence of associated objects or locations along with named objects were noted when they were taken to be part of the child's focus of attention. That is, when a child plays with any particular object many others (some associated and some not) may be lying on the floor next to the child, and the object is in some location. We considered the child's focus to be on those objects and locations included in an activity. Others, while perhaps in the child's visual field, were considered peripheral. Thus, while putting a shoe on a doll and saying "baby," the child's focus was assumed to be on both the doll and the shoe; while putting a doll to bed in a crib, the focus was assumed to be on both the doll and the crib. Where named objects were not present, associated objects and/or locations were the only focus of the child's attention, and these were recorded. Associated room size locations (e.g., kitchens for bottles, backyards for big balls, etc.) were also recorded, although it is unclear to what extent these are actually the focus of attention.

The reliability of recording utterances and context was assessed using two observers (one trained and one in training) during one session for each of two children midway through their single-word periods. At this point in the observations, tape-recordings were not yet being used. Agreement on what utterances occurred for the two children was 87 and 83 percent, respectively; agreement on occurrences for small object words was 87 and 100 percent. Omissions occurred for all word types. (Of the disagreements on occurrences, 75 percent were utterances recorded by the experienced observer but not by the inexperienced one.) Agreement on context coding was very high. For the two children, agreement on context across all words was 95 and 90 percent, respectively; agreement on context for small object words was 92 and 100 percent. Thus, the experienced observer recorded more utterances, perhaps because she was used to the particular child's way of articulating or because she was quicker, but even the inexperienced observer could apply the method of recording context.

The contexts of all nonimitative utterances were analyzed except for utterances which were elicited rather than spontaneous. Elicited utterances are those made in response to questions by adults (e.g., "What's that?"). These utterances may be context restricted by virtue of the way adults draw attention to particular objects (e.g., the child's bib in Barrett, 1986). Examining spontaneous utterances allows us to determine what the child considers appropriate contexts for word use, and hence to evaluate the possibility of complexive meanings.

The data presented here include the object names used during the period of single-word speech, starting with the children's first word uses and continuing until the month when more than 5 per cent of utterances were multiword. A multiword utterance is one in which each word in the utterance is used in combination with other words or alone (cf. Braine, 1963). While each child utterance was recorded, some speech sounds produced by the youngest children were not treated as utterances. We excluded any sound repeated three or more times (*dadada*), singsong vowel sounds, and apparently random sounds made when the child's attention did not appear to be focused on anything, such as an object or an action he was carrying out. The children sometimes produced single words embedded in inarticulate speech sounds, as well as strings of two or more single words separated by short time intervals. The words occurring in these contexts were treated as separate single-word utterances.

Results

Table 2.4.1 presents certain basic data on each child: In the first three columns are shown the age span of the single-word period, the number of months after the onset of speech when the first object name appeared, and the number of object names acquired. The single-word period ranged from five to twelve months in duration, and began, for all but one child, by fourteen months. Only three children had an object name in their first month of speaking, but all had one by their third month. Nine of the ten children used between about twenty and fifty different words for objects during the single-word period, but there was one child who used only six object names. Many of the words acquired by each child are acquired by others as well. The number of words in common with at least three other children is given in Column 4. Only these object names are analyzed here because they provide a sufficient number of contexts to examine. In fact, the object names used by several children were generally used with greater frequency by each child. (The words used by fewer than four children are discussed at the end of Results.)

Table 2.4.2 presents these object names in order of decreasing frequency of use. The three left-hand columns show the number of children using a word, the median month of speech at which that word was first produced, and the total number of uses across children. The remaining columns show the various aspects of context that were common to uses of the words. The interpretable contexts are of two types: first, the predominant usage pattern, namely uses where the objects named in the adult language (or similar ones, as defined below) are present, and second, uses where such instances are absent, but where spatiotemporal associates are present. (In Table 2.4.4 these are broken down into the different subtypes described in the introduction.)

Table 2.4.1 *Production of small object words during the single-word period*

Child	Age span of single-word period	Month of speech of first object word	Number of object words acquired	Number of object words used by four or more children
G_1	14–18 months	2	33	19
G_2	13–18	2	19	16
G_3	13–19	1	31	18
G_4	13–20	3	24	13
G_5	11–20	1	36	17
B_1	21–25	3	6	4
B_2	13–19	2	40	17
B_3	13–21	1	44	18
B_4	13–23	3	30	21
B_5	13–24	3	49	21

Table 2.4.2 *Small object word use*

Word	No. of children using	Median first month of use	Number of uses	Contexts of use							
				Object present				Object absent		?	
				Appropriate	High similar	Low similar	% of total	Associated objects or locations	Search, request	Dissimilar object	No focus
Ball	10	3.0	580	389	82	15	84	57	22	6	9
Baby	9	5.0	456	332	31	15	83	64	8	3	3
Shoe	9	4.5	264	248	1	0	94	12	2	0	1
Dog	10	3.5	197	146	35	0	92	6	1	1	8
Truck	4	7.0	150	106	26	0	88	12	4	0	2
Car	8	6.0	143	122	6	0	90	4	6	5	0
Bottle	7	4.0	138	92	2	0	68	15	24	4	1
Cookie	7	5.0	128	48	5	0	41	56	15	3	1
Kitty, cat	8	7.0	90	72	14	1	97	2	0	1	0
Book	9	5.0	88	84	2	0	98	1	1	0	0
Hat	7	5.0	77	65	8	0	95	3	0	1	0
Doll	5	4.0	68	62	0	0	91	4	1	0	1
Keys	5	5.0	65	55	0	0	85	9	1	0	0
Light	7	7.0	62	57	1	0	94	4	0	0	0
Horsey	7	7.0	56	51	1	0	93	4	0	0	0
Eye	7	6.0	53	50	1	0	96	1	0	1	0
Block	6	7.0	44	44	0	0	100	0	0	0	0
Duck	5	4.0	38	29	8	0	97	1	0	0	0
Sock	6	9.0	38	35	0	0	92	3	0	0	0
Apple	5	6.0	33	17	5	4	79	3	3	1	0
Banana	5	5.0	30	26	1	0	90	1	2	0	0
Flower	4	7.5	27	21	4	0	93	1	0	1	0
Nose	7	7.0	27	25	2	0	100	0	0	0	0
Peas	4	4.5	18	13	4	0	94	1	0	0	0
Cheese	4	5.0	11	7	0	2	82	2	0	0	0

The last three columns on the right show the uninterpretable uses: cases where requests or searches are made for absent objects but not in the context of an associated object or location; cases where an object is present that is perceptually dissimilar to the named object and whose relation to the named object is not apparent; and cases where no object is present, the child is in some nondistinctive location, and/or his attention seems unfocused. Uses during searches or requests generally occur after the children have produced many present object uses. For a few words (*ball*, *baby*, *car*, and *apple*), children produced search/request uses in the first month; even for these cases, the words were used for appropriate objects that month as well. Still, on their own merits, these search/request uses add no positive information about word meaning. For uses to dissimilar objects or uses with no focus it is impossible to tell what the child had in mind. For example, different children used *ball* for a blanket, for a fish, while sitting in a high chair, or pointing in a mirror. One might have expected many of these utterances, since the child might often have conceived of contextual relations that were not evident in the situations, but these actually constitute a very small proportion of the total.

In certain important respects, the pattern of usage was constant during the single-word period. First, words were used with both request intonation (i.e., a whining or demanding voice) and with "declarative" intonation from the start. While requests were frequent for only a few kinds of objects when present (e.g., balls, shoes, bottles, cookies), some of these requests always occurred in the first two months of use. Second, in cases where overgeneral uses of words to similar instances occurred, they continued throughout the period studied. However, the ratio of appropriate to overgeneral uses for object words across children increases from about four to one in the first half of the single-word period to about nine to one in the second half. (The continuation of overgeneral uses has also been noted by Bowerman, 1980, and by Rescorla, 1980.) Finally, uses when the named objects are absent occurred throughout the period studied; the ratio of present to absent uses for object words across children is about 5:1 in the first half of the period and 6:1 in the second half. Since usage changes little over the single-word period, especially in the occurrence of the object absent uses with which we are particularly concerned, the striking correspondences between child and adult extensions we report below are present from the start. A few shifts in word use do occur within the single-word period; for example, as described below, certain names were initially restricted to toy models and later applied to real objects.

For the words in Table 2.4.2, the overwhelming majority of uses were in the presence of objects of a particular kind. Further, the objects named were almost all small and inanimate. While some of the words acquired do name large objects in adult speech, for example, *car* and *truck*, they were used mainly for toys until the last one or two months of the single-word period, when a few children also used them for real vehicles: Several other names that were used by fewer than four children could also potentially refer to large objects, including vehicles and furniture. The seven vehicle names (e.g., *bus, train*) showed the same pattern of usage. The three words for furniture (e.g., *chair*) were used for large objects from the start but were always acquired late in the single-word period. In short, until the last months of the single-word period, the objects named were small objects. Some of the words in Table 2.4.2 can also name animate creatures in the adult language, namely *baby, dog, kitty,* and *duck*. However, three of these are most often used for toys, and *duck* is used solely for toys. Of the small number of uses for animate creatures, several were to the sounds rather than the appearance of those creatures, i.e., to the bark of a dog or the cry of a baby.

Finally, there is one word, *door,* which was used by four children, yet is not included in Table 2.4.2. Like the vehicle and furniture words, it names a large object in adult language and was acquired late in the single-word period. *Door* was used almost exclusively for real doors (94 percent). However, it is not included in Table 2.4.2 since it fits our criteria for a word that encodes an event involving movement/change, as we discuss later.

The uses when objects are present are given in the left half of Table 2.4.2. First, there are uses for appropriate category instances. Second, there are uses for perceptually similar instances. Uses for perceptually dissimilar instances are included in the "object absent" section and we discuss these later. Uses for perceptually similar objects are broken down into two subtypes—high similar instances and low similar instances. Highly similar objects share many perceptual features with the appropriate object and generally belong to the same immediately superordinate category (e.g., a pear for the word *apple*). For only a few words, high similarity uses were based only on perceptual features; e.g., *ball* was used for a wide variety of spherical, oval, or flat round objects, and *hat* was used for bowls and buckets. All the other high similar instances shared superordinate category membership as well. Low similar objects share some perceptual features but are more distantly related (e.g., a block for the word *ball* or a stuffed animal for the word *baby*).

The percentage of object present uses that are for the appropriate object is very high (80 percent to 100 percent). (The only exception is *apple*; only 65 percent of its object present uses are for appropriate objects.) When object names are used for similar rather than appropriate objects, high similar instances outnumber low similar ones on average almost seven to one (Kay and Anglin, 1982, report similar findings). Present object uses for appropriate or similar objects are 90 percent or more for seventeen of the twenty-five object words, and approximately 80 percent to 90 percent for the other six object words (see Column 4 under "Object present"). Two words, *bottle* and *cookie,* had fewer positive instances; uses for these edibles were often requests in the absence of the object.

The finding that object names are used mainly for objects of a particular kind suggests that they are names for objects per se. However, although object names are consistently associated with objects having particular characteristics, they might only be used when those objects appear in particular action or locational contexts. That is, they might have undergeneral childlike meanings. In addition, while a minority of uses occur when the named or a similar object is absent, these uses might include aspects of context that for the child are appropriately named with the word. That is, they might have overgeneral complexive meanings. We take up these issues in order below.

Is action relevant?

To determine whether object words encode object-in-action, we tabulated the actions that occur (whether the child or another is acting) during the naming of present objects. Table 2.4.3 differentiates object-specific acts, like throwing for *ball* or putting on the head for *hat*, from object-general acts like getting, giving, pointing, showing, etc. For twenty of the twenty-five words, a varied set of actions predominates, and actions specific to particular objects are infrequent (less than 20 percent of all contexts). Clearly, these twenty object names are not words for objects involved in particular actions. Further, for the five words with a higher proportion of uses during object-specific actions (*light, hat, shoe, apple,* and *sock*), such uses are still in the minority (less than 45 percent), indicating that not even these are words for objects in particular actions.

For the five words frequently used during object-specific actions, the high proportion of such uses may reflect the existence of childlike complexes (e.g., *hat* may mean either hat or lowering an object on the head). But this interpretation would be plausible only if the range of objects named during specific actions were broader than the range of stationary objects named. Such uses are reported by Gruendel (1977); in her data *hat* and *baba* are used for a variety of objects that serve similar functions before they are restricted to category-appropriate objects. No such findings emerged in our data. For three of the five words (*light, shoe,* and *sock*), the object-specific acts *always* involved the appropriate object. For *hat* and *apple*, the object-specific acts never involved low similar objects; object-specific acts sometimes involved high similar objects, but the percentages of high similar objects involved in object-specific acts versus object-general acts were similar (17 percent versus 10 percent for *hat* and 17 percent versus 12 percent for *apple*). Gruendel does not report the frequency of similar objects involved in object-general acts.

Across children, we found no cases of restriction of use to objects in particular actions. However, such constraints might be found in individual children in their very early uses. Therefore, we examined the earliest uses of the children's first two object names during the month by which they had been used at least twice. These twenty words were used between two and thirty-one times, with a median of 3.5 uses. Despite the low frequency of most of the twenty words, none of the words was used only for instances involved in a particular action. In addition, comprehension of most of these words was tested during or prior to the first month of production. The comprehension task involved new exemplars of objects presented in sets of contrasting but similar kinds (e.g., a

Table 2.4.3 *Actions during present object uses*

Word	Total frequency	Object specific No.	Object specific %	Give	Take	Get	Try get	Touch	Point	Show	Other acts	Other attempts	No action
Ball	486	75	16	11	17	77	27	15	89	22	71	7	75
Baby	378	54	14	29	12	44	4	8	53	11	84	2	77
Shoe	249	66	27	28	4	17	1	15	41	19	29	1	28
Dog	181	5	3	5	3	14	3	7	65	9	19	1	50
Truck	132	24	18	3	0	18	1	5	21	4	23	3	30
Car	128	14	11	3	5	13	6	17	10	2	27	2	29
Bottle	94	4	4	5	3	15	6	2	9	6	25	0	25
Cookie	53	6	11	2	4	6	4	1	10	3	12	0	5
Kitty	87	4	5	0	2	2	2	6	37	2	12	0	20
Book	86	10	12	21	0	9	4	4	7	1	19	0	11
Hat	73	29	40	9	3	6	2	3	11	1	6	0	3
Doll	62	3	5	1	1	12	0	0	14	7	15	1	8
Keys	55	9	16	1	3	12	0	0	4	6	10	0	10
Light	58	25	43	0	0	0	1	2	20	0	2	1	7
Horse	52	4	8	2	4	4	2	1	12	4	8	1	10
Eye	51	0	0	0	0	0	0	5	41	0	3	0	2
Block	44	4	9	6	0	8	1	1	2	6	10	0	6
Duck	37	0	0	1	0	4	1	2	18	2	0	0	9
Sock	35	7	20	2	0	5	0	0	3	3	7	0	8
Apple	26	6	23	1	2	2	3	0	9	1	0	0	2
Banana	27	2	7	0	1	4	4	0	0	2	6	0	8
Flower	25	2	8	0	0	0	0	2	14	2	3	0	2
Nose	27	2	7	0	0	0	1	5	18	1	0	0	0
Peas	17	2	12	1	0	4	1	0	5	3	0	0	1
Cheese	9	1	11	0	0	3	0	0	0	2	2	0	1

set of toy animals) and they were not involved in action during testing. Only two individual errors were found; one child selected a dog for *cat* and one child the opposite.

Finally, let us consider production of certain other words which name objects in the adult language, but occurred primarily in action contexts for these children. These include *door*, which was used by four children, and a group of words, e.g., *slide, swing,* and *drink*, which were used by fewer than four children. Examining the commonalities across uses, for *door*, we found that doors were present during all uses. and for the other words as a group, the named objects were present 85 percent of the time. As for other object words, we noted when the objects were acted on in an object-specific or object-general way. For these objects, every time an action took place it involved object-specific movements of opening or closing, sliding, etc. In addition, we noted the occurrence of a type of context that did not characterize other object word use but did appear during use of words for events (Huttenlocher and Smiley, 1986). In these cases the child did not act on the object, and did not simply look at and name the object. Rather, he or she said the word in conditions where the action on that object was anticipated or requested (e.g., "door" while standing by the closed front door). Together, object-specific acts and conditions for such acts account for 81 percent of all uses of *door* and 68 percent of all uses of the other word group. These proportions are similar to those for event words (e.g., *up, sit*) as discussed in Huttenlocher and Smiley (1986). Thus, even though *door* encodes an object category in the adult language, and *slide*, etc., encode categories of object-or-act in the adult language, for our subjects they all seem to encode events involving particular objects.

Are associated objects or locations relevant?

To determine whether these object names encode undergeneral notions of object-in-habitual-context, we tabulated the number of uses where associated objects and locations occur together with the named objects. The presence of associated objects or locations was coded by the observer and an independent coder, working from the context notes. Coders agreed on the presence of an associate and its type 94 percent of the time. Disagreements were distributed across words. The good agreement is probably due to the fact that the natural variation in distribution of objects with other objects and in locations is limited. Thus, children may get baby dolls from their toy chests and use them along with blankets and bottles, but there are few other habitually associated contexts. Other objects are often used alone (e.g., cars); still others are always in their associated location (e.g., lamps or ceiling fixtures).

Uses with associated objects or locations are shown in the left portion of Table 2.4.4 for the most frequent words. (We list only the most frequent since the other words have too few instances to examine.) The uses where an object is present along with an habitually associated object or location are subdivided into

Table 2.4.4 Associated objects or locations present during object word use

Word	Named object present			Named object absent			
	Habitual associates		% of object present uses	Habitual associates		Rare, salient associates	% of object absent uses
	Symmetric	Asymmetric		Symmetric	Asymmetric		
Ball	0	2	0	0	27	30	72
Baby	0	64	17	0	29	35	89
Shoe	100	5	42	7	3	2	86
Dog	0	8	4	0	2	4	86
Truck	0	4	3	0	1	11	75
Car	0	1	1	0	1	3	40
Bottle	0	29	31	1	7	7	39
Cookie	4	15	36	21	29	6	79
Kitty	0	0	0	0	1	1	100
Book	0	7	8	0	1	0	50
Hat	42	1	59	2	1	0	100
Doll	0	4	6	0	3	1	80
Keys	0	12	22	0	9	0	90
Light	46	12	100	0	4	0	100
Horse	0	16	31	0	2	2	100

symmetric (e.g., a hat on a head) and asymmetric (e.g., a bottle in the kitchen). The total percentage of such uses is shown in the third column; it is under 10 percent for seven of the fifteen frequent object words. The small percentages indicate that these object concepts are not context bound. For *baby*, several kinds of small objects were often present with dolls. Of the other seven words, all refer to objects which, just by their nature, are often found in fixed or typical locations. Thus, lamps and horses for riding are stationary; shoes and hats are often juxtaposed with a foot or a head; cookies and bottles are often in the kitchen or on the high chair tray; and keys are often left in doors or particular drawers. Even with natural environmental constraints, naming in associated contexts accounts for at most about half the uses (for all words except *light*) and thus, these are not words for objects-in-habitual-location either.

While we found no cases of restriction of use to objects in particular locations across children, restrictions might be found in early uses by individual children. Examination of the uses of each child's first two object words during the month when they first appear shows that, as for actions, there are no cases where objects were in the same distinctive location across the instances named. In addition, our comprehension testing of these early words, as described above, involved presentation of new exemplars from object categories in a spatial array—i.e., in nonhabitual locations. As we noted, there were almost no errors in this task by the earliest month of production of the words.

The total number of interpretable object absent uses, namely uses to objects or locations known to be associated with the named object, is shown on the right in Table 2.4.2. The percentage of object absent uses that are interpretable is generally high—over 70 percent for twelve of the fifteen words with the most absent object uses. These interpretable object absent uses are broken down into the three types discussed in the introduction in Table 2.4.4 on the right— symmetric and asymmetric habitual contexts, and rare salient contexts. As for the present object uses, both the observer and another coder identified the types of associated contexts. Again, in 95 percent of cases coders agreed on the type of relation between the present context and the named object. As for present object uses, variation in context across children was limited. For example, of the twenty-nine asymmetric habitual associates for *baby*, twenty-six were items of clothing, cups, or bottles; the others were habitual locations in homes. Variation in the types of rare associates was limited because many of these were pairings introduced by the observer (e.g., a purse that had had a ball in it). Of the thirty-five rare associates for *baby*, thirty-two were of this sort; the other three were locations where the child had recently seen babies. The latter were easily noted when following children around and recording situations to which they attended.

We examined the type of associates present for the most frequently used words—as we did for the contexts of object present uses—to determine whether or not object names encode a complexive notion of object or associated context. The results were striking. Most of the contexts of object absent uses involve rare salient associates or habitual asymmetric associates of the absent object; these are the cases where the objects or locations present could not reasonably be part of the child's word meanings. That is, they provide evidence against complexive meanings. Instead, these uses probably reflect the child's memory that a particular object is sometimes found in a certain location or along with another object.

Note that the likelihood of having asymmetric versus symmetric habitual associates varies with object type. Balls and other toys are found throughout the house; thus, associated contexts for these objects are more likely to be distinctive asymmetrically associated contexts where they sometimes occur than recurring symmetrically associated contexts. Shoes and hats, in contrast, are found in only a few contexts, and these are symmetrically related. This natural distribution of object types makes it inherently difficult to assess the extensions of words like *shoe* and *hat* from production data. Many of the object present uses and a few object absent uses of *shoe* and *hat* were in the same symmetrically associated contexts. Since these contexts are named whether the object is present or not, *shoe* and *hat* might have complexive meanings; e.g., *shoe* could encode shoe, foot, or both. On the other hand, they may well name objects as the other object names do, but we lack positive evidence from production that this is the case. It should be noted, however, that six of the eight subjects who used *shoe* were tested in comprehension tasks where shoes were presented outside of these symmetrically related contexts, all six chose the correct object.

Finally, to assure ourselves that less frequently used object words do not constitute a class of complexes, we examined contexts of use for object names produced by fewer than four children. These data are comparable to those described above. Ninety-nine small object words were used by fewer than four children: *Bear, bird, cow, cup, fish, man,* and *teeth* were used by three children; twenty-six words were used by two children each, and sixty-three words by one child each. An average of 85 percent of all uses are for positive instances; only 11 percent of these uses occur during object-specific acts, and only 10 percent of these uses are for objects in habitual locations. Further, the object absent uses are similar to those for the frequent object words. Thus, the less frequent object words also encode concepts of small objects and not complexes that include these small objects.

Discussion

Our results show that, from the earliest uses, the extensions of children's object names are like those of adults. The finding that object names encode categories of particular sorts of objects should lay to rest long-standing claims that object names initially encode complexive groupings that incorporate actions or locations associated with objects. While the index of concepts in the present study, as in earlier studies, is the child's use of words, our conclusions are based on more systematic data gathering and analysis. We obtained samples of several hours of speech each month, systematically recorded context, and analyzed all instances of word–context pairings. On the basis of this analysis we found no evidence of restriction of word use to objects in particular locational or action contexts. Further, while words are sometimes used in the absence of concept instances, we have presented evidence that these utterances do not reflect overgeneral complexive meanings.

Most important to establishing the extensions of children's object names is the set of criteria we developed for interpreting utterances in the presence of spatiotemporal associates of named objects that were themselves absent. Using these criteria, we exploited the naturally occurring variations in the types of associations among objects and locations to explore the possibility that the child uses words for communicative functions other than naming (e.g., commenting). We found that the spatiotemporal associates present when children use object names are most often rare or asymmetric associates of those objects. Such utterances are not consistent with the view that these words are complexes, used for any of a set of frequently co-occurring features of situations. Only a few words (*shoe*, *hat*) are used for symmetric associates (feet, heads) a high proportion of the time. For these words, usage is not inconsistent with complexive categories, although it provides no positive evidence for complexive categories.

The nature of conceptual categories can be explored not only with word use, but with nonverbal behavior as well. Using a sorting task, Piaget found that children place objects into "thematic" (complexive) rather than similarity groupings until four or five years; e.g., given toy people and furniture, they group the baby with the crib rather than the people (Inhelder and Piaget, 1964). However, the results of two other types of studies show that children produce similarity groupings much earlier. First, twelve- to eighteen-month-olds initiate appropriate differential uses of objects (e.g., using new brooms to sweep and new knives to cut); this behavior provides evidence that these new exemplars are treated as category members on the basis of perceptual similarity. In the first year of life, children treat all sorts of objects similarly, mouthing, grasping, or transferring them from hand to hand (Fenson *et al.*, 1976; Hutt, 1967); their actions become specific and appropriate to particular objects between twelve and eighteen months (Fenson *et al.*, 1976; Lowe, 1975).

Second, by twelve months, children who are exposed to category members (even for superordinate categories of food and furniture) differentially attend to noncategory objects (Ross, 1980). Further, children presented with an array of two contrasting types of simple forms sequentially touch similar shapes by nine months, and sequentially touch first one type and then the contrasting type by shortly after 1 year of age (Ricciuti, 1965; Starkey, 1981). With realistic objects, by eighteen months, all children group at least one of two contrasting sets (Nelson, 1973a; Sugarman, 1982), and by twenty-four months, both contrasting classes (Sugarman, 1982). Moreover, Gelman and Baillargeon (1983) argue that spatial groupings are probably not a product of the persistence of a common motor response to like items, especially in the case where both classes are grouped. Thus, in forming thematic groupings, Piaget's subjects were probably displaying their knowledge of spatiotemporal or functional relations among objects, not their lack of knowledge of similarity groups. After all, possessing similarity-based object categories does not necessarily entail possessing a rule that similar objects should be placed in spatial proximity, especially when a competing form of grouping (thematic) is also possible. In fact, 3-year-olds apparently possess a rule that a continuous surface such as a table top is more appropriate for thematic sorting while separate containers are more appropriate for taxonomic sorting (Markman, Cox, and Machida, 1981).

The claim that children's initial groupings of experience are spatiotemporal clusters extends to the words themselves. That is, especially for Piaget and Vygotsky, words are said to be features of situations, not symbols whose function is to call to mind particular categories. If the child's words in the single-word period were simply features of situations, and not symbols, there would be no reason to expect them to appear in both receptive and productive language, or to be used in productive language for a variety of communicative purposes. Instead, a word might be a discriminative response said at the sight of a particular object, or it might be an instrumental response said with the expectation of the delivery of a desired object (cf. Huttenlocher and Higgins, 1978). In examining the contexts of single-word use and their intonation contours, we have seen that object names in the single-word period are produced for a range of communicative functions—naming, requesting, and commenting on absent objects and events. We also have seen that all of the words produced that were also tested in our comprehension tasks were understood. Thus, the flexibility in the communicative functions of words, and their appearance in receptive as well as productive language, strongly suggest that even early single words are symbols.

There are reports in the literature which suggest the possibility of nonsymbolic uses of words. For example, Reich (1976) reports that, for one eight-month-old, *shoes* functioned only in receptive language in a particular situation. In production, Bloom (1973) reports that her nine-month-old used *car* only for moving cars seen from the living room; usage of the word disappeared completely after ten months. Barrett (1986) reports that a thirteen-month-old used *dog* for a few weeks solely in response to an eliciting question about a picture on his bib. These examples may indeed reflect nonsymbolic functions of words. In each of these examples, the words may be discriminative responses to particular situations. Moreover, in the Reich and Barrett examples, the contexts involve verbal and/or exemplar structuring by adults. Our findings from early spontaneous speech fail to show early restrictions. If these exist at all, they must be rare and short-lived. In short, the evidence is that even in very early spontaneous production, children's object names are symbols which encode object categories and can serve a variety of communicative functions.

Taken as a group, the object words acquired in the single-word period form a broad semantic class which contrasts with other semantic classes emerging at the same time. That is, the pattern of usage for object words contrasts with that of words for events (Huttenlocher and Smiley, 1986); words for persons (Huttenlocher, Smiley, and Prohaska, 1986); words for temporary states, greetings, negation, and so on. The presence of these contrasting types of word classes in the single-word period has implications for the course of syntactic development.

It is generally agreed that syntactic rules in adults are best described as applying to grammatical categories of words—nouns, verbs, etc. The developmental issue is how children come to treat the particular words they acquire as members of such grammatical categories. One possibility is that children's early word combinations are based not on syntactic categories, but rather on semantic categories such as agent, action, patient, etc. In one view, grammatical categories subsequently emerge on the basis of the similarities in the distributional properties of new words to those of the words in early multiword utterances (e.g., Maratsos and Chalkley, 1980). An alternative view holds that grammatical categories are innately available but that semantic categories provide the basis for linking particular words to those grammatical categories (Pinker, 1984). Such accounts rest on the assumption that children's interpretations of the world are roughly consistent with those of adults, so that the semantic categories that underlie early word combinations can be subsumed by grammatical categories.

The evidence in the present paper indicates that syntax acquisition theories that have a semantic basis are plausible, since children's object concepts are adultlike notions of small objects that constitute part of the class of nouns. Moreover, the ways children use these words in the single-word period suggest that when word combinations begin to be produced, a variety of relational meanings into which small objects enter might be encoded. Object words are used singly in relation to spatiotemporal associates of those objects, and we have argued that these uses are comments on the relation of the present objects or locations to the named objects. As words for these associated objects and locations are acquired, they could be combined with small object names to encode spatiotemporal relations. Event words also emerge in this period and could combine with small object words to describe movement or change in those objects. Finally, the early words *no* and *more* are used to encode negation and recurrence in situations involving small objects (cf. Bloom, 1973). Words for particular objects could be combined with *no* and *more* to produce specific relational meanings. In short, since children's notions of small objects in the single-word period are of classes of objects that can enter into various action and spatial relations, their earliest word combinations should encode these relations, as indeed they do (cf. Brown, 1973).

We have shown that, from the start, children, like adults, group objects into categories of similar objects. However, adults and older children not only possess extensional rules that allow them to select objects—distinguishing dogs from nondogs—they possess other defining information as well—that dogs have hearts and livers, that they reproduce and die, etc. Such information, often potentially extensional itself, is an important aspect of adult conceptual knowledge, but there is evidence to suggest it develops only in somewhat older children (Keil, 1983). In addition, adults possess information about the relation of a particular object category to other related categories. They know that *dog* contrasts with coordinate categories such as *cat*, etc., that *dog* belongs to such superordinate categories as *pet* and *mammal*, and that *dog* has subtypes such as *collie* and *poodle*.

It has been argued that the formation of coherent sets of related categories is essential to the formulation of particular "true concepts." Thus Piaget (1962) claims that "true concepts" emerge only when the child possesses sets of related concepts which specify the necessary and sufficient conditions for category membership. He presents evidence that information about such categorical relations is not available until 4 to 5 years of age. In his view, word meanings should be complexive prior to this age, since their boundaries are not firmly established. More recently, Clark (1973) proposed that words initially have only a few features of meaning (e.g., *dog* initially includes only the feature "four legs") and that proper extensions only become established through the gradual accretion of features which differentiate a particular concept from other related concepts. In this view, all concepts should be overgeneral until the set of contrasting concepts in a domain are formed.

The notion that individual word meanings are acquired via the establishment of sets of concepts with shared and/or contrasting features is associated with the theory that the basic elements involved in conceptual development are subconceptual features. In this view, the child acquires concepts by learning how these features combine to form sets of related categories. However, Fodor (1972) has argued that featural analysis is not a good model even of adult concept learning, and the present study shows that sets of related words need not have been acquired for early object words to have proper extensions. Thus, Piaget's claim that early word meanings are complexive because they are not part of related sets is not supported. Clark's claim that word meanings develop through a gradual accretion of features was shown earlier by other investigators to lack empirical support (cf. Barrett, 1982; Carey, 1982; Richards, 1979), and she has now abandoned this view herself (Clark, 1983).

Surely, as sets of related concepts are acquired, they become organized according to their contrasting and hierarchical relations. Assembling related sets of concepts and analyzing their constituent features may be integrally related; indeed, Shipley and Kuhn (1983) find that 4-year-olds use similar features in order to make comparisons among related classes of objects. At any rate, the process is well underway by about 4 years, as Piaget suggested (see review by

Gelman and Baillargeon, 1983; Rosch *et al.*, 1976). However, this process is not essential in order to develop individual concepts, and the featural view of acquisition should be discarded, at least for object concepts.

Any coherent model of conceptual development must posit biologically available mechanisms—conceptual primitives—that operate at the start. If the primitives in the emergence of the child's conceptual scheme are not subconceptual features, perhaps they are entire concepts. Fodor *et al.* (1980) have proposed such a view. In fact, they have argued that *all* concepts are biologically available primitives, i.e., unanalyzable gestalts "triggered" by input and not definable as combinations of other elements. Without taking a stand on this general view, we would suggest that object categories are primitive concepts in just this sense; that is, that the child acquires gestalt notions of objects on the basis of experiences with objects of particular sorts.

The view that object categories are primitive notions of objects as things-of-a-kind is supported by the fact that they emerge early and probably do not depend on other categories for their formation. Further, object words are the first to emerge for children with very different perceptual experience and language input. Blind children acquire object names first (Landau and Gleitman, 1985), as do learners of several non-English languages, even when, in those languages, object words are as morphologically complex as predicate words or are not salient in input sentences (Gentner, 1982). In sum, our evidence shows that the object categories children acquire are not complexive; they support proper extensions, even though they are not organized into sets of related categories. Moreover, these early notions of objects are present at the start of speech, beginning shortly after a year of age.

Acknowledgments

The study reported in this paper was supported by a grant from the Spencer Foundation to the senior author. The authors thank Rochel Gelman and Mary C. Potter for their helpful comments on the manuscript.

References to 2.4

Anglin, J. (1977). *Word, Object, and Conceptual Development*. New York: Norton.
Barrett, M. (1982). "Distinguishing between prototypes: The early acquisition of the meaning of object names." In S. Kuczaj II (ed.), *Language Development: Vol. 1, Syntax and semantics*. Hillsdale, NJ: Erlbaum.
Barrett, M. (1986). "Early semantic representations and early word-usage." In S. Kuczaj and M. Barrett (eds), *The Development of Word Meaning*. New York: Springer-Verlag.

Bates, E., Camaioni, L., and Volterra, V. (1975). "The acquisition of performatives prior to speech." *Merrill–Palmer Quarterly*, **21**, 205–26.

Bloom, L. (1973). *One Word at a Time*. The Hague: Mouton.

Bowerman, M. (1980). "The structure and origin of semantic categories in the language-learning child." In M. L. Foster and S. Brandes (eds), *Symbol as Sense*. New York: Academic Press.

Braine, M. D. S. (1963). "The ontogeny of English phrase structure." *Language*, **39**, 1–13.

Bretherton, I., McNew, S., Snyder, L., and Bates, E. (1983). "Individual differences at 20 months: Analytic and holistic strategies in language acquisition." *Journal of Child Language*, **10**, 293–320.

Brown, R. (1973). *A First Language: The early stages*. London: Allen & Unwin.

Carey, S. (1982). "Semantic development: The state of the art." In E. Wanner and L. Gleitman (eds), *Language Acquisition*, Cambridge: Cambridge University Press.

Clark, E. (1973). "What's in a word? On the child's acquisition of semantics in his first language." In T. Moore (ed.), *Cognitive Development and the Acquisition of Language*. New York: Academic Press.

Clark, E. (1983). "Meanings and concepts." In J. Flavell and E. Markman (eds), *Handbook of Child Psychology* (Vol. 3). New York: Wiley.

Edwards, D. (1978). "The sources of children's early meanings." In I. Markova (ed.), *The Social Context of Language*. Chichester: Wiley.

Fenson, L., Kagan, J., Kearsley, R. and Zelazo, P. (1976). "The developmental progression of manipulative play in the first two years." *Child Development*, **47**, 232–6.

Fodor, J. (1972). "Some reflections on L. S. Vygotsky's *Thought and Language*." *Cognition*, **1**, 83–95.

Fodor, J., Garrett, M., Walker, E., and Parkes, C. (1980). "Against definitions." *Cognition*, **8**, 263–367.

Fremgen, A. and Fay, D. (1980). "Overextensions in production and comprehension: A methodological clarification." *Journal of Child Language*, **7**, 205–11.

Gelman, R. and Baillargeon, R. (1983). "A review of some Piagetian concepts." In J. Flavell and E. Markman (eds), *Handbook of Child Psychology* (Vol. 3). New York: Wiley.

Gentner, D. (1982). "Why nouns are learned before verbs: Linguistic relativity versus natural partitioning." In S. A. Kuczaj II (ed.), *Language Development* (Vol. 2). Hillsdale, NJ: Erlbaum.

Goodman, N. (1955). *Fact, Fiction, and Forecast*. Cambridge, MA: Harvard University Press.

Griffiths, P. and Atkinson, M. (1978). "A 'door' to verbs." In N. Waterson and C. Snow (eds). *The Development of Communication*. Chichester: Wiley.

Gruendel, J. (1977). "Referential extension in early language development." *Child Development*, **48**, 1567–76.

Guillaume, P. (1973). " [First stages of sentence formation in children's speech.] " In C. A. Ferguson and D. I. Slobin (eds), *Studies of Child Language Development*, New York: Holt, Rinehart and Winston (originally published, 1923).

Hutt, C. (1967). "Effects of stimulus novelty on manipulatory exploration in an infant." *Journal of Child Psychology and Psychiatry*, **8**, 241–7.

Huttenlocher, J. (1974). "The origins of language comprehension." In R. L. Solso (ed.), *Theories in Cognitive Psychology*. Potomac, MD: Erlbaum.

Huttenlocher, J. and Higgins, E. T. (1978). "Issues in the study of symbolic development." In A. Collins (ed.), *Minnesota Symposia on Child Psychology* (Vol. 10). Hillsdale, NJ: Erlbaum.

Huttenlocher, J. and Smiley, P. (1986). *Origins of Event Categories: Evidence from speech*. Unpublished manuscript.

Huttenlocher, J., Smiley, P., and Prohaska, V. (1986). *Origins of the Category of Person: Evidence from speech*. Unpublished manuscript.

Inhelder, B. and Piaget, J. (1964). *The Early Growth of Logic in the Child*. New York: Norton.

Kay, D. and Anglin, J. (1982). "Overextensions and underextensions in the child's expressive and receptive speech." *Journal of Child Language*, **9**, 83–98.

Keil, F. (1983, November). *The Acquisition of Natural Kind and Artifact Terms*. Paper presented at the 24th Annual Meeting of the Psychonomic Society, San Diego.

Landau, B. and Gleitman, L. (1985). *Language and Experience*, Cambridge, MA: Harvard University Press.

Lowe, M. (1975). "Trends in the development of representational play in infants from one to three years: An observational study." *Journal of Child Psychology and Psychiatry*, **16**, 33–47.

Macnamara, J. (1982). *Names for Things*. Cambridge, MA: MIT Press.

Maratsos, M. and Chalkley, M. (1980). "The internal language of chidren's syntax: The ontogenesis and representation of syntactic categories." In K. E. Nelson (ed.), *Children's Language* (Vol. 2). New York: Gardner.

Markman, E., Cox, B., and Machida, S. (1981). "The standard object-sorting task as a measure of conceptual organization." *Developmental Psychology*, **17**, 115–17.

Nelson, K. (1973a). "Some evidence for the cognitive primacy of categorization and its functional basis." *Merrill–Palmer Quarterly*, **19**, 21–39.

Nelson, K. (1973b). "Structure and strategy in learning to talk." *Monographs of the Society for Research in Child Development*, **38** (1–2, Serial No. 149).

Nelson, K. (1974). "Concept, word and sentence: Interrelations in acquisition and development." *Psychological Review*, **81**, 267–85.

Nelson, K. (1983). "The conceptual basis for language." In T. Seiler and W. Wannenmacher (eds). *Concept Development and the Development of Word Meaning*. Berlin: Springer-Verlag.

Nelson, K. and Bonvillian, J. (1973). "Concepts and words in the 18-month-old: Acquiring concept names under controlled condition." *Cognition*, **2**, 435–50.

Piaget, J. (1962). *Play, Dreams and Imitation in Childhood*. New York: Norton.

Pinker, S. (1984), *Language Learnability and Language Development*. Cambridge, MA: Harvard University Press.

Quine, W. V. (1969). *Ontological Relativity and Other Essays*. New York: Cambridge University Press.

Reich, P. (1976). "The early acquisition of word meaning." *Journal of Child Language*, **3**, 117–23.

Rescorla, L. (1980). "Overextension in early language development." *Journal of Child Language*, **7**, 321–35.

Ricciuti, H. (1965). "Object grouping and selective ordering behavior in infants 12 to 24 months old." *Merrill–Palmer Quarterly*, **11**, 129–48.

Richards, M. M. (1979). "Sorting out what's in a word from what's not: Evaluating Clark's semantic features acquisition theory." *Journal of Experimental Child Psychology*, **27**, 1–47.

Rosch, E., Mervis, C., Gray W., Johnson, D., and Boyes-Braem, P. (1976). "Basic objects in natural categories." *Cognitive Psychology*, **8**, 382–439.

Ross, G. (1980). "Categorization in 1- to 2-year-olds." *Developmental Psychology*, **16**, 391–6.

Shipley, E. and Kuhn, I. (1983). "A constraint on comparisons: Equally detailed alternatives." *Journal of Experimental Child Psychology*, **35**, 195–222.

Snyder, L., Bates, E. and Bretherton, I. (1981) "Content and context in early lexical development." *Journal of Child Language*, **8**, 565–82.

Starkey, D. (1981). "The origins of concept formation: Object sorting and object preference in early infancy." *Child Development*, **52**, 489–97.

Sugarman, S. (1982). "Developmental change in early representational intelligence: Evidence from spatial classification strategies and related verbal expressions." *Cognitive Psychology*, **14**, 410–49.

Thomson, J. R. and Chapman, R. S. (1977). "Who is 'Daddy' revisited: The status of two-year-olds' overextended words in use and comprehension." *Journal of Child Language*, **4**, 359–75.

Vygotsky, L. (1962). *Thought and Language*. Cambridge, MA: MIT Press.

—PART 3 —————————

Syntax and Semantics

3.1

The Notion of Source in Language Acquisition

Eve V. Clark and Kathie L. Carpenter

Introduction

In English, when 2- and 3-year-olds talk about agents that are not subjects, they often rely on *from* where adults would not mark agents at all, or would use conventional *by* in passives. We list some typical examples in 1:[1]

1. (a) Damon (2;2,3, looking at pieces of sandwich he'd pushed off the edge of his plate): *These fall down from me.*
   (b) Julia (2;2, recounting a visit to the doctor): *I took my temperature from the doctor.*
   (c) Chris (3;0, talking about a character in a favorite book): *He's really scared from Tommy.*
   (d) Duncan (5;10,15, announcing a finger-puppet show to be performed by his younger sister, Helen): *Ken, Ken! Another puppet show! From Helen!*
   (e) Jessica (5;11, during a chase-game at a party, to the child who had just caught her): *I was caught from you before.*

The same children may also produce *from* to introduce clauses that describe the cause of a previously mentioned effect, as in 2:

2. (a) Damon (2;6,12, recalling what he had done three months earlier when his mother had left him with his grandmother while she fetched his father): *When gran'ma'ancy was here, you go fetch Herb.* [pause] *Then I cried a bit from you go get him.*

251

(b) Shem (2;8,7, explaining why his fire-engine was stuck on the roof of his toy garage): *That's fro—that's from I put a thing on it.*

(c) Walt (3;3,25, explaining how to tell mean hawks from nice hawks): *Maybe from they—hawks eat sea-shells. Some hawks eat sea-shells.*

We take these to be evidence for a general category of source. The argument is the following. Children have a category of source that encompasses not only locations but also agents, causes, possessors, standards of comparison, and prior events. When children need to mark sources in oblique arguments, they use the most available term to mark the category. They therefore choose *from* to introduce agents and causes because it expresses the notion of locative source. SOURCE, we propose, is an emergent category with even broader membership than appears in English alone, where agents, for example, are not conventionally marked as sources.[2] But if source is an emergent category, we would expect its members to be marked both in the speech of young children and in other languages.

The notion of source

Spatial terms are used to express not only spatial relations but also many protections of space onto nonspatial domains. In different languages spatial terms are commonly used for time, change of state, temperature, musical pitch, mood, and attitude, among many other domains. Philosophers, psychologists, and linguists alike have analyzed uses of spatial terms for nonspatial domains,[3] and have argued that reliance on spatial terms in language—terms originally devised to talk about space itself—goes far beyond the domain of space. As Jackendoff (1983: 210) noted:

> If there is any primacy to the spatial field, it is because this field is so strongly supported by nonlinguistic cognition; it is the common ground for the essential faculties of vision, touch, and action. From an evolutionary perspective, spatial organization had to exist long before language.

Conceptions of space, in other words, serve as a basis for organizing both nonlinguistic and linguistic information.

In Modern English, spatial expressions have commonly been categorized as sources, goals, or locations (e.g. Anderson, 1971; DeLancey, 1981; Gruber, 1976; Jackendoff, 1972). Sources are defined by Gruber as the initial position of the theme. With verbs of motion, the theme is the entity undergoing motion (*Dan* in *Dan ran from his house to the school*); otherwise the theme is the entity located (*that vase* in *That vase comes from Lugano*). The source, then, is a relation linking a theme to a place and a direction. The place is the origin or starting point, and the direction is "away from" that place. The place and direction may, but need not, be associated with an explicit motion. The locative source may also encompass people as long as person and place (the starting point) coincide, as in *The book is from grandma* and *You'll hear from his lawyer next week*.

Modern English offers considerable evidence for the notion of source. The primary preposition for marking source is the locative *from*. Other prepositions such as *out (of)* and *off (of)* serve this function too, but they are more specialized in meaning. *Out of* specifies an enclosure and *off of* a surface, whereas *from* is unmarked for these distinctions (e.g., *He took the books from his suitcase* and *He knocked the butter from the table*).[4] *From* also forms complex prepositions to specify the source, as in *He moved the umbrella from beside the desk; He took the box from underneath the shelf*.

From marks starting points in time, as in *From now until four o'clock* and *From the age of ten*, as well as events that serve as starting points, as in *From World War II on, their fortunes failed*.[5] Another use of the starting-point sense of *from* is for intermediary instruments, where a new state or creation results, as in *The lock was marked with scratches from a screwdriver*. Notice that where no new state results *from* is taken to be locative, as in *hinges from a door*—which can only refer to detached hinges, with the *from* phrase identifying their spatial origin.

From is used for states. So just as typical motion events contain a theme that moves from source to goal, as in *Kate drove from Cincinnati to Chicago*, so do events without motion, notably events with changes of state. In *His mood changed from despair to anger*, the source phrase indicates the starting state. Changes of state, then, have a source and a goal, just as motion events do (*from Cincinnati, from despair*); but instead of a displacement in space, changes of state involve a displacement from one state to another.

From can mark certain causes as sources, where these distinguish earlier from later activities, as in *From his silence/from the look on his face/from what he just said, they guessed the truth*. One subtype of cause is disease, as in *to collapse from a heart attack, to suffer from hives, to die from starvation* (see DeLancey, 1984). *From* is also used to mark prior activities or states that have since ceased, as in *He stopped her from complaining* and *Their father prevented them from climbing*. Here the prior state or activity is the source. Only a handful of verbs, typically *stop, prevent,* and *keep,* allow this construction.

Agents are also a kind of source, but this can be seen only in certain constructions. In *Jane sold the book to Ken*, the agent and source are the same (*Jane*), although there is no explicit marking of the source. But in constructions with *get* the agent is explicitly marked with *from*, as in *He got a book from Jill, He got a black eye from Mel,* and *He got a good scolding from his father*. The agent in *get ... from* constructions may otherwise appear in the *by* phrase of passives.[6] This suggests that agents in general are sources, even though they are not usually marked with *from*. One reason for considering them as sources is that they are the origins of actions. In causative actions, they are the instigators of subsequent change. Agents, of course, are not normally marked with a preposition except when they appear as oblique arguments.[7]

The identification of agents in Modern English as sources may be obscured by conventional *by* (rather than *from*), as in *Tom was tripped by his brother*. But in Old English (OE) and Middle English (ME), uses of *from* were much broader and encompassed agents and natural forces as well as places. In OE texts, 80 percent of oblique personal agents were marked by *fram* "from," 2 percent by *of*, 15 percent by *through*, and 3 percent by *mid* (Van Dam, 1957). Natural forces such as wind or snow were also marked by *fram*, as were animal agents. These uses of *fram* show that agents used to be marked explicitly as sources in English (see also Anderson, 1971; DeLancey, 1984).

Yet over time, *from* has been replaced with *by*, and *by* in turn may alternate with *with* in certain environments. To understand how the distributions of these three prepositions have changed, we need to look briefly at their histories. All three have been called on at one time or another to express causality, and the traces remain in Modern English. In ME agentive *from* was gradually ousted by *of* (still used today with an ablative or source meaning) which in turn gave way to *by* around 1600. At that time, the locative *by* had the meaning of "via," a meaning now less accessible to speakers than the static meaning of "proximity." Agentive *by* first emerged towards the end of the fourteenth century, and by the fifteenth to sixteenth century it rivaled *of* in frequency. *By*, in OE and ME, marked direction "via" (*go to Norwich by London*), "in the presence of" in oaths (*by God*), and later the notion of "alone" (*by himself*) (Green, 1914; Mitchell, 1985; Mustanoja, 1960; Visser, 1963–73).[8]

While *from* for oblique agents was being replaced first by *of* and then by *by*, instrumental *mid* was entirely replaced by *with*, which took over all its functions. *Mid* in OE carried the meanings of association, connection, and accompaniment, and hence of instrument, which were all later taken on by *with*.[9] In OE, *with* itself expressed the notions of "against" (as in Modern English *argue with*, *quarrel with*) and "proximity." Between 1250 and 1350 it took over the senses of *mid* to such an extent that *mid* was obsolete by the end of the fourteenth century (Visser, 1963–73). From then on, *with* was used in five main senses: (a) in its original sense of opposition in verbs of conflict; (b) in a locative sense for accompaniment (*with his brother*, meaning "in the company of"), taken over from *mid*; (c) in the sense of manner or attribute (*walk with a limp*, *with a nod*); (d) for instruments (*hit with a stick*, *break with a hammer*, *pick up with tongs*, where the instrument enables the action); and (e) for some kinds of causes (*tremble with fear*, *be at home with the flu*) (cf. Mitchell, 1985; Quirk *et al.*, 1972; Schlesinger, 1979). The instrumental and causal meanings of *with* appear to have arisen from the notion of accompaniment and the consequent participation of instrument or cause in an action.

All three prepositions were originally locative in meaning, but only *from* marks the notion of locative source. The causal senses of both *by* and *with* seem to have arisen from meanings where instruments or intermediaries enabled actions, rather than through a direct connection with the notion of source. And, in fact, intermediaries in an action—elements that accompany the action—are not, by nature, the direct sources of the action. Within causative events, then, both *from* and *by*, at different times, have served to mark oblique agents as agents; *with* has consistently been used to mark instruments as instruments since the fifteenth century, and, over time, all three prepositions have come to be used with both causal and noncausal constructions.

In this brief account we have indicated the range of English constructions in which sources have been marked with *from*, sources which in Modern English include spatial and temporal origins, certain prior events, and certain kinds of cause. We have also outlined ways in which *from*, *with*, and *by* are connected historically as well as in modern usage. We turn now to children's uses of *from* for further evidence for SOURCE, and show that this category is considerably broader for children than in contemporary conventional usage.

The data

In our analyses of children's uses of *from* we draw on several kinds of data. The first corpus we have used is an extensive diary kept on Damon, the son of the first author. Damon is an only child growing up in Northern California with English as his first language. The diary consists of daily notes, with detailed contexts that include day, time, who was present, and the linguistic and nonlinguistic setting of each utterance recorded. Daily observations such as these offer a particularly fine-grained basis for analysis compared to recordings based on one hour a week or every two weeks, as in many longitudinal studies. Diaries offer more detail in part because the observer (typically a parent) has access to the child's daily routine as well as to special events and experiences (Braunwald and Brislin, 1979; Dromi, 1987). Some entries contain only the child's utterance; others contain segments of conversations between Damon and his adult or child interlocutors. The diary contains some 15,000 observations made between the ages of 1;0 and 6;0.

The other longitudinal data we draw on come from the CHILDES Archive (MacWhinney and Snow, 1985). They consist of the transcriptions of thirty–sixty-minute recordings made weekly or biweekly over the age range of 1;6 to 5;1. We included the following corpora from English-speaking children: Adam (2;3–4;6), Sarah (2;3–5;1), Eve (1;6–2;3), Shem (2;2–3;4), Walt (2;4–5;0), and Naomi (1;1–5;1) (see Brown, 1973; Clark, 1978a; Sachs, 1983). In these corpora the child's interlocutor is sometimes a parent and sometimes an observer; the recording sessions are an hour every week (Sarah, Shem), an hour every two weeks (Adam, Eve), half an hour twice a week (Walt), or less regular than this (Naomi). The transcripts often lack the detail about physical context available in the diary notes, but the surrounding utterances usually offer enough information for interpretation of what the child is talking about. In all, there

Table 3.1.1 *Number of uses of* from, with, *and* by *in each longitudinal child corpus*

Name	Age	*from*	*with*	*by*
Damon	1;6–5;11	198	249	84
Adam	2;0–4;11	142	638	74
Sarah	2;6–5;5	62	171	14
Eve	1;6–2;5	19	83	19
Shem	2;2–3;5	60	62	20
Naomi	1;6–4;11	18	56	15
Walt	2;0–5;5	119	576	76

were 618 uses of *from*, 1,835 uses of *with*, and 302 uses of *by*. The numbers for each child are given in Table 3.1.1.

From *in acquisition*

Children's uses of *from* fell into several categories. Their first uses were all locative, but these were soon followed by uses of *from* for nonlocative domains. The main categories children used are described below.[10]

Location and time

Locative uses of *from* included all uses for the origin in space of an object or event.[11] Damon's earliest recorded use appeared in a question addressed to his father: *Herb, where that came from?* (2;1.28). Later locative uses included *That came from my toe* (2;2,5, as his mother picked up a sock), *Look, look, I found the book what we got from the library* (2;6,24), *I think Eve hears this from Washington* (2;8,29, when making a noise while his mother was away), and *I'll get something from my Lego box* (2;10,18). The other six children, like Damon, all began with locative *from*, as in *What dat from?* (Adam 2;5), *Hey, ge' down from house* (Sarah 3;2), or *An' it come from in the bathroom* (Shem 2;3,16). The children's locative uses of *from* resembled adult uses in their range and in the kinds of verbs with which they occurred.

From was also used for time in referring to events or activities, as in *back from fishing* (Walt 2;8,22) or *and when I wake up from my nap* (Eve 2;2). These uses emerged after locative ones and typically accounted for less than 10 percent of uses in any six-month period. Again, most uses resembled adult usage. This extension of *from* from space to time is particularly common across languages (e.g. Traugott, 1978).

Agents and natural forces

The first instances of agentive *from* consisted of nonconventional uses in which the animate instigator of an event appeared in an oblique noun phrase marked by *from*, as in *This fall down from me* (Damon 2;2,3, knocking pieces of sandwich off his plate), *They scared from me* (Damon 2;5,10, after rushing at some starlings), or *No, he isn't going to get hurt from those bad guys* (Damon 2;7,11, fantasizing). Oblique agents like this appeared after a variety of verbs (e.g. *catch, arrest, send,* and *allow*) and after *be scared, be afraid,* and *be tired,* as in *Some women were arrested from the soldiers* (Damon 4;2,23, reporting what he had heard on the radio); *I'm tired from her* (Sarah 3;8, complaining about another child); or *He comed from me* (Shem 3;0,0, explaining that he had been the one to put the doll on the bed). Every child who produced *from* to mark the animate instigator of an event had already used *from* for locative starting points. The agent in each instance is the source of the action being talked about. These child uses, however, have no conventional counterpart in adult English.

From was also used to mark nonanimate natural forces that played a causal role in provoking an event, as in *Look at that knocked down tree from the wind* (Damon 2;11,12, looking at a fallen tree), or *Daddy, the pigs have been marooned from a flood* (Damon 4;6,9, filling in the story his father was about to continue reading). In such instances the natural force itself was the source of the event. Included in this category were *wind, sun, rain, dark, flood, cold,* and *snow.* These uses, like the agentive uses, emerged after locative *from.* Natural forces share with agents several properties of agenthood, even though they lack the volitional element common to animate (typically human) agents (Cruse, 1973).[12]

Cause, means, and instrument

In causal uses of *from,* the preposition *from* introduces a noun phrase or clause that designates the cause of the effect or result just mentioned. Causes introduced in this way appeared quite common, as in *I not tired from my games* (Adam 2;8); *That's fro' ... [repair] that's from I put a thing on it* (Shem 2;8,3, explaining how his fire-truck had got stuck in his toy garage); *If I talk too much, I be tired from doing that* (Damon 2;10,23); *Who gets sick from eating seeds?* (Walt 3;1,8, after being told seeds were hard to digest); *I'm gon' faint from that* (Sarah 4;8, talking about a play she had seen the night before); or *I think it was from the wood of the storage box* (Walt 4;8,2, discussing how he had cut his finger).

On rare occasions *from* was also used for talking about the means or intermediary object by which an action was accomplished, as in *I opened my door from my wooden box* (Damon 2;5,25, after he opened the door and then propped it open with a wooden box). Also rare were uses of *from* to mark instruments, typically inanimate objects used as auxiliaries in an event, as in *I drawed the lines from the pencil* (Walt 4;0,3).[13]

Possession

Children's possessive constructions with *from* use the preposition to mark the possessor, as in *That's a finger from him* (Shem 3;0,13, pointing at a picture of someone patting a horse); *I see boats from Mommy* (Adam 3;0); *You can be a mum from two babies* (Damon 3;7,5, assigning roles in a game); *Do you know there's two next door neighbors from us?* (Walt 4;1,15, talking to his father about their having neighbors on both sides); or *Here's the father-whale from this tiny whale* (Damon 4;3,17, as he was drawing). Jackendoff (1983), like Gruber (1976), argued that possessors are sources, with the notion of "motion away" being derived from the notion of transfer from possessor A to possessor B. Note that the possessor need not be engaged in an actual transfer to be considered a source.

Identification of the possessor with the notion of source is found in many languages, whether the source is marked with a preposition (as in French *de*, Dutch *van*, and German *von*) or with the genitive or ablative case.[14] But many languages rely instead on the dative case for the possessor (Ultan, 1978). This suggests that languages may favor one of two possible viewpoints: The possessor is viewed either as the course from which the possessed object comes (genitive/ablative, from/of) or as the goal to which the object goes (dative, to).[15] Children who opt for *from* would then be conceiving of the possessor as a source.

Comparison

From was also used at times to mark the standard of comparison. Consider such child uses as Damon's *This seat is getting too small from me* (2;8,15, climbing into his car-seat), *Herb's the tallest from me and you're the tallest from me* (3;7,1, comparing his height to that of his parents), and *Do you know what hours are for giants from other people? Years! They have twelve years every day!* (4;5,27), or Walt's *See? This ear is longer from the other ear* (3;1,15, talking about a toy rabbit).[16]

Comparison, like possession, can be conceived of as requiring (abstract) movement away from a standard toward the element being compared to that standard (e.g., Jackendoff, 1983). In *Jan is taller than Chris*, *Chris* is the standard and *Jan* the entity being compared to it. This analysis equates the standard in a comparison with a place analogous to the places in *Jan is from London* or *Chris lives two miles from here*. That is, the standard is a SOURCE (see also Joly, 1967).[17] But notice that the standard could also be conceived of as static location (*at, on*) or as a goal (*to*), and is so marked in some languages (see Stassen, 1985). So marking with *from* reflects just one perspective on comparison.

Cessation

From was also used for cessation in nonconventional ways, and children did this before they began to use it conventionally in this domain. Adults use *from* here only after a limited set of verbs, notably *stop, prevent,* and *keep,* as in *They prevented the dogs from getting out, Tam stopped the boys from climbing on the wall,* and *Jack kept the door from opening.* In each case, the current event either puts an end to the earlier one or forestalls its occurrence. Thus, the dogs were going out or about to do so, but were stopped or forestalled; the boys were climbing on the wall and then were stopped; and the door was going to open, or was already opening, and Jack intervened to stop it. Whether the prior event has really taken place may not always be determinate, but the current event has the effect of causing a change of activity from the actual or expected prior event. The prior event, then, is the source, and as such is marked with *from.*[18]

Nonconventional uses appear after such verbs as *get, shoot, fix, be careful,* and *wake up,* none of them verbs that conventionally license a *from* complement. Typical early uses included *I'm going to dive in and get people from getting into trouble* (2;7,18, pretending to be a lifeguard); *Don't wake me up from sleeping* (2;9,23, in the car, pretending to go to sleep); and *I can't fix it from breaking* (3;3,1, a slide he had constructed with wooden blocks).[19]

Only after these nonconventional uses do children begin to use apparently conventional forms as well. But at this point children may distinguish actual from hypothetical prior events by adding a *not* to the complement of the latter. Typical examples from Damon include: *I'm keeping Duncan from not getting my boat* (2;10,26, as he placed his toy boat out of the reach of his 1-year-old cousin); *The motor in the back prevents the wheels from not stopping so that's why they don't go* (3;1,27, of his train);[20] *They're to keep the wind from not blowing it down* (3;7,29, of some pointed bricks on a house he had built); and *My hands are to keep the baby from not falling out* (3;8,14, as he made a crib on his knee for a doll). That is, for some months the conventionally appropriate verbs for introducing *from* complements carried along with them an added negative that specified the purpose expressed in the complement, where, for example, the aim was for Duncan not to get the boat, for the newly built house not to be blown down, or for the doll not to fall. The nonconventional addition of *not* serves to mark the prior event of getting hold of the boat, or of the doll falling, as hypothetical.[21]

The added *nots* in these constructions, then, distinguish hypothetical from actual prior events. Whether this solution is tried by all children is unclear. Damon continued to use such *from* complements without an added *not* alongside those that did contain *not.* The difference between the two, aside from the main-clause verbs, seems to reside precisely in the realis/irrealis status of the prior event. By age 4, however, he appears to have realized that the status of the prior event need not be specified in English, and he stopped using *not* in these constructions.

The categories of *from* used by the children are summarized in Table 3.1.2. The order in which *from* emerged for use with different members of the source category was very consistent. Locative *from* always appeared before any other

Table 3.1.2 *Categories of* from *uses produced at each age*

Category	1;6–1;11	2;0–2;5	2;6–2;11	3;0–3;5	3;6–3;11	4;0–4;5	4;6–4;11	5;0–5;5	5;6–5;11
Location	X	X	X	X	X	X	X	X	X
Time		X	X	X	X	X	X		X
Agent		X	X	X	X	X	X	X	
Force		X	X	X	X	X	X		
Cause		X	X	X	X	X	X	X	X
Means		X		X	X				
Instrument	X	X	X	X	X	X	X	X	X
Possess		X	X	X	X	X			
Compare		X	X	X	X	X	X	X	X
Cease		X	X	X	X	X	X	X	X
Total Uses	6	36	132	141	119	95	63	17	9

uses: agent *from* appeared before possess, compare, and cease constructions, as did causal *from*. Whenever children produced only one of the two constructions being compared, it was nearly always the one that was the earlier of the two for the other children. The only apparent exception was that some children who did not produce any instances of *from* for natural forces did use it for possession, comparison, or cessation. The consistency in ordering for each pair of constructions with *from* is shown in Table 3.1.3, which summarizes the numbers

Table 3.1.3 *Consistency in order of acquisition for* from

	Number of children				
From	Dominant order	Other order	Simultaneous emergence	Only one construction	Neither construction
Location before time	5	0	0	2 (Location)	0
Location before agent	5	0	0	2 (Location)	0
Location before natforce	2	0	0	5 (Location)	0
Location before cause	5	0	0	2 (Location)	0
Location before means	3	0	0	4 (Location)	0
Location before instr	4	0	0	3 (Location)	0
Location before possess	4	0	0	3 (Location)	0
Location before compare	3	0	0	4 (Location)	0
Location before cease	4	0	0	3 (Location)	0
Agent before possess	2	1	1	1 (Agent)	2
Agent before compare	2	1	0	2 (Agent)	2
Agent before cease	2	1	1	1 (Agent)	2
NatForce before possess	2	0	0	2 (Possess)	3
NatForce before compare	2	0	0	1 (Compare)	4
NatForce before cease	2	0	0	2 (Cease)	3
Cause before possess	3	0	1	1 (Cause)	2
Cause before compare	3	0	0	2 (Cause)	2
Cause before cease	2	0	2	1 (Cause)	2

Table 3.1.4 *Percentages of* from *uses in each category, summed over age, for each child*

Category	Child							
	Damon	Adam	Sarah	Eve	Shem	Walt	Naomi	Mean
Location	26	86	50	68	63	50	100	53
Time	3	0	5	32	6	9	0	6
Agent	16	6	24	0	4	9	0	12
Force	5	0	2	0	0	2	0	3
Cause	11	4	10	0	10	6	0	4
Means	1	0	0	0	0	0	0	0.2
Instrument	2	1	5	0	3	6	0	6
Possess	11	0	2	0	8	6	0	5
Compare	9	0	3	0	0	8	0	5
Cease	13	2	0	0	5	3	0	6

Note: Percentages do not always sum to 100 because of rounding.

of children who used each *from* construction relative to the predominant orderings observed in the data.

Nonconventional uses of *from* for agents, natural forces, and causes became rare after age 4;0 (see further "Experimental data from children" below). The order in which particular extensions of *from* emerged was consistent across children ($r = .51$), but the correlation was lowered because some of the children extended *from* to only one or two categories during the period in which they were recorded. (Recall that not all the children were followed over the whole period from about 2 to 5 or 6 years, as indicated in Table 3.1.1.) The percentages of uses that fell into each category overall, for each child, are shown in Table 3.1.4.

With *and* by

How are children's uses of *from* related to those of *with* and *by*? Overall, *with* and *by* are connected to *from* through their roles in causal events. These three constitute the main causal prepositions in English, and historically they have all been used at one time or another to express the roles of agent, cause, means, and instrument. Here we examine early productions of *with* and *by* to see whether children produce nonconventional uses here too.

With

With had three main uses—comitative, instrumental, and attributive. Comitative uses referred to accompaniment, as in *Damon take doll with you* [= Damon] (Damon 2;0,1) or *I want my jacket with me* (Walt 2;6,10). These emerged at about the same time as the earliest uses of *from*. Instrumental uses of *with* introduced the instrument used in the performance of an action. Instruments were inanimate, e.g., pencils, sticks, and spoons, but they included body parts, as in *I getting rings out my bib with my hand* (Damon 2;1,12, picking cheerios out of the lip of his bib) and *I paint with my arms* (Shem 2;5,23). Five of the seven children produced comitative or instrumental *with* first, with the other type emerging within a few days. The other two children produced *with* first in what was probably an unanalyzed form, in the idiom *play with* (Adam at 2;6 and Eve at 1;7). The verb *play with* was very frequent for all the children, but it appears to have been used as a single lexeme—*play* was never separated from its particle *with*—and so may not have been associated with other uses of *with* until later. Because of its frequency, we tallied uses of *play with* separately from other idioms (*be through with, done with, okay with*, etc.).[22] Both Adam and Eve produced comitative and instrumental *with* within a few weeks of *play with*. For all seven children, comitative and instrumental uses of *with* predominated at all ages.

Attributive uses of *with* introduced characteristics that served to describe or identify entities, as in *An' vans to move, with wheels on it* (Shem 2;7,18, specifying the drawing he wanted done) or *You see that man with a pipe?* (Damon 3;8,18). The children's attributive uses generally emerged after both comitative and instrumental ones.

Other uses of *with*, besides those categorized as idioms, were rare. For example, Damon produced *with* on just seven occasions to mark a cause, as in *It's very trippy with these shoes* (3;11,17, as he ran across a stretch of gravel), and on just three occasions to mark an agent, as in *It might be stealed away with the robbers* (4;0, fantasizing as he played with his smurfs). One other child, Walt, used one instance of agentive *with*. (Since these agentive uses were so rare, accounting for less than 1 percent and 0.2 percent respectively of the children's *with*s, they are not included in the summary table.) These rare nonconventional uses of *with* seemed to stem from its comitative and instrumental meanings.[23]

The order of emergence of different uses of *with* was very stable across the children ($r = .86$). The percentages of uses in each category for each child are summarized in Table 3.1.5. For all seven children, comitative and instrumental uses of *with* emerged before attributive uses. Uses of *with* for agent (two children, with four uses between them) and cause (three children, with seventeen uses in all) emerged later still. The remaining uses of *with* were nearly all idioms not easily included in other categories, e.g. *start with, be done with*, and *be all through with*. As Table 3.1.5 shows, the three categories of comitative, instrumental, and attributive together accounted for 62 percent of all the children's uses. Nearly all the remaining uses, including *play with*, are idioms (38 percent).

Table 3.1.5 *Percentages of* with *uses in each category, summed over age, for each child*

Category	Child							
	Damon	Adam	Sarah	Eve	Shem	Walt	Naomi	Mean
Comitative	14	17	29	31	24	22	27	21
Attribute	22	10	17	2	14	16	7	11
Material	2	2	0.6	0	5	5	0	3
Manner	4	0	0	0	0	0	0	0.6
Instrument	42	16	20	34	27	19	20	23
Cause	3	0.5	0	0	0	0.4	0	1
Play with	3	38	19	23	19	21	36	26
Idiom	13	12	14	1	6	17	11	14

By

By was first produced either as a locative to indicate proximity in space or in some version of *by myself*, meaning "alone, without help." It was used to mark an instrument or a causal event, or to mark the agent of a passive verb, only long after these initial uses, if at all. Five of the children used *by* first as a locative to mark proximity, as in *Man by you* (Eve 1;7), *There's food by the 'frigerator* (Shem 2;3,2), or *Sit by me* (Sarah 2;5). These children all began to use *by* in combination with *self* (*self, myself, yourself, itself*), meaning "alone," within a few months. The other two children, Damon and Adam, used *by* first with this sense, as in *I get down by self* (Damon 2;0,12) or *Put it by self* (Adam 2;6). Locative and *self* uses were the only two types to appear in the speech of Eve (to age 2;5), Shem (to age 3;4), and Naomi. These two uses also accounted for nearly all the early uses from the other children as well.

Four of the children also used *by* to introduce natural forces (Damon and Walt), instruments (all four), causes (Damon and Sarah), means (Adam and Walt), or agents (Damon, Adam, and Walt). The natural forces included wind and rain, as in *The branches come off by the wind* (Damon 2;2,3)[24] or—in response to the adult question *How did it get buried?—I don't know. By the rain or some dirt* (Walt 3;7,5). Natural forces appeared to emerge alongside two other elements in causal events: Instruments and causes in Damon and Sarah, and instruments and means in Adam and Walt. Instruments were inanimate objects or body parts that contributed to the outcome of an event. Typical of the children's uses were *I tied it by my hand* (Damon 2;7,5) and *Grandma, see how I covered the dots. By the pencil* (Walt 4;0,3). Instances of means were often close to instruments in the role they played in events, but they were characterized as having an intermediary role in accomplishing an action, as in *Why'd you carry it by de handle?* (Adam 3;3) or *I hanged by one leg* (Walt 2;9,23, reporting on his gymnastics class). In causes, the cause of an event or result already mentioned is introduced with *by*, as in

Table 3.1.6   *Percentages of* by *uses in each category, summed over age, for each child*

Category	Child							
	Damon	Adam	Sarah	Eve	Shem	Walt	Naomi	Mean
Location	14	22	64	79	60	16	27	28
Time	0	3	0	0	0	0	0	0.4
X-self	7	65	21	21	40	36	67	34
Agent	19	4	0	0	0	17	0	11
Force	14	0	0	0	0	5	0	6
Cause	12	0	0	0	0	0	0	6
Instrument	16	1	3	0	0	7	0	10
Idiom	1	4	7	0	0	0	7	4

I feel tired by running—all done in! (Damon 3;6,7) or *It explodes by a bomb hitting it* (Damon 3;6,28). Agentive uses of *by* were produced by only three children, Damon, Adam (two instances only), and Walt. Typical examples include *I caught by a fish* (Adam 4;0), *And the lion got eaten by a hippo* (Walt 4;1,0), and *He'll get killed by the dragon* (Walt 4;1,15, answering a question about a knight in a story). Agentive *by* uses emerged only after some other causal uses (instrument, means, cause) had been produced, and few instances occurred before 3;0.

The percentage of *by* uses overall in each category is shown for all the children in Table 3.1.6. There was again a high correlation across children for the order in which different uses emerged in their spontaneous speech ($r = .61$). Either locative or *self* uses emerged first, with the other use appearing within weeks. Both these uses emerged before the more obviously causal uses of *by* for instruments, natural forces, causes, and agents. *Self* uses may in fact be precursors to some form of agentive meaning, since they emerge in contexts where children are trying to take on activities and carry them out independently (see also Horgan, 1978). The overall number of *by* uses was low, especially compared to uses of *from* and *with* (see Table 3.1.1). Finally, the vast majority of *with* and *by* uses were conventional, unlike children's uses of *from*.

Parental input

Does parental input offer a basis for children's nonconventional uses of *from*? We first considered whether adult input could account for the patterns observed in children's spontaneous uses of all three prepositions. To examine this possibility, we tallied all the adult uses of the three prepositions in the input to Adam, Sarah, and Eve (the Brown corpus), where the speech addressed to the children came from one or the other parent and an observer; the input to Walt, where most of the speech was from his parents; and the input to Shem, where most of the speech was from an observer.[25]

Adult *from*

Most adult uses of *from* (82 percent on average) were locative, just as they were in the children's speech. Adults, like most of the children, used *from* for time as well (8 percent). But although children used *from* to mark agents, adults never did so. Adults did make use of *from* for cause, but these uses were rare—only twenty-three out of a total of 565 instances of *from*, and five of the twenty-three were adult echoes of nonconventional child uses. Although children used *from* to mark the possessor, adults never did. The only adult uses of *from* in comparative constructions occurred after the adjective *different*, with six instances in all (versus five instances of *than*). Finally, the uses of *from* for cessation were fairly rare, were all conventional, and occurred only after such verbs as *stop* or *keep*. These findings are summarized in Table 3.1.7. The adult input on *from* showed no discernible shifts in usage as the children got older. The correlation between adults, based on the frequency of each category, was .55, but the correlation between adult frequency and child order of acquisition (correlated for each adult–child pair) was considerably lower, with $r = .36$.

Adult *with*

The major adult uses of *with* fell into three categories: comitative (21 percent),

Table 3.1.7   *Percentage of* from *uses in input for each category, summed over age*

Category	Input to					
	Adam	Sarah	Eve	Shem	Walt	Mean
Location	89	85	71	74	75	82
Time	3	6	22	6	11	8
Agent	0	0.5*	0	0	0	0.2*
Force	0	0.5	0	0	0	0.2
Cause	1*	6	2	6	5*	4
Means	0	0	0	0	0	0
Instrument	0	0	0	0	0	0
Possess	0	0	0	0	0	0
Compare	0.7	0	2	3	5	1
Cease	4	1	0	9	4	3
Change	0.7	0.5	0	3	0	0.6
Idiom	2	0.5	4	0	0	1

Note: The * indicates at least one repeat of a nonconventional child form.

instrumental (16 percent), and attributive (10 percent), as shown in Table 3.1.8. Across all ages, to all five children, these categories in the input accounted for over two-thirds of adult *with* uses (compare the children's uses in Table 3.1.5).

Most of the other adult uses fell in the category of idioms, mainly uses of *play with* (21 percent, e.g., *D'you want to play with that?*) or *do with* (15 per cent, e.g., *What are you going to do with that?*). Means and cause were rare in adults' speech, just as they were in the children's. The agreement between adults was high (*r* = .91), but the correlation between adult frequency and child order of acquisition was not so high (*r* = .70). At the same time, the parallels between adult and child categories for *with* were stronger than for either *from* or *by*.

Adult *by*

The two most frequent categories of *by* in adult speech were locative (36 percent), for talking about proximity (e.g., *It's over there by the box*), and *self* uses (30 percent, e.g., *Oh, can you carry that by yourself?*), as shown in Table 3.1.9. The only other categories used with any frequency were means (11 percent, e.g., *He went by bike, yes*), used to all five children; temporal *by* (8 percent, e.g., *By the time you have lunch it'll be cool*), used to four of the five; and agent *by* (10 percent, e.g., *You got stung by a bee* and *It's made by Indians*), used to all five children. The only other uses, for instrument and cause, were very rare (less than 2 percent).

Adult uses of *by*, like those of *with*, were highly consistent from one person to the next, so the correlation for frequency of use for each category across adults was high (*r* = .67). The correlation between adult frequency and child order of acquisition was again lower, at *r* = .59, than the correlation among adults, but not reliably so.

Table 3.1.8 *Percentage of* with *uses in input for each category, summed over age*

Category	Adam	Sarah	Eve	Shem	Walt	Mean
			Input to			
Comitative	14	29	17	18	26	21
Attribute	7	12	8	12	8	10
Material	2	0	2	1	2	1
Manner	0.2	1	1	2	1	1
Instrument	19	10	21	18	16	16
Cause	0.4	1	0.3	0.4	0.4	0.5
Means	0	0	0	2	0.2	0.3
Play with	29	26	22	14	18	21
Do with	10	17	20	17	14	15
Idiom	14	18	8	15	14	14

Table 3.1.9 *Percentage of* by *uses in input for each category, summed over age*

Category	Input to					
	Adam	Sarah	Eve	Shem	Walt	Mean
Location	21	7	65	36	33	36
Time	4	28	5	0	14	8
X-self	43	21	24	25	34	30
Agent	11	24	2	11	8	10
Force	0	0	0	0	0	0
Cause	0	7	0	2	0	0.4
Means	16	10	5	17	8	11
Instrument	2	0	0	2	0	1
Idiom	4	10	0	6	3	4

Summary

It seems unlikely that children's NONCONVENTIONAL uses are based on adult uses. In the speech addressed to Adam, Sarah, Eve, Walt, and Shem, adult uses of the three prepositions—*from, with,* and *by*—were all conventional, except on the few occasions where an adult echoed a nonconventional child form. Otherwise adults never provided models for children's nonconventional uses. But they made use of all three prepositions for conventional categories NOT represented as well as for ones that WERE represented in the children's speech. Only in the case of *with* did child and adult usage match. *From* was used by children where it was not expected, and *by* was not used where it was expected. Children's uses of these prepositions, we therefore argue, can only be accounted for by (a) the conceptual notion of source, and (b) children's reliance on this notion to mark sources with *from* despite the conventions of the language they hear around them. Before we expand on this, we will consider some additional data, from a larger sample of children, that offer further systematic evidence that *from* is often favored early on to mark oblique agents.

Experimental data from children

The forms children produce in spontaneous speech should also appear in elicitation tasks that focus on constructions where children make errors, namely in the agent phrases of passive sentences. And there are scattered mentions of this phenomenon in earlier studies (e.g., Horgan, 1978 and Maratsos and Abramovitch, 1975; see further E. Clark and Carpenter, 1989). The present longitudinal data suggest that younger children should prefer *from* over *by* in agent phrases, and that older children should prefer the reverse. All ages, though, should prefer *with* for instrument phrases. We therefore asked children to imitate various kinds of sentences, and to repair them to "make them better." Since younger children listen to and then reproduce structures filtered through their own current system, we expected their imitations to reflect preferences of the kind observed in spontaneous speech, particularly between age 2;0 and 3,0. Older children, though, are better able to imitate verbatim regardless of the form they hear, so their imitations probably yield less information about preferences for *from* versus *by*. But if older children are asked to repair a sentence they have imitated, they are likely to do so in terms of what they think that form ought to have been. So it is older children's repairs, rather than their imitations, that should reflect their preferences.

We gave forty children between 2;5 and 6;1 a set of sentences to imitate and repair, with equal numbers containing each preposition—*from, with,* and *by*. The sentences we used were all based on spontaneous utterances produced by children in the same age range. Half the sentences were grammatical and half ungrammatical. Grammatical *from* appeared in locative sentences, as in *Molly took some Legos from my box,* while ungrammatical *from appeared with agents and natural forces, as in *Birds are scared from big cats or *The tree blew down from the wind. Grammatical *with* introduced instruments, as in *Josh is eating with Daddy's spoon,* and ungrammatical *with introduced agents and natural forces, as in *The treasure might be stolen with the pirates or *The leaves might be burned with the fire. Grammatical *by* appeared with passive agents, as in *The dog was patted by the little girl,* while ungrammatical *by appeared with instruments or natural forces, as in *Jill can fix toys by a hammer or *The shells wash up by the waves. Two-year-olds imitated only; 3-, 4-, and 5-year-olds both imitated and repaired such sentences.

The results attested to the generality of the findings from the longitudinal observations. The youngest children, aged 2, retained ungrammatical *from for agents and natural forces in their imitations 80 percent and 70 percent of the time respectively, and also substituted *from* for grammatical *by* 30 percent of the time (e.g., changing *The dog was patted by the little girl* to *The dog was patted from the little girl). Such changes were made by nine of the ten 2-year-olds tested, but by only two of the ten 5-year-olds.[26] In addition, 2-year-olds substituted *from* for ungrammatical *with 40 percent of the time where it introduced oblique agents (as in *The treasure might be stolen with the pirates) and natural forces, as well as for ungrammatical *by where the latter introduced natural forces (30 percent). These patterns of retention and substitution in 2-year-olds for different kinds of oblique arguments are summarized in Table 3.1.10. From age 3 onwards, however, children showed less reliance on *from* to mark agent phrases, and instead repaired ungrammatical *from to *by* 44 percent of the time. They also repaired ungrammatical *with to *by* 40 percent of the time (again, when it marked agents).

Overall, our data showed that the 2-year-olds assigned *from* to mark locative sources and chose *from* more often than *by* to mark oblique agents. They chose

Table 3.1.10 *Percentage of retentions and substitutions in 2-year-olds' imitations (based on E. Clark and Carpenter, 1989)*

	Produced:		
Given	*From*	*With*	*By*
From (locative)	**60**	2	8
*From (agent)	**80**	0	10
*From (natforce)	**70**	0	20
With (instrument)	12	**72**	2
*With (agent)	40	**0**	50
*With (natforce)	40	**0**	10
*With (means)	15	**35**	10
By (agent)	30	8	**58**
*By (natforce)	30	10	**40**
*By (instrument)	25	35	**40**

Note: Retentions of input forms are shown in boldface.

with to mark instruments. Older children reserved *from* for locative sources, *with* for instruments, and *by* for agents. Only at age 3 or later do children switch their allegiance to *by* for marking an oblique agent as the agent. These cross-sectional observations from forty children offer strong statistical support to the longitudinal findings (see further E. Clark and Carpenter, 1989).

Contrasts among from, with, *and* by

In Modern English *from*, *with*, and *by* may be partitioned ideally as follows, with each preposition deriving its primary causal sense from its locative one to mark a different role in causal events:

PREPOSITION	LOCATIVE SENSE	CAUSAL ROLE
from	starting point	cause
with	accompaniment	instrument
by	proximity	agent

But the paths children follow in acquisition are complex. The uses of *from* have shown that some children take the locative sense of source or starting point and use it for agents and causes before they master conventional *by* for the agentive role. It is because *from* is mastered earlier than *by* for expressing causal meaning that it gets assigned functions that must later be reassigned to *by*. *With* emerges at much the same time as *from*, though, and takes on the sense of instrument very early, an assignment that requires little later revision.

Instruments are as much a part of causal events as agents, but they lack almost all the properties of agents: they are not agentive, volitional, effective, or instigative (Cruse, 1973). So instruments should be differentiated from agents. They are. Instruments are consistently marked by *with*, while agents are initially marked by *from* and later by *by*. In English *by* may mark either agents or instruments, but *with* can mark only instruments. And *with* must be used for the instrument if the sentence contains an agent.[27] Children's usage was generally consistent with this: *By* marked agents and instruments in the causal chain, and *with* marked instruments and, on four occasions only, agents. Bowerman (1983) noted that instrumental *with* was used by two children around age three to mark causes, as in *You made me cry with putting that up there* (C 3;6, after her mother had put a desired object out of reach) or *I'm making a rug with cutting little lines* (E 3;1, as she cut a fringe into the end of a rectangular piece of paper). These uses later gave way to conventional *by*, as in *He opened the door by kicking it*. (The same children subsequently also used *by* inappropriately for instruments, e.g. in imperatives such as **Open the door by the key*.) Because both *with* and *by* can mark instruments, children may find it hard to discern the conditions that govern each kind of use in causal constructions.

Why do children not use *by* for agents and instruments from the start? We suggest that children are observing the Principle of Contrast (E. Clark, 1987). Since *from* marks sources, *with* and *by* should contrast with it and pick out other meanings: *With* is assigned to instruments (along with accompaniment and attribute) and *by* to location, independence, and, only later, agency. For those children who mark agents as sources with *from*, *from* will contrast, in causal events, with both *with* (instruments) and *by* (independence).[28] Such contrasts are sometimes quite explicit in the children's usage, as when Damon (2;2,3) looked at pieces of his sandwich he had knocked off the edge of his plate:

It fall down *from me*. I knock it down *with my fingers*.

Children's early assignment of distinct meanings to *from*, *with*, and *by* in the causal domain requires certain adjustments as they begin to take account of overlaps among the contrasting meanings. Adjustments, though, may take time, since all three prepositions have several senses. All three have conventional senses for space, and all three overlap at certain points in their uses for causal roles.

Why did children choose *from* rather than some other locative source marker for other sources? The children we studied did use *out of* to identify locative sources, but they never used it for other kinds of source. *Out of* typically emerged after the first uses of *from*, and its uses were split between locative verb particles with the meaning of "removal from a place," as in *take X out*, *pull X out* or *go out*, and material meanings, in combination with *of*, as in *made out of playdough*. When *out* appears as a verb particle, the location itself is unspecified but must be some kind of locative enclosure. This suggests that *from* is the preposition of choice in large part because the other source prepositions, such as *out of*, are too specific in meaning.

The only other prepositions besides *from* (and later *by*) that marked oblique agents were *with* and *of*. Uses of *with* for agents were very rare (only four instances in all), as we have already indicated, and appeared only at around 3;6–4;0, after *from* uses had already emerged (see also E. Clark and Carpenter, 1989). *Of* for agents appeared first around age 3;0 and never occurred after age 5;0. Overall these uses, like those of *with*, were rare (less than 1 percent of the total), and the major function of *of*, from its first appearance onwards, was partitive. It was typically used after quantifiers such as *some, a bit, kind*, and *sort* in the children's speech.

In talking about causes, children also used *from* initially instead of *because*. To see why, we examined all Damon's uses of *because*. Although he first produced *because* at 2;3, only 12 percent of his *because* uses before 4;0 actually marked the cause in relation to a result, as when he explained how he'd known the newspaper was upside down: *Because I saw the letters upside down* (3;2,22). This compared with 62 percent of his *because* uses that expressed reasons, as in *Could I have another gingersnap 'cos I want to put it in my mouth and drink at the same time* (3;4.19).[29] That is, *from* to introduce causes contrasted with *because* to introduce reasons. At the stage when *from* marked causes as sources, *because* was not yet available as a clausal conjunction to mark the causing event as the cause. Such causal uses of *because* did not appear with any frequency until around age 4.

Lastly, notice that the notion of source is not in itself a causal one. The starting point for motion in space bears no causal relation to the subsequent motion. It simply marks the origin. Equally, agents appear to be identified as sources because they are starting points for the (causal) action, just as possessors are starting points for objects possessed. And prior states in cease constructions simply mark temporal priority, again with no causal link. The point is that agents and causes, for example, are sources, but sources are not necessarily causal. The category of source contains several members, all of them on occasion marked explicitly as sources, and only some of these have causal roles.

Source as a conceptual category

Children, we have proposed, form a category of source. Sources are explicitly marked as such only when they are in oblique positions and are not canonical subjects or topics.[30] It is only then that agents must be marked in some way AS AGENTS. The option children take is to use the source marker *from*. They choose it because they identify agents as a kind of source—the starting point for the action.[31] They also identify whole events as sources for subsequent events, and use *from* to introduce them as well. Some of these are the causes of other events; others simply precede them in time. Identification of a category as a source, then, licenses the use of the preferred preposition for sources. This accounts for children's using *from* for possessors and standards of comparison as well. The marking of agents and causes as sources with *from* is widespread among 2- to 3-year-olds.

Emergent categories

Children typically assume that language is more regular than it is and readily overregularize as they build paradigms of words and structures. The consistent errors in these regularizations are informative because they reveal the generalizations children have made en route to the adult system. Consistent errors may also be diagnostic of what we will call EMERGENT CATEGORIES in language. Such categories resemble what Whorf (1956) termed covert categories, which reflect some underlying conceptual distinction that plays little or no overt role in the grammatical structure of the language. One such covert category in English can be found in the restrictions on verbs prefixed by *un-* to convey the meaning of reversal: *un-* may be added only to verbs of attaching, enclosing, and surface contact (Marchand, 1973; Whorf, 1956).[32] But unlike covert categories, emergent categories reflect the conceptual similarities perceived by children among paradigms or structures, even where these similarities are obscured by the conventional forms of the language. Emergent categories offer evidence for the conceptual representations that underlie linguistic categories and that have linguistic consequences. Where emergent categories do not match conventional linguistic categories, children have to re-form such categories as they learn the conventional system. On the other hand, where emergent categories do match linguistic conventions, children can simply move ahead on the basis of their initial analysis. Emergent categories, we propose, respect universals of conceptual representation.

Such universals have often been claimed to account for facts of acquisition (e.g., Andersen, 1978; Bowerman, 1978, 1983; E. Clark, 1977). Slobin (1973, 1985a, 1985b) surveyed extensive crosslinguistic evidence for acquisition and concluded that all children construct very similar early grammars. These early grammars, he argued, stem from a common set of basic notions on which all children build. These notions represent the categories children select first for grammatical expression. But before children use grammatical forms in conventional ways, they may use them nonconventionally. And when children do this, their nonconventional uses, in many cases, identify emergent categories.

Nonconventional usage has identified other emergent categories, among them NUMBER, as when children opt for nonconventional *more* or *two*—e.g., *more shoe* or *two spoon* prior to acquisition of the conventional plural morpheme *-s;*

LOCATION in Serbo-Croatian when children use a single case or preposition for a specific location in lieu of conventional preposition-plus-case combinations (Mikeš, 1967); COMPLETION (or result) in Italian and English, where children use tense markers such as English -*ed* initially for aspect instead of for tense (Antinucci and Miller, 1976); CAUSATIVE when children initially express "cause to VERB" by using just the intransitive verb base, as in *I fell it down* (Bowerman, 1974, 1982c); and AGENCY when children initially contrast first-person pronoun forms to mark degree of control, as in *My cracked those eggs* versus *I like peas* for high and low control respectively (Budwig, 1986; also Deutsch and Budwig, 1983). Children's uses of locative *from*, then, are likewise evidence for an emergent category of source. Children produced not only conventional uses of *from*, but also a range of nonconventional ones where conventional usage would expect *by* or *with* (agents and causes), *because* (also causes), or *than* (comparisons). All these uses picked out kinds of sources. They suggest that the notion of source is available as a conceptual category before it is available as a linguistic one.[33]

The emergent-category view is that children start with universal conceptual notions and only later arrive at the conventional expressions for the corresponding grammatical categories. The principal alternative view is that children's earliest uses of grammatical forms are semantically appropriate (e.g., Bowerman, 1978). For *from*, however, the evidence favors the emergent-category view. Nonconventional uses of *from* appear around age 2, with no evidence of an earlier period of adultlike usage. Nor does the adult input offer any model for the nonconventional uses of *from*. It does, of course, provide the locative term *from*, but once that is available children use it, sometimes almost immediately, for agents and causes as well as places. Budwig (1986) documented a similar phenomenon for the emergent category of agency. As soon as children began to produce first-person pronoun forms (e.g., *I* and *me* or *my*), from just before age 2 on, they differentiated them nonconventionally to mark degrees of agency and control. Input provided them with the pronoun forms, but they then used those forms nonconventionally to construct their own grammatical system, prior to acquisition of the conventional one.

What is source?

There are three ways of viewing the notion of source. The first one might be called the taxonomic view, according to which places, agents, possessors, and the rest bear the same relation to the category SOURCE as dogs and cats do to the category ANIMAL. Each is a subtype of source in a taxonomy. These subtypes may also participate in a family-resemblance structure, such that locative sources are "better sources" than others are, in the same way that robins are "better birds" than penguins are (e.g., Rosch, 1973). This would account for the early marking of locatives as sources and for the later uses of *from* to mark other sources that were farther from the center, or prototype.

The second is the metaphorical view, namely that locative sources are primary and all other uses are metaphorical extensions of *from*, just as in the extensions of *foot* to *at the foot of the cliff* or *at the foot of the bed*. In each instance, the extension works because of similarities in the properties of the new situation to those of the original one. The main property extended in the case of *from* should probably be named [+ source]. This account, like one based on taxonomic relations, would predict that locative sources should be marked first, but would not predict any particular order to children's extensions.

The third view is the property view, and it claims simply that entities may have a property we will call [+ source]. But what is this property? The notion of source itself is really an abstract temporal relation between two entities, A and B. A and B are both places, or both people, or both events. The crucial property is that A is first at time t_1, and B is second at t_2, so when considering A one is considering the source, and when considering B one is considering the goal. With locative sources, A is a place; with agentive ones, A is a person; with temporal ones, A is a point in time or an event; with causal ones, A is an event (the cause); with possessive ones. A is a (prior) possessor; and with comparatives, A is a standard. Source, then, is a PROPERTY that initial locations bear to final locations, that agents bear to patients or themes, that causes bear to effects, and so on. Under this view, the notion of source is an abstract property that may be associated with a variety of roles or event types.

The present data are consistent with all three views. All three depend on some similarity holding among the different kinds of source. And it is unclear what would allow us to distinguish them.

Conclusion

Emergent categories in acquisition tell us about the initial concepts on which children build as they select grammatical devices to encode their meanings. In particular, emergent categories should offer information about universal conceptual categories that underlie languages, even though they are frequently obscured by language-specific conventions of expression (Bowerman, 1983, 1985; Budwig, 1986; H. Clark, 1973; Clark and Clark, 1978; Jackendoff, 1983; Slobin, 1985a, 1985b). Children's choices of *from* in English provide evidence that agents and causes are related conceptually to notions of origin or starting point, direction, and change. We have argued for an emergent category of SOURCE that is realized in places, agents, causes, possessors, standards of comparison, and prior events in time. Evidence for it comes from earlier forms of English, from other languages, and from children's acquisition of language.

An emergent category such as SOURCE may surface in linguistic expressions for oblique agents and for noninitial causal clauses. The marking of sources has syntactic consequences for children who wish to talk about things out of canonical order—about agents that are not subjects, or causes subordinated to their consequences.[34] That is, while children's earliest expressions for causative events are based on canonical or prototypical event-schemata, these syntactic options are complemented by syntactic options that present such events from different perspectives—with the focus of attention on the object affected or on the activity itself, for example, rather than on the agent as causer. Such options vary from language to language, but discourse typically demands both canonical and noncanonical perspectives on events (see also Croft, 1986; Talmy, 1985).

Children's emergent categories may fit some conventions of some languages from the start. Where this is not the case, as for agents and causes in English, children must replace earlier nonconventional uses with conventional ones. In effect, children's initial uses of locative *from* in nonlocative domains fit Slobin's (1973) characterization of the use of an old form—locative *from*—for new functions: The expression of agency, cause, possession, and so on. Later, as children become aware that their forms do not match the conventional ones, they adopt new forms from the input (for instance, *by* for oblique agents) to express old functions already in their repertoires.

Appendix: Coding categories

The following categories were used to code all child and adult instances of *from*, *with*, and *by* for analysis; in many cases, we relied on the nonlinguistic or linguistic context to make decisions. There was a high level of agreement on the initial coding, and the few instances of disagreement were resolved through discussion.

Location

This included all uses with NPs for the origin (*from*) or static location (*by*) in space of an object or event, as in *It came from my book-box* (Eve 2;2) or *There's food by the 'frigerator* (Shem 2;3,2). *From* with an animate NP after another NP or after a form of *be* was also counted as locative, as in *All of 'em are from Karen* (Walt 3;11,25, of presents under the tree).

Time

Temporal uses of *from*, *with*, and *by* referred to events or activities, encoded as NPs or clausal constructions, as in *back from fishing* (Walt 2;8,22) and *with your turn* (Sarah 3;6), or passage of time, as in *I haven't noticed that from years* (Damon 3;9,29) and *It'll be open by the time I finish* (Adam 4;4).

Cause

In these uses, the cause of an event is introduced by *from, with,* or *by,* followed either by a NP, as in *I not tired from my games* (Adam 3;0), *Hey, my hands are greasy from all the egg* (Sara 4;2), and *Fell down with shoes* (Adam 2;8), or by a clausal construction, as in *I feel tired by running—all done in* (Damon 3;6,7) and *Ooh, I have a tummy ache from drinking all of it* (Adam 4;4).

Means

These uses of *by,* and occasionally *from,* signal the means (sometimes called the intermediary instrument) by which an action is accomplished, with either a NP or a clausal construction, as in *Oh the milkman is coming . . . by a horse* (Adam 3;4) or as in Sarah's response to a *how* question: *Um, by put 'em in straight* (5;0). They also include rare uses of *from* and *with* with the discrete units (blocks, Legos) or the substance making up an object, as in *Show me make a bridge with—with these blocks* (Shem 2;6,27) and *I don't know how to make that with mine kind of clay* (Walt 3;4,1).

Manner and attribute

Manner uses of *with* describe or identify the mode of action but do not contribute directly to its accomplishment, as in *I can cut with two in one place* (Walt 3;1,15) and *It comes up from a great big hole with a big blow* (Damon 3;7,7). Manner is thus distinct from Means in that the latter contributes directly to the accomplishment of the action. Manner is also distinguished from Attribute (also marked by *with*): Manner picks out characteristics of action and Attribute picks out characteristics of entities, as in *An' vans to move, with wheels on it* (Shem 2;7,18) and *You see that man with a pipe?* (Damon 3;8,18).

Agent

Only animate initiators of events in PPs following verbs other than *be* were coded as agents. Agent *from* consisted of unconventional uses, as in *He isn't going to get hurt from those bad guys* (Damon 2;7,18) or *Who is dis made from?* (Adam 4;7). There were also some agent *by* uses, as in *I caught by a fish* (Adam 4;0), and a few agent *with* uses.

Natural forces

These *from* and *by* uses were for nonanimate forces such as the wind, sun, rain, and electricity, as in *I'm scary-ed from the dark* (Damon 2;5,14, as the light was turned off) and *Now the rainbow is getting higher from the rain* (Sarah 5;1).

Instrument

These uses of *from*, *with*, and *by* referred to inanimate objects (including body parts) used as auxiliaries in an activity, as in *I paint with my arms* (Shem 2;5,23), *I drawed the lines from the pencil* (Walt 4;0,3), and *I think by tape we could fix it* (Walt 3;6,16).

Comitative

Comitative uses, only with *with*, referred to accompaniment, as in *Lemme sit down with you* (Adam 2;11) or *I want my jacket with me* (Walt 2;6,10). To distinguish these *with* uses from instrumental ones, the accompanying entity had to be incidental to, rather than contributing directly to, the outcome of the action or event.

Possession

These uses of *from* referred to both inalienable and alienable possession, as in *That's a finger from him* (Shem 3;0,13) and *D'you know there's two next-door neighbors from us?* (Walt 4;1,15).

Comparison

These uses of *from* included four adultlike uses of *different from* as well as nonconventional comparisons such as *I'm gonna show you what's the same from that one* (Walt 3;1,22) or *She's three years older from me* (Damon 3;6,23).

Cessation

These uses, again only with *from*, included a variety of verbs never used in this construction by adults (e.g. *fix*, *get*, *wave*), as in *I can't fix it from breaking* (Damon 3;3,1), as well as some adultlike uses after the verbs *stop* and *keep*.

Idioms

These uses of *from*, *with*, and *by* comprised a large set of collocations, including many verb–particle combinations (e.g. *play with*), adjectives (e.g. *wrong with*), and adverbial phrases (e.g. *by accident*). A few of them were counted separately in our analyses, e.g. *by X + self*, as in *I put dat by self* (Adam 2;6), and *play with*.

Acknowledgments

This research and the preparation of this paper were supported in part by a grant from the National Institute of Child Health and Human Development (NICHHD 5 R01 HD18908) and in part by the Sloan Foundation. We thank Brian MacWhinney of Carnegie Mellon University for providing tapes from the CHILDES archive, and we are grateful to Melissa Bowerman, Herbert H. Clark, and Scott DeLancey for their invaluable comments on an earlier draft.

Notes to 3.1

1. Children's ages are reported in years; months, and, where known, days.
2. We will return in "Source as a conceptual category" below to what it means to be a MEMBER of the category SOURCE.
3. See, for example Bennett (1975), H. Clark (1973), Fauconnier (1985), Gruber (1976), Jackendoff (1975, 1983), Miller and Johnson-Laird (1976), Talmy (1983), and Urban (1939); for nonspatial uses of deictic terms, see E. Clark (1974), Fillmore (1971), and Sinha (1972); for localistic theories of case, see Anderson (1971, 1977) and Hjelmslev (1935–37); for historical shifts in meaning from space to other domains, see Traugott (1978, 1986), and for the acquisition of spatial meanings before nonspatial ones, see Bowerman (1982a) and E. Clark (1972).
4. *Out* and *off* also serve as adverbials (e.g., *He went out* and *He climbed off*) and verb particles (e.g., *He took off his socks*), in addition to marking locative sources (e.g. *He ran out of the house* and *He knocked the jug off the table*).
5. Not all source prepositions are used this way: In English, neither *out* nor *off* applies to time, presumably because they specify the dimensionality of the source as container (three-dimensional) or surface (two-dimensional), respectively. *From* is used for time, we suggest, precisely because it does not specify the dimensionality of the source in question.
6. Consider the passive analogues to the sentences just cited: *He was given a book by Jill*, *He was given a black eye by Mel*, and *He was given a good scolding by his father*.
7. In some dialects of English *from* may also mark natural forces, as in *The branch broke from the snow* and *The ice-cream melted from the sun*. However, native speakers often reject *from* here in favor of *in*, as in *The ice-cream melted in the sun*. When we asked adults to judge whether such sentences were okay—and, if not, to fix them up—we found that *from* after intransitive *blow down* or *melt* was retained 45 percent of the time, but changed to *in*, *because*, or *by* with the passive 55 percent of the time (E. Clark and Carpenter, 1989).
8. *By* also appeared on a few occasions in OE to mark instruments, but even in ME instrument uses continued to be rare.
9. Van Dam (1957) reported that, of 577 instrument phrases in OE texts, 84 percent were marked by *mid*. (A further 8 percent were marked by *through* instead, and 2 percent by *from*.) None was marked by *with*.

10. All the categories identified in our analyses are listed with examples in the Appendix.
11. The origin in space may also be designated with an animate noun phrase if the spatial origin and the person's location coincide, as in e.g. *a letter from my uncle*. Forms like this were coded as locative, not agentive, uses in the children's data (see Appendix).
12. According to Cruse, natural forces share with human agents the feature "agentive," exemplified in sentences referring to actions performed by objects that are regarded as using their own energy in carrying out the actions (as in *The wind opened the door*). They also often share with them the feature "effective," characteristic of something that exerts force because of its position or motion (as in *That column supports the roof*). But natural forces differ from agents in lacking the feature "volitive" which marks an act of will, either stated or implied (see further Cruse, 1973. Natural forces were also grouped with human agents in OE: in oblique NPs, both were marked by *from* (Van Dam, 1957).
13. Forms as rare as this have not been included in the summary tables unless they make up 1 percent or more of a child's uses.
14. Possessive constructions in general tend to rely on locative elements to mark the possessor (see E. Clark, 1978b; Lyons, 1967, 1968; Ultan, 1978).
15. Compare DeLancey's 1981, 1984, and 1985 discussions of agency. Notice also that the use of static prepositions such as *on* or *at* to mark the possessor may offer a third viewpoint, neutral between source and goal.
16. See also examples cited by Gathercole (1979), e.g., *I think these are the smallest ones from that one* (CB 4;1, comparing sizes of pancakes) or *It means you're biggest from the rest* (RG 6;3, explaining what "biggest" meant).
17. While English conventionally uses *than* to introduce the standard in comparisons, one adjective, *different*, also allows *from* for this purpose. However, inspection of adult uses to children (see "Parental input" below) showed that, out of 164 uses of *different*, only six were followed by *from* and five by *than*. The availability of *different from*, then, is unlikely to account for children's uses of *from* in comparative constructions with other adjectives.
18. Jackendoff (1983:199) characterized constructions with *stop* as "circumstantial GO" constructions because they involve movement away from a prior state. But he characterized *prevent* and *keep* constructions as "circumstantial STAY" constructions, with *from* represented as NOT-AT. This amounts to the claim that *from* has a source meaning after *stop* but not after *prevent* or *keep*. However, Jackendoff himself pointed out that *from* should probably not be analyzed in two different ways here. While *prevent* and *keep*, unlike *stop*, may be used when the intended action is forestalled or blocked completely, we would argue that, had the intended action been carried out, it would have preceded any subsequent action. In the case of *stop*, the subsequent action is the act of stopping the ongoing activity. In the case of *prevent* and *keep*, where the prior activity has been forestalled before it occurred, the subsequent activity remains unspecified. While these constructions present some unresolved problems, it is important to note that children's forms appear not to be based on either *prevent* or *keep* as a model. None of their early cessation constructions contain these verbs (or the verb *stop*). We have therefore analyzed them for present purposes as all marking cessation.
19. These are similar to utterances reported by Bowerman (1977) for her two daughters: *I'll hit he from doing that* (Eva 2;11); *The birdies will find the squirrel and spank the squirrel from eating their bird seed . . . with their feet* (Eva 3;0, after the squirrel got into the bird-feeder); and *Will this squeeze the blood from going through?* (Christy 4;0, of a rubber band on her wrist). Bowerman proposed that these constructions were borrowed from conventional adult *keep FROM verbing* constructions, with the children's forms reflecting an extension of a common cause-result construction involving manner in English, as in *squeeze the blood through* = "by squeezing, cause the blood to go through." We argue for an alternative account in view of the fact that the verbs children use in these constructions have no analogues in adult input.
20. The *so* clause makes explicit the intended purpose meaning of the complement after *from*.
21. This account would cover such "cease" constructions as Shem's *That's a handle that keeps the water from not coming out* (2;9,27, identifying the parts of a fire-hydrant). However, there were not enough instances in the CHILDES data for detailed comparisons with the diary observations.
22. It is conceivable that *with* in *play with* carries an accompaniment sense, or even an instrumental one. Since these two senses are the first to emerge for all seven children, the exclusion of collocations like *play with* from our primary analysis does not affect our claims about order of

emergence for the different categories of *with*. One other verb, *do with*, was also frequent in the speech of some of the children. This too was counted as an idiom.

23. The primacy of comitative and instrumental *with* sometimes resulted in miscomprehension of adult uses, as in (i), where Damon (2;2,26) interpreted an attributive use as a comitative:

> (i) H: Let's go watch the news with Dan Rather.
> D: *Not with Dan Rather. Dan Rather on the news.*

On another occasion Damon (4;2,4) inappropriately treated an idiom as if it had instrumental meaning, when he explained to a visitor (EB) how he usually cut cauliflower:

> (ii) D: *I just take a bite and it falls apart.*
> EB: It doesn't work with many other things.
> D: *It'll work with knifes.*

24. This early use of *by* for a natural force as agent was an isolated one, with other instances from Damon only appearing after age 3;0.

25. The data on Damon and Naomi did not contain enough information about adult usage to be included in this analysis.

26. Maratsos and Abramovitch (1975) reported one pilot study where they asked 2-year-olds to imitate ungrammatical passives (containing *of* instead of *by*), but only three of their ten children imitated the preposition at all, and eight deleted the *is* of the passive verb. This was rare among the 2-year-olds in the present study: They all either imitated the prepositions they heard or substituted other prepositions most of the time.

27. Compare *The man opened the box with a key* and **The man opened the box by a key*. For further discussion of instrument phrases, see Wojcik (1976).

28. Since children seem to keep the three prepositions quite distinct from each other at first, they may also be relying on an added assumption about word meaning, over and above Contrast, namely that words do not overlap in meaning (E. Clark, 1987, 1988). This assumption, however, is typically abandoned quite early as children discover that many meanings do in fact overlap.

29. The remaining uses of *because* either introduced consequences and so were equivalent to *so* or *so then* (only used up to 3;6), or appeared in metalinguistic definitions in the analysis of words, e.g., *It's a runway because you run on it* (Damon 3;0). For comparable observations, see Hood, (1977), and, for further discussion of children's expressions of causality, Donaldson, (1986).

30. All the children we studied produced canonical subjects, as in *The man hit the ball* and *The dog chased the cat*, prior to their first attempts to talk about agents that were not subjects.

31. Some children may not use *from* in this way because they simply do not talk about agents when their attention is on the entity affected by the action. In diary data from another child, A (1;11–3;0), we found no instances of agents being mentioned when the theme/patient was the grammatical subject. During the same period, A produced *by* only for location. The few "passive" constructions A produced were typically indeterminate between an adjectival and a verbal meaning (Levin and Rappaport, 1986; Wasow, 1977; see also Horgan, 1978).

32. For example, *un-* may be used to reverse the meanings of verbs like *tie*, *wrap*, and *staple*, but not verbs like *dry*, *spread*, or *set*, even though the actions denoted by these verbs are all equally reversible. This tendency is so strong that when *un-* is used with verbs that have an inherently restrictive meaning it merely intensifies their inherent meanings instead, e.g. *unloosen*, *unthaw*. Children may take some time to discover this covert category (Bowerman, 1982b, 1983).

33. Infants in the later sensorimotor stages of development (roughly eight–fourteen months) will not search for objects in a new location once they have been hidden from sight; instead they first look in the original location (Bower, 1982). This suggests that children may organize their early knowledge of displacements in space around sources rather than goals.

34. For further discussion of canonical or prototypical events, see Croft (1986), Hopper and Thompson (1980), Lakoff (1977), and Rice (1987). Slobin (1979, 1981) suggested that prototypical events provide the basic event-schemata to which children first try to match grammatical expressions (see also de Villiers, 1980). Bever (1970) and Slobin and Bever (1982) discussed the role of canonical transitive clauses in acquisition and processing, and E. Clark (1971), Clark and Clark (1968) and Ferreiro (1971) have argued that canonical clause order affects how children (and adults) represent events in time.

References to 3.1

Andersen, E. S. (1978). "Lexical universals of body-part terminology." In *Universals of human language, vol. 3: Word structure*. Joseph H. Greenberg (ed.), Stanford: Stanford University Press, 335–68.

Anderson, J. M. (1971). *The Grammar of Case: Towards a localistic theory*. Cambridge: Cambridge University Press.

Anderson, J. M. (1977). *On Case Grammar: Prolegomena to a theory of grammatical relations*. London; Croom Helm.

Antinucci, F. and Miller, R. (1976). "How children talk about what happened." *Journal of Child Language*, **3**, 167–89.

Bennett, D. C. (1975). *Spatial and Temporal Uses of English Prepositions: An essay in stratificational semantics*. London: Longman.

Bever, T. G. (1970). "The cognitive basis for linguistic structures." In *Cognition and the Development of Language*, John R. Hayes. (ed.), New York: John Wiley & Sons, 279–352.

Bower, T. G. R. (1982). *Development in Infancy* (2nd edn). San Francisco: W. H. Freeman.

Bowerman, M. (1974). "Learning the structure of causative verbs: A study in the relationship of cognitive, semantic, and syntactic development." *Papers and Reports on Child Language Development* [Department of Linguistics, Stanford University], **8**, 142–78.

Bowerman, M. (1977). "The acquisition of rules governing 'possible lexical items': Evidence from spontaneous speech errors." *Paper and Reports on Child Language Development* [Department of Linguistics, Stanford University] **13**, 148–56.

Bowerman, M. (1978). "Systematizing semantic knowledge: Changes over time in the child's organization of word meaning." *Child Development*, **49**, 977–87.

Bowerman, M. (1982a). "Starting to talk worse: Clues to language acquisition from children's late speech errors." In *U-shaped Behavioral Growth*, Sidney Strauss (ed.). New York: Academic Press, 101–45.

Bowerman, M. (1982b). "Reorganizational processes in lexical and syntactic development." In *Language Acquisition: The state of the art*, Eric Wanner and Lila R. Gleitman (eds), Cambridge: Cambridge University Press, 319–46.

Bowerman, M. (1982c). "Evaluating competing linguistic models with language acquisition data: Implications of developmental errors with causative verbs." *Quaderni di Semantici*, **3**, 5–66.

Bowerman, M. (1983). "Hidden meanings: The role of covert conceptual structures in children's development of language." In *Acquisition of Symbolic Skills*. Don R. Rogers and John A. Sloboda (eds), New York and London: Plenum Press, 445–70.

Bowerman, M. (1985). "What shapes children's grammars?" In *The Crosslinguistic Study of Language Acquisition, vol. 2: Theoretical issues*, Dan I. Slobin (ed.), Hillsdale, NJ: Lawrence Erlbaum, Associates, 257–319.

Braunwald, S. R. and Brislin, R. W. (1979). "The diary method updated." In *Developmental Pragmatics*, Elinor Ochs and Bambi B. Schieffelin (eds), New York: Academic Press, 21–42.

Brown, R. (1973). *A First Language: The early stages*. Cambridge, MA: Harvard University Press.

Budwig, N. A. (1986). *Agentivity and Control in Early Child Language*. University of California at Berkeley dissertation.

Clark, E. V. (1971). "On the acquisition of the meaning of *before* and *after*." *Journal of Verbal Learning and Verbal Behavior*, **10**, 266–75.

Clark, E. V. (1972). "On the child's acquisition of antonyms in two semantic fields." *Journal of Verbal Learning and Verbal Behavior*, **11**, 750–8.

Clark, E. V. (1973). "How children describe time and order." In *Studies of Child Language Development*, Charles A. Ferguson and Dan I. Slobin. (eds), New York: Holt, Rinehart & Winston, 585–606.

Clark, E. V. (1974), "Normal states and evaluative viewpoints." *Language*, **50**, 316–32.

Clark, E. V. (1977). *Universal Categories: On the semantics of classifiers and children's early word meanings*. Linguistic studies offered to Joseph H. Greenberg on the occasion of his sixtieth birthday, vol. 1, Alphonse Juilland. (ed.), Saratoga, CA: Anma Libri, 449–62.

Clark, E. V. (1978a). "Discovering what words can do." *Papers from the Parasession on the Lexicon*, Donka Farkas, Wesley M. Jacobsen, and Karol W. Todrys. (eds.), Chicago: Chicago Linguistic Society, 34–57.

Clark, E. V. (1978b). "Locationals: Existential, locative, and possessive constructions." In *Universals of Human Language, vol. 4: Syntax* Joseph H. Greenberg (ed.), Stanford: Stanford University Press, 85–126.

Clark, E. V. (1987). "The Principle of Contrast: A constraint on acquisition." *Mechanisms of Language Acquisition*. Brian MacWhinney. (ed.), Hillsdale, NJ: Lawrence Erlbaum Associates, 1–33.

Clark, E. V. (1988). "On the logic of Contrast." *Journal of Child Language*, **15**, 317–35.

Clark, E. V. and Carpenter, K. L. (1989). "On children's uses of *from*, *by*, and *with* in oblique noun phrases." *Journal of Child Language*, **16**, 349–64.

Clark, H. H. (1973). "Space, time, semantics, and the child." *Cognitive Development and the Acquisition of Language*, Timothy E. Moore (ed.), New York: Academic Press, 27–63.

Clark, H. H. and Clark, E. V. (1968). "Semantic distinctions and memory for complex sentences." *Quarterly Journal of Experimental Psychology*, **20**, 129–38.

Clark, H. H. and Clark, E. V. (1978). "Universals, relativity, and language processing." In *Universals of Human Language, vol. 1: Method and theory*, Joseph H. Greenberg (ed.), Stanford: Stanford University Press, 225–77.

Croft, W. A. (1986). *Categories and Relations in Syntax: The clause-level organization of information*. Stanford University dissertation.

Cruse, D. A. (1973). "Some thoughts on agentivity." *Journal of Linguistics*, **9**, 11–23.

DeLancey S. (1981). "An interpretation of split ergativity and related patterns." *Language*, **57**, 626–57.

DeLancey S. (1984). "Notes on agentivity and causation." *Studies in Language*, **8**, 181–213.

DeLancey S. (1985). "Categories of non-volitional actor in Lhasa Tibetan." *Proceedings of the Conference on Participant Roles: South Asia and adjacent areas*, Arlene R. K. Zide, David Magier, and Eric Schiller (eds), Bloomington: Indiana University Linguistics Club, 58–70.

Deutsch, W. and Budwig, N. (1983). "Form and function in the development of possessives." *Papers and Reports on Child Language Development* [Department of Linguistics, Stanford University] **22**, 36–42.

de Villiers, J. G. (1980). "The process of rule learning in child speech: A new look." In *Children's Language*, vol. 2, Keith E. Nelson (ed.), New York: Gardner Press, 1–44.

Donaldson, M. L. (1986). *Children's Explanations: A psycholinguistic study*. Cambridge: Cambridge University Press.

Dromi, E. (1987). *Early Lexical Development*. Cambridge: Cambridge University Press.

Fauconnier, G. (1985). *Mental Spaces: Aspects of meaning construction in natural language*. Cambridge, MA: MIT Press.

Ferreiro, E. (1971). *Les relations temporelles dans le language de l'enfant*. Paris: Librairie Droz.

Fillmore, C. J. (1971). *Lectures on Deixis*. (University of California Summer Program in Linguistics.) Bloomington: Indiana University Linguistics Club.

Gathercole, V. C. M. (1979). *Birdies Like Birdseed the Bester than Buns: A study of relational comparatives and their acquisition*. University of Kansas dissertation.

Green, A. (1914). "The analytic agent in Germanic." *Journal of English and German Philology*, **13**, 514–52.

Gruber, J. S. (1976). *Lexical Structure in Syntax and Semantics*. (North-Holland Linguistic Series 25.) Amsterdam: North-Holland.

Hjelmslev, L. (1935–37). "La catégorie des cas: Etude de grammaire générale." *Acta Jutlandica*, **7**, 1–184, **9**, 1–78.

Hood, L. H. (1977). *A Longitudinal Study of the Development of the Expression of Causal Relations in Complex Sentences*. Columbia University dissertation.

Hopper, P. J. and Thompson, S. A. (1980). "Transitivity in grammar and discourse." *Language*, **56**, 251–99.

Horgan, D. M. (1978). "The development of the full passive." *Journal of Child Language*, **5**, 65–80.

Jackendoff, R. S. (1972). *Semantic Interpretation in Generative Grammar*. Cambridge, MA: MIT Press.

Jackendoff, R. S. (1975). "Morphological and semantic regularities in the lexicon." *Lg*, **51**, 639–71.

Jackendoff, R. S. (1983). *Semantics and Cognition*. Cambridge, MA: MIT Press.

Joly, A. (1967). "Negation and the comparative particle in English." (*Cahiers de psychomécanique du langage*. No. 9) Québec: Les Presses de l'Université Laval.

Lakoff, G. (1977). "Linguistic Gestalts." *Papers from the Thirteenth Regional Meeting*. Woodford A. Beach, Samuel E. Fox, and Shulamith Philosoph (eds), Chicago: Chicago Linguistic Society, 236–87.

Levin, B. and Rappaport, M. (1986). "The formation of adjectival passives." *Linguistic Inquiry*, **17**, 623–61.

Lyons, J. (1967). "A note on possessive, existential, and locative sentences." *Foundations of Language*, **3**, 390–6.

Lyons, J. (1968) "Existence, location, possession and transitivity." In *Logic, Methodology, and Philosophy of Science*, vol. III. Bob van Rootselaar and Frits Staal (eds), Amsterdam: North-Holland, 495–509.

MacWhinney, B. and Snow, C. E. (1985). "The child language data exchange system (CHILDES)." *Journal of Child Language*, **12**, 271–94.

Maratsos, M. P. and Abramovitch, R. (1975). "How children understand full, truncated, and anomalous passives." *Journal of Verbal Learning and Verbal Behavior*, **14**, 145–57.

Marchand, H. (1973). "Reversative, ablative, and privative verbs in English, French, and German." In *Issues in Linguistics: Papers in honor of Henry and Renée Kahane*. Braj B. Kachru, R. B. Lees, Y. Malkiel, A. Pietrangeli, and S. Saporta (eds), Urbana: University of Illinois Press, 636–43.

Mikes, M. (1967). "Acquisition des catégories grammaticales dans le langage de l'enfant." *Enfance*, **20**, 289–98.

Miller, G. A. and Johnson-Laird, P. N. (1976). *Language and Perception*. Cambridge, MA: Harvard University Press.

Mitchell, B. (1985). *Old English Syntax. vol. 1: Concord, the parts of speech, and the sentence*. Oxford: Clarendon Press.

Mustanoja, T. F. (1960). "A Middle English syntax." (*Mémoires de la Société Néophilologique de Helsinki*, **23**.) Helsinki: Société Néophilologique.

Quirk, R., Greenbaum, S., Leech, G,. and Svartvik, J. (1972). *A Grammar of Contemporary English*. New York: Seminar Press.

Rice, S. (1987). "Towards a transitive prototype: Evidence from some atypical English passives." *Proceedings of the Thirteenth Annual Meeting*. Berkeley: Berkeley Linguistics Society, 422–34.

Rosch, E. H. (1973). "On the internal structure of perceptual and semantic categories." In *Cognitive Development and the Acquisition of Language*. Timothy E. Moore (ed.), New York: Academic Press, 111–44.

Sachs, J. S. (1983). "Talking about the there and then: The emergence of displaced reference in parent–child discourse." In *Children's Language*, vol. 4, Keith E. Nelson (ed.), Hillsdale, NJ: Lawrence Erlbaum Associates, 1–28.

Schlesinger, I. M. (1979). "Cognitive structures and semantic deep structures: The case of the instrumental." *Journal of Linguistics*, **15**, 307–24.

Sinha, A. K. (1972). "On the deictic use of *coming* and *going* in Hindi." *Papers from the Eighth Regional Meeting*. Paul Peranteau, Judith N. Levi, and Gloria C. Phares (eds.), Chicago: Chicago Linguistic Society, 351–8.

Slobin, D. I. (1973). "Cognitive prerequisities for the development of grammar." In *Studies of Child Language Development*. Charles A. Ferguson and Dan I. Slobin (eds), New York: Holt, Rinehart and Winston, 175–208.

Slobin, D. I. (1979). "The role of language in language acquisition." Invited address, Fiftieth Annual Meeting of the Eastern Psychological Association, Philadelphia.

Slobin, D. I. (1981). "The origins of grammatical encoding of events." In *The Child's Construction of Language*. Werner Deutsch. (ed.), London: Academic Press, 187–99.

Slobin, D. I. (1985a). "Introduction: Why study acquisition crosslinguistically?" In *The Crosslinguistic Study of Language Acquisition. vol. 1: The data*, Dan I. Slobin (ed.), Hillsdale, NJ: Lawrence Erlbaum Associates, 3–24.

Slobin, D. I. (1985b). "Crosslinguistic evidence for the language-making capacity." In *The Crosslinguistic Study of Language Acquisition. vol. 2: Theoretical issues*, Dan I. Slobin (ed.), Hillsdale, NJ: Lawrence Erlbaum Associates, 1157–256.

Slobin, D. I. and Bever, T. G. (1982). "Children use canonical sentence schemas: A crosslinguistic study of word order and inflections." *Cognition*, **12**, 229–65.

Stassen, L. (1985). *Comparison and Universal Grammar*. Oxford: Basil Blackwell.

Talmy, L. (1983). "How language structures space." In *Spatial Orientation: Theory, research, and application*. Herbert Pick and Linda Acredolo (eds), New York: Plenum Press, 225–82.

Talmy, L. (1985). "Lexicalization patterns: Semantic structure in lexical forms." In *Language Typology* and Syntactic Description, vol. III: Grammatical categories and the lexicon. Timothy Shopen (ed.), Cambridge: Cambridge University Press, 57–149.

Traugott, E. C. (1978). "On the expression of spatio-temporal relations in language." In *Universals of Human Language, vol. 3: Word structure*, Joseph H. Greenberg (ed.), Stanford: Stanford University Press, 369–400.

Traugott, E. C. (1986). "On the origins of 'and' and 'but' connectives in English." *Studies in Language*, **10**, 137–50.

Ultan, R. (1978). "Toward a typology of substantival possession." In *Universals of Human Language, vol. 4: Syntax*, Joseph H. Greenberg (ed.), Stanford: Stanford University Press, 11–49.

Urban, W. M. (1939). *Language and Reality: The philosophy of language and the principles of symbolism*. London: Allen & Unwin.

Van Dam, J. (1957). *The Causal Clause and Causal Prepositions in Early Old English Prose*. Groningen and Djakarta: Wolters.

Visser, F. T. (1963–73). *An Historical Syntax of the English Language, vol. 3*. Leiden: Brill.

Wasow, T. (1977). *Transformations and the Lexicon. Formal syntax*. Peter Culicover, Thomas Wasow, and Adrian Akmajian (eds), New York: Academic Press, 338–53.

Whorf, B. L. (1956). *Language, Thought, and Reality*. In John B. Carroll (ed.), Cambridge, MA: MIT Press.

Wojcik, R. H. (1976). "Where do instrumental NPs come from." In *Syntax and Semantics, vol. 6: The grammar of causative constructions*. Masayoshi Shibatani (ed.), New York: Academic Press, 165–80.

Affectedness and Direct Objects:
The role of lexical semantics in the acquisition of verb argument structure

Jess Gropen, Steven Pinker, Michelle Hollander
and Richard Goldberg

Introduction

There is a strong correlation in English between a verb's semantic properties and its syntactic properties, and it seems obvious that speakers can sometimes exploit this pattern to predict form from meaning. Knowing that a verb *to glip* means "to shove with one's elbow," an English speaker can confidently guess that it is a transitive verb whose agent argument is mapped onto the subject role and whose patient ("acted upon") argument is mapped onto the object role. Thus the speaker would use the verb in *John glipped the dog* but not *The dog glipped John* or *John glipped to the dog*. There is evidence that children can do this as well (see Gropen *et al.*, 1989; Pinker, 1984). Furthermore this procedure of *linking* (or *canonical mapping*; see Pinker, 1984) would work not only in English but in most other languages; agents of actions are generally subjects (Keenan, 1976), and patients are generally objects (Hopper and Thompson, 1980). What is not so obvious, however, is exactly what these linking regularities are or how they are used.

Early theories: Lists of primitive thematic roles

The list theories of linking, developed by Fillmore (1968), Gruber (1965), and Jackendoff (1972), shared certain assumptions. Each posited a list of primitive "thematic roles"—such as agent, patient, theme (moving entity in a motion

285

event), goal, source, and location—that specified the role played by the argument with respect to the event or state denoted by the predicate. These thematic roles were linked to "grammatical relations" (subject, direct object, and oblique object) according to some canonical scheme. Usually grammatical relations are arranged in a hierarchy like "subject–object–oblique" and thematic relations are arranged in a hierarchy like "agent–patient/theme–source/location/goal." Then the thematic relations specified by the verb are linked to the highest available grammatical relation (see Bowerman, 1990; Grimshaw, 1990; Pinker, 1984; for reviews). Thus a verb with an agent and a theme would have a subject and an object; a verb with an agent and a goal, or a theme and a goal, would have either a subject and an object (e.g., *enter*) or a subject and an oblique object (e.g., *go*); and a verb with an agent, a theme, and a goal (e.g., *put*) would have a subject, an object, and an oblique object.

Theories of linking based on lists of primitive thematic roles were influential in both linguistic theory (e.g., Bresnan, 1982; Chomsky, 1981) and language acquisition research (e.g., Bowerman, 1982a; Marantz, 1982; Pinker, 1984) through the first half of the 1980s, until a number of problems became apparent.

First, the early theories predict that all verbs denoting a kind of event with a given set of participant types should display the same linking pattern, and that is not true. This is especially notable among "locative" verbs that refer to an agent causing an entity (the "content" or "figure" argument, usually analyzed as a patient and theme) to move to a place (the "container" or "ground" argument, usually analyzed as a location or goal). There are some locative verbs, which we will call "figure-object" verbs, that display the standard linking pattern, where the moving entity gets mapped onto the direct object (e.g., *pour*, as in *pour water into the glass*/*pour the glass with water*). Others, which we will call "ground-object" verbs, violate it (e.g., *fill*, as in *fill water into the glass*/*fill the glass with water*). Some others, which we will call "alternators," permit both patterns (e.g., *brush*, as in *brush butter onto the pan*/*brush the pan with butter*).

In some versions of the list-of-primitives theory, verbs that violate the standard linking pattern would be noncanonical or "marked" and presumably would be rarer in the language and harder to learn. Not only does this reduce the predictive power of the theory, but its predictions do not seem to be true. Supposedly noncanonical ground-object forms may in fact be more numerous than those with the supposedly canonical figure-object syntax (Gropen *et al.*, 1991; Rappaport and Levin, 1985), and both kinds are acquired at the same time (Bowerman, 1990; Pinker, 1989). Similarly, many analyses of the dative alternation take the prepositional form (e.g., *give the book to him*) as unmarked because the theme is the object and goal is an oblique object, and the double-object form (e.g., *give him the book*) as marked because the goal is the surface object and the theme assumes a "lower" grammatical relation of second object. However, verbs taking the double-object construction are extremely common, and children do not learn the construction any later than they learn the prepositional construction (Bowerman, 1990; Gropen *et al.*, 1989; Pinker, 1984, 1989).

A third problem with the list-of-primitives assumption is that it does not naturally explain systematic semantic differences between two forms of an alternating verb that involve the same kinds of thematic roles but different linking patterns. For example, *John loaded the cart with apples* implies that the cart is completely filled with apples, but *John loaded apples into the cart* does not. This *holistic interpretation* (Anderson, 1971) is puzzling under the list-of-primitives assumption because the arguments are labeled with the same thematic roles in both forms. This phenomenon is widely seen across constructions and languages. Across constructions we see similar semantic shifts in the difference between *Kurt climbed the mountain* and *Kurt climbed up the mountain*, only the first implying that the entire mountain has been scaled, and *Sam taught Spanish to the students* versus *Sam taught the students Spanish*, the latter suggesting that the students successfully learned Spanish (see Green, 1974; Gropen et al., 1989; Hopper and Thompson, 1980; Levin, 1985; Moravscik, 1978; Pinker, 1989; for reviews). Comparing languages we frequently find homologues to the locative alternation that involve the same kinds of verbs that alternate in English, and the holistic interpretation accompanying the ground-object form, many in languages that are genetically and areally distinct from English (Foley and Van Valin, 1985; Gropen, 1989; Moravscik, 1978; Pinker, 1989; Rappaport and Levin, 1988).

A fourth problem involves the productivity of patterns of alternation. Children and adults notice that some verbs alternate between linking patterns and extend the alternation to novel verbs. This can be seen in children's errors (e.g., *Can I fill some salt into the bear?*; Bowerman, 1982a, 1988), adults' neologisms (e.g., *fax me those data*), and children's and adults' behavior in experiments, where they are presented with sentences like *pilk the book to her* and are willing to extend it to *pilk her the book* (Gropen et al., 1989, 1991; Pinker, 1984, 1989). In standard theories this productivity is thought to be accomplished by *lexical rules*, which take a verb with its canonical linking pattern and substitute new grammatical relations (or syntactic positions) for old ones; for example, $\text{NP-V-NP}_{\text{theme}}\text{-}into\text{-}\text{NP}_{\text{goal}} \rightarrow \text{NP-V-NP}_{\text{goal}}\text{-}with\text{-}\text{NP}_{\text{theme}}$ (e.g. Bresnan, 1982; Pinker, 1984).

The problem is that the verb's semantic information relevant to linking should be exhaustively captured in its list of thematic roles. But the patterns of alternation (i.e., alternative linking patterns for one verb) vary among verbs with identical lists of thematic roles. While novel *fax me the message* sounds natural, equally novel *shout me the message*, with the same list of thematic roles according to the early theories, does not. Presumably some property of the individual verbs allows speakers to distinguish the alternating verbs, which can be input to a lexical rule relating it to a second linking pattern, from the nonalternating verbs, which cannot. But whatever this property is, the straightforward list-of-primitives approach is failing to capture it. It is important to know what these properties are and why they influence linking patterns. Since children are not reliably corrected for making errors like *fill salt into the bear* or *she said me nothing*, it would be mysterious how they unlearn the errors they do make and avoid the countless tempting ones they never make, unless they can detect the diagnostic properties and use them to constrain lexical rules (Baker, 1979; Gropen *et al.*, 1989; Pinker, 1984, 1989).

Recent theories: Semantic structure

Recent theories aimed at solving these and other problems have abandoned the assumption that a verb's syntactically relevant semantic properties can be captured in a list of thematic role labels. Instead a verb is said to have a structured semantic representation that makes explicit the agentive, causal, and temporal properties of the event to which the verb refers. Thematic roles are not primitive types but are argument positions in these multidimensional structures; though certain traditional thematic labels like "agent" and "theme" can serve as mnemonics for some of these positions, the actual roles are more finely differentiated and the verb's interaction with syntax can be sensitive to such distinctions. For example, as we shall see there may be several kinds of "themes," and there may be roles that do not have traditional thematic labels. Examples of the newer theories may be found in Dowty (1991), Grimshaw (1990), Jackendoff (1987, 1991), Levin (1985), Levin and Rappaport Hovav (1991), Pinker (1989), Pustejovsky (1991), and Tenny (1988). See Levin (1985) for a review of how these theories are related to earlier theories of semantic decomposition such as generative semantics and the work of Miller and Johnson-Laird (1976).

Moreover, whereas the content of the thematic role labels in the early theories was dictated by the physical properties of the event, usually motion (so that the "theme" was always defined as the moving entity if there was one), semantic structure theories cross-classify thematic roles in terms of more elementary and abstract relations. Since the early analyses of Gruber (1965) and Jackendoff (1972) it has been apparent that events involving physical motion and events involving more abstract changes are expressed using parallel syntactic structures. For example, *John went from sickness to health* parallels *John went from Boston to Chicago*, presumably reflecting a common level of mental representation underlying physical motion and more abstract "motion" in state space, that is, change of state. Although early theories could capture these parallels by assigning the same thematic labels to concrete and abstract motion events (e.g., *John* would be a "theme" in both of the preceding examples), they were not equipped to capture the parallels when a *single* argument of a single verb simultaneously played several kinds of roles. This is because the semantic content of each argument was exhaustively summarized in its role label, which corresponded to its role in physical motion if it participated in a motion event. The ability of an argument to play two roles simultaneously—one motional, one nonmotional—is the key to understanding constructions such as the locative, which present such severe problems for the list-of-primitives theory.

Semantic structure and the locative alternation

In their analyses of the locative alternation, Rappaport and Levin (1985, 1988) and Pinker (1989) show how the problematic noncanonicity of verbs like *fill* disappears under a more subtle analysis of their semantic structure and a more abstract theory of linking.

Say the semantic structure of *fill the glass with water* can be rendered as something like (1), which contrasts with the semantic structure of *pour water into the glass*, rendered in (2) (see Pinker, 1989, for a more formal representation):

1. Cause the glass to become full of water by means of causing water to be in the glass.
2. Cause water to go downward in a stream into the glass.

In (1), the semantic roles of *glass* and *water* cannot be exhaustively captured by any single thematic label. *Glass* is both an abstract "theme" or affected entity in a change-of-state event (changing from not full to full) and the "goal" in a change of location event. *Water* is both the "theme" or affected entity in a change-of-location event and helps define the state in the change-of-state event (it is what the glass becomes full of).

Furthermore the two events are related in a specific way. The state change is the "main event" and the location change is a subsidiary "means" of achieving it. This asymmetry between main and subsidiary events is motivated by dimensions of meaning that are closely related to thematic structure. In the realm of pragmatics, the choice of *fill* over *pour* serves to make the change of fullness of the glass, rather than the motion of the water, the highlighted feature of the event. (This effect is reinforced by the fact that within the rigid word order of English, the choice of *fill* focuses the content as the "new" entity by putting it at the end of the sentence, backgrounding the "given" container by putting it immediately after the verb, and vice versa, if *pour* is used.)[1] In the realm of aspect, the event of *filling* is understood as temporally delimited at the moment that the main event is over with, namely, when the container becomes full (see Dowty, 1991; Gropen, 1989; Tenny, 1988).

Now say that there is a linking rule such as the one in (3):

3. Link the argument that is specified as "caused to change" in the main event of a verb's semantic representation to the grammatical object.

The change or "affectedness" that is caused can either be a change of location (i.e., a motion) *or* a change of state.[2] This would correctly map the container argument of *fill* onto the object position; it is caused to change state from not full to full. The fact that it also in some sense bears the thematic role "goal" does not disrupt this mapping; since the semantic representation is a multi-dimensional structure rather than a single list, the "goal" relation is specified within the "means" substructure where it does not trigger the object linking rule, which distinguishes main events from means. (Instead, the goal relation triggers a linking rule for the object of the preposition *with*; the fact that it does not have a traditional thematic role label is irrelevant.)[3]

Psychologically speaking, the "semantic structure" theory renders both *pour* (traditionally canonical) and *fill* (traditionally noncanonical) as canonical, thanks to the lexicalization of a "gestalt shift" that is possible when conceptualizing locative events. An event of filling a glass by pouring water into it can be conceptualized either as "causing water to go into a glass" (water affected) or "causing a glass to become full" (glass affected). English provides the speaker with a different verb for each perspective, and the objects of both verbs are linked to arguments with the same linking rule. The rule always picks out the affected entity in the main event, whether the affectedness involves a change of location (water for *pour*) or a change of state (glass for *fill*).

The semantic structure theory in its strongest form holds that the linking pattern of a verb is fully predictable from its meaning. At first glance this may seem circular. Since every act of moving an object to a goal is also an act of affecting the goal by forcing it to accommodate an object in some way, one might worry that the "predictability" is attained post hoc by looking at the verb's linking pattern and asserting that it means "cause to change location" just in case the moving entity is seen to be the object and "cause to change state" just in case the goal is seen to be the object. The circle is broken by a key semantic property that classifies verbs a priori as referring to change of location or change of state. Most verbs do not simply mean "move" or "change"; if they did we would have hundreds of synonyms. Rather, particular verbs mean "move in such-and-such a way" or "change in such-and-such a way." If a verb specifies *how* something moves in a main event, it must specify *that* it moves; hence we predict that for verbs that are choosy about manners of motion (but not change of state), the moving entity should be linked to the direct object role. In contrast, if a verb specifies *how* something changes state in a main event, it must specify *that* it changes state; this predicts that for verbs that are choosy about the resultant state of a changing entity (but not manner of motion), the changing entity should be linked to the direct object role. By assessing speakers' judgments about the kinds of situations to which a verb can naturally refer, we can identify which feature of the verb's meaning is specified as its main event, and predict which of its arguments is the direct object.

For example, the meaning of the verb *pour* specifies the particular manner in which a substance changes location—roughly, in a downward stream. For now it does not matter exactly how we characterize the manner in which a *poured* substance moves; what is crucial is that *some* particular manner of motion is specified in the meaning of the verb. This specificity becomes clear when we compare *pour* to closely related verbs such as *drip* and *dribble*, where equally specific, yet distinct, manners of location change are specified: An event counts as *dripping* or *dribbling*, but not *pouring*, if one drop at a time changes location. Although *pour* is choosy about how a substance moves, it is *not* choosy about the resultant state of the container or goal: one may *pour* water down the drain, out the window, into a glass, and so on. This tells us that the semantic representation of *pour* (and *drip* and *dribble*) specifies a change of location as its main event, and the affectedness linking rule, operating on the semantic representation, therefore licenses only the figure-object form of the verb. In contrast, the meaning of the verb *fill* specifies the particular way in which the ground is affected: A container must undergo a change of state from being not full to being full. Yet *fill* does *not* specify anything about the manner in which a substance is transferred: One may *fill* a container by pumping liquid into it, by pouring liquid into it, by dripping liquid into it, by dipping it into a bathtub, and so on. Hence, the affectedness linking rule maps the semantic representation for *fill* onto the ground-object form, but not the figure-object form. Verbs like *cover, saturate,* and *adorn* also specify only a change of state of a ground, and they, too, can only encode the ground as direct object.

Advantages of the semantic structure theory of locative verbs

Aside from accounting for the equal naturalness and acquirability of verbs like *pour* and verbs like *fill*, the semantic structure theory has several additional advantages over the list-of-primitives theory.

For one, it jointly predicts which syntactic forms are related in an alternation, and how the verb's interpretation changes when it is linked to one form or another. In the semantic structure theory, a lexical rule is an operation on a verb's semantic structure.[4] A rule for the locative alternation converts a verb's main effect representation from "cause X to go to Y" to "cause Y to change by means of causing X to be in Y." For example, when applied to the semantic representation of *splash* in which the liquid argument is specified as affected (moving in a particular manner), the rule would generate a new semantic representation in which the target of the motion is specified as affected (covered in a particular way). The syntactic effects need not be specified directly; the linking rules automatically specify *splash water onto the wall* for the first meaning, and *splash the wall with water* for the second. The main advantage of dividing the labor of argument structure alternations between meaning-altering lexical rules and general linking rules is that the *form* of each alternative is explained. It is no longer an arbitrary stipulation that *splash water onto the wall* alternates with *splash the wall with water* rather than *splash the wall the water, splash onto the wall against water,* or countless other possibilities (and indeed, such forms are not to be found among children's errors; Pinker, 1989). Rather, the construability of surfaces as affected or "caused to change" entities renders the ground-object form predictable.

Moreover, because the two forms related in the alternation have similar, but not identical, semantic representations, subtle meaning differences between them—such as the holism effect—are to be expected. An alternating verb like *splash* has a slightly different meaning in the ground-object form, asserting a state change of the ground. Since the most natural interpretation of a state change is that it is the entire object that undergoes the change, rather than one part, the ground is interpreted holistically in this form. (The effect may in turn be related to the fact that themes in general are treated as dimensionless points in semantic structures, without any representation of their internal geometry; see Gropen, 1989; Jackendoff, 1983, 1990; Pinker, 1989; Talmy, 1983; for discussion.) This predicts that the holism requirement, because it is just a consequence of the most natural conceptualization of state changes, can be abrogated when the addition of the figure to one part of the ground can be construed as changing its state. Indeed *a vandal sprayed the sculpture with paint* is compatible with only a splotch of paint having been sprayed, presumably because here even one splotch is construed as ruining the sculpture (Dowty, 1991; Foley and Van Valin, 1984; Rappaport and Levin, 1985).

Another advantage is that the new linking theory can be applied to a variety of constructions in a variety of languages. Besides the ubiquity of the holism effect, noted above, there is a strong cross-linguistic tendency for affected entities to be encoded as direct objects. Verbs expressing events that are naturally construed as involving an agent that brings about a direct effect on a patient, such as verbs of causation of change of position (e.g., *slide*) or state (e.g., *melt*), or verbs of ingestion (e.g., *eat*), are almost invariably transitive across languages, with patients/themes as direct objects. In contrast, verbs that fall outside this broad semantic class, and allow different arguments to be construed as affected, show more variation within and across languages. For example, either argument can appear as the direct object of verbs of emotion (e.g., *fear* vs. *frighten*), and particular arguments waffle between direct and prepositional objects across verbs of perception (e.g., *see* vs. *look at*) and verbs of physical contact without a change in the contacted surface (*hit* vs. *hit at*); see Levin (1985), Hopper and Thompson (1980), and Talmy (1985). Even in these more ambiguous verbs, the new theory predicts that there should be a correlation between the linking pattern and the construal underlying the verb meaning, and this too seems to be true. For example, Grimshaw (1990) reviews evidence that *fear* and *frighten* are not synonymous but that the latter involves causation of a change in the object argument and hence its linking pattern is predictable. In sum, although languages differ as to which verb meanings they have, the linking rule for objects and affected entities may be universal. (See Pinker, 1989, for reviews of cross-linguistic surveys that suggest that abstract linking rules for subject and second object, as well as object, and the meaning changes that accompany alternations involving them, have very wide cross-linguistic applicability.)

Finally, the semantic structure theory helps explain which verbs undergo alternations. Consider the verb *stuff*, which can alternate between *Mary stuffed mail into the sack* and *Mary stuffed the sack with mail*. In order for an action to be an instance of *stuffing*, it cannot be the case (e.g.) that Mary simply dropped letters into the sack until it was full. In fact, it would not count as *stuffing* even if Mary had wadded up a few letters before dropping them in. Instead, the mail must be forced into the sack *because* the sack is being filled to a point where its remaining capacity is too small, or just barely big enough, relative to the amount of mail that is being forced in. The semantic representation of *stuff* jointly constrains the change of location that the figure undergoes and the change of state the ground undergoes. That is why the object of *stuff* can be linked either to the figure or to the ground. (We shall return to the issue of precisely how linking applies to alternating verbs.) Other alternators also denote changes or effects simultaneously specified in terms of figure and ground. For verbs like *brush* and *dab*, force is applied pushing the figure against the ground; for *load*, the insertion of a kind of contents specific to the container enables the container to act in a designated way (e.g., a camera, or a gun). See Pinker (1989) for formal semantic representations for these and other kinds of locative verbs, for evidence motivating the form of such representations, and for a discussion of precisely how they interact with linking rules.

Developmental evidence from children's errors with existing verbs

As mentioned, one of the prime challenges of the list-of-primitives theory is that children acquire the supposedly noncanonical verbs with no more difficulty than the supposedly canonical ones. The semantic structure theory is consistent with the developmental facts noted earlier because all the verbs in question are canonical. However, these data do not rule out the possibility that children create verb argument structures solely in response to examples of use of the verbs in the parental input, without deploying general mapping patterns between meaning and form. (In that case the regularities found in the adult lexicon would have to be attributed to the accumulation of individual words coined by one-time analogies during the history of the language, possibly coupled with adults noticing redundancies in their lexicons.) Better evidence concerning children's linking mechanisms comes from the study of children's errors in using verbs in syntactic structures, because errors by definition could not have been recorded directly from the input and must be the output of some productive mechanism.

Bowerman (1982a) found that children between the ages of 4 and 7 often overuse the figure-object form, as in *Can I fill some salt into the bear?* [referring to a bear-shaped salt shaker]. Errors involving incorrect ground-object forms (e.g., *I poured you with water*) also occur, but far less frequently. Both kinds of errors, and the difference in their likelihood, were also found in experiments by Gropen *et al.* (1991), in which 3–8-year-old children were asked to describe pictures of locative events using verbs like *pour*, *fill*, and *dump*.

Bowerman (1982a, 1988, 1990) has drawn parallels between such errors and inflectional overregularizations of irregular verbs such as *breaked*. The child is thought to acquire many irregular verb forms from parental speech before abstracting the regular "add -*ed*" rule from pairs like *walk*/*walked*, and then overapplying it to the previously correct irregulars (see Marcus *et al.*, 1990). Similarly in acquiring locative verbs the child would acquire individual verbs of both the figure-object and ground-object types with the correct parental syntax, before noticing that most of them had the figure-object linking pattern. This pattern would be distilled into linking rules (of the list-of-primitives variety, though restricted to locative events) and overapplied to the ground-object verbs, resulting in errors like *fill salt*. Errors in which the opposite pattern is overapplied are presumably rarer for the same reason that inflectional errors like *brang* are less common than overregularization errors.

According to the semantic structure theory the observed asymmetry in syntactic errors could have a different source. If children are prone to making systematic mistakes about verb meaning, such as the misspecification of which entity is affected, the affectedness linking rule, even when applied correctly, would yield syntactic errors. Moreover, consistent patterns in mislearning verb meanings should lead to consistent patterns in misusing verb syntax.

Gentner (1975, 1978, 1982) has gathered evidence that children do make errors in acquiring verbs' meanings (see also Pinker, 1989, for a literature review). Furthermore some of the errors fall into a systematic pattern: Children have more difficulty acquiring meaning components relevant to changes of state than components relevant to changes of location. In one experiment, Gentner (1978) tested the ability of children aged 5–9 and adults to understand common cooking terms, such as *mix*, which specifies a particular change of state ("an increase in homogeneity"), and *stir*, *shake*, and *beat*, which specify particular manners of motion. Subjects were asked to verify whether each of these verbs applied to events in which a mixable substance (a combination of salt and water) or a nonmixable substance (cream, already homogeneous) was shaken or stirred. Gentner found that the youngest children, but not the older children or adults, had difficulty in distinguishing appropriate from inappropriate instances of *mixing*: The 5–7-year-olds applied the verb on 48 percent of the trials involving mixable substances (where it is appropriate) and on 46 percent of the trials involving nonmixable substances (where it is not appropriate). In contrast, the same children applied the three manner-of-motion verbs on 97 percent of the trials in which it is appropriate, but only on 6 percent of the trials in which it is inappropriate.

This asymmetry in the acquisition of verb meaning components, together with the affected-entity linking rule in (3), could explain the asymmetry in syntactic error types with locative verbs noted by Bowerman (1982a) and Gropen *et al.* (1991): If children frequently misinterpret a state change verb as a location change verb, they will map the wrong changing entity onto the object position, resulting in figure-object errors. For example, *fill the water* might be due to the child erroneously thinking that verbs like *fill* specify a particular manner of motion of the content argument (e.g., pouring). The prediction was tested in two experiments in Gropen *et al.* (1991). We showed that children between the ages of 2;6 and 8;9 not only have a tendency to make more *fill the water* (figure-object) than *pour the glass* (ground-object) errors in their speech, but they are also more likely to misrepresent the meaning of *fill* than the meaning of *pour* in comprehension. Unlike adults, they often interpreted *fill* as implying that something must be poured, even if the container ended up not full. Furthermore, there was a small tendency for the individual children who misinterpreted verbs like *fill* to be more likely to make syntactic errors with such verbs—errors in which the figure was used as the direct object.

Of course, if children are misled by the salience (to them) of the moving entity in certain locative events and mistakenly encode its manner of motion as part of the verb's meaning, they must possess a learning mechanism that at some point in development replaces the incorrect feature with the correct one. This mechanism could operate by monitoring the application of the verb *across* situations in parental speech. Sooner or later *fill* will be used by an adult to refer to an event in which there is no pouring (e.g., when a cup is filled by dripping or bailing or leaving it out during a rainstorm), so the incorrect "pouring manner" component can be expunged. But *fill* will always be used to refer to becoming full, so the state change meaning component, once hypothesized, will remain with the verb (see Pinker, 1989, for a theory outlining mechanisms of verb learning in children). If these two influences on verb learning—salience and cross-situation consistency—can be manipulated experimentally to affect speakers' construals of new verb meanings, the predictions of the semantic structure theory can be tested directly. That is the goal of the present investigation.

Developmental predictions about children's acquisition of novel verbs

We present three experiments assessing whether speakers use a verb's meaning, specifically, which argument is specified as caused to change (affected), to predict the verb's syntax. Children and adults are taught novel verbs for actions involving the transfer of objects to a surface or container. The participants are then tested on their willingness to express the figure (content) or the ground (container) argument as the direct object of the verb. The verbs are taught in a neutral syntactic context (e.g., *this is mooping*), but the meanings of the verbs are varied according to whether the figure or the ground is saliently and consistently affected in a particular way (e.g., whether the figure moves in a zig-zagging fashion, or whether the ground changes color).

According to the list-of-primitives theory, the child should assign a single thematic role to each participant in the event, drawing from the list of available primitives. This would be "theme" for the moving entity or figure, and "goal" or "location" for the destination or ground, and they would be invariably linked to object and oblique object, respectively.

In contrast, in the semantic structure theory the child would notice the thematic roles related to motion for each of the arguments, but these roles would not exhaust the syntactically relevant semantic representation of the verb. Arguments' semantic roles could be specified on several levels of semantic representation, only one of which would correspond to the motion relations, and the linking mechanism could be sensitive to the full structure of the verb. For the events with a specific manner of motion, the figure (moving entity) and ground (destination) would be encoded as theme and goal and linked to object and *to*-object respectively, as in the primitives theory. But for events with a specific state change but without a specific manner of motion, the causation of a change of the ground would be specified in the main event, and the ground would be linked to object position by the affectedness linking rule in (3). The motion of the figure would still be specified, but in a subsidiary "means" structure, as in (1), where it would not trigger the object linking rule.[5]

The predictions of Bowerman's overregularization analogy are similar, but not identical, to those of the list-of-primitives theory. Irregular forms by definition are *unpredictable*, and can be learned only by direct exposure. For example when one comes across the archaic verb *to shend*, one cannot know that its correct past tense form is *shent* unless one actually hears it in the past tense; the regular form *shended* would be offered as the default. According to the overregularization analogy, this would be true for ground-object verbs as well, and it predicts that a child should generally assign figure-object syntax to a novel locative verb if it is heard without syntactic cues, regardless of the kind of locative event to which it refers. In addition, the analogy predicts some smaller proportion of uses of ground-object syntax, matching the asymmetry of errors observed in spontaneous speech, which in turn would be related to the smaller fraction of existing verbs in the language that display the ground-object pattern.

Experiment 1

In the first experiment we teach children one novel verb with the intended construal "cause X to move to Y in a zig-zagging manner," and another with the intended construal "cause Y to sag by means of placing X on it." We did not invent verbs with both a manner and a state change. On the one hand, if such a verb involved an unrelated manner and state change (e.g., "to cause X to zig-zag over to Y, causing Y to sag") it would not be linguistically possible and psychologically natural, because real verbs cannot specify multiple events unless they also specify some causal relation between them (Carter, 1976; Pinker, 1989, Chapter 5). On the other hand, if the verb involved an interpredictable manner of motion and resulting state change, the theory predicts it should alternate, and thus any mixture of figure-object and ground-object responses would be compatible with the theory and its prediction would be unclear.

The verbs are presented in a context like "this [acting out] is keating." Note that this construction involves a gerund form rather than an intransitive use of the verb, and that gerunds do not require arguments to be expressed. For example, English verbs that are obligatorily transitive can easily appear in the gerund form, as in "This [acting out or pointing] is devouring." Thus the grammatical context does not leak any grammatically relevant information to the subjects.

Method

Subjects

Sixty-four native English speakers participated: Sixteen children between 3;4 and 4;5 (mean 3;11); sixteen between 4;7 and 5;11 (mean 5;1); sixteen between 6;5 and 8;6 (mean 7;5); and sixteen paid undergraduate and graduate students at MIT. The children were drawn from middle-class day-care and after-school programs in the Boston area. Eight children who failed to understand the taught verbs or were confused, distracted, or shy, were replaced in the design.

Materials

In a pretest, we used a cup and some marbles. In the experiment, to discourage subjects from making rote responses we used two separate pairs of materials: A clear packet of pennies was moved to a 20cm felt square, or a packet of marbles was moved to a plastic square. During the teaching and testing phases, the cloth or plastic was placed on a stand consisting of either a solid square, which supported its entire surface, or a hollow frame, supporting only its perimeter.

Two verb meanings were created. In the *manner* condition, a packet was moved to a fully supported piece of material in a zig-zagging manner. In the *endstate* condition, the packet was moved in a direct path to an unsupported piece of material, which sagged under the weight of the packet. By using the same pairs of materials for both actions (within subject), we ensured that any differences in performance were not due to the salience of the materials. Corresponding to these two novel actions were two verb roots, *pilk* and *keat*. The pairing of one of the meanings with one of the roots that defined each verb was counterbalanced across subjects within each age group.

Procedure

Children were tested in a quiet area by two experimenters, one eliciting responses, the other recording data. Each novel verb was introduced to children by a puppet as a "puppet word."

Pretest After being introduced to the materials, subjects were pretested on sentences with the verbs *pour* and *fill*. They were shown examples of pouring and filling, and descriptions were elicited; the experimenter recorded whether they used the figure (marbles) or ground (cup) as the direct object. For example, the experimenter would say: "do you know the word *fill*? . . . when I do this [moving marbles, a few at a time, into a cup] . . . and it ends up like that [the cup filled] . . . it's called *filling*." After doing this three times, the experimenter asked, "using the word *fill*, can you tell me what I'm doing?" If a subject failed to produce a sentence with an unambiguous direct object, we followed up with a prompt: "filling what?" or "filling_____?"[6] Regardless of the subject's final response, the experimenter modeled a correct sentence with *fill* (i.e., I'm *filling the cup with marbles*), and had the subject repeat it. The analogous protocol was followed for *pour*. The order of pretesting the two verbs was counterbalanced across subjects within an age group.

Teaching the novel verbs   Each subject was then taught two novel verbs: One specifying a manner (zig-zagging) and the other specifying an endstate (sagging). The verbs were taught and elicited one at a time, order counter-balanced across subjects in an age group. The experimenter first asked, "Can you say *keat*? . . . say *keat*," and then said, "let me show you what *keating* is . . . when I do this [moving a packet directly towards an unsupported square] . . . and it ends up like that [placing the packet onto the square, causing it to sag] . . . it's called *keating*." After repeating the demonstration, the experimenter said, "now let me show you something that's *not keating* . . . when I do this [moving a packet towards a *supported* square] . . . and it ends up like that [placing the packet onto the square, without changing its shape] . . . it's *not* called *keating*." The experimenter then asked, "Can you show me what keating is?" and then "Can you show me something that's not keating?" If children failed, the experimenter again showed examples and non-examples of the verb's meaning, and had the child act out the verb again, using the same materials. The teaching protocol was repeated with the second pair of materials.

   The same teaching procedure was used when teaching the manner-of-motion verb. The experimenter moved a packet onto a supported square in a zig-zagging manner, saying, "when I do this . . . and it ends up over there . . . it's called *pilking*." To illustrate what the verb was not, the experimenter then moved the packet in a bouncing manner.[7]

Testing the novel verbs   After each verb was taught, sentences containing it were elicited. The experimenter reverted to the original set of materials, asked the child to act out the verb again, asked him or her for the name of the figure (marbles or pennies), supplying it if the child did not, and asked him or her to say the verb. Then the experimenter asked, "Can you tell me, with the word *keating*, what I'm doing with the *marbles*?" while performing the action. The experimenter then verified that the child knew the names of the second set of materials, and elicited a sentence with it with a slightly different question: "Can you tell me, using the verb *keating*, what I'm doing with the *cloth*?" We posed the question these two ways to guard against the possibility that the subjects had a constant preference for either the figure-object or ground-object form, masking any potential effect of verb meaning. The figure question is a discourse context that makes the figure-object sentence pragmatically natural as a reply, and similarly the ground question makes a ground-object sentence natural (this technique was also used in Gropen *et al.*, 1989, 1991, and in Pinker, Lebeaux, and Frost, 1987). Since both questions were asked with both verbs, order counterbalanced, this did not introduce any confound. In those trials where a subject failed to provide an unambiguous direct object, we followed up with a prompt: "keating what?" or "keating _____?"

The second verb was then taught and tested with the same protocol. Both pairs of materials were used in the teaching and syntactic testing of each verb, with the sequence of materials switched for the second verb (within subject) and balanced across subjects within an age group. In addition, we also switched the order of question types so that the sequence of items mentioned in the questions was either figure–ground–ground–figure or ground–figure–figure–ground. Together, these switches guaranteed that the same two items (i.e., marbles and felt or pennies and plastic) were mentioned in questions for both verbs within subject, so that the focusing of different materials in the questions could not account for any differences in a subject's performance with the two meanings. Furthermore, the combination of verb meaning, question order, and material order was counterbalanced across subjects in each age group.

Scoring

Responses containing the appropriate verb and an unambiguous direct object were scored according to whether the object consisted of the figure or the ground in the action. Responses that were made only in response to the follow-up prompt (e.g., "keating what?") were also tallied separately. When subjects used a pronoun (e.g., "you're keating it"), utterances were counted only if the referent was disambiguated by the presence of an oblique object or particle (e.g., "you keated it onto the felt" or "You keated it on"), or if the referent could be pinned down via the subsequent prompt. In addition, we noted spontaneous intrusions of English verbs and unsolicited descriptions of the actions.

Results and discussion

Table 3.2.1 presents the proportions of figure-object and ground-object responses for the manner and endstate verbs, broken down by the type of eliciting question. Responses to the original question and to the subsequent prompt are combined in the proportions reported in this and other tables

Table 3.2.1 *Experiment 1: likelihood of choosing figure or ground arguments as the direct object of manner and endstate verbs*

	Age									
	3;4–4;5		4;7–5;11		6;5–8;6		Adult		Mean	
Object argument:	Figure	Ground	Figure	Ground	Figure	Ground	Figure	Ground	Figure	Ground
Manner verbs										
Figure question	1.00	0.00	1.00	0.00	1.00	0.00	0.88	0.06	0.97	0.02
Ground question	0.88	0.12	0.94	0.06	0.69	0.31	0.62	0.31	0.78	0.20
Mean	0.94	0.06	0.97	0.03	0.84	0.16	0.75	0.19	0.88	0.11
No prompt/prompt	6/24	2/0	8/23	0/1	17/10	5/0	20/4	6/0		
Endstate verbs										
Figure question	0.94	0.06	0.88	0.12	0.75	0.19	0.69	0.31	0.81	0.17
Ground question	0.56	0.38	0.69	0.31	0.38	0.62	0.44	0.56	0.52	0.47
Mean	0.75	0.22	0.78	0.22	0.56	0.41	0.56	0.44	0.66	0.32
No prompt/prompt	7/17	4/3	12/13	3/4	11/7	10/3	16/2	14/0		

A small number of unscorable responses caused some sets of proportions not to add up to 1.00 and some sets of frequencies not to add up to 32.

presented in this paper. The actual frequencies of unprompted and prompted responses (collapsed across question types) are also reported in the tables.

As predicted, children in all age groups, and adults, produced more figure-object responses when using manner verbs than when using endstate verbs, and produced more ground-object responses when using endstate verbs than when using manner verbs.

In principle, the frequencies of figure-object and ground-object responses are independent because children could fail to provide an unambiguous sentence of either type; this calls for separate analyses of the proportions of figure-object and of ground-object responses. In practice, however, ambiguous responses were rare (less than 0.5 percent across the three experiments), so a single number for each condition suffices to summarize the subjects' behavior. The number we chose to enter into the analyses of variance is the proportion of trials in which a figure-object form was produced. Subjects produced significantly more figure-object responses in the manner condition (mean proportion = 0.88) than in the endstate condition (0.66), $F(1, 60) = 20.59$, $p < .001$. The difference was also significant for the mid-aged children, $F(1, 15) = 5.87$, $p < .03$, and the oldest children, $F(1, 15) = 6.36$, $p < .03$, and marginally so for the youngest children, $F(1, 15) = 4.36$, $p < .06$, and the adults, $F(1, 15) = 4.36$, $p < .06$. Finally, because of a set carried over from the first verb taught to the second, the verb type effect was stronger (between subjects within each age group) for the first verb taught ($F(1, 56) = 22.40$, $p < .001$) than for the second ($F(1, 56) < 1$).

The analysis of variance also revealed a significant main effect of question type, showing that subjects were sensitive to discourse influences on object choice. They produced more figure-object sentences (and thus fewer ground-object sentences) when the figure was mentioned in the question than when the ground was mentioned, $F(1, 60) = 31.68$, $p < .001$. No other effect or interaction was statistically significant.

Although we have shown that the choice of direct object is influenced by the aspect of the situation that the verb meaning specifies, with more figure-object responses and fewer ground-object responses for manner-of-motion verbs than change-of-state verbs, figure-object responses were in the majority for both types of verbs. We found a similar overall preference in the pretest using existing verbs: Eleven of the youngest children, three of the middle group, and four of the oldest group (but no adults) produced ungrammatical sentences in which the direct object of *fill* was the content argument, and none made the converse error with *pour* (see also Bowerman, 1982a; Gropen *et al.*, 1991). Part of this preference may be attributed to an overall bias for young children to attend to manners over endstates, as documented by Gentner (1978) and Gropen *et al.* (1991): The linking rule would translate a bias towards the manner components of verb meaning into a preference for figure-object sentences. Indeed our choice of endstate verb may, inadvertently, have fostered such a bias. The experimenter often had to nudge the packet into the unsupported material in order to initiate the sagging, and subjects may have noticed this, thereby interpreting the action that we have been calling "change of state" as involving a particular manner as well. That is, the verb may inadvertently have been given the interconnected motion-and-state-change semantics of an alternator like *stuff* or *brush*. In fact, of the sixteen children who provided overt descriptions of the meaning of the endstate verb by focusing on one of the arguments, ten mentioned what happened to the figure (most often, that it moved downward), contrary to our intentions.

Experiment 2

In this experiment we teach children and adults a purer endstate verb. The problem with the endstate verb in Experiment 1 was that the state change was a change of shape, and by definition whenever an object changes shape its local parts must change position. To cause a change in the position of the local parts of the ground object, the figure object had to impinge on it in a particular way, and that particular way (nudging) may have been interpreted by the subjects as part of the verb meaning, rendering it an alternator and diluting the predicted effect. Here we will teach a verb in which the ground changes color, not configuration, and furthermore the proximal cause of the change is chemical, not the motion of an impinging figure. If the linking hypothesis is correct, ground-object constructions should be the response of choice in using these endstate verbs.

Method

Subjects

Sixty-four native English speakers, drawn from the same sources as in Experiment 1, participated: Sixteen between 3;5 and 4;5 (mean 3;10); sixteen between 4;7 and 5;8 (mean 5;1); sixteen between 6;7 and 8;5 (mean 7;3); and sixteen adults. We replaced one child in the design for being unresponsive in the syntactic task, three children because of experimenter error, and one adult who was color-blind.

Materials

As in Experiment 1, two separate pairs of materials were used with each subject, though in this experiment the pairing of objects (figures) and surfaces (grounds) was balanced across subjects in an age group. The surface was either a 6×10cm piece of absorbent paper or a piece of white felt; the object was either a 2cm square piece of sponge or a cotton ball. All materials were kept damp: The surface was saturated with cabbage juice; the object was saturated with either water, lemon juice, or a baking soda solution. As in Experiment 1, a cup and some marbles were used in a pretest.

Two verb meanings were created, both involving taking a damp object and patting it against a damp surface. For the endstate verb, the surface changed color in an acid-base reaction from purple (the color of unadulterated cabbage juice) to either pink (when the object contained lemon juice) or green (when the object contained baking soda solution). In the manner condition, an object was moved to a surface in a particular manner, either zig-zagging or bouncing; the object was saturated with water so no color change resulted. The color of the change and the particular manner were consistent for each subject and counterbalanced across subjects. As in the previous experiment, we used the same pairs of materials for both actions (within subjects). Corresponding to these two novel actions were two verb roots, *moop* and *keat*. The pairing of verb meanings and verb roots was counterbalanced across subjects in an age group.

Procedure

The procedure and scoring were the same as in Experiment 1, except that when providing a demonstration of what the endstate verb did not refer to, the experimenter used the solution that produced the other color. In addition, in order to reduce the carry-over effects in Experiment 1 caused by questioning the same materials for both verbs, we made the following changes: The sequence of materials for the first verb was counterbalanced with the sequence for the second verb, the order of question types for the first verb was counterbalanced with the order for the second verb, and the total sequence of materials and the total sequence of question types were combined so that each material (object or surface) was mentioned in only one question per session, and each material (in a given pairing) was mentioned an equal number of times in a question within meaning condition (all counterbalancings are over subjects within each age group).

Results and discussion

Results are shown in Table 3.2.2. As predicted, subjects responded with more figure-object sentences for manner verbs than for endstate verbs. An analysis of variance on the proportion of figure-object responses reveals a significant difference for the two verb types, $F(1, 60) = 115.52$, $p < .001$. (The effect is even larger when examined between subjects using only the first verb taught, eliminating carry-over effects.) The difference between the two verb types does not just arise from responses to the follow-up prompts, but is observed for full sentence responses to the original question; $F(1, 60) = 17.55$, $p < .001$. The effect of verb type is significant within each age group: Youngest children, $F(1, 15) = 9.00$, $p < .01$; middle children, $F(1, 15) = 90.00$, $p < .001$; oldest

Table 3.2.2 *Experiment 2: likelihood of choosing figure or ground arguments as the direct object of manner and endstate verbs*

| | Age | | | | | | | | | |
| | 3;4–4;5 | | 4;7–5;8 | | 6;7–8;5 | | Adult | | Mean | |
Object argument:	Figure	Ground	Figure	Ground	Figure	Ground	Figure	Ground	Figure	Ground
Manner verbs										
Figure question	0.62	0.38	0.88	0.12	0.81	0.19	0.69	0.31	0.75	0.25
Ground question	0.44	0.56	0.62	0.38	0.69	0.31	0.62	0.38	0.59	0.41
Mean	0.53	0.47	0.75	0.25	0.75	0.25	0.66	0.34	0.67	0.33
No prompt/prompt	1/16	5/10	1/23	1/7	9/15	4/4	15/6	11/0		
Endstate verbs										
Figure question	0.19	0.75	0.00	1.00	0.25	0.75	0.00	1.00	0.11	0.88
Ground question	0.12	0.81	0.00	1.00	0.06	0.94	0.00	1.00	0.05	0.94
Mean	0.16	0.78	0.00	1.00	0.16	0.84	0.00	1.00	0.08	0.91
No prompt/prompt	3/2	5/20	0/0	5/27	2/3	14/13	0/0	29/3		

A small number of unscorable responses caused some sets of proportions not to add up to 1.00 and some sets of frequencies not to add up to 32.

children, $F(1, 15) = 27.21$, $p < .001$; adults, $F(1, 15) = 30.77$, $p < .001$. We also replicated the effect of discourse focus seen in Experiment 1, in which subjects produced relatively more figure-object forms when the figure was mentioned in the question than when the ground was mentioned, $F(1, 60) = 10.00$, $p < .005$.

What is noteworthy in these data is that in each age group figure-object sentences were in the majority for the manner verb whereas ground-object sentences were in the majority for the endstate verb. (Indeed the 4–5-year-old children and the adults expressed the stationary entity as the direct object 100 percent of the time when it was observed to change state.) The results show that when a change of state is salient enough, children will usually express this affected entity as a direct object, even though it would traditionally be analyzed as a "goal" to which some other "theme" in the scene is moving. (Indeed, it is possible that when children correctly grasp that the meaning of a verb involves a change of state, they *always* choose the ground-object form: The thirty-three children [69 percent] who spontaneously used a color name to explain the meaning of the endstate verb produced nothing but ground-object sentences, though we cannot rule out the possibility that both phenomena are due to general precociousness.) Interestingly, the pretest revealed the same kind of error patterns with existing verbs that have been found in previous studies: Seventeen children out of forty-eight (ten, four, and three from the respective age groups) incorrectly used *fill* with the ground as direct object, and only one child made the complementary error with *pour*. Thus the tendency to make errors like *fill water* does not reflect the operation of a general requirement that figures be linked to the direct object position.

Experiment 3

In this experiment we attempt to explain the holistic interpretation that accompanies alternating locative verbs such as *load* and *spray*, whereby in ground-object sentences like *John loaded the cart with apples* the ground is interpreted as being affected over its entire surface or capacity, whereas in figure-object sentences like *John loaded apples into the cart* no such interpretation is forced (Anderson, 1971; Schwartz-Norman, 1976). If the holism effect is a consequence of the fact that a state change is naturally conceptualized as applying to an entire entity, and of a rule that links entities changing state to the grammatical object, then surfaces or containers that are completely covered or filled should be more likely to be construed as affected, and thus more likely to be expressed as direct objects, than those that are only partly covered or filled.

We contrast a "partitive" condition, in which (e.g.) a peg is inserted into a hole on a board, with a "holistic" condition, in which the same action is repeated until all of the holes on the board are plugged with pegs. We predict that children and adults should produce more ground-object sentences with the verb in the holistic condition than with the verb in the partitive condition.

Method

Subject

Sixty-four native English speakers, drawn from the same sources as in the previous two experiments, participated: Sixteen between 3;5 and 4;10 (mean 4;0); sixteen between 5;0 and 6;11 (mean 5;7); sixteen between 7;0 and 9;4 (mean 7;10); and sixteen adults. We replaced five children in the design for being uncooperative, inattentive, or shy, one child because of experimenter error, one child for having received contaminating intervention, and one adult for misinterpreting the task as a request to imitate a child.

Materials

Two sets of materials were used with each subject, each consisting of two types of objects and two containers. One set consisted of beads, 0.6cm plastic eggs, a flatbed cart with six holes in its 8 × 20cm surface, and a 10cm square cube with four holes on one of its sides. The second set consisted of marbles, small plastic balls, an 8 × 20cm bench with six holes, and an 8 × 60cm board with four holes. Both kinds of objects in a set could be inserted part way into the holes of either container in that set. Each subject saw the same pairings of objects and containers, counterbalanced across subjects in an age group. In addition, two (non-interchangeable) pairs of materials were used in the teaching phase: 5cm styrofoam disks and a muffin tray with eight cavities; and 3 × 3cm Duplo pieces and a candy mold with twelve indentations.

Because the comparison in this experiment involves a single kind of action, performed either once or enough times to fill all the holes in a container, a between-subjects design was necessary: Each subject was taught and tested on one verb meaning. Across subjects in an age group, the partitive meaning was taught and tested as often as the holistic meaning, and the mean ages of the children in different meaning conditions were matched to ±2 months for each age group. In addition, we counterbalanced the four possible combinations of objects and containers with verb meaning so that each combination of object–container pairs occurred as often in the partitive condition as it did in the holistic condition, across the subjects in an age group. The verb root *keat* was used throughout.

Procedure

After introducing the subject to the materials and verb form, the experimenter taught the verb by performing the holistic or partitive action once, using either the styrofoam and muffin tray or the Duploes and candy mold. In the partitive condition, the experimenter inserted (e.g.) a piece of styrofoam into a hole in the tray while saying "I am keating." In the holistic condition, the experimenter inserted (e.g.) styrofoam pieces into the tray, one at a time, until all of the holes in the tray were plugged. The description "I am keating" was uttered only once, but the utterance was stretched out while the experimenter inserted several pieces. The experimenter then asked the subject to "show me what keating is." The teaching sequence was repeated on the rare occasions when it was necessary .

In eliciting sentences, we sought to increase the number of prepositional phrases uttered by making it pragmatically informative to include them (see Crain, Thornton, and Murasugi, 1987; Gropen *et al.*, 1991). Subjects saw two types of objects or two types of containers, only one of which actually participated in the event, and had to describe the action to a blindfolded puppet. For example, when asking a ground question in the holistic condition, the experimenter would say "Here is a board . . . I can have either some marbles [pointing] . . . or some balls [pointing]. Now watch this: I am keating [filling the board with the marbles] . . . Tell Marty the puppet, using the word *keat*, what I did to the *board*." The most natural response in this context is a full ground-object form, (e.g.) "You keated the board with the *marbles*," where the old information (topic) is encoded as the direct object and the new information is encoded as the prepositional object. Similarly, when asking a figure question in the holistic condition, the experimenter would say (e.g.) "Here are some marbles . . . I can have either a board [pointing] . . . or a bench [pointing]. Now watch this: I am keating [filling the bench with the marbles] . . . Tell Marty, using the word *keat*, what I did to the *marbles*." The order of presentation of the two materials was balanced within subject so that the chosen material was first as often as it was second. The same procedure was used for the partitive action except that single objects were moved and named. As before, the question was followed, if necessary, with the prompt "keating_____?" or "keating what?"

Four of these questions were asked in each of two blocks of elicitation trials, in the order figure–ground–figure–ground or ground–figure–ground–figure. Each presentation of the novel action was performed with a new pair of materials, so that after four trials each of the four objects and containers had been used once. The procedure for the second block was the same as for the first, except that the experimenter reinforced the temporal end point of the events by saying, "I am done keating. I keated" after each presentation of an action. We counterbalanced the sequence of question types for the first and second blocks, and coordinated the total sequence of question types with the total sequence of material pairs so that each of the eight materials was mentioned in a question exactly once per session, and each material (in a given pairing) was mentioned as often in the partitive condition as it was in the holistic condition (all counterbalancings are over subjects within each age group). After each block of trials, the experimenters administered several procedures designed to assess and train children's understanding of the temporal unfolding of the event. Since the results of these procedures had no measurable effect on the second block of elicitation trials, we will not discuss them; details are reported in Gropen (1989).

The responses were scored as in Experiments 1 and 2. Acceptable ground-object forms included one passive (*the block was keated*) and two sentences in which the figure was encoded as an instrumental subject (e.g., *the bead keated the block*).

Results and discussion

Table 3.2.3 shows the proportions of figure-object and ground-object responses (collapsing across both blocks of elicitation trials) for the partitive and holistic verbs. As predicted, subjects used more ground-object forms when the verb referred to a holistic action (ground completely filled) than when referring to a partitive action (ground partly filled). The comparison is significant in an analysis of variance whose dependent variable is the proportion of figure-object responses; $F(1, 56) = 4.36$, $p < .05$. The actual effect consists of subjects strongly preferring the figure-object sentence with partitive verbs, but being indifferent between figure-object and ground-object sentences with holistic verbs. This can be seen in a set of two-tailed t-tests: For partitive verbs, the difference between proportions of figure-object and ground-object responses is significantly different from zero in every age group except the oldest children: Young children, $t(7) = 3.29$, $p < .02$; middle children, $t(7) = 3.00$, $p < .025$; oldest children, $t(7) = 1.69$, $p = .14$; adults, $t(7) = 2.61$, $p < .05$. In contrast, the difference between proportions of figure-object and ground-object responses in the holistic condition is not significantly different from zero for any of the age groups.

As in previous experiments, subjects produced relatively more figure-object forms when the figure was mentioned in the question than when the ground was mentioned, $F(1, 56) = 16.55$, $p < .001$. A significant interaction of verb meaning and question type indicates that the effect of question type is greater in the holistic condition than in the partitive condition, $F(1, 56) = 5.33$, $p < .05$. This reflects a tendency for subjects to avoid the ground-object form of the partitive verb, even in response to a ground question, but to respond to the ground question with a ground response for holistic verbs.

We have shown that children interpret completely filled or covered surfaces as more worthy of being expressed as the direct object of a novel verb. This manifests itself most strongly as an outright avoidance of ground-object sentences when the surface is only partly filled. This is exactly what we would expect if speakers respected the holism constraint, according to which ground-object sentences imply holistic effects, and hence partitive effects imply the avoidance of ground-object sentences. In other words, subjects should avoid saying (e.g.) *you keated the board with the ball* in the partitive condition for the

Table 3.2.3 Experiment 3: likelihood of choosing figure or ground arguments as the direct object of partitive and holistic verbs

Object argument:	Age									
	3;5–4;10		5;0–6;11		7;0–9;4		Adult		Mean	
	Figure	Ground	Figure	Ground	Figure	Ground	Figure	Ground	Figure	Ground
Partitive verbs										
Figure question	0.88	0.12	0.88	0.12	0.78	0.22	0.84	0.16	0.84	0.16
Ground question	0.84	0.16	0.88	0.12	0.69	0.31	0.72	0.28	0.78	0.22
Mean	0.86	0.14	0.88	0.12	0.73	0.27	0.78	0.22	0.81	0.19
No prompt/prompt	5/50	4/5	40/16	7/1	45/2	13/4	45/5	11/3		
Holistic verbs										
Figure question	0.81	0.19	0.59	0.41	0.69	0.31	0.84	0.16	0.73	0.27
Ground question	0.47	0.53	0.31	0.69	0.69	0.31	0.56	0.44	0.51	0.49
Mean	0.64	0.36	0.45	0.55	0.69	0.31	0.70	0.30	0.62	0.38
No prompt/prompt	25/16	18/5	16/13	30/5	42/2	18/2	45/0	18/1		

same reason that English speakers avoid saying *Mary loaded the cart with the apple(s)* in the situation where most of the cart remains empty. In contrast, it is not unnatural to say *Mary loaded apples into the cart* or *Mary put apples into the cart* even when she fills it. This is consistent with our finding that subjects did not avoid uttering figure-object sentences in either condition.

General discussion

The three experiments clearly show that children (from 3 to 9) and adults, when faced with a locative verb and no syntactic information about how to use it, show no across-the-board tendency to express the caused-to-move or figure entity as the direct object. Rather, when the goal of the motion changes state, whether it be shape (Experiment 1), color (Experiment 2), or fullness (Experiment 3), speakers are more likely to select that goal as the direct object.

These findings add developmental evidence to the list of problems recently recognized as plaguing earlier theories of linking such as those of Fillmore (1968), Gruber (1965), and Jackendoff (1972), where a verb's syntactically relevant semantic argument structure consists of a single set of thematic roles drawn from a fixed list and determined on the basis of motion if the verb refers to motion. It supports the more recent theories (e.g., Dowty, 1991; Grimshaw, 1990; Jackendoff, 1987, 1990; Pinker, 1989; Rappaport and Levin, 1985, 1988; see Levin, 1985, for a review) that posit a multilayered semantic structure in which information about motion, other changes, and their causal relations are specified, and in which linking rules are triggered by arguments in specific semantic substructures. Specifically, we have demonstrated the operation of a linking rule that interprets "themes" as entities that are "caused to change" or "affected" as part of the verb's main event representation, and maps them onto the direct object position, whether the change be location, state, or something else. Thus even when a learner registers that a verb can refer to a salient motion along a path to a goal, this motion event does not exhaust his or her syntactically relevant semantic representation of the verb; if there is a consistent state change serving as the end to which the motion is merely a means, the motion can be represented in this subordinate role, and the state change, as superordinate main event, can trigger the linking to direct object.

The results reinforce a theory that helps to explain many properties of English and other languages: Why different verbs (e.g., *pour* and *fill*) have seemingly different linking patterns, the prevalence and lack of markedness of verbs whose moving entities are not objects, and the nonsynonymity (holism effect) of constructions with alternating verbs. Indeed the psycholinguistic foundation of the holism effect—that a state is most naturally predicated of the object considered in its entirety—was directly demonstrated in Experiment 3, where subjects, knowing only that a surface was holistically affected, were likely to describe the event with novel verbs using ground-object syntax.

In its strongest form the semantic structure theory predicts that verbs' syntactic argument structures are completely predictable from their semantic representations, for all verbs, speakers, ages, and languages. For many years this proposition has seemed clearly false, given the seemingly arbitrary differences between verbs within and across languages, and the existence of children's errors. The semantic structure theory, however, posits a richness and fine grain to verbs' semantic representations that might render the extreme claim defensible. All differences in syntactic argument structures should be accompanied by subtle, though measurable differences in semantic structure. In the next section we discuss how the theory would characterize such an interplay between syntax and semantics.

How are linking rules used in language?

According to the version of semantic structure theory discussed here, linking rules are not isolable bits of knowledge particular to a language, like a vocabulary item or rule of morphology, but are an inherent part of the interface between lexical semantics and syntactic argument structure. Thus they should have pervasive (though indirect) effects coordinating the semantics and syntax of predicates. In this section we examine these effects as they might operate in the experiments reported here and in the language acquisition process.

1. In the experiments

In all three experiments we influenced the syntactic privileges that subjects assigned to a novel verb presented with no syntactic information: Children (in each age group) and adults were more likely to express the stationary goal entity as direct object (and less likely to express the moving entity as direct object) when the goal entity underwent a change of shape, color, or fullness than when it stayed the same and an entity moved to it in a characteristic fashion.

However, one might wonder (as did one of the reviewers of an earlier version of this paper) whether the semantic structure theory should predict that *all* of the uses of state-change verbs should have the ground as the direct object, and all of the uses of the manner verbs should have the figure as the direct object. This would be true only if we could have controlled subjects' construal of the verb *completely* in the few demonstrations of its meaning we were able to present (and, of course, if we could have prevented all lapses of attention, forgetting, idiosyncratic interest in the nonspecifically changing entity, response bias, and carry-over effects), which is not practical. In a person's real-life experience, any inappropriate construal of a verb's meaning as including some irrelevant semantic dimension (e.g., manner for an endstate verb or vice versa) can be expunged as the person witnesses the verb being used in circumstances that lack that feature, as noted. But even with our brief teaching situations, we were able to find a consistent significant effect in the predicted direction superimposed on the various uncontrollable factors. Moreover, the partial dilution of the effect, especially in Experiment 1, is understandable from independent sources of evidence, such as the manner bias demonstrated by Gentner (1978) and Gropen *et al.* (1991) and the partially faulty, alternator-like semantics of the verb we designed. In Experiment 2, where the endstate verb was better designed, children of all ages and adults preferred to express the stationary ground surface as the direct object, a preference that was absolute for two of the groups. (Of course, since subjects are literally free to construe a wetted surface as "affected" even if it does not change color or any other feature, we could not prevent them from ever using the ground-object form in the manner condition.) In Experiment 3, previous examination of the range of meanings allowed by existing alternating verbs helped make sense of the magnitudes of effects obtained: Both figure-object and ground-object forms are compatible with a holistic event, but a partitive event lacking any obvious state change should strongly bias a choice of the figure-object form.

Furthermore, an experiment reported in Gropen (1989) is consistent with our conjecture that some nonpredicted sentences in these studies were lawful consequences of subjects' construing events in ways we could not completely control. The experiment was similar to the holistic condition of Experiment 3 except that subjects were also asked whether the event was best described as *putting* or *covering*. This was thought to assess in part their uncontrolled personal construals of the event as kinds of motions (for which *put* would be the most appropriate existing verb) or kinds of changes (for which *cover* would be most appropriate). Subjects (3;7 to adult) who chose *cover* preferred the ground-object form 91 percent of the time when using the novel verb; subjects who chose *put* preferred it only 61 percent of the time.

2. *Novel coinages*

The real-life case closest to our experiments is one where a speaker coins a novel verb (or interprets such a novel coinage by another speaker for the first time). Such coinages can occur when stems are invented out of the blue, perhaps influenced by phonetic symbolism: Such as the recent verbs *snarf* (retrieve a computer file), *scarf* (devour), *frob* (randomly try out adjustments), *mung* (render inoperable), and *ding* (reject). They can also occur when a stem is borrowed from another lexical category (e.g., *He tried to Rosemary-Woods the tape*; *He nroffed and scribed the text file*; see Clark and Clark, 1979). In all such cases the argument structure of the novel verb is not predictable from existing forms in the language and must be created from the verb's meaning by linking rules.

3. Recording a verb used in a sentence

Whenever a verb is heard in a grammatical syntactic construction, there is, strictly speaking, no need to use a linking rule to predict that the verb can appear in that construction; that fact can be recorded directly from the input. However, the fact that verbs obey linking regularities so uniformly suggests that linking rules do play a role in their acquisition, unlike genuinely input-driven memorization such as irregular morphology or the association between a word's sound and its meaning.

The prediction of the semantic structure theory discussed in this paper is that the child must make a verb's syntax (observed from syntactic analyses of parental sentences) compatible with its semantics (observed from the sets of situations in which the verb is used) according to the linking rules. Thus children should have trouble learning verbs whose hypothesized semantic representations are incompatible with their syntax, such as an English verb meaning something like "pour" but with the syntax of *fill* or vice versa.

Furthermore, when a child hears a verb used in a full sentence, he or she could use the linking rule in the reverse direction, to guide the acquisition of the verb's meaning by directing attention to features of meaning that reliably accompany the verb but that may otherwise have gone unnoticed. For example, if an argument is heard in direct object position, the child may try out the hypothesis that the verb specifies that it is affected. The child would verify whether the referent reliably changes when used with the verb, and if it does, he or she could look for some characteristic manner if it moves, or state change if it does not, and would add it to the semantic representation of the verb. See Gleitman (1990) and Pinker (1989) for discussion and evidence.[8]

Finally, note that even when a child witnesses the syntactic privileges of a verb, he or she may forget them, but if the meaning is remembered the linking rules can reconstruct them. See Pinker (1989: 330–41) for a discussion of verb errors in children's spontaneous speech that suggests that this process does occur.

4. Generalizing a verb from one construction to another

The most common setting where a speaker may be expected to apply linking rules productively is in generalizing from one construction that a verb is heard in to a new, related construction. For example, a learner might be faced with generalizing from a figure-object form of an alternating verb like *daub paint on the board* to a ground-object verb form like *daub the board with paint*, or vice versa, in the absence of having heard one of the two forms. See Gropen *et al.* (1989), Bowerman (1988), and Pinker (1984, 1989) for reviews of experimental and naturalistic evidence that adults and children frequently make such generalizations.

Within the semantic structure theory, these generalizations are enabled not by a single lexical rule specifying the syntactic linking of the new form (as in the list-of-primitives theory), but by a combination of a specific lexical rule and general linking rules (Pinker, 1989; Rappaport and Levin, 1988). The lexical rule is reduced to a simple manipulation of a verb's semantic structure, effecting a gestalt shift: The rule takes a semantic representation like "cause X to go into/onto Y" and generates a new, related representation like "cause Y to change by means of causing X to be in/on Y" (or vice versa). The linking rules would create the corresponding syntactic structures automatically. As mentioned in the Introduction, this division of labor helps explain the forms of the syntactic structures that are related by an alternation, the change of interpretation (e.g., holism) that accompanies it, and its verbwise selectivity. If this characterization of a lexical rule as a simple semantic operation is correct, it would mean that linking rules are used whenever a verb is extended to a new construction for the first time.

Note, though, that the lexical rule cannot be applied freely to just any locative verb. If it could, a nonalternating motion verb like *pour* could be the basis for the creation of a similar verb predicating a state change resulting from pouring (something like "be poured upon"), and the linking rule would generate the ungrammatical *pour the glass with water. True, we pointed out in the Introduction that alternating verbs like *stuff* and *spray* are generally different from nonalternators in simultaneously constraining properties of the figure and ground arguments in their definitions, but this raises the question of why non-alternators like *pour* and *fill* cannot have secondary meanings, involving simultaneous figure and ground constraints, that would make them eligible for the construction in which they do not, in fact, appear.

Pinker (1989) and Gropen *et al.* (1989), drawing on Levin (1985) and Green (1974), suggest that lexical rules apply freely only within narrowly circumscribed subclasses of verbs within the broad class that is generally associated with an alternation. For example, the English locative rule applies freely not to all verbs involving motion of contents to a container or surface, but only to verbs of simultaneous contact and motion (e.g., *smear, brush, dab*), vertical arrangement (*heap, pile, stack*), ballistic motion of a mass (e.g, *splash*, spray, *inject*), scattering (e.g., *scatter, strew, sow*), overfilling (e.g., *stuff, cram, pack, wad*), and insertion of a designated kind of object (*load, pack, stock*). Virtually all other locative verbs, those that fall outside of these subclasses, are confined to one syntactic form or the other. For example verbs of enabling the force of gravity (e.g., *pour, dump, drip, spill*) are confined to the figure-object construction, and verbs of exact covering, filling, or saturating (e.g., *fill, cover, line, coat, soak, drench*) are confined to the ground-object form.[9]

Presumably the child learns the subclasses by focusing on a verb that he or she hears alternate in parental speech, and generalizing its meaning to a minimal extent. This has the effect that a subsequently encountered verb that is highly similar in meaning will be allowed to alternate as well. See Pinker (1989) for a precise definition of "highly semantically similar" and for formal details of the generalization mechanism and how it interacts with verbs' semantic representations.

5. Development of alternating subclasses in acquisition and history

There is one effect of linking rules on the language whose mode of psychological operation is not clear, and this is in motivating the *kinds* of semantic subclasses that are freely subjectable to lexical rules in a given language, that is, the kind of constraints discussed in the immediately preceding passage. It seems that which subclasses of verbs actually alternate in the language correlates with the cognitive content of the notion "affectedness": The easier it is to construe both the figure and the ground as directly "affected" by a given action, the more likely English is to allow verbs of that type to alternate. For example in verbs like *brush* and *dab*, force is applied simultaneously to the figure and the ground, an action easily construable as affecting them both. Similarly, what makes an event an instance of *stuffing, cramming*, or other verbs in the overfilling subclass is that force is applied to the contents in opposition to resistance put up by the container. The difference between the gravity-enabled motion subclass (*pour, spill, drip*, etc., which cannot be used in the ground-object form) and the imparted-force subclass (*splash, spray, inject, splatter*, etc., which alternate) may be related to the fact that when force is imparted to a substance the location and shape of the goal object is taken into account by the agent in how the force is imparted (e.g., in aiming it), and the particular pattern of caused motion defining the verb also predicts the effect on the goal (e.g., the kind of motion that makes an act *splattering* or *injecting* also dictates how a sprayed surface or injected object has changed. See Pinker, 1989, and Gropen, 1989, for explicit semantic representations of all these verbs.)

Why do English constraints on alternation show signs of having hints of a cognitive motivation? It is certainly not true that the ease of construing an event as simultaneously affecting figure and ground is the *direct* cause of a speaker's willingness to allow a verb to alternate. That is because there are stable constraints within a dialect, and differences between dialects, in the specifications of the exact subclasses of verbs that can alternate. (For example, we cannot say *drip the cake with icing* even if we construe the cake as directly affected, though some English speakers can; see Pinker, 1989; Rappaport and Levin, 1985.) Instead, presumably the psychology of affectedness interacts with psycholinguistic rules of the locative alternation in more indirect ways. Over historical timespans innovative speakers may be more likely to extend a verb subclass to a new construction for the first time if the intrinsic semantics of the verbs in the subclass is cognitively compatible with the semantics of the construction (e.g., if the object argument in the new construction is easily conceptualized as being affected). And perhaps these innovations are more likely to spread through a linguistic community if many members of the community find it tempting to construe the event in the multiple ways originally entertained by the innovator. Finally, once the subclass becomes entrenched as a possible domain of a rule, it might be more easily learned by each generation if the construals it forces on the speakers are cognitively natural (see Pinker, 1989, for discussion).

6. *Bootstrapping the first rules involving grammatical relations*

A final implication of the semantic structure theory of linking concerns the semantic bootstrapping hypothesis (see Grimshaw, 1981; Macnamara, 1982; Pinker, 1982, 1984, 1987, 1989; Wexler and Culicover, 1980). According to this hypothesis, young children at the outset of language acquisition (younger than those studied here) might use linking regularities and word meanings to identify examples of formal syntactic structures and relations in parental speech and hence to trigger syntactic rule learning for their particular language. (This is logically independent of the claim that linking rules are used to predict *individual* verbs' syntactic privileges from their meanings after the rules of syntax for their language have been acquired.) For example, if the patient argument of a verb comes after the verb in an input sentence, the child can deduce that it is a VO language, even if the child had no way of knowing prior to that point what counted as an object in that language.

A major sticking point for the hypothesis has been the existence of seeming counter-examples to any proposed set of linking rules: For example, passives, in which the agent is not expressed as a subject, and double-object datives and ground-object locatives, where the argument traditionally analyzed as the "theme" or "patient" is not expressed as the verb's first object. The hypothesis required that parents avoid using the supposedly exceptional constructions in their speech, that the child recognizes them as exceptional by various cues, or that the child weighs and combines multiple sources of evidence to settle on the most concordant overall analysis of the construction (see Pinker, 1982, 1984, 1987, for discussion).

But if linking rules, when properly formulated, are exceptionless, the burden of filtering "marked" or "noncanonical" or "exceptional" constructions out of the input to rule-learning mechanisms is shifted. If objects are linked from "affected" or "caused to change" entities, not necessarily "moved" ones (and if subjects can be linked not only from agents but from themes in agentless semantic structures; see Pinker, 1989), then neither the child nor the parent would have to pay special attention to using or analyzing the supposedly "marked" constructions. The restriction instead is that the parent would have to use predicates whose semantic structures meshed with the young child's construal of the situation; the universal linking rules, shared by parent and child, would yield the correct syntactic analysis for the child as long as the child could identify (e.g.) which entities counted as "affected." Obviously, it is not realistic to expect that the lexical semantics of a parent's verb matches the child's cognitive representation of the described event for all situations and languages.

But the fact that the new linking theory allowed us to predict the syntactic frames that children assigned to novel verbs in specific kinds of situations, including frames often treated as "marked," suggests that some sharing of construals between child and adult is plausible.

Appendix: A comparison of the semantic structure theory of linking with Melissa Bowerman's overregularization analogy

Bowerman (1990) presents an interesting discussion of the possible operation of linking rules in children's first word combinations (the two–five word strings produced before the age of 2). She first points out that though word-order errors are not infrequent in the speech of her two daughters (about 11 percent of the utterances she reproduces in her tables) the errors do not seem to occur more often for verb argument structures that would be harder according to the list-of-primitives theory (e.g., double-object datives or ground-object locatives). Nor do the first correct uses of these marked constructions appear later than their supposedly unmarked counterparts. These data were among those we mentioned in the Introduction as posing a challenge to the list-of-primitives theory.

Bowerman notes that the semantic structure theory defended in this paper does not predict the same asymmetry. But she presents additional tests that, she claims, refute the newer theory as well—in particular, the hypothesis that the child's language system is innately organized to link verbs' syntactic and semantic representations in particular ways. Instead, she argues that children are not predisposed to follow any particular pattern of linking. At first they acquire verbs' syntactic properties individually from the input, and they are capable of acquiring any linking pattern between arguments and syntactic positions with equal ease. When the child notices statistically predominant linking patterns in the verbs thus acquired, the patterns are extracted as rules and possibly overextended, like inflectional overregularizations (e.g., *breaked*). As support for this proposal she cites evidence that children's use of linking rules appears only late in development (presumably after the child has had enough time to tabulate the linking patterns) and that their errors mirror the relative frequencies of the linking patterns among verbs in the language.

In this Appendix we will first outline the logic of testing for the existence of linking rules, then turn to Bowerman's two empirical tests (one claimed to refute the existence of innate linking rules, the other claimed to support the overregularization analogy); finally, we examine the overregularization analogy itself.

The logic of testing for linking rules in early speech

Linking rules, under the conception outlined here and in Pinker (1989) and Gropen (1989), are internal pointers between lexical semantic structures and grammatical relations, and hence cannot be tested directly against children's behavior, but only together with independently motivated hypotheses about each of the structures that the linking rules would link. In the experiments reported in this paper and in Gropen *et al.* (1991), such motivation was readily available. It seems safe to assume that in experimental subjects 3;4 and older, basic grammatical relations like object and oblique object are well developed. In the experiments reported here, we attempted to control lexical semantic structures directly, as part of our experimental manipulations; in Gropen *et al.* (1991), we exploited the bias previously demonstrated by Gentner (1978) and others (see Pinker, 1989, for a review) whereby children acquire manner-of-motion components of meaning more easily than change-of-state components.

Bowerman's data are far more problematic as tests for the existence of linking rules, because neither of the two entities that the linking rules would link is reliably present in the children's speech. First, there is some evidence from Bowerman herself that the girls' first meanings for several common verbs were not true semantic representations but could be quite context-bound. In Bowerman (1978: 982) she argues that their first uses of *put, take, bring, drop,* and *make go* "were restricted to relatively specific, and different, contexts" with the result that each child "may be at a loss when she wants to refer to a new act that does not fit clearly into any of these categories." This raises the possibility that many early verbs (including "nonprototypical" verbs) could be used correctly simply because they were memorized as referring to stereotyped situations and kinds of arguments. Linking rules, which apply to more schematic verb semantic structures that can refer to a particular range of situations, may not be applicable until such semantic structures are acquired, which Bowerman (1978) suggests often comes later. Second, the errors in this early state do not appear to involve linking per se, where the wrong arguments would be linked to particular grammatical positions like subject, object, or the object of particular prepositions. Rather, the errors include every possible distortion of the grammatical positions themselves: SOV, VOS, VSO, OSV, and OVS orders all occur. The ordering of subject, verb, and object is not a linking phenomenon (specific verbs do not call for SVO order; it is general across the English language), and so these errors probably reflect noisy processing or incomplete acquisition in components of the child's language system involving phrase structure and grammatical relations.[10]

But for now, let us assume that the correct utterances in Bowerman's sample involve properly represented grammatical relations and semantic structures, so that we can focus on the logic of her tests comparing different kinds of verbs.

Bowerman does not outline any specific proposals about young children's semantic representations, but points to a discussion in Pinker (1989) on the mechanisms by which verb meanings are acquired. Pinker (1989) describes three plausible (and not mutually exclusive) mechanisms. One is called event-category labeling: The child would take a preexisting concept of a particular kind of event or state (e.g., seeing, or breaking) and use it as a hypothesis about the meaning of a verb inferred to express an instance of such an event. In general this mechanism can serve as no more than a source of first or default hypotheses, however, because many verbs corresponding to a general cognitive category like "moving an object" or "fright" vary in their precise semantic representations across languages (Gentner, 1982; Pinker, 1989; Talmy, 1985). The second learning mechanism is called semantic structure hypothesis testing: The child would add or delete substructures to his or her current representation of a verb meaning to make it conform with instances of its use. (For example, if a child incorrectly represented *fill* as requiring a pouring manner, that meaning component would be dropped when the verb was heard in connection with bailing.) The third learning mechanism is called syntactic cueing, in which the child would create semantic substructures with a set of inferences including the use of linking rules in reverse. That is, when the child hears a verb used in a sentence at a point at which enough syntax has been acquired to parse the sentence, the child would adjust the semantic representation of the verb to make it compatible with the grammatical relations of the verb's arguments, in conformity with the linking rules. For example a child who thought that *fill* meant "to pour" would change its semantics upon hearing *fill* used with a direct object referring to a full container, which implies that the verb expresses the change undergone by the container argument. Note that the subsequent use of linking rules does not care about which (if any) of these procedures was used to acquire a verb's semantic representation, as long as the verb has one.

Bowerman extracts a prediction from the operation of these mechanisms. She first lists verbs for which event-category labeling would be a sufficient learning mechanism; in particular, "prototypical agent–patient verbs" such as *open*, *fix*, *throw away*, *wash*, and *eat* should be prominent examples of such "cognitively-given" verbs. These verbs are then contrasted with stative transitive verbs such as *like*, *scare* (with an inanimate subject), *see*, *hear*, *need*, and *want*, where general cognitive concepts are associated with verbs that show variation in linking within and across languages (e.g., fright can be expressed with either *fear* or *scare*). She notes, "Regardless of which technique the child uses to determine the mapping of 'non-cognitively-given' verbs, it is clear that these verbs will require more effort than verbs whose meanings are cognitively transparent. Cognitively transparent verbs can in principle be mapped immediately (because there is only one candidate Agent, Patient, etc.); in contrast, 'something more' is needed for ambiguous verbs, and this will take extra time." But her two daughters did not use prototypical agent–patient verbs any sooner, or with fewer errors, than the "non-cognitively-given" verbs.[11]

Note, however, that Bowerman's prediction relies on an extra and gratuitous assumption. While it is true that "something more" is needed to acquire ambiguous verbs compared to unambiguous ones, that something more is not, as she suggests, "effort," or even time, but *information*. The semantic representation of an unambiguous verb could be acquired as a default by category labeling even if the child did no more than witness the verb itself expressing a single instance of the relevant event or state; for ambiguous verbs, a syntactic context or a disambiguating situation or situations would be required. But the difference is simply one of availability of information, not of inherent difficulty or time consumption other than that entailed by the difference between no information and some information. And crucially, because these are naturalistic data, the child surely *has* had access to relevant information. If a child is uttering *scare* or *like* at all she has necessarily heard those verbs used previously. If she has heard them used previously she has almost certainly heard them in contexts providing information that resolves their thematic ambiguity. One kind of context is situational: While the general event/state category pertaining to fright may be ambiguous, *to scare* involves an event and *to fear* a state (Dowty, 1991; Grimshaw, 1990; Pesetsky, 1990), and a situation in which *scare* is used to refer to an event can disambiguate them. The other kind of context is sentential: The child surely has not learned the verb from sentences like "this is scaring" but from sentences where the verb appears with a subject and an object, identifiable on many occasions as referring to either the experience or the stimulus. Here the syntax could cue the child, via reverse linking, to select a semantic representation of *scare* involving a causal stimulus argument. Similarly, there is no reason why it should be hard to acquire consistent semantic and syntactic representations for other "non-cognitively-given" verbs in Bowerman's list, like *ride, hold, spill, drop, wear, see, hear,* and *like,* as long as the child does not hear them in isolation but in correct sentences with their usual referents.

Thus Bowerman has not tested linking rules by themselves (which is generally impossible) but in conjunction with the extra assumption that *even with information sufficient to resolve thematic ambiguities* verbs whose meanings require the use of hypothesis testing or syntactic cueing have a lasting disadvantage compared to verbs that could have been acquired by category labeling. Note that Bowerman needed this extra assumption so that she could use her naturalistic data to test a hypothesis that is inherently better suited to being tested experimentally. According to the semantic structure theory of linking, together with the assumption that category labeling exists as one of the mechanisms for acquiring semantic structure, the ambiguous and unambiguous verbs should differ only when no disambiguating information is available. This situation is impossible to achieve in everyday life, but easy to achieve (at least in principle) in an experiment: An experimenter can present novel verbs without any syntactic context, controlling the events and states it refers to, and test whether children use the verbs with predictable syntax. Of course, that is exactly what we did in this paper with older children. A related experiment can be done by presenting novel verbs in syntactic contexts that linking rules render flatly incompatible with any reasonable semantic representation (verbs with "anticanonical" linking, where, for example, the direct object is an agent and hence not construable as "affected"), and seeing if children have more trouble learning them. This has been done with older children by Marantz (1982) and Pinker, Lebeaux, and Frost (1987).

If verbs without a preexisting concept corresponding precisely to their meanings can develop through experience without measurable disadvantage, one might wonder whether the role of linking, especially in semantic bootstrapping, has been minimized, or worse, defines a vicious circle (verbs' syntactic properties are deduced by linking rules applied to their semantic representations, verbs' semantic representations are acquired by reverse linking from syntax). The issues are discussed in detail in Pinker (1987, 1989, Chapter 6). The circle is easily broken by the fact that the verbs that inspire the hypothesization of grammatical rules are not the *same* verbs that need to be acquired with the help of their grammatical contexts; even a few unambiguous verbs would be sufficient in principle to get grammar acquisition started.[12] Moreover, no matter what the relative contributions are of nonlinguistic concepts, patterns of use across situations, and syntactic cues in how a verb was originally acquired, linking rules will govern its syntactic expression and semantic interpretation thereafter in a variety of spheres, such as refinement of its semantic representation, participation in lexical alternations, innovative uses including those leading to historical change, and holistic interpretation, as outlined in the General discussion.

Are children's linking errors strongly input driven?

Bowerman presents independent evidence in support of her claim that linking regularities must be acquired completely from parental speech. She suggests that errors attributable solely to linking rules (i.e., where the language does not contain lexical alternations, like the locative, that allow the appearance of a verb in one construction to predict its appearance in a related one via a lexical rule) occur only late in development, presumably after the child has tabulated enough data. Specifically, errors where experiencer-subject psychological verbs are used with stimulus subjects (e.g., *It didn't mind me very much*), reflecting the majority pattern in English, do not occur until the 6–11-year age range in Bowerman's two daughters.

Upon wider examination the data pattern provides little if any support for the hypothesis, however. Because lexical alternations are ubiquitous in English, Bowerman was able to rule out many possible examples of linking on the grounds that an existing English alternation might have been the source. But this does not mean that the alternation in fact was the source. In Hebrew, there are no verbs that can be used in identical form in causative and intransitive constructions, but Berman (1982) notes that 2-year-old children acquiring

Hebrew use intransitive verb forms as causative transitives with agent subjects and theme objects, just as English-speaking children do. Moreover, even in English young children use verbs with nonadult but appropriate linking patterns that could not have been analogized from existing alternations. For example, Bowerman herself (1982b) presents fourteen examples where children, as young as 2, causativized transitive verbs to form double-object structures (e.g., *I want to watch you this book*). This pattern of alternation is for all practical purposes nonexistent in English (Pinker, 1989). Most strikingly, the particular transitive verbs that children incorrectly link to the double-object construction are just the kinds of verbs that legitimately appear in that construction in a great variety of languages (Pinker, 1989), suggesting a common underlying psychological bias in linking. (See Pinker, 1984, Chapter 8, and Pinker, 1989, Chapters 1 and 7, for other examples of linking errors that are not based on existing English lexical alternations.)

Finally, let us examine Bowerman's data on psychological verbs, consisting of nine errors from her two daughters. One has an experiencer subject, the minority pattern in English. Of the eight with stimulus subjects, one consists of a sequence of two incorrect forms and a correct form: *I am very fond. Everyone's fond of me. I am very fonded.* Note that the second incorrect form in this sequence is a passive whose active verb source would *not* differ in linking from the correct English form (experience subject); the error is in converting an adjective to a passive. The other incorrect form in the sequence may also have been intended as a passive, given that the child followed it with nonpassive and clearly passive recastings of the predicate with the linking pattern it would have if it were indeed a passive, and given children's tendency to leave forms ending in *t* or *d* unmarked in past and participle forms (see Pinker and Prince, 1988). Even if it was intended as a nonpassive adjective, its experiencer subject follows no common English linking pattern for such predicates. A third example is a double-object form (*You know what pictures me uncle*?), which does not occur at all in English with stimulus subjects verbs. Three others are intransitive with prepositionally marked stimulus arguments (*approved to you; reacted on me; picture to me like*), of which the great majority in English actually have experiencer subjects; there are only a tiny number with stimulus subjects (*appeal, matter*; Talmy, 1985; Beth Levin, personal communication). This leaves only three errors containing transitive usages with stimulus subjects, reportedly the majority pattern in English, out of the nine linking errors with psych verbs listed. Thus when the grammatical properties of the errors and of English verbs are examined with more precision, one finds no clear evidence for Bowerman's assertion that most children's errors follow the statistically dominant linking pattern for English psychological verbs.

Do alternative linking patterns act like irregular inflection?

Bowerman gives no explicit account of how her alternative learning mechanism works or how its operation predicts developmental patterns or linguistic regularities. But the guiding analogy, inflectional overregularization, seems more misleading than helpful when examined in detail (see Marcus *et al.*, 1990; Pinker and Prince, 1988). First, whereas irregularly inflected verbs are fewer in number and higher in average token frequency than regular ones, the exact opposite may be true of ground-object and figure-object locative verbs (Rappaport and Levin, 1985; Gropen *et al.*, 1991). Second, verbs fall into inflectional paradigms specifying a past-tense form for every verb, in which the presence of an irregular is sufficient to block the regular rule. This allows the child to recover from inflectional overregularization when he or she hears the irregular a sufficient number of times. But no such paradigm organization is apparent for locative argument structures and the overregularization analogy leaves the unlearning of such errors unexplained (Gropen *et al.*, 1991; Pinker, 1989). Third, whereas any particular irregular pattern occurs with an unpredictable set of verbs (by definition), the ground-object linking pattern occurs *predictably* with verbs having a particular kind of meaning (in children as well as adults). Fourth, whereas any particular irregular pattern is an arbitrary memorization and supports no further grammatical inferences, the ground-object form is lawfully associated with a particular shift in interpretation (in children as well as adults), the one we have referred to as "holistic." Fifth, whereas the child's course of acquiring irregular verbs is mainly governed by frequency of exposure (since the verbs' unpredictability requires them to be memorised by rote; see Marcus *et al.*, 1990), the developmental course of ground-object forms is influenced by specific, independently measurable aspects of their semantic development (Gropen *et al.*, 1991). Sixth, while particular irregular patterns and the verbs they take vary radically from language to language, the ground-object form and the verbs that use it show highly similar patterns across unrelated languages. A learning mechanism that recorded any statistically predominant linkage between figure versus ground and direct versus oblique object predicts that these widespread and mutually consistent patterns should not occur. In contrast, it would be shocking to find an *i–a* alternation in the past tense inflection of the translations of *sing* in language after language, other than those historically close to English. The fact that these linking patterns do occur counts as evidence against Bowerman's claim that children learn the syntactic argument structure of verbs like *fill* in the same way that they learn the past tense forms of verbs like *sing*.

In sum, we find Bowerman's data interesting in suggesting that, in the presence of linguistic and nonlinguistic contextual information, young children can acquire verb representations even if the verbs do not unambiguously label preformed concepts for kinds of events, states, and arguments. But we see two problems in her claim that children learn all aspects of linking from the statistics of parental speech, with all possible linking patterns being equally easy to acquire. Methodologically, she tries to exploit her naturalistic data to test a hypothesis that can only be tested clearly with experimental materials in which a verb's semantic and syntactic contexts can be manipulated. Theoretically she appeals to the metaphor of irregular morphology; we have shown that when one examines the linguistic and psychological facts in detail, the metaphor falls apart. The ground-object form is just not an example of linguistic irregularity.

Note that we are not suggesting that learning plays a small role in the acquisition of argument structure. The child must learn details of the semantic structures of individual verbs, the kinds of verb structures permitted in the language, and which kinds of verbs lexical rules apply to. But the evidence suggests that linking rules, which show little or no cross-linguistic variation and which enforce pervasive systematicities among these learned structures, are more plausibly seen as one of the causes of such learning rather than as one of its products.

Acknowledgments

We thank Kay Bock, Melissa Bowerman, Susan Carey, Eve Clark, Adele Goldberg, Jane Grimshaw, Beth Levin, Ken Wexler, and an anonymous reviewer for their helpful comments on an earlier draft. We are also grateful to the directors, parents, and especially children of the following centers: Angier After School Program, Bowen After School Care Program, Children's Village, Creative Development Center, MIT Summer Day Camp, Needham Children's Community Center, Newton Community Service Center, Newton-Wellesley Children's Corner, Plowshares Child Care Program, Recreation Place, Red Barn Nursery School, Rosary Academy Learning Center, Second Church Nursery School, Leventhal-Sidman Jewish Community Center, Temple Beth Shalom, Underwood After School Program, and the Zervas Program. This research is part of the first author's MIT doctoral dissertation. It was supported by NIH grant HD 18381 to the second author, a grant from the Alfred P. Sloan Foundation to the MIT Center for Cognitive Science, and by an NIH NRSA Postdoctoral Fellowship to the first author, which he held at the Department of Linguistics, Stanford University.

Notes to 3.2

1. Note, however, that differences between the versions of an alternating verb cannot be *reduced* to properties of pragmatic focus. The speaker can use alternative verb structures to express differences in focus *only* to the extent that the particular verbs in the language permit it; he

cannot push verbs around at will to satisfy pragmatic intentions. For example, even if the listener already knows all about a bucket becoming full and only needs to know how and with what it became full, an English speaker still may not use the semantically interpretable and pragmatically appropriate *I dripped it with maple syrup. Conversely if the listener has background knowledge that paint has been used up but does not know how or onto what, grammar prevents the speaker from using the pragmatically natural *I coated it onto the chair. Only for alternating verbs like sprayed paint/sprayed the wall can the speaker avail himself or herself of either form, depending on the discourse context. Details of the semantic representation of the phrase will necessarily differ between the forms, but will generally be consistent with the discourse difference, because differences in which entity is being asserted to be "affected" are compatible with differences in which entity is focused as "new" information.

2. There are several other "semantic fields" such as possession, existence, or knowledge, in which a theme can be caused to change; see Jackendoff (1983, 1987, 1990) and Pinker (1989), both of which use the mnemonic "GO" to correspond to all such changes.

3. In addition, there is a linking rule mapping the agent onto the subject; a linking rule that, in combination with other rules, maps the main event theme onto the subject if the subject has not already been linked or onto the direct object otherwise; a linking rule mapping the main event patient (i.e., an acted-upon entity, whether or not it changes) onto the direct object; and linking rules that map places, paths, and certain subordinated arguments onto oblique (prepositional) objects (see Pinker, 1989). Linking rules do not specify individual prepositions; the preposition's own semantic representation selects the appropriate kind of oblique object that it can be inserted into (Jackendoff, 1987, 1990; Pinker, 1989).

4. An essentially similar formulation can be found in Pesetsky (1990), who suggests that lexical alternations are morphological operations that affix a null morpheme onto a verb. The morpheme, though phonologically empty, has a semantic representation, which thereby alters the meaning of the whole affixed form.

5. The subordinated figure argument can either be left unexpressed, as an "understood" argument, or expressed as the object of the preposition with. The distinction, not studied in this investigation, is discussed in Jackendoff (1987), Rappaport and Levin (1988), and Pinker (1989).

6. If subjects still failed to respond, the procedure called for a forced-choice question (e.g.), "Am I filling the cup or filling the marbles?" order counterbalanced. However, we had to resort to a forced-choice question on only four occasions in this investigation (0.2 percent), so we have grouped these data with those given in response to the fill-in-the-blank prompt.

7. Note that the difference in instructions between manner and state-change verbs does not provide syntactic information that the child can use to predict the syntactic differences between the verbs. In most grammatical theories, over there and like that are both prepositional phrases. In particular, like in this context is not an adjective: Adjectives do not take direct objects, only prepositional phrases and clauses; prepositions do take direct objects, but do not take the comparative -er suffix; cf. *A is liker B than C. The fact that over there refers to a location (semantics typical of a PP) and like that refers to a state (semantics typical of an AP) is syntactically irrelevant: PPs can refer to states (e.g., in this state; with red paint all over it; in a mess) and APs can refer to locations (e.g., very close to the edge; closer to the edge). Of course, children could be attending to the semantics of the phrases in the instructions, instead of or in addition to their real-world referents, but this is fully compatible with the intention that the independent variable be one of verb semantics. Crucially, the syntactic difference between the instructions provides no information of use to the child.

8. Note that this is distinct from the proposal of Landau and Gleitman (1985) and Gleitman (1990) that the child must use a set of argument structures to deduce the idiosyncratic semantic content of the verb (e.g., whether the verb refers to opening, closing, breaking, or melting) from those argument structures, without having to note the contexts in which the verb is used. Pinker (1989, in press) and Grimshaw and Pinker (1990) examine this particular proposal in detail, and discuss evidence suggesting that it is unlikely be an important factor in learning lexical semantics.

9. Goldberg (1992) suggests that once one specifies narrow subclasses of verbs belonging to a construction, one can eliminate lexical rules. The speaker could note that a verb has an intrinsic meaning that is compatible with more than one possible subclass and could use it in both accompanying constructions; constraints on alternations would reduce to constraints on possible verb meanings. See Pinker (1989, Chapter 4) for three reasons why lexical rules seem

to be necessary. (1) They specify morphological changes accompanying certain alternations (e.g., English passive). (2) They dictate the semantic composition of verb meaning and construction meaning (e.g., distinguishing whether the semantic representation of a verb in one construction is a "means" or an "effect" in the representation in another construction). (3) They specify pairs of compatible semantic subclasses that are allowed to share verb roots, distinguishing them from pairs of compatible semantic subclasses that are confined to disjoint sets of verb roots. For example, verbs of "removing stuff from a surface" and "making a surface free of stuff" can share roots, as in *clean (clear, strip) the table of crumbs/crumbs from the table,* presumably because of a lexical rule. But verbs of "removing possessions from a person" and "making a person bereft of possessions," though both possible in English, must be expressed by different roots as in *seize (steal, recover, grab) money from John/*John of his money; bilk (rob, relieve, unburden) John of his money/*money from John* (see Talmy, 1985), presumably because of the absence of a lexical rule.

10. Bowerman notes that the errors occur more often for prototyical agent–patient verbs than for "other" verbs, but this pattern, if general, would be difficult to explain in any theory.

11. In some cases, Bowerman's assignment of verbs to her "prototypical agent–patient" class may not exactly fit the criterion of verbs that show little variation in linking: *hit* and *cover* are classified as prototypical agent–patient verbs, though they do vary across languages (see her Note 7); for some excluded verbs, such as *hold* and *draw*, it is not clear that they do vary. Still, the patterns shown by the two children would not change much if a few verbs were recategorized.

12. Note that Bowerman's data also do not test the semantic bootstrapping hypothesis, which asserts the prototypical semantic relations are cues used to hypothesize rules involving grammatical relations (which can then be used for all verbs, regardless of semantics), not that the rules themselves are specific to particular kinds of semantic relations. Semantic bootstrapping, like linking, is best tested experimentally: Children hearing a language containing only situationally ambiguous or anticanonical verbs would have trouble learning its grammar; see Pinker (1984, Chapter 2).

References to 3.2

Anderson, S. R. (1971). "On the role of deep structure in semantic interpretation." *Foundations of Language,* **6**, 197–219.

Baker, C. L. (1979). "Syntactic theory and the projection problem." *Linguistic Inquiry,* **10**, 533–81.

Berman, R. A. (1982). "Verb-pattern alternation: The interface of morphology, syntax, and semantics in Hebrew child language." *Journal of Child Language,* **9**, 169–91.

Bowerman, M. (1978). "Systematizing semantic knowledge: Changes over time in the child's organization of word meaning." *Child Development,* **49**, 977–87.

Bowerman, M. (1982a). "Reorganizational processes in lexical and syntactic development." In E. Wanner and L. R. Gleitman (eds), *Language Acquisition: The state of the art.* New York: Cambridge University Press, 319–46.

Bowerman, M. (1982b). "Evaluating competing linguistic models with language acquisition data: Implications of developmental errors with causative verbs." *Quaderni di Semantica,* **3**, 5–66.

Bowerman, M. (1988). "The 'no negative evidence' problem: How do children avoid constructing an overly general grammar?" In J. A. Hawkins (ed.), *Explaining Language Universals.* Oxford: Blackwell, 73–101.

Bowerman, M. (1990). "Mapping thematic roles onto syntactic functions: Are children helped by innate 'linking rules'?" *Journal of Linguistics,* **28**, 1253–89.

Bresnan, J. (1982). "The passive in lexical theory." In J. Bresnan (ed.), *The Mental Representation of Grammatical Relations.* Cambridge, MA: MIT Press, 3–86.

Carter, R. J. (1976). "Some constraints on possible words." *Semantikos,* **1**, 27–66.

Chomsky, N. (1981). *Lectures on Government and Binding.* Dordrecht: Foris Publications.

Clark, E. V. and Clark, H. H. (1979). "When nouns surface as verbs." *Language,* **55**, 767–811.

Crain, S., Thornton, R., and Murasugi, K. (1987). "Capturing the evasive passive." Paper presented at the Twelfth Annual Boston University Conference on Language Development. October, 23–5.

Dowty, D. R. (1991). "Thematic proto roles and argument selection." *Language*, **67**, 547–619.

Fillmore, C. J. (1968). "The case for case." In E. Bach and R. J. Harms (eds), *Universals in Linguistic Theory*. New York: Holt. Rinehart, and Winston, 1–90.

Foley, W. A. and Van Valin, R. D. (1984). *Functional Syntax and Universal Grammar*. New York: Cambridge University Press.

Foley, W.A. and Van Valin, R. D. (1985). "Information packaging in the clause." In T. Shopen (ed.), *Language Typology and Syntactic Description. Vol 1: Clause structure*. New York: Cambridge University Press, 282–364.

Gentner, D. (1975). "Evidence for the psychological reality of semantic components: The verbs of possession." In D. A. Norman and D. E. Rumelhart (eds), *Explorations in Cognition*. San Francisco: W.H. Freeman, 211–46.

Gentner, D. (1978). "On relational meaning: The acquisition of verb meaning." *Child Development*, **49**, 988–98.

Gentner, D. (1982). "Why nouns are learned before verbs: Linguistic relativity vs. natural partitioning." In S. A. Kuczaj II (ed.), *Language Development. Vol. 2: Language, thought, and culture*. Hillsdale, NJ: Erlbaum, 301–34.,

Gleitman, L. R. (1990). "Structural sources of verb meaning." *Language Acquisition*, **1**, 3–55.

Goldberg, A. (1992). "The inherent semantics of argument structure: The case of the English ditransitive construction." *Cognitive Linguistics*, **3**, 37–74.

Green G. M. (1974). *Semantics and Syntactic Regularity*. Bloomington: Indiana University Press.

Grimshaw, J. (1981). "Form, function, and the language acquisition device." In C. L. Baker and J. J. McCarthy (eds), *The Logical Problem of Language Acquisition*. Cambridge, MA: MIT Press, 165–82.

Grimshaw, J. (1990). *Argument Structure*. Cambridge, MA: MIT Press.

Grimshaw, J. and Pinker, S. (1990). "Using syntax to deduce verb meaning." Paper presented to the Fifteenth Annual Boston University Conference on Language Development, 19–21 October.

Gropen, J. (1989). *Learning Locative Verbs: How universal linking rules constrain productivity*, Ph.D. dissertation, MIT.

Gropen, J., Pinker, S., Hollander, M., and Goldberg, R. (1991). "Syntax and semantics in the acquisition of locative verbs." *Journal of Child Language*, **18**, 115–51.

Gropen, J., Pinker, S., Hollander, M., Goldberg, R., and Wilson, R. (1989). "The learnability and acquisition of the dative alternation in English." *Language*, **65**, 203–57.

Gruber, J. (1965). *Studies in Lexical Relations*. Ph.D. dissertation, MIT.

Hopper, P. J. and Thompson, S. A. (1980). "Transitivity in grammar and discourse." *Language*, **56**, 251–99.

Jackendoff, R. S. (1972). *Semantic Interpretation in Generative Grammar*. Cambridge, MA: MIT Press.

Jackendoff, R. S. (1978). "Grammar as evidence for conceptual structure." In M. Halle, J. Bresnan, and G. Miller (eds), *Linguistic Theory and Psychological Reality*. Cambridge, MA: MIT Press, 201–28.

Jackendoff, R. S. (1983). *Semantics and Cognition*. Cambridge, MA: MIT Press.

Jackendoff, R. S. (1987). "The status of thematic relations in linguistic theory." *Linguistic Inquiry*, **18**, 369–411.

Jackendoff, R. S. (1990). *Semantic Structures*. Cambridge, MA: MIT Press.

Jackendoff, R. S. (1991). "Parts and boundaries." *Cognition*, **41**, 9–45.

Keenan, E. O. (1976). "Towards a universal definition of 'subject'." In C. Li (ed.), *Subject and Topic*. New York: Academic Press, 303–33.

Landau, B. and Gleitman, L. R. (1985). *Language and Experience*. Cambridge, MA: Harvard University Press.

Levin, B. (1985). "Lexical semantics in review: An introduction." In B. Levin (ed.), *Lexical Semantics in Review*. Lexicon Project working Papers No. 1, MIT Center for Cognitive Science, 1–62.

Levin B. and Rappaport Hovav (1991). "Wiping the slate clean: A lexical semantic exploration." *Cognition*, **41**, 123–51.

Macnamara, J. (1982). *Names for Things: A study of human learning*. Cambridge, MA: MIT Press.

Marantz, A. P. (1982). "On the acquisition of grammatical relations." *Linguistic Berichte: Linguistik als Kognitive Wissenschaft*, **80/82**, 32–69.

Marcus, G., Ullman, M., Pinker, S., Hollander, M., Rosen, T. J., and Xu, F. (1990). *Overregularization*. MIT Center for Cognitive Science Occasional Paper No. 41.

Miller, G. A. and Johnson-Laird, P. N. (1976). *Language and Perception*. Cambridge, MA: Harvard University Press.

Moravscik, E. A. (1978). "On the case marking of objects." In J. H. Greenberg *et al.* (eds), *Universals of Human Language, Vol. 4: Syntax*. Stanford, CA: Stanford University Press, 249–89.

Pesetsky, D. (1990). "Psych predicates, universal alignment and lexical decomposition." Unpublished manuscript, Department of Linguistics and Philosophy, MIT.

Pinker, S. (1982). "A theory of the acquisition of lexical interpretive grammars." In J. Bresnan (ed.), *The Mental Representation of Grammatical Relations*. Cambridge, MA: MIT Press, 655–726.

Pinker, S. (1984). *Language Learnability and Language Development*. Cambridge, MA: MIT Press.

Pinker, S. (1987). "The bootstrapping problem in language acquisition." In B. MacWhinney (ed.), *Mechanisms of Language Acquisition*. Hillsdale, NJ: Erlbaum, 399–441.

Pinker, S. (1989). *Learnability and Cognition: The acquisition of argument structure*. Cambridge, MA: MIT Press.

Pinker, S. (in press). "How could a child use verb syntax to learn verb semantics?" *Lingua*.

Pinker, S., Lebeaux, D. S., and Frost L. A. (1987). "Productivity and constraints of the acquisition of the passive." *Cognition*, **26**, 195–267.

Pinker, S. and Prince, A. (1988). "On language and connectionism: Analysis of a parallel distributed processing model of language acquisition." *Cognition*, **28**, 73–193.

Pustejovsky, J. (1991). "The syntax of event structure." *Cognition*, **41**, 47–81.

Rappaport, M. and Levin, B. (1985). "A case study in lexical analysis: The locative alternation." Unpublished manuscript, MIT Center for Cognitive Science.

Rappaport, M. and Levin, B. (1988). "What to do with theta-roles." In W. Wilkins (ed.), *Thematic Relations*. New York: Academic Press.

Schwartz-Norman, L. (1976). "The grammar of 'content' and 'container.'" *Journal of Linguistics*, **12**, 279–87.

Talmy, L. (1983). "How language structures space." In H. Pick and L. Acredolo (eds), *Spatial Orientation: Theory, research and application*. New York: Plenum.

Talmy, L. (1985). "Lexicalization patterns: Semantic structure in lexical forms." In T. Shopen (ed.), *Language Typology and Syntactic Description. Vol. 3: Grammatical categories and the lexicon*. New York: Cambridge University Press, 57–149.

Tenny, C. (1988). "The aspectual interface hypothesis." *Proceedings of the North East Linguistics Society*, **18**.

Wexler, K. and Culicover, P. (1980). *Formal Principles of Language Acquisition*. Cambridge, MA: MIT Press.

Learning a Semantic System:

What role do cognitive predispositions play?

Melissa Bowerman

[. . .] The question of what is innate and what is learned has long been the most fundamental theoretical issue in the study of language acquisition. Following Chomsky's influential arguments for an inborn "Language Acquisition Device" (e.g., Chomsky, 1965), controversy initially focused on whether there is innate knowledge of syntactic structure (and of course this is still hotly debated). Although many researchers were persuaded by Chomsky's arguments that the then-reigning theory of learning, behaviorism, was incapable of accounting for the acquisition of grammar, they did not, like him, necessarily assume that this meant that grammar was not learned. Instead, they suspected that children's developing cognitive understanding, together with their general capacity to detect and mentally represent regularities, might be a sufficient basis on which to acquire grammar.

One important line of theorizing pursued by cognitively minded investigators gave a major role in language acquisition to children's growing conceptual knowledge. This approach held that a critical foundation for language learning is laid during the prelinguistic period, as the infant builds up an understanding of such basic notions as objects, actions, causality, and spatial relations. As children begin to want to communicate, they search for the linguistic forms (content words, grammatical morphemes, word order or intonation patterns, etc.) that will allow them to encode their ideas. Initial lexical, morphological, and syntactic development, according to this view, is a process of learning to map linguistic forms onto pre-established concepts, and these concepts, in turn, at first serve to guide the child's generalization of the forms to new contexts.

Although this approach was at first fueled partly by the desire to provide a "learning" alternative to Chomsky's innatism, it has gradually developed some important nativist tendencies of its own. In particular, researchers point to growing evidence that the initial semantic categories of children learning the same or different languages show many intriguing similarities. These similarities can be accounted for if we assume that the way children conceptualize and classify the elements of their experience is not free to vary arbitrarily, but rather is shaped and constrained by the inherent properties of the human perceptual and cognitive system. According to this hypothesis, children's early categories may be "learned" in the sense that experience is required to set their development in motion, but they will develop in a relatively uniform way despite exposure to different linguistic and nonlinguistic environments.

The goal of this chapter is to evaluate this important proposal. First I review the rise of the hypothesis that children's early language maps onto a universally constrained set of meanings that emerges independently of experience with any particular language. Following this, I argue that although there is good evidence that children do have cognitive biases with respect to the organization of meaning, the position has been overstated. In particular, I present evidence that recent theorizing has overestimated the strength and specificity of children's cognitive predispositions for semantic organization, and, conversely, underestimated the extent to which, even from a very young age, children are sensitive to language-specific principles of semantic categorization that are implicitly displayed in the linguistic input. In concluding, I suggest some possible implications for children's language disorders.

Evidence suggesting cognitive predispositions for semantic organization

In the modern era of the child language research, the belief that children come to the task of acquiring language equipped with prestructured categories has developed only over the last twenty years or so (although of course the idea that humans apprehend the world with innate categories of mind has a much longer philosophical tradition).[1] In the 1950s and 1960s, researchers generally assumed the opposite, that the meanings children associate with linguistic forms are constructed through linguistic experience, for example, by a process of abstracting the properties of objects, events, relationships, and the like that remain constant across successive uses of a form by fluent speakers (see Brown's [1958, Chapter 6] characterization of "The Original Word Game"). Interest was also strong in the extreme statement of this position, associated with Whorf (1956), that not only is children's understanding of the world shaped by the categories provided by their language ("linguistic determinism"), but also that languages differ so radically in the way they classify reality that learners of different languages end up with essentially noncomparable systems of thought ("linguistic relativity").

What happened to change these ideas? Interrelated developments in several different disciplines contributed to the shift, and it is worth reviewing them briefly.

Linguistics

During the earlier part of the twentieth century linguists were fascinated by evidence from newly described American Indian languages for the apparently endless ways that languages could differ from one other. By the 1960s, however, interest began to turn away from diversity and toward similarity. Underlying all the apparent differences, were languages in some respects all alike?

Inspired by Chomsky, initial work on language universals was aimed primarily at formal syntactic properties of language. Gradually, however, semantics came in for attention as well. Comparative studies such as Berlin and Kay's (1969) classic work on color terminology began to show that languages are indeed more similar in their semantic structure than had previously been supposed (see also Heider, 1972); other examples include Allan's (1979) study of the semantics of classifier systems, Talmy's (1975, 1976) work on the semantics of motion and causation, and chapters in Greenberg (1978) on a variety of semantic domains. For some domains, particularly color, there was also evidence linking cross-linguistic similarities to properties of human physiology (see Bornstein, 1979, for a review). It began to seem as if the semantic organization of language, far from influencing or determining speakers' categories of thought, was itself a reflection of deep-seated properties of human perceptual and cognitive organization.

Psychology

In the late 1960s, interest increased enormously among American developmental psychologists in the work of Piaget (1954, 1970), who attributed little role to language in children's more general cognitive development. According to Piaget, children acquire a basic grasp of concepts of space, causality, object permanence, and so forth in the first eighteen to twenty-four months of life, when language is still absent or rudimentary.

An additional influence was new approaches to the fundamental psychological process of categorization, including in particular research on prototype structure and "basic level categories" by Rosch (1973; Rosch *et al.*, 1976). This work suggested that natural language categories are less arbitrary than had often been thought, and more "given" in the correlational structure of reality. This meant that reliable clues to categorization were available to children independently of language, and, indeed, Rosch and Mervis (1977) demonstrated that children can categorize objects at the "basic level" before they learn names for them.

On still another front, new work on infant cognitive and perceptual development began to show that babies have less to learn than had previously been assumed. Rather than experiencing the world as a "blooming, buzzing confusion," infants appear to come "prewired" to interpret their experiences in certain ways, for example, to pick out objects from their background (Spelke 1985), to infer causality (Leslie and Keeble, 1987), and to perceive changes along certain physical continua in a discontinuous or "categorical" way (see Bornstein, 1979, and Quinn and Eimas, 1986, for reviews).

Language acquisition

Studies of language acquisition both fed into the developing "nonlinguistic meanings first" view of the relationship between language and thought and were influenced by it. Three important lines of early research were: (1) studies of the semantic properties of children's first word combinations, (2) work on determinants of the order in which children within and across languages acquire the members of a set of linguistic forms, and (3) analyses of children's overextensions of words.[2]

Semantic relations and early word combinations

An important finding of research of the late 1960s and early 1970s was that regardless of the language being learned, children's first sentences revolve around a restricted set of meanings to do with agency, action, location, possession, and the existence, recurrence, nonexistence, and disappearance of objects (Bloom, 1970; Bowerman, 1973; Brown, 1973; Schlesinger, 1971; Slobin, 1970). These semantic commonalities led several researchers (e.g., Bowerman, 1973; Brown, 1973, Schlesinger, 1971) to hypothesize that early syntactic development consists of children's discovery of regular patterns for positioning words whose referents are understood by the child as playing relational roles like "agent," "action," and "location." The relational roles are not learned through language according to this view, but instead reflect the way children come to conceptualize the structure of events during the sensorimotor period of development (see Brown, 1973). This hypothesis was the starting point for a more general idea that developed over the 1970s: That children initially link not only word-order patterns but also many other grammatical forms and construction patterns to categories of meaning and pragmatic function that have developed prior to, and independently of, language.

Order of acquisition

A second important line of research was initiated by Slobin's (1973) proposal that the order in which children acquire linguistic items is jointly determined by two factors: The order in which the relevant meanings are understood and the relative formal linguistic complexity of the items themselves. The time of emergence of the meaning expressed by a language form sets the lower boundary: The form will not emerge until the child has a grasp of the relevant concept. However, acquisition can be delayed beyond this point if the formal means of expression are difficult. A fundamental tenet of Slobin's approach was that the semantic basis for acquisition is universal: "the rate and order of development of the semantic notions expressed by language are fairly constant across languages, regardless of the formal means of expression employed" (1973: 187).

Subsequent work has strongly confirmed that relative difficulty of meaning plays an important role in the time of acquisition of linguistic forms, and there is evidence for a few semantic domains that the sequence of cognitive mastery is similar across children learning different languages. For example, Johnston and Slobin (1979) established that the order of acquisition of locative markers is remarkably consistent across languages, and Johnston (1979) showed further that the order in which English-speaking children acquire locative prepositions mirrors the order in which the underlying concepts are grasped, as determined by nonlinguistic testing (see also Corrigan *et al.*, 1981; Halpern, Corrigan, and Aviezer, 1981). An analogous cross-linguistically shared sequence was established by Clancy, Jacobsen, and Silva (1976) for the emergence of the meanings underlying the use of connectives like *and, but, when,* and *if.*

Overextensions and other nonadultlike uses

A third early impetus for the "meanings first" position was the approach to children's early acquisition of word meaning pioneered by Eve Clark in her (1973b) publication, "What's in a word?" In this chapter Clark called attention to the phenomenon of overextension—children's use of words for a broader range of referents than is appropriate in adult speech. After reviewing and classifying reported overextensions from a variety of languages, Clark concluded that children at first link words to perceptual properties of objects that are salient to them prior to language, and that possibly reflect biologically given ways of viewing and organizing the world (Bierwisch, 1967, 1970).

Clark's claims engendered much debate about the relative importance of overextension versus underextension, overlap, and "mismatch" of children's word meanings relative to those of adults, about whether children's early word use reflects perceptual or functional concepts, and about whether early categories are based on necessary-and-sufficient conditions or have a prototype or family resemblance structure (e.g., Anglin, 1977; Bowerman, 1978a; Nelson,

1974). Throughout these controversies, however, most researchers agreed with Clark that early words are mapped to meanings that arise in the child before the words themselves are learned. The reasoning behind this assumption was that if the meanings were learned from observing how adults use the words, the range of referents for which children use the words should be closely similar to those for which adult speakers use them, not persistently larger, smaller, or "different."

Cognitive pretuning for language: Still stronger evidence

The various kinds of evidence I have outlined strongly support the hypothesis that cognitive/perceptual understanding of some sort must be established before certain linguistic forms are acquired. However, with the exception of E. Clark's proposals, they are not very specific about the exact properties of this understanding. In particular, they do not indicate that, at any given level of cognitive development, children are biased to *categorize* the situations they understand in one way rather than another, nor do they show that their early preferred categorization principles are universally important across languages.[3] However, additional research shows that, in applying linguistic forms to referents, children often classify spontaneously on the basis of categorization principles that play a role in the semantic systems of natural languages.

Overextensions revisited

Several researchers have noted that children's overextensions and word substitution errors are often strikingly well motivated from a linguistic point of view. That is, although the perceived similarities and differences among objects, events, and the like that guide the child's use of a form may be incorrect for that particular form, they often define semantic categories that are important in languages, sometimes even in connection with translation-equivalent forms in other languages.

For instance, consider again children's initial overextensions of words for objects, which, according to E. Clark's (1973b) analysis, are based primarily on salient perceptual properties of objects. In a later study, Clark (1977) showed that the categories that guide children's object-word overextensions are strikingly similar to the meanings encoded by noun classifiers in languages that have classifier systems (noun classifiers are a system of obligatory markers that must accompany or can often replace nouns in specific syntactic contexts, such as after numerals, e.g., *two ROUND-THINGS balls/stones/gourds, five LONG-THINGS pencils/poles, three FLAT-THINGS rugs/newspapers*). In both children and classifier systems, according to Clark, "objects are categorized primarily on the basis of shape, and the same properties of shape appear to be relevant in acquisition and in classifier systems. Roundness and length . . . appear to be very salient" (1977: p. 263 in 1979 reprint). Clark concludes that the categories defined by children's overextensions of object words are similar to the meanings of classifiers because both reflect, and are constrained by, fundamental properties of the human perceptual system.

Errors with body-part terms and related words provide a second example of spontaneous classifications that are linguistically "sensible." English-speaking children sometimes make overextensions like *hand* for "foot," *ankle* for "wrist," *sleeve* for "pantleg," and *kick* for an action of throwing (Bowerman, 1980). Although the everyday vocabulary of English has separate words for body parts and actions involving upper and lower extremities, many other languages have words that collapse the distinction; for example, the word for "finger" is often also used for "toe" (see Andersen, 1978, for a discussion of cross-linguistic constraints on body part terms and further evidence that these constraints play a role in language acqusition). English-speaking children's errors indicate that even though they are learning a language that models a differentiated classification scheme, they are still able to recognize parallels between upper and lower extremities, and so command a mode of categorizing body parts that is often important for language.

For a third example, consider periphrastic causative constructions. In these sentences English makes an obligatory distinction between "active" and "permissive" causation, as illustrated by the meaning difference between *MAKE John sing* (active: do something to bring John's singing about) and *LET John sing* (permissive: do not do something that, if done, would prevent John from singing). Although English-speaking children respect this distinction most of the time, they occasionally substitute *make* and *let* for each other: For example, "I don't want to go to bed yet; don't LET me go to bed" (= don't MAKE me go to bed; said after the child has been told to go to bed), and "MAKE me watch it" (= LET me watch it; said as the child begs to be allowed to watch a TV program) (Bowerman, 1978c). These errors suggest that the meanings of *make* and *let* in periphrastic causatives are closely related for children, even though they are learning a language that does not encourage this classification. And this sensitivity to the similarity in meaning between the two forms is linguistically well founded: Many languages make no obligatory distinction between active and permissive causation, but construct causative sentences with a single causative morpheme that can mean either MAKE or LET, according to context (Comrie, 1981).

Basic child grammar

Scattered evidence that there is a close relationship between children's spontaneous ways of organizing meaning and classification schemes that are common in the world's languages has been assembled and marshalled into a strong hypothesis by Slobin (1985). Slobin's proposal concerns the acquisition of forms that constitute the closed-class or "grammaticized" portion of language; that is, inflections and other bound affixes, prepositions and postpositions, connectives, negative markers, and so on. Following Talmy (1978, 1983, 1985), Slobin proposes that there is a difference between the kinds of meanings expressed by open-class and closed-class forms: The former are essentially unbounded, while the latter are quite constrained. As Talmy puts it:

> [Grammatical forms] represent only certain categories, such as space, time (hence, also form, location, and motion), perspective-point, distribution of attention, force, causation, knowledge state, reality status, and the current speech event, to name some main ones. And, importantly, they are not free to express just anything within these conceptual domains, but are limited to quite particular aspects and combinations of aspects, ones that can be thought to constitute the "structure" of those domains. (1983: 227)

After reviewing cross-linguistic evidence concerning the meanings that children initially associate with a variety of different grammatical forms and constructions, Slobin (1985) concludes that children, like languages, are constrained in the meanings they assign to the grammaticized portions of language. Specifically, he proposes that children approach the language acquisition task with a prestructured "semantic space" in which meanings and clusters of meanings (which include pragmatic as well as semantic notions) constitute a "privileged set of grammaticizable notions" onto which functors and other grammatical constructions are initially mapped. The particular forms that get mapped vary from language to language, of course, but the basic meanings are constant. The outcome of this initial mapping process (which, in addition to the basic "grammaticizable" meanings, includes certain constraints on the co-occurrence and positioning of forms) is a "universally specifiable 'Basic Child Grammar' that reflects an underlying ideal form of human language" (p. 1160).[4]

Slobin's specific proposals about the core meanings that constitute children's initial "semantic space" are based primarily on evidence for typical patterns of overextending and underextending inflections and other grammatical forms. A paradigm illustration concerns children's acquisition of markers associated with transitivity. In many languages, the direct objects of transitive verbs must be marked with an accusative ending (e.g., *John opened the box*-ACC.) In some languages, it is the subject of a transitive sentence rather than the direct object that requires special marking. According to Slobin (1982, 1985), when children learning a language of either kind begin to use the relevant markers, they at first restrict them to the objects or subjects of verbs that specify a *direct physical manipulation* of an object, such as *break*, *take*, and *throw*. Only later is the marker extended to the objects or subjects of nonmanipulative verbs like *see, read,* and *call (to).*

To explain this pattern Slobin proposes that children are initially sensitive to an experiential gestalt that he terms the "prototypical transitive event" (1982) or the "manipulative activity scene" (1985): A causal event in which an animate agent intentionally brings about a physical and perceptible change of state in a patient by means of direct bodily contact or with an instrument under the agent's control. This category of events serves as a core meaning that initially attracts markers associated with transitivity in the language the child is learning. Slobin notes that the "manipulative activity scene" is important not only to children but also to the structure of language more generally. For example, Hopper and Thompson (1980) have identified it as the core conceptual notion associated with markers of transitivity in all languages, and in many languages it has served as the historical starting point for forms that eventually spread to become general markers of transitivity (Givón, 1975; Lord, 1982).

Although English lacks general markers for the objects or subjects of transitive verbs, children learning English also seem to be sensitive to the "manipulative activity scene." In an analysis of self-referent forms (*I, me, my,* name) in the spontaneous speech of six children between twenty and thirty-two months of age, Budwig (1985, 1986) found that, for the three children who referred only to themselves and never to others in sentence-subject position, selection among pronouns correlated with degree of agentivity of the subject. Thus, *my* tended to occur in utterances expressing events in which the child acted as a prototypical agent bringing about a physical change (*My blew the candles out, My cracked the eggs*), whereas *I* was used primarily in utterances expressing the child's experiential states and intentions, or activities that did not result in change (*I like peas, I no want those, I wear it*).

Summary

To summarize, the various lines of evidence sketched above all indicate that children can spontaneously categorize objects, events, situations, and the like for purposes of linguistic expression. Further, these spontaneous categories are often of "the right kind"—that is, categories that are important in the semantic/grammatical systems of languages, even though perhaps not in connection with the particular forms to which children have linked them. This evidence testifies to an impressive contribution from nonlinguistic cognitive and perceptual development in children's formation of language-relevant concepts. But does it show that the meanings children initially link to words and grammatical morphemes are entirely provided by nonlinguistic cognitive and perceptual development, as is currently often assumed? Or does the linguistic input also direct young language learners' attention to ways of classifying that they would not have hit upon otherwise?

Cross-linguistic semantic variation

One problem that affects attempts to understand the relative balance between nonlinguistic cognition and linguistic experience in children's early semantic development is methodological. When children's use of language forms is guided by categories that have been generated independently of linguistic experience, the result is often errors from the adult point of view. Errors are salient, and they demand an explanation.[5] In contrast, when children extend forms on the basis of categorization principles they have induced by observing how the forms are used in adult speech, their usage is more conventional. Correct use where in principle there might have been errors is easy to overlook. If even only 10 percent (for example) of children's early forms were used in connection with self-generated categories, whereas 90 percent were linked to concepts constructed partially or entirely with the help of the linguistic input, our attention and explanatory efforts would immediately be drawn to the 10 percent, since this is where the errors would be concentrated.

Even when we recognize that children use a given form more or less correctly, we rarely interpret this as evidence that they have been attending to the linguistic input in their construction of the governing concept. This is because— at least if the language is our own—the categories involved seem to us so "natural" that it is easy to imagine that they could be formed directly on the basis of nonlinguistic cognition.

In the current era of interest in linguistic universals, researchers have tended to deemphasize or neglect cross-linguistic differences in semantic categorization. However, even though recent research has shown that languages are semantically less varied than had previously been supposed, they are by no means uniform. In most conceptual domains there are significant options from among which languages can "choose" in structuring the categories of meanings to which words, grammatical morphemes, or construction patterns are linked (see, e.g., Lakoff, 1987; Langacker, 1987; Plunkett and Trosberg, 1984; Talmy, 1975, 1976, 1985).[6]

To the extent that a particular semantic domain is partitioned differently across languages, human cognition is correspondingly flexible in how it can construe the to-be-classified actions, events, and so forth. In this case there is no a priori reason to assume that just one mode of construal should be easiest or most obvious for children—that is, that one is somehow "basic" (Brown, 1965: 317). In such situations children, like human beings more generally, may be sensitive to a number of different similarities and differences among referents, and they may be relatively easily influenced by classification schemes introduced by their language.

Spatial relationships

To make the significance of cross-linguistic variation in semantic categorization more concrete, let us compare how certain spatial relationships are classified in a few languages. Variability in spatial categorization provides a particularly striking demonstration that children have more to learn than is at first obvious, because spatial relationships are often taken as quintessential examples of concepts that children can acquire purely on the basis of their nonlinguistic manipulations and observations. After all, what could be more sensorimotor than an understanding of space?

I do indeed take it as well established that the development of a nonlinguistic understanding of space is an important prerequisite to the acquisition of spatial words (e.g., E. Clark, 1973b; H. Clark, 1973; Corrigan *et al.*, 1981; Halpern, Corrigan, and Aviezer, 1981; Johnston, 1979; Johnston and Slobin, 1979; Levine and Carey, 1982). However, it is not clear exactly what this nonlinguistic understanding consists of. Many investigators, I think, have assumed that it takes the form of concepts such as "containment," "support," and "lower than in vertical alignment," which correspond relatively directly to words such as *in*, *on*, and *under* and their translation equivalents in other languages. This knowledge would allow children to distinguish among the three situations shown in Figure 3.3.1 in a straightforward way, and to assign a different locative market to the category of spatial relations that each one represents. However, an inspection of how different languages solve the problem of categorizing spatial relationships for linguistic expression suggests that the match between

An apple IN a bowl

A cup ON a table

A cat UNDER a table

Figure 3.3.1 *Three spatial configurations.*

nonlinguistic spatial knowledge and the concepts underlying spatial words in particular languages must be less direct than this.

Although all languages make categorical distinctions among spatial configurations for the purpose of referring to them with a relatively small set of expressions such as the spatial prepositions of English, they do not do so in exactly the same way. That is, what "counts" as an instance of a particular spatial relationship varies from one language to another. For example, in English, the distinction between "containment" and "noncontainment" is critical: Although an object in contact with the surface of a reference-point object may be "contained" within a curvature of that surface to varying degrees (picture a button resting against the palm of a slowly closing hand), speakers of English must decide categorically if the object is *on* or *in* (Brown, 1973: 328, 330). In Spanish, in contrast, a single preposition, *en*, can be used for the entire range of spatial relations that English obligatorily splits into *on* versus *in*. Unless they want to be very explicit, Spanish speakers do not have to worry about the breakdown of the "on-to-in" continuum; thus, the spatial relations shown in the top and middle parts of Figure 3.3.1 are routinely described as "an apple EN a bowl" and "a cup EN a table."

Before being tempted to dismiss this as a case of homonymy—use of the same name for two clearly distinct meanings—let us look at some languages that make distinctions that English does not make. Consider Figure 3.3.2, which shows

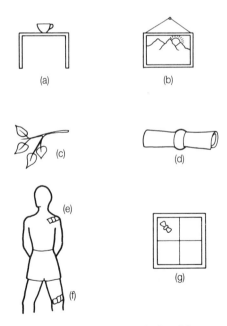

Figure 3.3.2 *Some to-be-classified "support" relationships.*

some instances of the "support" relationship that English encodes with the preposition *on*: (*a*) a cup ON a table, (*b*) a picture ON the wall, (*c*) leaves ON a twig, (*d*) a napkin ring ON a napkin, (*e*) a Band-Aid ON a man's shoulder, (*f*) a Band-Aid ON a man's leg, and (*g*) a fly ON a window.

In German, this array of spatial configurations is broken down for linguistic encoding into three different categories, expressed by *auf* (cup AUF table, Band-Aid AUF shoulder), *an* (picture AN wall, leaves AN twig, Band-Aid AN leg, fly AN window), and *um* (napkin ring UM napkin). German is sensitive, in a way that English is not, to whether a relationship of contact between two objects involves a relatively horizontal surface (table, shoulder: *auf*), a vertical or otherwise nonhorizontal surface or contact point (wall, twig, leg, window: *an*), or encirclement (napkin: *um*. *Um* is usually translated as *around*. English speakers can also say "the napkin ring is AROUND the napkin," but *on* is typically preferred when an encircling object is in close contact with, and supported by, the object it encircles; cf. also "the ring *on* my finger," "a diaper *on* a baby," and "a pillowcase *on* a pillow".)

Dutch, like German, describes the spatial configurations of Figure 3.3.2 with three different prepositions, but although these words—*op*, *aan*, and *om*—are cognate with German *auf*, *an*, and *um*, the semantic categories they encode are slightly different. As in German, "cup on table" and "Band-Aid on shoulder" (*op*) are differentiated from "picture on wall" and "leaves on twig" (*aan*), and "napkin ring on napkin" must also be given separate marking (*om*). However, whereas in German, "Band-Aid on leg" and "fly on window" are described with *an*, and hence classed together with, for example, "picture on wall" (all involve nonhorizontal surfaces), in Dutch they are encoded with *op* rather than *aan*, and thus fall together with "cup on table." For Dutch, the distinction between *op* and *aan* has less to do with orientation than with *method of attachment*: If a surface is not horizontal, an object is described as *aan* it if it is attached (often hanging or projecting) by one or more fixed points ("picture on wall," "leaves on twig," "clothes on line," "coathook on wall," "handle on pan"). In contrast, if it is a living creature like a fly (whose means of support are not perceptually obvious) or a flattish object attached over its entire base ("Band-aid on leg," "sticker on refrigerator," "pimple on chin") the relationship is called *op*.

Although English, German, and Dutch differ in their classification of "on" relationships, they also share certain features. For example, they are not terribly fussy about the overall shape of the reference-point object (although the orientation and concave versus convex curvature of its surfaces may be important). On the other hand, they *are* particular about whether the located object is *in contact with* the reference-point object, or only adjacent to it. For example, an object like a cup or a lamp can only be described as *on*, *auf*, or *op* a table if it is actually resting on the table. A different preposition (e.g., *over*, or *above* in English) is needed if the two objects are not touching.

A markedly different set of contrasts is found in Chalcatongo Mixtec, an Otomanguean language of Mexico. Mixtec has no prepositions (or other locative markers) devoted to expressing spatial relationships. Instead, it classifies spatial configurations via an extended and systematic body-part metaphor (Brugman, 1983, 1984; see also Lakoff, 1987). For example, consider the spatial configurations shown in Figure 3.3.3. These would all be encoded as *on* in English (and as *auf, op,* and *en* in German, Dutch, and Spanish, respectively); note that they all involve a relatively horizontal supporting surface: (*a*) "the man is ON the roof of the house," (*b*) "the cat is ON the mat," (*c*) "the tree is ON (the top of) the mountain," and (*d*) "the boy is ON the tree branch." In Mixtec, these configurations fall into four different categories, as suggested by the loose translations: (*a*) "the man is-located the house's ANIMAL-BACK" (there are separate words for a human back and an animal's back; the word for human back is used for expressing "behind" relations—cf. English *in back of*); (*b*) "the cat is-located the mat's FACE"; (*c*) "the tree is-located the mountain's HEAD"; and (*d*) "the boy is-located the tree's ARM."

At first glance it might seem that by metaphorically projecting human and animal body parts onto reference-point objects, Mixtec differs from the other languages we have looked at in classifying more finely. This is not the case, however: The total number of categories appears to be similar, but they are partitioned according to *cross-cutting criteria of similarity and difference* among spatial configurations.

For instance, in contrast to descriptions with *on* (*auf,* etc.), the Mixtec descriptions of configurations *a–d* in Figure 3.3.3 could also be applied to situations in which the located objects are hovering in the air above the reference-point objects, since the appropriate use of locating expressions like

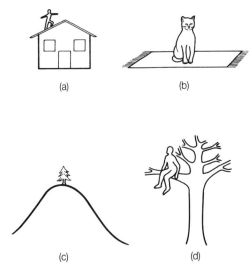

Figure 3.3.3   *Further spatial relationships involving "support."*

ANIMAL-BACK, FACE, and ARM does not require contact and support, but only adjacency.[7] Further, consider the two spatial configurations shown in Figure 3.3.4. In Mixtec, these fall together into the same category: (*a*) "the owl is-located the tree's BELLY" and (*b*) "the ball is-located the table's BELLY." (The tree's "belly" is positioned analogously to a human belly by virtue of the tree's overall resemblance in shape to a person; the table's "belly" is positioned analogously to the [downward-facing] belly of a four-legged animal.) In contrast, in English, configurations *a* and *b* clearly fall into two different spatial categories, which are encoded with *in* and *under*, respectively.

As speakers of English we may protest that the spatial relations shown in parts *a* and *b* of Figure 3.3.4 are "really" fundamentally very different, hence that BELLY in the two uses must be homonymous for Mixtec speakers. But this is no more logical than for a Mixtec speaker to argue that configurations *a–d* of Figure 3.3.3 are "really" fundamentally different; hence that English *on* in the four uses is obviously homonymous. Spatial categorization in both languages involves classifying referents that are dissimilar in some ways on the basis of properties they share. However, the shared properties on which the two languages focus—and the dissimilarities they choose to disregard—are different.

Cora, a second Mexican Indian language, takes still another approach to spatial classification (Casad, 1977; Casad and Langacker, 1985). For example, in referring to one object that is (from the English point of view) "on" another object—for example, a tail on a dog—speakers must choose between two expressions on the basis of whether, from their viewing perspective, the located object projects beyond the plane of the object on which it is located ("outside-slope") or is visually contained within that plane ("inside-slope"); compare the dog's tail in *a* and *b* of Figure 3.3.5.

By now, I hope that readers who a few paragraphs ago were untroubled by the assumption that nonlinguistic cognitive development provides children with

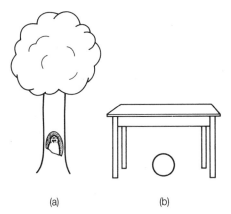

(a)   (b)

Figure 3.3.4 *Spatial relationships* in *and* under *(English) versus "belly" (Mixtec).*

(a)

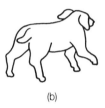

(b)

Figure 3.3.5 *Spatial classification according to viewing perspective in Cora.*

spatial concepts suitable for fairly direct mapping to the English words *on*, *in*, *under* and the like are somewhat less certain. What seemed such an obvious— "natural"—linguistic classification of spatial relationships may be widespread, but it is by no means universal.[8]

I do not, with these examples, intend to imply that the way we think is necessarily influenced by the categories of our language (although I would not rule this out either; see Kay and Kempton, 1984, and Lucy, 1987, for positive evidence on this persistent Whorfian question, and discussion in Lakoff, 1987, Chapter 18). I assume that all human beings have the same basic perceptual and cognitive capacities and can in principle recognize the same similarities and differences among spatial configurations or other to-be-categorized referents. However, to the extent that languages use different criteria for classifying referents, semantic categories cannot be viewed as a direct reflection of the structure of nonlinguistic thought. Instead, they constitute a level of organization in which, from among all the possible ways human beings can classify the elements of their experience, a language selects and combines certain options and not others. It is therefore a level of organization that children must *learn*, through experience with the way linguistic forms are used in the speech around them.

Characteristics of the learning process

We are still far from understanding how and when this learning takes place. With respect to "how," however, it is worth emphasizing that the obligatory nature of linguistic distinctions has important consequences for the learning process.

First, notice that the notion of "communicative intentions" provides little help in explaining how children acquire language-specific ways of partitioning a semantic domain such as space. Proponents of the view that early linguistic forms map onto nonlinguistic meanings often assume that children acquire forms to express meanings they have come to want to communicate. While it is probably true that children start to acquire spatial forms as they begin to want to talk about the locations of objects, it is unlikely that their communicative intentions are conveniently cast in terms of the particular categories of spatial relations their language employs. (For example, it is improbable that Dutch children are intent on expressing the method of attachment of one object to another, whereas German children are more interested in orientation and English-speaking children do not care about either one.) Part of learning to talk is learning what meaning distinctions *must* be attended to, regardless of whether one is interested in those distinctions at the moment of speech (Bowerman, 1983, 1985a; Slobin, 1979, 1982).

Some of the obligatory meaning distinctions a language makes may coincide with similarities and differences among referents that children find naturally salient; presumably this results in rapid learning (E. Clark, 1973a, explains the early emergence of *in* among spatial prepositions in English-speaking children in these terms). In other cases, however, the criteria will be relatively unsalient: Children then must learn to notice properties of referent events, relationships, and so forth that do not naturally attract their attention, and they also may have to learn to suppress their sensitivity to linguistically irrelevant properties that are more immediately salient. In this case arriving at the right categories will take longer, and children may for a time classify according to principles that are incorrect from the adult point of view. The situation may often lie between these two extremes: Children are spontaneously sensitive to several different properties of referents that might or might not be relevant to semantic classification in their language, and they find it equally easy to learn to categorize on the basis of any one of these properties (Bowerman, 1985b).[9]

Finally, it is important to note that learners' attention to properties of referents that are critical to semantic categorization in their language must become highly *automatic*: That is, speakers must continually and unconsciously scan for the relevant features and note their values if they are to choose correctly among contrasting forms. Registration of obligatory distinctions cannot be left under voluntary control, since a speaker's attention may often be elsewhere at the moment of speech.[10]

When does language-directed semantic learning begin?

I have argued that the existence of cross-linguistic differences in semantic classification means that semantic development requires considerably more of the child than simply working out concepts on a nonlinguistic basis and then matching them up with the words and grammatical morphemes of the language being acquired. The child must figure out, by observing how forms are distributed in the input, what the needed classification principles are. When does the process of attending to language for clues to categorization begin?

To the extent that researchers have been concerned with cross-linguistic semantic differences, they have generally assumed that the process of learning categories from the linguistic input begins relatively late. According to current theorizing, the concepts that drive the early use of words, grammatical morphemes, and construction patterns are nonlinguistic and more or less universal. With linguistic experience, however, children begin to diverge in the direction of the category structure of their particular language (see Slobin, 1985, for a strong statement of this position with respect to the categories underlying grammatical marking and early construction patterns). For example, a form that is at first linked to a universal core meaning that is too narrow may gradually be extended to situations that are increasingly dissimilar to the core, until language-appropriate boundaries have been reached (Schlesinger, 1974; Slobin, 1985). Conversely, a form associated with a too-broad meaning may gradually have its range of application cut back. Change toward language specificity could also involve collapsing categories that are too finely differentiated by effacing unnecessary distinctions, or splitting categories that are too broad by introducing new distinctions (Slobin, 1985).

These proposals about the course of early semantic development from universal to language specific remain largely conjectural. Little empirical research has been carried out on the problem of when and how children learn language-specific modes of categorization. It is likely that further work will confirm that semantic development does at times follow the hypothesized path from universal to language specific. However, recent research suggests that this is only part of the story. Children are also able to home in on the categories of the particular language they are learning from an astonishingly early age, sometimes before there is evidence for a preceding, "universal" stage (Bowerman, 1985b). Let us look at two examples, one concerning early words encoding spatial actions and the other to do with the grammatical treatment of subjects and objects.

Early relational words: Talking about spatial actions

In an earlier section I illustrated the problem of cross-linguistic semantic variation with examples of different systems of categorizing spatial relationships. In recent work, together with colleagues and students, I have been exploring how young children talk about certain spatial relations in different languages. Here I would like to summarize some findings that are emerging from an ongoing comparative study that Soonja Choi (San Diego State

University) and I are conducting of the way children learning English or Korean talk about space during and just beyond the one-word stage of development.[11] In particular, I want to compare the way these children describe actions involving putting things on or in other things, and taking them off or out.

Spatial manipulations of objects are salient and interesting to young children, and they begin to talk about them early, often—if they are learning English— with particles like *on, off, in,* and *out.*[12] Some or all of these words are typically found among the small set of relational words acquired during the one-word period (Bloom, 1973; Bowerman, 1978a; Farwell, 1976, 1977; Gopnik, 1982; Gopnik and Meltzoff, 1986; McCune-Nicholich, 1981; Tomasello, 1987), and they also often figure prominently in children's first two-word combinations (Miller and Ervin, 1964).

The early acquisition of spatial particles and certain other relational words, along with similarities in the way different children use them, has led many investigators to hypothesize that these words map directly onto rational concepts that children form on a nonlinguistic basis during the second year of life (Bloom, 1973: 112; McCune-Nicholich, 1981; Nelson, 1974).[13] For example, McCune-Nicholich proposed that relational words encode operative knowledge (knowledge of transformations) attained in the late sensorimotor period (Piaget, 1970), and she predicted that "since operative intelligence is a universal aspect of cognition, the same categories of meaning would be expected for all children, although various lexical items might be used to encode these" (p. 18).

This hypothesis can be tested by comparing English-speaking children's use of words like *on, in, off,* and *out* with what Korean children say in similar contexts. Actions of "putting on," "taking off," and the like are categorized differently by the semantic systems of English and Korean. However, if it is sensorimotor concepts rather than experience with the categories of language that guides children's generalization of early relational words to new contexts, the situations in which children learning English say *in,* for example, should correspond closely to the situations in which Korean children say some Korean word; similarly for *out* and so on.

The English words *in, out, on, off,* and the like are part of a larger, closed-class system of spatial morphemes that factor out what Talmy (1975, 1976, 1983, 1985) terms the Path of Motion ("Motion" is defined in such a way that it also includes static location) and gives it constant expression, regardless of whether the verb is transitive or intransitive (e.g., *put in* versus *go in* or *be in*) and regardless of the specific manner expressed by the main verb (e.g., *take/pull/push/cut off;* *go/fly/run/crawl in*). Similar systems are found in most or all Indo-European languages except Romance languages, according to Talmy's analyses, and also in Chinese. However, many languages, including Romance and Semitic languages, lack a system of Path morphemes and instead incorporate the spatial meanings encoded by these words directly into the verb (analogous to *enter* [= go IN], *exit* [= go OUT], *ascend* [= go UP], etc., which have been borrowed from Romance into English). Korean presents a somewhat mixed picture, but it patterns in the Romance way with respect to verbs specifying spatial manipulations of objects.

In English the choice among particles is governed by the nature of the Path (or what we might loosely call the "geometry" of the spatial relationship). For example, if one object is seen as moving toward another more stable (and usually larger) object such that it ends up (partially) contained by the reference-point object, *in* is selected ("put the apple IN the bowl/the cassette IN its case/the cigarette IN your mouth/your finger IN this ring I'm holding"). In contrast, *on* is the morpheme of choice if the moving object ends up in flat surface contact with the reference-point object ("put the cup ON the table/the sticker ON the wall"), (partially) covering or encircling it ("put the cap ON the pen/hat, shoes, coat ON [the relevant body part]/ring ON your finger"; *over* can be used in some contexts of this type as well), or attached to it by a fixed point ("put the ear ON Mr. Potatohead"). When two (or more) objects are similar in size and move roughly equally, *together* is appropriate and the *on* versus *in* contrast is lost: "put TOGETHER two Lego pieces/two Pop-beads/two toy train cars/two tables." The set of contrasts encoded by *take OUT*, *take OFF*, and *take APART* is similar, but for the opposite direction or motion.

The categories associated with everyday Korean verbs for actions of putting in, on, or together, and their reversals, cross-cut the contrasts drawn by the English particles. Consider the two verbs *kki-ta* and *ppay-ta*, which are very frequent in the speech of young children. In one way these verbs seem very tolerant: *kki-ta* is used indiscriminately across actions that English obligatorily distinguishes as *put IN*, *put ON*, and *put TOGETHER*. Similarly, *ppay-ta*, its opposite, collapses the distinctions between *take OUT/OFF/APART*. In another way, however, *kki-ta* and *ppay-ta* are much more restricted than *put IN/ON/TOGETHER* and *take OUT/OFF/APART*. Specifically, they can be used ONLY for actions in which objects are brought into or out of a relationship of *tight fit* or *attachment*. Thus, *kki-ta* is used for both putting a ring ON a finger and a finger IN a ring, a glove ON a hand and a hand *IN* a glove, a screw-on or click-down lid ON a jar, a cassette IN its case, and two Lego pieces or two Pop-beads TOGETHER, also for buttoning a button, snapping a snap, closing a tight-fitting drawer, pan lid, or door, and wedging a book between other books. *Ppay-ta* describes the reversal of all these actions.

Kki-ta and *ppay-ta* cannot be used for "loose-fit" or "no-fit" actions like putting an apple IN a bowl or taking it OUT, putting a blanket ON a bed or taking it OFF, putting ON or taking OFF clothing (with a few exceptions, like gloves), putting two tables TOGETHER or moving them APART, or opening and closing drawers and other objects that do not attach tightly. Nor can they be used in connection with magnets, Band-Aids, or stickers: To qualify for *kki-ta* and *ppay-ta*, attachment should involve some degree of three-dimensional meshing, not completely flat surfaces. For these various non-*kki-ta/ppay-ta* actions, Korean uses a number of different verbs. Some are specific to clothing that goes on different parts of the body. There are also verbs to describe putting objects into containers where they do not fit tightly, for putting objects onto surfaces, for attaching or juxtaposing flat surfaces, and for the reverse actions.

The relationship between Korean *kki-ta* and English *put in*, *put on*, and *put together* is shown schematically in Figure 3.3.6.

These differences between English and Korean mean that children who listen to English-speaking adults are exposed to a distribution of words that instructs them, in effect, that tightness of fit is unimportant but that the geometry of the spatial relationship (e.g., containment, flat contact or covering, (a)symmetrical movement) is critical. In contrast, children who listen to Korean-speaking adults are told, in effect, that tightness of fit is important, and that when tightness of fit obtains, the geometry of the relationship is irrelevant. If the early use of relational words is guided by universal sensorimotor schemes, children should be unaffected by these differences—that is, the categories of actions to which they extend particular words should look very similar. However, Choi and I are finding that English- and Korean-speaking children in fact classify actions of putting in, on, and so forth, and their reversals, in profoundly different and language-specific ways for purposes of talking about them. These differences are present by at least twenty to twenty-two months of age, and probably earlier, to judge from the English data (we do not yet have Korean data from a younger age).

Korean children by this age clearly grasp the importance of the notion of tight fit or attachment for *kki-ta* and *ppay-ta*, and they do not extend these verbs to "loose-fit" or "no-fit" situations such as putting objects into paper bags or other large containers, putting on clothing (except for gloves, where it is appropriate), and reversals of these actions. Additionally, children grasp that the precise geometry of the spatial relationship is irrelevant to *kki-ta* and *ppay-ta*, and they extend the words indiscriminately, as is appropriate, to spatial actions that in English must be distinguished on the basis of whether the Path of motion is "on," "in," or "together," or their opposites.

In the data we looked at, for example, *kki-ta* was used to describe both putting gloves ON hands and hands IN gloves, a toy shovel IN a narrow hole, putting ON rings, BUTTONING buttons, and so on. *Ppay-ta* was used for taking a nail OUT of a hole, an object OUT of an envelope, a book OUT of a bookcase (where it was wedged in), the cap OFF a pen, and the lid OFF a can, for taking a flute or Lego pieces APART, and so on. Actions of putting objects into bags and other loose-fitting containers and taking them out, putting objects onto surfaces and taking them off, and donning or doffing clothing were described with other, generally appropriate verbs.

Our English-speaking subjects differed from the Korean children in several important respects at this age. First, they used *on* and *off* in connection with clothing of all sorts, regardless of which body part was involved; the Korean children, in contrast, used different verbs, as is appropriate, for putting things on the head, the feet, and the trunk. Second, unlike the Korean children, the English-speaking children also applied the words they used in connection with

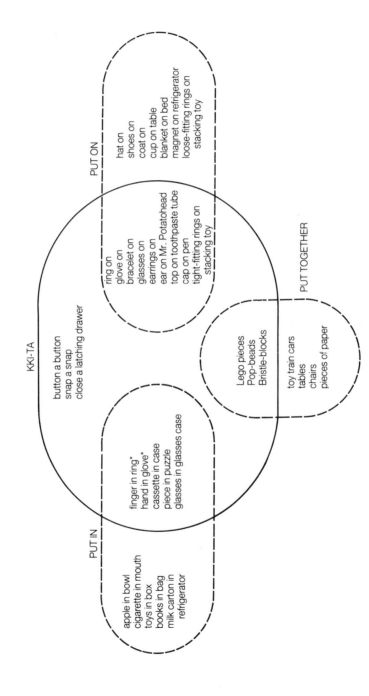

Figure 3.3.6   *Relationships between Koran kki-ta and English put in, put on, and put together. * Canonically, rings are put on fingers and gloves on hands, but envision here a situation in which the ring or glove is held stable and the finger or hand moves towards it.*

clothing to other actions, most typically those involving "attaching" and "detaching" objects to and from other objects (see also Gopnik and Meltzoff, 1986).[14]

Third, the critical English distinction between *on/off* situations (those involving covering or flat surface contact, or fixed-point-of-attachment) and *in/out* situations (those in which the moving object is contained) emerged very early (e.g., by 18½ months for my daughter Eva). Thus, *on* and *off* were used, for example, in connection with caps on pens, lids on jars, tops on bottles, doll clothes on hangers, clip-on sunglasses, magnets or tape stuck on surfaces at any angle, and ears, nose, and so forth on the Mr. Potatohead doll. In contrast, *in* and *out* were said in connection with putting books into a tiny, fitted container and removing them, putting a picture in a wallet, and the like. Recall that the Korean children encoded both "in/out" and "on/off" situations involving "tight fit" with *kki-ta* ("put on/in/together") or *ppay-ta* ("take off/out/apart").

Fourth, the English-speaking children also differed from the Korean children in that they used the same words for both tight- *and* loose-fitting containment relationships. For example, they said *in* both for putting books into a fitted container and a piece into a puzzle (tight fit) and for dropping a key into a glasses case and putting blocks into a pan (loose fit); similarly, they said *out* both for removing books from a fitted container and a piece from a puzzle (tight fit) and extracting toys from bags and large boxes (loose fit). In contrast, the Korean children distinguished between tight and loose containment—they applied *kki-ta* and *ppay-ta* only to the former, and used other verbs for the latter.

Finally, the English-speaking children used *in* and *out* (and, very occasionally, *on* and *off*) in connection with *intransitive* movements of themselves or other people (e.g., getting in and out of a bathtub, going in and out of a house or a room, climbing on or off laps). In contrast, the Korean children did not extend words for either "tight-fit" or "loose-fit" manipulations of objects to intransitive spatial actions, but instead used completely different (intransitive) verbs, as is appropriate in Korean.

It is not clear whether Korean children perceive a similarity between "tight-fit" and "loose-fit/no-fit" containment or contact, or between causative actions of putting things into containers and taking them out and noncausative motions of animate beings into and out of containers. At any rate, they do not use these similarities as a basis for extending their early words. This means that the concepts that children learning English associate with *in*, *out*, *on*, and *off* in the second half of their second year do not directly reflect nonlinguistic sensorimotor concepts (because then Korean children would extend words according to the same concepts), but instead reflect experience with the categories picked out by the abstract Path morphemes of English.[15]

Although Korean and English-speaking children clearly identity the major cleavages in their language's system of talking about spatial manipulations at a remarkably early age, they still make certain errors. These errors are important for two reasons. First, they demonstrate that children are not simply parroting back the words they have heard in specific contexts (which would make apparent early language specificity less significant), but rather are linking the words to concepts that can guide generalization to new referent situations. Second, the errors reveal which distinctions are difficult for children and provide interesting clues to their efforts to work out the needed categories.

For example, although the Korean children were quick to determine that attachment or tight fit is important for *kki-ta* and *ppay-ta*, they were apparently unclear about exactly what "counts" as attachment or tight fit. Sometimes they overextended *kki-ta* to putting magnets on surfaces to which they stick, and *ppay-ta* to peeling stickers off surfaces. Similarly, although the English-speaking children mastered the obligatory contrast between *on/off* and *in/out* situations early, they found the "symmetrical movement" property relevant for *together/apart* difficult, and they often overextended *off* or *open* to actions involving the separation of Lego pieces, Pop-beads, and stuck-together Frisbees.[16]

The patterns of correctness and errors I have described testify to a complex interaction between linguistic input and nonlinguistic cognitive development. Clearly children in the age range eighteen–twenty-four months are not simply mapping words directly onto nonlinguistically developed concepts of surface contact or support, containment, and so on. Already at this age they have analyzed the distribution of words in the speech they hear to discover which classification principles are important. On the other hand, not all classification principles are equally accessible to them. For example, "tight fit/attachment" versus "loose fit/no attachment" is relatively easy, but three-dimensional versus two-dimensional attachment (e.g., Lego pieces versus magnets) is more difficult. Similarly, "containment" versus "noncontainment" (covering, surface attachment, etc.) is straightforward, but the distinction between asymmetrical and symmetrical movement is more problematic.

In sum, the categories of the input language clearly have an important effect on children's early semantic categorization, but their influence is not absolute: Input distinctions must coincide with distinctions that are readily accessible to children, or they will not be picked up.

What to do with intransitive subjects?

As a second example of early language-specific categorization, let us look at how children determine the correct grammatical handling of the major noun arguments of verbs and other predicates. The three most basic grammatical roles associated with arguments are subject of a transitive verb ("transitive subject"; e.g., *JOHNNY opened a box*), object of a transitive verb ("object"; e.g., *Mary hit SUSIE*), and subject of an intransitive verb ("intransitive subject"; e.g., *DADDY went [to the store]*). Some languages (e.g., Takelma, an American Indian language) mark nouns in all three roles distinctly. However, most languages reduce the three categories to two by marking nouns in two of the roles identically.

Transitive subjects and objects are always distinguished in such systems. Where languages differ is in whether they treat intransitive subjects like transitive subjects or like objects (e.g., whether intransitive subjects behave like transitive subjects or like objects with respect to typical positioning in the sentence, type of case marking they can receive, and ability—or lack of it—to govern verb agreement). Languages that opt for the first solution, like English, Spanish, and Hungarian, are called "nominative" or "nominative-accusative" languages, whereas those that choose the second, like Eskimo and Samoan, are called "ergative" or "ergative-absolutive" languages (Dixon, 1979; Haiman, 1979).

Both classifications can be considered well motivated, since intransitive subjects share certain properties with both transitive subjects and objects. For example, the grouping of intransitive subjects with transitive subjects by nominative languages is responsive to the shared tendency of noun arguments in these roles (as opposed to in the object role) to be *animate agents* and/or *topics*. Conversely, the grouping of intransitive subjects with objects by ergative languages reflects the shared tendency for noun arguments in these roles (but not in the transitive subject role) to express *new information* (Du Bois, 1985, 1987; see also Keenan, 1976, 1984, for additional properties shared by intransitive and transitive subjects but not objects, on the one hand, and by intransitive subjects and objects, but not subjects, on the other).

Children acquiring languages of either type are faced with an intriguing language-specific learning problem. Once they realize that distinctions are to be made at all among major sentence constituents, they should treat transitive subjects and objects differently, since this pattern is shared by both nominative and ergative languages. But what should they do with intransitive subjects? Should they treat them like transitive subjects, like objects, or like neither one?

If children indeed start out in a uniform, universal way, and only later diverge in the direction of language-specific categorization schemes, they should wait to take a stand on intransitive subjects. When they learn case markers and word-order patterns in connection with transitive subjects or objects, they should at first withhold marking for intransitive subjects or treat them inconsistently. Only later should they begin to extend the grammatical privileges of either transitive subjects or of objects—depending on the language they are learning— to intransitive subjects. This unbiased, universal beginning point is also what we would predict on the basis of Slobin's (1985) proposal, discussed earlier, that subject and object markers are at first restricted to sentences expressing "prototypical transitive events," since sentences with intransitive subjects fall outside of this set.

Yet the prediction is incorrect. From their earliest two-word sentences, children learning nominative languages treat intransitive subjects—as is appropriate—like transitive subjects, and not like objects. For example, when they learn a word-order pattern for positioning the agents of transitive verbs such as *open* and *push,* this pattern is also immediately applied to the agents of intransitive verbs like *go, walk,* and *cough* (Braine, 1976; see Bowerman 1985b, for discussion of this and other evidence). Conversely, children learning ergative languages never overextend the so-called ergative marker from transitive to intransitive subjects (Schieffelin, 1985, on Kaluli; Pye, 1980, on Quiché); in addition (although the data are sparser on this point), they seem to treat intransitive subjects like objects rather than like transitive subjects with respect to word order patterns (Ochs, 1985, on Samoan).

The uniform treatment of agents by children learning English and other languages that happen to be nominative led many researchers in the early 1970s to hypothesize that the concept of "agent"—the one who initiates and carries out an action, whether transitive or intransitive—emerges spontaneously in the sensorimotor period, and is used as a core meaning to which word-order patterns and other grammatical privileges are mapped (e.g., Bowerman, 1973; Schlesinger, 1971). However, the more recent evidence from children learning ergative languages shows that agent is *not* a universal cognitive organizer for early grammatical development (see also Slobin, 1982). Instead, it is a semantic category that reflects experience with a language that treats transitive and intransitive agents alike (see Schlesinger, 1977, for independent speculation that agent is a category learned from language). If children are exposed to a language that makes a fundamental grammatical distinction between transitive and intransitive agents, they respect this distinction from the beginning.

Conclusions: Implications for language disorders

The evidence just discussed indicates that children are highly sensitive, even in the very earliest stages of language acquisition, to the way the words, grammatical forms, and construction patterns of their language are used by fluent speakers. Although learners may sometimes match language forms to concepts generated independently of linguistic experience, they are also capable, at least from the late one-word period and possibly earlier, of building language-specific categories by observing the distribution of forms in adult speech and making inferences about the categorization principles that might underlie this distribution.

This evidence for early language specificity in semantic categorization may seem surprising, given the heavy emphasis on innate principles of conceptual and perceptual structuring in recent theorizing about semantic and syntactic development. However, it is compatible with several recent studies of other aspects of language acquisition that also demonstrate strikingly early effects of experience with a particular language—for example, on children's early phonemic inventories (Pye, Ingram, and List, 1987), on infants' ability to discriminate speech sounds (Streeter, 1976; Werker and Tees, 1984; see also Bornstein, 1979), and on 2-year-olds' reliance on word order versus noun animacy to interpret who does what to whom when they are confronted with simple strings containing two nouns and a verb (Bates *et al.*, 1984).

Recognizing the importance of semantic learning in early language acquisition does not mean devaluing the progress that has been made within the cognitivist framework. There can be little doubt that nonlinguistic conceptual and perceptual development is an important prerequisite to many aspects of language acquisition, including acquiring the meanings associated with particular linguistic forms. However, having a general nonlinguistic understanding of particular situations (e.g., certain spatial configurations) does not automatically mean having a preference for *classifying* these situations in certain ways and not others.

In some cases (e.g., for "basic level objects" and for colors) initial cognitive/perceptual understanding probably does include recognition of, or sensitivity to, certain "natural" cleavages among referent entities. However, for many conceptual domains—including "spatial actions," as discussed earlier—children seem to be prepared from the beginning to classify in different ways (although this plasticity unquestionably has limits; see Bowerman, 1985b). Whatever form children's nonlinguistic understanding of these domains may take, it does not supply the initial semantic categories directly. Rather, categorization is influenced, from the outset, by the distribution of forms in the speech the child hears: The evidence is that the categories differ across children acquiring different languages.

Do the linguistic and developmental phenomena discussed in this chapter have any relevance for the assessment or treatment of children with language disorders? It seems to me that they may.

It is possible that some children experience special difficulties in bridging the gap between nonlinguistic understanding and the formation of semantic categories. Although their conceptual development may be normal, they have trouble discovering the grouping principles that would allow them to make sense of the adult use of linguistic forms. Several potential sources of difficulty can be imagined.

1. A prerequisite to adopting language-specific modes of categorization is the ability to let one's attention be guided to potential classification principles by the linguistic input. That is, the learner must be alert to similarities among actions, relationships, and so on, to which the same linguistic forms are applied, and to differences among referents to which different forms are applied. Language-disordered children often suffer from attentional deficits (Johnston, 1982) that may cause reduced sensitivity to the details of form–meaning pairings in the input they receive.

2. Some children may have a normal ability to scan the input for clues to categorization, but nevertheless be limited in their ability to make sensible

guesses about what the needed grouping principles might be. Alternatively or in addition, they may have trouble suppressing attention to distinctions that, although irrelevant for the particular language forms they are working on, are naturally highly salient to them, in order to focus on critical distinctions that are relatively less salient.

3. For some children, the requirement that attention to obligatory distinctions becomes fully automatic may present special difficulties. That is, they may succeed in identifying certain critical distinctions and be able to choose correctly among linguistic forms part of the time, but have trouble in establishing and maintaining the continual, unconscious scanning for these distinctions that fluent speech requires.

Awareness of these potential sources of trouble that a child might experience in classifying the world for purposes of language use may be useful in diagnosis, and it also might help in targeting deficits for particular attention in the design of training programs.

On a more general note, I would like to suggest that even though clinicians and researchers concerned with children's language disorders may deal only with children learning one particular language, they could potentially benefit from information about similarities and differences in semantic structure across languages. As I pointed out earlier, speakers internalize the semantic system of their native language so thoroughly that its categories feel like a direct reflection of the structure of thought. We are not aware—at least until we try to learn a second language—that distinctions that we think of as fundamental might be irrelevant in some languages, or, conversely, that distinctions that seem minor or exotic to us may play a major role in the structure of other languages. One consequence of our having learned our language lesson so well is that when language-disordered children have trouble grasping the meanings of certain forms, we may be too quick to assume that the problem lies in their nonlinguistic understanding of the relevant situations.

In some cases this assumption will no doubt be warranted. But in other cases the problem may lie purely in the mapping between nonlinguistic knowledge and the categories of the language being learned. When this is so, no amount of nonlinguistic training with the relevant situations (e.g., with objects in containers or on surfaces for a child who has trouble with the words *in* and *on*) is likely to help. What the child needs is guidance in identifying which, out of the various cross-linguistically possible ways of classifying spatial relations, is the way his language does it.

It is likely that children will have more trouble with classification principles that are uncommon cross-linguistically than with those that turn up frequently in the languages of the world, since frequency is likely to correlate with degree of cognitive "naturalness" or ease for human beings (Bowerman, 1985b). It is also possible that children will have more difficulty identifying the needed semantic principles for conceptual domains that are classified in widely different ways across languages than for those that are classified very similarly. This is because cross-linguistic variation suggests a basic flexibility in human cognitive structure—with a concomitant need for children to *learn* the locally appropriate categories—whereas similarity suggests strong nonlinguistic conceptual or perceptual constraints on categorization. Thus, knowledge of how the particular semantic categories a child is trying to acquire are related to the categories with which other languages partition the same domain may provide valuable cues to the kinds of problems the child may experience.

At present, our understanding of cross-linguistic similarities and differences in semantic structure is still quite limited, as is our knowledge of how these are reflected in the ease or difficulty of particular semantic distinctions for children. However, future research on these questions may well lead to information with direct relevance for the treatment of children with language disorders.

Acknowledgments

I am grateful to Soonja Choi for her comments on an earlier draft of this chapter and to Pauline Draat and Inge Tarim for their help with the figures.

Notes to 3.3

1. A few remarks about terminology: In this chapter, the words "category" and "concept" are often used interchangeably. Traditionally, a "category" has been defined as a (potentially infinite) group of items (objects, actions, relationships, etc.) that, although distinguishably different, are responded to as if at some level they are "the same" (e.g., the same word is applied to them). "Concept" is the term for the mental representation that provides the grouping principle for a category (it is also used to refer to mental constructs in a more general way, as in "the concept of object permanence"). For present purposes, this distinction is often unimportant. By the "meaning" of a word or other linguistic form is intended the concept that guides the form's use, or, more loosely, the associated category. Still more loosely, "meaning" is sometimes used to refer to a prelinguistic concept that is a candidate for being linked to a form. The term "semantic" is used in connection with concepts, categories, distinctions, and so on, that *make a difference* in the structure of the language under consideration (e.g., that govern the choice between two contrasting forms). It is not equivalent to "cognitive" or "conceptual," since aspects of nonlinguistic understanding may often have no consequences for the structure of a particular language.
2. Equally important was research on the more general relationship between cognitive and linguistic development, such as studies of whether linguistic advances can be linked to the establishment of the concept of object permanence or other cognitive milestones. I omit these here in the interests of concentrating on the problem of categorization, but see, for example, Bowerman (1978b), Cromer (1987), and Johnston (1985) for reviews.
3. See Bowerman (1976, 1987), Labov (1978), Newport (1982), Plunkett and Trosberg (1984), and Schlesinger (1977) on the difference between the ability to understand and interpret experiences on a nonlinguistic basis and the ability to categorize them.

4. This proposal has close correspondences with Bickerton's (1981) claim, based on creole studies, that there is an innate universal cognitive/semantic substratum for language—the "language bio-program." More distantly, it is also related to Pinker's (1984) "semantic bootstrapping" hypothesis, according to which children use certain nonlinguistic concepts to identify instances of the grammatical categories or roles with which they are most highly correlated (e.g., "if a word names a concrete object, it must be a noun," or "if a word names an entity that performs the role of agent, it must be the subject of the sentence").

5. As Anglin (1979) has pointed out, overt errors occur only when children's categories are too broad (e.g., *doggie* applied to horses as well as dogs). Too-narrow categories lead to usage that is correct on any particular occasion, but underextended with respect to the adult range of application. Brown, Cazden, and Bellugi (1969) term these obvious versus more subtle departures from adult usage "errors of commission" and "errors of omission," respectively. Errors of omission can be detected by careful comparison of children's usage patterns with those of adults.

6. It is likely that some conceptual domains are subject to more cross-linguistic variation in semantic partitioning than others. For example, Gentner (1981, 1982) presents evidence that, in general, relational concepts are less "given" by the structure of reality and hence more variable from one language to another than are concepts of concrete objects.

7. Some other languages that work like Mixtec in this respect are Korean, Japanese, and Chinese.

8. For some other interesting examples of cross-linguistic differences in spatial classification, see Denny (1978), Hill (1978), Zubin and Choi (1984), and Zubin and Svorou (1984).

9. Research traditions in developmental psychology that might profitably be brought to bear on how children identify language-specific principles of semantic categorization include work on acquired cue distinctiveness and selective attention (e.g., Gibson, 1966; Lane and Pearson, 1982; Odom, 1982).

10. The automaticity requirement probably accounts for many of the problems experienced by adult second language learners in trying to achieve fluency in their new language. When faced with a meaning distinction that is not obligatory in their native language, learners may (sometimes) be able to grasp it intellectually, but they often cannot register it fast enough or they fail to notice that it is relevant in all the contexts in which it must be marked. Some clues to how automatization takes place in the context of first and second language acquisition may come from the literature on controlled search versus automatic processing (e.g., Schneider and Shiffrin, 1977; Shiffrin and Dumais, 1981; Shiffrin and Schneider, 1977).

11. The English data come from detailed diary records of my two daughters from the start of the one-word stage; these are generally consistent with published reports of the acquisition of spatial expressions by other English-speaking children. For Korean, longitudinal spontaneous speech samples from four children between 1;8 and 3;0 were used. One child was followed by Choi; for the additional materials, we are grateful to Pat Clancy (two children) and Youngjoo Kim (one child).

12. These particles are used for some time only in the context of action, where they seem to have a verbal force suggested by glosses like "put on" and "take off." Use of the same words to encode static spatial configurations emerges somewhat later, although still during the one-word period for many children. I here ignore the syntactic distinction between these words as particles and as prepositions, and simply call them "particles."

13. Gopnik and Meltzoff (1986) present interesting arguments for a somewhat different position: That new relational words in the sensorimotor period do not map onto concepts that have already been established but, rather, concepts that children find "problematic" and are still in the process of working out. They speculate that hearing a word such as *gone* or *down* in a variety of contexts could help draw children's attention to what these contexts share. However, they do not take up the question, raised here, of whether exposure to different kinds of input could cause concepts to develop differently.

14. Our English-speaking subjects, like those of other researchers, used *on* and *off* for "attachment" and "detachment" relationships before they used them in connection with horizontal supporting surfaces like tables. Also like other children, they used these words very early in connection with lights and other electrical appliances. Although there is a metaphorical basis for the extension of *on* and *off* from spatial to "activation" meanings (Lindner, 1982), it seems most likely that children initially learn these different uses independently, that is, the words are homonyms.

15. Berman and Slobin (1987), who studied narratives from children learning English, German, Spanish, or Hebrew, found profound cross-linguistic differences in the encoding of Path meanings from as early as 3 years (their youngest group), with English- and German-speaking children clearly in control of the Path morphemes by then. The present study indicates that these differences are well established even at a very much younger age.
16. *Open* is also sometimes used for certain "off" and "out" situations, and for situations where more specific verbs are needed like *unbutton* and *unfold*; see Bowerman (1978a).

References to 3.3

Allan, K. (1979). "Classifiers." *Language*, **53**, 285–311.
Andersen, E. S. (1978). "Lexical universals of body-part terminology." In J. H. Greenberg (ed.), *Universals of Human Language, Vol. 3: Word Structure*. Stanford: Stanford University Press.
Anglin, J. (1977). *Word, Object, and Conceptual Development*. New York: W. W. Norton.
Anglin, J. (1979). "The child' first terms of reference." In N. R. Smith and M. B. Franklin (eds), *Symbolic Functioning in Childhood*. Hillsdale, NJ: Lawrence Erlbaum.
Bates, E., MacWhinney, B., Caselli, C., Devescovi, A., Natale, F., and Venza, V. (1984). "A cross-linguistic study of the development of sentence interpretation strategies." *Child Development*, **55**, 341–54.
Berlin, B. and Kay, P. (1969). *Basic Color Terms*. Berkeley: University of California Press.
Berman, R. and Slobin, D. I. (1987). *Five Ways of Learning How to Talk About Events: A crosslinguistic study of children's narratives*. Berkeley Cognitive Science Report No. 46. Berkeley: University of California.
Bickerton, D. (1981). *Roots of Language*. Ann Arbor, MI: Karoma.
Bierwisch, M. (1967). "Some semantic universals of German adjectivals." *Foundations of Language*, **5**, 153–84.
Bierwisch, M. (1970). "Semantics." In J. Lyons (ed.), *New Horizons in Linguistics*. Harmondsworth, England: Penguin.
Bloom, L. (1970). *Language Development: Form and function in emerging grammars*. Cambridge, MA: MIT Press.
Bloom, L. (1973). *One Word at a Time*. Amsterdam: Mouton.
Bornstein, M. H. (1979). "Perceptual development: Stability and change in feature perception." In M. H. Bornstein and W. Kessen (eds), *Psychological Development from Infancy*. Hillsdale, NJ: Lawrence Erlbaum Associates.
Bowerman, M. (1973). *Early Syntactic Development: A cross-linguistic study with special reference to Finnish*. Cambridge, England: Cambridge University Press.
Bowerman, M. (1976). "Semantic factors in the acquisition of rules for word use and sentence construction." In D. M. Morehead and A. E. Morehead (eds), *Normal and Deficient Child Language*. Baltimore: University Park Press.
Bowerman, M. (1978a). "The acquisition of word meaning: An investigation into some current conflicts." In N. Waterson and C. Snow (eds), *The Development of Communication*. New York: John Wiley & Sons.
Bowerman, M. (1978b). "Semantic and syntactic development: A review of what, when, and how in language acquisition." In R. L. Schiefelbusch (ed.), *Bases of Language Intervention*. Baltimore: University Park Press.
Bowerman, M. (1978c). "Systematizing semantic knowledge: Changes over time in the child's organization of word meaning." *Child Development*, **49**, 977–87.
Bowerman, M. (1980). "The structure and origin of semantic categories in the language-learning child." In M. L. Foster and S. H. Brandes (eds), *Symbol as Sense: New approaches to the analysis of meaning*. New York: Academic Press.
Bowerman, M. (1983). "Hidden meanings: The role of covert conceptual structures in children's development of language." In D. R. Rogers and J. A. Sloboda (eds), *Acquisition of Symbolic Skills*. New York: Plenum.

Bowerman, M. (1985a). "Beyond communicative adequacy: From piecemeal knowledge to an integrated system in the child's acquisition of language." In K. E. Nelson (ed.), *Children's Language* (Vol. 5). Hillsdale, NJ: Lawrence Erlbaum Associates.

Bowerman, M. (1985b). "What shapes children's grammars?" In D. I. Slobin (ed.), *The Crosslinguistic Study of Language Acquisition* (Vol. 2). Hillsdale, NJ: Lawrence Erlbaum Associates.

Bowerman, M. (1987). "Inducing the latent structure of language." In F. S. Kessel (ed.), *The Development of Language and Language Researchers*. Hillsdale, NJ: Lawrence Erlbaum Associates.

Braine, M. D. S. (1976). "Children's first word combinations." *Monographs of the Society for Research in Child Development*, **41**(1), Serial no. 164.

Brown, R. (1958). *Words and Things*. New York: Free Press.

Brown, R. (1965). *Social Psychology*. New York: Free Press.

Brown, R. (1973). *A First Language: The early stages*. Cambridge, MA: Harvard University Press.

Brown, R., Cazden, C., and Bellugi, U. (1969). "The child's grammar from I to III." In J. P. Hill (ed.), *Minnesota Symposium on Child Development* (Vol. 2). Minneapolis: University of Minnesota Press.

Brugman, C. (1983). "The use of body-part terms as locatives in Chalcatango Mixtec." *Report No. 4 of the Survey of California and Other Indian Languages*. Berkeley: University of California, 235–90.

Brugman, C. (1984). *Metaphor in the Elaboration of Grammatical Categories in Mixtec*. Unpublished manuscript, Linguistics Department, University of California, Berkeley.

Budwig, N. (1985). "'I, me, my and 'name': Children's early systematizations of forms, meanings and functions in talk about the self." *Papers and Reports on Child Language Development* (Stanford University Department of Linguistics), **24**.

Budwig, N. (1986). *Agentivity and Control in Early Child Language*. Unpublished doctoral dissertation, University of California, Berkeley.

Casad, E. (1977). "Location and direction in Cora discourse." *Anthropological Linguistics*, **19**, 216–41.

Casad, E. and Langacker, R. (1985). "'Inside' and 'outside' in Cora grammar." *International Journal of American Linguistics*, **51**, 247–81.

Chomsky, N. (1965). *Aspects of the Theory of Syntax*. Cambridge, MA: MIT Press.

Clancy, P., Jacobsen, T., and Silva, M. (1976). "The acquisition of conjunction: A cross-linguistic study." *Stanford Papers and Reports on Child Language Development* (Stanford University Department of Linguistics), **12**, 71–80.

Clark, E. V. (1973a). "Nonlinguistic strategies and the acquisition of word meanings." *Cognition*, **2**, 161–82.

Clark, E. V. (1973b). "What's in a word? On the child's acquisition of semantics in his first language." In T. E. Moore (ed.), *Cognitive Development and the Acquisition of Language*. New York: Academic Press.

Clark, E. V. (1977). "Universal categories: On the semantics of classifiers and children's early word meanings." In A. Juilland (ed.), *Linguistic Studies Presented to Joseph Greenberg*. Saratoga, CA: Anma Libri. (Reprinted in Clark, E. V. [1979]. *The Ontogenesis of Meaning*. Wiesbaden: Akademische Verlagsgesellschaft Athenaion.)

Clark, H. H. (1973). "Space, time, semantics, and the child." In T. E. Moore (ed.), *Cognitive Development and the Acquisition of Language*. New York: Academic Press.

Comrie, B. (1981). *Language Universals and Linguistic Typology*. Chicago: University of Chicago Press.

Corrigan, R., Halpern, E., Aviezer, O., and Goldblatt, A. (1981). "The development of three spatial concepts: In, on, under." *International Journal of Behavioral Development*, **4**, 403–19.

Cromer, R. (1987). "The cognition hypothesis revisited." In F. S. Kessel (ed.), *The Development of Language and Language Researchers*. Hillsdale, NJ: Lawrence Erlbaum Associates.

Denny, J. P. (1978). "Locating the universals in lexical systems for spatial deixis." In D. Farkas, W. M. Jacobsen, and K. W. Todrys (eds), *Papers from the Parasession on the Lexicon*. Chicago: Chicago Linguistic Society.

Dixon, R. (1979). "Ergativity." *Language*, **55**, 59–138.

Du Bois, J. W. (1985). "Competing motivations." In J. Haiman (ed.), *Iconicity in Syntax*. Amsterdam: John Benjamins.

Du Bois, J. W. (1987). "The discourse basis of ergativity." *Language*, **63**, 805–55.

Farwell, C. (1976). *The Early Expression of Motion and Location*. Paper presented at the First Annual Boston University Conference on Language Development.

Farwell, C. (1977). "The primacy of *Goal* in the child's description of motion and location." *Papers and Reports on Child Language Development* (Stanford University Department of Linguistics), **13**, 126–33.

Gentner, D. (1981). "Some interesting differences between verbs and nouns." *Cognition and Brain Theory*, **4**, 161–78.

Gentner, D. (1982). "Why nouns are learned before verbs: Linguistic relativity versus natural partitioning." In S. Kuczaj (ed.), *Language Development: Language, cognition and culture*. Hillsdale, NJ: Lawrence Erlbaum Associates.

Gibson, J. J. (1966). *The Senses Considered as Perceptual Systems*. Boston: Houghton Mifflin.

Givón, T. (1975). "Serial verbs and syntactic change: Niger-Congo." In C. N. Li (ed.), *Word Order and Word Order Change*. Austin: University of Texas Press.

Gopnik, A. (1982). "Words and plans: Early language and the development of intelligent action." *Journal of Child Language*, **9**, 303–18.

Gopnik, A. and Meltzoff, A. N. (1986). "Words, plans, things, and locations: Interactions between semantic and cognitive development in the one-word stage." In S. A. Kuczaj II and M. D. Barrett (eds), *The Development of Word Meaning*. Berlin: Springer-Verlag.

Greenberg, J. (ed.). (1978). *Universals of Human Language* (four volumes). Stanford, CA: Stanford University Press.

Haiman, J. (1979). "Hua: A Papuan language of New Guinea." In T. Shopen (ed.), *Languages and Their Status*. Cambridge, MA: Winthrop Publishers.

Halpern, E., Corrigan, R., and Aviezer, O. (1981). "Two types of 'under'? Implications for the relationship between cognition and language." *International Journal of Psycholinguistics*, **8–4**(24), 36–57.

Heider, E. (1972). "Universals in color naming and memory." *Journal of Experimental Psychology*, **93**, 10–20.

Hill, C. A. (1978). "Linguistic representation of spatial and temporal orientation." *Berkeley Linguistics Society*, **4**, 524–38.

Hopper, P. J. and Thompson, S. A. (1980). "Transitivity in grammar and discourse." *Language*, **56**, 251–99.

Johnston, J. R. (1979). *A Study of Spatial Thought and Expression*: In back and in front. Unpublished doctoral dissertation, University of California, Berkeley.

Johnston, J. R. (1982). "The language disordered child." In N. Lass, J. Norther, D. Yoder, and L. McReynolds (eds), *Speech, Language and Hearing* (Vol. 2). Philadelphia: W. B. Saunders.

Johnston, J. R. (1985). "Cognitive prerequisites: The evidence from children learning English." In D. I. Slobin (ed.), *The Crosslinguistic Study of Language Acquisition* (Vol. 2). Hillsdale, NJ: Lawrence Erlbaum Associates.

Johnston, J. R. and Slobin, D. I. (1979). "The development of locative expressions in English, Italian, Serbo-Croatian and Turkish." *Journal of Child Language*, **6**, 529–45.

Kay, P. and Kempton, W. (1984). "What is the Sapir-Whorf hypothesis?" *American Anthropologist*, **86**, 65–79.

Keenan, E. (1976). "Toward a universal definition of 'subject'." In C. N. Li (ed.), *Subject and Topic*. New York: Academic Press.

Keenan, E. (1984). "Semantic correlates of the ergative/absolutive distinction." *Linguistics*, **22**, 197–223.

Labov, W. (1978). "Denotational structure." In D. Farkas, W. M. Jacobsen, and K. W. Todrys (eds), *Papers from the Parasession on the Lexicon*. Chicago: Chicago Linguistic Society.

Lakoff, G. (1987). *Women, Fire, and Dangerous Things: What categories reveal about the mind*. Chicago: University of Chicago Press.

Lane, D. M. and Pearson, D. A. (1982). "The development of selective attention." *Merrill–Palmer Quarterly*, **28**, 317–37.

Langacker, R. W. (1987). *Foundations of Cognitive Grammar. Vol. I: Theoretical prerequisites*. Stanford: Stanford University Press.

Leslie, A. M. and Keeble, S. (1987). "Do six-month-old infants perceive causality?" *Cognition*, **27**, 265–88.

Levine, S. C. and Carey, S. (1982). "Up front: The acquisition of a concept and a word." *Journal of Child Language*, **9**, 645–57.

Lindner, S. (1982). "What goes up doesn't necessarily come down: The ins and outs of opposites." *Papers of the Chicago Linguistic Society*, **18**, 305–23.

Lord, C. (1982). "The development of object markers in serial verb languages." In P. J. Hopper and S. A. Thompson (eds), *Syntax and Semantics, Vol. 15: Studies in transitivity*. New York: Academic Press.

Lucy, J. A. (1987). *Grammatical Categories and Cognitive Processes: An historical, theoretical, and empirical re-evaluation of the linguistic relativity hypothesis.* Unpublished doctoral dissertation, University of Chicago.

McCune-Nicholich, L. (1981). "The cognitive bases of relational words in the single word period." *Journal of Child Language*, **8**, 15–34.

Miller, W. and Ervin, S. (1964). "The development of grammar in child language." In U. Bellugi and R. Brown (eds), "The acquisition of language." *Monographs of the Society of Research in Child Development*, **29**(1) (Serial No. 92).

Nelson, K. (1974). "Concept, word, and sentence: Interrelations in acquisition and development." *Psychological Review*, **81**, 267–85.

Newport, E. L. (1982). "Task specificity in language learning? Evidence from speech perception and American Sign Language." In E. Wanner and L. R. Gleitman (eds), *Language Acquisition: The state of the art*. Cambridge, England: Cambridge Univeristy Press.

Ochs, E. (1985). "Variation and error: A sociolinguistic approach to language acquisition in Samoa." In D. I. Slobin (ed.), *The Crosslinguistic Study of Language Acquisition* (Vol. 1). Hillsdale, NJ: Lawrence Erlbaum Associates.

Odom, R. D. (1982). "Lane and Pearson's inattention to relevant information: A need for the theoretical specifications of task information in developmental research." *Merrill–Palmer Quarterly*, **28**, 339–45.

Piaget, J. (1954). *The Construction of Reality in the Child*. New York: Basic Books.

Piaget, J. (1970). *Genetic Epistomology*. New York: W. W. Norton.

Pinker, S. (1984). *Language Learnability and Language Development*. Cambridge, MA: Harvard University Press.

Plunkett, K. and Trosberg, A. (1984). "Some problems for the cognitivist approach to language." In C. L. Thew and C. E. Johnson (eds), *Proceedings of the Second International Congress for the Study of Child Language* (Vol. 2). Lanham, MD: University Press of America.

Pye, C. (1980). "The acquisition of person markers in Quiché Mayan." *Papers and Reports on Child Language Development* (Stanford University Department of Linguistics), **19**, 53–9.

Pye, C., Ingram, D., and List, H. (1987). "A comparison of initial consonant acquisition in English and Quiché." In K. E. Nelson and A. Van Kleeck (eds), *Children's Language* (Vol. 6). Hillsdale, NJ: Lawrence Erlbaum Associates.

Quinn, P. C. and Eimas, P. D. (1986). "On categorization in early infancy." *Merrill–Palmer Quarterly*, **32**, 331–63.

Rosch, E. (1973). "On the internal structure of perceptual and semantic categories." In T. E. Moore (ed.), *Cognitive Development and the Acquisition of Language*. New York: Academic Press.

Rosch, E. and Mervis, C. B. (1977). "Children's sorting: A reinterpretation based on the nature of abstraction in natural categories." In R. C. Smart and M. S. Smart (eds), *Readings in Child Development and Relationships* (2nd edn). New York: Macmillan.

Rosch, E., Mervis, C., Gray, W., Johnson, D., and Boyes-Braem, P. (1976). "Basic objects in natural categories." *Cognitive Psychology*, **8**, 382–439.

Schieffelin, B. B. (1985). "The acquisition of Kaluli." In D. I. Slobin (ed.), *The Crosslinguistic Study of Language Acquisition* (Vol. 1). Hillsdale, NJ: Lawrence Erlbaum Associates.

Schlesinger, I. M. (1971). "Production of utterances and language acquisition." In D. I. Slobin (ed.), *The Ontogenesis of Grammar*. New York: Academic Press.

Schlesinger, I. M. (1974). "Relational concepts underlying language." In R. L. Schiefelbusch and L. L. Lloyd (eds), *Language Perspectives: Acquisition, retardation, and intervention*. Baltimore: University Park Press.

Schlesinger, I. M. (1977). "The role of cognitive development and linguistic input in language acquisition." *Journal of Child Language*, **4**, 153–69.

Schneider, W. and Shiffrin, R. M. (1977). "Controlled and automatic human information processing: I. Detection, search, and attention." *Psychological Review*, **84**, 1–66.

Shiffrin, R. M. and Dumais, S. T. (1981). "The development of automatism." In J. R. Anderson (ed.), *Cognitive Skills and Their Acquisition*. Hillsdale, NJ: Lawrence Erlbaum Associates.

Shiffrin, R. M. and Schneider, W. (1977). "Controlled and automatic human information processing: II. Perceptual learning, automatic attending, and a general theory." *Psychological Review*, **84**, 127–90.

Slobin, D. I. (1970). "Universals of grammatical development in children." In W. J. M. Levelt and G. B. Flores d'Arcais (eds), *Advances in Psycholinguistic Research*. Amsterdam: North-Holland.

Slobin, D. I. (1973). "Cognitive prerequisites for the development of grammar." In C. A. Ferguson and D. I. Slobin (eds), *Studies of Child Language Development*. New York: Holt, Rinehart & Winston.

Slobin, D. I. (1979). *The Role of Language in Language Acquisition*. Unpublished manuscript, University of California, Berkeley.

Slobin, D. I. (1982). "Universal and particular in the acquisition of language." In E. Wanner and L. R. Gleitman (eds), *Language Acquisition: The state of the art*. Cambridge, England: Cambridge University Press.

Slobin, D. I. (1985). "Crosslinguistic evidence for the language-making capacity." In D. I. Slobin (ed.), *The Crosslinguistic Study of Language Acquisition*. Hillsdale, NJ: Lawrence Erlbaum Associates.

Spelke, E. (1985). "Perception of unity, persistence, and identity: Thoughts on infants' conceptions of objects." In J. Mehler and R. Fox (eds), *Neonate Cognition: Beyond the blooming buzzing confusion*. Hillsdale, NJ: Lawrence Erlbaum Associates.

Streeter, L. A. (1976). "Language perception of two-month-old infants shows effects of both innate mechanism and experience." *Nature*, **259**, 39–41.

Talmy, L. (1975). "Semantics and syntax of motion." In J. P. Kimball (ed.), *Semantics and Syntax* (Vol. 4). New York: Academic Press.

Talmy, L. (1976). "Semantic causative types." In M. Shibatani (ed.), *Syntax and Semantics, Vol. 6: The grammar of causative constructions*. New York: Academic Press.

Talmy, L. (1978). "Relation of grammar to cognition." In D. Waltz (ed.), *Proceedings of TINLAP-2* (Theoretical Issues in Natural Language Processing). Champaign, IL: Coordinated Science Laboratory, University of Illinois.

Talmy, L. (1983). "How language structures space." In H. Pick and L. Acredolo (eds), *Spatial Orientation: Theory, research, and application*. New York: Plenum Press.

Talmy, L. (1985). "Lexicalization patterns: Semantic structure in lexical form." In T. Shopen (ed.), *Language Typology and Syntactic Description, Vol. 3: Grammatical categories and the lexicon*. Cambridge, England: Cambridge University Press.

Tomasello, M. (1987). "Learning to use prepositions: A case study." *Journal of Child Language*, **14**, 79–98.

Werker, J. F. and Tees, R. C. (1984). "Cross-language speech perception: Evidence for perceptual reorganization during the first year of life." *Infant Behavior and Development*, **7**, 49–63.

Whorf, B. L. (1956). *Language, Thought, and Reality* (J. B. Carroll, ed.), Cambridge, MA: MIT Press.

Zubin, D. A. and Choi, S. (1984). "Orientation and gestalt: Conceptual organizing principles in the lexicalization of space." *Papers from the Parasession on Lexical Semantics*. Chicago: Chicago Linguistic Society.

Zubin, D. A. and Svorou, S. (1984). "Perceptual schemata in the spatial lexicon: A cross-linguistic study." *Papers from the Parasession on Lexical Semantics*. Chicago: Chicago Linguistic Society.

Language Acquisition in the Absence of Experience

Stephen Crain

The acquisition puzzle

It is a remarkable fact that, without special training or carefully sequenced linguistic input, every normal child acquires a natural language. The universality of language in our species stands in glaring contrast to the much more selective attainment of comparable cognitive skills, such as the ability to perform arithmetic calculations. A related fact is that every child in a linguistic community succeeds in converging on a grammatical system that is equivalent to everyone else's, despite considerable variability in linguistic experience. Moreover, children acquire language quite rapidly and with few wrong turns, considering the number of potential pitfalls that exist. This picture of the course of acquisition has been observed so often across the diversity of natural languages that its validity seems firmly established. It nevertheless remains astonishing for a parent to watch the process unfold and difficult for a scientific theory to explain it. What is so special about natural language, or about children, that guarantees that, almost without fail, they master a rich and intricate system of rules for language production and comprehension by the time they reach school age, that is, at a time when they are receiving their earliest instruction in other complex cognitive skills?

Linguistic theory has set itself the task of explaining this remarkable acquisitional scenario. In the broadest terms, what must be explained is how adult grammar is achieved on the basis of the linguistic input available to the learner. The knowledge the learner brings to that task (including procedures for learning) is often called the *language acquisition device* (LAD). The linguistic input from parents and others is called the *primary linguistic data* (PLD). On the basis of these data, the LAD hypothesizes a series of grammars, the last of which is the adult grammar, or *final state*. The entire process is represented schematically in (1):

(1) Input (PLD) → LAD → Final State

The problem of language acquisition is just one instance of the general problem of knowledge acquisition. Probably the main difficulty is to explain how different learners converge on similar mental representations on the basis of dissimilar environments. In the literature on conceptual development, as in the literature on language acquisition, it is common to approach the solution to the problem of induction by invoking constraints on hypothesis formation. As Keil (1990) remarks, "It is now relatively commonplace to advocate the need for some sorts of constraints" on knowledge acquisition. Although the need for constraints might be commonplace, there is disagreement about their exact nature and source. One question is whether constraints are borrowed across domains or whether some at least are dedicated to a single cognitive function, such as language. Another unanswered question is whether constraints are "innately" specified or result from general principles of cognitive growth. Another question concerns the way constraints interact with environmental inputs. Constraints are sometimes viewed as "filters" that close off certain choices from consideration in the learner's hypothesis search space. An alternative conception would have them play a more active role, directing a search through the environment for particular "triggering" experiences that promote the unfolding of latent knowledge. (Markman, 1989, discusses constraints on the acquisition of lexical knowledge and presents relevant empirical data. For a broader discussion of the nature of constraints on knowledge acquisition, see the papers in Gelman, 1990.)

In linguistics, one finds a near consensus on the need for constraints in explaining the development of linguistic knowledge. In addition, linguists generally find it reasonable to suppose that constraints are innate, domain-specific properties. A distinguishing feature of recent linguistic theory, at least in the tradition of generative/transformational grammar, is that it postulates universal (hence, putatively innate) principles of grammar formation, rather than characterizing the acquisition of language as the product of general cognitive growth (Chomsky, 1971, 1975). This theoretical framework is often referred to as the theory of universal grammar, a theory of the internal organization of the mind/brain of the language-learner.

Although there remain many disagreements about the exact specification of the principles of universal grammar, most linguists have reached the conclusion that at least some properties of human language are innately determined. To understand why, it is useful to introduce some notation. The final state of language development can be viewed as a mapping between an unbounded set of sentences and their potential meanings. This is represented in (2):

(2) Input → LAD → Final State
                  ⟨sentence 1, meaning 1⟩
                  ⟨sentence 2, meaning 2⟩
                  ⟨sentence 3, meaning 3⟩
                  ⟨sentence 4, meaning 4⟩

Another, perhaps less obvious fact about linguistic development is that every child comes to know facts about language for which there is no decisive evidence from the environment. In some cases, there appears to be no evidence at all; in others the evidence is compatible with a number of alternative hypotheses (including false ones). In still other cases the evidence that is available appears to be misleading at best. Aspects of linguistic knowledge for which decisive evidence is not available are generally inferred to be encoded in constraints. To a first approximation, constraints fall into two classes. One class informs the learner that a sentence, although grammatical, cannot have a particular interpretation. For example, consider the interpretations that can be given to the pronoun *he* in the sentences in (3).

(3) a. The Ninja Turtle danced while he ate pizza.
     b. He danced while the Ninja Turtle ate pizza.
     c. While he danced, the Ninja Turtle ate pizza.

Note that the first sentence (*"The Ninja Turtle danced while he ... "*) the pronoun may be interpreted as referring to the Ninja Turtle: *He* and the *Ninja Turtle* are *coreferential*. In the second sentence, however, (*"He danced while the Ninja Turtle ... "*) the referent of *he* cannot be the Ninja Turtle. The third sentence shows that this restriction on coreference in the second example does not depend solely on the fact that the pronoun appears before the name. In (3c), the pronoun *he* again comes before *the Ninja Turtle*, yet coreference is possible. Coreference is ruled out in the second example because the pronoun and the definite description are in a particular structural relationship, as we will discuss below. For now the point is that the final state of linguistic development includes knowledge that certain sentences cannot have certain meanings assigned to them. This knowledge is represented as in (4), where the * indicates that some meaning is not permitted by the grammar.

(4) Input → LAD → Final State
                  ⟨sentence, *meaning⟩

In another class of examples, it is the form rather than the content that is excluded by the grammar. Consider the paradigm in (5) and (6), where the deviant sentence is marked by the * to indicate that this means of expression is not allowed by the grammar, although the intended meaning seems clear.

(5) a. Who do you want to help?
     b. Who do you wanna help?
(6) a. Who do you want to help you?
     b. *Who do you wanna help you?

Every English-speaking adult is (implicitly) aware that contraction is permitted in (5b), but not in (6b). Knowledge of facts of this kind can be represented as follows:

(7) Input → LAD → Final State
                  ⟨*sentence, meaning⟩

In the case of *wanna contraction*, there is a strong tendency for speakers to contract in ordinary speech, at least in dialects of American English. Consequently, learners might well be tempted to form the false generalization that *want* and *to* may contract in sentences like (6b), if this were not ruled out by the grammar. Several of the studies discussed later in this article were designed to investigate whether learners resist the temptation to "complete" partial syntactic generalizations such as this. Clearly, an appeal to induction by general procedures of analogy could actually hinder the acquisition process in these cases.

To summarize, universal grammar views the task of language learning as the acquisition of mappings of sentences and meanings. The adult mapping, or final state, includes knowledge of certain restrictions on the meanings that can be mapped onto sentences as well as restrictions on the utterances that can be used to express meanings. Both kinds of knowledge are encoded in constraints.

In recent years there has been a concerted effort to reduce as far as possible the number of rules of universal grammar. This has resulted in the postulation of highly general rules such as *Move alpha* (move anything, anywhere.) As a consequence, some measure is needed to prevent these highly general rules from overgenerating, that is, from licensing constructions that do not occur in the target language. The solution that has been advanced is to hold overgeneration in check by constraints. Constraints spell out the specific circumstances in which the general rules are not operative. As we have seen, constraints can either be sanctions on the form a message can take (⟨*sentence, meaning⟩), or they can be sanctions on the meanings that can be given to certain sentences (⟨sentence, *meaning⟩). Constraints are *negative* in the sense that adding a constraint to a grammar results in an overall *reduction* in the language that can be generated.[1] Since introducing constraints into a grammar restricts the language, constraints have the desired effect of handling the "overgeneration" problem that would otherwise arise from highly general rules.

Constraints are one of the main ingredients in the solution to the acquisition puzzle offered by the theory of universal grammar.

From the standpoint of acquisition, constraints reduce the number and kind of hypotheses children can entertain in response to their linguistic experience. By circumscribing the hypotheses children must contend with, constraints make direct, rapid acquisition less mysterious. This does not exclude the possibility, however, that constraints themselves are learned or follow from the same basic principles of learning that govern other aspects of cognitive development. Not surprisingly, there are those who reject the view that there are domain-specific constraints on grammar formation (e.g. Arbib and Hill, 1988; Lee, 1988; MacWhinney, 1987; Rumelhart and McClelland, 1987). The search for domain-general principles that can explain language universals is hindered, however, by the arbitrariness of the properties of natural language. This should become apparent from the sample of constraints examined later in this article. Another complicating factor for this approach, also discussed later, is the early emergence of knowledge of linguistic contraints, as compared to other cognitive abilities.

Proponents of the theory of universal grammar have argued that constraints are innately encoded prescriptions specific to grammar formation. The argument for innateness rests on two observations in addition to the arbitrariness of their linguistic properties. First, as we saw, constraints are negative, that is, they are sanctions against hypotheses of certain sorts. The second observation is an empirical one—it is widely held that the data available to the learner for grammar construction do not include "negative evidence" (Bowerman, 1988; Braine, 1971; Brown and Hanlon, 1970; Grimshaw and Pinker, 1988; Morgan and Travis, 1989; Wexler and Culicover, 1980). Negative evidence refers to information about which sentences are ungrammatical. This information could, for example, take the form of parental feedback in response to children's incorrect productions. Negative evidence could be used by a learner to avoid constructing an overly general grammar. In the case of *wanna contraction*, for example, the learner might benefit from outside information about which utterances are *not* well formed, such as (6b) above. Reviewing the literature on this topic, Pinker (1990) concludes, "When parents are sensitive to the grammaticality of their children's speech at all, the contingency between their behavior and that of their children is noisy, indiscriminate, and inconsistent from child to child and age to age" (p. 217).

These observations invite the inference that constraints are innately specified. In a nutshell, the argument is based on "the poverty of the stimulus": The adult grammar contains a set of constraints, which are negative, and the only apparent source of data by which they could be learned, negative evidence, is not available.[2] The argument is graphically depicted in (8).

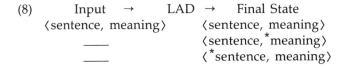

(8)   Input   →   LAD   →   Final State
       ⟨sentence, meaning⟩   ⟨sentence, meaning⟩
       ____   ⟨sentence, *meaning⟩
       ____   ⟨*sentence, meaning⟩

As we have seen, the data available during the course of language development underdetermine the knowledge that learners attain, both in production and in comprehension.

As a solution to this problem, universal grammar supposes that the constraints characterizing the final state also characterize the initial state of the language acquisition device. That is, the constraints are not learned; rather, they are innately specified as part of universal grammar. This circumvents the problem of learning negative facts without negative evidence. Assuming that this argument is valid, it is worth remarking further on two other sources of data that can be marshalled in support of the innateness of constraints (besides their appearance in the absence of corresponding experience).

A second hallmark of innateness is universality. If constraints are part and parcel of the human genetic program, we should also expect them to appear in all of the world's languages.[3] A caveat should be noted, however. Even an innate linguistic property could fail to show up in every language. An innate principle might not appear because the language in question does not offer the ingredients necessary for its application. (For example, we should not expect to observe the effects of a constraint on the "movement" of Wh-phrases in languages that do not have syntactic Wh-movement.)[4] Any principle that does appear universally, however, is a prime candidate for consideration as an innate linguistic property.

A third hallmark of innateness is early emergence. Although it is not logically necessary, it is reasonable to expect the early emergence of innate properties in the course of language development. Some explanation would clearly be called for if a principle is respected in all adult languages but not in the language of children until well after the relevant lexical items and structures have been mastered (Otsu, 1981). This is one reason why language acquisition provides a good testing ground for the theory. In addition, even in languages that appear to go against the grain with respect to principles of universal grammar, children should respect its inherent principles, at least initially.

The discussion has so far focused on aspects of linguistic theory that limit the possible wrong turns a child can take in the course of language acquisition. We have seen that innate constraints provide a rationale for expecting direct and rapid acquisition of syntax. Efficient acquisition and rapid acquisition are not the same thing, but a theory that provides children with innate capabilities certainly suggests that acquisition should be rapid. Appearances suggest otherwise, however. The kind of direct, rapid acquisition anticipated by the theory of universal grammar does not appear to square with the facts. Rather, children are seen to spend a considerable number of years in the acquisition of syntactic principles (Borer and Wexler, 1987; Phinney, 1981; Roeper, 1986; Solan and Roeper, 1978; Wexler and Chien, 1985). Worse still, some researchers have uncovered apparent violations of universal syntactic principles (Aitchison, 1989; Matthei, 1982; Wilson and Peters, 1984). Some errors might not have shown up in children's spontaneous productions, but were revealed in studies that used more analytic comprehension tasks to probe for linguistic knowledge. These studies unearthed apparent deficiencies in knowledge of complex syntactic structures even by children as old as 10 or 11.

Based on these observations, some researchers believe that children do not advance rapidly in grammatical competence. Rather, they are seen to proceed slowly and, in the process, to settle at stages along the way. Since this acquisition scenario does not cohere well with the predictions of universal grammar outlined above, it might be helpful to pause and consider why language acquisition seems to take so long and why children make mistakes along the way. We will first consider two hypotheses that are consistent with the innateness of syntactic principles. One is that certain principles, though innate, are nevertheless inaccessible to a child's grammar induction routines until a critical maturational stage is reached. The other hypothesis explains gradual acquisition in terms of a parameter-setting model of language acquisition.

Maturation

There have recently been detailed proposals to the effect that some aspects of syntactic knowledge, though innate, are not yet developed at birth, taking some years to mature (Borer and Wexler, 1987; Radford, 1990). Let us call this the *maturation hypothesis*. The maturation hypothesis correctly points out that even if the acquisition of some structures is slow in developing, with long stops along the way, this does not disconfirm the strong innateness hypothesis. Like aspects of physical development of the body (e.g., the secondary sex characteristics), linguistic principles may lie dormant for many years, biologically timed to become effective at a certain maturational stage.

Borer and Wexler, for example, propose that the principles underlying the emergence of full verbal passives undergo maturational change. They maintain that before a critical level of maturation is reached, children will be unable to produce or comprehend verbal passives with *by*-phrases. They argue that A-chains, which are involved in the derivation of verbal passive constructions, are not available to children in the first few years.[5] They also assert that knowledge of A-chains is innate but becomes accessible only after the language faculty undergoes maturational change.

There are reasons to question the maturation hypothesis as it pertains to passives. One source of data invoked in its support is the absence of full verbal passives in the spontaneous speech of young children. It has been found recently, however, that children learning Sesotho, an African language, use full passives (with the equivalent of "*by*-phrases") before the age of 3 (Demuth, 1989). Even if passives were entirely absent from children's speech, however, this would not be incontrovertible evidence that children's grammars are *incapable* of generating them. In English, full passives are rarely observed in adults' spontaneous speech, or in adult speech to children (Pinker, Lebeaux, and Frost, 1987). The paucity of passives in adult speech is not interpreted as revealing a lack of grammatical knowledge. Instead, it is attributed to *performance* factors weighing in favor of the reduced form or an alternative structure that is permissible in the same discourse settings. That is, the absence of full verbal passives in adult speech is assumed to be a consequence of the fact that situations in which the full passive is uniquely appropriate are rare. But the same logic that explains why adults produce so few full passives would seem to apply to children. Perhaps they too have knowledge of this construction but do not use it unless the communicative situation is appropriate.

This question was pursued in a test of English-speaking children by Crain, Thornton, and Murasugi (1987). In this study, one experimenter had each child pose questions to another experimenter. The pragmatic context was carefully controlled so that questions containing a full verbal passive would be felicitous. In this experiment, 50 percent of the children's responses were full passives (with *by*-phrases) and all but two of the children tested used a full passive, including those as young as 3 years, four months. Children's considerable success in producing passive sentences appropriate to the circumstances (i.e., their correct pairing of sentence forms and meanings) constitutes compelling evidence of their grammatical competence with this construction. The finding that young children evince mastery of the passive obviates the need to appeal to maturation to account for its absence in early childhood language. Maturation cannot be absolutely excluded, but a maturational account is motivated only where a construction is acquired later than would be expected on the basis of processing complexity, pragmatic usefulness in children's discourse, and so forth. The results on production in Sesotho and English suggest that the age at which the passive is acquired falls well within a timespan that is compatible with these other factors. Therefore, maturation need not be invoked.

It might eventually turn out that the strong innateness hypothesis must be augmented by maturation in certain cases. But unless some motivated predictions can be made about exactly when latent knowledge will become effective, adding maturation into the equation for language acquisition only introduces additional degrees of freedom, making the hypothesis compatible with a wider range of data. The strong innateness position, that is, that children abide by universal principles at *all* stages of language development, is more restricted and should be adopted until clear evidence is presented to the contrary.

Parameter theory

Another explanation has been offered for the gradualness of language development. It is sometimes suggested that it takes some months, even years, to fix all the parameters appropriate for a language (Roeper, 1986). It is important to appreciate, however, that parameter-setting models do *not* entail slow, piecemeal acquisition of linguistic knowledge (Hyams, 1989; Lasnik and Crain, 1985).

Parameter-setting models have been offered to explain the fact that clusters of syntactic properties appear to vary systematically across languages. For example, one variable is the presence or absence of a null element in the subject position of tensed clauses. English does not allow superficially empty subjects, but Italian and Spanish do. Other properties seem to covary with this one across languages, including the presence or absence of expletive pronouns and the use of Subject/AUX inversion.[6]

Parameter-setting models contribute another ingredient to the solution to the problem of language learnability. Parameters, like constraints, exert limits on the ways languages may differ, thereby reducing the number of grammatical hypotheses a child might consider in the course of language acquisition. Each parameter is a purported universal syntactic principle. A parameter consists of a limited, ordered set of hypotheses (or values) that may be entertained for some linguistic phenomenon. In acquisition, it is supposed that children abandon the initial setting of a parameter only in response to positive evidence that it is incorrect, thereby changing to a setting that is appropriate for the target language.[7]

At first glance, it might seem that parameter-setting models do entail gradual, staged acquisition, for the following reason: Since parameters must sometimes be reset, a child must remain at some parameter setting until positive data indicate that a change of values is necessary. But the question is: Why would the setting of parameters take months or even years, as some researchers seem to believe?[8] One possibility is that the relevant linguistic evidence that would permit a child to reset a parameter is not readily available. (Other possible explanations of gradual acquisition are discussed in Crain and Fodor, in press; Hamburger and Crain, 1984; Hyams, 1989; Lasnik and Crain, 1985.) This proposal will not do, however, because if the necessary input for resetting a parameter were not readily available, some children would never encounter it, and would never advance to the adult grammar. Because this does not happen, we must infer that the requisite data are plentiful. This in turn suggests that the acquisition of syntax will indeed be nearly instantaneous, once the relevant lexical items and sentence structures are in place.

It may be helpful to think of parameterized language acquisition as a kind of scavenger hunt in which the child knows in advance what sentences to look for (namely, the ones that are relevant to setting parameters). Recall that in a scavenger hunt one can gather the requisite items in any order whatsoever, unlike in a treasure hunt, where the order is imposed. If parameters are free to be fixed independently of each other, the result could be called "scavenger acquisition": The same final state is reached irrespective of how the data in the child's language environment are ordered. In short, acquisition would be *as if* instantaneous.[9]

Competence versus performance

There is a different approach to the question of why language acquisition takes so long. This approach emphasizes the nonsyntactic demands of the tasks of sentence production and comprehension. To remove the sting from data that are unaccommodating to the theory of universal grammar, this approach asks whether the errors children have been found to make might not reflect one or more of the nonsyntactic factors that are interleaved with syntactic processing.

The interpretation of imperfect performance in any psycholinguistic experiment is complicated by the existence of a variety of factors extraneous to syntax. Successful comprehension requires children to parse the test sentence, to plan and execute an appropriate response, to accommodate any unmet presuppositions, and so on. Unless we are cognizant of these factors in both production and comprehension, we might infer, for example, that a child has a syntactic deficit, when in fact the real culprit is the child's inability to correctly plan an action-response, or to attend to the pragmatic presuppositions of the test sentences. It is therefore important, when children perform poorly in some psycholinguistic task, to consider the possibility that one of these aspects of language processing may be at the heart of the problem, rather than their imperfect knowledge of syntactic principles.

To assess children's linguistic knowledge, we must not only develop our understanding of the nature of these nonsyntactic factors, but we must devise experimental paradigms that minimize their impact on linguistic processing. To substantiate the claim that nonsyntactic factors play an important role in many psycholinguistic tasks, several experimental studies with 2- to 5-year-old children have successfully disentangled performance errors from knowledge of syntax. These experiments demonstrate that the source of children's performance errors in several previous studies was the failure to control the nonsyntactic demands of experimental tasks, since the errors disappeared or were greatly reduced in tasks that simplified these additional burdens on language processing (Crain and Fodor, in press; Fodor and Crain, 1987; Goodluck and Tavakolian, 1982; Hamburger and Crain, 1982, 1984). When sufficient attention is paid to nonsyntactic processes such as presupposition and sentence parsing, we find that children produce and understand syntactic structures of considerable complexity. Their performance failures previously imputed to lack of syntactic knowledge are better explained in terms of the relative complexity of processing factors associated with the test sentences. From the standpoint of language learnability, the demonstration that nonsyntactic factors are responsible for some of the problems children have in sentence comprehension raises the possibility that there may be considerably less divergence than is commonly believed between child and adult grammars. If so, children's uniform transition to the correct grammar is rendered less mysterious.

To sum up so far: We began by stating the primary goal of research on language development—to explain children's rapid and uniform mastery of a richly articulated system of linguistic knowledge that is shared by other members of a speech community. Developments in linguistic theory have reinforced the view that children are guided through the course of language acquisition by knowledge that is in large part predetermined. Much of this knowledge is encoded in constraints. Constraints are likely candidates for innateness because (i) they appear universally and (ii) they could not be learned from experience. A third hallmark of innateness is early emergence. This is the subject of the next section, which presents the results of experimental investigations of young children's knowledge of constraints.

Empirical research

The empirical studies presented in this section were designed to assess young children's knowledge of purportedly innate constraints on what can be said, and on what meanings can be assigned to sentences. Assessing children's knowledge of constraints has called for new experimental methods and new research strategies. For illustrative purposes, the examples are chosen from my own research and that of colleagues. It should be understood that space limitations do not allow a discussion of related findings from the research literature (e.g., de Villiers, Loeper, and Vainikka, 1990; Hyams and Sigurjonsdottir, 1990; McDaniel, Cairns, and Hsu, 1990; Wexler and Chien, 1985).

Studies of production

Three studies examined how children obey purportedly innate constraints on sentence production. All three adopted an elicited production methodology. This method requires the delicate manipulation of situations to elicit the construction that is being targeted. In each study we tried to devise a situation that was uniquely appropriate for a particular sentence meaning; we then observed the utterances children used to describe that situation. Successful production by children is a strong indicator of underlying competence because there are so many ways to combine words incorrectly. Children's repeated correct combinations in appropriate contexts are therefore not likely to come about by accident.

The first experiment was designed to see whether children would apply structure-dependent or structure-independent operations in forming Yes/No questions. In the acquisition of this construction, much of the data available to children is compatible with hypotheses of either kind. It has long been claimed that children invariably apply structure-dependent rules at every stage of language development, even at stages where their linguistic experience is limited such that it is also amenable to structure-independent hypotheses. We subjected this claim to an empirical test in the first experiment. The two studies that follow provide an even stronger test of children's knowledge of purportedly innate principles. These experiments investigate constructions involving linguistic principles for which there is no corresponding input from the environment. These are examples of partial syntactic generalizations involving contraction. The method of elicited production is used to assess children's knowledge of a constraint that prohibits words from contracting across a Wh-trace.

A constraint on structure-dependence

The parade case of an innate constraint is structure-dependence. It is a basic tenet of universal grammar that grammatical rules are structure-dependent (Chomsky, 1971, 1975). A linguistic hypothesis is structure-dependent if it applies to the hierarchical structure of sentences. A structure-independent hypothesis, on the other hand, operates on sentences construed as strings of words rather than on their structural representations. Because structure-independent hypotheses apply to ordered strings, they invoke such linear relations as "first," "left-most," and so on. A revealing example is the formation of Yes/No questions, where a linear (structure-independent) strategy might be as follows:

(9) Move the *first* "is" (or "can," "will," etc.) to the front of the sentence.

This principle produces correct question forms for many simple declarative sentences, as in (10). Indeed, as Chomsky (1971) points out, what is so striking about the constraint of structure-dependence is that it rules out hypotheses that appear to be computationally simpler than are necessary to capture the facts about question formation in simple sentences.

(10) John is tall.   Is John tall?
      Mary can sing very well   Can Mary sing very well?

Given the reasonable assumption that children encounter simple sentences first, at least some children might be expected to adopt the structure-independent hypothesis were it not precluded by universal grammar. Notice, though, that these children would produce incorrect question forms when they began to ask more complex questions, such as questions that contain a relative clause. Consider sentence (11) below. Applying the structure-independent rule results in the ungrammatical question (12). The correct question form (13) comes from the application of a structure-dependent rule, which treats *the man who is running* as a single constituent. It is this constituent, the entire subject-noun phrase, that must be inverted with the first auxiliary verb in the main clause to give the correct question forms in all cases. This transformational operation is an example of Subject/AUX inversion.

(11) The man who is running bald.
(12) *Is the man who __ running is bald?
(13) Is the man who is running __ bald?

To test whether children give structure-independent responses such as (12), we used a simple experimental procedure to elicit Yes/No questions from them. The procedure was to preface a declarative like (11) with the carrier phrase "Ask (someone) if . . . ," as in (14).

(14) Ask Jabba if the man who is running is bald.

In an elicitation study, thirty 3- to 5-year-old children responded to requests like (14) (Crain and Nakayama, 1987). In response, children posed Yes/No questions to Jabba the Hutt, a figure from *Star Wars* who was being manipulated by one of the experimenters. Following each question, Jabba was shown a picture and would respond "yes" or "no." This game was used to see whether children would produce incorrect Yes/No questions in response to declaratives that contained a relative clause.

The outcome was as predicted: Children never produced incorrect sentences like (12). Therefore, a structure-independent strategy was not adopted in spite of its simplicity and the fact that it produces the correct question forms in many instances. The findings of this study, then, lend support to one of the central claims of universal grammar, that the initial state of the language faculty contains structure-dependence as an inherent property (see also further studies by Nakayama, 1987).

It is worth emphasizing that system-internal constraints like structure-dependence are efficacious in forestalling wrong turns a child might otherwise take. These constraints obviate the need for detailed corrective feedback that would otherwise be required to inform children of their grammatical errors. In the absence of negative evidence such as this, it is hard to see how children who err in grammar construction might "unlearn" the incorrect hypothesis, to realign their grammars so as to converge on a system that is equivalent to that of adult members of the linguistic community.

A constraint on wanna *contraction*

The research strategy followed in the next two experiments is to set up situations in which the overriding temptation for children is to violate the grammatical constraint under investigation. Children's adherence to the grammar in this situation, shown by their resistance to the preferences they exhibit in other contexts, is interpreted as evidence of their knowledge of the constraint under investigation. Before we review the experiments, however, some linguistic preliminaries are in order.

The theory of generative/transformational grammar postulates that Wh-questions (i.e., questions beginning with Wh-phrase like "who," "what," "which man," and so on) are formed by movement of the Wh-phrase from an underlying level of representation (D-structure) to its surface position (at S-structure). The theory also postulates that an empty category is left behind as a record of the movement of a Wh-phrase. The empty category is called a *trace*, abbreviated as *t* in the examples that follow.

One source of evidence for the psychological reality of the trace comes from agreement facts. In ordinary declarative sentences, number agreement is established *locally* between a noun phrase and a verb, as the examples in (15) indicate.

(15)   Diane thinks Quayle is the best looking.
       Diane thinks the Democrats are the best looking.

Observe that, following Wh-movement, the Wh-phrase that has been moved agrees in number with the verb that is next to its trace.

(16)   Which candidate does Diane think *t* is the best looking?
       Which candidates does Diane think *t* are the best looking?

The local nature of agreement is maintained in Wh-questions by copying the agreement features of the moved Wh-phrase onto its trace. This allows agreement to remain a strictly local relation even in Wh-questions like (16), where the Wh-phrase has moved some distance from its site of origin. In these questions agreement holds between the trace of the moved Wh-phrase and the verb that is adjacent to the trace in the lower clause.

Children's knowledge of the trace of movement can be tested by seeing whether they obey the constraints to which a Wh-trace is subject (in the adult grammar). One constraint prohibits contraction across a trace, as illustrated in the *wanna contraction* paradigm:

(17)   a. Who do you want to help *t*?
       b. Who do you wanna help?
(18)   a. Who do you want *t* to help you?
       b. *Who do you wanna help you?
Cf.   a. I want to help make salsa.
       b. I wanna help make salsa.

The inadmissibility of contraction in (18b) is assumed to derive from fundamental principles of grammar, which prohibit two words from contracting together when a trace intervenes (Chomsky, 1976). In (18), "who" has been moved from the subject position of the subordinate clause, leaving behind a trace between "want" and "to." The trace between them blocks contraction. Note that in (17) the trace of "who" is in the object position of the subordinate clause, after "help." Therefore, the trace does not block contraction.

Assuming that the linguistic input to children consists only of possible sentence/meaning pairs, however, it is difficult to see how knowledge about the ungrammaticality of sentences like (18b) could have been acquired through exposure to environmental input at any age. It is accordingly important to ask when children know that a trace blocks contraction. The logic of the situation would suggest they must know it innately. Otherwise, they might make the wrong generalization—that contraction is permitted in sentences like (18b). This would be an easy mistake to make, because contraction is permitted in so many other contexts. If corrective feedback is not available to children who err in this way, however, children who make the false generalization would not be informed of their mistake, and would not attain the adult grammar. Because this does not happen (i.e., since everyone does achieve the same, correct final state), it seems that children never make this error. The only way this could be possible, given the absence of relevant experience, is if they know that Wh-trace blocks contraction. Here, then, is a partial syntactic generalization of grammar that clearly calls for assistance from innate linguistic principles.

To test for the early emergence of knowledge of this restriction on *wanna contraction* we developed an elicitation task that encourages children to ask questions like (18b) if these are compatible with their grammars (Crain and Thornton, in press; Thornton, 1990). Using this technique, we have elicited long-distance Wh-questions like those in the paradigm in (17) and (18) from twenty-one 2- to 5-year-old children.

We hypothesized that children would exhibit a preference for contraction of *want* and *to* whenever this was consistent with their grammars. In the present case, a preference for reduced forms would be revealed in the frequency count of contracted forms in extracting from the object position of the infinitival clause. Comparing this result with the proportion of contracted forms in extracting from the subject position would indicate whether or not children's grammars contained the constraint on the *wanna contraction*.

Two experimenters were needed to elicit the relevant Wh-questions. One solicited the child's help in finding out information about rats. Help was sought in this task because the rat (puppet) in the experimental workspace was too timid to talk to grown-ups. One set of contexts was designed to evoke object extraction questions; another set required children to ask subject extraction questions. Examples of the protocols are given below.

Protocol for eliciting object extraction questions
Experimenter: The rat looks hungry. I bet he wants to eat something. Ask
                 Ratty what he wants.
Child: *What do you wanna eat?*
Rat: Some cheese would be good.

Although we could often get away with simple protocols like this, sometimes we had to resort to more complex situations with a number of characters. Notice that an appropriate response to the scenario above would consist of a partial question such as "What do you want?" This partial question would not give the information needed to test our hypothesis. To avoid this uninformative question, we had to complicate the situation, to make it pragmatically necessary for the child to produce a "full" question such as, "Who do you want to take a walk?" The pragmatics of the complex situations, such as the one below, demand a full question.

Complex protocol: Subject extraction questions
Experimenter: There are three guys in this story: Cookie Monster, a dog, and this baby. One of them gets to take a walk, one gets to take a nap, and one gets to eat a cookie. And the rat gets to choose who does each thing. So, *one* gets to take a walk, right? Ask Ratty who he wants.
Child: *Who do you want to take a walk?*
Rat: I want the dog to take a walk.

Using this technique, we elicited both subject and object extraction questions from twenty-one children, who ranged in age from 2 years, ten months, to 5 years, five months (mean = 4 years, three months). The results were clearly in accord with the theory of universal grammar. The results were, first, that children's productions of object-extraction questions, which permit contraction in the adult grammar, contained contracted forms 59 percent of the time; they produced uncontracted forms 18 percent of the time. By contrast, children's production of subject-extraction questions, where contraction is illicit, contained contracted forms only 4 percent of the time and uncontracted forms 67 percent of the time. Out of the seventy-five opportunities children had to contract in the subject-extraction contexts, one child (K.M., 3 years, nine months) accounted for all three violations of the constraint. It was found, therefore, that children prefer to contract in asking questions like (17b), but correctly resist this preference when they should. As a result they ask questions such as (18a), but not ones like (18b), which are in violation of the constraint on contraction across a Wh-trace. Although children's systematic control of this subtle contrast might appear in spontaneous production data, the crucial situations that call for the long-distance questions we elicited from children probably occur quite rarely in their experience. Analyses of children's spontaneous productions reveal relatively few instances of long-distance movement. For example, de Villiers, Roeper, and Vainikka (1990) report that there were only sixteen instances of long-distance Wh-movement in the Brown corpus of Adam (MacWhinney and Snow, 1985) between the ages of 2 and 4. Moreover, all of Adam's long-distance questions are instances of object extraction. By contrast, nineteen of the twenty-one children in the *wanna contraction* experiment produced questions with extraction from both the subject and object positions.

A constraint on rightward contraction

Crain and Thornton (1991) elicited another kind of long-distance question like (19), which permits contraction.

(19) Who do you think's in the box?

Sentences like this represent an apparent counter-example to the generalization that the trace of Wh-movement blocks contraction. Example (19) is clearly a well-formed sentence, so contraction must be admissible. This means, however, that *is-contraction* is permitted when the trace of a Wh-phrase appears to the left of *is*, as indicated in (20). If so, this would be a violation of the constraint mentioned above, that prohibits *wanna contraction*.

(20) Who do you think *t* is in the box?

This apparent conflict between principles has received critical attention in the literature. A particularly insightful explanation was offered by Bresnan (1978), who proposed that contraction occurs to the left in some cases and to the right in others. According to Bresnan, *wanna contraction* is an instance of leftward contraction, where *to* contracts with the preceding word *want*. Bresnan argues that, by contrast, *is* contracts with material to its right, despite orthographic appearances to the contrary. An orthography that conforms with Bresnan's proposal would represent *is-contraction* as in (21), with *is* contracting onto the word *in*.

(21) Who do you think s' in the box?

The following examples provide further support for Bresnan's treatment of *is-contraction*. These examples show that when the trace of a Wh-phrase intervenes between *is* and material to its right, contraction is inhibited.

(22) a. Do you know what that is doing *t* up there?
      b. Do you know what that's doing up there?
(23) a. Do you know what that is *t* up there?
      b. *Do you know what that's up there?

If it could be shown that children are treating questions such as (21) as instances of *rightward contraction*, this would reinforce the conclusion that they respect the prohibition on contraction across a Wh-trace. It is important to establish, then, that children know that *is-contraction* cannot occur if a trace intervenes between *is* and a lexical item that follows it.

To test this aspect of children's linguistic knowledge, we designed an experiment that encouraged children to formulate questions like those in (22) and (23) (Crain and Thornton, 1988, 1991). As in the previous studies, the prediction of universal grammar is that children will not produce such ungrammatical questions as (23b), despite the absence of relevant evidence from the environment. The target productions were evoked using protocols such as those given below. Notice that the experimenter is careful not to use contracted forms, to avoid providing any clues about where contraction is and is not permitted.

Protocols for rightward contraction
Experimenter: Ask Ratty if he knows what that is doing up there.
Child: *Do you know what that's doing up there?*
Rat: It seems to be sleeping.

Experimenter: Ask Ratty if he knows what that is up there.
Child: *Do you know what that is up there?*
Rat: A monkey.

Twelve children were tested. They ranged in age from 2 years, eleven months to 4 years, five months, with an average of 3 years, eight months. The findings are completely in accord with the expectations of linguistic theory. Questions involving rightward contraction were elicited from all of the children, and there was not a single instance of contraction where it is ruled out in the adult grammar (see [24] below). It is reasonable to conclude that children's questions with contractions in the previous experiment should not be counted as violations of the constraint prohibiting contraction across a trace. By overriding their strong tendency to use reduced forms wherever their grammars permit, the present study offers further evidence of children's early knowledge of a linguistic principle for which they have no corresponding experience.

(24) Do you know what that black thing on the flower is? (4 years, three months)
      Squeaky, what do you think that is? (3 years, eleven months)
      Do you know what that is on the flower? (4 years, five months)
      Do you know what that is, Squeaky? (3 years, two months)

Studies of comprehension

The experiments described so far were concerned with the studies of children's production. Grammatical knowledge was tested by presenting situations that suggest a unique interpretation, and observing the utterances children use to describe those situations. We turn now to tests of children's comprehension, which proceed in the other direction. The input to the child is a statement and a situation, and the behavior we observe is the child's judgment about the truth of the statement as it pertains to the situation.

A constraint on backwards anaphora

Our concern now is with the kinds of constraints that apply to the *meanings* of sentences, rather than to the sentences themselves. The notation ⟨sentence, *meaning⟩ was introduced earlier to capture this idea. An example of the application of this kind of constraint is illustrated in the following examples:

(25)   a. Sajak thinks he should get a free spin of the wheel.
       b. He thinks Sajak should get a free spin of the wheel.

The first sentence could mean that Sajak thinks that he, himself, should get a free spin. This may not be the preferred interpretation, but it is permissible. In the second example, however, this interpretation is impossible. We do not interpret the pronoun *he* as referring to Sajak. We also saw earlier that the constraint in question applies to full noun phrases such as *the Ninja Turtle*. Following Chomsky (1981, 1986) we will use the term *r-expression* (suggesting that the NP in question is a *referring expression*), to cover both full NPs and names.

Since the pronoun precedes the noun phrase in example (25b), this phenomenon is called *backwards anaphora*. As indicated in the previous section, the constraint on coreference in cases of backwards anaphora is based on structure rather than simply on the order relation between the pronoun and an r-expression. To see this, note that coreference is permitted in the following sentence, yet the pronoun precedes the r-expression (i.e., the speaker can intend that *he* is Sajak).

(26)   While he talks, Sajak likes to spin the wheel.

The constraint in question turns on the configurational relation between pronouns and r-expressions, first discovered by Lasnik (1976). This constraint is now called Principle C, because it is the third principle of Binding Theory—that part of the theory concerned with the coreference relations among different kinds of noun phrases (Chomsky, 1981). Principle C is specifically about r-expressions. According to this principle, if there is a particular structural relation between a pronoun and an r-expression, it suffices to rule out coreference. The structural relation is called *c-command*, which stands for *constituent command*. The exact formulation of c-command has been subject to a great deal of controversy, but the following rough definition will do for our purposes:

(27)   A pronoun c-commands an r-expression if there is a route that goes up to the first branching node above the pronoun, and then down to the r-expression.

It is important to recall that knowledge of noncoreference (i.e., the ungrammaticality of certain cases of backwards anaphora) is knowledge that some well-formed sentences cannot receive certain interpretations. (This was represented earlier as ⟨sentence, *meaning⟩). Notice that this makes Principle C another candidate for innate linguistic knowledge and, by hypothesis, we should expect its early emergence in child grammar, as pointed out by Solan (1983).

Let us turn, then, to the results of experimental investigations designed to see whether young children respect Principle C. The first study on this topic concerns the phenomenon of backwards anaphora. This phenomenon is of special concern because, in light of studies with young children, several researchers have raised the possibility that children initially apply a purely linear prohibition against backwards anaphora. Data that might suggest this interpretation were obtained in an experiment by Tavakolian (1978). Tavakolian found that two-thirds of the 3- to 5-year-old subjects in an act-out study selected an animal that was not mentioned in the sentence, but one that was present in the experimental workspace, as the referent of the pronoun in sentences like (28) and (29).

(28)   For him to kiss the lion would make the duck happy.
(29)   That he kissed the lion made the duck happy.

Of the twenty-four subjects tested, fourteen consistently acted out these sentences in this fashion.

Should we conclude from these data that children use direction rather than structural principles in restricting anaphora? This is not a valid conclusion (see Lasnik and Crain, 1985, for further discussion). For one thing, a third of the subjects' responses indicated acceptance of backwards anaphora, so the conclusion that children do not allow backwards anaphora is clearly too strong. But suppose that every child has chosen an unnamed referent on every opportunity. At most, this would be evidence of a strong preference for interpreting pronouns in one way rather than another, that is, as having a referent not mentioned in the sentence. Indeed, such a preference can be expected as a result of children's limited memory capacity (Crain *et al.*, 1989; Hamburger and Crain, 1984). Hence, children's extrasentential interpretation of pronominals is not by itself convincing evidence that they disallow backwards anaphora.

The question of children's knowledge of the alternative, backwards anaphora interpretation, was pursued in a comprehension experiment reported in Crain and McKee (1985). The experiment used a truth value judgment task. On a typical trial a child heard a sentence following a staged event acted out by one of two experimenters. The second experimenter manipulated a puppet: Kermit the Frog. Following each event Kermit said what he thought had happened. The child's task was to indicate whether or not the sentence uttered by Kermit accurately described the event that had taken place. Children were asked to feed Kermit a cookie when he said the right thing, that is, when what he said was what really happened. But sometimes, Kermit was not paying close attention and said the wrong thing. When this happened the child made Kermit eat a rag. These procedures made it fun for children to reward or punish Kermit. Without the rag ploy children were reluctant to say that Kermit has said anything wrong. Notice that both the acted-out events and the test sentences were provided for the children. This allowed unparalleled experimental control and at the same time reduced extraneous processing demands that are present in comprehension tasks in which children are required to act out the events themselves.

Using this technique, sixty-two children between 2 and 5 years old were asked to respond to sentences like (30) and (31). Since sentences like (30) are ambiguous, they were presented on two separate occasions. For example, in one scenario for (30) the Smurf ate the hamburger while inside the box; in the other, another character, Gargamel, ate the hamburger while the Smurf was in the box.

(30)   When he ate the hamburger, the Smurf was in the box.
(31)   He ate the hamburger when the Smurf was in the box.

Following each situation, Kermit said the same thing, and the children indicated in each case whether or not what he said was true. The results were that the children accepted sentences like (30) about 75 percent of the time in either context. Only one child consistently rejected backwards anaphora.

More important, sentences like (31) were uttered by the puppet in contexts that corresponded to the interpretation that is ruled out by the structural constraint on coreference. For example, (31) was presented in a context in which the Smurf ate the hamburger, but Gargamel, who hates hamburgers, did not. In this situation, children who were abiding by the constraint should have rejected these utterances by making Kermit the Frog eat the rag. This is precisely what happened: Children correctly rejected sentences of this form 87 percent of the time.[10] Even 2- and 3-year olds prohibit backwards anaphora only when Principle C dictates that they should.

A constraint on strong crossover

Principle C crops up again in Wh-questions and embedded questions, as in (32). It can be invoked to explain the restriction on coreference between pronouns and Wh-phrases following Wh-movement (Chomsky, 1986; Freidin and Lasnik, 1981).

(32)   a. Who does he think has big feet?
         b. I know who he thinks has big feet.

Notice that when one asks question (32a) or asserts (32b), one intends the

Wh-phrase and the pronoun to refer to different people. By convention, distinct indices are used to show that two linguistic expressions refer to different individuals. For example, the noncoreferential interpretation of question (32a) is represented in (33).

(33) Who$_i$ does he$_j$ think has big feet?

Question (32a) is therefore about an individual who thinks that someone else (possibly several other people) has big feet. If *who* and *he* refer to the *same* person, the result is ungrammatical, as indicated in (34).

(34) *Who$_i$ does he$_i$ think has big feet?

The examples in (32) can be contrasted with the following ones.

(35) a. Who thinks he has big feet?
       b. I know who thinks he has big feet.

In (35), the speaker may intend coreference between the Wh-phrase and the pronoun. So, (35a) may be asking who thinks that he, himself, has big feet. This is indicated by the fact that the two noun phrase (NPs) share indices in (36).

(36) Who$_i$ thinks he$_i$ has big feet?

It is important to note, moreover, that the question may be asking about several people who think they have big feet. This is called the *multiple reference interpretation* of the question. By contrast, a multiple reference interpretation is not possible for the examples in (32), where the referent of *he* must be a single individual.

To explain the fact that noncoreference is required in examples such as those in (32), we might expect to focus on the structural relationship between the Wh-phrase and the pronoun (cf. Sportiche, 1985). Chomsky (1986) suggests, however, that Principle C is at work in this case, too. This proposal stems from the observation that although the pronoun does not c-command the Wh-phrase in examples like (32), it does c-command the *trace* of the Wh-phrase. It is interesting to note that when a Wh-phrase is moved, leaving behind a trace that is c-commanded by a pronoun, the Wh-phrase and the pronoun are intended to be disjoint in reference. Obviously, a trace does not have reference in-and-of-itself, but it seems to act just like a name or definite description with respect to the coreference relation that holds between itself and a pronoun. By hypothesis, then, a Wh-trace is an r-expression. And, as with other r-expressions, the fact that a trace must be disjoint in reference from any pronoun that c-commands it is indicated by the assignment of different indices to these constituents. (See Wasow, 1972, for the first trace theoretic analysis of strong crossover.)

Another way of looking at the situation is this: If a Wh-phrase "crosses over" a pronoun as it moves from its underlying position to its surface position, the pronoun and the Wh-phrase must be disjoint in reference (see Postal, 1971, for the original discussion of crossover phenomena in generative grammar). Chomsky (1986) suggested that Principle C can account for this so-called *strong crossover* effect and explain the illegitimacy of intended coreference between the pronoun and moved Wh-phrase that has crossed over it, as illustrated in (37) below. Example (38) illustrates that when the movement of the Wh-phrase does not align the pronoun in a position to c-command the trace, Principle C does not apply. It is accordingly predicted that coreference (and multiple reference) should be permitted between the Wh-phrase and the pronoun.

(37)   *Who$_i$ did he$_i$ say t_i has big feet?   Crossover

(38)   Who$_i$ t_i said he$_i$ has big feet?   No crossover

A recent study was conducted to assess children's knowledge of Principle C as it applies to Wh-movement (Crain and Thornton, 1991; Thornton 1990). This experiment included embedded questions in which a Wh-phrase "crossed over" a pronoun, to see whether children exhibit the same strong crossover effects as adults. Some previous findings have led some investigators to conclude that children lack some aspect of syntactic knowledge relevant for strong crossover (Roeper *et al.*, 1985; Roeper, 1986). We were not convinced, however.[11]

This experiment used a variant of the truth value judgment task described in the last study (Crain and McKee, 1985). The subjects were twelve children ranging in age from 3 years, seven months to 4 years, eight months, with an average age of 4 years, 2 months. On different trials Kermit would utter different questions involving Principle C. The materials for the experiment included both one- and two-clause crossover trials. This permitted us to investigate whether the constraint of strong crossover might emerge first on simpler sentences. What follows are some examples of the one-clause crossover sentences. As indicated, the sentences were presented twice, once with a singular pronoun, and once with a plural pronoun.[12]

(39)   a. I know who he/they washed.
       b. I know who he/they dressed.
       c. I know who she/they scratched.

The stories for these sentences all had certain features in common. The storyline for trials with a plural pronoun, for example, all involved five characters who have some kind of adventure. The story ends with one character needing help. This "helpless" character is aided by two of the other characters who are "merciful" in disposition. The remaining two characters in the party are "self-reliant," and take care of their own needs. In fact, the self-reliant characters tell the merciful ones they do not need their help. In this way, the merciful characters are made prominent and are the natural referents for the pronoun in the test question. Figure 3.4.1 illustrates a typical situation. This particular protocol was used in testing example (39c), with the plural pronoun. The story tells of a group of friends who go for a hike in the woods and get bitten by mosquitoes. Big Bird needs help scratching all his bites, RoboCop and Batman come to his rescue, while Bert and Huckleberry Hound refuse to help and scratch their own bites. We also included simple declarative counterparts to the embedded questions, as in (40).

(40)   They scratched Bert and Huckleberry Hound.

Principle C applies to sentences (39) and (40) equally, since both are inappropriate descriptions of a situation in which Bert and Huckleberry Hound scratched themselves, but were not scratched by someone else. Of course, in the experiment this is precisely the situation that Kermit describes, as indicated in the following protocol.

Protocol for one-clause strong crossover
Experimenter: This is a story with Big Bird, Bert, and Huckleberry Hound.
                In this story they take a walk with RoboCop and Batman just

Figure 3.4.1   *The mosquito bite story.*

before dark. The problem is that mosquitoes come out at dark, and bite everyone except for RoboCop and Batman because they are wearing special suits. Big Bird gets the most bites and is having trouble scratching them. RoboCop and Batman say, "We'll help you. We don't have any bites." Bert says, "I don't need RoboCop and Batman to help me. I can reach my bites." And Huckleberry Hound says, "Me neither. I don't need RoboCop and Batman to help me."

Kermit: I know who they scratched—Bert and Huckleberry Hound.

Or, They scratched Bert and Huckleberry Hound.

Child feeds Kermit the rag, then:

Kermit: No? I said the wrong thing? What about Bert and Huckleberry Hound?
Child: *They are scratching theirself.*

The last mentioned event in each scenario consisted of the reflexive actions of the two characters that are named by Kermit. This was done to put the pragmatic focus on the reflexive action of the "self-reliant" characters. Ending the story in this way biased the protocols towards the "multiple reference" interpretation, which, as we saw, is permitted for questions such as (35), but not for crossover questions such as (32). The question was whether children's knowledge of Principle C would cause them to override this pragmatic bias and reject the incorrect interpretation of the crossover examples. Questions like (35) were also included to establish the children's level of acceptance of the multiple reference interpretation in cases where it should be permitted by their grammars. The control questions were presented in exactly the same kinds of situations.

Another important feature of this experiment is that it provides a reason for children to say "no." We call this feature *plausible denial*. Notice how plausible denial is built into the scenario above, by making it apparent why Kermit is wrong in saying, "I know who they scratched—Bert and Huckleberry Hound." It is clear in the situation that this is wrong, because RoboCop and Batman scratched someone else, Big Bird. On the other hand, if the child misinterpreted "I know who he scratched" as "I know who scratched himself," this would be true because the two characters named by Kermit, Bert and Huckleberry Hound, had in fact scratched themselves. The only thing to stop a child subject from allowing this interpretation would be knowledge of Principle C. Finally, there were many trials on which Kermit said the right thing and trials on which he said the wrong thing, to guard against any bias children might develop toward rewarding or punishing Kermit.

Two-clause crossover questions

There were also two-clause crossover sentence/answer pairs testing the strong crossover constraint. These materials were included to evaluate the proposal by Roeper *et al.* (1985) that children correctly interpret one-clause crossover questions before they are able to correctly interpret two-clause questions, in which movement is from a lower clause. Only the singular pronoun was used in the two-clause sentences, but two different verbs were tested, as indicated in (41).

(41) a. I know who he said/thinks has the best food.
      b. I know who he said/thinks is the best flyer.
      c. I know who he said/thinks is the best color.
      d. I know who he said/thinks has the best smile.

The stories for two-clause crossover were also alike in all important aspects. Each story depicted some kind of competition. There were four characters: A judge and three contestants. The judge checked all the contestants, openly rejecting two of them and settling on a "winner." The "would-be" winners disputed the judge's decision by pointing out to him that they would have been better choices, and that he was mistaken. In this way the judge was made salient as the referent for "he" in the crossover question. In the typical protocol that follows, the Joker judges which contestant has the best smile.

Protocol for two-clause strong crossover

Experimenter: Last year's winner of the best smile contest was the Joker. That makes him this year's judge of the best smile. Here are the three people in the contest: Grover, one of the Teenage Mutant Ninja Turtles, and Yogi Bear. The Joker walks over to each contestant in turn. To Grover, he says "Pretty good, big mouth." To Yogi Bear, "Not the best." Then he looks at the Ninja Turtle and says, "Look at those teeth. You've definitely got the best smile." But Grover says "Joker, You're wrong. I have the best smile. Look at how big my mouth is." And Yogi Bear says "No, I have the best smile."

Kermit: I know who he said has the best smile. Grover and Yogi Bear.

Child: No. (feeds Kermit the rag)

As in the one-clause crossover stories, the condition of plausible denial is satisfied. The child has reason to deny Kermit's assertion that Grover and Yogi Bear have the best smiles because it was clear in the story that the Joker chose the Ninja Turtle as having the best smile. The protocol also parallels the one-clause protocol in its bias for the multiple reference interpretation. The story ends with the action that corresponds to the incorrect interpretation of the question: The two would-be winners of the contest, Grover and Yogi Bear both dispute the Joker's judgment about who has the best smile. If the child understood, "I know who *he said* has the best smile," to mean "I know who *said he* has the best smile," the answer "Grover and Yogi Bear" would have been correct. Figure 3.4.2 illustrates the situation corresponding to example (41d), with the verb *said*. Also included in the study were control sentences such as (42), which allow coreference.

(42)   I know who said he has the best smile—Grover and Yogi Bear.

This sentence was presented in situations exactly like the one above.

Now we can turn to the findings. The main result was that the children in this study were steadfast in their adherence to Principle C, in both one-clause and two-clause crossover questions, in contrast to previous findings by Roeper *et al.* (1985). For one-clause crossover questions, children correctly rejected the multiple reference interpretation more than 95 percent of the time, for both singular and plural pronouns. They performed equally well on the nonmovement sentences, which replicated the Crain and McKee (1985) finding. In two-clause questions, the multiple reference interpretation was rejected over 92 percent of the time. Collapsing the results across one- and two-clause crossover questions, we find that children rejected the multiple reference response on 131/138 opportunities. This gives an overall correct rejection rate of 95 percent. By contrast, children *accepted* such sentences as (42) 87 percent of the time.

It is worth asking again whether children could have learned to prohibit coreference in crossover sentences. This would require them to have access to the right kind of linguistic experience. In the present case, this would presumably be information about what sentences cannot mean. As in the case of negative evidence, it is highly unlikely that this source of data is available to children in sufficient abundance to explain their early acquisition of the

Figure 3.4.2   *The best smile story.*

constraint. This underscores the contention of universal grammar that linguistic constraints are not something children must learn. The finding that children as young as 3 have mastered the prohibition on coreference in the absence of relevant experience invites us to consider the alternative solution advanced by current linguistic theory, that knowledge of the constraint on coreference is built into the human biological blueprint for language acquisition.

A constraint on prenominal modifiers

One prominent proposal about the way-stations children stop at on the path to adult grammar is called the *flat-structure hypothesis*. According to this hypothesis, children's intermediate grammars are characterized by flat constituent structure, where the adult grammar assigns hierarchical structural analyses. On this account, children's intermediate grammars comprise a subset of the rules and principles that characterize later stages. At the core of the flat-structure hypothesis is the view that children advance in a stepwise fashion in making the transition to the adult system—small steps for small feet. From a learnability perspective, small steps are advantageous in that they safeguard against overgeneration.

The flat-structure hypothesis was applied to Matthei's (1982) and Roeper's (1972) observations that 4- to 6-year-olds have difficulty interpreting phrases such as *the second striped ball*. They observed that children who were confronted with arrays like the one in Figure 3.4.3 often selected the ball that was second in the array and was also striped, rather than the second of the striped balls (counting from the left). The empirical finding, then, is that children assign an interpretation that is not the one an adult would assign to expressions of this kind. Matthei attributes this difference to children's failure to adopt the hierarchical phrase structure of noun phrases that characterizes the adult grammar. Instead, he argues that they adopt a flat structure analysis for phrases of this kind:

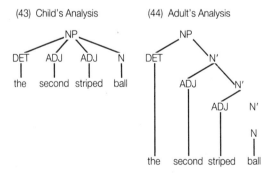

From the standpoint of language acquisition, however, any divergence like this between children's and adults' grammars poses the problem of explaining how

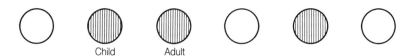

Figure 3.4.3   *Array for "second striped ball".*

the child ultimately converges on the adult grammar. In the present case, the problem of transition has received critical attention in the linguistic literature. Hornstein and Lightfoot (1981) argue that if children adopted nonadult phrase structure rules that generate trees like (43) rather than an adult tree like (44), evidence would not be readily available in the environment to purge their grammars of the incorrect analysis. The evidence that would justify the abandonment of the illicit analysis could, in principle, be supplied by negative data but, as we have seen, these are generally believed to be unavailable to children. (Note that the negative data needed in this case would have to consist of sentence/meaning pairs, since the phrase itself is well formed.)

To avoid this problem, Hornstein and Lightfoot propose as an innate principle of universal grammar that children initially hypothesize rules that establish intermediate level syntactic constituents like N'. They argue on the basis of learnability considerations that the rules generating (43) are not part of children's early grammars. Note that the flat-structure account of children's errors is based on rules that generate such trees as (43) without intermediate level categories. If Hornstein and Lightfoot are right, an explanation of children's errors invoking a flat phrase marker runs headlong into the "negative data problem," that is, the absence of the kind of evidence that would be needed to abandon an erroneous structural analysis.

Fortunately, there is an alternative component of the language processor in which the errors might have arisen. The logical structure of the necessary plan for finding the *second striped ball* in an array is quite complex. This raises the possibility that plan complexity and not syntactic complexity is the source of children's errors. Differences in the task demands associated with planning sometimes spell the difference between success and failure in comprehension. An explanation of children's errors in terms of plan complexity has received empirical support. A dramatic improvement in children's responses to the target phrases resulted from two changes in methode, implemented in successsive experiments (Hamburger and Crain, 1984). One change was the inclusion of a pretask session in which the children handled and counted homogeneous subsets of the items that that were subsequently used in the test arrays. This experience is assumed to prime some of the planning required in the main experimental task. In addition, a dramatic improvement in performance on phrases like *second striped ball* resulted from first asking children to identify the *first* striped ball, thus forcing them to plan and execute part of the plan used in interpreting the target phrase. Facilitating the planning aspects of the task with these simplifying maneuvers made it possible for children to reveal mastery of the syntax and semantics of such expressions.

A positive result from the standpoint of learnability theory was also obtained in the Hamburger and Crain study. On the Hornstein and Lightfoot account, the proform *one* can substitute for an intermediate level constituent like N' but, crucially, it cannot substitute for a lexical constitutent like N. Based on this analysis, we are led to expect that as soon as children understood the meaning of ordinals, they would permit "one" to corefer with "striped ball" in response to arrays like the one in Figure 3.4.4, following the request to "point to the first striped ball; point to the second one." That is, they would sometimes point to the fifth object in the array. This is precisely what was found. In fact, children *consistently* used the proform "one" to corefer with expressions like "striped ball." Notice that using "one" in this way is incompatible with the flat-structure account, given the standard assumption in linguistics that proforms corefer with a syntactic constituent. Because "striped ball" does not form a constituent on this account, children should only have been able to interpret "the second one" to mean the second *ball*, not the second *striped ball*. The finding of the Hamburger and Crain experiment suggests that children, like adults, use proforms to corefer with intermediate level syntactic constituents, as Hornstein and Lightfoot predicted.

Another example of the flat-structure hypothesis is the *conjoined-clause analysis* of relative clauses (Tavakolian, 1981). The proposal is that children go through a stage of development at which they have mastered the "flat" phrase structure of conjoined clauses but not the recursive rules that are needed to generate hierarchical structures such as relative clauses. Having only a (proper) subset of the rules of the target grammar at their disposal, children at this stage of development incorrectly apply their existing rules to sentences that their grammar does not yet properly generate. The result is an incorrect interpretation of certain sentences. For example, consider sentence (45), which contains a relative clause modifying the direct object. According to the conjoined clause analysis, this type of sentence would be assigned a structural analysis that is appropriate for two conjoined clauses, as in (46). This would explain why many children who are asked to act out (45) make the dog push the sheep and then jump over the fence, a response that would be appropriate for (46), but is not appropriate in response to (45).

(45) The dog pushed the sheep that jumped over the fence.
(46) The dog pushed the sheep and jumped over the fence.

Figure 3.4.4 *Array for one substitution experiment.*

Despite widespread acceptance of the conjoined-clause analysis, there are hidden dangers within it. As with prenominal modifiers, there is the problem of unlearning. Children whose grammars contain a conjoined-clause analysis would require access to special input to inform them of their error. Access to positive data, that is, a normal language environment containing chiefly grammatical sentences, will not suffice. Like the flat-structure account of prenominal modifiers, the conjoined-clause analysis of relative clauses constitutes a mistaken mapping between sentences and meanings, which must be purged from children's grammars. What sort of evidence will tell the child that an error has been made? As before, the learner cannot identify the error solely on the basis of information about which strings of words are grammatical or ungrammatical. Rather, what is needed to jettison the conjoined-clause analysis is negative evidence of a different sort, namely, evidence that certain sentence/meaning pairs are illicit. It is highly questionable whether these data appear with sufficient regularity to ensure that every child receives them.

Fortunately, further experimental evidence indicates that the source of children's errors in performance is not a lack of syntactic knowledge. This was shown in a study by Hamburger and Crain (1982). By constructing pragmatic contexts in which the presuppositions of restrictive relative clauses were satisfied, we were able to demonstrate mastery of relative clause structure by children as young as 3 years. Consider sentence (45) again.

(45) The dog pushed the sheep that jumped over the fence.

There are two presuppositions in (45). One is that there are least two sheep in the context; the other is that one (but only one) of the sheep jumped over a fence prior to the utterance. We suspected that the reason previous studies failed to demonstrate early knowledge of relative clause constructions is that they did not pay scrupulous attention to these pragmatic presuppositions. For example, subjects were required to act out the meaning of a sentence such as (45) in contexts in which only one sheep was present. The typically poor performance by young children in these experiments was attributed to their ignorance of the linguistic properties of relative clause constructions. But suppose a child did know the linguistic properties, but was also aware of the associated presuppositions. Such children might be unable to relate their correct understanding of the sentence structures to the inappropriate circumstances provided by the experiment. Adult subjects may be able to "see through" the unnaturalness of an experimental task to the intentions of the experimenter, but it is often not realistic to expect this of young children.

Following this line of reasoning, Hamburger and Crain (1982) made the apparently minor change of adding more sheep to the acting-out situation for sentence (45), a change that resulted in a much higher percentage of correct responses. The most frequent remaining "error" was failure to act out the event described by the relative clause. This was called the *assertion only* response. Since appropriate usage presupposes that the event described in a relative clause has already occurred, the *assertion only* response is not really an error, but precisely the kind of response that is compatible with perfect comprehension of the sentence. This interpretation of the data is supported by the fact that there was a positive correlation between the incidence of this response type and the child's age.

Other researchers have questioned this interpretation of the *assertion only* response. Goodluck (1990) and de Villiers and de Villiers (1986) suggests that if earlier work had counted this response as correct, children would have been seen as performing better in those studies, too. This objection is unwarranted, for several reasons. First, responses of this type did not appear in previous studies, presumably because these studies failed to meet the presuppositions of the restrictive relative clause. Moreover, in the Hamburger and Crain study this response was not evinced by any of the 3-year-old children and accounted for only 13 percent of the responses of the 4-year-olds. Nevertheless, even the 3-year-olds acted out sentences with relative clauses at a much higher rate of success than in earlier studies.

Comprehension data aside, the most compelling evidence that young children possess the structural knowledge underlying relative clause formation comes from a second experiment, overlooked by critics of the Hamburger and Crain study. Using an elicited production task, we constructed pragmatic contexts in which the presuppositions of restrictive relatives were satisfied. As we saw in the comprehension study, a context that is uniquely appropriate for a relative clause is one that requires the speaker to restrict from a set of objects, identifying to an observer which of two objects is to perform some action. In the elicitation experiment, the child is asked to identify one of several toys to a blindfolded observer. This is done to prevent the child from identifying the toy to the observer merely by pointing to it or saying *this/that one*. The property that differentiates between the toys is not one that can be encoded merely with a noun (e.g. *the guard*) or a prenominal adjective (e.g. *the big guard*) or a prepositional phrase (e.g., *the guard with the gun*), but involves a more complex state or action (e.g., *the guard that is shooting Darth Vader*). Young children reliably produce meaningful utterances with relative clauses when these felicity conditions are met. For example:

(47)   Jabba, please come over to point to the one that's asleep.
        (3 years, five months)
        Point to the one that's standing up. (3 years, nine months)
        Point to the guy who's going to get killed. (3 years, nine months)
        Point to the kangaroo that's eating the strawberry ice cream. (3 years, eleven months)

It should be noted that the possibility of imitation is excluded by the experimenter's care not to use any relative clause constructions in the elicitation situation. Also worth mentioning is the fact that the elicitation technique has been extended to younger children (as young as thirty-two months) and to the elicitation of a wider array of relative clause constructions, including relatives with object gaps (e.g., *the guard that Princess Leia is standing on*). Comparable findings with 2- and 3-year-old children have been obtained in Italian, in a study by Crain, McKee and Emiliani (1990).

The discovery that children produce sentences with relative clauses in appropriate circumstances supports the claim that children's performance failures reflect processing limitations and not a lack of structural knowledge. In the past few years, several other unaccommodating findings have been reinterpreted as reflecting the influence of task factors, and not an indication of lack of structural competence. When questions about syntactic knowledge are asked in a different way, by adopting tasks that reduce as far as possible the *nonsyntactic* demands in a comprehension test, children were found to succeed. (For a review, see Crain and Fodor, in press.) We conclude that the failure in previous research to control for these nonsyntactic contributors to the total task of sentence comprehension has led to underestimates of the grammatical capabilities of children in some cases. As a consequence of the new findings, the timetable for the acquisition of syntax has been brought more in line with the expectations of the theory of universal grammar, which, as we saw, anticipates rapid acquisition of full knowledge without stages of successive approximation.

Conclusion

We began by observing that recent developments in linguistic theory (the postulation of universal constraints of language acquisition), together with the observation that children's linguistic experience is quite limited (the absence of carefully sequenced input or negative evidence), reinforce the view that syntactic knowledge is in large part innately specified. What is innately given is knowledge of certain restrictions on the meanings that can be mapped onto sentences as well as restrictions on the sentences that can be used to express meanings. This knowledge is encoded in constraints. The problem for the learner is that there are no data available in the environment corresponding to the kinds of negative facts that constraints explain.

The force of this argument from the ''poverty of the stimulus'' is blunted somewhat by an emphasis in the literature on what has been achieved by the time the learner has reached the final state of acquisition. Because adults have had years of exposure to language, one might suppose that some of the complex facts that characterize the adult system emerge only after much fine tuning— statements about the poverty of the stimulus notwithstanding. A dyed-in-the-wool skeptic might be left wondering about the extent to which empirical data from child language support specific proposals about triggering data, innate knowledge, and the relation between them.

The purpose of the second section of the paper was to put these doubts to rest, by surveying a sample of the growing body of evidence evaluating the proposals of linguistic theory. The research reviewed consisted of an interlocking series of empirical tests of children's knowledge of constraints, both in production and comprehension. In the broadest terms, this research was concerned with testing the hypothesis that linguistic knowledge of considerable complexity emerges in child grammars without decisive evidence from experience. Empirical evidence was presented showing children's adherence to constraints at early stages of language acquisition. There has been a steady increase in recent years in the number of empirical demonstrations of children's mastery of syntactic facts for which they have little, if any, corresponding experience. These data clearly reinforce the bridge between linguistic theory and language acquisition research.

Acknowledgments

The research reported in this paper was supported in part by NSF Grant BNS 84-18537, and by a Program Project Grant to Haskins Laboratories from the National Institute of Child Health and Human Development (HD-01994). I wish to thank the following friends and colleagues for their contributions: Janet Dean Fodor, Bob Freiden, Paul Gorrell, Henry Hamburger, Stevan Harnad, Howard Lasnik, Cecile McKee, Keiko Murasugi, Mineharu Nakayama, Jaya Sarma, Don Shankweiler, Carole Tenny, Rosalind Thornton, and Ken Wexler. The author is also affiliated with Haskins Laboratories.

Notes to 3.4

1. In this respect, constraints contrast with *rules*. Unlike constraints, rules added to a grammar generally extend the language that could otherwise be generated.
2. To take an example, it would be possible for children to learn the constraint on a *wanna contraction* if parents were to inform them whenever they illicitly contracted *want* and *to*. On the assumption that the input to children consists only of the grammatical sentences in the paradigm (and their associated meanings), it is difficult to see how children could learn where contraction is *not* admissible. To make matters worse, children might well be tempted to produce ungrammatical utterances based on analogies with the grammatical ones, if these were not ruled out by some aspect of universal grammar. Evidence that children resist this temptation is presented in "The constraint on *wanna contraction*."
3. Obviously, this is an idealized position. It would not be prudent to disavow any influence of genetic variation in language acquisition and use. Some researchers would no doubt claim this to be the true hallmark of innateness. In the absence of any clear indications of which aspects of language are subject to genetic variation, however, it seems reasonable to use universality as one criterion for innateness, while not forgetting that this will be too stringent for some linguistic properties.

4. An innate linguistic property could also fail to characterize the adult grammar of a language if it is overidden on the basis of positive evidence (i.e., sentence/meaning pairs that are present in the input to learners). Suppose, for example, that in some dialect of English learners actually hear adults using the contracted form *wanna*. This could lead the learners to abandon the constraint on contraction. From that time on, they might disregard the constraint, since that is what adults have come to do.

5. An A-chain associates an empty category, called *NP-trace*, with a moved noun phrase in an Argument (A) position, such as Subject or Object. For example, in *The ball was kicked by Bill*, there is an A-chain consisting of *the ball* and its associated trace following *kicked*.

6. There are a number of candidates for the so-called *null subject parameter*, which ties this constellation of facts together. One of these, proposed by Hyams (1986), is noteworthy both empirically and theoretically (see also Hyams, 1989. Rizzi, 1982). Hyams's account of the parameter takes null subjects as the unmarked value. This predicts restructuring for languages like English, which have overt subjects in tensed clauses. According to Hyams, restructuring occurs when children encounter sentences containing expletives (i.e., "it" and "there"). Hyams suggests that productive use of expletives will be closely followed by the emergence of modals, which may then undergo Subject/AUX inversion. This means that expletives, modals, and interrogatives with modals should all emerge at about the same time in the acquisition of overt subject languages like English. For further discussion and relevant empirical findings, see Crain and Nakayama (1987).

7. Two general types of parameter models have been entertained. In one, choosing a more marked value for a parameter is like setting a switch which in turn sets other switches. Setting a single parameter may therefore have widespread repercussions throughout the child's grammatical system. An alternative view is that each parameter is set independently, to avoid ordering paradoxes (Wexler and Manzini, 1987).

8. The idealization of instantaneous acquisition was introduced by Chomsky (1965) as a working assumption to be made in the absence of evidence one way or the other about the effect of experience on language development. Not knowing *what* data are available to children and *when*, linguists made the simplifying assumption that all of the primary linguistic data needed for grammar construction were available all at once. Abstracting away from the unknown effects of experience is justified to the extent that it does not hinder subsequent developments in theory or empirical testing of hypotheses. It is worth asking whether ignoring the sequential aspects of acquisition has significantly impeded progress in the theory of grammar. Working under the assumption of instantaneous acquisition, linguists have made great strides in uncovering candidates for universal principles of natural language as well as for boundary conditions within which languages may differ (for a review, see Newmeyer, 1986). The consequence of this development in theory has been a corresponding reduction in the amount of primary linguistic data learners should need. That is, the idealization to instantaneous acquisition has not hindered progress; instead, it has led to a net reduction in the potential impact of experience on the final state.

9. If the term "stage" simply means whatever time it takes (however brief) to encounter the requisite data, then parameter models do indeed entail staged acquisition.

10. A variety of control sentences were also tested to rule out other, less interesting explanations of the children's performance. For example, the children rejected sentence (i) following a situation in which Strawberry Shortcake did eat ice cream, but not while she was outside playing. This shows that they were not simply ignoring the subordinated clauses of sentences in deciding whether to accept or reject them.

(i) When she was outside playing, Strawberry Shortcake ate ice cream.

11. McDaniel and McKee (in press) also reject the proposal that children lack the constraint on strong crossover. They attempted to investigate children's knowledge of the constraint using a comprehension methodology that, unlike the Roeper *et al.* study, confronted children with the multiple reference interpretation of crossover questions. Unfortunately, there were other problems with the task, resulting in poor performance by both children and adults.

12. The trials with singular and plural pronouns were intended to enable us to evaluate children's knowledge of accidental coreference, which can be assigned only when a plural pronoun appears in the target sentence. As it turned out, there was no difference in children's responses to singular or plural pronouns.

References to 3.4

[Ed. note: These references include both the sources cited by Crane and those cited by commentators who were responding to Crane's original *Behavioral and Brain Sciences* article.]

Aitchison, J. (1989). *The Articulate Mammal: An introduction to psycholinguistics.* Unwin Hyman.

Alcock, J. (1988). "Singing down a blind alley." *Behavioral and Brain Sciences*, **11**, 630–1

Amidon, A. and Carey, P. (1972). "Why five-year-olds cannot understand before and after." *Journal of Verbal Learning and Verbal Behavior*, **11**, 417–23.

Andersen, R. (1987). "Inferior parietal lobule function in spatial perception and visuomotor integration." In V. Mountcastle, F. Plum and S. Geiger (eds), *Handbook of Physiology*, vol. 5: *Higher functions of the brain*. American Physiological Society.

Aoki, C. and Siekevits, P. (1988). "Plasticity in brain development." *Scientific American*, **259**, 56–64.

Aram, D. and Hall, N. (1989). "Longitudinal follow-up of children with preschool communication disorders: Treatment implications." *School Psychology Review*, **18**, 487–501.

Arbib, M. A. and Hill, J. C. (1988). "Language acquisition: Schemas replace universal grammar." In J. Hawkins (ed.), *Explaining Language Universals*. Blackwell.

Astington, J., Harris, P. L., and Olson, D. (1988). *Developing Theories of Mind.* Cambridge University Press.

Baker, C. L. (1979). "Syntactic theory and the projection problem." *Linguistic Inquiry*, **10**, 533–81.

Baker, M. (1988). *Incorporation: A theory of grammatical function changing.* University of Chicago Press.

Baker, N. D. and Nelson, K. E. (1984). "Recasting and related conversational techniques for triggering syntactic advances by young children." *First Language*, **5**, 3–22.

Bates, E. A. and MacWhinney, B. (1982). "Functionalist approaches to grammar." In E. Wanner and L. R. Gleitman (eds), *Language Acquisition: The state of the art.* Cambridge University Press.

Bellugi, E., Marks, S., Bihrle, A. M., and Sabo, H. (1988). "Dissociation between language and cognitive functions in Williams Syndrome." In D. Bishop and K. Mogford (eds), *Development in Exceptional Circumstances*. Churchill Livingstone.

Bellugi, U. and Klima, E. S. (1966). "Syntactic regularities in the speech of children." In J. Lyons and R. Wales (eds), *Psycholinguistic Papers*, Edinburgh University Press.

Berman, R. A. (1985). "The place of grammar in language acquisition." Presented to 10th Annual Boston University Conference on Language Development, October.

Berman, R. A. (1986). *A Step-by-Step Model of Language Learning. Stage and structure: Re-opening the debate.* I. Levin, (ed.), Ablex.

Berman, R. A. (1987). "A developmental route: Learning about the form and use of complex nominals." *Linguistics*, **27**, 1057–85.

Berman, R. A. (1988). "On the ability to relate events in narrative." *Discourse Processes*, **11**, 469–97.

Berman, R. A. (1989). "Children's knowledge of substructure." Data from Hebrew paper given at Boston University Conference on Language and Development, Boston, MA, October.

Berman, R. A. (1990a). "The role of 'and' in developing narrative skills." Presented to International Pragmatics Conference, Barcelona, July.

Berman, R. A. (1990b). "Acquiring an (S)VO language: Subjectless sentences in children's Hebrew." *Linguistics*, **28**(4); 1135–66.

Berman, R. A. (1991). (submitted) "Marking of verb transitivity by Hebrew-speaking children." *Journal of Child Language* (orig. "Acquisition of transitivity distinctions: A confluence of cues." Manuscript submitted to Tel Aviv University).

Bernstein, B., Brandeis, B., and Henderson, D. (1969). "Speech of lowerclass children" (Letter to the editor). *Developmental Medicine and Child Neurology*, **11**, 113–16.

Berwick, R. (1985). *The Acquisition of Syntactic Knowledge.* MIT Press.

Bloom, L., Miller, P., and Hood, L. (1975). "Variation and reduction as aspects of competence in language development." In A. Pick (ed.), *The 1974 Minnesota Symposia on Child Psychiatry*, University of Minnesota Press.

Bloom, P. (1990a). "Subjectless sentences in child language." *Linguistic Inquiry*, **21**(4), 491–504.

Bloom, P. (1990b). "Syntactic distinctions in child language." *Journal of Child Language*, **17**, 343–55.

Bohannon, J. N. and Stanowicz, L. (1988). "The issue of negative evidence: Adult responses to children's language errors." *Developmental Psychology*, **24**(5), 684–9.

Bolinger, D. (1977). *Meaning and Form.* Longmans.

Borer, H. and Wexler, K. (1987). "The maturation of syntax." In T. Roeper and E. Williams (eds), *Parameter Setting*. Reidel.

Bowerman, M. (1974). "Learning the structure of causative verbs: A study in the relation of cognitive, semantic, and syntactic development." *Papers and Reports on Child Language*, **8**, Stanford University Press.

Bowerman, M. (1982). "Evaluating competing linguistic models with language acquisition data: Implications of developmental errors with causative verbs." *Quaderni di Semantica*, **3**, 5–66.

Bowerman, M. (1987). "Commentary: Mechanisms of language acquisition." In B. MacWhinney (ed.), *Mechanisms of Language Acquisition*. Erlbaum.

Bowerman, M. (1988). "The 'no negative evidence' problem: How do children avoid constructing an overly general grammar?" In J. Hawkins (ed.), *Explaining Language Universals*. Blackwell. 73–101.

Bowerman, M. (1990). "Mapping thematic roles onto syntactic functions: Are children helped by innate linking rules?" *Linguistics*, **28**, 1253–90.

Braine, M. D. S. (1971). "On two types of models of the internalization of grammars." In D. I. Slobin (ed.), *The Ontogenesis of Grammar*. New York: Academic Press.

Braine, M. D. S. (1988). "Modeling the acquisition of linguistics structure." In Y. Levy, I. M. Scheslinger, and M. D. S. Braine (eds), *Categories and Processes in Language Acquisition Theory*. Erlbaum.

Bresnan, J. (1978). *Contraction and the Transformational Cycle in English*. The Indiana University Linguistics Club.

Bresnan, J. (ed.) (1982). *The Mental Representation of Grammatical Relations*. MIT Press.

Brown, R. (1973). *A First Language: The early stages*. Harvard University Press.

Brown, R. and Hanlon, C. (1970). "Derivational complexity and the order of acquisition in child speech." In J. R. Hayes, (ed.), *Cognition and the Development of Language*. Wiley.

Bruner, J. S. (1966). "On cognitive growth, I and II." In J. S. Bruner, R. R. Olver, and P. M. Greenfield, (eds), *Studies in Cognitive Growth*. Wiley.

Bruner, J. S. (1972). "Nature and uses of immaturity." *American Psychologist*, **27**(8).

Cairns, H. S. and McDaniel, D. (forthcoming). "The notion of 'innateness' in language acquisition: Some empirical consequences." *CUNY Forum*.

Cazden, C. B. (1966). "Subcultural differences in child language: An interdisciplinary review." *Merrill–Palmer Quarterly*, **12**, 185–218.

Chance, M. R. A. and Mead, A. P. (1953). "Social behavior and primate evolution." *Symposia of the Society for Experimental Biology*. **7**, 395–439.

Changeux, J. (1980). "Genetic determinism and epigenesis of the neuronal network: Is there a biological compromise between Chomsky and Piaget?" In M. Piattelli-Palmarini (ed.), *Language and Learning: The debate between Jean Piaget and Noam Chomsky*. Harvard University Press.

Cheney, D. and Seyfarth, R. (1990). *How Monkeys see the World: Inside the mind of another species*. University of Chicago Press.

Chien, Y. C. and Wexler, K. (1990). "Children's knowledge of locality conditions in binding as evidence for the modularity of syntax and pragmatics." *Language Acquisition: A Journal of Developmental Linguistics*, **1**(3), 225–95.

Chomsky, N. (1957). *Syntactic Structures*. Mouton.

Chomsky, N. (1965). *Aspects of the Theory of Syntax*. MIT Press.

Chomsky, N. (1971). *Problems of Knowledge and Freedom*. Pantheon Books.

Chomsky, N. (1975). *Reflections on Language*. Pantheon Books.

Chomsky, N. (1976). "Conditions on rules of grammar." *Linguistic Analysis*, **2**.

Chomsky, N. (1981). *Lectures on Government and Binding*. Foris.

Chomsky, N. (1986a). *Knowledge of Language: Its nature, origin and use*. Praeger.

Chomsky, N. (1986b). *Barriers*. MIT Press.

Chomsky, N. (1991). *Lectures on Government and Binding*. Foris

Chomsky, N. and Lasnik, H. (1977). "Filters and control." *Linguistic Inquiry*, **8**, 425–504.

Clahsen, H. and Smolka, K. (1986). "Psycholinguistic evidence and the description of V-second phenomena in German." In H. Haider and M. Prinzhorn (eds), *V-2 Phenomena in Germanic Languages*. Foris Publications.

Corder, P. (1967). "The significance of learners' errors." *International Review of Applied Linguistics*, **5**, 161–70.

Cordier, J. and Lowenthal, F. (1973). "Can new maths help disturbed children?" (Letter to the editor). *The Lancet*, August, **18**, 383–84.

Cordier, J., Lowenthal, F., and Heraux, C. (1975). "Enseignement de la mathématique et exercices de verbalisation chez les enfants caractériels." *Enfance*, **1**, 111–24.

Crain, S. (1982). "Temporal terms: Mastery by age five." In *Papers and Reports on Child Language Development*. Proceedings of the 14th Annual Stanford Child Language Research Forum, Stanford University, Palo Alto, CA.

Crain S. and Fodor, J. D. (1985). "On the innateness of subjacency." In *The Proceedings of the First Eastern States Conference on Linguistics*, Ohio State University, Columbus, OH.

Crain, S. and Fodor, J. D. (in press) "Competence and performance in child language." E. Dromi (ed.). In *Language and Cognition: A developmental perspective*. Albex.

Crain, S. and McKee, C. (1985). "Acquisition of structural restrictions on anaphora." *Proceedings of NELS*, **16**, University of Massachusetts, Amherst, MA.

Crain, S., McKee, C., and Emiliani, M. (1990). "Visiting relatives in Italy." In L. Frazier and J. de Villiers (eds), *Language Processing and Language Acquisition*. Kluwer.

Crain, S. and Nakayama, M. (1987). "Structure dependence in grammar formation." *Language*, **63**, 522–43.

Crain, S., Shankweiler, D., Macaruso, P., and Bar-Shalom, E. (1989). "Repercussions of working memory limitations on sentence comprehension by poor readers." In G. Vallar and T. Shallice (eds), *Neuropsychological Impairments of Short-term Memory*. Cambridge University Press.

Crain, S. and Thornton, R. (1988). "Innateness and Wh-movement." Paper presented at the 13th Annual Boston University Conference on Language Development, Boston, MA.

Crain, S. and Thornton, R. (1990). "Levels of representation in child grammar." Paper presented at 13th GLOW Colloquium, Cambridge, England.

Crain, S. and Thornton, R. (1991). "Recharting the course of language acquisition: Studies in elicited production." In N. Krasnegor, D. Rumbaugh, R. Schiefelbusch, and M. Studdert-Kennedy (eds), *Biobehavioral Foundations of Language Development*. Erlbaum.

Crain, S., Thornton, R., and Murasugi, K. (1987). "Capturing the evasive passive." Paper presented at the 12th Annual Boston University Conference on Language Development, Boston, MA.

Cromer, R. F. (in press). "A case study of dissociation between language and cognition." In H. Tager-Flusberg (ed.), *Constraints on Language Acquisition: Studies of atypical children*.

Culicover, P. W. and W. Wilkins (1984). *Locality in Linguistic Theory*. Academic Press.

Dawkins, M. S. (1986). *Unravelling Animal Behavior*. Longman.

Dawkins, R. (1986). *The Blind Watchmaker*. Norton.

Demetras, M., Post, K., and Snow, C. (1986). "Feedback to first-language learners." *Journal of Child Language*, **13**, 275–92.

Demuth, K. (1989). "Maturation and the acquisition of Sesotho passive." *Language*, **65**(1), 56–81.

Dent, C. H. (1990). "An ecological approach to language development: An alternative functionalism." *Developmental Psychobiology*, **23**, 679–704.

de Villiers, J. (1990). "Why questions?" Paper presented at the Linguistic Association of Great Britain, Cambridge, England.

de Villiers, J. G. and de Villiers, P. A. (1986). "The acquisition of English." In D. Slobin (ed.), *The Crosslinguistic Study of Language Acquisition*, vol. 1: *The data*. Erlbaum.

de Villiers, J. and Roeper, T. (1991). "Introduction". In T. Maxfield and B. Plunkett (eds), *Proceedings of the Workshop on the Acquisition of Wh-movement*. University of Massachusetts Occasional Papers.

de Villiers, J., Roeper, T., and Vainikka, A. (1990). "The acquisition of long-distance rules." In L. Frazier and J. de Villiers (eds), *Language Processing and Language Acquisition*. Kluwer.

de Waal, F. B. M. (1989). "Dominance 'style' and primate social organization." In V. Standen and R. Foley (eds), *Comparative Socioecology: The behavioral ecology of humans and other mammals*. Blackwell.

Edmonson, W. H. (1990). "Poverty of stimulus or poverty of theory?" University of Birmingham, Cognitive Science Research Paper 90-19.

Farrar, M. (1990). "Discourse and the acquisition of grammatical morphemes." *Journal of Child Language*, **17**, 607–24.

Fodor, J. A., Bever, T., and Garrett, M. (1974). *The Psychology of Language: An introduction to psycholinguistics and generative grammar*. McGraw-Hill.

Fodor, J. D. and Crain, S. (1987). "Simplicity and generality of rules in language acquisition." In B. MacWhinney (ed.), *Mechanisms of Language Acquisition*. Erlbaum.

Fogel, A. and Thelen, E. (1987). "Development of early expressive and communicative action: Reinterpreting the evidence from a dynamic systems perspective." *Developmental Psychology*, **23**, 747–61.

Frazier, L. and de Villiers, J. (eds.) (1990). *Language Processing and Language Acquisition*. Kluwer.

Freidin, R. (1978). "Cyclicity and the theory of grammar." *Linguistic Inquiry*, **9**(4), 519–49.

Freidin, R. and Lasnik, H. (1981). "Disjoint reference and Wh-trace." *Linguistic Inquiry*, **12**, 39–53.

Gallistel, R. (1990). *The Organization of Learning*. Bradford Books.

Garner, W. R. (1974). *The Processing of Information and Structure*. Erlbaum.

Gazdar, G. (1982). "Phase structure grammar." In P. Jacobson and G. Pullum (eds), *The Nature of Syntactic Representation*. Reidel.

Gazdar, G., Klein, E., Pullum. G., and Sag, I. (1985). *Generalized Phrase Structure Grammar*. Harvard University Press.

Gelman, R. (ed). (1990a). Special issue of *Cognitive Science*, **14**.

Gelman, R. (1990b). "Structural constraints on cognitive development: Introduction to a special issue of *Cognitive Science*." *Cognitive Science*, **14**, 3–9.

Givon, T. (1979). *On Understanding Grammar*. Academic Press.

Givon, T. (1984). *Syntax: A functional-typological introduction*, vol. 1. J. Benjamins.

Givon, T. (1989). *Mind, Code and Context: Essays in pragmatics*. Erlbaum.

Gold, E. (1967). "Language identification in the limit." *Information and Control*, **16**, 447–74.

Goldin-Meadow, S. (1982). "The resilience of recursion: A study of a communicative system developed without a conventional language model." In E. Wanner and L. R. Gleitman (eds), *Language Acquisition: The state of the art*. Cambridge University Press.

Goldin-Meadow, S. (1987). "Underlying redundancy and its reduction in a language developed without a language model: The importance of conventional linguistic input." In B. Lust (ed.), *Studies in the Acquisition of Anaphora: Applying the constraints*. vol. 2. Reidel.

Goldin-Meadow, S. and Mylander, C. (1984). "Gestural communication in deaf children: The effects and non-effects of parental input on early language development." *Monographs of the Society for Research in Child Development*, **49**, 1–121.

Goldin-Meadow S. and Mylander, C. (1990a). "Beyond the input given: The child's role in the acquisition of language." *Language*, **66**, 323–55.

Goldin-Meadow S. and Mylander, C. (1990b). "The role of parental input in the development of a morphological system." *Journal of Child Language*, **17**, 527–63.

Goodluck, H. (1981). "Children's grammar of complement subject interpretation." In S. Tavakolian (ed.), *Language Acquisition and Linguistic Theory*. MIT Press.

Goodluck, H. (1989). "When grammar wins over sense: Children's judgments of extraposed relative clauses." *Journal of Psycholinguistic Research*, **18**, 389–416.

Goodluck, H. (1990). "Knowledge integration in processing and acquisition: Comments on Grimshaw and Rosen." In L. Frazier and J. de Villers (eds), *Language Processing and Language Acquisition*. Kluwer.

Goodluck, H., Foley, M., and Sedivy, J. (1990). "Adjunct islands and acquisition." In H. Goodluck and M. Rochemont (eds), *Island Constraints: Theory, acquisition and processing*. Kluwer (in press).

Goodluck, H. and Tavakolian, S. (1982). "Competence and processing in children's grammar of relative clauses." *Cognition*, **11**, 1–27.

Gorrell, P., Crain, S., and Fodor, J. D. (1989). "Contextual information and temporal terms." *Journal of Child Language*, **16**, 623–32.

Gottlieb, G. (1976). "Early development of species-specific auditory perception in birds." In G. Gottlieb (ed.), *Neural and Behavioral Specificity*. Macmillan.

Gottlieb, G. (1991a). "Experiential canalization of behavioral development: Theory." *Developmental Psychology*, **27**, 4–13.

Gottlieb, G. (1991b). "Experiential canalization of behavioral development: Results." *Developmental Psychology*, **27**, 35–39.

Grimshaw, J. and Pinker, S. (1988). "Positive and negative evidence in language acquisition." *Behavioral and Brain Sciences*, **12**, 341.

Grimshaw, J. and Rosen S. T. (1990). "Knowledge and obedience: The development status of the Binding Theory." *Linguistic Inquiry*, **21**(2), 187–223.

Guilfoyle, E. and Noonan, M. (1988). "Functional categories and language acquisition." Paper presented at the Boston University Conference on Language Acquisition.
Haiman, J. (ed.) (1985a). *Iconicity in Syntax*. John Benjamins.
Haiman, J. ed. (1985b). *Natural Syntax: Iconicity and erosion*. Cambridge University Press.
Halliday, M. (1975). *Learning How to Mean: Explorations in the development of language*. Edward Arnold.
Hamburger, H. and Crain, S. (1982). "Relative acquisition." In S. Kuczaj (ed.), *Language Development*, vol. I. Erlbaum.
Hamburger, H. and Crain, S. (1984). "Acquisition of cognitive compiling." *Cognition*, **17**, 85–136.
Hammouda, S. (1988). "Learnability issues in the acquisition of the dative alternation in English." Unpublished Ph.D. dissertation, University of Connecticut.
Harnad, S. (1987). *Categorical Perception: The groundwork of cognition*. Cambridge University Press.
Harris, C. L. and Bates, E. A. (1990). "Functional constraints on backwards pronominal reference." *Proceedings of the Twelfth Annual Meeting of the Cognitive Science Society*. Erlbaum.
Harris, C. L. and Bates, E. A. (1991). "Correlations between form and function in cases of allowed and prohibited pronominal reference." Unpublished mansucript.
Hawkins, J. (1983). *Word Order Universals*. Academic Press.
Hecht, B. F. (1985). "Situations and language: Children's use of plural allomorphs in familiar and unfamiliar settings." Doctoral dissertation, Stanford University.
High, C., DiPaolo, M., and Dodd, D. (unpublished). "The development of relativization in English."
Hirsh-Pasek, K., Golinkoff, R., Braidi, S., and McNally, L. (1986). "'Daddy Throw': On the existence of implicit negative evidence for subcategorization errors." Paper presented at the Boston University Conference on Child Language Development.
Hirsh-Pasek, K., Treiman, R., and Schneiderman, M. (1984). "Brown and Hanlon revisited: Mother's sensitivity to ungrammatical forms." *Journal of Child Language*, **11**, 81–8.
Hoekstra, T. and Mulder, R. (1990). "Unergatives as copular verbs: Locational and extensional predication." *The Linguistic Review*, **7**(1).
Hoji, H. (forthcoming). "Theories of anaphora and aspects of Japanese syntax." MIT Press.
Hopper, P. J. (1979). "Aspect and foregrounding in discourse." In T. Givon (ed.), *Discourse and Syntax: Syntax and semantics*, vol. 12. Academic Press.
Hopper, P. J. (1982). *Tense-Aspects: Between semantics and pragmatics*. John Benjamins.
Hopper, P. and Thomson, S. (1980). "Transitivity in grammar and discourse." *Language*, **56**, 251–99.
Hornstein, N. and Lightfoot, D. (1981). "Introduction." In N. Hornstein and D. Lightfoot (eds), *Explanation in Linguistics: The logical problem of language acquisition*. Longman.
Hyams, N. (1986). *Language Acquisition and the Theory of Parameters*. Reidel.
Hyams, N. (1989). "The null subject parameter in language acquisition." In O. Jaeggli and K. J. Safir (eds), *The Null Subject Parameter*. Kluwer.
Hyams, N. and Sigurjonsdottir, S. (1990). "The development of 'long-distance anaphora': A cross-linguistic comparison with special reference to Icelandic". *Language Acquisition*, **1**(1), 57–95.
Hyams, N. and Wexler, K. (1991). "On the grammatical basis of null subjects in child language." (unpublished manuscript).
Inkelas, S. and Zec, D. (1990). "Auxiliary reduction without empty categories: A prosodic account." (unpublished manuscript).
Jackendoff, R. (1983). *Semantics and Cognition*. MIT Press.
Johnson, J. I., Hamilton, T. C., Hsung, J. C., and Ulinski, P. S. (1972). "Gracile nucleus absent in adult opossums after leg removal in infancy." *Brain Research*, **38**, 421–4.
Johnston, J. (1988). "Specific language disorders in the child." In N. Lass, L. McReynolds, J. Northern, and D. Yoder (eds), *Handbook of Speech-language Pathology and Audiology*. B. C. Decker.
Johnston, T. D. (1988). "Developmental explanation and the ontogeny of birdsong: Nature/nurture redux." *Behavioral and Brain Sciences*, **11**, 617–63.
Jusczyk, P. W. and Bertoncini, J. (1988). "Viewing the development of speech perception as an innately guided learning process." *Language and Speech*, **31**, 217–38.
Kaisse, E. (1983). "The syntax of auxiliary reduction in English." *Language*, **59**, 93–122.
Karmiloff-Smith, A. (1979). *A Functional Approach to Language Acquisition*. Cambridge University Press.
Karmiloff-Smith, A. (1986a). "From meta-processes to conscious access: Evidence from children's metalinguistic and repair data." *Cognition*, **23**, 95–147.

Karmiloff-Smith, A. (1986b). "Stage/structure versus phase/process in modelling linguistic and cognitive development." In I. Levin (ed.), *Stage and Structure: Re-opening the debate*. Ablex.

Karmiloff-Smith, A. (1990). "Piaget and Chomsky on language acquisition: Divorce or marriage?" *First Language*, **10**, 255–61.

Karmiloff-Smith, A. (1991). "Beyond modularity: Innate constraints and developmental change." In S. Carey and R. Gelman (eds), *Epigenesis of the Mind: Essays in biology and knowledge*. Erlbaum.

Keenan, E. (1985). "Passive in the world's languages." In T. Shopen (ed.), *Language Typology and Syntactic Description*, vol. I., Cambridge University Press.

Keil, F. (1990). "Constraints on constraints: Surveying the epigenetic landscape." *Cognitive Science*, **14**(1):135–69.

Kitagawa, Y. (1986). "Subjects in Japanese and English." Doctoral dissertation, University of Massachusetts.

Klima, E. and Bellugi, U. (1966). "Syntactic regularities in the speech of children." In J. Lyons and R. Wales (eds), *Psycholinguistic Papers*. Edinburgh University Press.

Koopman, H. and Sportiche, D. (1990). "Subjects." *Lingua*, (in press).

Koster, J. (1978). *Locality Principles in Syntax*. Foris.

Koster, J. (1987). *Domains and Dynasties: The radical autonomy of syntax*. Foris.

Kucjaz, S. A. and Brannick, N. (1979). "Children's use of the Wh: Question modal auxiliary placement rule." *Journal of Experimental Psychology*, **28**, 43–67.

Kummer, H. (1974). "Rules of dyad and group formation among captive gelada baboons (*Theropithecus gelada*)." Symposium, 5th Congress of the International Primatology Society.

Kuroda, Y. (1988). "Whether we agree or not: A comparative syntax of English and Japanese." In W. Poser (ed.), *Papers on the Second International Workshop on Japanese Syntax*. Center for the Study of Language and Information. Stanford University.

Labelle, M. (1989). "Predication et mouvement: L'acquisition de la relative chez les enfants francophones." Ph.D. dissertation, University of Ottawa.

Labov, W. and Labov, T. (1978). "Learning the syntax of questions." In R. Campbell and P. Smith (eds), *Recent Advances in the Psychology of Language: Formal and experimental approaches*. Plenum.

Landercy, A. and Renard, R. (1977). *Eléments de phonétique*. Didier.

Langacker, R. W. (1969). "On pronominalization and the chain of command." In W. Reibel and S. Schane (eds), *Modern Studies in English*. Prentice Hall.

Langacker, R. W. (1986). *Foundations of Cognitive Grammar*, vol. 1. Standford University Press.

Langer, J. (1980). *The Origin of Logic: Six to twelve months*. Academic Press.

Langer, J. (1986). *The Origin of Logic: One to two years*. Academic Press.

Langer, J. (1990). "Early cognitive development: Basic functions." In C.-A. Hauert (ed.), *Developmental Psychology: Cognitive, perceptuo-motor, and neuropsychological perspectives*. Elsevier.

Lasnik, H. (1976). "Remarks on coreference." *Linguistic Analysis*, **2**, 1–22.

Lasnik, H. (1989). *Essays on Anaphora*. Reidel.

Lasnik, H. and Crain, S. (1985). "On the acquisition of pronominal reference." *Lingua*, **65**, 135–54.

Lasnik, H. and Kupin, J. (1976). "A restrictive theory of transformational grammar." *Theoretical Linguistics*, **4**, 173–96. (Reprinted in H. Lasnik, *Essays on Restrictiveness and Learnability*. Kluwer.)

Lebeaux, D. (1987). "Comments on Hyams." In T. Roeper and E. Williams (eds), *Parameter Setting*. Reidel.

Lebeaux, D. (1988). "Language acquisition and the form of the grammar." Doctoral dissertation, University of Massachusetts.

Lee, M. (1988). "Language, perception and the world." In J. Hawkins (ed.), *Explaining Language Universals*. Blackwell.

Lehrman, D. S. (1979). "Semantic and conceptual issues in the nature-nurture problem." In L. R. Aronson, E. Tobach, D. S. Lehrman, and J. S. Rosenblatt (eds), *Development and Evolution of Behavior*. Freeman.

Leonard, L. (1979). "Language impairment in children." *Merrill–Palmer Quarterly*, **25**, 205–32.

Leonard, L. (1989). "Language learnability and specific language impairment in children." *Applied Psycholinguistics*, **10**, 179–202.

Levy, Y. and Schlesinger, I. M. (1988). "The child's early categories: Approaches to language acquisition theory." In Y. Levy, I. M. Schlesinger and M. D. S. Braine (eds), *Categories and Processes in Language Acquisition Theory*. Erlbaum.

Lightbown, P. (1978). "Consistency and variation in the acquisition of French." Doctoral dissertation, Columbia University.

Lowenthal, F. (1972). "Enseignement de la mathématique à 2 groupes d'enfants caractériels." *NICO*, **10**, 33–44.

Lowenthal, F. (1973). "La mathématique peut-elle être une thérapeutique?" *NICO*, **13**, 98–104.

Lowenthal, F. (1982). "Example of auxiliary formalisms used to help the development of children's logical thinking." In F. Lowenthal, F. Vandamme, and J. Cordier (eds), *Language and Language Acquisition*. Plenum Press.

Lowenthal, F. (1985). "Non-verbal communication devices in language acqusition." *Revue de Phonétique Appliquée*, **73/74/75/**, 155–66.

Lowenthal, F. (1987). "Représentation concrète de systèmes formels et structuration d'une communication." *Revue de Phonétique Appliquée*, **82/83/84**, 231–45.

Lowenthal, F. and Saerens, J. (1982). "Utilisation de formalismes logiques pour l'examen d'enfants aphasiques." *Acta Neurological Belgica*, **8**, 215–23..

Lowenthal, F. and Saerens, J. (1986). "Evolution of an aphasic child after the introduction of NVCDs." In F. Lowenthal and F. Vandamme (eds), *Pragmatics and Education*. Plenum Press.

McCawley, J. D. (1984). "Anaphora and notions of command." Proceedings of the 10th Annual Meeting of the Berkeley Linguistics Society.

McCawley, J. D. (1988). "Review of Chomsky. *Knowledge of Language*." *Language*, **64**, 355–65.

McClintock, M. K. (1980). "Innate behavior is not innate." *Signs*, **4**, 703–10.

McDaniel, D. (1987). "Partial and multiple Wh-movement." *Natural Language and Linguistic Theory*, **7**, 565–604.

McDaniel, D., Cairns, H. S. and Hsu, J. R. (1990). "Binding principles in the grammars of young children." *Language Acquisition*, **1**(1), 121–38.

McDaniel, D. and McKee, C. (in press). "Which children did they show obey strong crossover?" In H. Goodluck and M. Rochemont (eds), *The Psycholinguistics of Island Constraints*. Kluwer.

McNeill, D. (1966). "Developmental psycholinguistics." In F. Smith and G. A. Miller (eds), *The Genesis of Language*. MIT Press.

McNeill, D. (1987). *Psycholinguistics*. Harper & Row.

MacWhinney, B. (1987). "The competition model." In B. MacWhinney (ed.), *Mechanisms of Language Acquisition*. Erlbaum.

MacWhinney, B. and Bates, E. (1990). *Crosslinguistic Studies of Sentence Processing*. Cambridge University Press.

MacWhinney, B., Leinbach, J., Taraban, R., and McDonald, J. (1989). "Language learning: Cues or rules." *Journal of Memory and Language*, **28**(3), 255–77.

MacWhinney, B. and Snow, C. (1985). "The child language data exchange system." *Journal of Child Language*, **12**, 271–96.

Markman, E. M. (1989). *Categorization and Naming in Children: Problems of induction*. Bradford Books/MIT Press.

Marler, P. (1970). "A comparative approach to vocal learning: Song development in white-crowned sparrows." *Journal of Comparative Physiological Psychology*, **71**, 1–25.

Marshall, J. C. (1984). "Multiple perspectives on modularity." *Cognition*, **17**, 209–42.

Matthei, E. M. (1981). "Children's interpretation of sentences containing reciprocals." In S. Tavakolian (ed.), *Language Acquisition and Linguistic Theory*. MIT Press.

Matthei, E. M. (1982). "The acquisition of prenominal modifier sequences." *Cognition*, **11**, 201–332.

Matthei, E. M. and Roeper, T. (1974). "On the acquisition of some and every." *Stanford Papers in Language Acquisition*.

Maxfield, T. and Plunkett, B. (1991). "Proceedings of the University of Massachusetts Conference on the Acquisition of Wh-Movement." University of Massachusetts GLSA.

Mayr, E. (1974). "Behavioral programs and evolutionary strategies." *American Scientist*, **52**, 650–69.

Mazurkiewicz, I. and White, L. (1984). "The acquisition of the dative alternation: Unlearning overgeneralizations." *Cognition*, **16**, 261–83.

Mehler, J., Jusczyk, P., Lambertz, G., Halsted, N., Bertoncini, J., and Amiel-Tison, C. (1988). "A precursor of language acquisition in young infants." *Cognition*, **29**, 143–78.

Meisel, J. and Muller, N. (1990). "On the position of finiteness in early child grammar: Evidence from simultaneous acquisition of two first languages, French and German." Paper presented at the Boston University Conference on Language Development, October.

Miller, G. A. (1956). "The magical number seven, plus or minus two: Some limits on our capacity for processing information." *Psychological Review*, **63**, 81–97.

Moreau, M.-L. and Richelle, M. (198•) *L'Acquisition du Language*. Mardaga.

Morehead, D. M. and Ingram, D. (1976). "The development of base syntax in normal and linguistically deviant children." In D. M. Morehead and A. E. Morehead (eds), *Normal and Deficient Child Language*. University Park Press.

Morgan, J. L. and Travis, L. L. (1989). "Limits on negative information in language input." *Journal of Child Language*, **16**, 531–52.

Mundinger, P. (1988). "Conceptual errors, different perspectives, and genetic analysis of song ontogeny." *Behavioral and Brain Sciences*, **11**, 643–44.

Nakayama, M. (1987). "Performance factors in Subject-Aux inversion by children." *Journal of Child Language*, **14**.

Nelson, K. (1977). "Facilitating children's syntax acquisition." *Developmental Psychology*, **13**(2), 101–7.

Nelson, K. E., Carskaddon, G., and Bonvillian, J. D. (1973). "Syntax acquisition: Impact of experimental variation in adult verbal interaction with the child." *Child Development*, **44**, 497–504.

Nelson, K. E., Denninger, M. S., Bonvillian, J. D., Kaplan, B. J., and Baker, N. D. (1984). "Maternal input adjustments and non-adjustments as related to children's linguistic advances and to language acquisition theories." In A. D. Pellegrini and T. D. Yawkey (eds), *The Development of Oral and Written Language in Social Contexts*. Ablex.

Newmeyer, F. (1986). *Linguistic Theory in America*. Academic Press.

Newport, E. L. (1990). "Maturational constraints on language learning." *Cognitive Science*, **14**, 11–28.

Newport, E. L., Gleitman, H., and Gleitman, L. (1977). Mother, I'd Rather Do it Myself: Some effects and non-effects of maternal speech style. In C. E. Snow and C. A. Ferguson (eds), *Talking to Children: Language input and acquisition*. Cambridge University Press.

Otsu, Y. (1981). "Universal grammar and syntactic development in children: Toward a theory of syntactic development." Unpublished Ph.D. dissertation. Massachusetts Institute of Technology.

Oyama, S. (1990). "The idea of innateness: Effects on language and communication research." *Developmental Psychobiology*, **23**, 741–50.

Perner, J. (1991). *Understanding the Representational Mind*. MIT Press.

Petitto, L. A. (1987). "On the autonomy of language and gesture: Evidence from the acquisition of personal pronouns in American Sign Language." *Cognition*, **27**, 1–52.

Philips, W. and Takahashi, M. (1991). "Acquisition of quantifiers." In B. Plunkett and T. Maxfield (eds), *UMOP Proceedings of the Conference on Acquisition of Wh-Movement*.

Phinney, M. (ed.) (1981). "Syntactic constraints and the acquisition of embedded sentences." Unpublished Ph.D. dissertation, University of Massachusetts, Amherst.

Piaget, J. and Inhelder, B. (1959) *La genèse des structures logiques élémentaires—Classifications et sériations*. Delachaux et Niestlé.

Piattelli-Palmarini, M. (1979). *Language and Learning: The debate between Jean Piaget and Noam Chomsky*. Routledge and Kegan Paul.

Piattelli-Palmarini, M. (1980). *Language and Learning: The debate between Jean Piaget and Noam Chomsky*. Harvard University Press.

Pierce, A. (1989). "On the emergence of syntax: A crosslinguistic study." Doctoral dissertation, Massachusetts Institute of Technology.

Pike, K. L. (1954). *Language in Relation to a Unified Theory of the Structure of Human Behavior*. Mouton.

Pike, K. L. and Pike, E. G. (1977). *Grammatical Analysis*. Summer Institute of Linguistics and University of Texas at Arlington, Dallas, TX.

Pinker, S. (1984). *Language Learnability and Language Development*. Harvard University Press.

Pinker, S. (1989). *Learnability and Cognition: The acquisition of argument structure*. MIT Press.

Pinker, S. (1990a). *Learnability and Cognition: The acquisition of argument structure*. MIT Press.

Pinker, S. (1990b). "Language acquisition." In D. Otherson and H. Lasnik (eds), *An Invitation to Cognitive Science*, vol. 1, MIT Press.

Pinker, S. and Bloom, P. (1990). "Natural language and natural selection." *Behavioral and Brain Sciences*, **13**, 707–84.

Pinker, S., Lebeaux, D., and Frost, L. (1987). "Productivity and constraints in the acquisition of the passive." *Cognition*, **26**, 195–267.

Plunkett, K. and Marchman, V. (in press) "U-shaped learning and frequency effects in a multi-layered perceptron: Implications for child language acquisition." *Cognition*.

Poizner, H., Klima, E. S., and Bellugi, U. (1987). *What the Hands Reveal about the Brain*. MIT Press.

Pollard, C. and Sag. I. (1987). "Information-based syntax and semantics, vol. 1: *Fundamentals*." CSLI Lecture Notes, Stanford University.

Postal, P. (1971). *Cross-over Phenomena*. Holt, Rinehart and Winston.

Powers, D. M. W. (1983). "Neurolinguistics and psycholinguistics as a basis for computer acquisition of natural language." *SIGART*, **84**, 29–34.

Powers, D. M. W. (1991). "How far can self-organization go? Results in unsupervised language learning." AAAI Spring Symposium on Machine Learning of Natural Language and Ontology, Stanford, CA, March.

Powers, D. M. W. and Turk, C. (1989). *Machine Learning of Natural Language*. Springer-Verlag.

Pullum, G. and Postal, P. (1982). "The contraction debate." *Linguistic Inquiry*, **13**, 122–38.

Pye, C. and Poz, P. (1988). "Precocious passives (and antipassives) in Quiché Mayan." *Papers and Reports on Child Language Development*, **27**, 71–80.

Radford, A. (1990). *Syntactic Theory and the Acquisition of English Syntax*. Blackwell.

Randall, J. (1987). *Indirect Positive Evidence: Overturning generalizations in language acquisition*. Indiana Linguistics Club.

Read, C. (1975). "Children's categorization of speech sounds in English (NCTE Report No. 17)." National Council of Teachers of English. Urbana, IL.

Reinhart, T. (1976) "The syntactic domain of anaphora." Ph.D. dissertation, Massachusetts Institute of Technology.

Reinhart, T. (1981). "Definite NP anaphora and c-command domains." *Linguistic Inquiry*, **12**(4), 605–35.

Reinhart, T. (1983a). *Anaphora and Semantic Interpretation*. Croom Helm.

Reinhart, T. (1983b). "Coreference and bound anaphora: A restatement of the anaphora questions." *Linguistics and Philosophy*, **6**, 47–88.

Rice, M. (1991). "Children with specific language impairment: Toward a model of teachability." In N. Krasnegor, M. Studdert-Kennedy, and R. Schiefelbusch (eds), *Biobehavioral Foundations of Language Development*. Erlbaum.

Rizzi, L. (1982). *Issues in Italian Syntax*. Foris.

Rizzi, L. (1990). *Relativized Minimality*. MIT Press.

Roeper, T. W. (1972). "Approaches to a theory of language acquisition with examples from German children." Unpublished Ph.D. dissertation, Harvard University.

Roeper, T. W. (1986). "How children acquire bound variables." In B. Lust (ed.), *Studies in the Acquisition of Anaphora*, Vol. 1. Reidel.

Roeper, T. and de Villiers, J. G. (1991). "Ordered decisions in the acquisition of Wh-movement." In H. Goodluck, J. Weissenborn, and T. Roeper (eds), *Theoretical Issues in Language Acquisition*. Erlbaum.

Roeper, T., Rooth, M., Mallis, T., and Akiyama, S. (1985). "The problem of empty categories and bound variables in language acquisitions." Unpublished manuscript, University of Massachusetts, Amherst.

Rondal, J.-A. (1983). *L'Interaction Adulte-enfant et la Construction du Langage*. Mardaga.

Ross, J. (1967). "Constraints on variables in syntax." Unpublished Ph.D. dissertation, Massachusetts Institute of Technology.

Ross, J. (1969). "On the cyclic nature of English pronominalization." In D. A. Reibel and S. A. Schance (eds), *Modern Studies in English*. Prentice-Hall.

Rumelhart, D. and McClelland, J. (1986). "On learning the past tense of English verbs." In J. L. McClelland and D. E. Rumelhart (eds), *Parallel-distributed Processing: Explorations in the microstructure of cognition*. MIT Press.

Rumelhart, D. and McClelland, J. (1987). "Learning the past tenses of English verbs: Implicit rules on parallel distributed processing." In B. MacWhinney (ed.), *Mechanisms of Language Acquisition*. Erlbaum.

Schlesinger, I. M. (1982). *Steps to Language: Toward a theory of language acquisition*. Erlbaum.

Sereno, M. (in press). "Four analogies between biological and culture/linguistic evolution." *Journal of Theoretical Biology*.

Shallice, T. (1988). *From Neuropsychology to Mental Structure*. Cambridge University Press.

Shatz, M. (1982). "On mechanisms of language acquisition: Can features of the communicative environment account for development?" In E. Wanner and L. R. Gleitman (eds), *Language Acquisition: The state of the art*. Cambridge University Press.

Siegel, L. S. (1978). "The relationship of language and thought in the preoperational child: A reconsideration of nonverbal alternatives to Piagetian tasks." In L. S. Siegel and C. J. Brainerd (eds), *Alternatives to Piaget—Critical Essays on the Theory*. Academic Press.

Siegel, L. S. (1982). "The discrepancy between cognitive and linguistic abilities in the young child." In F. Lowenthal, R. Vandamme, and J. Cordier (eds), *Language and Language Acquisition*. Plenum Press.

Simon, H. (1962). "The architecture of complexity." *Proceedings of the American Philosophical Society*, **106**(6), 467–82.

Sinclair, H. (1971). "Sensori-motor action patterns as the condition for the acquisition of syntax." In R. Huxley and E. Ingrams (eds), *Language Acquisition: Models and methods*. Academic Press.

Sinclair, H. (1987). "Language: A gift of nature or a home-made tool?" In S. Modgil and C. Modgil (eds), *Noam Chomsky: Consensus and controversy*. Falmer Press.

Singleton, J. L. (1987). "When learners surpass their models: The acquisition of American Sign Language from impoverished input." Unpublished master's thesis, University of Illinois, Champaign-Urbana.

Singleton, J. L. (1989). "Restructuring of language from impoverished input: Evidence for linguistic compensation." Unpublished doctoral dissertation, University of Illinois, Champaign-Urbana.

Singleton, J. L. and Newport, E. L. (1987). "When learners surpass their models: The acquisition of American Sign Language from impoverished input." Paper presented at the Society for Research in Child Development, Baltimore, MD.

Slobin, D. I. (1988). "Confessions of a wayward Chomskyan." *Papers and Reports on Child Language Development*, **27**, 131–36.

Smyth, R. (1985). *Cognitive Aspects of Anaphora Judgment and Resolution*. Indiana University Linguistics Club.

Snow, C. (1989). "Understanding social interaction and language acquisition: Sentences are not enough." In M. H. Bornstein and J. S. Bruner (eds), *Interaction in Human Development*. Erlbaum.

Sokolov, J. L. (1988). "Cue validity in Hebrew sentence comprehension." *Journal of Child Language*, **15**, 129–55.

Sokolov, J. L. (1991). "A reverse analysis of implicit negative feedback: Expanded, reduced, and exact parental responses." Paper presented at the Biannual meeting of the Society for Research in Child Development, Seattle, WA.

Solan, L. (1983). *Pronominal Reference: Child language and the theory of grammar*. Reidel.

Solan, L. and Roeper, T. W. (1978). "Children's use of syntactic structure in interpreting relative clauses." In H. Goodluck and L. Solan (eds), *Papers in the Structure and Development of Child Language*. University of Massachusetts Occasional Papers in Linguistics, vol. 4.

Spelke, E. (1990). "Principles of object perception." *Cognitive Science*, **14**, 29–56.

Sportiche, D. (1985). "Remarks on crossover." *Linguistic Inquiry*, **16**(3).

Stemmer, N. (1981). "A note on empiricism and structure dependence." *Journal of Child Language*, **8**, 649–63.

Studdert-Kennedy, M. (1990). "Language development from an evolutionary perspective." Haskins Laboratories Status Report on Speech Research. SR-101, 14–27.

Studdert-Kennedy, M. (forthcoming). In R. Hoffman and D. Palermo (eds), *Cognition and the Symbolic Processes*. Erlbaum.

Takashashi, M. (1991). "The acquisition of echo questions." In T. Maxfield and B. Plunkett (eds), *Proceedings of the Workshop on the Acquisition of Wh-movement*. University of Massachusetts Occasional Papers.

Tallal, P. (1988). "Developmental language disorders." In J. Kavanaugh and T. Truss (eds), *Learning Disabilities: Proceedings of the national conference*. York Press.

Tanenhaus, M., Carlson, G., and Seidenberg, M. (1985). "Do listeners compute representations?" In D. R. Dowty, L. Karttunen, and A. M. Zwicky (eds), *Natural Language Parsing*. Cambridge University Press.

Tavakolian, S. (1978). "Children's comprehension of pronominal subjects and missing subjects in complicated sentences." In H. Goodluck and L. Solan (eds), *Papers in the Structure and Development of Child Language*. University of Massachusetts Occasional Papers in Linguistics, vol. 4.

Tavakolian, S. (1981). "The conjoined-clause analysis of relative clauses." In S. Tavakolian (ed.), *Language Acquisition and Linguistic Theory*. MIT Press.

Tew, B. (1979). "The 'cocktail party syndrome' in children with hydrocephalus and spina bifida." *British Journal of Disorders of Communication*, **14**, 89–101.

Thal, D., Bates, E., and Bellugi, E. (1989). "Language and cognition in two children with Williams Syndrome." *Journal of Speech and Hearing Research*, **32**, 489–500.

Thornton, R. (1990). "Adventures in long-distance moving: The acquisition of complex Wh-questions." Unpublished Ph.D. dissertation, University of Connecticut.

Thornton, R. (1991). "Successful cyclic movement." Presentation of the 14th GLOW Colloquium Workshop on Acquisition of Syntax, Leiden, The Netherlands.

Travis, L. (1984). "Parameters and effects of word order variation." Unpublished Ph.D. dissertation, Massachusetts Institute of Technology.

Udwin, O., Yule, W., and Martin, N. (1987). "Cognitive abilities and behavioral characteristics of children with idiopathic infantile hypercalcaemia." *Journal of Child Psychology and Psychiatry*, **28**, 297–309.

Waddington, C. H. (1957). *The Strategy of the Genes*. Allen and Unwin.

Warren-Leubecker, A., Bohannon, J., Stanowicz, L., and Ness, J. (1986). "New evidence about negative evidence." Paper presented at the Teachability of Language Conference, Kansas City, MO.

Wasow, T. (1972). "Anaphoric relations in English." Unpublished Ph.D. dissertation, Massachusetts Institute of Technology.

Weinberg, A. (1990). "Markedness vs. maturation: The case of subject-auxiliary inversion." *Language Acquisition*, **1**(2), 165–94.

Weiner, P. (1985). "The value of follow-up studies." *Topics in Language Disorders*, **5**, 78–92.

Weissenborn, J. (1990). "Functional categories and verb movement in early German." Paper presented at the 5th International Congress for the Study of Child Language, Budapest, Hungary, July 15–21.

Wellman, H. M. and Somerville, S. C. (1980). "Quasi-naturalistic tasks in the study of cognition: The memory-related skills of toddlers." In M. Perlmutter (ed.), *Children's Memory*. Jossey-Bass.

Werker, J. F. (1989). "Becoming a native listener." *American Scientist*, **77**, 54–59.

Wexler, K. (1979). Presentation at the Workshop on Learnability, Laguna Beach, CA. June 4–8.

Wexler, K. and Chien, Y.-C. (1985). "The development of lexical anaphors and pronouns." *Papers and Reports on Child Language Development*, **24**, 138–49. Stanford University Press.

Wexler, K. and Culicover, P. (1980). *Formal Principles of Language Acquisition*. MIT Press.

Wexler, K. and Manzini, R. (1987). "Parameters and learnability in binding theory." In T. Roeper and E. Williams (eds), *Parameter Setting*. Reidel.

Wilson, B. and Peters, A. M. (1984). "What are you cookin' on a hot? A blind child's 'violation' of universal constraints." Paper presented at the 9th Boston University Conference on Language Development, Boston, MA.

Wimsatt, W. C. (1986). "Developmental constraints, generative entrenchment and the innate-acquired distinction." In W. Bechtel (ed.), *Integrating Scientific Disciplines*. Martinus Nijhoff.

Zaidel, D. (1986). "Memory for scenes in stroke patients: Hemisphere processing of semantic organization in pictures." *Brain*, **109**, 547–60.

3.5

Language Growth with Experience without Feedback

Richard F. Cromer

One of the major difficulties in developmental psycholinguistics is to go beyond mere descriptions of child language behavior and to develop theories of language change and language growth. One trend in observational research has been to study closely caretaker—child interactions and to attempt to account for the acquisition of particular language features in terms of input (see, e.g., papers in Snow and Ferguson, 1977). In the more sophisticated accounts, the child is viewed as an active, hypothesis-testing individual who relies for language change on the confirmation or disconfirmation of particular hypotheses. In such theories the force for change is seen as being due to feedback. This feedback can be thought of either as being highly specific, with the child noting discrepancies between its own grammar and the language being produced by others (also cf. learnability theory approaches, e.g., Pinker, 1984), or merely as a generalized failure to communicate or comprehend, thereby necessitating changes in the grammar in less directly specified ways. It may be, however, that some aspects of language acquisition occur in a different way than previous input studies have assumed. Perhaps the child merely needs experience of particular language forms for internal organizational processess to operate. In addition, if one views language as a highly interrelated set of structures and assumes a motivation within the child to acquire that highly structured system (Karmiloff-Smith, 1979; Slobin, 1982), then changes in one part of the grammatical system may trigger changes in other parts of the system. Thus, it may be that changes in the child's grammatical system may occur for reasons other than the noting of particular grammatical discrepancies or to the failure to communicate or comprehend. It may be instead (or in addition to other acquisition processes) that experience stimulates language organizational processes and that these affect other linguistic structures that are internally related.

The following study consisted of an experimental task on a difficult linguistic structure administered longitudinally to children over the course of a year. The purpose was to give the child repeated experience of this structure but with no feedback of having performed correctly or incorrectly in its interpretation. Results were compared with those obtained cross-sectionally to examine whether this experience affected the age at which comprehension of this linguistic structure was attained. The linguistic structure of which comprehension was investigated was that rendered by the contrast pair "John is eager/easy to please." Hand puppets of the heads of a wolf and a duck were employed. The child's task was to show which animal did the biting for a series of sentences, such as "The wolf is glad to bite" versus "The wolf is fun to bite." Earlier studies (e.g., Cromer, 1970) had shown that at about 6 years of age children become aware that the nonnamed animal in such sentences can be the actor, but they have not yet learned which adjectives (such as *glad* and *fun*) require the recovery of which underlying structure. Thus, in performing on a series of sentences of this type, they sometimes show the named animal and sometimes the nonnamed animal as the actor, but their interpretations do not consistently match adult interpretations. Cross-sectional studies (e.g., Cromer, 1972) had shown that correct adult performance was not achieved by a majority of children until after 10 or 11 years of age. The purpose of the present study was to trace for one year the acquisition of adult competence on this structure by children currently in the intermediate stage—i.e., the extended period between immature performance (under age 6, where children always show the named animal as the actor for this linguistic structure) and adult performance.

Method

Subjects

Sixty normal, monolingual English-speaking children participated in the study. At the beginning of the study, there were seventeen 7-year-olds, thirty-three 8-year-olds, and ten 9-year-olds. Their verbal IQs as measured on the PPVT ranged from 70 to 155, with a median of 115.

Procedure

Each child was tested individually. At the initial testing session, the child was shown how to operate the two puppets, a wolf and a duck, one on each hand,

and was allowed a few minutes to play with these puppets. During this time, the child was asked to make the wolf bite the duck, and also to make the duck bite the wolf. In the course of this warm-up, the experimenter indicated that the animal doing the biting should bite the other on the ear so that the experimenter could clearly see which animal was doing the biting. The actual study itself consisted of ten instances of the structure—five requiring the named animal and five requiring the nonnamed animal to do the biting according to adult interpretation (see Table 3.5.1 for the sentences used). The wolf and the duck were counterbalanced across sentence types. Details can be found in Cromer (1983), where an analysis of the changes in interpretations of the particular lexical items used has previously been reported. All answers by the child were treated as correct; no indication was given to the child as to whether any interpretation accorded with adult expectations or not. The same test was repeated the next day. The child was similarly tested two days in a row on the succeeding visits, these visits occurring at three-month intervals for one year. It should be noted that not only was no feedback given as to the correct adult interpretation of these words but no indication was even given that some of the answers by the children were in fact wrong. It was predicted that significantly more of these children who experienced this structure for a year would perform in the adult manner than children of the same age without such concentrated exposure and experience (i.e., children of that same age on initial testing at the beginning of the longitudinal study, and children of that same age tested cross-sectionally in earlier experiments), in spite of the fact that no feedback was given either of the correct interpretations of specific lexical items or even that they had performed incorrectly on the comprehension tests.

Table 3.5.1 *Sentences used in the study*

	Correct answer to "Who does the biting?"	
Warm-up		
1. The wolf bites the duck.	wolf	
2. The duck bites the wolf.	duck	
Test sentences		
1. The wolf is *happy* to bite.	wolf	named animal
2. The duck is *keen* to bite.	duck	named animal
3. The wolf is *easy* to bite.	duck	nonnamed animal
4. The duck is *exciting* to bite.	wolf	nonnamed animal
5. The wolf is *delightful* to bite.	duck	nonnamed animal
6. The duck is *anxious* to bite.	duck	named animal
7. The wolf is *willing* to bite.	wolf	named animal
8. The duck is *hard* to bite.	wolf	nonnamed animal
9. The wolf is *glad* to bite.	wolf	named animal
10. The duck is *fun* to bite.	wolf	nonnamed animal

Results

The percentages of children in the various groups who performed the sentences in the adult manner are shown in Table 3.5.2. The 7- and 8-year-old groups, who performed similarly, have been combined in order to make more meaningful comparisons to the earlier cross-sectional study that had few subjects at those ages. It can be seen that at the beginning of the present longitudinal study, on their first exposure to this structure, seven of the fifty 7- and 8-year-olds (14.0 percent) already performed all ten test sentences in the adult manner. Two of the ten 9-year-olds (20.0 percent) performed at the adult level. These percentages are close to those found cross-sectionally in the past. In Cromer (1972), three of the thirteen 7- and 8-year-olds (23.1 percent) and two of the fourteen 9-year-olds (14.3 percent) performed like adults on initial testing. None of these percentages differed significantly from any other. In the cross-sectional study, only in 10- and 11-year-old groups did 50.0 percent of the children attain adultlike performance.

In the present longitudinal study, after experiencing this linguistic structure every three months for one year, seventeen of the thirty-one children who were now 9 years old (54.8 percent) showed adultlike performance. This is significantly greater than the two of ten 9-year-olds (20.0 percent) in this same group one year earlier at the beginning of the longitudinal study ($Z = 1.92$, $p < .05$, one-tailed) and significantly greater than the two of fourteen 9-year-olds (14.3 percent) in the earlier cross-sectional study ($Z = 2.55$, $p < .01$, one-tailed). If one considers only the 8-year-olds at the beginning of the present study, five of thirty-three (15.2 percent) performed like adults. At the end of one year, of the thirty-one of these children who completed the entire course of testing and who were now 9 years old, seventeen (54.8 percent) showed adult performance. These percentages are significantly different ($Z = 3.33$, $p < .001$, one-tailed).

Discussion

In the longitudinal study, children merely performed the actions in the

Table 3.5.2 *Percentage of children performing in the adult manner on the "easy to please" structure*

	At 7 and 8 years	At 9 years
One-year longitudinal study	14.0% (start of study)	54.8% (end of study)
One-year longitudinal study	—	20.0% (start of study)
Previous cross-sectional study	23.1%	14.3%

sentences and all of their answers were treated as correct. Nevertheless, experience of this linguistic structure every three months for one year appears to have led many children to reorganize their linguistic knowledge. Exposure to and concentration on this linguistic structure by 8-year-olds led to levels of performance by 9 years of age that not only were significantly improved but also are not typically found until age 10 or 11 in cross-sectional studies. What are the implications of this for theories of language acquisition?

Acquisition of a particular language obviously requires exposure to that language, but mere exposure is not sufficient to account for growth and change. While it may be that those who focus on universal grammar often undervalue the influence of environmental factors on language acquisition, researchers who concentrate on environmental input often fail to take into account adequately the nature of the organism registering, manipulating, and making use of that input. A better understanding of language acquisition must somehow take into account both perspectives. That is, whatever may be innate about universal grammar must interact with specific language input to the child, but that input can be understood only in relation to how the child understands and makes use of it. Some recent research addresses itself to both parts of this complex issue. The cross-cultural studies of language acquisition by Slobin and his associates (Slobin, 1982) and the experimental studies by Newport, Gleitman, and Gleitman (1977) and by Karmiloff-Smith (1978, 1979) detail the interactions between what the child brings to the language acquisition task and the particularities of the language to which the child is exposed. It should be noted that children in the present task were not merely exposed to the linguistic structure under study. Instead, they were required to make judgments about it in the comprehension task, even though all of these judgments were treated as correct. Thus, these children were forced to concentrate on and "experience" this linguistic structure.

The study reported here seems to indicate that children built some portions of their own linguistic systems without direct feedback. In other words, the path to adult performance may not be as directly dependent on feedback on particular structures as various hypothesis-testing models have supposed. However, linguistic exposure can play an important part by encouraging children to concentrate on one or another aspect of the grammar. Exposure to particular linguistic forms—if it causes the child to "work on" and thus to experience particular aspects of the grammar—may accelerate specific acquisitions. Furthermore, language is a highly structured system, and changes in one part of the system will cause changes to occur in other parts of the system. Thus, specific acquisitions may have ramifications in the child's overall system that are not directly related to the language input. It is not clear how children move from one stage to another in their acquisition of specific linguistic structures, but there is evidence from this longitudinal study that some language growth can occur with experience without feedback.

Addendum

An incident illustrating rapid linguistic change without feedback in unusual circumstances

After the results reported here were analyzed, our Medical Research Council research unit was paid a royal visit by Princess Diana. Each member of staff was given about ten minutes to explain some aspect of cognitive development research to her. We invited several children to take part in our various experimental demonstrations. I thought it would be fun to demonstrate the wolf/duck experiment that formed the basis of the longitudinal study above. Since children younger than 6 years almost invariably show the named animal as doing the biting for all of the sentences in Table 3.5.1, we obtained the cooperation of a 5-year-old girl, whom we will call Judy, who lived in the neighborhood of one of my colleagues. Since we wanted the children to be familiar with us and our laboratory so that they would not be nervous on the day of Princess Diana's visit, we had a "run-through" one week before the actual visit.

Judy was given the set of sentences used in the study, as shown in Table 3.5.1. She happily carried out the task and showed the named animal as doing the biting for the sentences. Our intention was that once she left the room, we would turn to the princess and say something like "You see, she gives these answers with great assurance, and no one tells her that some are wrong; yet within a year she will move into an intermediate stage where she will no longer always show the named animal, but neither will she perform as an adult would. It will take her several years to organize her knowledge of which of the words requires the recovery of which abstract structure. ..." The practice demonstration went very smoothly. In fact, we were so pleased that she was indeed at the stage of showing the named animal, we did something that we do not do during a real experiment: We gave feedback. But it was positive, not negative, feedback. We said how wonderfully she had done and in effect communicated, "Just do the same thing next week when Princess Diana is here."

The big day arrived. Seated across from the princess, I began the set of sentences: "Show me 'The wolf is happy to bite'" and Judy showed the wolf biting the duck. "Now show me 'The duck is keen to bite'"; Judy duly showed the duck as the actor. "Now show me 'The wolf is easy to bite'"—but now Judy showed the duck as doing the biting. "Oh, maybe she's entered the intermediate stage," I thought as I went on to "Now show me 'The duck is exciting to bite.'" She showed the wolf as doing the biting. Through the rest of the test she rapidly and with great ease and assurance proceeded to give the adult interpretation for all of the sentences, a behavior not usually seen in a majority of children until 10 or 11 years of age. How, in one week, could a 5-year-old child initially still at the most primitive stage of behavior on this linguistic test suddenly completely skip an intermediate stage of behavior that normally lasts four or more years and interpret this structure consistently in the adult manner? In increasing desperation I tried to account for what we had observed:

The "royal touch" hypothesis

In ancient, but said to be reliable, sources, it has been reported that the mere touch of a royal hand has had beneficial effects on people suffering from a variety of incurable maladies. If we conceive of child grammar as a form of illness, with the achievement of adult competence constituting the cure, perhaps we can account for the sudden transition in Judy's case as being due to Princess Diana's presence. (To those skeptics who ridicule the "royal touch" hypothesis for language acquisition, we would point out that even Chomsky (1966) makes frequent reference to the Port-Royal Grammar.) However, this hypothesis fails for two reasons. First, reliable witnesses report that the princess was not observed ever to have touched the child. Second, it is probable that Princess Diana has not been a member of the royal family long enough for the curative "royal touch" properties to have fully developed.

The negative–positive reinforcement exchange hypothesis

In most theories of learning, including those that stress the importance of hypothesis-testing, crucial effects are attributed to negative reinforcement. In the incident under study, however, only positive reinforcement was given. The child was commended for her excellent performance when she showed the named animal as the actor for all sentences in the initial testing session. However, many parents have reported that their children show negativistic attitudes in which negative reinforcement (in these cases in the form of punishment) appears to be cognitively converted by the child into positive reinforcement, so that the child continues to engage in the annoying behavior. We may hypothesize, then, that during this negativistic stage, some children equally convert positive reinforcement into negative reinforcement. Thus, Judy may have cognitively converted the praise she was given after her initial testing into its opposite, and this in turn may have led her to change her performance when tested one week later. Unfortunately, this hypothesis too appears to fail. Most parents report that the negativistic stage in children occurs at two points in development: At about 2 years of age and at adolescence. Judy, however, was 5 years of age at the time of the observation, and so we must rule out the likelihood of the "negative–positive reinforcement exchange hypothesis" as providing an adequate explanation for the observed change in linguistic behavior in this case.

418   *Richard F. Cromer*

Serious hypothesis

None.

Serious conclusions

It is not easy to account for the extraordinary behavior observed on this occasion. Could the mere exposure to a concentrated set of instances of this linguistic structure under emotionally charged circumstances trigger a reorganization of linguistic competence? The longitudinal study showed that linguistic change can apparently occur with experience without feedback. But that experiment concerned children at the intermediate stage on this linguistic form who were already struggling to work out which adjectives call for the recovery of which abstract linguistic structure. The acceleration of change during that period might be interpreted as being on the order of one year (9-year-olds who have been exposed to this linguistic structure for one year since age 8, behaving the way uninitiated 10-year-olds behave). But the acceleration in Judy's case was phenomenal, with a 5-year-old performing like a normal 5-year-old one week and like a 10-year-old the next. It is not at all clear what factors are crucial for the occurrence of such acceleration. But if the behavior observed in this case is reliable and can be replicated, then language change with experience without feedback may be a more important factor in language acquisition than anyone previously supposed.

References to 3.5

Chomsky, N. (1966). *Cartesian Linguistics*. New York: Harper & Row.
Cromer, R. F. (1970). "'Children are nice to understand': Surface structure clues for the recovery of a deep structure." *British Journal of Psychology*, **61**, 397–408.
Cromer, R. F. (1972). "The learning of surface structure clues to deep structure by a puppet show technique." *Quarterly Journal of Experimental Psychology*, **24**, 66–76.
Cromer, R. F. (1983). "A longitudinal study of the acquisition of word knowledge: Evidence against gradual learning." *British Journal of Developmental Psychology*, **1**, 307–16.
Karmiloff-Smith, A. (1978). "The interplay between syntax, semantics, and phonology in language acquisition processes." In R. N. Campbell and P. T. Smith (eds), *Recent Advances in the Psychology of Language: Language development and mother–child interaction*. New York: Plenum Press, 1–23.
Karmiloff-Smith, A. (1979). *A Functional Approach to Child Language: A study of determiners and reference*. Cambridge: Cambridge University Press.
Newport, E. L., Gleitman, H., and Gleitman, L. R. (1977). "Mother, I'd rather do it myself: Some effects and non-effects of maternal speech style." In C. E. Snow and C. A. Ferguson (eds), *Talking to Children: Language input and acquisition*. Cambridge: Cambridge University Press, 109–50.
Pinker, S. (1984). *Language Learnability and Language Development*. Cambridge, MA: Harvard University Press.

Slobin, D. I. (1982). "Universal and particular in the acquisition of language." In E. Wanner and L. R. Gleitman (eds), *Language Acquisition: The state of the art*. Cambridge: Cambridge University Press, 128–70.

Snow, C. E. and Ferguson, C. A. (eds). (1977). *Talking to Children: Language input and acquisition*. Cambridge: Cambridge University Press.

—PART 4—

Morphology

— 4.1

On Learning the Past Tenses of English Verbs

D. E. Rumelhart and J. L. McClelland

The issue

Scholars of language and psycholinguistics have been among the first to stress the importance of rules in describing human behavior. The reason for this is obvious. Many aspects of language can be characterized by rules, and the speakers of natural languages speak the language correctly. Therefore, systems of rules are useful in characterizing what they will and will not say. Though we all make mistakes when we speak, we have a pretty good ear for what is right and what is wrong—and our judgments of correctness—or grammaticality—are generally even easier to characterize by rules than actual utterances.

On the evidence that what we will and will not say and what we will and will not accept can be characterized by rules, it has been argued that, in some sense, we "know" the rules of our language. The sense in which we know them is not the same as the sense in which we know such "rules" as "*i* before *e* except after *c*," however, since we need not necessarily be able to state the rules explicitly. We know them in a way that allows us to use them to make judgments of grammaticality, it is often said, or to speak and understand, but this knowledge is not in a form or location that permits it to be encoded into a communicable verbal statement. Because of this, this knowledge is said to be *implicit*.

So far there is considerable agreement. However, the exact characterization of implicit knowledge is a matter of great controversy. One view, which is perhaps extreme but is nevertheless quite clear, holds that the rules of language are stored in explicit form as propositions, and are used by language production,

423

comprehension, and judgment mechanisms. These propositions cannot be described verbally only because they are sequestered in a specialized subsystem which is used in language processing, or because they are written in a special code that only the language processing system can understand. This view we will call the *explicit inaccessible rule* view.

On the explicit inaccessible rule view, language acquisition is thought of as the process of inducing rules. The language mechanisms are thought to include a subsystem—often called the *language acquisition device* (LAD)—whose business it is to discover the rules. A considerable amount of effort has been expended on the attempt to describe how the LAD might operate, and there are a number of different proposals which have been laid out. Generally, though, they share three assumptions:

● The mechanism hypothesizes explicit inaccessible rules.
● Hypotheses are rejected and replaced as they prove inadequate to account for the utterances the learner hears.
● The LAD is presumed to have *innate* knowledge of the possible range of human languages and, therefore, is presumed to consider only hypotheses within the constraints imposed by a set of *linguistic universals*.

The recent book by Pinker (1984) contains a state-of-the-art example of a model based on this approach.

We propose an alternative to explicit inaccessible rules. We suggest that lawful behavior and judgments may be produced by a mechanism in which there is no explicit representation of the rule. Instead, we suggest that the mechanisms that process language and make judgments of grammaticality are constructed in such a way that their performance is characterizable by rules, but that the rules themselves are not written in explicit form anywhere in the mechanism. An illustration of this view, which we owe to Bates (1979), is provided by the honeycomb. The regular structure of the honeycomb arises from the interaction of forces that wax balls exert on each other when compressed. The honeycomb can be described by a rule, but the mechanism which produces it does not contain any statement of this rule.

In our earlier work with the interactive activation model of word perception (McClelland and Rumelhart, 1981; Rumelhart and McClelland, 1981, 1982), we noted that lawful behavior emerged from the interactions of a set of word and letter units. Each word unit stood for a particular word and had connections to units for the letters of the word. There were no separate units for common letter clusters and no explicit provision for dealing differently with orthographically regular letter sequences—strings that accorded with the rules of English—as opposed to irregular sequences. Yet the model did behave differently with orthographically regular nonwords than it behaved with words. In fact, the model simulated rather closely a number of results in the word perception literature relating to the finding that subjects perceive letters in orthographically regular letter strings more accurately than they perceive letters in irregular, random letter strings. Thus, the behavior of the model was lawful even though it contained no explicit rules.

It should be said that the pattern of perceptual facilitation shown by the model did not correspond exactly to any system of orthographic rules which we know. The model produced as much facilitation, for example, for special nonwords like *SLNT*, which are clearly irregular, as it did for matched regular nonwords like *SLET*. Thus, it is not correct to say that the model exactly mimicked the behavior we would expect to emerge from a system which makes use of explicit orthographic rules. However, neither do human subjects. Just like the model, they showed equal facilitation for vowelless strings like *SLNT* as for regular nonwords like *SLET*. Thus, human perceptual performance seems, in this case at least, to be characterized only approximately by rules.

Some people have been tempted to argue that the behavior of the model shows that we can do without linguistic rules. We prefer, however, to put the matter in a slightly different light. There is no denying that rules still provide a fairly close characterization of the performance of our subjects. And we have no doubt that rules are even more useful in characterizations of sentence production, comprehension, and grammaticality judgments. We would only suggest that parallel distributed processing models may provide a mechanism sufficient to capture lawful behavior, without requiring the postulation of explicit but inaccessible rules. Put succinctly, our claim is that PDP models provide an alternative to the explicit but inaccessible rules account of implicit knowledge of rules.

We can anticipate two kinds of arguments against this kind of claim. The first kind would claim that although certain types of rule-guided behavior might emerge from PDP models, the models simply lack the computational power needed to carry out certain types of operations which can be easily handled by a system using explicit rules. We believe that this argument is simply mistaken. The second kind of argument would be that the details of language behavior, and, indeed, the details of the language acquisition process, would provide unequivocal evidence in favor of a system of explicit rules.

It is this latter kind of argument we wish to address in the present chapter. We have selected a phenomenon that is often thought of as demonstrating the acquisition of a linguistic rule. And we have developed a parallel distributed processing model that learns in a natural way to behave in accordance with the rule, mimicking the general trends seen in the acquisition data.

The phenomenon

The phenomenon for which we wish to account is actually a sequence of three stages in the acquisition of the use of past tense by children learning English as their native tongue. Descriptions of development of the use of the past tense may be found in Brown (1973), Ervin (1964), and Kuczaj (1977).

In Stage 1, children use only a small number of verbs in the past tense. Such verbs tend to be very high-frequency words, and the majority of these are irregular. At this stage, children tend to get the past tenses of these words correct if they use the past tense at all. For example, a child's lexicon of past-tense words at this stage might consist of *came, got, gave, looked, needed, took,* and *went*. Of these seven verbs, only two are regular—the other five are generally idiosyncratic examples of irregular verbs. In this stage, there is no evidence of the use of the rule—it appears that children simply know a small number of separate items.

In Stage 2, evidence of implicit knowledge of a linguistic rule emerges. At this stage, children use a much larger number of verbs in the past tense. These verbs include a few more irregular items, but it turns out that the majority of the words at this stage are examples of the *regular* past tense in English. Some examples are *wiped* and *pulled*.

The evidence that the Stage 2 child actually has a linguistic rule comes not from the mere fact that he or she knows a number of regular forms. There are two additional and crucial facts:

- The child can now generate a past tense for an invented word. For example, Berko (1958) has shown that if children can be convinced to use *rick* to describe an action, they will tend to say *ricked* when the occasion arises to use the word in the past tense.
- Children now *incorrectly* supply regular past-tense endings for words which they used correctly in Stage 1. These errors may involve either adding *ed* to the root as in *comed* /k^md/, or adding *ed* to the irregular past tense form as in *camed* /kʌmd/[1] (Ervin, 1964; Kuczaj, 1977).

Such findings have been taken as fairly strong support for the assertion that the child at this stage has acquired the past-tense "rule." To quote Berko (1958):

> If a child knows that the plural of *witch* is *witches*, he may simply have memorized the plural form. If, however, he tells us that the plural of *gutch* is *gutches*, we have evidence that he actually knows, albeit unconsciously, one of those rules which the descriptive linguist, too, would set forth in his grammar. (p. 151)

In Stage 3, the regular and irregular forms coexist. That is, children have regained the use of the correct irregular forms of the past tense, while they continue to apply the regular form to new words they learn. Regularizations persist into adulthood—in fact, there is a class of words for which either a regular or an irregular version are both considered acceptable—but for the commonest irregulars such as those the child acquired first, they tend to be rather rare. At this stage there are some clusters of exceptions to the basic, regular past-tense pattern of English. Each cluster includes a number of words that undergo identical changes from the present to the past tense. For example, there is a *ing/ang* cluster, an *ing/ung* cluster, an *eet/it* cluster, etc. There is

Table 4.1.1   *Characteristics of the three stages of past-tense acquisition*

Verb type	Stage 1	Stage 2	Stage 3
Early verbs	Correct	Regularized	Correct
Regular	—	Correct	Correct
Other irregular	—	Regularized	Correct or regularized
Novel	—	Regularized	Regularized

also a group of words ending in /d/ or /t/ for which the present and past are identical.

Table 4.1.1 summarizes the major characteristics of the three stages.

Variability and gradualness

The characterization of past-tense acquisition as a sequence of three stages is somewhat misleading. It may suggest that the stages are clearly demarcated and that performance in each stage is sharply distinguished from performance in other stages.

In fact, the acquisition process is quite gradual. Little detailed data exists on the transition from Stage 1 to Stage 2, but the transition from Stage 2 to Stage 3 is quite protracted and extends over several years (Kuczaj, 1977). Further, performance in Stage 2 is extremely variable. Correct use of irregular forms is never completely absent, and the same child may be observed to use the correct past of an irregular, the base + ed form, and the past + ed form, within the same conversation.

Other facts about past-tense acquisition

Beyond these points, there is now considerable data on the detailed types of errors children make throughout the acquisition process both from Kuczaj (1977) and more recently from Bybee and Slobin (1982). We will consider aspects of these findings in more detail below. For now, we mention one intriguing fact: According to Kuczaj (1977) there is an interesting difference in the errors children make to irregular verbs at different points in Stage 2. Early on, regularizations are typically of the base + ed form, like *goed*; later on, there is a large increase in the frequency of past + ed errors, such as *wented*.

The model

The goal of our simulation of the acquisition of past tense was to simulate the three-stage performance summarized in Table 4.1.1, and to see whether we could capture other aspects of acquisition. In particular, we wanted to show that the kind of gradual change characteristic of normal acquisition was also a characteristic of our distributed model and we wanted to see whether the model would capture detailed aspects of the phenomenon, such as the change in error type in later phases of development and the change in differences in error patterns observed for different types of words.

We were not prepared to produce a full-blown language processor that would learn the past tense from full sentences heard in everyday experience. Rather, we have explored a very simple past-tense learning environment designed to capture the essential characteristics necessary to produce the three stages of acquisition. In this environment, the model is presented, as learning experiences, with pairs of inputs—one capturing the phonological structure of the root form of a word and the other capturing the phonological structure of the correct past-tense version of that word. The behavior of the model can be tested by giving it just the root form of a word and examining what it generates as its "current guess" of the corresponding past-tense form.

Structure of the model

The basic structure of the model is illustrated in Figure 4.1.1. The model consists of two basic parts: (a) a simple *pattern associator* network similar to those studied by Kohonen (1977, 1984) which learns the relationships between the base form and the past-tense form, and (b) a decoding network that converts a featural representation of the past-tense form into a phonological representation. All learning occurs in the pattern associator; the decoding network is simply a

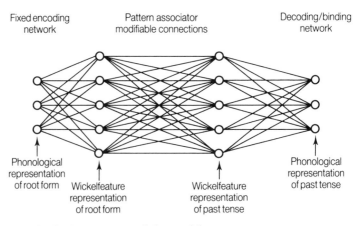

Figure 4.1.1   *The basic structure of the model.*

mechanism for converting a featural representation which may be a near miss to any phonological pattern into a legitimate phonological representation. Our primary focus here is on the pattern associator. We discuss the details of the decoding network in the Appendix.

Units

The pattern associator contains two pools of units. One pool, called the input pool, is used to represent the input pattern corresponding to the root form of the verb to be learned. The other pool, called the output pool, is used to represent the output pattern generated by the model as its current guess as to the past tense corresponding to the root form represented in the inputs.

Each unit stands for a particular feature of the input or output string. The particular features we used are important to the behavior of the model, so they are described in a separate section below.

Connections

The pattern associator contains a modifiable connection linking each input unit to each output unit. Initially, these connections are all set to 0 so that there is no influence of the input units on the output units. Learning, as in other PDP models in McClelland and Rumelhart (1986), involves modification of the strengths of these interconnections as described below.

Operation of the model

On test trials, the simulation is given a phoneme string corresponding to the root of a word. It then performs the following actions. First, it encodes the root string as a pattern of activation over the input units. The encoding scheme used is described below. Node activations are discrete in this model, so the activation values of all the units that should be on to represent this word are set to 1, and all the others are set to 0. Then, for each output unit, the model computes the net input to it from all of the weighted connections from the input units. The net input is simply the sum over all input units of the input unit activation times the corresponding weight. Thus, algebraically, the net input to output unit i is

(1) $\quad net_i = \sum_j a_j w_{ij}$

where a_j represents the activation of input unit j, and w_{ij} represents the weight from unit j to unit i.

Each unit has a threshold, θ, which is adjusted by the learning procedure that we will describe in a moment. The probability that the unit is turned on depends on the amount the net input exceeds the threshold. The *logistic* probability function is used here as in the Boltzmann machine and in harmony theory to determine whether the unit should be turned on. The probability is given by

(2) $p(a_i = 1) = \dfrac{1}{1 + e^{-(net_i - \theta_i)/T}}$

where T represents the temperature of the system. The logistic function is shown in Figure 4.1.2. The use of this probabilistic response rule allows the system to produce different responses on different occasions with the same network. It also causes the system to learn more slowly so the effect of regular verbs on the irregulars continues over a much longer period of time. The temperature, T, can be manipulated so that at very high temperatures the response of the units is highly variable; with lower values of T, the units behave more like *linear threshold units*.

Since the pattern associator built into the model is a one-layer net with no feedback connections and no connections from one input unit to another or from one output unit to another, iterative computation is of no benefit. Therefore, the processing of an input pattern is a simple matter of first calculating the net input to each output unit and then setting its activation probabilistically on the basis of the logistic equation given above. The temperature T only enters in setting the variability of the output units; a fixed value of T was used throughout the simulations.

To determine how well the model did at producing the correct output, we simply compare the pattern of output Wickelphone activations to the pattern that the correct response would have generated. To do this, we first translate the correct response into a target pattern of activation for the output units, based on the same encoding scheme used for the input units. We then compare the

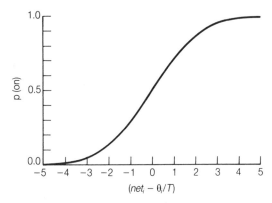

Figure 4.1.2 *The logistic function used to calculate probability of activation. The x-axis shows values of (net$_i$ − θ$_i$/T), and the y-axis indicates the corresponding probability that unit* i *will be activated.*

obtained pattern with the target pattern on a unit-by-unit basis. If the output perfectly reproduces the target, then there should be a 1 in the output pattern wherever there is a 1 in the target. Such cases are called *hits*, following the conventions of signal detection theory (Green and Swets, 1966). There should also be a 0 in the output whenever there is a 0 in the target. Such cases are called *correct rejections*. Cases in which there are 1s in the output but not in the target are called *false alarms*, and cases in which there are 0s in the output that should be present in the input are called *misses*. A variety of measures of performance can be computed. We can measure the percentage of output units that match the correct past tense, or we can compare the output to the pattern for any other response alternative we might care to evaluate. This allows us to look at the output of the system independently of the decoding network. We can also employ the decoding network and have the system synthesize a phonological string. We can measure the performance of the system either at the featural level or at the level of strings of phonemes. We shall employ both of these mechanisms in the evaluation of different aspects of the overall model.

Learning

On a learning trial, the model is presented with both the root form of the verb and the target. As on a test trial, the pattern associator network computes the output it would generate from the input. Then, for each output unit, the model compares its answer with the target. Connection strengths are adjusted using the classic *perceptron convergence procedure* (Rosenblatt, 1962). The perceptron convergence procedure is simply a discrete variant of the delta rule. The exact procedure is as follows: We can think of the target as supplying a teaching input to each output unit, telling it what value it ought to have. When the actual output matches the target output, the model is doing the right thing and so none of the weights on the lines coming into the unit is adjusted. When the computed output is 0 and the target says it should be 1, we want to increase the probability that the unit will be active the next time the same input pattern is presented. To do this, we increase the weights from all of the input units that are active by a small amount η. At the same time, the threshold is also reduced by η. When the computed output is 1 and the target says it should be 0, we want to decrease the probability that the unit will be active the next time the same input pattern is presented. To do this, the weights from all of the input units that are active are reduced by η, and the threshold is increased by η. In all of our simulations, the value of η is simply set to 1. Thus, each change in a weight is a unit change, either up or down. For nonstochastic units, it is well known that the perceptron convergence procedure will find a set of weights that will allow the model to get each output unit correct, provided that such a set of weights exists. For the stochastic case, it is possible for the learning procedure to find a set of weights that will make the probability of error as low as desired. Such a set of weights exists if a set of weights exists that will always get the right answer for nonstochastic units.

Learning regular and exceptional patterns in a pattern associator

In this section, we present an illustration of the behavior of a simple pattern associator model. The model is a scaled-down version of the main simulation described in the next section. We describe the scaled-down version first because in this model it is possible actually to examine the matrix of connection weights, and from this to see clearly how the model works and why it produces the basic three-stage learning phenomenon characteristic of acquisition of the past tense. Various aspects of pattern associator networks are described in McClelland and Rumelhart (1986) and elsewhere (Anderson, 1973, 1977; Anderson *et al.*, 1977; Kohonen, 1977, 1984). Here we focus our attention on their application to the representation of rules for mapping one set of patterns into another.

For the illustration model, we use a simple network of eight input and eight output units and a set of connections from each input unit to each output unit. The network is illustrated in Figure 4.1.3. The network is shown with a set of connections sufficient for associating the pattern of activation illustrated on the input units with the pattern of activation illustrated on the output units. (Active

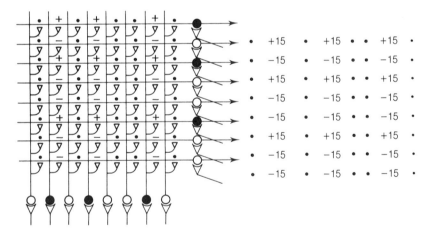

Figure 4.1.3 *Simple network used in illustrating basic properties of pattern associator networks; excitatory and inhibitory connections needed to allow the active input pattern to produce the illustrated pattern are indicated with + and −. Next to the network, the matrix of weights indicating the strengths of the connections from each input unit to each output unit. Input units are indexed by the column they appear in; output units are indexed by row.*

units are darkened; positive and negative connections are indicated by numbers written on each connection.) Next to the network is the matrix of connections abstracted from the actual network itself, with numerical values assigned to the positive and negative connections. Note that each weight is located in the matrix at the point where it occurred in the actual network diagram. Thus, the entry in the ith row of the jth column indicates the connection w_{ij} from the jth input unit to the ith output unit.

Using this diagram, it is easy to compute the net inputs that will arise on the output units when an input pattern is presented. For each output unit, one simply scans across its rows and adds up all the weights found in columns associated with active input units. (This is exactly what the simulation program does!) The reader can verify that when the input pattern illustrated in the left-hand panel is presented, each output unit that should be on in the output pattern receives a net input of $+45$; each output unit that should be off receives a net input of -45.[2] Plugging these values into Equation 1, using a temperature of 15,[3] we can compute that each output unit will take on the correct value about 95 percent of the time. The reader can check this in Figure 4.1.2; when the net input is $+45$, the exponent in the denominator of the logistic function is 3, and when the net input is -45, the exponent is -3. These correspond to activation probabilities of about .95 and .05, respectively.

One of the basic properties of the pattern associator is that it can store the connections appropriate for mapping a number of different input patterns to a number of different output patterns. The perceptron convergence procedure can accommodate a number of arbitrary associations between input patterns and output patterns, as long as the input patterns form a linearly independent set. Table 4.1.2 illustrates this aspect of the model. The first two cells of the table show the connections that the model learns when it is trained on each of the two indicated associations separately. The third cell shows connections learned by the model when it is trained on both patterns in alternation, first seeing one and then seeing the other of the two. Again, the reader can verify that if either input pattern is presented to a network with this set of connections, the correct corresponding output pattern is reconstructed with high probability; each output unit that should be on gets a net input of at least $+45$, and each output unit that should be off gets a net input below -45.

The restriction of networks such as this to linearly independent sets of patterns is a severe one since there are only N linearly independent patterns of length N. That means that we could store at most eight unrelated associations in the network and maintain accurate performance. However, if the patterns all conform to a general rule, the capacity of the network can be greatly enhanced. For example, the set of connections shown in Table 4.1.2D is capable of processing all of the patterns defined by what we call the *rule of 78*. The rule is described in Table 4.1.3. There are eighteen different input/output pattern pairs corresponding to this rule, but they present no difficulty to the network. Through repeated presentations of examples of the rule, the perceptron

Table 4.1.2 *Weights in the 8-unit network after various learning experiences*

A. Weights acquired in learning
   (2 4 7) → (1 4 6)

```
.   15   .    15   .   .   15
.  -16   .   -16   .   .  -16
.  -17   .   -17   .   .  -17
.   16   .    16   .   .   16
.  -16   .   -16   .   .  -16
.   17   .    17   .   .   17
.  -16   .   -16   .   .  -16
.  -17   .   -17   .   .  -17
```

B. Weights acquired in learning
   (3 4 6) → (3 6 7)

```
.   .   .  -16  -16   .  -16   .   .
.   .   .  -17  -17   .  -17   .   .
.   .   .   17   17   .   17   .   .
.   .   .  -16  -16   .  -16   .   .
.   .   .  -17  -17   .  -17   .   .
.   .   .   16   16   .   16   .   .
.   .   .   17   17   .   17   .   .
.   .   .  -17  -17   .  -17   .   .
```

C. Weights acquired in learning A
   and B together

```
.   24  -24    .     . -24   24
.  -13  -13  -26     . -13  -13
.  -23   24    1     .  24  -23
.   24  -25   -1     . -25   24
.  -13  -13  -26     . -13  -13
.   13   13   26     .  13   13
.  -25   24   -1     .  24  -25
.  -12  -13  -25     . -13  -12
```

D. Weights acquired in learning the rule
   of 78

```
.   61  -37  -37   -5   -5   -3   -6   -7
.  -35   60  -38   -4   -6   -3   -5   -8
.  -39  -35   61   -4   -5   -4   -7   -6
.   -6   -4   -5   59  -37  -37   -8   -7
.   -5   -5   -4  -36   60  -38   -7   -7
.   -5   -4   -6  -37  -38   60   -8   -7
.    .    1    .    1    .    .  -50   51
.    .   -1   -2    1    .   49  -50
```

Table 4.1.3 *The rule of 78*

Input patterns consist of one active unit from each of the following sets:	(1 2 3) (4 5 6) (7 8)
The output pattern paired with a given input pattern consists of:	The same unit from (1 2 3) The same unit from (4 5 6) The other unit from (7 8)
Examples:	2 4 7→2 4 8 1 6 8→1 6 7 3 5 7→3 5 8
An exception:	1 4 7→1 4 7

convergence procedure learned the set of weights shown in cell D of Table 4.1.2. Again, the reader can verify that it works for any legal association fitting the rule of 78. (Note that for this example, the "regular" pairing of (1 4 7) with (1 4 8) was used rather than the exceptional mapping illustrated in Table 4.1.3.)

We have, then, observed an important property of the pattern associator: If there is some structure to a set of patterns, the network may be able to learn to respond appropriately to all of the members of the set. This is true, even though the input vectors most certainly do not form a linearly independent set. The model works anyway because the response that the model should make to some of the patterns can be predicted from the responses that it should make to others of the patterns.

Now let us consider a case more like the situation a young child faces in learning the past tenses of English verbs. Here, there is a regular pattern, similar to the rule of 78. In addition, however, there are exceptions. Among the first words the child learns are many exceptions, but as the child learns more and more verbs, the proportion that are regular increases steadily. For an adult, the vast majority of verbs are regular.

To examine what would happen in a pattern associator in this kind of a situation, we first presented the illustrative 8-unit model with two pattern pairs. One of these was a regular example of the 78 rule [(2 5 8) → (2 5 7)]. The other was an exception to the rule [(1 4 7) → (1 4 7)]. The simulation saw both pairs twenty times, and connection strengths were adjusted after each presentation. The resulting set of connections is shown in cell A of Table 4.1.4. This number of learning trials is not enough to lead to perfect performance; but after this much experience, the model tends to get the right answer for each output unit close to 90 percent of the time. At this point, the fact that one of the patterns is an example of a general rule and the other is an exception to that rule is irrelevant to the model. It learns a set of connections that can accommodate these two patterns, but it cannot generalize to new instances of the rule.

This situation, we suggest, characterizes the situation that the language-learner faces early on in learning the past tense. The child knows, at this point,

Table 4.1.4 *Representing exceptions: Weights in the 8-unit network*

A. After 20 exposures to (1 4 7)→(1 4 7),(2 5 8)→(2 5 7)

12	−12	.	12	−12	.	12	−12
−11	13	.	−11	13	.	−11	13
−11	−11	.	−11	−11	.	−11	−11
12	−12	.	12	−12	.	12	−12
−11	11	.	−11	11	.	−11	11
−11	−12	.	−11	−12	.	−11	−12
12	11	.	12	11	.	12	11
−11	−13	.	−11	−13	.	−11	−13

B. After 10 more exposures to all 18 associations

44	−34	−26	−2	−10	−4	−8	−8
−32	46	−27	−11	2	−4	−9	−4
−30	−24	43	−5	−5	−1	−2	−9
−1	−7	−7	45	−34	−26	−4	−11
−8	−3	−3	−31	44	−27	−7	−7
−6	−8	−3	−31	−28	42	−7	−10
11	−2	−6	11	−2	−6	−35	38
−9	−4	7	−13	1	6	36	−42

C. After 30 more exposures to all 18 associations

61	−38	−38	−6	−5	−4	−6	−9
−38	62	−39	−6	−5	−4	−8	−7
−37	−38	62	−5	−5	−3	−7	−6
−4	−6	−6	62	−40	−38	−8	−8
−5	−5	−4	−38	62	−38	−7	−7
−6	−4	−5	−38	−39	62	−8	−7
20	−5	−4	22	−5	−6	−50	61
−19	8	5	−18	5	7	54	−60

D. After a total of 500 exposures to all 18 associations

64	−39	−39	−5	−4	−5	−7	−7
−39	63	−39	−5	−5	−5	−7	−8
−39	−40	64	−5	−5	−5	−8	−7
−5	−5	−5	64	−40	−39	−8	−7
−5	−5	−5	−39	63	−39	−7	−8
−5	−5	−5	−39	−39	63	−8	−7
71	−28	−29	70	−28	−28	−92	106
−70	27	28	−70	27	28	91	−106

only a few high-frequency verbs, and these tend, by and large, to be irregular, as we shall see below. Thus each is treated by the network as a separate association, and very little generalization is possible.

But as the child learns more and more verbs, the proportion of regular verbs increases. This changes the situation for the learning model. Now the model is faced with a number of examples, all of which follow the rule, as well as a smattering of irregular forms. This new situation changes the experience of the network, and thus the pattern of interconnections it contains. Because of the predominance of the regular form in the input, the network learns the regular pattern, temporarily "overregularizing" exceptions that it may have previously learned.

Our illustration takes this situation to an extreme, perhaps, to illustrate the point. For the second stage of learning, we present the model with the entire set of eighteen input patterns consisting of one active unit from (1 2 3), one from (4 5 6), and one from (7 8). All of these patterns are regular except the one exception already used in the first stage of training.

At the end of ten exposures to the full set of eighteen patterns, the model has learned a set of connection strengths that predominantly captures the "regular pattern." At this point, its response to the exceptional pattern is *worse* than it was before the beginning of Phase 2; rather than getting the right output for Units 7 and 8, the network is now *regularizing* it.

The reason for this behavior is very simple. All that is happening is that the model is continually being bombarded with learning experiences directing it to learn the rule of 78. On only one learning trial out of eighteen is it exposed to an exception to this rule.

In this example, the deck has been stacked very strongly against the exception. For several learning cycles, it is in fact quite difficult to tell from the connections that the model is being exposed to an exception mixed in with the regular pattern. At the end of ten cycles, we can see that the model is building up extra excitatory connections from input Units 1 and 4 to output Unit 7 and extra inhibitory strength from Units 1 and 4 to Unit 8, but these are not strong enough to make the model get the right answer for output Units 7 and 8 when the (1 4 7) input pattern is shown. Even after forty trials (panel C of Table 4), the model still gets the wrong answer on Units 7 and 8 for the (1 4 7) pattern more than half the time. (The reader can still be checking these assertions by computing the net input to each output unit that would result from presenting the (1 4 7) pattern.)

It is only after the model has reached the stage where it is making very few mistakes on the seventeen regular patterns that it begins to accommodate to the exception. This amounts to making the connection from Units 1 and 4 to output Unit 7 strongly excitatory and making the connections from these units to output Unit 8 strongly inhibitory. The model must also make several adjustments to other connections so that the adjustments just mentioned do not cause errors on regular patterns similar to the exceptions, such as (1 5 7), (2 4 7), etc. Finally, in panel D, after a total of 500 cycles through the full set of eighteen patterns, the weights are sufficient to get the right answer nearly all of the time. Further improvement would be very gradual since the network makes errors so infrequently at this stage that there is very little opportunity for change.

It is interesting to consider for a moment how an association is represented in a model like this. We might be tempted to think of the representation of an association as the difference between the set of connection strengths needed to represent a set of associations that includes the association and the set of strengths needed to represent the same set excluding the association of interest. Using this definition, we see that the representation of a particular association is far from invariant. What this means is that learning that occurs in one situation (e.g., in which there is a small set of unrelated associations) does not necessarily transfer to a new situation (e.g., in which there are a number of regular associations). This is essentially why the early learning our illustrative model exhibits of the (1 4 7) → (1 4 7) association in the context of just one other association can no longer support correct performance when the larger ensemble of regular patterns is introduced.

Obviously, the example we have considered in this section is highly simplified. However, it illustrates several basic facts about pattern associators. One is that they tend to exploit regularity that exists in the mapping from one set of patterns to another. Indeed, this is one of the main advantages of the use of distributed representations. Second, they allow exceptions and regular patterns to coexist in the same network. Third, if there is a predominant regularity in a set of patterns, this can swamp exceptional patterns until the set of connections has been acquired that captures the predominant regularity. Then further, gradual tuning can occur that adjusts these connections to accommodate both the regular patterns and the exception. These basic properties of the pattern associator model lie at the heart of the three-stage acquisition process, and account for the gradualness of the transition from Stage 2 to Stage 3.

Featural representations of phonological patterns

The preceding section describes basic aspects of the behavior of the pattern associator model and captures fairly well what happens when a pattern associator is applied to the processing of English verbs, following a training schedule similar to the one we have just considered for the acquisition of the rule of 78. There is one caveat, however: The input and target patterns—the base forms of the verbs and the correct past tenses of these verbs—must be represented in the model in such a way that the features provide a convenient basis for capturing the regularities embodied in the past-tense forms of English verbs. Basically, there were two considerations:

- We needed a representation that permitted a differentiation of all of the root forms of English and their past tenses.
- We wanted a representation that would provide a natural basis for generalizations to emerge about what aspects of a present tense correspond to what aspects of the past tense.

A scheme which meets the first criterion, but not the second, is the scheme proposed by Wickelgren (1969). He suggested that words should be represented as sequences of context-sensitive phoneme units, which represent each phone in a word as a triple, consisting of the phone itself, its predecessor, and its successor. We call these triples *Wickelphones*. Notationally, we write each Wickelphone as a triple of phonemes, consisting of the central phoneme, subscripted on the left by its predecessor and on the right by its successor. A phoneme occurring at the beginning of a word is preceded by a special symbol (#) standing for the word boundary: Likewise, a phoneme occurring at the end of a word is followed by #. The word /kat/, for example, would be represented as $_\#k_a$, $_ka_t$, and $_at_\#$. Though the Wickelphones in a word are not strictly position specific, it turns out that (a) few words contain more than one occurrence of any given Wickelphone, and (b) there are no two words we know of that consist of the same sequence of Wickelphones. For example, /slit/ and /silt/ contain no Wickelphones in common.

One nice property of Wickelphones is that they capture enough of the context in which a phoneme occurs to provide a sufficient basis for differentiating between the different cases of the past-tense rule and for characterizing the contextual variables that determine the subregularities among the irregular past-tense verbs. For example, the word-final phoneme that determines whether we should add /d/, /t/ or /ˆd/ in forming the regular past. And it is the sequence $_iN_\#$ which is transformed to $_aN_\#$ in the *ing → ang* pattern found in words like *sing*.

The trouble with the Wickelphone solution is that there are too many of them, and they are too specific. Assuming that we distinguish thirty-five different phonemes, the number of Wickelphones would be 35^3, or 42,875, not even counting the Wickelphones containing word boundaries. And, if we postulate one input unit and one output unit in our model for each Wickelphone, we require rather a large connection matrix (4.3×10^4 squared, or about 2×10^9) to represent all their possible connections.

Obviously, a more compact representation is required. This can be obtained by representing each Wickelphone as a distributed pattern of activation over a set of feature detectors. The basic idea is that we represent each phoneme, not by a single Wickelphone, but by a pattern of what we call *Wickelfeatures*. Each Wickelfeature is a conjunctive, or context-sensitive, feature, capturing a feature of the central phoneme, a feature of the predecessor, and a feature of the successor.

Details of the Wickelfeature representation

For concreteness, we will now describe the details of the feature coding scheme we used. It contains several arbitrary properties, but it also captures the basic principles of coarse, conjunctive coding. First, we will describe the simple feature representation scheme we used for coding a single phoneme as a pattern of features without regard to its predecessor and successor. Then we describe how this scheme can be extended to code whole Wickelphones. Finally, we show how we "blur" this representation, to promote generalization further.

To characterize each phoneme, we devised the highly simplified feature set illustrated in Table 4.1.5. The purpose of the scheme was (a) to give as many of the phonemes as possible a distinctive code, (b) to allow code similarity to reflect the similarity structure of the phonemes in a way that seemed sufficient for our present purposes, and (c) to keep the number of different features as small as possible.

The coding scheme can be thought of as categorizing each phoneme on each of four dimensions. The first dimension divides the phonemes into three major types: Interrupted consonants (stops and nasals), continuous consonants (fricatives, liquids, and semivowels), and vowels. The second dimension further subdivides these major classes. The interrupted consonants are divided into plain stops and nasal; the continuous consonants into fricatives and sonorants (liquids and semivowels are lumped together); and the vowels into high and low. The third dimension classifies the phonemes into three rough places of articulation—front, middle, and back. The fourth subcategories the consonants into voiced vs. voiceless categorizes and subcategorizes the vowels into long and short. As it stands, the coding scheme gives identical codes to six pairs of phonemes, as indicated by the duplicate entries in the cells of the table. A more

Table 4.1.5 *Categorization of phonemes on four simple dimensions*

		Place					
		Front		Middle		Back	
		V/L	U/S	V/L	U/S	V/L	U/S
Interrupted	*Stop*	b	p	d	t	g	k
	Nasal	m	-	n	-	N	-
Cont. Consonant	*Fric.*	v/D	f/T	z	s	Z/j	S/C
	Liq/SV	w/l	-	r	-	y	h
Vowel	*High*	E	i	O	ˆ	U	u
	Low	A	e	I	a/α	W	*/o

Key: N = ng in *sing*; D = th in *the*; T = th in *with*; Z = z in *azure*; S = sh in *ship*; C = ch in *chip*; E = ee in *beet*; i = i in *bit*; O = oa in *boat*; ˆ = u in *but* or schwa; U = oo in *boot*; u = oo in *book*; A = ai in *bait*; e = e in *bet*; I = i_e in *bite*; a = a in *bat*; α = a in *father*; W = ow in *cow*; * = aw in *saw*; o = o in *hot*.

adequate scheme could easily be constructed by increasing the number of dimensions and/or values on the dimensions.

Using the above code, each phoneme can be characterized by one value on each dimension. If we assigned a unit for each value on each dimension, we would need ten units to represent the features of a single phoneme since two dimensions have three values and two have two values. We could then indicate the pattern of these features that corresponds to a particular phoneme as a pattern of activation over the ten units.

Now, one way to represent each Wickelphone would simply be to use three sets of feature patterns: One for the phoneme itself, one for its predecessor, and one for its successor. To capture the word-boundary marker, we would need to introduce a special eleventh feature. Thus, the Wickelphone $_\#k_a$ can be represented by

$$[(000)\ (00)\ (000)\ (00)\ 1]$$
$$[(100)\ (10)\ (001)\ (01)\ 0]$$
$$[(001)\ (01)\ (010)\ (01)\ 0].$$

Using this scheme a Wickelphone could be represented as a pattern of activation over a set of thirty-three units.

However, there is one drawback with this. The representation is not sufficient to capture more than one Wickelphone at a time. If we add another Wickelphone, the representation gives us no way of knowing which features belong together.

We need a representation, then, that provides us with a way of determining which features go together. This is just the job that can be done with detectors for Wickelfeatures—triples of features, one from the central phoneme, one from the predecessor phoneme, and one from the successor phoneme.

Using this scheme, each detector would be activated when the word contained a Wickelphone containing its particular combination of three features. Since each phoneme of a Wickelphone can be characterized by eleven features (including the word-boundary feature) and each Wickelphone contains three phonemes, there are $11 \times 11 \times 11$ possible Wickelfeature detectors. Actually, we are not interested in representing phonemes that cross word boundaries, so we only need ten features for the center phoneme.

Though this leaves us with a fairly reasonable number of units ($11 \times 10 \times 11$ or 1,210), it is still large by the standards of what will easily fit in available computers. However, it is possible to cut the number down still further without much loss of representational capacity since a representation using all 1,210 units would be highly redundant; it would represent each feature of each of the three phonemes sixteen different times, one for each of the conjunctions of that feature with one of the four features of one of the other phonemes and one of the four features of the other.

To cut down on this redundancy and on the number of units required, we simply eliminated all those Wickelfeatures specifying values on two different dimensions of the predecessor and the successor phonemes. We kept all the Wickelfeature detectors for all combinations of different values on the same dimension for the predecessor and successor phonemes. It turns out that there are 260 of these (ignoring the word-boundary feature), and each feature of each member of each phoneme triple is still represented four different times. In addition, we kept the 100 possible Wickelfeatures combining a preceding word-boundary feature with any feature of the main phoneme and any feature of the successor; and the 100 Wickelfeatures combining a following word boundary feature with any feature of the main phoneme and any feature of the successor. All in all then, we used only 460 of the 1,210 possible Wickelfeatures.

Using this representation, a verb is represented by a pattern of activation over a set of 460 Wickelfeature units. Each Wickelphone activates sixteen Wickelfeature units. Table 4.1.6 shows the sixteen Wickelfeature units activated by the Wickelphone ₖAₘ, the central Wickelphone in the word *came*. The first Wickelfeature is turned on whenever we have a Wickelphone in which the preceding contextual phoneme is an interrupted consonant, the central phoneme is a vowel, and the following phoneme is an interrupted consonant. This Wickelfeature is turned on for the Wickelphone ₖAₘ since /k/ and /m/, the context phonemes, are both interrupted consonants and /A/, the central phoneme, is a vowel. This same Wickelfeature would be turned on in the representation of ᵦi𝒹, ₚˆt, ₘaₚ, and many other Wickelfeatures. Similarly, the sixth Wickelfeature listed in the table will be turned on whenever the preceding phoneme is made in the back, and the central and following phonemes are both

Table 4.1.6   *The sixteen Wickelfeatures for the Wickelphone* ₖAₘ

Feature	Preceding context	Central phoneme	Following context
1	Interrupted	Vowel	Interrupted
2	Back	Vowel	Front
3	Stop	Vowel	Nasal
4	Unvoiced	Vowel	Voiced
5	Interrupted	Front	Vowel
6	Back	Front	Front
7	Stop	Front	Nasal
8	Unvoiced	Front	Voiced
9	Interrupted	Low	Interrupted
10	Back	Low	Front
11	Stop	Low	Nasal
12	Unvoiced	Low	Voiced
13	Interrupted	Long	Vowel
14	Back	Long	Front
15	Stop	Long	Nasal
16	Unvoiced	Long	Voiced

made in the front. Again, this is turned on because /k/ is made in the back and /A/ and /m/ are both made in the front. In addition to $_k A_m$ this feature would be turned on for the Wickelphones $_g i_v$, $_g A_p$, $_k A_p$, and others. Similarly, each of the sixteen Wickelfeatures stands for a conjunction of three phonetic features and occurs in the representation of a large number of Wickelphones.

Now, words are simply lists of Wickelphones. Thus, words can be represented by simply turning on all of the Wickelfeatures in any Wickelphone of a word. Thus, a word with three Wickelphones (such as *came*, which has the Wickelphones $_\#k_A$, $_k A_m$, and $_a m_\#$) will have at most forty-eight Wickelfeatures turned on. Since the various Wickelphones may have some Wickelfeatures in common, typically there will be less than sixteen times the number of Wickelfeatures turned on for most words. It is important to note the temporal order is entirely implicit in this representation. All words, no matter how many phonemes in the word, will be represented by a subset of the 460 Wickelfeatures.

Blurring the Wickelfeature representation

The representational scheme just outlined constitutes what we call the *primary* representation of a Wickelphone. In order to promote faster generalization, we further blurred the representation. This is accomplished by turning on in addition to the sixteen primary Wickelfeatures, a randomly selected subset of the similar Wickelfeatures, specifically, those having the same value for the central feature and one of the two context phonemes. That is, whenever the Wickelfeature for the conjunction of phonemic features f_1, f_2, and f_3 is turned on, each Wickelfeature of the form $\langle ?f_2f_3\rangle$ and $\langle f_1f_2?\rangle$ may be turned on as well. Here "?" stands for "any feature." This causes each word to activate a larger set of Wickelfeatures, allowing what is learned about one sequence of phonemes to generalize more readily to other similar but not identical sequences.

To avoid having too much randomness in the representation of a particular Wickelphone, we turned on the same subset of additional Wickelfeatures each time a particular Wickelphone was to be represented. Based on subsequent experience with related models, we do not believe this makes very much difference.

There is a kind of trade-off between the discriminability among the base forms of verbs that the representation provides and the amount of generalization. We need a representation which allows for rapid generalization while at the same time maintains adequate discriminability. We can manipulate this factor by manipulating the probability p that any one of these similar Wickelfeatures will be turned on. In our simulations we found that turning on the additional features with fairly high probability (.9) led to adequate discriminability while also producing relatively rapid generalization.

Although the model is not completely immune to the possibility that two different words will be represented by the same pattern, we have encountered no difficulty decoding any of the verbs we have studied. However, we do not claim that Wickelfeatures necessarily capture all the information needed to support the generalizations we might need to make for this or other morphological processes. Some morphological processes might require the use of units that were further differentiated according to vowel stress or other potential distinguishing characteristics. All we claim for the present coding scheme is its sufficiency for the task of representing the past tenses of the 500 most frequent verbs in English and the importance of the basic principles of distributed, coarse (what we are calling blurred), conjunctive coding that it embodies.

Summary of the structure of the model

In summary, our model contained two sets of 460 Wickelfeature units, one set (the input units) to represent the base form of each verb and one set (the output units) to represent the past-tense form of each verb.

The model is tested by typing in an input phoneme string, which is translated by the fixed encoding network into a pattern of activation over the set of input units. Each active input unit contributes to the net input of each output unit, by an amount and direction (positive or negative) determined by the weight on the connection between the input unit and the output unit. The output units are then turned on or off probabilistically, with the probability increasing with the difference between the net input and the threshold, according to the logistic activation function. The output pattern generated in this way can be compared with various alternative possible output patterns, such as the correct past-tense form or some other possible response of interest, or can be used to drive the decoder network described in the Appendix.

The model is trained by providing it with pairs of patterns, consisting of the base pattern and the target, or correct, output. Thus, in accordance with common assumptions about the nature of the learning situation that faces the young child, the model receives only correct input from the outside world. However, it compares what it generates internally to the target output, and when it gets the wrong answer for a particular output unit, it adjusts the strength of the connection between the input and the output units so as to reduce the probability that it will make the same mistake the next time the same input pattern is presented. The adjustment of connections is an extremely simple and *local* procedure, but it appears to be sufficient to capture what we know about the acquisition of the past tense, as we shall see in the next section.

The simulations

The simulations described in this section are concerned with demonstrating three main points:

- That the model captures the basic three-stage pattern of acquisition.
- That the model captures most aspects of differences in performance on different types of regular and irregular verbs.
- That the model is capable of responding appropriately to verbs it has never seen before, as well as to regular and irregular verbs actually experienced during training.

In the sections that follow we will consider these three aspects of the model's performance in turn.

The corpus of verbs used in the simulations consisted of a set of 506 verbs. All verbs were chosen from the Kučera and Francis (1964) word list and were ordered according to frequency of their gerund form. We divided the verbs into three classes: Ten high-frequency verbs, 410 medium-frequency verbs, and eighty-six low-frequency verbs. The ten highest frequency verbs were: *come* (/kˆm/), *get* (/get/), *give* (/giv/), *look* (/luk/), *take* (/tʌk/), *go* (/gO/), *have* (/hav/), *live* (/liv/), and *feel* (/fEl/). There is a total of eight irregular and two regular verbs among the top ten. Of the medium-frequency verbs, 334 were regular and seventy-six were irregular. Of the low-frequency verbs, seventy-two were regular and fourteen were irregular.

The three-stage learning curve

The results described in this and the following sections were obtained from a single (long) simulation run. The run was intended to capture approximately the experience with past tenses of a young child picking up English from everyday conversation. Our conception of the nature of this experience is simply that the child learns first about the present and past tenses of the highest frequency verbs; later on, learning occurs for a much larger ensemble of verbs, including a much larger proportion of regular forms. Although the child would be hearing present and past tenses of all kinds of verbs throughout development, we assume that he is only able to learn past tenses for verbs that he has already mastered fairly well in the present tense.

To simulate the earliest phase of past-tense learning, the model was first trained on the ten high-frequency verbs, receiving ten cycles of training presentations through the set of ten verbs. This was enough to produce quite good performance on these verbs. We take the performance of the model at this point to correspond to the performance of a child in Phase 1 of acquisition. To simulate later phases of learning, the 410 medium-frequency verbs were added to the first ten verbs, and the system was given 190 more learning trials, with each trial consisting of one presentation of each of the 420 verbs. The responses of the model early on in this phase of training correspond to Phase 2 of the acquisition process; its ultimate performance at the end of 190 exposures to each of the 420 verbs corresponds to Phase 3. At this point, the model exhibits almost errorless performance on the basic 420 verbs. Finally, the set of eighty-six lower-frequency verbs were presented to the system and the transfer responses to these were recorded. During this phase, connection strengths were not adjusted. Performance of the model on these transfer verbs is considered in a later section.

We do not claim, of course, that this training experience exactly captures the learning experience of the young child. It should be perfectly clear that this training experience exaggerates the difference between early phases of learning and later phases, as well as the abruptness of the transition to a larger corpus of verbs. However, it is generally observed that the early, rather limited vocabulary of young children undergoes an explosive growth at some point in development (Brown, 1973). Thus, the actual transition in a child's vocabulary of verbs would appear quite abrupt on a time-scale of years so that our assumptions about abruptness of onset may not be too far off the mark.

Figure 4.1.4 shows the basic results for the high-frequency verbs. What we see is that during the first ten trials there is no difference between regular and irregular verbs. However, beginning on Trial 11 when the 410 midfrequency verbs were introduced, the regular verbs show better performance. It is important to notice that there is no interfering effect on the regular verbs as the midfrequency verbs are being learned. There is, however, substantial interference on the irregular verbs. This interference leads to a dip in performance on the irregular verbs. Equality of performance between regular and irregular verbs is never again attained during the training period. This is the

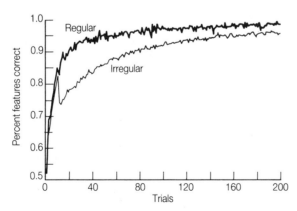

Figure 4.1.4 *The percentage of correct features for regular and irregular high-frequency verbs as a function of trials.*

so-called U-shaped learning curve for the learning of the irregular past tense. Performance is high when only a few high-frequency, largely irregular verbs are learned, but then drops as the bulk of lower-frequency regular verbs are being learned.

We have thus far only shown that performance on high-frequency irregular verbs drops; we have not said anything about the nature of the errors. To examine this question, the response strength of various possible response alternatives must be compared. To do this, we compared the strength of response for several different response alternatives. We compared strengths for the correct past tense, the present, the base + ed and the past + ed. Thus, for example with the verb *give* we compared the response strength of /gʌv/, /gɪv/, /gɪvd/, and /gʌvd/. We determined the response strengths by assuming that these response alternatives were competing to account for the features that were actually turned on in the output. The details of the competition mechanism, called a *binding network*, are described in the Appendix. For present purposes, suffice it to say that each alternative gets a score that represents the percentage of the total features that it accounts for. If two alternatives both account for a given feature, they divide the score for that feature in proportion to the number of features each accounts for uniquely. We take these response strengths to correspond roughly to relative response probabilities, though we imagine that the actual generation of overt responses is accomplished by a different version of the binding network, described below. In any case, the total strength of all the alternatives cannot be greater than 1, and if a number of features are accounted for by none of the alternatives, the total will be less than 1.

Figure 4.1.5 compares the response strengths for the correct alternative to the combined strength of the regularized alternatives.[4] Note in the figure that

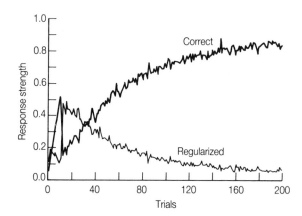

Figure 4.1.5   *Response strengths for the high-frequency irregular verbs. The response strengths for the correct responses are compared with those for the regularized alternatives as a function of trials.*

during the first ten trials the response strength of the correct alternative grows rapidly to over .5 while that of the regularized alternative drops from about .2 to .1. After the midfrequency verbs are introduced, the response strength for the correct alternative drops rapidly while the strengths of regularized alternatives jump up. From about Trials 11 through 30, the regularized alternatives together are stronger than the correct response. After about Trial 30, the strength of the correct response again exceeds the regularized alternatives and continues to grow throughout the 200-trial learning phase. By the end, the correct response is much the strongest with all other alternatives below .1.

The rapidity of the growth of the regularized alternatives is due to the sudden influx of the medium-frequency verbs. In real life we would expect the medium-frequency verbs to come in somewhat more slowly so that the period of maximal regularization would have a somewhat slower onset.

Figure 4.1.6 shows the same data in a slightly different way. In this case, we have plotted the ratio of the correct response to the sum of the correct and regularized response strengths. Points on the curve below the .5 line are in the region where the regularized response is greater than the correct response. Here we see clearly the three stages. In the first stage, the first ten trials of learning, performance on these high-frequency verbs is quite good. Virtually no regularization takes place. During the next twenty trials, the system regularizes and systematically makes errors on the verbs that it previously responded to correctly. Finally, during the remaining trials the model slowly eliminates the regularization responses as it approaches adult performance.

In summary, then, the model captures the three phases of learning quite well, as well as the gradual transition from Phase 2 to Phase 3. It does so without any explicit learning of rules. The regularization is the product of the gradual tuning

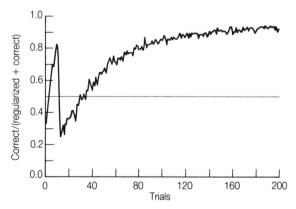

Figure 4.1.6 *The ratio of the correct response to the sum of the correct and regularized response. Points on the curve below the .5 line are in the region where the regularized response is greater than the correct response.*

of connection strengths in response to the predominantly regular correspond-ence exhibited by the medium-frequency words. It is not quite right to say that individual pairs are being stored in the network in any simple sense. The connection strengths the model builds up to handle the irregular forms do not represent these items in any separable way; they represent them in the way they must be represented to be stored along with the other verbs in the same set of connections.

Before discussing the implications of these kinds of results further, it is useful to look more closely at the kinds of errors made and at the learning rates of the medium-frequency regular and irregular verbs.

Learning the medium-frequency verbs

Figure 4.1.7A compares the learning curves for the regular verbs of high and

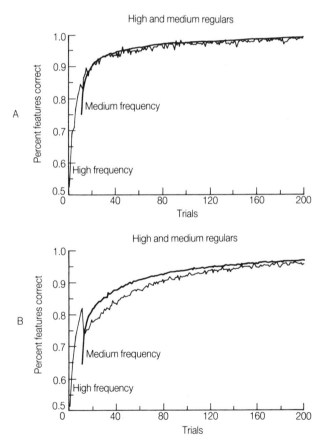

Figure 4.1.7 *The learning curves for the high- and medium-frequency verbs.*

medium frequency, and Figure 4.1.7B compares the learning curves for the corresponding groups of irregular verbs. Within only two or three trials the medium-frequency verbs catch up with their high-frequency counterparts. Indeed, in the case of the irregular verbs, the medium-frequency verbs seem to surpass the high-frequency ones. As we shall see in the following section, this results from the fact that the high-frequency verbs include some of the most difficult pairs to learn, including, for example, the *go/went* pair which is the most difficult to learn (aside from the verb *be*, this is the only verb in English in which the past and root form are completely unrelated). It should also be noted that even at this early stage of learning there is substantial generalization. Already, on Trial 11, the very first exposure to the medium-frequency verbs, between 65 and 75 percent of the features are produced correctly. Chance responding is only 50 percent. Moreover, on their first presentation, 10 percent more of the features of regular verbs are correctly responded to than irregular ones. Eventually, after 200 trials of learning, nearly all of the features are being correctly generated and the system is near asymptotic performance on this verb set. As we shall see below, during most of the learning period the difference between high- and medium-frequency verbs is not important. Rather, the differences between different classes of verbs is the primary determiner of performance. We now turn to a discussion of these different types.

Types of regular and irregular verbs

To this point, we have treated regular and irregular verbs as two homogeneous classes. In fact, there are a number of distinguishable types of regular and irregular verbs. Bybee and Slobin (1982) have studied the different acquisition patterns of each type of verb. In this section we compare their results to the responses produced by our simulation model.

Bybee and Slobin divided the irregular verbs into nine classes, defined as follows:[5]

I. Verbs that do not change at all to form the past tense, e.g., *beat, cut, hit*.

II. Verbs that change a final /d/ to /t/ to form the past tense, e.g., *send/sent, build/built*.

III. Verbs that undergo an internal vowel change and also add a final /t/ or /d/, e.g., *feel/felt, lose/lost, say/said, tell/told*.

IV. Verbs that undergo an internal vowel change, delete a final consonant, and add a final /t/ or /d/, e.g., *bring/brought, catch/caught*.[6]

V. Verbs that undergo an internal vowel change whose stems end in a dental, e.g., *bite/bit, find/found, ride/rode*.

VIa. Verbs that undergo a vowel change of /i/ to /a/ e.g., *sing/sang, drink/drank*.

VIb. Verbs that undergo an internal vowel change of /i/ or /a/ to /^/ e.g., *sting/stung, hang/hung*.[7]

VII. All other verbs that undergo an internal vowel change, e.g., *give/gave*, *break/broke*.

VIII. All verbs that undergo a vowel change and that end in a diphthongal sequence, e.g., *blow/blew*, *fly/flew*.

A complete listing by type of all of the irregular verbs used in our study is given in Table 4.1.7.

In addition to these types of irregular verbs, we distinguished three categories of regular verbs: (a) those ending in a vowel or voiced consonant, which take a /d/ to form the past tense; (b) those ending in a voiceless consonant, which take a /t/; and (c) those ending in /t/ or /d/, which take a final /^d/ to form the past tense. The number of regular verbs in each category, for each of the three frequency levels, is given in Table 4.1.8.

Type I: No-change verbs

A small set of English verbs require no change between their present- and past-

Table 4.1.7 *Irregular verbs*

Type	High	Medium	Low
		Frequency	
I		beat fit set spread hit cut put	thrust bid
II		build send spend	bend lend
III	feel	deal do flee tell sell hear keep leave sleep lose mean say sweep	creep weep
IV	have make	think buy bring seek teach	catch
V	get	meet shoot write lead understand sit mislead bleed feed stand light find fight read meet hide hold ride	breed wind grind
VIa		drink ring sing swim	
VIb		drag hang swing	dig cling stick
VII	give take come	shake arise rise run become bear wear speak brake drive strike fall freeze choose	tear
VIII	go	throw blow grow draw fly know see	

Table 4.1.8 *Number of regular verbs of each type*

| Type | Suffix | Example | Frequency | | |
			High	Medium	Low
End in detail	/ˆd/	start	0	94	13
End in voiceless consonant	/t/	look	1	64	30
End in voiced consonant or vowel	/d/	move	1	176	29

tense forms. One factor common to all such verbs is that they already end in /t/ or /d/. Thus, they superficially have the regular past-tense form—even in the present tense. Stemberger (1981) points out that it is common in inflectional languages not to add an additional inflection to base forms that already appear to have the inflection. Not all verbs ending in /t/ or /d/ show no change between present and past (in fact the majority of such verbs in English do show a change between present and past tense), but there is a reasonably large group—the Type I verbs of Bybee and Slobin—that do show this trend. Bybee and Slobin (1982) suggest that children learn relatively early on that past-tense verbs in English tend to end in /t/ or /d/ and thus are able to correctly respond to the no-change verbs rather early. Early in learning, they suggest, children also incorrectly generalize this "no-change rule" to verbs whose present and past tenses differ.

The pattern of performance just described shows up very clearly in data Bybee and Slobin (1982) report from an elicitation task with preschool children. In this task, preschoolers were given the present-tense form of each of several verbs and were asked to produce the corresponding past-tense form. They used the set of thirty-three verbs shown in Table 4.1.9.

The results were very interesting. Bybee and Slobin found that verbs not ending in *t/d* were predominately regularized and verbs ending in *t/d* were predominately used as no-change verbs. The number of occurrences of each kind is shown in Table 4.1.10. These preschool children have, at this stage, both

Table 4.1.9 *Verbs used by Bybee and Slobin*

Type of verb	Verb list
Regular	walk smoke mɔ̣ ̣at smile climb
Vowel change	drink break run swim throw meet shoot ride
Vowel change +*t/d*	do buy lose sell sleep help teach catch
No change	hit hurt set shut cut put beat
Other	go make build lend

Table 4.1.10 *Regular and no change responses to t/d and other verbs (Data from Bybee and Slobin, 1982)*

Verb ending	Regular suffix	No change
Not *t/d*	203	34
t/d	42	157

learned to regularize verbs not ending in *t/d* and, largely, to leave verbs ending in *t/d* without an additional ending.

Interestingly, our simulations show the same pattern of results. The system learns both to regularize and has a propensity *not* to add an additional ending to verbs already ending in *t/d*. In order to compare the simulation results to the human data we looked at the performance of the same verbs used by Bybee and Slobin in our simulations. Of the thirty-three verbs, twenty-seven were in the high- and medium-frequency lists and thus were included in the training set used in the simulation. The other six verbs (*smoke, catch, lend, pat, hurt* and *shut*) were either in the low-frequency sample or did not appear in our sample at all. Therefore, we will report on twenty-seven out of the thirty-three verbs that Bybee and Slobin tested.

It is not clear what span of learning trials in our simulation corresponds best to the level of the preschoolers in Bybee and Slobin's experiment. Presumably the period during which regularization is occurring is best. The combined strength of the regularized alternatives exceeds correct response strength for irregulars from about Trial 11 through Trials 20 to 30 depending on which particular irregular verbs we look at. We therefore have tabulated our results over three different time-ranges—Trials 11 through 15, Trials 16 through 20, and Trials 21 through 30. In each case we calculated the average strength of the regularized response alternatives and of the no-change response alternatives. Table 4.1.11 gives these strengths for each of the different time-periods.

The simulation results show clearly the same patterns evident in the Bybee and Slobin data. Verbs ending in *t/d* always show a stronger no-change

Table 4.1.11 *Average simulated strengths of regularized and no-change responses*

Time-period	Verb ending	Regularized	No change
11–15	not *t/d*	0.44	0.10
	t/d	0.35	0.27
16–20	not *t/d*	0.32	0.12
	t/d	0.25	0.35
21–30	not *t/d*	0.52	0.11
	t/d	0.32	0.41

response and a weaker regularized response than those not ending in t/d. During the very early stages of learning, however, the regularized response is stronger than the no-change response—even if the verb does end with t/d. This suggests that the generalization that the past tense of t/d verbs is formed by adding /ˆd/ is stronger than the generalization that verbs ending in t/d should not have an ending added. However, as learning proceeds, this secondary generalization is made (though for only a subset of the t/d verbs, as we shall see), and the simulation shows the same interaction that Bybee and Slobin (1982) found in their preschoolers.

The data and the simulations results just described conflate two aspects of performance, namely, the tendency to make no-change *errors* with t/d verbs that are not no-change verbs and the tendency to make *correct* no-change responses to the t/d verbs that are no-change verbs. Though Bybee and Slobin did not report their data broken down by this factor, we can examine the results of the simulation to see whether in fact the model is making more no-change errors with t/d verbs for which this response is incorrect. To examine this issue, we return to the full corpus of verbs and consider the tendency to make no-change errors separately for irregular verbs other than Type I verbs and for regular verbs.

Erroneous no-change responses are clearly stronger for both regular and irregular t/d verbs. Figure 4.1.8A compares the strength of the erroneous no-change responses for irregular verbs ending in t/d (Types II and V) versus those not ending in t/d (Types III, IV, VI, VII, and VIII). The no-change response is erroneous in all of these cases. Note, however, that the erroneous no-change responses are stronger for the t/d verbs than for the other types of irregular verbs. Figure 4.1.8B shows the strength of erroneous no-change responses for regular verbs ending in t/d versus those not ending in t/d. Again, the response strength for the no-change response is clearly greater when the regular verb ends in a dental.

We also compared the regularization responses for irregular verbs whose stems end in t/d with irregulars not ending in t/d. The results are shown in Figure 4.1.8C. In this case, the regularization responses are initially stronger for verbs that do not end in t/d than for those that do. Thus, we see that even when focusing only on erroneous responses, the system shows a greater propensity to respond with no-change to t/d verbs, whether or not the verb is regular, and a somewhat greater tendency to regularize irregulars not ending in t/d.

There is some evidence in the literature on language acquisition that performance on Type I verbs is better sooner than for irregular verbs involving vowel changes—Types III through VIII. Kuczaj (1978) reports an experiment in which children were to judge the grammaticality of sentences involving past tenses. The children were given sentences involving words like *hit* or *hitted* or *ate* or *eated* and asked whether the sentences sounded "silly." The results, averaged over three age groups from 3;4 to 9;0 years, showed that 70 percent of the responses to the no-change verbs were correct whereas only 31 percent of

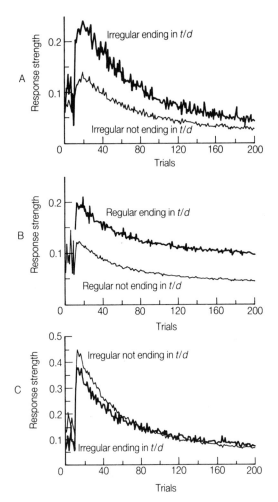

Figure 4.1.8   A: *The strength of erroneous no-change responses for irregular verbs ending in a dental versus those not ending in a dental. B: The strength of erroneous no-change responses for regular verbs ending in a dental versus those not ending in a dental. C: The strength of erroneous regularization responses for irregular verbs ending in a dental versus those not ending in a dental.*

the responses to vowel-change irregular verbs were correct. Most of the errors involved incorrect acceptance of a regularized form. Thus, the results show a clear difference between the verb types, with performance on the Type I verbs superior to that on Type III through VIII verbs.

The simulation model too shows better performance on Type I verbs than on any of the other types. These verbs show fewer errors than any of the other irregular verbs. Indeed, the error rate on Type I verbs is equal to that on the most difficult of the regular verbs. Table 4.1.12 gives the average number of Wickelfeatures incorrectly generated (out of 460) at different periods during the learning processes for no-change (i.e. Type I) irregular verbs, vowel-change (i.e., Type III–VIII) irregular verbs, regular verbs ending in t/d, regular verbs not ending in t/d, and regular verbs ending in t/d whose stem is a CVC (consonant-vowel-consonant) monosyllable. The table clearly shows that throughout learning, fewer incorrect Wickelfeatures are generated for no-change verbs than for vowel-change verbs. Interestingly, the table also shows that one subset of regulars are no easier than the Type I irregulars. These are the regular verbs which look on the surface most like Type I verbs, namely, the monosyllabic CVC regular verbs ending in t/d. These include such verbs as *bat, wait, shout, head*, etc. Although we know of no data indicating that people make more no-change errors on these verbs than on multisyllabic verbs ending in t/d, this is a clear prediction of our model. Essentially what is happening is that the model is learning that monosyllables ending in t/d sometimes take no additional inflection.[8] This leads to quicker learning of the no-change verbs relative to other irregular verbs and slower learning of regular verbs which otherwise look like no-change verbs. It should be noted that the two regular verbs employed by Bybee and Slobin which behaved like no-change verbs were both monosyllables. It would be interesting to see whether no-change errors actually occur with verbs like *decide* or *devote*.

Types III–VIII: Vowel-change verbs

To look at error patterns on *vowel-change* verbs (Types III–VIII), Bybee and Slobin (1982) analyzed data from the spontaneous speech of preschoolers ranging from 1½ to 5 years of age. The data came from independent sets of data collected by Susan Ervin-Tripp and Wick Miller, by Dan Slobin, and by Zell Greenberg. In all, speech from thirty-one children involving the use of sixty-nine irregular verbs was studied. Bybee and Slobin recorded the percentages of regularizations for each of the various types of vowel-change verbs. Table 4.1.13 gives the percentages of regularization by preschoolers, ranked from most to

Table 4.1.12 *Average number of Wickelfeatures incorrectly generated*

Trial Number	Irregular verbs		Regular verbs		
	Type I	Types III–VIII	Ending in t/d	Not Ending in t/d	CV$t/d$
11–15	89.8	123.9	74.1	82.8	87.3
16–20	57.6	93.7	45.3	51.2	60.5
21–30	45.5	78.2	32.9	37.4	47.9
31–50	34.4	61.3	22.9	26.0	37.3
51–100	18.8	39.0	11.4	12.9	21.5
101–200	11.8	21.5	6.4	7.4	12.7

Table 4.1.13   *Percentage of regularization by preschoolers (Data from Bybee and Slobin, 1982)*

Verb type	Example	Percentage regularizations
VIII	blew	80
VI	sang	55
V	bit	34
VII	broke	32
III	felt	13
IV	caught	10

fewest erroneous regularizations. The results show that the two verb types which involve adding a t/d plus a vowel change (Types III and IV) show the least regularizations, whereas the verb type in which the present tense ends in a diphthong (Type VIII) shows by far the most regularization.

It is not entirely clear what statistic in our model best corresponds to the percentage of regularizations. It will be recalled that we collected response strength measures for four different response types for irregular verbs. These were the correct response, the no-change response, the base + ed regularization response, and the past + ed regularization response. If we imagine that no-change responses are, in general, difficult to observe in spontaneous speech, perhaps the measure that would be most closely related to the percentage of regularizations would be the ratio of the sum of the strengths of the regularization responses to the sum of the strengths of regularization responses and the correct response—that is,

$$\frac{(base + ed \ + \ past + ed)}{(base + ed \ + \ past + ed \ + \ correct)}.$$

As with our previous simulation, it is not entirely clear what portion of the learning curve corresponds to the developmental level of the children in this group. We therefore calculated this ratio for several different time periods around the period of maximal overgeneralization. Table 4.1.14 shows the results of these simulations.

The spread between different verb classes is not as great in the simulation as in the children's data, but the simulated rank orders show a remarkable similarity to the results from the spontaneous speech of the preschoolers, especially in the earliest time period. Type VIII verbs show uniformly strong patterns of regularization whereas Type III and Type IV verbs, those whose past tense involves adding a t/d at the end, show relatively weak regularization responses. Type VI and Type VII verbs produce somewhat disparate results. For Type VI verbs, the simulation conforms fairly closely to the children's speech data in the earliest time period, but it shows rather less strength for regularizations of these

Table 4.1.14 *Strength of regularization responses relative to correct responses*

Rank order	Data		Trials 11–15		Trials 16–20		Trials 21–30		Average trials 11–30	
	Type	Percent	Type	Ratio	Type	Ratio	Type	Ratio	Type	Ratio
1	VIII	80	VIII	.86	VIII	.76	VIII	.61	VIII	.71
2	VI	55	VII	.80	VII	.74	VII	.61	VII	.69
3	V	34	VI	.76	V	.60	IV	.48	V	.56
4	VII	32	V	.72	IV	.59	V	.46	IV	.56
5	III	13	IV	.69	III	.57	III	.44	III	.53
6	IV	10	III	.67	VI	.52	VI	.40	VI	.52

verbs in the later time periods and in the average over Trials 11–30. For Type VII verbs, the model errs in the opposite direction: Here it tends to show rather greater strength for regularizations of these verbs than we see in the children's speech. One possible reason for these discrepancies may be the model's insensitivity to word frequency. Type VI verbs are, in fact, relatively low-frequency verbs, and thus, in the children's speech these verbs may actually be at a relatively earlier stage in acquisition than some of the more frequent irregular verbs. Type VII verbs are, in general, much more frequent—in fact, on the average they occur more than twice as often (in the gerund form) in the Kučera–Francis count than the Type VI verbs. In our simulations, all medium-frequency verbs were presented equally often and the distinction was not made. A higher-fidelity simulation including finer gradations of frequency variations among the verb types might lead to a closer correspondence with the empirical results. In any case, these verbs aside, the simulation seems to capture the major features of the data very nicely.

Bybee and Slobin attribute the pattern of results they found to factors that would not be relevant to our model. They proposed, for example, that Type III and IV verbs were more easily learned because the final t/d signaled to the child that they were in fact past tenses so the child would not have to rely on context as much in order to determine that these were past-tense forms. In our simulations, we found these verbs to be easy to learn, but it must have been for a different reason since the learning system was always informed as to what the correct past tense really was. Similarly, Bybee and Slobin argued that Type VIII verbs were the most difficult because the past and present tenses were so phonologically different that the child could not easily determine that the past and present tenses of these verbs actually go together. Again, our simulation showed Type VIII verbs to be the most difficult, but this had nothing to do with putting the past and present tense together since the model was always given the present and past tenses together.

Our model, then, must offer a different interpretation of Bybee and Slobin's findings. The main factor appears to be the degree to which the relation between the present and past tense of the verb is idiosyncratic. Type VIII verbs are most difficult because the relationship between base form and past tense is most idiosyncratic for these verbs. Thus, the natural generalizations implicit in the population of verbs must be overcome for these verbs, and they must be overcome in a different way for each of them. A very basic aspect of the mapping from present to past tense is that most of the word, and in particular everything up to the final vowel, is unchanged. For regular verbs, all of the phonemes present in the base form are preserved in the past tense. Thus, verbs that make changes to the base form are going against the grain more than those that do not; the larger the changes, the harder they will be to learn. Another factor is that past tenses of verbs generally end in /t/ or /d/.

Verbs that violate the basic past-tense pattern are all at a disadvantage in the model, of course, but some suffer less than others because there are other verbs that deviate from the basic pattern in the same way. Thus, these verbs are less idiosyncratic than verbs such as *go/went*, *see/saw*, and *draw/drew* which represent completely idiosyncratic vowel changes. The difficulty with Type VIII verbs, then, is simply that, as a class, they are simply more idiosyncratic than other verbs. Type III and IV verbs (e.g., *feel/felt*, *catch/caught*), on the other hand share with the vast bulk of the verbs in English the feature that the past tense involves the addition of a *t/d*. The addition of the *t/d* makes these verbs easier than, say, Type VII verbs (e.g., *come/came*) because in Type VII verbs the system must not only learn that there is a vowel change, but it must also learn that there *is not* an addition of *t/d* to the end of the verb.

Type VI verbs (*sing/sang*, *drag/drug*) are interesting from this point of view, because they involve fairly common subregularities not found in other classes of verbs such as those in Type V. In the model, the Type VI verbs may be learned relatively quickly because of this subregularity.

Types of regularization

We have mentioned that there are two distinct ways in which a child can regularize an irregular verb: The child can use the base + ed form or the past + ed form. Kuczaj (1977) has provided evidence that the proportion of past + ed forms increases, relative to the number of base + ed forms, as the child gets older. He found, for example, that the nine youngest children he studied had more base + ed regularizations than past + ed regularizations whereas four out of the five oldest children showed more past + ed than base + ed regularizations. In this section, we consider whether our model exhibits this same general pattern. Since the base form and the past-tense form are identical for Type I verbs, we restrict our analysis of this issue to Types II through VIII.

Figure 4.1.9 compares the average response strengths for base + ed and past + ed regularizations as a function of amount of training. The results of this

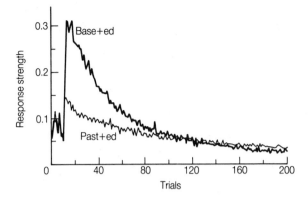

Figure 4.1.9   *Average response strength for base + ed and past + ed responses for verb Types II through VIII.*

analysis are more or less consistent with Kuczaj's findings. Early in learning, the base + ed response alternative is clearly the stronger of the two. As the system learns, however, the two come together so that by about 100 trials the base + ed and the past + ed response alternatives are roughly equally strong. Clearly, the simulations show that the percentage of regularizations that are past + ed increases with experience—just as Kuczaj found in children. In addition, the two curves come together rather late, consistent with the fact, reported by Kuczaj (1977), that these past + ed forms predominate for the most part in children who are exhibiting rather few regularization errors of either type. Of the four children exhibiting more past + ed regularizations, three were regularizing less than 12 percent of the time.

A closer look at the various types of irregular verbs shows that this curve is the average of two quite different patterns. Table 4.1.15 shows the overall percentage of regularization strength due to the base + ed alternative. It is clear from the table that the verbs fall into two general categories, those of Types III, IV, and VIII which have an overall preponderance of base + ed strength (the

Table 4.1.15   *Percentage of regularization strength due to base + ed*

Verb type	Percent base + ed	Examples
III	0.77	sleep/slept
IV	0.69	catch/caught
VIII	0.68	see/saw
II	0.38	spend/spent
VII	0.38	come/came
V	0.37	bite/bit
VI	0.26	sing/sang

percentages are all above .5) and Types II, VII, V, and VI which show an overall preponderance of past + ed strength (the percentages are all well below .5). The major variable which seems to account for the ordering shown in the table is the amount the ending is changed in going from the base form to the past-tense form. If the ending is changed little, as in *sing/sang* or *come/came*, the past + ed response is relatively stronger. If the past tense involves a greater change of the ending, such as *see/saw*, or *sleep/slept*, then the past + ed form is much weaker. Roughly, the idea is this: To form the past + ed for these verbs *two operations* must occur. The normal past tense must be created, and the regular ending must be appended. When these two operations involve very different parts of the verb, they can occur somewhat independently and both can readily occur. When, on the other hand, both changes occur to the same portion of the verb, they conflict with one another and a clear past + ed response is difficult to generate. The Type II verbs, which do show an overall preponderance of past + ed regularization strength, might seem to violate this pattern since it involves some change to the end in its past-tense form. Note, however, that the change is only a one feature change from /d/ to /t/ and thus is closer to the pattern of the verbs involving no change to the final phonemes of the verb. Figure 4.1.10A shows the pattern of response strengths to base + ed and past + ed regularizations for verb Types II, VII, V, and VI which involve relatively little change of the final phonemes from base to past form. Figure 4.1.10B shows the pattern of response strengths to base + ed and past + ed for verb Types III, IV, and VIII. Figure 4.1.10A shows very clearly the pattern expected from Kuczaj's results. Early in learning, base + ed responses are by far the strongest. With experience the past + ed response becomes stronger and stronger relative to the base + ed regularizations until, at about Trial 40, it begins to exceed it. Figure 4.1.10B shows a different pattern. For these verbs the past + ed form is weak throughout learning and never comes close to the base + ed regularization response. Unfortunately, Kuczaj did not present data on the relative frequency of the two types of regularizations separately for different verb types. Thus for the present, this difference in type of regularization responses remains an untested prediction of the model.

Transfer to novel verbs

To this point we have only reported on the behavior of the system on verbs that it was actually taught. In this section, we consider the response of the model to the set of eighty-six low-frequency verbs which it never saw during training. This test allows us to examine how well the behavior of the model generalizes to novel verbs. In this section we also consider responses to different types of regular verbs, and we examine the model's performance in generating unconstrained responses.

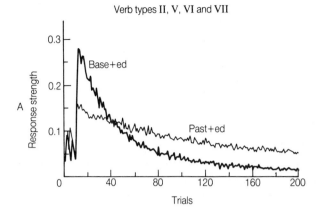

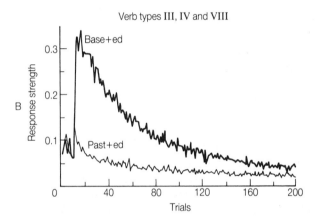

Figure 4.1.10 A: *The pattern of response strengths to base + ed and past + ed regularizations for verb Types II, V, VI, and VII. B: The pattern of response strengths to base + ed and past + ed for verb Types III, IV, and VIII.*

Overall degree of transfer

Perhaps the first question to ask is how accurately the model generates the correct features of the new verbs. Table 4.1.16 shows the percentage of Wickelfeatures correctly generated, averaged over the regular and irregular verbs. Overall, the performance is quite good. Over 90 percent of the Wickelfeatures are correctly generated without any experience whatsoever with these verbs. Performance is, of course, poorer on the irregular verbs, in which the actual past tense is relatively idiosyncratic. But even there, almost 85 percent of the Wickelfeatures are correctly generated.

Table 4.1.16 *Proportion of Wickelfeatures correctly generated*

Regular	.92
Irregular	.84
Overall	.91

Unconstrained responses

Up until this point we have always proceeded by giving the model a set of response alternatives and letting it assign a response strength to each one. This allows us to get relative response strengths among the set of response alternatives we have provided. Of course, we chose as response alternatives those which we had reason to believe were among the strongest. There is the possibility, however, that the output of the model might actually favor some other, untested alternative some of the time. To see how well the output of the model is really doing at specifying correct past tenses or errors of the kind that children actually make, we must allow the model to choose among all possible strings of phonemes.

To do this, we implemented a second version of the binding network. This version is also described in the Appendix. Instead of a competition among alternative strings, it involves a competition among individual Wickelphone alternatives, coupled with mutual facilitation between mutually compatible Wickelphones such as $_{\#}k_A$ and $_kA_m$.[9]

The results from the free-generation test are quite consistent with our expectations from the constrained alternative phase, though they did uncover a few interesting aspects of the model's performance that we had not anticipated. In our analysis of these results we have considered only responses with a strength of at least .2. Of the eighty-six test verbs, there were sixty-five cases in which exactly one of the alternatives exceeded .2. Of these, fifty-five were simple regularization responses, four were no-change responses, three involved double marking of regular verbs, (e.g., *type* was responded to with /tɪpˆ d/), and there was one case of a vowel change (e.g., *slip/slept*). There were fourteen cases in which two alternatives exceeded threshold and one case in which three exceeded threshold. Finally, in six cases, no response alternative exceeded threshold. This occurred with the regular verbs *jump, pump, soak, warm, trail,* and *glare.* In this case there were a number of alternatives, including the correct past-tense form of each of these verbs, competing with a response strength of about .1.

Table 4.1.17 shows the responses generated for the fourteen irregular verbs. The responses here are very clear. All of the above-threshold responses made to an irregular verb were either regularization responses, no-change responses (to Type I and V verbs as expected) or correct vowel-change generalizations. The

Table 4.1.17 *The model's responses to unfamiliar low-frequency irregular verbs*

Verb type	Presented word	Phonetic input	Phonetic response	English rendition	Response strength
I	bid	/bɪd/	/bɪd/	(bid)	0.55
	thrust	/Trˆst/	/Trˆstˆd/	(thrusted)	0.57
II	bend	/bend/	/bendˆd/	(bended)	0.28
	lend	/lend/	/lendˆd/	(lended)	0.70
III	creep	/krEp/	/krEpt/	(creeped)	0.51
	weep	/wEp/	/wEpt/	(weeped)	0.34
			/wept/	(wept)	0.33
IV	catch	/kaC/	/kaCt/	(catched)	0.67
V	breed	/brEd/	/brEdˆd/	(breeded)	0.48
	grind	/grɪnd/	/grɪnd/	(grind)	0.44
	wind	/wɪnd/	/wɪnd/	(wind)	0.37
VI	cling	/klɪN/	/klɪNd/	(clinged)	0.28
			/klˆN/	(clung)	0.23
	dig	/dig/	/digd/	(digged)	0.22
	stick	/stik/	/stikt/	(sticked)	0.53
VII	tear	/ter/	/terd/	(teared)	0.90

fact that *bid* is correctly generated as the past for *bid*, that *wept* is correctly generated as the past for *weep*, and that *clung* is correctly generated as a past tense for *cling* illustrates that the system is not only sensitive to the major regular past-tense pattern, but is sensitive to the subregularities as well. It should also be noted that the no-change responses to the verbs *grind* and *wind* occurs on monosyllabic Type V verbs ending in t/d, again showing evidence of a role for this subregularity in English past-tense formation.

Of the seventy-two regular verbs in our low-frequency sample, the six verbs mentioned above did not have any response alternatives above threshold. On forty-eight of the remaining sixty-six regular verbs, the only response exceeding threshold was the correct one. The threshold responses to the remaining eighteen verbs are shown in Table 4.1.18.

Note that for twelve of the eighteen verbs listed in the table, the correct response is above threshold. That means that of the sixty-six regular verbs to which any response at all exceeded threshold, the correct response exceeded threshold in sixty cases. It is interesting to note, also, that the model never chooses the incorrect variant of the regular past tense. As shown in Table 4.1.8, verbs ending in a /t/ or /d/ take /ˆd/ in the past tense; verbs ending in unvoiced consonants take /t/, and verbs ending in vowels or voiced consonants take /d/. On no occasion does the model assign a strength greater than .2 an incorrect variant of the past tense. Thus, the model has clearly learned the substructure of the regular correspondence and adds the correct variant to all different types of base forms. These results clearly demonstrate that the model acts in

Table 4.1.18 *System responses to unfamiliar low-frequency regular verbs*

Verb type	Presented word	Phonetic input	Phonetic response	English rendition	Response rendition
End in t/d	guard	/gɑrd/	/gɑrd/	(guard)	0.29
			/gɑrdˆd/	(guarded)	0.26
	kid	/kid/	/kid/	(kid)	0.39
			/kidˆd/	(kidded)	0.24
	mate	/mʌt/	/mʌtˆd/	(mated)	0.43
			/mʌdˆd/	(maded)	0.23
	squat	/skwˣt/	/skwˣtˆd/	(squated)	0.27
			/skwˣt/	(squat)	0.22
			/skwˣkt/	(squawked)	0.21
End in unvoiced consonant	carp	/kɑrp/	/kɑrpt/	(carped)	0.28
			/kɑrptˆd/	(carpted)	0.21
	drip	/drip/	/driptˆd/	(dripted)	0.28
			/dript/	(dripped)	0.22
	map	/map/	/maptˆd/	(mapted)	0.24
			/mapt/	(mapped)	0.22
	shape	/sʌp/	/sʌpt/	(shaped)	0.43
			/sipt/	(shipped)	0.27
	sip	/sip/	/sipt/	(sipped)	0.42
			/sept/	(sepped)	0.28
	slip	/slip/	/slept/	(slept)	0.40
	smoke	/smOk/	/smOktˆd/	(smokted)	0.29
			/smOk/	(smoke)	0.22
	snap	/snap/	/snaptˆd/	(snapted)	0.40
	step	/step/	/steptˆd/	(stepted)	0.59
	type	/tɪp/	/tɪptˆd/	(typted)	0.33
End in voiced consonant or vowel	brown	/brwn/	/brwnd/	(browned)	0.46
			/brˣnd/	(brawned)	0.39
	hug	/hˆg/	/hˆg/	(hug)	0.59
	mail	/mʌˆl/	/mʌˆld/	(mailed)	0.38
			/membˆld/	(membled)	0.23
	tour	/tʊr/	/tʊrdˆr/	(toureder)	0.31
			/tʊrd/	(toured)	0.25

accordance with the regular pattern for English verbs and that it can apply this pattern with a high level of success to novel as well as familiar verbs.

In addition to the regular responses, five of the responses were no-change responses. In three cases the no-change response was to a verb ending in t/d. Four of the responses followed the pattern of Type III verbs, modifying the vowel and adding a final /t/. Thus, for example, we have the past of *sip* rendered as *sept*, presumably on the model of *sleep/slept, keep/kept, sweep/swept,* etc. Interestingly, three of the four cases involved verbs whose base form ended in /p/ just as in the models listed above. Even though these last responses are, strictly speaking, incorrect, they all indicate a sensitivity to the regular and subregular patterns of the English past tense.

Perhaps the most surprising result evident from the table is the occurrence of a double past marker on the responses to seven of the verbs. Although we know of no references to this phenomenon in the literature, we expect that children (and adults) do occasionally make this kind of error. It is interesting, and possibly significant, that all seven of these responses occurred to verbs whose correct past tense is the addition of a /t/. It would be interesting to see whether children's errors of this type follow a similar pattern.

Finally, there were just four responses that involved the addition or modification of consonants. These were *maded* as a past tense of *mate*, *squawked* as a past tense for *squat*, *membled* as a past tense for *mail*, and *toureder* as a past tense for *tour*. It is unlikely that humans would make these errors, especially the last two, but these responses are, for the most part, near threshold. Furthermore, it seems likely that many of these responses could be filtered out if the model incorporated an auto-associative network of connections among the output units. Such a network could be used to clean up the output pattern and would probably increase the tendency of the model to avoid bizarre responses. Unfortunately, we have not yet had the chance to implement this suggestion.

Summary

The system has clearly learned the essential characteristics of the past tense of English. Not only can it respond correctly to the 460 verbs that it was taught, but it is able to generalize and transfer rather well to the unfamiliar low-frequency verbs that had never been presented during training. The system has learned about the conditions in which each of the three regular past-tense endings are to be applied and it has learned not only the dominant, regular form of the past tense, but many of the subregularities as well.

It is true that the model does not act as a perfect rule-applying machine with novel past-tense forms. However, it must be noted that people—or at least children, even in early grade-school years—are not perfect rule-applying machines either. For example, in Berko's classic (1958) study, though her kindergarten and first-grade subjects did often produce the correct past forms of novel verbs like *spow*, *mott*, and *rick*, they did not do so invariably. In fact, the rate of regular past-tense forms given to Berko's novel verbs was only 51 percent.[10] Thus, we see little reason to believe that our model's "deficiencies" are significantly greater than those of native speakers of comparable experience.

Conclusions

We have shown that our simple learning model shows, to a remarkable degree, the characteristics of young children learning the morphology of the past tense in English. We have shown how our model generates the so-called U-shaped learning curve for irregular verbs and that it exhibits a tendency to overgeneralize that is quite similar to the pattern exhibited by young children. Both in children and in our model, the verb forms showing the most regularization are pairs such as *know/knew* and *see/saw*, whereas those showing the least regularization are pairs such as *feel/felt* and *catch/caught*. Early in learning, our model shows the pattern of more no-change responses to verbs ending in t/d whether or not they are regular verbs, just as young children do. The model, like children, can generate the appropriate regular past-tense form to unfamiliar verbs whose base form ends in various consonants or vowels. Thus, the model generates an /^d/ suffix for verbs ending in t/d, a /t/ suffix for verbs ending in an unvoiced consonant, and a /d/ suffix for verbs ending in a voiced consonant or vowel.

In the model, as in children, different past-tense forms for the same word can coexist at the same time. On rule accounts, such *transitional* behavior is puzzling and difficult to explain. Our model, like human children, shows a relatively larger proportion of past + ed regularizations later in learning. Our model, like learners of English, will sometimes generate past-tense forms to novel verbs which show sensitivities to the subregularities of English as well as the major regularities. Thus, the past of *cring* can sometimes be rendered *crang* or *crung*. In short, our simple learning model accounts for all of the major features of the acquisition of the morphology of the English past tense.

In addition to our ability to account for the major *known* features of the acquisition process, there are also a number of predictions that the model makes which have yet to be reported. These include:

- We expect relatively more past + ed regularizations to irregulars whose correct past form *does not* involve a modification of the final phoneme of the base form.
- We expect that early in learning, a no-change response will occur more frequently to a CVC monosyllable ending in t/d than to a more complex base verb form.
- We expect that the double inflection responses (/dript^d/) will occasionally be made by native speakers and that they will occur more frequently to verbs whose stem is ends in /p/ or /k/.

The model is very rich and there are many other more specific predictions which can be derived from it and evaluated by a careful analysis of acquisition data.

We have, we believe, provided a distinct alternative to the view that children learn the rules of English past-tense formation in any explicit sense. We have shown that a reasonable account of the acquisition of past tense can be provided without recourse to the notion of a "rule" as anything more than a *description* of the language. We have shown that, for this case, there is no *induction problem*. The child need not figure out what the rules are, nor even that there are rules.

The child need not decide whether a verb is regular or irregular. There is no question as to whether the inflected form should be stored directly in the lexicon or derived from more general principles. There is not even a question (as far as generating the past-tense form is concerned) as to whether a verb form is one encountered many times or one that is being generated for the first time. A uniform procedure is applied for producing the past-tense form in every case. The base form is supplied as input to the past-tense network and the resulting pattern of activation is interpreted as a phonological representation of the past form of that verb. This is the procedure whether the verb is regular or irregular, familiar or novel.

In one sense, every form must be considered as being derived. In this sense, the network can be considered to be one large rule for generating past tenses from base forms. In another sense, it is possible to imagine that the system simply stores a set of rote associations between base and past-tense forms with novel responses generated by "on-line" generalizations from the stored exemplars.

Neither of these descriptions is quite right, we believe. Associations are simply stored in the network, but because we have a *superpositional* memory, similar patterns blend into one another and reinforce each other. If there were no similar patterns (i.e., if the featural representations of the base forms of verbs were orthogonal to one another) there would be no generalization. The system would be unable to generalize and there would be no regularization. It is statistical relationships among the base forms themselves that determine the pattern of responding. The network merely reflects the statistics of the featural representations of the verb forms.

We chose the study of acquisition of past tense in part because the phenomenon of regularization is an example often cited in support of the view that children do respond according to general rules of language. Why otherwise, it is sometimes asked, should they generate forms that they have never heard? The answer we offer is that they do so because the past tenses of similar verbs they are learning show such a consistent pattern that the generalization from these similar verbs outweighs the relatively small amount of learning that has occurred on the irregular verb in question. We suspect that essentially similar ideas will prove useful in accounting for other aspects of language acquisition. We view this work on past-tense morphology as a step toward a revised understanding of language knowledge, language acquisition, and linguistic information processing in general.

Acknowledgments

This research was supported by ONR Contracts N00014-82-C-0374, NR 667-483 and N00014-79-C-0323, NR 667-437, by a grant from the System Development

Foundation, and by a Research Scientist Career Development Award MH00385 to the second author from the National Institute of Mental Health.

Appendix

One important aspect of the Wickelfeature representation is that it completely suppressed the temporal dimension. Temporal information is stored implicitly in the feature pattern. This gives us a representational format in which phonological forms of arbitrary length can be represented. It also avoids an a priori decision as to which part of the verb (beginning, end, center, etc.) contains the past-tense inflection. This grows out of the learning process. Unfortunately, it has its negative side as well. Since phonological forms *do* contain temporal information, we need to have a method of converting from the Wickelfeature representation into the time-domain—in short, we need a decoding network which converts from the Wickelfeature representation to either the Wickelphone or a phonological representational format. Since we have probabilistic units, this decoding process must be able to work in the face of substantial noise. To do this we devised a special sort of decoding network which we call a *binding network*. Roughly speaking, a binding network is a scheme whereby a number of units *compete* for a set of available features—finally attaining a strength that is proportional to the number of features the units account for. We proceed by first describing the idea behind the binding network, then describing its application to produce the set of Wickelphones implicit in the Wickelfeature representation, and finally to produce the set of phonological strings implicit in the Wickelfeatures.

Binding networks

The basic idea is simple. Imagine that there are a set of input features and a set of output features. Each output feature is consistent with certain of the input features, inconsistent with certain other of the input features, and neutral about still other of the input features. The idea is to find a set of output features that accounts for as many as possible of the output features while minimizing the number of input features accounted for by more than one output feature. Thus, we want each of the output features to *compete* for input features. The more input features it *captures*, the stronger its position in the competition and the more claim it has on the features for which it accounts. Thus consider the case in which the input features are Wickelfeatures and the output features are Wickelphones. The Wickelphones compete among one another for the available Wickelfeatures. Every time a particular Wickelphone "captures" a particular Wickelfeature, that input feature no longer provides support for other

Wickelphones. In this way, the system comes up with a set of more or less nonoverlapping Wickelphones which account for as many as possible of the available Wickelfeatures. This means that if two Wickelphones have many Wickelfeatures in common (e.g., $_k\hat{}_m$ and $_kA_m$) but one of them accounts for more features than the other, the one that accounts for the most features will remove nearly all of the support for the very similar output feature which accounts for few if any input features uniquely. The binding network described below has the property that if two output units are competing for a set of input features, each will attain a strength proportional to the number of input features uniquely accounted for by that output feature divided by the total number of input features uniquely accounted for by any output feature.

This is accomplished by a network in which each input unit has a fixed amount of activation (in our case we assumed that it had a total activation value of 1) to be distributed among the output units consistent with that input feature. It distributes its activation in proportion to the strength of the output feature to which it is connected. This is thus a network with a dynamic weight. The weight from input unit j to output unit i is thus given by

$$(3) \qquad w_{ij} = \frac{a_i}{\sum_{k_j} a_{k_j}}$$

where k_j ranges over the set of output units consistent with input units j. The total strength of output unit k at time t is a linear function of its inputs at time $t-1$ and is thus given by

$$(4) \qquad a_k(t) = \sum_{j_k} i_{j_k}\, W_{kj_k}(t) = \frac{\sum_{j_k} i_{j_k} a_k\,(t-1)}{\sum_{l_{j_k}} a_{l_{j_k}}\,(t-1)}$$

where j_k ranges over the set of input features consistent with output feature k, l_{j_k} ranges over the set of output features consistent with input feature j_k, and i_j takes on value 1 if input feature j is present and is 0 otherwise.

We used the binding network described above to find the set of Wickelphones which gave optimal coverage to the Wickelfeatures in the input. The procedure was quite effective. We used as the set of output all of the Wickelphones that occurred anywhere in any of the 500 or so verbs we studied. We found that the actual Wickelphones were always the strongest when we had 80 percent or more of the correct Wickelfeatures. Performance dropped off as the percentage of correct Wickelfeatures dropped. Still when as few as 50 percent of the Wickelfeatures were correct, the correct Wickelphones were still the strongest most of the time. Sometimes, however, a Wickelphone not actually in the input would become strong and push out the "correct" Wickelphones. If we added the constraint that the Wickelphones must fit together to form an entire string (by having output features activate features that are consistent neighbors), we found that more than 60 percent of correct Wickelfeatures led to the correct output string more than 90 percent of the time.

The binding network described above is designed for a situation in which there is a set of input features that is to be divided up among a set of output features. In this case, features that are present, but not required for a particular output feature play no role in the evaluation of the output feature. Suppose, however, that we have a set of alternative output features, one of which is supposed to account for the entire pattern. In this case, input features that are present, but not consistent, with a given output feature must count against that output feature. One solution to this is to have input units *excite* consistent output units according to the rule given above and to *inhibit* inconsistent output units. In the case in which we tried to construct the entire phonological string directly from a set of Wickelfeatures we used the following activation rule:

$$(5) \qquad a_k(t) = \sum_{j_k} i_{j_k} \, w_{k j_k}(t) - \sum_{l_k} i_{l_k}$$

where l_k indexes the input features that are inconsistent with output feature k. In this case, we used as output features all of the strings of fewer than twenty phonemes which could be generated from the set of Wickelphones present in the entire corpus of verbs. This is the procedure employed to produce responses to the lowest frequency verbs as shown in Tables 4.1.17 and 4.1.18.

Notes to 4.1

1. The notation of phonemes used in this chapter is somewhat nonstandard. It is derived from the computer-readable dictionary containing phonetic transcriptions of the verbs used in the simulations. A key is given in Table 4.1.5.
2. In the examples we will be considering in this section, the thresholds of the units are fixed at 0. Threshold terms add an extra degree of freedom for each output unit and allow the unit to come on in the absence of input, but they are otherwise inessential to the operation of the model. Computationally, they are equivalent to an adjustable weight to an extra input unit that is always on.
3. For the actual simulations of verb learning, we used a value of T equal to 200. This means that for a fixed value of the weight on an input line, the effect of that line being active on the unit's probability of firing is much lower than it is in these illustrations. This is balanced by the fact that in the verb-learning simulations, a much larger number of inputs contribute to the activation of each output unit. Responsibility for turning a unit on is simply more distributed when larger input patterns are used.
4. Unless otherwise indicated, the regularized alternatives are considered the base + ed and past + ed alternatives. In a later section of the paper we shall discuss the pattern of differences between these alternatives. In most cases the base + ed alternative is much stronger than the past + ed alternative.
5. Criteria from Bybee and Slobin (1982: 268–9).
6. Following Bybee and Slobin, we included *buy/bought* in this class even though no final consonant is deleted.
7. For many purposes we combine Classes VIa and VIb in our analyses.

8. Though the model does not explicitly encode number of syllables, monosyllabic words are distinguished from multisyllabic words by the fact that the former contain no Wickelphones of the form $_vC_v$. There are no no-change verbs in English containing such Wickelphones.
9. The major problem with this method of generating responses is that it is tremendously computer intensive. Had we used this method to generate responses throughout the learning phase, we estimate that it would have taken *over three years* of computer time to complete the learning phase alone! This compares to the 260 hours of computer time the learning phase took with the response alternatives supplied. It took about twenty-eight hours to complete the response generation process in testing just the eighty-six low-frequency verbs used in this section of the study. Of course, in biological hardware, this would not be a problem since the processing would actually occur in parallel.
10. Unfortunately, Berko included only one regular verb to compare to her novel verbs. The verb was *melt*. Children were 73 percent correct on this verb. The two novel verbs that required the same treatment as *melt* (*mott* and *bodd*) each received only 33 percent correct responses.

References to 4.1

Anderson, J. A. (1973). "A theory for the recognition of items from short memorized lists." *Psychological Review*, **80**, 417–38.

Anderson, J. A. (1977). "Neural models with cognitive implications." In D. LaBerge and S. J. Samuels (eds), *Basic Processes in Reading: Perception and comprehension*. Hillsdale, NJ: Erlbaum, 27–90.

Anderson, J. A., Silverstein, J. W., Ritz, S. A., and Jones, R. S. (1977). "Distinctive features, categorical perception, and probability learning: Some applications of a neural model." *Psychological Review*, **84**, 413–51.

Bates, E. (1979). *Emergence of Symbols*. New York: Academic Press.

Berko, J. (1958). "The child's learning of English morphology." *Word*, **14**, 150–77.

Brown, R. (1973). *A First Language*. Cambridge, MA: Harvard University Press.

Bybee, J. L. and Slobin, D. I. (1982). "Rules and schemas in the development and use of the English past tense." *Language*, **58**, 265–89.

Ervin, S. (1964). "Imitation and structural change in children's language." In E. Lenneberg (ed.), *New Directions in the Study of Language*. Cambridge, MA: MIT Press.

Green, D. M. and Swets, J. A. (1966). *Signal Detection Theory and Psychophysics*. New York: Wiley.

Kohenen, T. (1977). *Associative Memory: A system theoretical approach*. New York: Springer.

Kohenen, T. (1984). *Self-organization and Associative Memory*. Berlin: Springer-Verlag.

Kučera, H. and Francis, W. (1964). *Computational Analysis of Present-day American English*. Providence, RI: Brown University Press.

Kuczaj, S. A. (1977). "The acquisition of regular and irregular past tense forms." *Journal of Verbal Learning and Verbal Behavior*, **16**, 589–600.

Kuczaj, S. A. (1978). "Children's judgments of grammatical and ungrammatical irregular past tense verbs." *Child Development*, **49**, 319–26.

McClelland, J. L. and Rumelhart, D. E. (1981). "An interactive activation model of context effects in letter perception: Part 1. An account of basic findings." *Psychological Review*, **88**, 375–407.

McClelland, J. L. and Rumelhart, D. E. (eds) (1986). *Parallel Distributed Processing*. Cambridge, MA: MIT Press.

Pinker, S. (1984). *Language Learnability and Language Development*. Cambridge, MA: MIT Press.

Rosenblatt, F. (1962). *Principles of Neurodynamics*. New York: Spartan.

Rumelhart, D. E. and McClelland, J. L. (1981). "Interactive processing through spreading activation." In A. M. Lesgold and C. A. Perfetti (eds), *Interactive Processes in Reading*. Hillsdale, NJ: Erlbaum.

Rumelhart, D. E. and McClelland, J. L. (1982). "An interactive activation model of context effects in letter perception: Part 2. The contextual enhancement effect and some tests and extensions of the model." *Psychological Review*, **89**, 60–94.

Stemberger, J. P. (1981). "Morphological haplology." *Language*, **57**, 791–817.

Wickelgren, W. A. (1969). "Context-sensitive coding, associative memory, and serial order in (speech) behavior." *Psychological Review*, **76**, 1–15.

4.2

Rules of Language

Steven Pinker

Every normal human can convey and receive an unlimited number of discrete messages through a highly structured stream of sound or, in the case of signed languages, manual gestures. This remarkable piece of natural engineering depends upon a complex code or grammar implemented in the brain that is deployed without conscious effort and that develops, without explicit training, by the age of four. Explaining this talent is an important goal of the human sciences.

Theories of language and other cognitive processes generally fall into two classes. Associationism describes the brain as a homogeneous network of interconnected units modified by a learning mechanism that records correlations among frequently co-occurring input patterns.[1] Rule-and-representation theories describe the brain as a computational device in which rules and principles operate on symbolic data structures.[2,3] Some rule theories further propose that the brain is divided into modular computational systems that have an organization that is largely specified genetically, one of the systems being language.[3,4]

During the last thirty-five years, there has been an unprecedented empirical study of human language structure, acquisition, use, and breakdown, allowing these centuries-old proposals to be refined and tested. I will illustrate how intensive multidisciplinary study of one linguistic phenomenon shows that both associationism and rule theories are partly correct, but about different components of the language system.

Modules of language

A grammar defines a mapping between sounds and meanings, but the mapping is not done in a single step but through a chain of intermediate data structures, each governed by a subsystem. Morphology is the subsystem that computes the forms of words. I focus on a single process of morphology: English past tense inflection, in which the physical shape of the verb varies to encode the relative time of occurrence of the referent event and the speech act. Regular past tenses marking (for example, *walk-walked*) is a rulelike process resulting in addition of the suffix *-d*. In addition there are about 180 irregular verbs that mark the past tense in other ways (for example, *hit-hit*, *come-came*, *feel-felt*).

Past-tense inflection is an isolable subsystem in which grammatical mechanisms can be studied in detail, without complex interactions with the rest of language. It is computed independently of syntax, the subsystem that defines the form of phrases and sentences: The syntax of English forces its speakers to mark tense in every sentence, but no aspect of syntax works differently with regular and irregular verbs. Past-tense marking is also insensitive to lexical semantics: The regular–irregular distinction does not correlate with any feature of verb meaning.[5,6] For example, *hit-hit*, *strike-struck*, and *slap-slapped* have similar meanings, but three different past-tense forms; *stand-stood*, *stand me up-stood me up*, and *understand-understood*, have unrelated meanings but identical past tense forms. Past marking is also independent of phonology, which determines the possible sound sequences in a language: The three pronunciations of the regular suffix (in *ripped*, *ribbed*, and *ridded*) represent not three independent processes but a single suffix *-d* modified to conform with general laws of English sound patterning.[5]

Rulelike processes in language

English inflection can illustrate the major kinds of theories used to explain linguistic processes. Traditional grammar offers the following first approximation: Regular inflection, being fully predictable, is computed by a rule that concatenates the affix *-d* to the verb stem. This allows a speaker to inflect an unlimited number of new verbs, an ability seen both in adults, who easily create past forms for neologisms like *faxed*, and in preschoolers, who, given a novel verb like *to rick* in experiments, freely produced *ricked*.[7] In contrast, irregular verb forms are unpredictable: Compare *sit-sat* and *hit-hit*, *sing-sang* and *string-strung*, *feel-felt* and *tell-told*. Therefore they must be individually memorized. Retrieval of an irregular form from memory ordinarily blocks application of the regular rule, although in children retrieval occasionally fails, yielding "overregularization" errors like *breaked*.[8,9,10]

The rule-rote theory, although appealingly straightforward, is inadequate. Rote memory, if thought of as a list of slots, is designed for the very rare verbs with unrelated past-tense forms, like *be-was* and *go-went*. But for all other irregular verbs, the phonological content of the stem is largely preserved in the past form, as in *swing-swung*.[5,11] Moreover, a given irregular pattern such as a vowel change is typically seen in a family of phonetically similar items, such as *sing-sang, ring-rang, spring-sprang, shrink-shrank,* and *swim-swam,* or *grow-grew, blow-blew, throw-threw,* and *fly-flew*.[5,9,11] The rote theory cannot explain why verbs with irregular past forms come in similarity families, rather than belonging to arbitrary lists. Finally, irregular pairs are psychologically not a closed list, but their patterns can sometimes be extended to new forms on the basis of similarity to existing forms. All children occasionally use forms such as *bring-brang* and *bite-bote*.[5,9] A few irregular past forms have entered the language historically under the influence of existing forms. *Quit, cost, catch* are from French, and *fling, sling, stick* have joined irregular clusters in the last few hundred years;[12] such effects are obvious when dialects are compared (for example, *help-holp, rise-riz, drag-drug, climb-clome*).[13] Such analogizing can be demonstrated in the laboratory: Faced with inflecting nonsense verbs like *spling,* many adults produce *splung*.[6,7,14,15]

The partial systematicity of irregular verbs has been handled in opposite ways by modern rule and associationist theories. One version of the theory of Generative Phonology[11] posits rules for irregular verbs (for example, change *i* to *a*) as well as for regular ones. The theory is designed to explain the similarity between verb stems and their past tense forms: If the rule just changes a specified segment, the rest of the stem comes through in the output untouched, by default, just as in the fully regular case. But the rule theory does not address the similarity among different verbs in the input set and people's tendency to generalize irregular patterns. If an irregular rule is restricted to apply to a list of words, the similarity among the words in the list is unexplained. But if a common pattern shared by the words is identified and the rule is restricted to apply to all and only the verbs displaying that pattern (for example, change *i* to *a* when it appears after a consonant cluster and precedes *ng*), the rule fails because the similarity to be accounted for is one of family resemblance rather than necessary or sufficient conditions:[5,9,14,18] Such a rule, while successfully applying to *spring, shrink, drink,* would incorrectly apply to *bring-brought* and *fling-flung* and would fail to apply to *begin-began,* and *swim-swam,* where it should apply.

Associationist theories also propose that regular and irregular patterns are computed by a single mechanism, but here the mechanism is an associative memory. A formal implementation in neural net terms is the "connectionist" model of Rumelhart and McClelland, which consists of an array of input units, an array of output units, and a matrix of modifiable weighted links between every input and every output.[16] None of the elements or links corresponds exactly to a word or rule. The stem is represented by turning on a subset of input nodes, each corresponding to a sound pattern in the stem. This sends a signal across each of the links to the output nodes, which represent the sounds of the past-tense form. Each output node sums its incoming signals and turns on if the sum exceeds a threshold; the output form is the word most compatible with the set of active output nodes. During the learning phase, the past-tense form computed by the network is juxtaposed with the correct version provided by a "teacher", and the strengths of the links and thresholds are adjusted so as to reduce the difference. By recording and superimposing associations between stem sounds and past sounds, the model improves its performance and can generalize to new forms to the extent that their sounds overlap with old ones. This process is qualitatively the same for regular and irregular verbs: *stopped* is produced because input *op* units were linked to output *opped* units by previous verbs; *clung* is produced because *ing* was linked to *ung*. As a result such models can imitate people's analogizing of irregular patterns to new forms.

The models, however, are inadequate in other ways.[5,17] The precise patterns of inflectional mappings in the world's languages are unaccounted for: The network can learn input–output mappings found in no human language, such as mirror-reversing the order of segments, and cannot learn mappings that are common, such as reduplicating the stem. The actual outputs are often unsystematic blends such as *mail-membled* and *tour-tourder*. Lacking a representation of words as lexical entries, distinct from their phonological or semantic content, the model cannot explain how languages can contain semantically unrelated homophones with different past-tense forms such as *lie-lied* (prevaricate) and *lie-lay* (recline), *ring-rang* and *wring-wrung*, *meet-met* and *mete-meted*.

These problems call for a theory of language with both a computational component, containing specific kinds of rules and representations, and an associative memory system, with certain properties of connectionist models.[5,6,10] In such a theory, regular past-tense forms are computed by a rule that concatenates an affix with a variable standing for the stem. Irregulars are memorized pairs of words, but the linkages between the pair members are stored in an associative memory structure fostering some generalization by analogy:[9,14,18] Although *string* and *strung* are represented as separate, linked words, the mental representation of the pair overlaps in part with similar forms like *sling* and *bring*, so that the learning of *slung* is easier and extensions like *brung* can occur as the result of noise or decay in the parts of the representation that code the identity of the lexical entry.

Because it categorically distinguishes regular from irregular forms, the rule–association hybrid predicts that the two processes should be dissociable from virtually every point of view. With respect to the psychology of language use, irregular forms, as memorized items, should be strongly affected by properties of associative memory such as frequency and similarity, whereas regular forms should not. With respect to language structure, irregular forms, as memory-listed words, should be available as the input to other word-formation processes, whereas regular forms, being the final outputs of such processes, should not. With respect to implementation in the brain, because regular and irregular verbs are subserved by different mechanisms, it should be possible to find one system impaired while the other is spared. The predictions can be tested with methods ranging from reaction time experiments to the grammatical analysis of languages to the study of child development to the investigation of brain damage and genetic deficits.

Language use and associative laws

Frequency

If irregular verbs are memorized items, they should be better remembered the more they are encountered. Indeed, children make errors like *breaked* more often for verbs their parents use in the past-tense forms less frequently.[9,10,19] To adults, low-frequency irregular past tense forms like *smote, bade, slew,* and *strode* sound odd or stilted and often co-exist with regularized counterparts such as *slayed* and *strided*.[5,18,20] As these psychological effects accumulate over generations, they shape the language. Old English had many more irregular verbs than Modern English, such as *abide-abode, chide-chid, gild-gilt*; the ones used with lower frequencies have become regular over the centuries.[18] Most surviving irregular verbs are used at high frequencies, and the thirteen most frequent verbs in English—*be, have, do, say, make, go, take, come, see, get, know, give, find*—are all irregular.[21]

Although any theory positing a frequency-sensitive memory can account for frequency effects on irregular verbs (with inverse effects on their corresponding regularized versions),[20] the rule–associative-memory hybrid model predicts that regular inflection is different. If regular past tense forms can be computed on-line by concatenation of symbols for the stem and affix, they do not require prior storage of a past-tense entry and thus need not be harder or stranger for low-frequency verbs than higher ones.[22]

Judgments by native English speakers of the naturalness of word forms bear this prediction out. Unlike irregular verbs, novel or low-frequency regular verbs, although they may sound unfamiliar in themselves, do not accrue any increment of oddness or uncertainty when put in the past tense: *infarcted* is as natural a past-tense form of *infarct* as *walked* is of *walk*.[5] The contrast can be seen clearly in idioms and clichés, because they can contain a verb that is not unfamiliar itself but that appears in the idiom exclusively in the present or infinitive form. Irregular verbs in such idioms can sound strange when put in the past tense: Compare *You'll excuse me if I forgo the pleasure of reading your paper before it's published* with *Last night I forwent the pleasure of reading student papers,* or *I don't know how she can bear the guy* with *I don't know how she bore the guy.* In contrast, regular verbs in nonpast idioms do not sound worse when put in the past: Compare *She doesn't suffer fools gladly* with *None of them ever suffered fools gladly*. Similarly, some regular verbs like *afford* and *cope* usually appear with *can't*, which requires the stem form, and hence have common stems but very low-frequency past tense forms.[21] But the uncommon *I don't know how he afforded it* (*coped*) does not sound worse than *He can't afford it* (*cope*).

These effects can be demonstrated in quantitative studies:[20] Subjects' ratings of regular past-tense forms of different verbs correlate significantly with their ratings of the corresponding stems ($r = 0.62$) but not with the frequency of the past form (-0.14, partialing out stem rating). In contrast, ratings of irregular past-tense forms correlate less strongly with their stem ratings (0.32), and significantly with past frequency (0.29, partialing out stem rating).

Experiments on how people produce and comprehend inflected forms in real time confirm this difference. When subjects see verb stems on a screen and must utter the past form as quickly as possible, they take significantly less time (16- to 29-msec difference) for irregular verbs with high past frequencies than irregular verbs with low past frequencies (stem frequencies equated), but show no such difference for regular verbs (< 2-msec difference).[23] When recognizing words, people are aided by having seen the word previously on an earlier trial in the experiment; their mental representation of the word has been "primed" by the first presentation. Presenting a regular past-tense form speeds up subsequent recognition of the stem no less than presenting the stem itself (181- versus 166-msec reduction), suggesting that people store and prime only the stem and analyze a regular inflected form as a stem plus a suffix. In contrast, prior presentation of an irregular form is significantly less effective at priming its stem than presentation of the stem itself (39- versus 99-msec reduction), suggesting that the two are stored as separate but linked items.[24]

Similarity

Irregular verbs fall into families with similar stems and similar past-tense forms, partly because the associative nature of memory makes it easier to memorize verbs in such families. Indeed, children make fewer overregularization errors for verbs that fall into families with more numerous and higher frequency members.[5,8–10,25] As mentioned above, speakers occasionally extend irregular patterns to verbs that are highly similar to irregular families (*brang*), and such extensions are seen in dialects.[13] A continuous effect of similarity has been measured experimentally: Subjects frequently (44 percent) convert *spling* to *splung* (based on *string*, *sling*, et cetera), less often (24 percent) convert *shink* to *shunk*, and rarely (7 percent) convert *sid* to *sud*.[14]

The rule–associative-memory theory predicts that the ability to generate regular past-tense forms should not depend on similarity to existing regular verbs: The regular rule applies as a default, treating all nonirregular stems as equally valid instantations of the mental symbol "verb." Within English vocabulary, we find that a regular verb can have any sound pattern, rather than falling into similarity clusters that complement the irregulars:[5] For example, *need-needed* co-exists with *bleed-bled* and *feed-fed*, *blink-blinked* with *shrink-shrank* and *drink-drank*. Regular–irregular homophones such as *lie-lay;lie-lied*, *meet-met;mete-meted*, and *hang-hung;hang-hanged* are the clearest examples. Moreover verbs with highly unusual sounds are easily provided with regular pasts. Although no English verb ends in *-ev* or a neutral vowel,[21] novel verbs with these patterns are readily inflectable as natural past-tense forms, such as *Yeltsin out-Gorbachev'ed Gorbachev* or *We rhumba'd all night*. Children are no more likely to overregularize an irregular verb if it resembles a family of similar regular verbs than if it is dissimilar from regulars, suggesting that regulars, unlike irregulars, do not form attracting clusters in memory.[10,25] Adults, when provided with novel verbs, do not rate regular past forms of unusual sounds like *ploamphed* as any worse, relative to the stem, than familiar sounds like *plipped* (similar to *clip*, *flip*, *slip*, et cetera), unlike their ratings for irregulars.[15,26] In contrast, in associationist models both irregular and regular generalizations tend to be sensitive to similarity. For example the Rumelhart–McClelland model could not produce any output for many novel regular verbs that did not resemble other regulars in the training set.[5,15,17]

Organization of grammatical processes

Grammars divide into fairly autonomous submodules in which blocks of rules produce outputs that serve (or cannot serve) as the input for other blocks of rules. Linguistic research suggests an information flow of lexicon to derivational morphology (complex word-formation) to regular inflection, with regular and irregular processes encapsulated within different subcomponents.[27,28] If irregular past-tense forms are stored in memory as entries in the mental lexicon, then like other stored words they should be the input to rules of complex word formation. If regular past-tense forms are computed from words by a rule acting as a default, they should be formed from the outputs of complex word formation rules. Two phenomena illustrate this organization.

A potent demonstration of the earlier point that regular processes can apply to any sound whatsoever, no matter how tightly associated with an irregular pattern, is "regularization-through-derivation": Verbs intuitively perceived as derived from nouns or adjectives are always regular, even if similar or identical to an irregular verb. Thus one says *grandstanded*, not *grandstood*; *flied out* in baseball (from a fly ball), not *flew out*; *high-sticked* in hockey, not *high-stuck*.[5,6,28] The explanation is that irregularity consists of a linkage between two word roots, the atomic sound–meaning pairings stored in the mental lexicon; it is not a link between two words or sound patterns directly. *High-stuck* sounds silly because the verb is tacitly perceived as being based on the noun root (*hockey*) *stick*, and noun roots cannot be listed in the lexicon as having any past-tense form (the past tense of a noun makes no sense semantically), let alone an irregular one. Because its root is not the verb *stick* there is no data pathway by which *stuck* can be made available; to obtain a past-tense form, the speaker must apply the regular rule, which serves as the default. Subjects presented with novel irregular-sounding verbs (for example *to line-drive*) strongly prefer the regular past tense form (*line-drived*) if it is understood as being based on a noun ("to hit a line drive"), but not in a control condition for unfamiliarity where the items were based on existing irregular verbs ("to drive along a line"); here the usual irregular form is preferred.[6]

The effect, moreover, occurs in experiments testing subjects with no college education[6] and in preschool children.[29] This is consistent with the fact that many of these lawful forms entered the language from vernacular speech and were opposed by language mavens and guardians of "proper" style.[6,13] "Rules of grammar" in the psycholinguists' sense, and their organization into components, are inherent to the computational systems found in all humans, not just those with access to explicit schooling or stylistic injunctions. These injunctions, involving a very different sense of "rule" as something that ought to be followed, usually pertain to minor differences between standard written and nonstandard spoken dialects.

A related effect occurs in lexical compounds, which sound natural when they contain irregular noun plurals, but not regular noun plurals: Compare *mice-infested* with *rats-infested*, *teethmarks* with *clawsmarks*, *men-bashing* with *guys-bashing*.[28] Assume that this compounding rule is fed by stored words. Irregulars are stored words, so they can feed compounding; regulars are computed at the output end of the morphology system, not stored at the input end, so they do not appear inside lexical compounds. This constraint has been documented experimentally in 3- to 5-year-old children:[30] When children who knew the word *mice* were asked for a word for a "monster who eats mice," they responded with *mice-eater* 90 percent of the time; but when children who knew *rats* were asked for a word for "monster who eats rats," they responded *rats-eater* only 2 percent of the time. The children could not have learned the constraint by recording whether adults use irregular versus regular plurals inside compounds. Adults do not use such compounds often enough for most children to have heard them: The frequency of English compounds containing any kind of plural is indistinguishable from zero.[21,30] Rather, the constraint may be a consequence of the inherent organization of the children's grammatical systems.

Developmental and neurological dissociations

If regular and irregular patterns are computed in different subsystems, they should dissociate in special populations. Individuals with undeveloped or damaged grammatical systems and intact lexical memory should be unable to compute regular forms but should be able to handle irregulars. Conversely, individuals with intact grammatical systems and atypical lexical retrieval should handle regulars properly but be prone to overregularizing irregulars. Such double dissociations, most clearly demonstrated in detailed case studies, are an important source of evidence for the existence of separate neural subsystems. Preliminary evidence suggests that regular and irregular inflection may show such dissociations.

Children

Most of the grammatical structure of English develops rapidly in the third year of life.[31] One conspicuous development is the appearance of overregularizations like *comed*. Such errors constitute a worsening of past marking with time; for months beforehand, all overtly marked irregular past forms are correct.[10] The phenomenon is not due to the child becoming temporarily overwhelmed by the regular pattern because of an influx of regular verbs, as connectionist theories[16] predict.[5,10,32] Instead it accompanies the appearance of the regular tense marking process itself: Overregularizations appear when the child ceases using bare stems like *walk* to refer to past events.[8,10] Say memorization of verb forms from parental speech, including irregulars, can take place as soon as words of any kind can be learned. But deployment of the rule system must await the abstraction of the English rule from a set of word pairs juxtaposed as nonpast and past versions of the same verb. The young child could possess memorized irregulars, produced probabilistically but without overt error, but no rule; the older child, possessing the rule as well, would apply it obligatorily in past-tense sentences whenever he failed to retrieve the irregular, resulting in occasional errors.

Aphasics

A syndrome sometimes called agrammatic aphasia can occur after extensive damage to Broca's area and nearby structures in the left cerebral hemisphere. Labored speech, absence of inflections and other grammatical words, and difficulty comprehending grammatical distinctions are frequent symptoms. Agrammatics have trouble reading aloud regular inflected forms: *smiled* is pronounced as *smile*, *wanted* as *wanting*. Nonregular plural and past forms are read with much greater accuracy, controlling for frequency and pronounceability.[33] This is predicted if agrammatism results from damage to neural circuitry that executes rules of grammar, including the regular rule necessary for analyzing regularly inflected stimuli, but leaves the lexicon relatively undamaged, including stored irregulars which can be directly matched against the irregular stimuli.

Specific language impairment (SLI)

SLI refers to a syndrome of language deficits not attributable to auditory, cognitive, or social problems. The syndrome usually includes delayed onset of language, articulation difficulties in childhood, and problems in controlling grammatical features such as tense, number, gender, case, and person. One form of SLI may especially impair aspects of the regular inflectional process.[34] Natural speech includes errors like "We're go take a bus; I play musics; One machine clean all the two arena." In experiments, the patients have difficulty converting present sentences to past (32 percent for SLI; 78 percent for sibling controls.) The difficulty is more pronounced for regular verbs than irregulars. Regular past forms are virtually absent from the children's spontaneous speech and writing, although irregulars often appear. In the writing samples of two children examined quantitatively, 85 percent of irregular pasts but 30 percent of regular pasts were correctly supplied. The first written regular past-tense forms are for verbs with past-tense frequencies higher than their stem frequencies; subsequent ones are acquired one at a time in response to teacher training, with little transfer to nontrained verbs. Adults' performance improves and their speech begins to sound normal but they continue to have difficulty inflecting nonsense forms like *zoop* (47 percent for SLI; 83 percent for controls). It appears as if their ability to apply inflectional rules is impaired relative to their ability to memorize words: Irregular forms are acquired relatively normally, enjoying their advantage of high frequencies; regular forms are memorized as if they were irregular.

SLI appears to have an inherited component. Language impairments have been found in 3 percent of first-degree family members of normal probands but 23 percent of language-impaired probands.[35] The impairment has been found to be 80 percent concordant in monozygotic twins and 35 percent concordant in dizygotic twins.[36] One case study[34] investigated a three-generation, thirty-member family, sixteen of whom had SLI; the syndrome followed the pattern of a dominant, fully penetrant autosomal gene. This constitutes evidence that some aspects of use of grammar have a genetic basis.

Williams syndrome

Williams syndrome (WS), associated with a defective gene expressed in the central nervous system involved in calcium metabolism, causes an unusual kind of mental retardation.[37] Although their Intelligence Quotient is measured at around 50, older children and adolescents with WS are described as hyperlinguistic with selective sparing of syntax, and grammatical abilities are close to normal in controlled testing.[37] This is one of several kinds of dissociation in which language is preserved despite severe cognitive impairments, suggesting that the language system is autonomous of many other kinds of cognitive processing.

WS children retrieve words in a deviant fashion.[37] When normal or other retarded children are asked to name some animals, they say *dog, cat, pig*; WS children offer *unicorn, tyrandon, yak, ibex*. Normal children speak of *pouring water*; WS children speak of *evacuating a glass*. According to the rule–associative-memory hybrid theory, preserved grammatical abilities and deviant retrieval of high-frequency words are preconditions for overregularization. Indeed, some WS children overregularize at high rates (16 percent), one of their few noticeable grammatical errors.[37,39]

Conclusion

For hundreds of years, the mind has been portrayed as a homogeneous system whose complexity comes from the complexity of environmental correlations as recorded by a general-purpose learning mechanism. Modern research on language renders such a view increasingly implausible. Although there is evidence that the memory system used in language acquisition and processing has some of the properties of an associative network, these properties do not exhaust the computational abilities of the brain. Focusing on a single rule of grammar, we find evidence for a system that is modular, independent of real-world meaning, nonassociative (unaffected by frequency and similarity), sensitive to abstract formal distinctions (for example, root versus derived, noun versus verb), more sophisticated than the kinds of "rules" that are explicitly taught, developing on a schedule not timed by environmental input, organized by principles that could not have been learned, possibly with a distinct neural substrate and genetic basis.

Acknowledgement

I thank my collaborators A. Prince, G. Hickok, M. Hollander, J. Kim, G. Marcus, S. Prasada, A. Senghas, and M. Ullman and thank T. Bever, N. Block, N. Etcoff, and especially A. Prince for comments. Supported by NIH grant HD18381.

References and notes to 4.2

1. D Hume, *Inquiry Concerning Human Understanding* (Bobbs-Merril, Indianapolis, 1955); D. Hebb, *Organization of Behavior* (Wiley, New York, 1949); D. Rumelhart and J. McClelland, *Parallel Distributed Processing* (MIT Press, Cambridge, 1986).
2. G. Leibniz, *Philosophical Essays* (Hackett, Indianapolis, 1989); A. Newell and H. Simon, *Science* **134**, 2011 (1961).

3. J. Fodor, *Modularity of Mind* (MIT Press, Cambridge, 1983).
4. N. Chomsky, *Rules and Representations* (Columbia University Press, New York, 1980); E. Lenneberg, *Biological Foundations of Language* (Wiley, New York, 1967).
5. S. Pinker and A. Prince, *Cognition* **28**, 73 (1988).
6. J. Kim, S. Pinker, A. Prince, S. Prasada, *Cognitive Science* **15**, 173 (1991).
7. J. Berko, *Word* **14**, 150 (1958).
8. S. Kuczaj, *Journal of Verbal Learning and Verbal Behavior* **16**, 598 (1977).
9. J. Bybee and D. Slobin, *Language* **58**, 265 (1982).
10. G. Marcus, M. Ullman, S. Pinker, M. Hollander, T. Rosen, F. Xu, *Centre for Cognitive Science Occasional Papers*. **41** (Massachusetts Institute of Technology, Cambridge, 1990).
11. N. Chomsky and M. Halle, *Sound Pattern of English* (MIT Press, Cambridge, 1990).
12. O. Jespersen, *A Modern English Grammar on Historical Principles* (Allen and Unwin, London, 1961).
13. H. Mencken, *The American Language* (Knopf, New York, 1936).
14. J. Bybee and C. Moder, *Language* **59**, 251 (1983).
15. S. Prasda and S. Pinker, unpublished data.
16. D. Rumelhart and J. McClelland, in *Parallel Distributed Processing*, J. McClelland and D. Rumelhart, Eds. (MIT Press, Cambridge, 1986), pp. 216–71.
17. J. Lachter and T. Bever, *Cognition* **28**, 197 (1988). More sophisticated connectionist models of past-tense formation employing a hidden layer of nodes have computational limitations similar to those of the Rumelhart–McClelland model (D. Egedi and R. Sproat, unpublished data).
18. J. Bybee, *Morphology* (Benjamins, Philadelphia, 1985).
19. In speech samples from nineteen children containing 9684 irregular past tense forms,[10] aggregate overregularizations rate for thirty-nine verbs correlated −0.37 with aggregate log frequency in parental speech. All correlations and differences noted herein are significant at $p = 0.05$ or less.
20. M. Ullman and S. Pinker, paper presented at the Spring Symposium of the AAAI, Stanford, 26 to 28 March 1991. Data represent mean ratings by ninety-nine subjects of the naturalness of the past and stem forms of 142 irregular verbs and fifty-nine regular verbs that did not rhyme with any irregular, each presented in a sentence in counterbalanced random order.
21. N. Francis and H. Kučera, *Frequency Analysis of English Usage* (Houghton Mifflin, Boston, 1982).
22. Such effects can also occur in certain connectionist models that lack distinct representations of words and superimpose associations between the phonological elements of stem and past forms. After such models are trained on many regular verbs, any new verb would activate previously trained phonological associations to the regular pattern and could yield a strong regular form; the absence of prior training on the verb itself would not necessarily hurt it. However, the existence of homophones with different past tense forms (*lie-lay* versus *lie-lied*) makes such models psychologically unrealistic; representations of individual words are called for, and they would engender word familiarity effects.
23. S. Prasada, S. Pinker, W. Snyder, paper presented at the 31st Annual Meeting of the Psychonomic Society, New Orleans, 16 to 18 November 1990. The effects obtained in three experiments, each showing thirty-two to forty subjects the stem forms of verbs on a screen for 300 msec and measuring their vocal response time for the past tense form. Thirty to forty-eight irregular verbs and thirty to forty-eight regular verbs were shown, one at a time in random order; every verb had a counterpart with the same stem frequency but a different past tense frequency.[21] In control experiments, forty subjects generated third-person-singular forms of stems, read stems aloud, or read past-tense forms aloud, and the frequency difference among irregulars did not occur; this shows the effect is not due to inherent differences in access or articulation times of the verbs.
24. R. Stanners, J. Neiser, W. Hernon, R. Hall, *Journal of Verbal Learning and Verbal Behavior* **18**, 399 (1979); S. Kempley and J. Morton, *British Journal of Psychology* **73**, 441 (1982). The effect was not an artifact of differences in phonological or othographic overlap between the members of regular and irregular pairs.
25. For seventeen of nineteen children studied in [10], the higher the frequencies of the other irregulars rhyming with an irregular, the lower its overregulation rate (mean correlation −0.07, significantly less than 0). For the corresponding calculation with regulars rhyming with an irregular, no consistency resulted and the mean correlation did not differ significantly from zero.
26. Twenty-four subjects read sixty sentences containing novel verbs, presented either in stem form, a past form displaying an English irregular vowel change, or a past form containing the regular

suffix. Each subject rated how good the verb sounded with a 7-point scale; each verb was rated in each of the forms by different subjects. For novel verbs highly similar to an irregular family, the irregular past form was rated 0.8 points worse than the stem; for novel verbs dissimilar to the family, the irregular past form was rated 2.2 points worse. For novel verbs resembling a family of regular verbs, the regular past form was rated 0.4 points better than the stem; for novel verbs dissimilar to the family, the regular past form was rated 1.5 points better. This interaction was replicated in two other experiments.

27. M. Aronoff, *Annual Review of Anthropology* **12**, 355 (1983); S. Anderson, in *Linguistics: The Cambridge Survey* (Cambridge University Press, New York, 1988), vol. 1, pp. 146–91.

28. P. Kiparsky, in *The Structure of Phonological Representations*, H. van der Hulst and N. Smith, Eds. (Foris, Dordrecht, 1982).

29. J. Kim, G. Marcus, M. Hollander, S. Pinker, *Papers and Reports in Child Language Development*, 1991.

30. P. Gordon, *Cognition* **21**, 73 (1985). The effect is not an artifact of pronounceability, as children were willing to say *pants-eater* and *scissors-eater*, containing s-final nouns that are not regular plurals.

31. R. Brown, *A First Language* (Harvard University Press, Cambridge, 1973).

32. The proportion of regular verb tokens in children's and parents' speech remains unchanged throughout childhood, because high frequency irregular verbs (*make*, *put*, *take*, et cetera) dominate conversation at any age. The proportion of regular verb types in children's vocabulary necessarily increases because irregular verbs are a small fraction of English vocabulary, but this growth does not correlate with overregularization errors.[3,8]

33. O. Marin, E. Saffran, M. Schwartz, *Annals of the N.Y. Academy of Sciences*, **280**, 868 (1976). For example, regular *misers, clues, buds* were read by three agrammatic patients less accurately than phonologically matched plurals that are not regular because they lack a corresponding singular, like *trousers, news, suds* (45 percent versus 90 percent), even though a phonologically well-formed stem is available in both cases. In another study, when verbs matched for past and base frequencies and pronounceability were presented to an agrammatic patient, he read 56 percent of irregular past forms and 18 percent of regular past forms successfully (G. Hickok and S. Pinker, unpublished data).

34. M. Gopnik, *Nature* **344**, 715, (1990); *Language Acquisition*, **1**, 139 (1990); M. Gopnik and M. Crago, *Cognition*, in press.

35. J. Tomblin, *Journal of Speech and Hearing Disorders*, **54**, 287 (1989); P. Tallal, R. Ross, S. Curtiss, ibid., p. 167.

36. J. Tomblin, unpublished data.

37. U. Bellugi, A. Bihrle, T. Jernigan, D. Trauner, S. Doherty, *American Journal of Medical Genetics Supplement* **6**, 115 (1990).

38. S. Curtiss, in *The Exceptional Brain*, L. Obler and D. Fein, Eds. (Guilford, New York, 1988).

39. E. Klima and U. Bellugi, unpublished data.

Level-ordering in Lexical Development

Peter Gordon

Introduction

To say that the child learns a set of rules in acquiring a grammar has become almost a truism in psycholinguistics. Such confidence is built on empirical observations of children who, for example, overgeneralize rules involving past tense or plural morphology (e.g., *goed, *tooths, etc.). Furthermore, children are able to apply such inflections to quite novel lexical items as in the "wug" test of Berko (1958). Going beyond these observations, one would like to show that the acquisition of such rules obeys certain underlying constraints. This approach is paralleled by current trends in linguistic theory away from listing sets of rules, toward more general, perhaps universal, principles that govern the form of those rules.

In the present paper I wish to consider the phenomenon of "level-ordering" with respect to lexical rules of word formation. The notion of ordered levels appears in the work of Allen (1978) and Siegel (1977) and more recently has been extended by Kiparsky (1982, 1983) and others. Ordering is implicit in the traditional phonological characterizations of boundary types as either primary (+) or secondary (#). Thus, consider *+ian* in *Darwin+ian*, and *#ism* in *Darwin#ism*. Since there is ordering of "+" affixes before "#" affixes, it is predicted that *Darwin+ian#ism* should be acceptable but not **Darwin#ism+ian* since the latter, but not the former, involves applying a secondary before a primary affix.

These and other properties of word formation can be coherently accounted for in lexical theory by positing ordered "levels" of rule application (see Kiparsky, 1982, 1983). For present purposes, I shall assume the three-level version of Kiparsky (1982). Level 1 is said to include primary (+) affixes (e.g., *+ian*, *+ous*, *+ion*) that characteristically deform their hosts phonologically by stress shifting, vowel reduction, alternation and so on, and are often semantically idiosyncratic in being noncompositional (e.g., the meaning of *populat+ion* appears to go beyond a simple semantic composite of *populate* and the nominalizing *+ion* affix). Also included are irregular inflections (e.g., *tooth → teeth*, *ox→oxen*), pluralia tantum (e.g., *clothes, scissors, alms*) and possibly others. Level 2 contains secondary (#) affixes of derivational morphology (e.g., *#er, #ism, #ness*) and is the site of compounding. The third level contains all of the regular inflectional morphology that characteristically shows neither semantic idiosyncrasy nor stem deformation (e.g., *car → cars*).

The three levels are schematized in Table 4.3.1 (adapted from Kiparsky, 1982). Rule application proceeds through the three levels such that rules at a later level may not be applied prior to those at a previous level. One very interesting prediction from this model, noted by Kiparsky (1982), is that one should not find regular plurals "inside" compounds. That is, once a compound is formed at level 2, its constituents cannot be inflected at level 3 (although the compound itself may be inflected to the right). However, since irregular inflections are at level 1, then they should be allowed inside compounds in certain cases. This prediction is supported by the difference in acceptability of *mice-infested* versus **rats-infested*, since the former includes a level 1 plural and the latter, a level 3 plural. Pluralia tantum (level 1) also find their way inside compounds in some cases (e.g., *clothes-basket*), although reduction is possible in other cases (e.g., *scissor-legs*).

Such results are quite surprising and combine with many others to provide support for the existence of level-ordering of some sort within the lexicon. What is more, many of these constraints appear to be motivated purely in terms of the

Table 4.3.1   *Examples and properties of level-ordered rules*

	Examples	Properties
Level 1	+ion, +ous, +ity, +th, in+ mice, oxen, scissors	Derivational, irregular, semantically idiosyncratic, host deforming, stress shift, vowel reduction, unproductive.
Level 2	#ness, #ism, #er, #ist, un# Compounding	Derivational, nondeforming, (more) semantically predictable, productive.
Level 3	#s, #ed, #ing	Regular inflections, nondeforming, semantically predictable.

SYNTAX

geometry of the system rather than by semantic considerations—although certainly semantic considerations are important in word formation itself (see Clark and Clark, 1979; Kiparsky, 1983). But, to take our example, there seems to be no semantic reason why *mice-infested* should be acceptable but not **rats-infested*.

Let us assume that level-ordering (or something like it) is the correct way of characterizing lexical structure and thus accounting for our intuitions. Consider how a child could ever learn such an organization. What evidence in the linguistic input would lead inductively to setting up this system? It would seem that of all the hypotheses available, there would be little to persuade an open-minded learner to choose this, rather than some other path. For example, most compounds that the child hears involve singular forms inside compounds. While this richly specifies the constraints with respect to reducing regular plurals inside compounds (e.g., for *rat-infested*), there appears to be little evidence available to the child regarding the possibility of placing irregular plurals inside compounds. For example, one finds forms such as *toothbrush*, *mouse-trap* and *man-eater*, but no *teethbrush*, *mice-trap* or *men-eater*.[1] In fact, an examination of certain high-frequency items with irregular plurals (*mouse*, *man*, *tooth*, *foot* and *goose*) was carried out using the Kučera and Francis (1967) word count of about one million words. This revealed that while these forms were listed in a total of twenty-eight compound types in non-head (left) position (token frequency: 153), in only two cases was the noun listed in its irregular plural form (token frequency: 3). This compares with a plural-to-singular ratio of 1181:1436 for the irregular nouns not occurring inside compounds.

Thus our intuitions regarding the acceptability of irregular forms inside compounds seem to arise primarily from cases that are quite novel. If it is true that, in general, the input underdetermines the child's induction of the appropriate ordering of rules in the lexicon, then one might suggest that such ordering does not come about through "learning" per se, but rather it is an a priori characteristic of the way the lexicon is structured to organize its word-formation rules. One might expect, therefore, to find evidence for the existence of level-ordering in the child's developing lexicon without finding evidence of the relevant learning having taken place. Strong support for this non-learning hypothesis would be if the child showed evidence for level-ordering as soon as particular morphological rules had been acquired.

Given this hypothesis, there are a number of developmental predictions that arise with respect to the appearance of plurals within compounds:

1. If rules of compounding and regular inflection are correctly assigned to levels 2 and 3 respectively, then as soon as the child acquires the regular plural morphology and shows evidence of regularization (e.g., by overgeneralization to irregular forms), the regular forms should be reduced to singulars inside compounds. For example, one should find *rat-infested* but not *rats-infested* being produced by the child.

2. As soon as the child stops overregularizing an irregular form (e.g., *mouses)
   and uses the appropriate plural (*mice*), then such forms should be (optionally)
   allowed inside compounds (e.g., *mice-infested*).
3. As soon as the child learns that pluralia tantum are irregular in the sense of
   having no singular form, then they too should optionally occur inside
   compounds (e.g., *clothes-dryer*).

These predictions constitute a very strong test of the nativist hypothesis. For
example, they assume that level assignment immediately falls out from the
phonological/semantic properties of particular forms or rules. That is, the
predicted synchrony between learning irregular forms and their allowability in
certain compound constructions assumes that the child essentially needs no
other data to "fine tune" the system. This, of course, could turn out to be an
oversimplification. For example, the child might require a certain amount of
distributional data regarding ordering of rules. Even if these data do not contain
direct evidence regarding the facts about compounding and pluralization (as
seems to be the case), other more indirect evidence may be required to trigger
the correct assignments (e.g., ordering of affixes in complex words, allomorphic
variation, amount of productivity). Be that as it may, the present experiment is
aimed at the strongest test as outlined in 1–3.

An opposing position would presumably claim that level-ordering is itself
learned from evidence in the linguistic input or, indeed, that there is no level-
ordering to be learned. In the former case, it is necessary to show that the child's
linguistic input is sufficiently rich to specify the existence of level-ordering for
a learning mechanism that is not already committed to searching for such
ordering. Given the kind of data alluded to in the examination of word counts
above, it would seem that arriving at such an account would not be trivial. There
is a similar problem in proposing that there is no such thing as level-ordering.
The acceptability of irregular plurals inside compounds would have to be
accounted for as a rule to be induced from little or no evidence.

On the assumption that the facts about pluralization inside compounds are
learned (rather than being a deductive consequence of innate structures), one
would not predict the immediate appearance of constraints on pluralization
within compounds. To illustrate this, let us compare another area in which
children must clearly learn restrictions on pluralization. For example, it has been
found that children are prone to make morphological errors involving
pluralization after certain distributive quantifiers that require singular nouns.
Errors of the form: *every cars and *each cars are very frequently made in tests
on 3- to 5-year-olds (Gordon, 1981, 1982) despite the fact that they never hear
such constructions in their input. Presumably such errors are at least partly a
result of the fact that *every* and *each* quantify over plural sets and the plurality
of the reference leads the child to produce an erroneous plural. If a similar
situation were to be presented for the case of compounding, one might also
expect pluralization errors. Thus, if the child were presented with a context in

which there were a number of rats being referred to, one might expect him or her to denote an eater of such animals as a *rats-eater rather than a *rat-eater*. However, if we assume that level-ordering constrains pluralization in this case, then such errors should never be found.

With respect to irregular plurals, there is also a different prediction on the hypothesis that constraints are learned. If the child has to learn that reduction of regular plurals is required within compounds, there is little reason to assume that this rule would apply only to regular plurals. This is especially true considering the fact that the child's input data tend not to include compounds containing irregular plurals. Thus, a natural induction from such evidence would be that irregular plurals are also subject to reduction inside compounds. There should be no necessary synchrony between the appearance of irregular plurals in the child's lexicon and their allowability inside compounds. In fact, if the child has to learn from the linguistic input that irregular plurals may occur inside compounds, the paucity of such data suggests that a fairly protracted period of time would be required before such forms as *mice-infested* would be generated by the child's grammar. Generally, the same arguments can be assessed for pluralia tantum, although the inability to reduce these forms to singulars in general might, on either account, lead one to expect their appearance inside compounds in the plural form.

Since there do seem to be quite different predictions for an account in which level-ordering is an innate constraint on word-formation and that in which the properties are learned, the following experiment was designed to test the two accounts. In the experiment, noun-agentive compounds (e.g., *rat-eater*) were elicited from children. The context was biased to predispose the child to use plural forms inside the compound. This was done by both having a plural referent for the non-head (left) noun, and also, by having the child produce the plural form (*rats*) prior to the compound form (*rat(s)-eater*). The three noun-types: (1) regular plural, (2) irregular plural, and (3) pluralia tantum, were examined.

Method

Subjects

Subjects included thirty-three children divided into three groups of eleven by age. Group I: 3;2 to 4;0 (mean age: 3;8); Group II: 4;1 to 4;11 (mean age: 4;6); Group III: 5;0 to 5;10 (mean age: 5;6). All subjects were of middle-class, mostly academic families.

Materials

Training items used to elicit compound production in subjects consisted of referents for non-pluralizable mass nouns. The stimuli included either real or toy examples of the following: rice, corn, paper, bread, wood, plastic, fruit, soup, cereal, money. Main test items were referents of pluralizable count nouns. These included teeth, beads, mice, rats, feet, hands, men, dolls, geese, ducks, clothes, toys (=airplane, ball, car), pants, shirts, (sun)glasses, shoes, scissors and knives. A "Cookie Monster" puppet was used in the testing and a cassette recorder was used to record responses as a back-up to manual scoring.

Procedure

The design for this task involved eliciting a singular, plural and compound form of each of a set of nouns that either had irregular plurals, were pluralia tantum or else were regularly pluralized nouns. There were five irregularly pluralized nouns including *mouse, man, tooth, foot* and *goose*. These nouns, respectively were (semantically) matched with the regular nouns *rat, baby, bead, hand* and *duck*. Semantically matching *tooth* required a noun whose referents exhibited similar configurational properties to a set of teeth (since we were dealing with pluralization). Beads on a necklace were chosen for this reason despite the lack of more obvious perceptual similarities. The stimuli for the pluralia tantum and their regular equivalents included *clothes/toy, pants/shirt, (sun)glasses/shoe, scissors/knife*. Again, the *clothes/toy* pair, while not semantically/perceptually similar, was chosen because it was felt that the superordinate term, *clothes*, should be paired with another superordinate, *toy*.

Subjects were tested individually by a female experimenter who had previously familiarized herself with the playgroup. Initially, the child was introduced to a Cookie Monster puppet and was told

> Do you know who this is? . . . It's the Cookie Monster. Do you know what he likes to eat? (Answer: Cookies.) Yes—and do you know what else he likes to eat?—He likes to eat all sorts of things . . .

Objects were then brought out and the child was asked if the Cookie Monster would like to eat X (where X was the name of the stimulus). They were then asked "What do you call someone who eats X?" (Answer: An X-eater.) With this procedure, it was possible to elicit compounds of the form *teeth-eater/rat-eater* and so on.[2] Initially, the subjects required some training in producing compounds. This was done using mass nouns such as *rice, corn* and *wood* (see Materials section). Since these do not have plural forms and children appear to know this by around 2½ years (Gordon, 1982), it was considered the least contaminating choice of noun class for training purposes. In this training condition, the child was asked what one would call someone who eats, say, rice. If there was no reply, or the child said something like "rice monster" (by analogy with "Cookie Monster") the appropriate form (*rice-eater*) would be given and the child would be asked to repeat it. The child was moved onto the main items after having successfully produced three consecutive compounds without assistance. Compounds of the form "X-monster" were produced quite frequently in the training, but rarely survived into the main test. If they were produced in the main test they were accepted as alternatives to X-eater compounds although correction again was given. Only three children produced such forms on the main items, once, twice and four times respectively. Thus, even these children produced "X-eater" on the majority of the eighteen items.

For the main items, singular, plural and compound forms were elicited from children. The first two were necessary to ascertain whether the child was overregularizing irregular forms (e.g., *mouses*). Or, even if the correct irregular form (*mice*) was being produced, it was necessary to ascertain that the irregular plural was a true plural. For example, Ervin (1964) has noted that irregular plural forms are often used by children as if they were singulars, thus producing *one mice, two mices* and so on. If the child were then to say *mice-eater*, it could not be concluded that an irregular plural was being used inside a compound since presumably, for the child, *mice* would be a singular in its function. To elicit a singular form, the child was shown a single object and asked to name it. For the plural, four of the objects[3] were presented and the child was told "Here we have a bunch of . . . what?" The child was required to complete the sentence with a plural form (cf. Berko, 1958). If she or he said "Mouses" or "Mices" in naming the plural referent, the experimenter continued to use that form in other questions involving *mouse*. Next the child was asked "What do you call someone who eats X?" where X was the form of the noun previously used by the child. The compound form produced by the child for this question indicated whether or not that type of plural was allowed inside compounds. The child was then asked if he thought the Cookie Monster was an X-eater and the puppet either consumed or rejected the objects in question.

Some adjustments were made in the procedure for *toy* and *clothes*, where it was very difficult to elicit a singular form of the superordinate term when, for example, a single ball or shirt was presented. Thus the experimenter attempted to elicit the superordinate by saying "What do you call something you play with?" or else, in the case of clothes, ". . . something you wear." Even with such measures, elicitation was very difficult for these cases. If the appropriate form was not forthcoming, it was supplied by the experimenter. This was also necessary for some of the basic-level nouns. Once the singular had been supplied, there was generally no problem in eliciting the plural and compound forms. Main items were presented in one of four predetermined random orders that were evenly distributed among the three age groups.

Results

All subjects remained in the test and completed all items without much difficulty. Occasionally subjects would change their responses spontaneously as if to correct themselves. For uniformity, it was decided to interpret such changes as corrections and score the "corrected" (second) version. For purposes of analysis, the data are represented in patterns of triplets [a-b-c] denoting forms produced for (a) the singular referent, (b) the plural referent and (c) the compound, respectively. A pattern such as [singular-plural-irregular + plural] would characterize responses of the form *mouse* (singular referent); *mouses* (plural referent) and *mices-eater* (compound). Thus, "plural" denotes either a regular or overregularized plural. "Irregular + plural" denotes a regularized plural using the irregular form as a base.

Irregular plurals

For the irregular plurals and their regular controls, there are two main predictions from the hypothesis that level-ordering is innate. First, subjects should consistently reduce regular plurals to singular forms inside compounds (e.g., *rat-eater*) thus producing the pattern [singular-plural-singular]. Compounds of the form **rats-eater* should not be found. Second, subjects should produce compounds containing irregular plurals (e.g., *mice-eater*) as soon as they start producing the irregular form (*mice*) in naming the plural referent. This would result in the pattern [singular-irregular-irregular]. Of course, since inclusion of the irregular plural is optional, one should also find [singular-irregular-singular] patterns (i.e., *mouse → mice → mouse-eater*). The degree to which the child produces an irregular plural inside the compound might well be subject to the amount of bias in the testing context. The fact that the child's previous utterance would contain *mice* could well lead to many *mice-eater* responses.

   If the child is overgeneralizing the regular plural to an irregular noun (e.g., **mouses*) then this should be a level 3 rule application and should not therefore occur inside the compound. The resulting pattern should therefore be identical to that of regular nouns, [singular-plural-singular]. Similarly, if the child overgeneralizes the plural but uses the irregular plural as a base (**mices*), then this rule application should again be at level 3 and not apply inside the compound. The resulting pattern should be [irregular-irregular + plural-irregular].

   The response patterns for irregular nouns and their regular controls are given in Table 4.3.2 and are broken down by age in Table 4.3.3. The column headings of the "Irregular" section represent the three patterns outlined above based on the first two responses: 1. Correct use of the irregular form [singular-irregular-X]; 2. Overregularization of the plural [singular-plural-X]; and 3. Use of the irregular form as a base [irregular-irregular + plural-X], where X is a variable for the form produced inside the compound. The "Regular" section contains only one pattern [singular-plural-X]. The row headings represent the form produced inside the compound (i.e., the value of X, the third member of the triplet). Main cell values represent the mean number of responses in that category with the

Table 4.3.2 *Mean response patterns for irregular and regular plurals (five responses per condition. Frequencies in parentheses)*

Regular nouns		Irregular nouns		
Compound form[*]	Regular plural [sg pl X[**]]	Irregular plural [sg IR X]	Overgeneralized plural [sg pl X]	Irregular base [IR IR + s X]
sg	4.9 (161)	0.12 (4)	2.6 (86)	0.03 (1)
pl	0.09 (3)	0	0.03 (1)	0
IR	—	1.09 (36)	0.03 (1)	0.24 (8)

[*] sg = singular form; pl = regular plural; IR = irregular plural; IR + s = irregular plural plus regular plural (e.g., *mices*).
[**] X = compound form given in row headings.

Table 4.3.3 *Mean response patterns for irregular and regular plurals by age (five responses per condition. Frequencies in parentheses)*

Regular nouns		Irregular nouns		
Compound form[*]	Regular plural [sg pl X[**]]	Irregular plural [sg IR X]	Overgeneralized plural [sg pl X]	Irregular base [IR IR + s X]
3 years				
sg	5 (55)	0	3.4 (37)	0
pl	0	0	0.09 (1)	0
IR	—	0.27 (3)	0	0.36 (4)
4 years				
sg	4.9 (54)	0.09 (1)	2.36 (26)	0.09 (1)
pl	0.09 (1)	0	0	0
IR	—	0.9 (10)	0	0.36 (4)
5 years				
sg	4.7 (54)	0.27 (3)	2.1 (23)	0
pl	0.18 (2)	0	0	0
IR	—	2.1 (23)	0.09 (1)	0

[*] sg = singular form; pl = regular plural; IR = irregular plural; IR + s = irregular plural plus regular plural (e.g., *mices*).
[**] X = compound form given in row headings.

absolute values in parentheses. There were a total of forty-three cases within these data in which the child had to be told the singular form rather than spontaneously coming up with the appropriate name. The majority of cases were for *bead* ($n = 19$) and *rat* ($n = 12$) for which children seemed to have problems producing the right name. While this fails to tap the children's knowledge of the singular form, these subjects did produce the plural and compound forms which were considered usable data. One item from a 5-year-old was discarded due to experimenter error.

With respect to the predictions, the data are quite unambiguous in supporting them. For regularly pluralized nouns, subjects overwhelmingly showed the correct pattern of reduction inside compounds (e.g., *rat-eater*) at all ages with 161/164 such patterns. Subjects were categorized as supporting the predicted pattern if all regular plurals were reduced inside compounds. The resulting chi-square value tested against chance expectation was extremely significant ($\chi^2(1, N = 33) = 132.5$, $p < .001$). When children overregularized an irregular noun (*mouse* → *mouses*) they similarly reduced to the singular form in compounding (*mouse-eater*) on 86/88 items ($\chi^2(1, N = 30) = 122$, $p < .001$). This pattern held for all ages although, quite naturally, 3-year-olds showed a greater tendency for such overregularizations (see Table 4.3.2). Also, when children treated the irregular form as a base (e.g., *mice* → *mices*) they reduced to the irregular form (*mice-eater*) 8/9 times ($\chi^2(1, N = 10) = 7.46$, $p < .01$). When subjects produced the correct irregular pattern (*mouse* → *mice*) they immediately showed evidence that these irregulars were allowable inside compounds. 36/40 responses in this category were of the form *mice-eater*. In this case, chi-square values were calculated for subjects showing greater than 50 percent inclusion of the irregular plural inside the compound, since such inclusion is optional. Again, results were very significant ($\chi^2(1, N = 20) = 15$, $p < .001$).

There were three other response patterns found in the data for irregular plurals. These included [singular-singular-singular] ($n = 10$); [irregular-irregular-irregular] ($n = 12$); [plural-plural-singular] ($n = 2$). The first two show no differentiation for singular versus plural and are therefore uninterpretable, except perhaps by analogy with *sheep* → *sheep* → *sheep-eater*. The third appears to be quite random. It is noteworthy, however, that the one type of response missing from the miscellaneous group is that in which regular plurals appear inside compounds. This suggests that even when responses appear somewhat random, they still obey the relevant constraints on compound formation. It is also noteworthy that the only subjects who did produce regular plurals inside compounds were two of the older 5-year-olds. One interpretation of this fact is that these subjects may have had superior metalinguistic skills and realized that pluralization was the relevant variable. This could possibly have interfered with their normal responding.

Pluralia tantum

For the pluralia tantum, it was predicted that these should be optionally allowed inside compounds in their plural form while their regular counterparts should be reduced (as in the previous case). As it turned out, the results differed among the items. Basically there were two patterns found among the pluralia tantum, one in which reduction to a singular form occurred (*scissor-eater*, *glass-eater*), and the other in which reduction was not prevalent (*clothes-eater*, *pants-eater*). Table 4.3.4 shows the responses for this condition. The column headings represent the two predominant response patterns for the pluralia tantum—[plural-plural-plural] and [plural-plural-singular]. As in the previous analysis, for the regular

Table 4.3.4 *Mean response patterns for pluralia tantum inside compounds (four responses per condition. Frequencies in parentheses)*

Pluralia tantum	Clothes		Pants		Glasses		Scissors	
Age (years)	pl	sg*	pl	sg	pl	sg	pl	sg
3	0.9 (10)	0	0.72 (8)	0.18 (2)	0.09 (1)	0.9 (10)	0	0.72 (8)
4	0.9 (10)	0.09 (1)	0.82 (9)	0.09 (1)	0.27 (3)	0.54 (6)	0	0.63 (7)
5	1 (11)	0	0.9 (10)	0.09 (1)	0.45 (5)	0.45 (5)	0.09 (1)	0.72 (8)
Total	0.94 (31)	0.09 (1)	0.82 (27)	0.12 (4)	0.27 (9)	0.64 (21)	0.09 (1)	0.69 (23)

Regular controls		
	Pattern	
Age (years)	[sg pl sg]	[sg pl pl]
3	4 (44)	0
4	3.9 (43)	0
5	3.7 (41)	0.27 (3)
Total	3.9 (128)	0.09 (3)

*sg = singular form; pl = regular plural.

control condition, the basic [singular-plural-singular] pattern predominated for 128/131 responses (χ^2 (1, $N = 33$) = 70.2, $p < .001$). The dichotomy in these data can be seen between, on the one hand, *clothes* and *pants*, which occurred 58/63 times as plurals inside compounds (χ^2 (2, $N = 33$) = 56.3, $p < .001$), and on the other hand, *glasses* and *scissors*, which occurred only 10/54 times as plurals inside compounds (χ^2 (2, $N = 32$) = 22.5, $p < .001$). While this latter pattern was consistent across ages for *scissors*, the reduction for *glasses* to *glass-eater* appeared to decline with age (though not significantly). That is, as children got older, they tended to be more likely to say *glasses-eater* rather than *glass-eater*. The reason for the dichotomy in results and the age trends will be discussed in the next section. However, it should be remembered that the prediction is that pluralia tantum should be optionally allowable inside compounds, not that they are obligatorily required inside compounds. Thus, an overall analysis shows that there was a significantly greater tendency to produce pluralia tantum inside compounds than regular plurals ($t(1) = 14.87$, $p < .001$).

There was a total of fifty-three cases in which the child was told the name for the singular referent. Most of these prompted cases were for the superordinate *clothes* in the pluralia tantum group (19/22) and for *toy* in the regular control group (26/29). This was because children usually named at the basic level (e.g., *dress* or *ball*) for a singular referent. Additional response patterns included nine cases in which *scissor* was used in naming the singular referent, and two cases in which *pant* was similarly used. The resulting pattern in all cases was [singular-plural-singular]—comparable to the regular items. Three responses were of the form, *glasses-eater*, and there was one reversal, *eater-clothes* (see Clark and Hecht, 1982, for similar examples). Two responses were discarded, one where the child failed to produce a compound and one due to experimenter error.

Discussion

The results for this experiment have been surprisingly clear-cut in the case of regular and irregular nouns. Also, for the most part, they are supportive of predictions in the case of pluralia tantum. They showed overwhelmingly that in forming compounds, regularly pluralized nouns are consistently reduced to singular forms. There was no evidence of any overpluralization errors that one finds in other domains where one does not expect rule application to be constrained by innate principles (e.g., quantifier agreement with *each* and *every*). In other words, where the child is required to *learn* the appropriate restrictions from input, errors occur; but where the restrictions follow deductively from the structural constraints, then one finds no errors.

For irregular plurals, as soon as children showed evidence of knowing the irregular forms, they produced them inside compounds. In fact the irregular plural appeared to be preferential inside the compound in the context of the present task, presumably due to the biases set up in the design. That is, children would probably not be so biased to produce a form such as *mice-eater* in an ordinary everyday context. This would be especially unlikely if, like adults, the reduced singular form is preferred. But the point is that such biasing was only effective in the allowable cases (i.e., irregulars and pluralia tantum). Also, there was no age at which children appeared to have assumed the hypothesis that irregular plurals behave just like regulars inside compounds. Such an hypothesis would be entirely reasonable given the kind of evidence available to the child in the form of such words as *toothbrush, mouse-trap* and so on. That this hypothesis never appears to be entertained supports the notion put forward here that it is not a "learning" process that we are examining, but rather, a process of filling out existing structures and deriving the consequences in an axiomatic fashion. It does not appear that the child is taking the linguistic input as primary data and inducing that rules are ordered on the basis of those data.

For the pluralia tantum, the results were in accord with our predictions to a large extent, although the dichotomy in the results was somewhat unexpected. Why children should reduce *scissors* and *glasses* to morphologically singular forms, but not *clothes* or *pants* has several possible explanations. In the case of *glasses*, one would predict that adults would not reduce to form *glass-eater*, since this would denote either drinking glasses or glass-material rather than sunglasses. However, since it may take some time for the child to learn that there is semantic pre-emption for this form, one might very well expect such erroneous responses early on. Note that responses of the form *glass-eater* did decline with age, suggesting some learning of the appropriate semantic restrictions in this case.[4] The preponderance of reductions in the case of *glasses* and *scissors* may also be due to clustering of sibilants (/s/ and /z/) within the word and in the plural perhaps causing the child to reduce the plural. This could be due to some general phonological principles acting to reduce clustering of similar features. An additional factor is syllabicity. Both *scissors* and *glasses* are bisyllabic whereas all of the other non-regular nouns tested were monosyllabic. Again, some general principles may be involved in simplifying multisyllabic compounded forms. Finally, one does find uses of *scissor* with some adults, and *glass* (in its other sense) is also a word, whereas *pant* and *clothe* are never used as nouns. The fact that a large number of children used *scissor* to refer to the singular object, further suggests a lexical entry for this word in its singular form. Whatever the explanation for these results, their dichotomous nature is not central to present concerns. The fact that at least some pluralia tantum were placed inside compounds suggests, along with the data on irregulars and regulars, that children are applying ordering of rules from very early on.

The force of the present data suggests that the young child's lexicon is richly structured in terms of the way in which rules are applied. The apparent lack of appropriate input to the child, and failure to find evidence of learning taking place, suggests that such structuring might be an innate property of the lexicon. What the child does presumably learn are particular words and morphological rules. From there, it is suggested that the constraints on word-formation follow deductively from the nature of the system. Of course, only a tiny part of the word-formation process has been examined here. In fact, the phenomenon of pluralization within compounds is really quite peripheral with respect to the theory of level-ordering and lexical theory in general. But, in a sense, its peripherality is what makes it interesting. It is a side-effect that seems totally unmotivated by considerations other than conformity to the structural constraints of the system. It is precisely the kind of phenomenon where one expects to find that properties of input are quite superfluous to acquisition.

One possibility that was mentioned only briefly is that the theory of level-ordering may itself be wrong, and therefore could not be an innate property of the lexicon. For example, Selkirk (1982) has argued for an alternative analysis whereby X-bar theory is extended into word structure and does not employ level-ordering per se (although some ordering effects are accounted for by positing differential affixation to "roots" vs. "words"). In her model, there is no constraint against affixation of regular plurals inside compounds. Examples such as *Parks Commissioner*, *drinks cabinet*, *Human Services Administration*, *weapons analysis* and so on appear to bear this out and also provide an embarrassment for level-ordering. However, as Selkirk herself points out, these examples tend to have idiosyncratic meanings for the plural forms. For example, the *drinks* in *drinks cabinet* does not denote any old drinks, but alcoholic drinks in particular. In a sense then, they are similar to the case of pluralia tantum in that one might consider the plural form in that particular usage to be a semantically idiosyncratic separate lexical form. Within the theory of level-ordering, such facts would be accounted for, since semantic idiosyncrasy is symptomatic of level 1 processes (see Table 4.3.1). This would allow for their presence inside compounds which are formed at level 2. Kiparsky (1982) has also suggested that there may be some recursion back into the lexicon. For example, *Human Services* may be formed at a first pass and then fed back into the lexicon to be compounded with *Administration*.

It is often hard to employ psychological data in adjudicating between linguistic theories. Even if such evaluations are warranted, it is not clear that psychological data should have any more prominence than purely linguistic data. However, it would seem that any psychologically plausible lexical theory would have to account, not only for the fact that we have different intuitions about *mice-infested* and **rats-infested*, but also for the fact that the same constraints appear to be present in very young children, with little or no evidence that any learning has taken place. Furthermore, the relevant constraints appear to operate productively for compounds that the child is very unlikely to have heard before (e.g., *feet-eater*). Thus, the least one would require is that the constraints should follow deductively from the theory. At present, level-ordering fits the bill and is adopted for these reasons.

Parenthetically, the existence of the exceptions noted above, actually serves to strengthen the argument against a learning account of ordering. If children do hear at least some regular plurals inside compounds (e.g., *drinks cabinet*) then this would appear to make learning the restrictions for **rats-eater* even harder. Furthermore, even if children hear some irregular plurals inside compounds, they are probably just as likely to hear regular plurals inside compounds. This would appear to make the present results quite inexplicable in terms of induction over the child's input.

If the present account is correct, then what remains is to specify a set of learning procedures that determine how the child decides at which level particular rules should be assigned. I have outlined certain properties that are symptomatic of the different levels, and presumably the child would use these in determining level-assignment (e.g., semantic compositionality, regularity, stem deformation, etc.). While such characteristics do guide one in determining level-assignment, they are often neither hard nor fast. Level 1 affixes sometimes produce semantically compositional forms or may not deform their stems. Level 2 affixes may produce non-compositional meanings and so on. Thus, properties for each of the levels tend to "cluster" rather than be absolute guides to level-assignment.

The process of rule formation in language acquisition presumably involves forming generalizations over semantically and/or phonologically related forms. In general, properties of level 1 rules serve to differentiate the derived form from its base to a greater extent than levels 2 or 3. By this, I mean that it is harder for the child to form a generalization between, for example, *derive* and *deriv + ation* [level 1] than, say, *open* and *open # er* [level 2] or *book* and *book # s* [level 3]. In other words, for both phonological and semantic reasons, level 1 derivations may not possess the kind of relatedness that the child requires to form productive rules. Consequently, the rules themselves turn out to be less productive (viz. being applicable to only a restrictive set of lexical items—those that the child has encountered in the input).

Linda Walsh (1984) has similarly proposed that level 1 derivations[5] are related to their bases only by redundancy rules that state the relationship between two forms rather than being productive morphological rules. If this were the case, then ordering would follow from the fact that the "derived" form of a level 1 process would be available as a separate lexical entry and could be compounded or affixed by rules applying at later levels. For example, if *mice* is simply a separate lexical item from *mouse*, related only by a redundancy rule, then it should be available for compounding. Thus, the issue of relatedness provides at least a partial account of how the child ends up with a distinguished set of level 1 rules.

The remaining question concerns how levels 2 and 3 are distinguished. Clearly this will turn on the child distinguishing between inflectional (level 3) and derivational (level 2) morphology. Anderson (1982), from the point of view of linguistic theory, suggests that the appropriate consideration here is relevance to syntax. That is, only inflectional processes can partake in such things as agreement over sentential constituents. Since the output of the lexicon is fed into the syntax (see Table 4.3.1), it is natural that elements that are required for syntactic processes should be affixed last—although, in some cases such as the irregular plural, phonological characteristics may pre-empt such assignment. Anderson (1982) actually proposes that inflection is a syntactic rather than a lexical process, although Jensen and Stong-Jensen (1984) provide some evidence to the contrary. Whatever the case, relevance to syntax could possibly be the appropriate property used by the child in distinguishing level 3 morphology, if indeed inflection is a lexical process. Otherwise the ordering of lexical rules before syntactic rules would again guarantee the appropriate ordering.

This does beg the question of how the child learns which morphological processes are relevant to syntax, but that is a question that must be addressed on any account either by co-occurrence phenomena or by semantically correlated properties (e.g., implicit plurality of quantifiers correlates with plural affixation). There might be a problem if it turns out that intrasentential agreement phenomena are acquired after there is evidence for level-ordering of inflectional versus derivational processes. If such were the case, it is possible that the child may use other additional strategies. For example, inflectional rules typically do not change category assignment whereas derivational processes often do. An alternative strategy might include a functional determination of level-assignment. It could be the case that the child has an innate set of hypotheses concerning possible inflectional functions, including number, gender, tense, mood, aspect, case and so on (cf. Pinker, 1982, 1984; Slobin,

1982). If this were the case, then the set of level 3 rules would be defined a priori. However, there is evidence that in some languages, functions such as pluralization are derivational rather than inflectional (Anderson, 1982).

The above is clearly just a sketch of various alternatives for what the process of level assignment may look like in acquisition. Considerable research will be required before any kind of evaluation of the proposals can be made. Furthermore, while I have adopted Kiparsky's three-level version of the lexical theory, there is by no means any clear consensus on just how many levels are required. For example, Halle and Mohanan (1985) propose that five levels are needed, although not all of these may be employed in every language. Thus if a certain amount of parametric variation exists, one major test of any acquisition theory will be its equipotentiality in acquiring word-formation rules across various languages.

In this regard, Melissa Bowerman (personal communication) has pointed out that Dutch differs significantly from English with respect to pluralization inside compounds. Whereas there are certain idiosyncratic cases of regular plurals occurring inside compounds in English (e.g., *Parks Commissioner*—see above discussion), Dutch appears to allow such cases quite freely in constructions that would be ungrammatical in English. For example, Bowerman has provided such examples as *tand-en # borstel* (= "tooth-[plural] # brush"); *muiz-en # vanger* (= "mouse-[plural] # catcher"); *paard-en # dief* (= "*horses # thief*"). In all cases, the plural (-*en*) is the most common regular form. Furthermore, it appears that such constructions are quite productive in Dutch.

This would appear to provide a considerable embarrassment to the present proposal for the innateness of level-ordering. It would seem that if a Dutch learner invoked the same strategy as the English learner, then the former would be at a considerable disadvantage. In particular, one might predict that the Dutch learner would start out like the English-speaking child and fail to use regular (-*en*) plurals inside compounds. There would then have to be a reorganization within the lexicon when forms such as *paardendief* were heard. In fact, they would have to be listed as some kind of exception to the principles of level-ordering. However, if such forms were to trigger a reorganization of the lexicon for the Dutch learner, why should cases like *Parks Commissioner* not cause a similar reorganization for the English learner?

I, like Bowerman, have little faith that such a reorganization would be found if tested on Dutch children. More persuasively, it does not make sense, linguistically, for Dutch to be exceptional in such a manner. A partial solution lies in the nature of the Dutch plural itself. Unlike English where there is basically one form of the plural (-*s*), Dutch has two basic forms: -*en*, as in the above examples, and -*s* as in *vleugel-s* (= "wing-s"). There is also a rarer form, -*eren* as in *been(d)-eren* (= "bone-s") plus other even less productive forms. While -*en* is the most common form of the plural, it appears that -*s* is not exactly rare. If -*en* is not sufficiently dominating in frequency, it could not in any sense be a "default" value for realization of the plural (as appears to be the case for -*s* in

English). Hence, the form of the plural would have to be listed with each lexical item rather than being applied productively in the strong sense (i.e., as an independently stated rule).

A second property of the Dutch plural is that it appears to have access to the internal phonology of the stem. That is, in certain cases, -*en* will change the vowel quality in the stem. This involves laxing of a tense vowel in such pairs as *dag-dagen* (= "day"-"days") where the change, though not reflected orthographically, involves /ɐ/ becoming /a/ after adding the plural. Occasionally, the vowel is changed altogether as in *schip-schepen* (= "ship"- "ships"); *stad-steden* (= "town"-"towns") (see Smit and Meijer, 1958, for other examples). Such vowel changes are quite characteristic of derivational rules as found in typical level 1 rules in English.

These two properties, lexical idiosyncrasy with respect to productivity, and phonological stem deformation, suggest that the organization of Dutch morphology and phonology is different from English in the case of pluralization. While there are insufficient data at present to propose the exact ordering of rules in Dutch, it would be quite surprising if "regular" (-*en*) plurals were not ordered before compounding which, presumably is productive, regular and non-deforming. In fact, Dutch plurals may be quite comparable to the English regular plurals in their level assignment. If true, then this would provide a natural explanation for how two quite similar languages could differ in such an odd way. Furthermore, let us suppose that phonological properties are given a greater weighting in the acquisition procedure than, say, relevance to syntax (which must in any case be abandoned for irregular plurals in English). This is not an ad hoc move, since it is the phonological properties that motivate much of the theory of level-ordering in the first place. In this case, the learner of Dutch should straightforwardly assign pluralization to a prior level than compounding. There is no need to posit reorganization and exceptional marking. Again, the ordering phenomena, or apparent lack thereof, should follow deductively from the theory.

There are clearly many gaps in the present account that will require patching with further empirical evidence and linguistic analyses. If the phenomenon of level-ordering does turn out to be correct in some form, then the results of the present study suggest that ordering, per se, may not be something for which we require a learning model. Level assignment, on the other hand, may be another matter.

Acknowledgments

The research reported here was carried out while the author was a Sloan Post-Doctoral Fellow at Stanford University. Many thanks to Susan Lierle for running subjects. I am also grateful to Melissa Bowerman, Susan Carey, Kathie

Carpenter, Eve Clark, Susan Gelman, Steven Pinker and Meg Withgot for helpful comments. A version of this paper was originally presented at the Ninth Annual Boston University Conference on Child Language Development, October 1984.

Notes to 4.3

1. The unacceptability of these forms is probably due to pre-emption by the standard singular form (cf. Clark and Clark, 1979, for a discussion of pre-emption in category shifting).
2. Eve Clark and Susan Gelman (personal communication) have previously used a similar procedure to elicit compounds from which I borrowed in designing the present study.
3. In the case of teeth and beads there were actually about twelve objects—the teeth were in an oral configuration and the beads on a string.
4. A reviewer has suggested that when one eats glasses one ipso facto eats glass and that this may also be a factor in children's errors.
5. While not using the terminology of level-ordering in her paper, the distinctions Walsh (1984) makes turn out to be equivalent to the levels.

References to 4.3

Allen M. (1978). *Morphological Investigations.* Unpublished doctoral dissertation, Department of Linguistics, University of Connecticut, Storrs, CT.

Anderson, S. R. (1982). "Where's morphology?" *Linguistic Inquiry,* **13**, 571–612.

Berko, J. (1958). "The child's learning of English morphology." *Word,* **14**, 150–77.

Clark, E. V. and Clark, H. H. (1979). "When nouns surface as verbs." *Language,* **55**, 767–811.

Clark, E. V. and Hecht, B. F. (1982). "Learning to coin agent and instrument nouns." *Cognition,* **12**, 1–24.

Ervin, S. M. (1964). "Imitation and structural change in children's language." In E. H. Lenneberg (ed.), *New Directions in the Study of Language.* Cambridge, MA: MIT Press.

Gordon, P. (1981). "Syntactic acquisition of the count/mass distinction." In *Papers and Reports on Child Language Development,* vol. 20, Department of Linguistics, Stanford University, Stanford, CA.

Gordon, P. (1982). *The Acquisition of Syntactic Categories: The case of the count/mass distinction.* Unpublished doctoral dissertation, Department of Psychology, MIT, Cambridge, MA.

Halle, M. and Mohanan, K. P. (1985). "Segmental phonology of Modern English." *Linguistic Inquiry,* **16**, 57–116.

Jensen, J. T. and Stong-Jensen, M. (1984). "Morphology is in the lexicon!" *Linguistic Inquiry,* **15**, 474–98.

Kiparsky, P. (1982). "From cyclic phonology to lexical phonology." In H. van der Hulst and N. Smith (eds), *The Structure of Phonological Representations* (part 1). Dordrecht, The Netherlands: Foris Publications.

Kiparsky, P. (1983). "Word-formation and the lexicon." In F. Ingemann (ed.), *Proceedings of the 1982 Mid-American Linguistics Conference.* University of Kansas, Lawrence, KS.

Kučera, H. and Francis, W. N. (1967). *Computational Analysis of Present-day American English.* Providence, RI: Brown University Press.

Pinker, S. (1982). "A theory of the acquisition of lexical-interpretive grammars." In J. Bresnan and R. Kaplan (eds), *The Mental Representation of Grammatical Relations.* Cambridge, MA: MIT Press.

Pinker, S. (1984). *Language Learnability and Language Development*. Cambridge, MA: Harvard University Press.

Selkirk, E. O. (1982). *The Syntax of Words*. Linguistic Inquiry Monograph, 7, Cambridge, MA: MIT Press.

Siegel, D. (1977). *Topics in English Morphology*. Unpublished doctoral dissertation, Department of Linguistics, MIT, Cambridge, MA.

Slobin, D. I. (1982). "Universal and particular in the acquisition of language." In E. Wanner and L. R. Gleitman (eds), *Language Acquisition: The state of the art*. Cambridge: Cambridge University Press.

Smit, J. and Meijer, R. P. (1958). *Dutch Grammar and Reader*. Melbourne: Melbourne University Press.

Walsh, L. (1984). *Possible Words*. Paper presented at the MIT Morphology Workshop, Jan. 26–7 1983. Cambridge, MA.

—PART 5———————

Acquisition in Special Circumstances

Beyond the Input Given:
The child's role in the acquisition of language

Susan Goldin-Meadow and Carolyn Mylander

This article describes our research program of the past fifteen years, which investigates a unique phenomenon in language acquisition—namely, the development of language-like behavior in children who lack normal linguistic input during their early stages of acquisition. The studies encompassed in our research program bear on a number of questions in linguistic and developmental theory, in particular the innate capabilities a child brings to the language-learning situation and the role of parental input in providing sufficient structure for those capabilities to flourish. We discuss our findings and relate them to other studies addressing the child's role in language acquisition.

The child's contribution to the language acquisition process

Linguistic input has an obvious impact on the child's acquisition of language—a child who hears Swahili learns Swahili, not French or Polish. It is equally clear, however, that children (but not dogs, cats, or even chimpanzees; cf. Seidenberg and Petitto, 1979) bring certain abilities to the language-learning situation that make language learning possible. A variety of approaches have recently been taken to the task of discovering the child's contribution to the language-learning process. For example, one approach explores the relationship between the linguistic input children receive and their output, in either semantic

507

(e.g., Huttenlocher, Smiley, and Latner, 1983) or structural domains (e.g., Furrow, Nelson, and Benedict, 1979; Gleitman, Newport, and Gleitman, 1984; Newport, Gleitman, and Gleitman, 1977). Another approach compares the spontaneous speech of children learning different languages, particularly languages that vary systematically in the semantic or structural models they provide for the learner (e.g., Clark, 1976; Slobin, 1985). Finally, a third approach derives conditions on the form of grammar that are then postulated to be part of the language-learning capacity of the child (e.g., Pinker, 1984; Wexler, 1982).

Perhaps the least ambiguous picture of the child's contribution to language learning can be obtained from situations where children go beyond the input given to them. Children routinely go beyond their input when they gain productive control of their language—that is when they can use language in ways they have never heard it used. However the child's creative contribution to the language-acquisition process is potentially most apparent in situations where the linguistic input available to the child is degraded, providing the child with ample opportunity to elaborate upon that input.

Bickerton (1981) proposes that creole genesis is one type of case in which children go beyond the degraded input they receive. Bickerton's proposal is controversial, in part because questions have been raised about the historical accuracy of the data upon which his claims are based (e.g. Goodman, 1984; Samarin, 1984; Seuren, 1984). There is, however, one well-documented example of the sort of process Bickerton hypothesizes for creoles. This case study, based on developmental data in a single individual, suggests that children can introduce complexity into the language system they receive from their parents. Singleton and Newport (1987), and Singleton (1987, 1989) have described the language of a deaf child whose deaf parents' signs provided an incomplete model of the morphological structure in American Sign Language (ASL). The child, exposed only to this imperfect model of ASL, nevertheless developed a sign language with morphological structure comparable to the morphological structure developed by other deaf children exposed to complete models of ASL. This example suggests that children can produce language output which exceeds language input, and also that children have the ability to organize the pieces of language they receive to produce a linguistic system which is governed by rules not used by the adults in their environment.

A similar situation arises when deaf children (typically deaf children of hearing parents) are exposed not to ASL but rather to Manually Coded English (MCE), sign systems which map English surface structure onto the visual/gestural modality. MCE systems were invented by educators to teach English to deaf children and thus are not "natural" language systems spontaneously developed by language users. MCE relies on a lexicon heavily borrowed from ASL. However, unlike ASL morphology, in which simultaneous spatial devices serve as morphological markers, morphology in MCE is sequential rather than simultaneous and utilizes invented signs that follow in a one-to-one fashion the morphological structure of English. There is some doubt that the structure of English can be successfully incorporated into the signed medium. Indeed, deaf children exposed only to MCE have been found to alter the code, innovating forms that systematically use space to convey meaning, as do many of the grammatical devices of ASL (Gee and Goodhart, 1985; Goodhart, 1984; Livingston, 1983; S. Supalla, 1990; Suty and Friel-Patti, 1982). Thus, when provided with an input that may be difficult to process, children are capable of altering that input and constructing a rule-governed system of their own.

An even more extreme example of the child's ability to go beyond the input comes from our work on children who are not exposed to usable input from any established language. The children we have studied are deaf with hearing losses so severe that they cannot naturally acquire oral language. In addition, these children are born to hearing parents who have chosen not to expose them to a conventional sign language such as ASL or MCE. Despite their lack of usable linguistic input, either signed or spoken, these deaf children develop gestural communication systems which share many—but not all—of the structural properties of the early linguistic systems of children exposed to established language models. A primary goal of our research has been to describe the structural properties of early child language that can be found in the gestural systems developed by deaf children without the benefit of a conventional language model.

At the outset, we recognize that, although the children in our studies are not exposed to a model of an established language, they are exposed to the spontaneous gestures their hearing parents use when speaking to them (as are children of hearing parents; cf. Shatz, 1982). These gestures could conceivably serve as input to the deaf children's gestural systems, so they must be the background against which the children's gestural accomplishments are evaluated. A second goal of our research, therefore, has been to determine the origin of the structural properties found in the deaf children's gestural systems—specifically, to discover which aspects of these structures can be traced to the gestural input provided by the children's hearing parents and which aspects go beyond this input.

The primary focus of this paper, then, is an assessment of the nature of the child's contribution to the language-acquisition process. We will begin by reviewing our own findings on the structural properties of the gesture systems produced by deaf children of hearing parents, and then by comparing the gestures produced by these deaf children to the gestures produced spontaneously by the children's own hearing parents. Finally, we will evaluate the structural properties found in our deaf children's gestures in the context of data gained from other approaches to the question of the child's language-making capacity.

Background on deafness and language learning

General background

The sign languages of the deaf are autonomous languages which are not based on the spoken languages of hearing cultures (Bellugi and Studdert-Kennedy, 1980; Klima and Bellugi, 1979; Lane and Grosjean, 1980). A sign language such as ASL is a primary linguistic system passed down from one generation of deaf people to the next and is a language in the full sense of the word. Like spoken languages, ASL is structured at syntactic (Fischer, 1974; Liddell, 1980; Lillo-Martin, 1986; Padden, 1983), morphological (Fischer, 1973; Fischer and Gough, 1978; Klima and Bellugi, 1979; Newport, 1981; T. Supalla, 1982; Supalla and Newport, 1978), and "phonological" levels of analysis (Battison, 1974; Coulter, 1986; Lane, Boyes-Braem, and Bellugi, 1976; Liddell, 1984; Liddell and Johnson, 1986; Padden and Perlmutter, 1987; Sandler, 1986; Stokoe, 1960; Wilbur, 1986).

Deaf children born to deaf parents and exposed from birth to a conventional sign language such as ASL have been found to acquire that language naturally; that is, these children progress through stages in acquiring sign language similar to those of hearing children acquiring a spoken language (Caselli, 1983; Hoffmeister, 1978; Hoffmeister and Wilbur, 1980; Kantor, 1982; Newport and Ashbrook, 1977; Newport and Meier, 1985). Thus, in an appropriate linguistic environment—in this case a signing environment—deaf children are not handicapped with respect to language learning.

However, 90 percent of deaf children are not born to deaf parents who could provide early exposure to a conventional sign language. Rather, they are born to hearing parents who, quite naturally, tend to expose their children to speech (Hoffmeister and Wilbur, 1980). Unfortunately, it is extremely uncommon for deaf children with severe to profound hearing losses to acquire the spoken language of their hearing parents naturally, that is, without intensive and specialized instruction. Even with instruction, deaf children's acquisition of speech is markedly delayed when compared either to the acquisition of speech by hearing children of hearing parents or to the acquisition of sign by deaf children of deaf parents. By age 5 or 6, and despite intensive early training programs, the average profoundly deaf child has only a very reduced oral linguistic capacity (Conrad, 1979; K. Meadow, 1968).

In addition, unless hearing parents send their deaf children to a school in which sign language is used, these children are not likely to receive conventional sign-language input. Under such inopportune circumstances, these deaf children might be expected to fail to communicate at all, or perhaps to communicate only in nonsymbolic ways. This turns out not to be the case.

Previous studies of deaf children of hearing parents have shown that these children spontaneously use gestures (referred to as "home signs") to communicate, even if they are not exposed to a conventional sign-language model (Fant, 1972; Lenneberg, 1964; Moores, 1974; Tervoort, 1961). Given a home environment in which family members communicate with each other through many different channels, one might expect that the deaf child would exploit the accessible modality (i.e. the manual modality) for purposes of communication. However, given that no language model is present in the child's accessible modality, one might *not* expect that the child's communication would be structured in language-like ways.

Our work has focused particularly on the structural aspects of deaf children's gestures and has attempted to determine whether any of the linguistic properties found in natural child language can also be found in those gestures. We have analyzed the gestures of ten deaf children of hearing parents and have found each child's gestures to be structured at several different levels. We focus here on three aspects of structure in the deaf child's gestures, describing each in turn: lexicon, syntax, and morphology.

Background on the sample

The ten children in our sample ranged in age from 1;4 (years;months) to 4;1 at the time of the first interview and from 2;6 to 5;9 at the time of the final interview. The children were videotaped in their homes during play sessions with their hearing parents or the experimenter every two to four months for as long as each child was available (the number of observation sessions per child ranged from two to sixteen). Six of the children lived in the Philadelphia area and four in the Chicago area.

The children were all born deaf to hearing parents and sustained severe (70–90dB) to profound (>90dB) hearing losses. Even when wearing a hearing aid in each ear, none of the children was able to acquire speech naturally. In general, a child with a severe hearing loss is unable to hear even shouted conversation and cannot learn speech by conventional means. A child with a profound loss can hear essentially no conversation and hears only occasional very loud sounds which may be perceived more as vibrations than sound patterns. Amplification serves to increase awareness of sound but often does not increase the clarity of sound patterns (Mindel and Vernon, 1971; Moores, 1982).

Two of the ten children were not attending any educational program at the time of our studies; the remaining eight were being educated in oral schools (two in one school, three in another, and the remaining three in three different schools). Each of the schools advocated an oral method of deaf education which offered early and intense training in sound sensitivity, lipreading (or speech-reading), and speech production, and which discouraged the use of conventional sign language with the child. It is important to note that the information one gets from reading visual cues off a speaker's lips is not enough to allow severely and profoundly deaf children to learn spoken language (see Conrad, 1979; Farwell, 1976; Summerfield, 1983). Visual cues are generally ambiguous with respect to speech: The mapping from visual cues to words is one to many. In order to constrain the range of plausible lexical interpretations, other higher-order classes of information (e.g. the phonological, lexical, syntactic, semantic, and pragmatic regularities of a language) must come into play during speechreading. The most proficient speechreaders are those who can use their knowledge of the language to interpret an inadequate visual signal (Conrad, 1977). In fact, postlingually deafened individuals (people who had knowledge of a language before losing their hearing) are generally more proficient speechreaders than individuals who have been deaf from birth (Summerfield, 1983). Since speechreading requires knowledge of a language to succeed, it cannot provide all the input necessary for a severely to profoundly deaf child to learn language. At the time of our studies, none of the children in our study had made significant progress in acquiring spoken English.[1]

In addition, none of the children in our sample had been exposed to conventional sign language. Consistent with the oral-education philosophy, sign language was not used in any of the schools these children attended (indeed, none of the teachers knew sign language, nor did any of the other children in the classroom). Moreover, neither the children's hearing parents nor their hearing siblings knew sign language.

The derivation of coding categories

How does one begin a description of the deaf child's gesture system? The problem lies in entering the system. Because there is no established language model toward which the deaf child's system is developing, there are no hints front a conventional system that might guide initial descriptions. Consequently, the description procedure necessarily becomes a bootstrap operation. It begins with preliminary decisions on how to categorize the gestures produced by deaf subjects (e.g., how to isolate gestures from the stream of motor behavior, how to segment those gestures, and how to assign them meanings).

Our preliminary coding categories were based on two sources. The first was the corpus of descriptions of spoken language, particularly child language, and the growing number of descriptions of conventional sign languages. The second source was our intuitions about the motoric forms and the meanings of the gestures produced by deaf subjects.

Having established preliminary coding categories (discussed below), we began to utilize them while transcribing videotapes. We tested the usefulness of our tentative categories in two ways. First, we asked if the categories were reliable, and we established reliability by comparing the judgments of one experimeter and a second coder who was not at the original taping sessions. The agreement scores between two coders were found to be quite high (between 87 percent and 100 percent, depending on the coding category), confirming category reliability.

In the second test of our category definitions, we asked if these particular categories resulted in coherent descriptions of the deaf child's gesture system. The claim made here is that, if a description based on these particular coding categories is coherent, this fact is evidence of the usefulness of the categories themselves. Consider the following example. Suppose we tentatively apply the semantic categories "patient" (object acted on) and "act" to the deaf child's gestures. If we then discover a pattern based on those categories (e.g., a gesture-ordering rule following, say, a patient-act pattern), we ask whether the pattern has both retrospective validity and prospective predictive value. If so, we have evidence that the particular categories PATIENT and ACT are useful in descriptions of the deaf child's system. The existence of the pattern confirms the utility of the categories, since the former is formulated in terms of the latter.

There is, of course, the possibility that these patterns and categories are products of the experimenter's mind rather than the child's. However, our study is no more vulnerable to this possibility than are studies investigating young hearing children who are learning spoken languages. Adult experimenters may be incapable of finding anything but language-like structures in a child's communication (for a discussion of this point, see Goldin-Meadow and Mylander, 1984a: 18–26). Although the problem can never be completely avoided, the following assumption allows us to proceed: If a category turns out to "make sense of," or organize, the child's communications (e.g., by forming the basic unit of a predictable pattern), we are then justified in isolating that category as a unit of the system and in attributing that category to the child. Thus, the consistency of the results described below and in our previous work lends credence to our coding categories.

Two final methodological points are worth noting in regard to our coding categories. First, the coding categories described below were devised on the basis of data from the Philadelphia children; however, these same categories, when applied to the Chicago data, continued to yield coherent and systematic structures. And second, our coding techniques do not inevitably unearth structure in spontaneous gestures (see "The role of parental gestures in guiding the deaf child's system," which shows that the spontaneous gestures produced by the deaf children's hearing mothers, when analyzed with the coding techniques described below, do not form a linguistic system comparable to the children's).

Identifying a gesture

Our first task is to isolate communicative gestures from the stream of ongoing motor behavior. The problem here is to discriminate acts that communicate indirectly (e.g., pushing a plate away, which indicates that the eater has had enough) from those acts whose sole purpose is to communicate symbolically (e.g., a "stoplike" movement of the hands produced in order to suggest to the host that another helping is not necessary). We do not consider every nudge or facial expression produced by the deaf subjects to be a communicative gesture (no matter how much information is conveyed). Consequently, we are forced to develop a procedure that isolates only those acts used for deliberate communication.

Lacking a generally accepted behavioral index of deliberate or intentional communication (see MacKay, 1972 for discussion), we decided that a communicative gesture must meet both of the following criteria. First, the motion must be directed to another individual. This criterion is satisfied if the child attempts to establish eye contact with the communication partner (the criterion was strictly enforced unless there had been recent previous communication with eye contact such that the child could assume the continued attention of the partner).[2] Second, the gesture must not be a direct motor act on the partner or on some relevant object. As an example, if the child attempts to twist open a jar, s/he is not considered to have made a gesture for "open," even if in some sense s/he is, by this act, trying to communicate to the experimenter that s/he needs help opening the jar. But if the child makes a twisting motion in the air, with eyes first on the experimenter to establish contact, we consider the motion to be a communicative gesture. Once isolated, gestures were recorded in terms of three dimensions commonly used to describe signs in ASL (Stokoe, 1960): Shape of the hand, movement of the hand or body, and location of the hand with respect to places on the body or in space.

Segmenting gesture strings

We next decided on the units appropriate for describing combinations of gestures. Here again we borrowed a criterion often used in studies of ASL: Relaxation of the hand after a gesture of series or gestures was taken to signal the end of a string, that is, to demarcate a sentence boundary. For example, if a child pointed to a toy and then, without relaxing the hand, pointed to a table, the two pointings were considered "within a string." The same two pointings, interrupted by a relaxation of the hand, would be classified as two isolated gestures.

This criterion received retrospective validation from our subsequent analyses. We determined the boundaries of gesture strings on the basis of relaxation of the hand, and then examined the resulting strings to see if they had sentence-like qualities. We found that the deaf children's gesture strings, when isolated according to this criterion, resembled the early sentences of children learning conventional languages in three respects: (1) the strings were used to express the same types of semantic relations as are typically expressed in early child language (see "Predicate structure"); (2) the strings were characterized by the same types of structural devices as are typically found in early child language ("Ordering and production probability rules"); and (3) the developmental onset of the strings used to express single propositions and multipropositions fits well with the onset of simple and complex sentences in early child language ("Developmental pattern"). We therefore felt justified in continuing to use relaxation of the hand to determine boundaries and in calling the deaf children's gesture strings "sentences."

Assigning meaning to gestures

Our subjects produced three types of gestures. DEICTIC gestures typically were pointing gestures that maintained a constant kinesic form in all contexts. These deictics were used predominantly to single out objects, people, places, and the like in the surroundings. In contrast, CHARACTERIZING gestures were stylized pantomimes whose forms varied with the intended meaning of each gesture (e.g., a fist pounded in the air as someone was hammering or two hands flapping in the presence of a pet bird). Finally, MARKER gestures were typically head or hand gestures (e.g., nods and headshakes or one finger held in the air signifying "wait") that are conventionalized in our culture and that the children used as modulators (e.g., to negate, affirm, and doubt.)

We next assigned lexical meanings to both deictic and characterizing gestures (markers are not included in the analyses presented here). The problems we faced were comparable to those that arise in assigning lexical meanings to a hearing child's words. Consider an English-speaking child who utters *duck walk* as a toy Donald Duck waddles by. Adult listeners assume that, since the child used two distinct phonological forms (*duck* and *walk*), s/he intended to describe two distinct aspects of the event (the feathered object and the walking action). Moreover, we assume that the child's noun *duck* refers to the object, and that the verb *walk* refers to the action of the object—that is, that the child's lexical meanings for the words *duck* and *walk* coincide with adult meanings for these words. In general, we tend to assume that nouns refer to objects, people, places, and the like, and that verbs refer to actions, processes, and so forth. This decision, although difficult to justify (for discussion, see Braine, 1976; Dromi, 1987), is bolstered by data from the child's language system taken as a whole. To the extent that the child has mastered other aspects of the adult system that are based on the noun–verb distinction (e.g., verb agreement), s/he can plausibly be said to have mastered the distinction in the instance of lexical meanings.

For our deaf subjects we must also make relatively arbitrary assumptions at this stage of assigning lexical meanings, but in this case we have no adult language model to guide us. As a result, we have chosen to use gesture FORM as a basis for assigning lexical meanings to the deaf children's gestures. We assume that deictic gestures (e.g., pointing at the duck) refer to objects, people, and places, and that characterizing gestures (e.g., walking motions produced by the hands) refer to actions and attributes. These decisions are elaborated in the next section and are justified in detail in Goldin-Meadow and Mylander (1984a: 19–26).

Although many of our coding decisions are arbitrary, they are not unmotivated. For example, in deciding that points denote objects, people, and places, we followed researchers of child language in ASL (e.g., Hoffmeister, 1978; Kantor, 1982) who treat points in the early sentences of deaf children acquiring ASL from their deaf parents as object-referring. Of course, it is likely that one could make a different set of coding decisions (equally arbitrary but motivated in their own right) that would result in a description of the deaf children's gestures that was less structured than the description presented below. In similar fashion, one could choose to describe the hearing child's sentences in such a way that they appear to be less structured. But what is to be gained by making a different set of coding decisions (for example, by excluding pointing gestures from the analyses, or by ignoring the boundaries demarcated by relaxation of the hands in the deaf children's gesture systems)? As we will show, structured patterns are undeniably present in the deaf children's gesture systems if the systems are described in terms of our coding categories. We believe that the reasonableness of the coding decisions we have made is supported by two facts: Our coding decisions yield coherent patterns with prospective validity, and these coherent structures resemble the structures of early child language, both spoken and signed.

Lexicon in the gestures of deaf children of hearing parents

Pointing gestures

At the outset, it is important to note that pointing gestures and words differ fundamentally in terms of the referential information each conveys. The deictic pointing gesture, unlike a word, serves to direct a communication partner's gaze toward a particular person, place, or thing; thus, the gesture explicitly specifies the location of its referent in a way that a word (even a pro-form) never can. The pointing gesture does not, however, specify what the object is; it merely indicates where the object is. That is, the pointing gesture is "location-specific" but not "identity-specific" with respect to its referent. Single words, by contrast, can be identity-specific (e.g., *lion* and *ball* serve to classify their respective referents into different sets), but not location-specific, unless the word is accompanied by a pointing gesture or other contextual support.

Despite this fundamental difference between pointing gestures and words, the deaf children's pointing gestures were found to function like the object-referring words of hearing children in two respects. First, the referents of the points in the deaf children's gestured sentences encompassed the same range of object categories (in approximately the same distribution) as the referents of nouns in hearing children's spoken sentences (Feldman, Goldin-Meadow, and Gleitman, 1978; Goldin-Meadow and Mylander, 1984a: 20).[3] Second, the deaf children combined their pointing gestures with other points and with characterizing gestures; if these points are considered to function like nouns and pronouns, the deaf children's gesture combinations turn out to be structured like the early sentences of children learning conventional languages (see "Ordering and production probability rules"). Thus, the deaf children's pointing gestures appear to function as part of a linguistic system.

In addition, the deaf children used their pointing gestures in ways that went beyond merely directing the gaze toward a particular object. The children primarily used their pointing gestures to refer to real-world objects in the immediate environment (e.g., the child pointed at a jar of bubbles, followed by a "blow" characterizing gesture, to request that the bubbles be blown). However, the children also used their pointing gestures to refer to objects that were not present in the here-and-now, and did so by pointing at a real-world object that was similar to the (absent) object they intended to refer to (e.g., the child pointed at an empty jar of bubbles, followed by a "blow" gesture, to request that the absent full jar of bubbles be blown). We examined pointing gestures in detail in one of our deaf subjects (Goldin-Meadow *et al.*, 1990), and found that this child could extend his use of points even farther beyond the here-and-now by pointing at an arbitrary location in space set up as a place-holder for an absent intended referent (e.g., the child pointed at a spot on his own gesture—a "round" gesture representing the shape of a Christmas-tree ball—to refer to the hook typically found at that spot on Christmas tree ornaments). This child was found to use points to indicate objects in the immediate context when he was first observed at age 2;10; he first used his points to indicate objects that were not present in the here-and-now at age 3;3, and began using points to indicate arbitrary locations set up as place-holders for objects at age 4;10. Hoffmeister (1978) reports a similar developmental pattern, from points at real-world objects to "semi-real-world" objects to arbitrary loci, in deaf children who have been exposed to a conventional sign language (ASL) from birth.

Moreover, the child whose points we have studied extensively was also found to use his pointing gestures to refer to his own gestures. For example, to request a Donald Duck toy that the experimenter held behind her back, the child pursed his lips to imitate Donald Duck's bill, then pointed at his own pursed lips and pointed toward the Donald Duck toy behind the experimenter's back. When offered a Mickey Mouse toy, the child shook his head, pursed his lips and again pointed at his own pursed lips (see also the above example in which he pointed at his own "round" gesture). Thus, the child was able to use his pointing gestures metalinguistically, suggesting not only that pointing gestures formed an integral part of his linguistic system, but also that he could distance himself from his own gestures and treat them as objects to be reflected on and referred to.

Characterizing gestures

The characterizing gesture, which is the lexical item the deaf children used to denote actions and attributes, also differs somewhat from the words or signs typically used by young language-learners exposed to conventional language models. The form of the deaf children's characterizing gesture captures an aspect of its referent and, in this respect, is distinct both from the far less transparent verb and adjective word forms that hearing children use to denote actions and attributes and from the early sign forms of deaf children acquiring ASL—since most of these are not iconic (Bonvillian, Orlansky, and Novack, 1983) or, if iconic from an adult's point of view, are not recognized as iconic by the child (Schlesinger, 1978). Note, however, that, in contrast to their location-specific pointing gestures, the deaf children's characterizing gestures resemble hearing children's words in that the characterizing gesture (via its iconicity) can specify the identity of its referent.

Although all of the deaf children's characterizing gestures were iconic, the gestures differed in the transparency of the relation between the form of the gesture and the intended referent. For example, the form of some of the gestures was based on an act associated with the act or attribute the child intended to refer to (e.g., the child arced a hand back and forth in the air as though conducting to refer to the act of singing, or put two palms together in front of the chest as though praying to refer to the act of going to school, which was an oral Catholic school where each day began with prayer). In other instances, the children used stereotyped actions commonly found in our culture as the basis for their gestures—e.g., one child held his nose to indicate that an object was smelly, or rubbed his belly to indicate that an object was tasty; another child held two fists together side-by-side and then broke the fists apart to indicate that an object was or had been broken, regardless of the motion that was actually used to break the objects; another extended her palm to request the transfer of an object, not just to her own hand, but to other people and to other locations. Lexical meaning for these less-transparent gestures was determined on the basis of extralinguistic context, which is the procedure followed in most studies of spoken language learning (cf. Bloom, 1970).

The majority of the deaf children's gestures were, however, quite transparent, with the motion or handshape of the gesture reflecting the action or attribute to which the child intended to refer. For these gestures we inferred a probable meaning on the basis of extralinguistic context but then used the form of the gesture further to constrain our meaning assignments. For example, one child held a fist near his mouth and made chewing movements to comment on his sister eating snacks; this gesture was assigned the meaning "eat." Another child moved her hand forward in the air to describe the path of a moving toy, and this gesture was assigned the meaning "go." Similarly for attribute gestures, as when one child formed a round shape with the hand to describe a Christmas-tree ornament; basing the meaning of the gesture on its form, we assigned the meaning "round" to the gesture.

The form of the gesture and its context were also used to classify action gestures as either transitive or intransitive. If the intended referent of a gesture involved action on an object (manipulating it, touching it, holding it, changing it, or moving it), the gesture was considered transitive. If, however, the intended referent of the gesture involved an action in which a person or object moved on its own (either moving in place or moving to a new location), the gesture was considered intransitive.[4] Often the form of the gesture was the crucial determinant in deciding about transitivity. For example, consider a situation in which the child pushed a toy truck and then watched the truck go forward on its own (a child learning English might describe this situation with the ambiguous word *move*, meaning either "I move the truck" or "the truck moves"). The way the deaf child chose to represent this event in a characterizing gesture determined whether we called that gesture a transitive act or an intransitive act. If the child moved a hand in a short arc representing the pushing action done on the truck, the gesture was classified as the transitive act "push." If, however, the child moved a hand forward in a linear path representing the action of the truck, the gesture was classified as the intransitive act "go."

Syntax in the gestures of deaf children of hearing parents

Predicate structure

The deaf children in our studies combined their gestures into strings that functioned in a number of respects like the sentences of early child language. First, the children's gesture sentences expressed the semantic relations typically found in early child language (in particular, action and attribute relations), with characterizing gestures representing the predicates and pointing gestures representing the arguments playing different thematic roles in those semantic relations (Goldin-Meadow and Mylander, 1984a: 26–9, 58–9). For example, one child produced a pointing gesture at a bubble jar (representing the argument playing the patient role) followed by the characterizing gesture "twist" (representing the act predicate) to request that the experimenter twist open the bubble jar. Another child produced a pointing gesture at a train (representing the argument playing the actor role) followed by the characterizing gesture "circle" (representing the act predicate) to comment on the fact that a toy train was circling on the track.

In addition, the predicates in the deaf children's sentences were comparable to the predicates of early child language in having underlying frames or structures composed of one, two, or three arguments (Goldin-Meadow, 1985: 215–19; Feldman, Goldin-Meadow, and Gleitman, 1978: 385–8). For example, all of the children produced "transfer" or "give" gestures with an inferred predicate structure containing three arguments—the actor, the patient, and the recipient[5] (e.g., you/sister give duck to her/Susan). The children also produced two types of two-argument predicates: Transitive gestures such as "eat" with a predicate structure containing the actor and patient (e.g., you/Susan eat apple), and intransitive gestures such as "go" with a predicate structure containing the actor and recipient (e.g., you/mother go upstairs). Finally, the children produced gestures such as "sleep" or "dance" with a one-argument predicate structure containing only the actor (e.g., you/father sleep).

We attributed these one-, two-, and three-argument predicate structures to the deaf children's gestures on the basis of two types of evidence. First, we found that each child, at some time in his or her repertoire, produced gestures for all of the arguments associated with a particular predicate structure (see Bloom [1970], who first used this procedure to justify assigning complex underlying structure to two-word strings in hearing children; see also Goldin-Meadow, 1985: 230–8 for further discussion of this procedure of "rich interpretation" and its application to the deaf children's gesture systems). For example, one child produced the following different two-gesture sentences, all conveying the notion of transfer of an object: "cookie give" (patient-act), "sister David" (actor-recipient), "give David" (act-recipient), "duck Susan" (patient-recipient). By overtly expressing the actor, the patient, and the recipient in this predicate context, the child exhibited knowledge that these three arguments are associated with the transfer predicate (see Goldin-Meadow, 1985: 216 for additional examples).

The second type of evidence for predicate structure in the deaf children's gestures came from the relative probability that a given argument or predicate would be gestured in a two-gesture sentence. Most of the children's sentences contained only two gestures; thus, for most sentences, the child was not likely to produce gestures for all of the arguments associated with a particular predicate. The likelihood that a gesture would be produced depicting any given argument should depend on the number of arguments that could be gestured in the predicate. If we are correct in assigning structures of one, two or three arguments to different predicates, the probability that a given argument, for example the actor, would be gestured in a three-argument predicate should be lower than the probability that the actor would be gestured in a two-argument predicate, simply because there is more "competition" for the limited number of surface slots for a three-argument predicate than there is for a two-argument predicate (so, for instance, the actor in a "give" predicate should be less likely to be gestured than the actor in an "eat" predicate). In turn, the probability that the actor would be gestured in a two-argument predicate should be lower than the probability that the actor would be gestured in a one-argument predicate (e.g., the actor in an "eat" predicate should be less likely to be gestured than the actor in a "dance" predicate). This predicted production-probability pattern was found for the actor, for the patient, and for the act in the gesture sentences of the six Philadelphia deaf children (Goldin-Meadow, 1979) and the four

Chicago deaf children (Goldin-Meadow, 1985), providing evidence for predicate structure in the gesture systems of all ten of our deaf subjects.

Ordering and production probability rules

The deaf children's gesture sentences were structured on the surface, as are the sentences of early child language (Goldin-Meadow and Feldman, 1975, 1977; Goldin-Meadow and Mylander, 1984a: 35–8). The sentences the children produced were found to conform to regularities of two types: Ordering regularities and production-probability regularities. Moreover, the particular structural regularities found in the children's sentences showed considerable consistency across the ten children in the sample.

Ordering regularities were based on the position that a gesture for a particular thematic role tended to occupy in a sentence. The children tended to order gestures for patients, acts, and recipients in a consistent way in their two-gesture sentences. The following three ordering patterns were found in many, but not all, of the children's two-gesture sentences (Goldin-Meadow and Mylander, 1984a: 35–6): PATIENT-ACT (e.g., the gesture for the patient "cheese" preceded the gesture for the act "eat"), PATIENT-RECIPIENT (e.g., the gesture for the patient "hat" preceded the gesture for the recipient "cowboy's head"), and ACT-RECIPIENT (e.g., the gesture for the act "move-to" preceded the gesture for the recipient "table"). In addition, although most of the children did not produce enough sentences containing gestures for the actor to enable us to discern a consistent order, two of the children did exhibit an ordering pattern for the actor (primarily for the intransitive actor, but also for the few transitive actors they produced): The gesture for the actor (e.g., "mother") preceded the gesture for the act (e.g., "goes").

As described above, production probability is the likelihood that a particular thematic role will be gestured in a sentence. Unlike the analysis in "Predicate structure" above, where we compared the production probability of a given thematic role (e.g., the patient) across different predicate frames, in this analysis we compare the production probability of different thematic roles (e.g., the patient vs. the actor) in predicate frames of the same size. If the children were randomly producing gestures for the thematic roles associated with a given predicate, they would, for example, be equally likely to produce a gesture for the patient as for the actor in a sentence about eating. We found, however, that the children were not random in their production of gestures for thematic roles—in fact, likelihood of production was found to distinguish among thematic roles. We found, in particular, that all ten of the children were more likely to produce a gesture for the patient e.g., "cheese" in a sentence about eating than to produce a gesture for the actor, "mouse" (Goldin-Meadow and Mylander, 1984a: 37). Note that this particular production probability pattern tends to result in two-gesture sentences that preserve the unity of the predicate, i.e., patient + act sentences (akin to OV in conventional systems) were more frequent in our deaf children's gestures than actor + act sentences (akin to SV in conventional systems).

In addition, nine of the ten children produced gestures for the intransitive actor (e.g., the mouse in a sentence describing a mouse running in his hole) as often as they produced gestures for the patient (e.g., the cheese in a sentence describing a mouse eating cheese), and far more often than they produced gestures for the transitive actor (e.g., the mouse in a sentence describing a mouse eating cheese; Goldin-Meadow and Mylander, 1984a: 36–8). This production-probability pattern is an analogue of the structural case-marking patterns of ergative languages in that the intransitive actor is treated like the patient rather than like the transitive actor. (Note, however, that in conventional ergative systems it is the transitive actor which is marked, whereas in the deaf children's gesture systems the transitive actor tends to be omitted and, in this sense, could be considered unmarked; cf. Dixon, 1979; Silverstein, 1976.)[6]

The ergative pattern found in the deaf children's gestures could reflect a bias on the part of the child toward the affected object of an action. In an intransitive sentence such as *you go to the corner*, the intransitive actor *you*, in some sense, has a double meaning. On the one hand, *you* refers to the goer, the actor, the effector of the going action. On the other hand, the *you* refers to the gone, the patient, the affectee of the going action. At the end of the action, *you* both *have gone* and *are gone*, and the decision to emphasize one aspect of the actor's condition over the other is arbitrary. By treating the intransitive actor like the patient, the deaf children appear to be highlighting the affectee properties of the intransitive actor over the effector properties.

Complex sentences

We determined the boundaries for a string of gestures on the basis of gesture form (using relaxation of the hand as the criterion, as described above in "Segmenting gesture strings") and then determined the number of propositions conveyed within that gesture string.[7] We found that all ten of the deaf children in our sample generated complex sentences containing at least two propositions (Goldin-Meadow, 1982; Goldin-Meadow and Mylander, 1984a: 39–42). The propositions conjoined in the children's complex sentences often had a temporal relationship to one another; these sentences either described a sequence of events or requested that a sequence of events take place. For example, one child pointed at a tower and produced a "hit" gesture and then a "fall" gesture to comment on the fact that he had hit [act$_1$] the tower and that the tower had fallen [act$_2$]. The children also produced complex sentences conveying propositions which were not ordered in time. For example, one child pointed at Mickey Mouse and produced a "swing" gesture and then a "walk" gesture to comment on the fact that Mickey Mouse both swings on the trapeze [act₁] and walks [act₂].

In English, when two propositions are conjoined, there is often at least one element of each of the propositions that is redundant or "shared" in both. For example, in the sentence *Mary cut the apples and John ate the apples, apples* is shared by both propositions (the second *apples* could of course be replaced by *them*; this overtly marks the property as shared in surface structure). Some of the complex sentences that the deaf children produced contained propositions with no redundant or shared elements (e.g., one child produced a "sip" gesture pointed at a toy cowboy, pointed at a toy soldier, and then produced a "beat" gesture, to comment on the fact that the cowboy sips a straw and the soldier beats a drum). However, the children also produced a number of complex sentences whose underlying propositions did contain shared or redundant elements. For example, in some of these sentences the actor was the same or shared across the two propositions (e.g., a "climb" gesture, followed by a "sleep" gesture, followed by a point at a horse, to comment on the fact that the horse climbed the house and then the horse slept), and in others the predicate was shared across the two propositions (e.g., a point at a toy pear, followed by a point at a toy banana and a side-to-side headshake, followed by a "roll" gesture, to indicate that the pear should roll forward but the banana should not roll forward).

Note that complex sentences with shared elements can be represented either as the conjunction of two full propositions, i.e., sentential conjunction, in which the shared element appears twice in the propositions underlying the sentence, once in each proposition (e.g., "Mickey Mouse swings and Mickey Mouse walks"), or as the conjunction of parts of propositions, i.e., phrasal conjunction, in this case predicate conjunction, in which the shared element appears only once (e.g., "Mickey Mouse swings and walks"). In an analysis of the complex sentences of the Philadelphia subjects, we found evidence for phrasal conjunction in the children's sentences with shared elements (Goldin-Meadow, 1982). In particular, we found that production probability of a particular thematic role, e.g., the actor, decreased systematically with an increase in the number of elements in the propositions underlying the sentence *only if* the shared element was allocated one slot in the propositional structure rather than two—that is, if Mickey Mouse were counted once (Mickey Mouse-swings-walks) rather than twice (Mickey Mouse-swings-Mickey Mouse-walks; see Goldin-Meadow, 1982, 1987 for further discussion).

Developmental pattern

Two of the ten children in our sample began producing two-gesture sentences sometime during our observations (the remaining eight children were already combining gestures into sentences when the study began). During their initial observation sessions these two children produced only one gesture at a time, either a single point or a single characterizing gesture. They began producing two-gesture sentences at 1;6 and 2;5—ages comparable to the onset of two-word sentences in hearing children learning English (Brown, 1973) and slightly later than the onset of two-sign sentences in deaf children learning ASL (Bonvillian, Orlansky, and Novack, 1983).

Moreover, four of the children in the sample began producing complex gesture sentences conveying more than one proposition (see "Complex sentences" above, for examples) sometime during our observations (the other six children were already producing complex sentences at the start of the study). Three of these children produced complex sentences for the first time at ages 2;2, 2;2, and 2;5; the fourth child began production sometime between 3;1 and 3;11 (we were not able to observe the child during this period). These ages are within the range for the onset of complex sentences in children learning conventional languages, both spoken (Brown, 1973) and signed (Hoffmeister, 1978).

Thus, the deaf children in our studies follow the same pattern with respect to early syntactic development as children learning languages from conventional language models. They first experience a one-word period during which they are limited to producing one gesture at a time. They then begin to combine those gestures into two-word sentences characterized by simple structural properties. Finally, they begin to produce longer sentences which convey two or more propositions.

Morphology in the gestures of deaf children of hearing parents

Derivational morphology

At this point in our studies, we have completed the investigation of morphological structure in the gestures of only one deaf child in our sample. (We do, however, have extensive preliminary evidence from two other children suggesting that the gesture systems of these children are also characterized by morphological structure; data from the remaining seven children in our sample have not yet been coded for morphological structure.) We first analyzed the child's characterizing gestures that were most transparent, i.e., the gestures whose form mirrored either the action or an attribute of the intended referent (see "Characterizing gestures").

We found that the corpus of transparent characterizing gestures that the child produced over a two-year period (from age 2;10 to 4;10) could be characterized as a system of handshape and motion morphemes (Goldin-Meadow and Mylander, 1984b, 1990). We began by coding handshapes and motions continuously along the dimensions typically used to code signs in ASL without establishing a priori either discrete categories or boundaries (e.g., we wrote down the distance between the fingers and thumb of a particular handshape as accurately as possible and did not try to force that handshape into a limited set of thumb–finger distances). We found that the child used only a restricted number of values on each of the dimensions we coded; in fact, five handshape and nine motion forms accounted for 99 percent of the forms the child produced.

We next asked whether these forms mapped in any systematic way onto categories of meanings. We listed all of the referents that the child represented with a particular form during the taping session at age 3;11, and determined whether those referents shared a common attribute or set of attributes. If they did, we took that common core to be the meaning of the particular form and used the resulting form/meaning pairing to code the videotapes of the remaining sessions. For example, the Fist handshape form was found to be associated with the meaning "handle a small, long object"; and the Short Arc motion form was found to be associated with the meaning "reposition". We found that 95 percent of the handshapes and 90 percent of the motions that the child produced could be classified into the form/meaning pairings established on the basis of the data from age 3;11.

Finally, we found that most of the child's handshape morphemes occurred in combination with more than one motion morpheme, and vice versa. Table 5.1.1 presents examples of the Fist handshape combined with three different motions—Short Arc, Arc To and Fro, and Circular—as well as examples of the Short Arc motion combined with three different handshapes—Fist, O-hand, and C-hand. As the table illustrates, the meaning of each gesture is predictable from the meaning of its handshape component and its motion component. For example, the Fist handshape (meaning "handle a small, long object") combined with a Short Arc motion (meaning "reposition") formed a gesture which meant "reposition a small, long object by hand" (e.g., scoop a spoon at mouth). Note that all the motions in the gestures presented in Table 5.1.1 represent transitive actions, with the handshapes of these gestures representing the hand of the actor as it is shaped around the patient. These handshape morphemes are comparable to Handle classifiers in ASL, which combine with motions to convey transitive actions (McDonald, 1982; Schick, 1987).

As in ASL, various handshapes were used not only to represent the handgrip around objects of varying sizes and shapes, but also to represent the objects themselves. For example, in addition to using the C-hand to mean "handle a large object of any length" (cf. Table 5.1.1), the child also used the C-hand to mean "a curved object."[8] These object handshape components similarly combined with motion components to create paradigms of meanings. For example, the C-hand, when combined with a Linear motion (meaning "change location"),[9] formed a gesture which meant "a curved object changes location" (e.g., a toy turtle moves forward); and, when combined with an Open and Close motion (meaning "open and/or close"), it formed a gesture which meant

Table 5.1.1   *Examples of hand and motion morphemes in the deaf child's gestures*

	Handshapes		
	Fist-hand (handle a small, long object)	O-hand (handle a small object of any length)	C-hand (handle a large object of any length)
Short Arc motion (reposition)	Reposition a small, long object by hand (e.g. scoop utensil)	Reposition a small, object of any length by hand (e.g. take out bubble wand)	Reposition a large object of any length by hand (e.g. pick up bubble jar)
Arc To and Fro motion (move to and fro)	Move a small, long object to and fro by hand (e.g. wave balloon string back and forth)	Move a small object of any length to and fro by hand (e.g. move crayon back and forth)	Move a large object of any length to and fro by hand (e.g. shake salt shaker up and down)
Circular motion (move in a circle)	Move a small, long object in a circle by hand (e.g. wave flag pole in circle)	Move a small object of any length in a circle by hand (e.g. turn crank)	Move a large object of any length in a circle by hand (e.g. twist jar lid)

Note: circular motions included those made by rotating the wrist, the elbow, and/or the shoulder.

"a curved object opens and/or closes" (e.g., a bubble expands). As these examples suggest, the object handshapes were typically combined with motions representing intransitive actions, with the handshape representing the size, shape, or semantic class of the actor. These object handshapes are comparable to Semantic-Class and Size-and-Shape classifiers in ASL, which combine with motions to create intransitive verbs of motion (T. Supalla, 1982; Schick, 1987).

The child in our morphological study at times also produced his object hand-shapes with motions representing transitive predicates. In these gestures the handshape represented the size, shape, or semantic class of the patient—omitting any representation of the actor entirely. For example, to represent placing a toy cowboy on a horse, the child produced a C-hand with his fingers pointed downward (meaning "a curved object"), combined with a Short Arc motion (meaning "reposition"), thereby focusing attention on the curved legs of the cowboy as they are placed around the horse. Gestures of this sort are comparable to Size-and-Shape classifiers in ASL, which combine with motions typically to represent instruments of transitive actions (Schick, 1987).

The morphemes in the deaf child's gestures were thus organized into a framework or system of contrasts. When he generated a gesture to refer to a particular object or action, the form of that gesture was determined not only by the properties of the referent object or action, but also by how that gesture fit with the other gestures in the lexicon. The child's gestures therefore appeared to reflect a morphological system, albeit a simple one, akin to the system that characterizes the productive lexicon in ASL.

We also analyzed the less transparent gestures that he produced and found that these gestures could not be broken up into morphemic parts, and thus appeared to be unanalyzed wholes in his system. For example, his "give" gesture consisted of a Palm handshape held in place (typically with the palm up). In his productive gestures, the Palm handshape meant "handle a flat surface"; however, the "give" gesture was used to represent the transfer not only of flat objects but also of round, angular, thin, curved, etc., objects. As a second example, the child's "break" gesture consisted of two Fist handshapes arced away from each other. In his productive gestures, the Fist handshape meant "handle a small, long object"; however the "break" gesture was used for a wide variety of objects of all shapes and sizes. Thus, this deaf child appeared to display a set of gestures which functioned as do the lexical items in ASL whose stems are unanalyzable and monomorphemic, that is, the so-called "frozen" lexicon of ASL (cf. Kegl, 1985; Newport, 1981; T. Supalla, 1982).

Inflectional morphology

Analyses of the deaf child's gestures suggest that the system also exhibits inflectional morphology (Goldin-Meadow *et al.*, 1990). Conventional sign languages such as ASL have inflectional systems in which spatial devices are used to modify verbs to agree with their noun arguments (e.g., the sign GIVE is moved from the signer to the addressee to mean "I give to you," but from the addressee to the signer to mean "You give to me"; Fischer and Gough [1978], Padden [1983]). The deaf child in our study could vary the placement of his characterizing gestures (all of them, both the more and the less transparent ones), producing gestures either in neutral space (e.g., a "twist" gesture performed at chest level) or oriented toward particular objects in the room (e.g., a "twist" gesture produced near a jar). In the latter case the placement of the gesture served to identify an entity playing a particular thematic role in the predicate represented by the gesture and, as such, served to modify the predicate to agree with one of its arguments.[10] As an example, for transitive predicates the characterizing gesture was typically displaced toward the object playing the patient role—the jar in the above example—thereby marking the jar as the patient of the predicate. In contrast, for intransitive predicates the characterizing gesture was typically displaced toward the object playing the recipient role; for example, the child moved his "go" gesture toward the open end of a car-trailer to indicate that cars go into the trailer, thereby marking the trailer as the recipient of the predicate. Gestures were very rarely displaced toward the actor of either transitive or intransitive predicates.

As in ASL (cf. Hoffmeister, 1978), it was not necessary that an object be in the room for the deaf child in our study to mark that object morphologically via displacement. He could produce his gestures near an object that was similar to the object he wished to refer to, e.g., a "twist" gesture produced near an empty jar of bubbles to indicate that he wanted the full jar of bubbles in the kitchen twisted open. Or, if the object the child wanted to indicate were animate, the child could indicate the object by producing his gestures on his own body, e.g. a "twist" gesture produced on the side of his body to indicate that he wanted the experimenter to twist a key on the side of a Mickey Mouse toy. Note that, in this example, the child is representing one individual with his hand (the experimenter) and a different individual with his body (Mickey Mouse): Thus, as is frequently the case in ASL, the child appears to be using his body as a stage for his own gestures.

In a developmental analysis, we found that he first began to displace his gestures toward objects that were similar to his intended-but-absent referents between the ages of 3;3 and 3;5—the age at which this same child began producing points at objects in the room to refer to objects that were not in the room (see "Pointing gestures" above). Thus, this child's morphological marking system began to be freed from the here-and-now situation at about the same moment in development as his system of pointing gestures.

Developmental pattern: Morphological reorganization

The developmental course of the deaf child's gestures was comparable to the development of words or signs in children acquiring conventional languages (Mylander and Goldin-Meadow, 1990). When first generating gestures, he created each gesture to map onto an individual event; that is, he used a particular handshape/motion combination, for example a C-hand combined with a Circular motion, to refer only to opening a jar and to no other actions or objects. This stage is reminiscent of the period during which children acquiring conventional languages treat their words or signs as unanalyzed wholes (MacWhinney, 1978; Newport, 1984; Peters, 1983). Later in development, between the ages of 3;3 and 3;5, this deaf child began to use a single gesture to refer to a class of events, with components of gesture form mapping onto components of gesture meaning, rather than the whole gesture form mapping onto a global, particular event. For example, he used the C-hand combined with a Circular motion to refer to opening a jar, rotating a wide knob, moving a train in a circle, etc.; that is, he used the C-hand in this and in other gestures to refer to a class of objects (objects with large diameters that can be grasped by hand), and he used the Circular motion in this and in other gestures to refer to a class of actions (rotating or moving objects around a center point). This latter stage is comparable to the period when children acquiring conventional languages begin to analyze the words they have learned as wholes and separate these words into meaningful components (Bowerman, 1982; MacWhinney, 1978; Newport, 1984).

The reorganization of the child's lexicon from an unorganized collection of gestures to a system of contrasting gestures may reflect a larger reorganization taking place across several parts of his linguistic system. For example, he began to analyze his gestures into component morphemes sometime between the age of 3;3 and 3;5—the age at which he began to refer (either via the placement of his characterizing, gestures [see "Inflectional morphology" above] or via his pointing gestures [see "Pointing gestures"]) to objects that were not present in the room. Thus, the child began to systematize his lexicon at the same time as he began to use his gestures in an increasingly symbolic fashion. The impetus for a reorganization of this sort might be the child's maturational state (i.e., the fact that he had reached a certain age), or perhaps the state of the gesture system itself (i.e., the fact that the system had become sufficiently cumbersome to require reorganization). Developmental analyses of the gesture systems of the remaining deaf children in our sample may help to pull apart these possibilities.

The role of parental gestures in guiding the deaf child's system

The deaf children in our studies were found to elaborate gestural communication systems characterized by a lexicon, a simple syntax, and a simple morphology without the benefit of a conventional language model. It is possible, however, that the children's hearing parents spontaneously generated their own structured gesture systems which their children saw and learned. The parents—not the children—would then be responsible for the emergence of structure in the children's gestures.

The hearing mothers of the deaf children in our studies all produced gestures as they spoke to their children.[11] Indeed, five of the six mothers whose gestures we analyzed in detail produced single gestures (as opposed to gesture strings) more often than their children. Moreover, the mothers produced both pointing and characterizing gestures, and they produced them in approximately the same proportions as their children. However, the mothers produced fewer different types of characterizing gestures than their children, and their lexicons of characterizing gestures were different from their children's, overlapping no more than 33 percent and as little as 9 percent (Goldin-Meadow and Mylander, 1984a: 78–9).

Despite the fact that the mothers were prolific producers of single gestures, they were not prolific producers of gesture strings: Five of the six mothers produced gesture strings less often than their children (Goldin-Meadow and Mylander, 1984a: 80). In addition, the mothers' gesture strings did not show the same structural regularities as their children's (Goldin-Meadow and Mylander, 1983, 1984a: 81–9). The mothers showed no reliable gesture-order patterns in their strings. Moreover, the production-probability patterns in the mothers' gesture strings differed from the production-probability patterns in the children's strings. Finally, the mothers began conveying two propositions in their gesture strings later in the study than their children did, and produced proportionately fewer sentences with conjoined propositions than their children did.

With respect to morphology, the mother of the single deaf child whose gestures we have analyzed for morphological structure was found to produce the same five handshape and nine motion forms as her child. In terms of form-meaning mapping, however, only 50 percent of the mother's handshapes and 51 percent of her motions could be described by the system developed to describe the child's form–meaning pairings for handshapes and motions; in contrast, recall that 95 percent of the child's handshapes and 90 percent of his motions could be described by this system. Moreover, the fit between the child's form–meaning mapping system and his mother's did not improve over the two-year period during which the child was observed. In addition, the child appeared to have generalized beyond his mother's gestures in two respects: (1) The child produced almost all of the different types of handshape/motion combinations that his mother produced (twenty of his mother's twenty-five), but, in addition, he produced another thirty-four combinations that were not found in his mother's repertoire. In order to go beyond his mother's gestures as he did, the child must have isolated the handshape and motion dimensions and used them as a basis for generating his novel combinations. (2) The mother used her gestures to refer to individual events (e.g., she used the C-hand combined with a Circular motion only to refer to opening a jar and to no other types of actions or objects), while the child used his to refer to classes of related events (Goldin-Meadow and Mylander, in press). Thus, at most, the mother's gestures may have served as a source for the handshape and motion components in the deaf child's gestures. However, it is important to note that, in order to utilize that source, the child would have had to search through considerable noise in order to arrive at the components. Moreover, he appeared to treat whatever structure he might have found in his mother's gestures as a starting point, using it to generalize to novel combinations and to novel referential uses.

With regard to the input issue in general, it is important to note that we are not claiming that deaf children develop their gesture systems in a vacuum. It is clear that the children receive input from their surroundings, which they undoubtedly put to good use. The crucial question, however, is this: How close is the mapping between this input and the child's output? We have looked for isomorphic patterns between the mother's gestures and the child's gestures on the assumption that the child might have been inclined to copy a model that was easily accessible. We found that the gesture systems developed by the deaf children in our studies had some obvious similarities to the gestures produced by their hearing mothers: Both the children and their mothers produced pointing and characterizing gestures which they used to express the action and attribute relations typical of early mother–child conversations. However, the children consistently surpassed their mothers by organizing these gestural elements into productive systems with patterns on at least two linguistic levels—the level of the sentence and the level of the word. All of the deaf children regularly combined the gestural elements into linear strings characterized by a syntactic structure, albeit a simple one. The one child studied so far analyzed the gestural elements into component parts characterized by a productive morphologic structure. Thus, our deaf children had indeed gone beyond their input, contributing linearization and componentialization to the gestures they received as input from their hearing mothers.[12]

Summary of the child's contributions to language learning

In this section we summarize the inferences we have drawn about the biases children bring to the task of communicating. We maintain that those properties of language which can be developed by deaf children without a language model are "resilient" (in the sense that their development is insensitive to wide variation in input conditions) and are therefore primarily contributed by the child. We will discuss the conclusions from our deaf children's data in relation to findings from other studies of children's language-making capacity, and consider the children's contributions in the context both of the semantic organization and of the structural organization of their communication systems.

Semantic organization: Organizing predicate frames

The deaf children's gesture systems were organized around different predicate types, each associated with a particular combination and number of arguments. This finding supports the hypothesis that children come to the language-learning situation equipped with a bias to organize their language around a predicate calculus. Indeed, on the basis of his review of the crosslinguistic literature Slobin (1985: 1192) suggests that children come equipped with "definitions of 'proposition types' in terms of some sort of presumably innate predicate calculus." Similarly, in his account of language learning Pinker (1984: 333) relies heavily on the child's giving the correct thematic analysis to verbs, and goes so far as to suggest that "the core of the thematic relations system does not require a special acquisition mechanism dedicated to inducing it from the input." Finally, Gleitman (1986: 22) has suggested that children come to the language-learning situation equipped with predicate types of the sort we have found in the deaf children's gesture systems, and that they use those predicate types as a starting place for extracting and differentiating verb meanings in the languages they are learning.

Focusing on the patient

The deaf children in our study appeared to organize their gestures in such a way as to highlight the patient role. They exhibited a focus on the patient in the organization both of their pointing gestures and of their characterizing gestures. On a syntactic level, all ten children were more likely to produce pointing gestures for objects playing the patient role than for objects playing the actor role in transitive actions; this particular production-probability pattern tends to result in two-gesture sentences that preserve the unity of the predicate, i.e., patient + act sentences rather than actor + act sentences. Moreover, the deaf children tended to treat the intransitive actor like the patient rather than like the actor of transitive actions, suggesting a focus on the affectee properties rather than the effector properties of the intransitive actor (see "Ordering and production probability rules" above). On a morphological level, all three of the deaf children whose data we have examined for morphological structure displaced their transitive characterizing gestures (when they marked those gestures) toward an object playing the patient role but rarely toward an object playing the actor role.

This patient-focus is reminiscent of the focus on transitivity and the results of actions that Slobin (1985) posits as part of the starting semantic space that children bring to the language-learning situation. In addition, children acquiring conventional language have been found to focus on the patient even if it means violating their input. For example, Ochs (1982) has shown that children acquiring Samoan adopt AVO or VOA word order for transitive sentences rather than the canonical adult VAO order. Thus, the Samoan children, like our deaf children, tended to preserve the unity of the predicate (i.e., VO appears as a unit) and to treat the intransitive actor like the patient (i.e., the position after the V, which is filled by S in the intransitive sentences of both adults and children, is filled by O in transitive sentences). As a second example, children learning English tend as a rule to omit words for the actors of their sentences (preserving the unity of the predicate; cf. Bloom, 1970) but to omit words for the actors of their intransitive sentences less often than words for the actors of their transitive sentences (Goldin-Meadow, 1979: 176).[13] In fact, for young children learning English, actors tend to appear in intransitive sentences about as often as patients appear in transitive sentences, a tendency which (as in our deaf children) highlights the affectee properties of the intransitive actor (Goldin-Meadow, 1979: 176).

Structural organization: Mechanisms for distinguishing thematic roles

The deaf children used a variety of devices that distinguished among different thematic roles (e.g., patient and actor). They varied the positions of the gestures in their two-gesture sentences according to the thematic roles of the objects represented by those gestures. They varied the probability with which they produced gestures for objects according to the thematic role played by that object. They varied the placement of their characterizing gestures, displacing gestures near objects playing particular thematic roles. The findings in our deaf children support the notions of Pinker (1984: 40), who argues that children come to the language-learning situation prepared to consider semantic notions such as agent and patient as linguistically relevant, and that they are prepared to use those semantic notions initially to identify grammatical entities such as subject and object in their input.

In terms of the particular devices used to distinguish among thematic elements, our data support Slobin's suggestion (1985: 1192) that the child comes to the language-learning situation with a disposition to notice and store sequential orders of classes of elements. Moreover, although perhaps forced to omit words from their sentences for processing reasons, young hearing children appear to omit words for particular classes of elements rather than omitting words on a random basis (cf. Bloom, 1970; Hyams, 1986). Finally, deaf children learning conventional sign languages have been found to generate spatial devices to mark their signs to agree with particular classes of elements, even if their input language does not provide evidence for such devices (Gee and Goodhart, 1985; Goodhart, 1984; Livingston, 1983; S. Supalla, 1990; Suty and Friel-Patti, 1982).

Introducing recursion

The deaf children in our study generated novel complex sentences (containing at least two propositions) from combinations of simple one-proposition sentences, thereby exhibiting the property of recursion in their gesture systems. These data are consistent with the observations of Newport, Gleitman, and Gleitman (1977), who found that the number of verbs that hearing children used in a sentence (a measure which corresponds approximately to the number of propositions in a sentence) was an environment-insensitive property of language. That is, maternal input did not affect the rate at which children developed this property in their language. These data suggest that child-centered factors (rather than environment-centered factors) may influence the development of the ability to conjoin propositions within a sentence.

Creating paradigms

Completed data from one deaf child and preliminary data from two others in our sample suggest that the children organized their gestures using paradigms or matrices which served as the basis for their morphological system. According to

Slobin (1985: 1213), the capacity to create paradigms is central to the child's language-making capacity. Moreover, paradigm construction is an important component of Pinker's (1984) account of language learning. In addition, Pinker (1984: 180) suggests that the child first creates word-specific miniparadigms and only later abstracts the patterns constrained within them to create general paradigms—a developmental pattern reminiscent of our deaf child's morphological development.

Gesture as an adjunct to speech vs. gesture as a primary communication system

Gesture development in children with linguistic input

Hearing children in the early stages of language acquisition exploit the manual modality for purposes of communication. In fact, prelinguistic hearing children use pointing gestures several months before they begin to speak (Bates, 1976) and continue to use gesture to support their verbal communications even after they learn to speak (Bates *et al.*, 1979; Carter, 1975; Goldin-Meadow and Morford, 1985; Greenfield and Smith, 1976).

However, it is important to note that, unlike the deaf children in our studies, hearing children do not elaborate their spontaneous gestures into linguistic systems. Not surprisingly, speech comes to dominate over gesture in the hearing child, and this domination typically occurs before the child's gestures become complex. For example, hearing children rarely produce their pointing gestures in combination with other gestures, even other points (Goldin-Meadow and Morford, 1985; Goldin-Meadow and Mylander, 1984a: 55; Masur, 1983), and they do not produce strings of characterizing gestures (Petitto, 1988; Volterra, 1981).

Moreover, young hearing children produce very few motor acts that would meet our criteria for characterizing gestures (i.e., motor acts that do not involve direct manipulation of objects and that are used for communication rather than symbolic play; cf. Goldin-Meadow and Mylander, 1984a: 54; Petitto, 1988). Even when hearing children produce the same characterizing gestures as the deaf children in our studies, they use those gestures differently. For example, one of the most common characterizing gestures that hearing children produce is the "give" gesture—open palm extended as though to receive an object. Hearing children use this gesture almost exclusively to request objects for themselves (Petitto, 1988), while the deaf children in our studies used the "give" gesture across a variety of semantic situations to request the transfer of objects to other people and locations as well as to themselves. In general, hearing children tend to use their characterizing gestures as names for particular objects (often nontransparent names developed in the context of interactive routines with parents, e.g., index fingers rubbed together to refer to a spider; Acredolo and Goodwyn, 1985, 1988), and their gestures therefore do not appear to have the internal handshape and motion structure characteristic of the deaf children's gestures. Unlike the deaf children's gestures, the gestures produced by hearing children do not seem to be organized in relation to one another and so do not form a system of contrasts.

Gesture with speech vs. gesture without speech

McNeill (1990: Chapter 6) has described the gestures that characteristically accompany speech in hearing children (and hearing adults as well) as less clear, less disciplined, less reproducible, and less schematic than the gestures used by the deaf children in our studies. The gestures that accompany speech in hearing individuals differ from the deaf children's gestures in that they do not stand on their own, but rather form an integrated system with the speech they accompany (McNeill, 1985; see also Church and Goldin-Meadow, 1986; Perry, Church, and Goldin-Meadow, 1988). Unlike the gestures produced by the deaf children in our studies, which tend to be linear and segmented, the gestures that accompany speech in hearing individuals are "GLOBAL in that the symbol depicts meaning as a whole (noncompositionally) and SYNTHETIC in that the symbol combines into one symbol meanings that in speech are divided into segments" (McNeill, 1987: 18).

The fact that gesture forms an integrated system with the speech it accompanies may explain why the hearing mothers of our deaf subjects produced gestures which were organized so differently from their deaf children's gestures. Since almost all of the mothers' gestures were accompanied by speech, it is likely that the mothers' gestures (like those of all hearing speakers) were influenced by the spoken utterances with which they occurred. Many of the mothers' gestures that appear unstructured and uninterpretable when analyzed with the techniques developed to analyze our deaf children's gestures—all primary communication systems—may in fact be quite structured and meaningful when analyzed in relation to the speech they accompany, i.e., with a system developed to code gesture as an adjunct to speech (cf. McNeill, in press). It goes without saying, however, that the structure of this combined speech/gesture communication is lost on our deaf children, for whom speech input is unavailable.

The fact that the gestures of hearing individuals do not, in general, exhibit inter-gesture and intra-gesture structure suggests that communication in the manual modality does not inevitably result in structure at the sentence and word levels. While gesture used as a primary communication system (as in our deaf subjects) appears to assume language-like structure, gesture used as an adjunct to speech does not necessarily do so.

We have previously referred to the language-like properties found in the deaf children's gestures as "resilient" (Goldin-Meadow, 1982)—properties that appear in children's communication despite extensive variation of the learning conditions (such as no exposure to an established language). Properties that show up under such extreme conditions are evidently among the most basic and indispensable for a structured system of human communication, and they should spontaneouly appear in any deliberate communication of meaning (cf. McNeill, in press: Chapter 6). That these same resilient properties are not systematically used in the spontaneous gestures accompanying the speech of both hearing children and hearing adults underscores (and continues to clarify by contrast) the "language-like" nature of the deaf children's gestures.

Conclusion

We have explored the child's contribution to the language-acquisition process by investigating a situation in which children have gone beyond the linguistic input they have experienced. We have shown that deaf children who are unable to use conventional spoken language models provided by their hearing parents and who are not exposed to conventional sign language models use gesture to communicate. These gestures exhibit simple structural properties at three levels: (1) LEXICON, consisting of pointing gestures which refer to objects either in the immediate environment or absent from the here-and-now, and characterizing gestures which refer to actions and attributes; (2) SYNTAX, consisting of predicate structure, ordering and production-probability rules, and recursion; and (3) MORPHOLOGY, consisting of both derivational and inflectional morphology.

Although the deaf children in our studies did not receive input from a conventional sign-language model, the children were clearly exposed to the spontaneous gestures that their hearing parents used as they spoke to their children. At the lexical level, the children's gestures were found to share properties with the spontaneous gestures produced by their mothers. However, the children surpassed their mothers in taking these gestures and organizing them into a productive linguistic system, combining them into structured linear strings characterized by a simple syntax, and analyzing them into hand and motion components characterized by a simple morphology. These properties of linearization and componentialization appear to distinguish gesture used as a primary communication system by a deaf child from gesture used as an adjunct to speech by hearing children and hearing adults.

The phenomena of gesture generation in deaf children of hearing parents suggests that children come to language predisposed to analyze and combine the words, signs, or gestures they use to communicate. Thus, with or without an established language as a guide, children appear to be "ready" to seek structure at least at word and sentence levels when developing systems for communication.

Acknowledgments

This research was supported by Grant No. BNS 8407041 from the National Science Foundation and Grant No RO1 NS26232 from the National Institutes of Health. We thank Rachel Mayberry, Bill Meadow, and the anonymous reviewers for their helpful comments on earlier drafts of the manuscript.

Notes to 5.1

1. For example, only 4 percent of the communications the children produced contained meaningful vocalizations; see Goldin-Meadow and Mylander (1984a:42–3) for further discussion of the children's progress in spoken English. Two additional deaf children of hearing parents were eliminated from the sample because they had been making good progress in acquiring spoken English, suggesting that speech was relatively accessible to these children.

2. Strict application of this criterion breaks down in the few instances where one of the children in our sample was found to gesture with no one else around, that is, as though he were gesturing to himself. The fact that this child was found to use his gestures to "talk" to himself indicates that gesture can take on other functions of language in addition to communication with others; see also "Pointing gestures" where evidence is presented that this same deaf child was able to use his gestures metalinguistically, that is, to refer to his own gestures.

3. One might object to coding a pointing gesture as though it were a noun rather than a pronoun, e.g., to coding a point as "dog" rather than "this". However, it is important to realize that whether a point is coded as "dog" or "this" makes no difference in our syntactic analyses (see "Ordering and production probability rules"); the crucial category for these analyses is the thematic role (e.g., patient or actor) played by the object indicated by the pointing gesture.

4. A number of activities cannot easily be classified as either transitive or intransitive using these criteria, e.g., the activity of seeing or noticing. However, the children rarely produced gestures for activities of this sort, and, when they did, the gestures were considered ambiguous with respect to this dimension. In addition, note that intransitive activities were defined in terms of spontaneous motion, a criterion which excludes more static activities that tend to be intransitive in English (e.g., "lying"). The few gestures the children produced for activities of this sort were classified as attributes because the form of each gesture reflected a static property of an object or person (e.g., a horizontal palm used to indicate lying flat).

5. We use the term RECIPIENT to refer to the destination of predicates such as "go" or "put," whether that destination is animate ("go to Mother") or inanimate ("go to the table"). The children do not appear to distinguish animate from inanimate recipients (i.e., both tend to occupy the same position in a two-gesture sentence). Traditionally, the term GOAL is used if a term encompassing both animate recipients and inanimate destination is needed. We continue to use the term recipient here to be consistent with previously-published descriptions of the deaf children's gesture systems.

6. In addition to an ergative-like pattern in production probability, the one child who produced a sufficient number of sentences with transitive actors to allow us to determine a pattern also showed an ergative pattern in the way he ordered his gestures. He tended to produce gestures for the patient and the intransitive actor *before* gestures for the act in his two-gesture sentences, but gestures for the transitive actor *after* gestures for the act. This one child thus treated patients and intransitive actors alike, and distinct from transitive actors, not only with respect to production probability but also with respect to gesture order (Goldin-Meadow and Mylander, 1984a: 39).

7. Note that, because we classify all characterizing gestures as predicates (See "Characterizing gestures"), when a characterizing gesture is combined with another characterizing gesture within a single string, two predicates (and therefore two propositions) are conveyed within that string, and the string is consequently classified as a complex sentence.

8. Thus, the children have two techniques for representing objects: They can incorporate a handshape which stands for the object into the gesture itself (a morphological device), or they can produce a deictic point at the object, or a similar object, along with the gesture (a syntactic device). In the analyses presented above, we relied exclusively on deictic gestures in determining the children's object lexicons ("Pointing gestures"), their predicate frames ("Predicate structure"), and their ordering and production-probability regularities ("Ordering and production probability rules"). In our future work we hope to describe the relationship between these two techniques for representing objects, and to determine whether that relationship is a systematic one.

9. The Linear motion was used to represent change of location from one place to another (e.g., moving a hammer from the floor to the table, or a duck moving from place 1 to place 2) and is distinct from the Short Arc motion, which was used to represent repositioning in place (e.g., swinging a hammer in place, or a duck flipping over in place).

10. Note that the children have a number of ways of indicating objects that play different thematic roles; for example, the children can displace the gesture for the predicate toward an object playing a particular role (e.g., they can displace the gesture "eat" toward the patient, "grape"), or they can produce a deictic gesture for the patient before the gesture for the predicate (e.g., they can produce a point at the grape before the gesture "eat"). Although these techniques serve the same function, we consider the displacement technique to be morphological because it deals with variations within a single gesture, while the ordering technique is syntactic because it deals with the relationship between gestures. Our future work will explore how these different marking devices work in relation to one another.

11. We studied the mothers' gestures rather than the fathers' gestures because in each instance the mother was the primary caretaker.

12. Of course, it is possible that the deaf child made use of other cues in the environment (such as speech) in conjunction with the mother's gesture model in order to make this model more functional. But note that this hypothesis necessitates attributing to the child a great deal of creative interpretation of the input. The child must take a 'mixed-mode' message (in which one signal—speech—is very severely degraded) and transform it into a structured single-mode output. If the child were indeed able to construct gesture patterns out of cues found in the mother's speech and gesture taken together, it merely reinforces our point: Since clues to structure were not at all obvious in the child's environment, the child was likely to have been predisposed to search for those kinds of structures in the first place.

13. Hyams (1986) argues that the tendency to omit words for actors at the beginning stages of language acquisition in English-learning children (and in Italian- and German-learning children as well) reflects the initial setting of the pro-drop parameter allowing subjects to be optional. Note, however, that the pro-drop explanation does not easily account for English-learning children's tendency to omit words for transitive actors more often than words for intransitive actors.

References to 5.1

Acredolo, L. P. and Goodwyn, S. W. (1985). "Symbolic gesturing in language development: A case study." *Human Development*, **28**, 40–9.

Acredolo, L. P., and Goodwyn, S. W. (1988). "Symbolic gesturing in normal infants." *Child Development*, **59**, 450–66.

Bates, E. (1976). *Language and Context: The acquisition of pragmatics*. New York: Academic Press.

Bates, E., Benigni, L., Bretherton, I., Camaioni, L., and Volterra V. (eds) (1979). *The Emergence of Symbols: Cognition and communication in infancy*. New York: Academic Press.

Battison, R. (1974). "Phonological deletion in American Sign Language." *Sign Language Studies*, **5**, 1–19.

Bellugi, U. and Studdert-Kennedy, M. (eds), (1980). *Signed and Spoken Language: Biological constraints on linguistic form*. Deerfield Beach, FL: Verlag Chemie.

Bickerton, D. (1981). *Roots of Language*. Ann Arbor, MI: Karoma.

Bloom, L. (1970). *Language Development: Form and function*. Cambridge, MA: MIT Press.

Bonvillian, J. D., Orlansky, M. D., and Novack, L. L. (1983). "Developmental milestones: Sign language acquisition and motor development." *Child Development*, **54**, 1435–45.

Bowerman, M. (1982). "Reorganizational processes in lexical and syntactic development." In Wanner and Gleitman (1982), 319–46.

Braine, M. (1976). "Children's first word combinations." *Monographs of the Society for Research in Child Development*, **41**(Serial No. 164).

Brown, R. (1973). *A First Language*. Cambridge, MA: Harvard University Press.

Carter, A. L. (1975). "The transformation of sensorimotor morphemes into words: A case study of the development of 'more' and 'mine'." *Journal of Child Language*, **2**:2, 233–50.

Caselli, M. C. (1983). "Communication to language: Deaf children's and hearing children's development compared." *Sign Language Studies*, **39**, 113–44.

Church, R. B. and Goldin-Meadow, S. (1986). "The mismatch betwen gesture and speech as an index of transitional knowledge." *Cognition*, **23**, 43–71.

Clark, E. (1976). "Universal categories: On the semantics of classifiers and children's early word meanings." *Linguistic Studies Offered to Joseph Greenberg*, Vol. 3: *Syntax*, Alphonse Juilland (ed.), Saratoga, CA: Anma Libri and Co., 449–62.

Conrad, R. (1977). "Lip-reading by deaf and hearing children." *British Journal of Educational Psychology*, **47**, 60–65.

Conrad, R. (1979). *The Deaf School Child*. London: Harper and Row.

Coulter, G. R. (1986). "One aspect of ASL stress and emphasis: Emphatic stress." Paper presented at the Conference on Theoretical Issues in Sign Language Research, Rochester, NY.

Dixon, R. M. W. (1979). "Ergativity". *Language*, **55**, 59–138.

Dromi, E. (1987). *Early Lexical Development*. New York: Cambridge University Press.

Fant, L. J. (1972). *Ameslan: An introduction to American Sign Language*. Silver Spring, MD: National Association of the Deaf.

Farwell, R. (1976). "Speech reading: A research review." *American Annals of the Deaf*, **121**, 19–30.

Feldman, H., Goldin-Meadow, S., and Gleitman, L. R. (1978). "Beyond Herodotus: The creation of language by linguistically deprived deaf children." In A. Luck, A. (ed.), *Action, Symbol, and Gesture: The emergence of language*. New York: Academic Press, 351–413.

Fischer, S. (1973). "Two processes of reduplication in American Sign Language." *Foundations of Language*, **9**, 469–80.

Fischer, S. (1974). "Sign language and linguistic universals." In C. Rohrer and N. Ruwet (eds), *Actes du Colloque franco-allemand de grammaire transformationnelle, Vol. 2, Études de sémantique et autres*. Tübingen: Niemeyer, 187–204.

Fischer, S. and Gough, B. (1978). "Verbs in American Sign Language." *Sign Language Studies*, **18**, 17–48.

Furrow, D., Nelson, K., and Benedict, H. (1979). "Mothers' speech to children and syntactic development: Some simple relationships." *Journal of Child Language*, **6**, 423–42.

Gee, J. P. and Goodhart, W. (1985). "Nativization, linguistic theory, and deaf language acquisition." *Sign Language Studies*, **49**, 291–342.

Gleitman, L. R. (1986). "Biological dispositions to learn language." In W. Demopoulos and A. Marras (eds), *Language Learning and Concept Acquisition*. Norwood, NJ: Ablex, 3–28.

Gleitman, L. R., Newport, E. L., and Gleitman, H. (1984). "The current status of the Motherese hypothesis." *Journal of Child Language*, **11**, 43–79.

Goldin-Meadow, S. (1979). "Structure in a manual communication system developed without a conventional language model: Language without a helping hand." In H. Whitaker and H. A. Whitaker (eds), *Language Without a Helping Hand: Studies in neurolinguistics*, Vol. 4. New York: Academic Press, 125–209.

Goldin-Meadow, S. (1982). "The resilience of recursion: A study of a communication system developed without a conventional language model." In Wanner and Gleitman (eds) (1982), 51–77.

Goldin-Meadow, S. (1985). "Language development under atypical learning conditions: Replication and implications of a study of deaf children of hearing parents." In K. Nelson (ed.), *Children's Language*, Vol. 5. Hillsdale, NJ: Lawrence Erlbaum, 197–245.

Goldin-Meadow, S. (1987). "Underlying redundancy and its reduction in a language developed without a language model." In B. Lust (ed.), *Studies in the Acquisition of Anaphora*, Vol. 2: *Applying the Constraints*. Boston, MA: D. Reidel, 105–34.

Goldin-Meadow, S., Butcher, C., Dodge, M., and Mylander, C. (1990). "Gestural communication in a deaf child: Lexical development without a language model." In H. Tager-Flusberg (ed.), *Constraints on Language Acquisition: Studies of atypical children*. Hillsdale, NJ: Lawrence Erlbaum, to appear.

Goldin-Meadow, S. and Feldman, H. (1975). "The creation of a communication system: A study of deaf children of hearing parents." *Sign Language Studies*, 8, 225–34.

Goldin-Meadow, S. and Feldman, H. (1977). "The development of language-like communication without a language model." *Science*, 197, 401–3.

Goldin-Meadow, S. and Morford, M. (1985). "Gesture in early child language: Studies of deaf and hearing children." *Merrill–Palmer Quarterly*, 31: 2, 145–76.

Goldin-Meadow, S. and Mylander, C. (1983). "Gestural communication in deaf children: The non-effect of parental input on language development." *Science*, 221, 372–74.

Goldin-Meadow, S. and Mylander, C. (1984a). "Gestural communication in deaf children: The effects and non-effects of parental input on early language development." *Monographs of the Society for Research in Child Development*, 49, 1–121.

Goldin-Meadow, S. and Mylander, C. (1984b). "The development of morphology without a conventional language model." *Papers from the Chicago Linguistic Society*, 20, 119–35.

Goldin-Meadow, S. and Mylander, C. (1990). "Levels of structure in a language developed without a language model." In K. Gibson and A. Peterson (eds), *The Brain and Behavioral Development: Biosocial dimensions*. Hawthorn, NY: Aldine Press, to appear.

Goldin-Meadow, S. and Mylander, C. (in press). "The role of parental input in the development of a morphological system." *Journal of Child Language*.

Goodhart, W. (1984). "Morphological complexity, ASL and the acquisition of sign language in deaf children." Boston: Boston University dissertation.

Goodman, M. (1984). "Are creole structures innate?" *Behavioral and Brain Sciences*, 7, 193–4.

Greenfield, P. M. and Smith, J. H. (1976). *The Structure of Communication in Early Language Development*. New York: Academic Press.

Hoffmeister, R. (1978). "The development of demonstrative pronouns, locatives and personal pronouns in the acquisition of American Sign Language by deaf children of deaf parents." Minneapolis: University of Minnesota dissertation.

Hoffmeister, R. and Wilbur, R. (1980). "Developmental: The acquisition of sign language." In H. Lane and F. Grosjean (eds), *Recent Perspectives on American Sign Language*. Hillsdale, NJ: Lawrence Erlbaum, 61–78.

Huttenlocher, J., Smiley, P., and Ratner, H. (1983). "What do word meanings reveal about conceptual development?" In T. B. Seiler and W. Wannenmacher (eds), *Concept Development and the Development of Word Meaning*. Berlin: Springer-Verlag, 210–33.

Hyams, N. M. (1986). *Language Acquisition and the Theory of Parameters*. Dordrecht, Holland: D. Reidel.

Kantor, R. (1982). "Communicative interaction: Mother modification and child acquisition of American Sign Language." *Sign Language Studies*, 36, 223–82.

Kegl, J. (1985). "Locative relations in ASL." Cambridge, MA: MIT dissertation.

Klima, E. and Bellugi, U. (1979). *The Signs of Language*. Cambridge, MA: Harvard University Press.

Lane, H., Boyes-Braem, P., and Bellugi, U. (1976). "Preliminaries to a distinctive feature analysis of handshapes in American Sign Language." *Cognitive Psychology*, 8, 263–89.

Lane, H. and Grosjean, F. (eds) (1980). *Recent Perspectives on American Sign Language*. Hillsdale, NJ: Lawrence Erlbaum.

Lenneberg, E. H. (1964). "Capacity for language acquisition." In J. A. Fodor and J. J. Katz (eds), *The Structure of Language: Readings in the philosophy of language*. Englewood Cliffs, NJ: Prentice-Hall, 579–603.

Liddell, S. (1980). *American Sign Language Syntax*. The Hague: Mouton.

Liddell, S. (1984). "'Think' and 'believe': Sequentiality in American Sign Language." *Lg.* 60, 372–99.

Liddell, S. and Johnson, R. (1986). "American Sign Language compound formation processes, lexicalization, and phonological remnants." *Natural Language and Linguistic Theory*, 4, 445–513.

Lillo-Martin, D. (1986). "Two kinds of null arguments in American Sign Language." *Natural Language and Linguistic Theory*, 4, 415–44.

Livingston, S. (1983). "Levels of development in the language of deaf children." *Sign Language Studies*, 40, 193–286.

MacKay, D. M. (1972). "Formal analysis of communicative processes." In R. A. Hinde (ed.), *Nonverbal Communication*. New York: Cambridge University Press, 3–25.

McNeill, D. (1985). "So you think gestures are nonverbal?" *Psychological Review*, **92**, 350–71.

McNeill, D. (1987). *Psycholinguistics: A new approach*. New York: Harper and Row.

McNeill, D. (in press). *Mirrors of Gesture*. Chicago: University of Chicago Press.

MacWhinney, B. (1978). "The acquisition of morphology." *Monographs of the Society for Research in Child Development*, **43**, 1–122.

Masur, E. F. (1983). "Gestural development, dual-directional signaling, and the transition to words." *Journal of Psycholinguistic Research*, **12:2**, 93–109.

McDonald, B. (1982). "Aspects of the American Sign Language predicate system." Buffalo, NY: State University of New York at Buffalo dissertation.

Meadow, K. (1968). "Early manual communication in relation to the deaf child's intellecutal, social, and communicative functioning." *American Annals of the Deaf*, **113**, 29–41.

Mindel, E. D., Vernon, M. (1971). *They Grow in Silence; The deaf child and his family*. Silver Spring, MD: National Association for the Deaf.

Moores, D. F. (1974). "Nonvocal systems of verbal behavior." In R. L. Schiefelbusch and L. L. Lloyd (eds), *Language Perspectives: Acquisition, retardation, and intervention*. Baltimore: University Park Press, 377–418.

Moores, D. F. (1982). *Educating the Deaf: Psychology, principles and practices*. 2nd ed. Boston: Houghton Mifflin.

Mylander, C. and Goldin-Meadow, S. (1990). "Home sign systems in deaf children: The development of morphology without a conventional language model." In P. Siple and S. Fischer (eds), *Theoretical Issues in Sign Language Research*, Vol. 2: *Acquisition*. Chicago: University of Chicago Press, to appear.

Newport, E. L. (1981). "Constraints on structure: Evidence from American Sign Language and language learning." In W. A. Collins (ed.), *Minnesota Symposium on Child Psychology*, Vol. 14. Hillsdale, NJ: Lawrence Erlbaum.

Newport, E. L. (1984). "Constraints on learning: Studies in the acquisition of American Sign Language." *Papers and Reports on Child Language Development*, **23**, 1–22.

Newport, E. L. and Ashbrook, E. F. (1977). "The emergence of semantic relations in American Sign Language." *Papers and Reports on Child Language Development*, **13**, 16–21.

Newport, E. L., Gleitman, H., and Gleitman, L. R. (1977). "Mother, I'd rather do it myself: Some effects and non-effects of maternal speech style." In C. E. Snow and C. A. Ferguson (eds), *Talking to Children*. New York: Cambridge University Press, 109–50.

Newport, E. L. and Meier, R. P. (1985). "The acquisition of American Sign Language." In D. I. Slobin (ed.), *The Cross-linguistic Study of Language Acquisition*, Vol. 1: *The Data*. Hillsdale, NJ: Lawrence Erlbaum, 881–938.

Ochs, E. (1982). "Ergativity and word order in Samoan child language." *Language*. **58**, 646–71.

Padden, C. (1983). "Interaction of morphology and syntax in American Sign Language." La Jolla: University of California at San Diego dissertation.

Padden, C. and Perlmutter, D. (1987). "American Sign Language and the architecture of phonological theory." *Natural Language and Linguistic Theory*, **5**, 335–75.

Perry, M., Church, R. B., and Goldin-Meadow, S. (1988). "Transitional knowledge in the acquisition of concepts." *Cognitive Development*, **3**, 359–400.

Peters, A. M. (1983). *The Units of Language Acquisition*. New York: Cambridge University Press.

Petitto, L. A. (1988). "'Language' in the pre-linguistic child." In F. Kessel (ed.), *The Development of Language and Language Researchers*. Hillsdale, NJ: Lawrence Erlbaum, 187–222.

Pinker, S. (1984). *Language Learnability and Language Development*. Cambridge, MA: Harvard University Press.

Samarin, W. J. (1984). "Socioprogrammed linguistics." *Behavioral and Brain Sciences*, **7**, 206–7.

Sandler, W. (1986). "The spreading hand autosegment of American Sign Language." *Sign Language Studies*, **50**, 1–28.

Schick, B. S. (1987). "The acquisition of classifier predicates in American Sign Language." *West Lafayette*, IN: Purdue University dissertation.

Schlesinger, H. (1978). "The acquisition of bimodal language." In I. Schlesinger (ed.), *Sign Language of the Deaf: Psychological, linguistic, and sociological perspectives*. New York: Academic Press, 57–93.

Seidenberg, M. S. and Petitto, L. A. (1979). "Signing behavior in apes: A criticial review." *Cognition*, **7**, 177–215.

Seuren, P. A. M. (1984). "The bioprogram hypothesis: Facts and fancy." *The Behavioral and Brain Sciences*, **7**, 208–9.

Shatz, M. (1982). "On mechanisms of language acquisition: Can features of the communicative environment account for development?" In Wanner and Gleitman (1982), 102–27.

Silverstein, M. (1972). "Hierarchy of features and ergativity." In R. M. W. Dixon (ed.), *Grammatical Categories in Australian Languages*. Canberra: Australian Institute of Aboriginal Studies, 112–71.

Singleton, J. L. (1987). "When learners surpass their models: The acquisition of American Sign Language from impoverished input." Champaign-Urbana: University of Illinois M.A. thesis.

Singleton, J. L. (1989). "Restructuring of language from impoverished input: Evidence for linguistic compensation." Champaign-Urbana: University of Illinois dissertation.

Singleton, J. L. and Newport, E. L. (1987). "When learners surpass their models: The acquisition of American Sign Language from impoverished input." Paper presented to the Society for Research in Child Development, Baltimore, MD.

Slobin, D. I. (1985). *The Cross-linguistic Study of Language Acquisition*. Hillsdale, NJ: Lawrence Erlbaum.

Stokoe, W. C. (1960). "Sign language structure: An outline of the visual communications systems." *Studies in Linguistics*. Occasional papers 8.

Summerfield, A. Q. (1983). "Audio-visual speech perception, lipreading and artificial stimulation." In M. E. Lutman and M. P. Haggard (eds), *Hearing Science and Hearing Disorders*, 132–79. New York: Academic Press.

Supalla, S. (1990). "Manually Coded English: The modality question in signed language development." In P. Siple and S. Fischer (eds), *Theoretical Issues in Sign Language Research*, Vol. 2: *Acquisition*. Chicago: University of Chicago Press, to appear.

Supalla, T. (1982). "Structure and acquisition of verbs of motion and location in American Sign language." La Jolla: University of California at San Diego dissertation.

Supalla, T. and Newport, E. L. (1978). "How many seats in a chair? The derivation of nouns and verbs in American Sign Language." In P. Siple (ed.), *Understanding Language Through Sign Language Research*. New York: Academic Press, 91–132.

Suty, K. A. and Friel-Patti, S. (1982). "Looking beyond Signed English to describe the language of two deaf children." *Sign Language Studies*, **35**, 153–68.

Tervoort, B. T. (1961). "Esoteric symbolism in the communication behavior of young deaf children." *American Annals of the Deaf*, **106**, 436–80.

Volterra, V. (1981). "Gestures, signs, and words at two years: When does communication become language?" *Sign Language Studies*, **33**, 351–62.

Wanner, E. and Gleitman, L. R. (eds) (1982). *Language Acquisition: The state of the art*. New York: Cambridge University Press.

Wexler, K. (1982). "A principle theory for language acquisition." In Wanner and Gleitman (1982), 288–318.

Wilbur, R. B. (1986). "Interaction of linguistic theory and sign language research." In P. C. Bjarckman and V. Raskin (eds), *The Real World Linguist: Linguistic applications for the 1980s*. Norwood, NJ: Ablex, 166–82.

Maturational Constraints on Language Learning

Elissa L. Newport

In this article, I will argue that the type of behavioral development I study—namely, language learning—operates under a set of internal constraints, without which it would be impossible to achieve adult competence. Language acquisition has been perhaps the earliest arena in which it has been widely argued that constraints on learning are required (Chomsky, 1965; Wexler and Culicover, 1980). This argument has been based primarily on two bodies of evidence: First, the logic of the language learning problem requires that some type of internal constraint exists in humans. Formal demonstrations have shown that the learning of systems like human languages cannot be based solely on the type of input data children receive (Gold, 1967; Wexler and Culicover, 1980). Second, a vast body of evidence showing common universal patterns in human languages likewise suggests that humans must be biased in particular ways to induce such similar outcomes, and fail to induce many apparently possible (nonhuman) languages (Chomsky, 1965, 1981).

In the present article I will present a third type of evidence. In particular, I will present some of our evidence that language acquisition occurs under *maturational* constraints, operating successfully only during a maturationally bounded period. Given similar input, learners in different maturational states do not achieve the same outcome. This finding suggests that at least some of the constraints insuring successful language acquisition do not remain constant even within the human lifespan. While such findings argue that internal constraints must exist, they do not dictate their precise nature. However, the shape and character of the function relating success in language learning to the maturational state of the learner may help in pointing toward viable classes of explanation. For example, in much of developmental psychology, insofar as there are maturational effects, an uncontroversial generalization is typically that big kids are better than little kids. In language acquisition (and possibly in other domains as well), however, the child, and not the adult, appears to be especially privileged as a learner. The correct account of such a phenomenon must therefore explain not only why children are successful language-learners, but also why adults, who have better capabilities than children at most things, are not.

I will begin by reviewing some of our evidence for the basic claim of a maturational effect, leaving aside the question of why this might be and whether the maturational constraint is particular to language or more general. After this review I will then suggest a possible account of the maturational constraints responsible for the findings, one which is rather different in character from most prior discussions of constraints on language learning.

Evidence of maturational constraints in first language learning

First, then, is the evidence that language learning is indeed subject to maturational constraints. Much of our work on this topic comes from studying the acquisition of American Sign Language (ASL). There are two main reasons why psycholinguists might study American Sign Language. One is that it is a language in a different modality than the usual one, and therefore offers the opportunity to examine the contributions of modality to the structure and acquisition of language. ASL has developed quite independently of English or any other spoken language, and has an entirely different grammar than that of English. At the same time, it is a natural language, in the sense that it has evolved within a human community of users rather than being devised or invented by technicians or educators. Linguistic research on ASL has demonstrated that it has the same degree of expressiveness and grammatical complexity as other languages of the world. Moreover, it displays the types of structural properties and developmental patterns shown by other natural languages (Klima and Bellugi, 1979; Newport and Meier, 1985; Supalla, 1982). These commonalities, despite independent evolution, thus suggest that such linguistic properties must not be linked in crucial ways to the particular modalities in which languages make their appearance.

The second reason why one might study ASL is that it is a language which is sometimes acquired under very different circumstances of time and input than the typical situation for spoken languages (Fischer, 1978; Newport, 1981). In particular, we have studied users of ASL to investigate whether there is a *critical period* for the acquisition of a first language. Although most profoundly deaf individuals in the United States use ASL as their primary language of communication (and are not highly fluent in any other language), they vary widely in when they were first exposed to the language. A small 5–10 percent of deaf signers are born to deaf parents and are exposed to ASL in the family from birth. The remainder of the deaf, signing community are born to hearing parents who, particularly until recently, did not know any sign language and were discouraged from learning any. These deaf children therefore often had no effective language exposure at all in infancy and early childhood. Although they may have been exposed to spoken English and even to training in lipreading and speech, for the congenitally and profoundly deaf this exposure is not highly effective and does not result in normal acquisition of English (Quigley and Kretschmer, 1982; Wilbur, 1979). Such individuals are then typically first exposed to ASL by being immersed with other deaf children in residential schools for the deaf, where ASL is not taught formally but is the language of everyday life among the children. Age of exposure to ASL is thus the age at which such children begin residential school: Usually age 4–6, but sometimes much later, depending on whether the parents first sent the children to nonresidential schools where signing is often intentionally and successfully prohibited among the children. ASL is then the everyday and primary language, from the time of first exposure on. In short, then, the deaf population offers the opportunity to observe the effects of age of exposure to a first language on the competence one achieves in that language.

Arguing for a maturational basis for language acquisition, Eric Lenneberg (1967) first hypothesized that there was a critical period for language acquisition, extending from infancy to perhaps puberty.[1] However, his argument lacked direct evidence of effects of age of exposure on the acquisition of a first language, since virtually all normal humans are routinely exposed to their first languages from birth. He therefore made his argument primarily by indirect evidence, particularly from data on the recovery of language after brain damage at varying ages: While children recover language quite well, adults do not. Although such evidence is certainly suggestive of a maturational constraint on language acquisition, it speaks most directly to a maturational change in the ability of nonlanguage areas of the brain to assume linguistic functions; it does not provide evidence concerning maturational changes in normal language learning abilities.

Since the publication of Lenneberg's important book, however, a number of other investigators have pursued his hypothesis. Most notably, studies of Genie, a girl isolated from linguistic input (and all other normal social and environmental stimulation) from around a year of age until after puberty, have suggested that first language acquisition during adulthood results in strikingly abnormal linguistic competence (Curtiss, 1977). A similar outcome has recently been reported for the case of Chelsea, a deaf woman isolated from linguistic input from birth to age 32, when her first exposure to spoken English was provided by successful auditory amplification (Curtiss, 1988). But, because of the (thankfully) rare occurrence of first language deprivation in otherwise normal individuals, little more has been discovered about the function relating age of exposure to linguistic competence.

Our own work on American Sign Language competence in the deaf community (Newport and Supalla, 1990; Newport *et al.*, 1990) has allowed us to investigate linguistic competence in a fairly large population of individuals who vary widely in age of exposure to their first full language, but who are socially, cognitively, and environmentally fairly normal. (See also Mayberry, Fischer, and Hatfield, 1983 for related findings on a measure of linguistic performance.) These studies, we believe, therefore approximate an experimental investigation of the effects of age of exposure on the acquisition of a first language.[2]

Our subject for these studies have been congenitally or prelingually deaf adults whose primary language is ASL, and who have only limited skills in English. All of our subjects attended the Pennsylvania School for the Deaf (PSD), and interact socially with one another within the deaf community of Philadelphia. At time of test all were approximately 35 to 70 years old. All attended PSD at a time when signing was prohibited in the classroom; they acquired ASL naturally, by immersion in the language within the dormitories at PSD and (for the Native group only) within their family homes. They are therefore quite a homogeneous population, except in when they were first exposed to ASL.

Most of our work has been performed on thirty subjects, who fall into three groups of age of first exposure to ASL: *Native* learners (exposed to ASL from birth by their deaf signing parents in the home and from ages 4–6 by deaf peers at PSD); *Early* learners (first exposed to ASL by deaf peers at age 4–6, when they entered PSD); and *Late* learners (first exposed to ASL by deaf peers after age 12, when they entered PSD or when they met friends or married spouses from PSD). Late learners first attended strict "oral" schools where they were not exposed to ASL; they entered PSD because the family moved to Philadelphia, or because their previous school did not include a high school. In sum, the subjects fall into one of these three groups by relatively random assignment, due to accidents of birth or family choice of schools, and are otherwise a highly homogeneous population. All subjects had a minimum of thirty years of daily exposure to ASL.

Our first study (Newport and Supalla, 1990) examined their elicited production and comprehension of the complex morphology of ASL verbs of motion; a subsequent study (Newport *et al.*, 1990), still in progress, included a battery of fifteen tests, both production and comprehension, of a variety of structures in ASL syntax and morphology. Altogether, the test battery examines such structures as basic and topicalized word order; agreement between subject, object, and verb; the use of verbal classifiers and associated motion morphemes; verb inflections for aspect and number; and derivational morphemes which distinguish related nouns and verbs. The production tasks each present a series of short videotaped events which the subjects are asked to describe, in ASL; the events are designed to elicit one sign or simple sentence responses which, over the test, contrast in the set of morphemes or syntactic forms required in ASL. The comprehension tasks each present a series of short videotaped ASL signs or sign sentences, which, over the test, contrast as in the production tasks; the subjects are asked to manipulate an object or to choose one of two pictures in correspondence with the meaning of the ASL form.

For example, linguistic analyses of ASL have revealed that ASL verbs of motion are composed of several components of form which vary independently, in accord with particular aspects of the event of motion (Supalla, 1982). The tests of these structures are designed to evaluate whether deaf subjects produce and comprehend each of these components correctly, according to the standards of native ASL grammar. In the Verbs of Motion Production test (VMP), each item shows an object (e.g., a car or a person) moving along a path (e.g., moving in a straight line or in a circle), with a manner of motion (e.g., bouncing or rolling). The subject is asked, in ASL, to say what happened. The appropriate response should include a verb with several morphemes, one for the category of the moving object, another for the path of motion traversed, and a third for the manner of motion used. In the Verbs of Motion Comprehension test (VMC), each item shows an ASL verb of motion, and the subject is asked to choose the appropriate object and make it perform the action. The response should involve making the correct object travel along the proper path, with the proper manner of motion. As another example, in ASL verbs "agree" in spatial location with their subjects and objects (that is, they move from the location of the subject to the location of the object). The Verb Agreement Production test (VAP) includes a series of events which vary in which of several videotaped participants is the subject, and which the object, of an action; signed responses should likewise vary in which participant the verb agrees with. The tests of the other linguistic structures are constructed similarly, in accord with analyses of native ASL usage. Scoring on each of the tests is performed by native signers, both quantitatively (with target responses predicted from linguistic analyses and verified by the test data from native signers) and qualitatively (internal analyses of the subject's responses, to determine the patterns of usage for non-native signers).

Figures 5.2.1A and 5.2.1B present the mean scores on eight of the tests from the ASL Test Battery, for the three groups of learners who vary in age of first exposure to ASL. (The other tests are either still in the final scoring stages or are inappropriate for quantitative presentation.) The test scores fall into two types. First, Figure 5.2.1A shows the scores on *ASL basic word order*. As can be seen, control over basic word order does not show effects of age of acquisition; subjects in all groups score virtually perfectly. Figure 5.2.1B shows the scores on seven tests of *ASL morphology*, with scores transformed into z-scores for comparability across the tests. In sharp contrast to the word-order data, the scores on morphology all show consistent and significant effects of age of

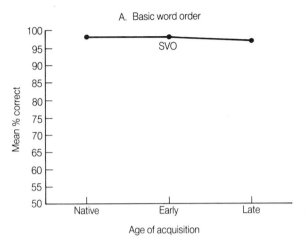

Figure 5.2.1A   *Score on ASL Basic word order for Native, Early, and Late learners of ASL.*

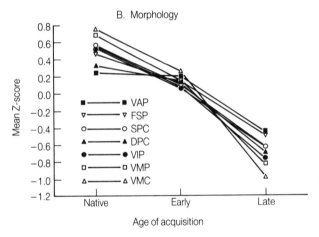

Figure 5.2.1B   *Z-scores on seven tests of ASL morphology for Native, Early, and Late learners of ASL.*

learning, with Natives outscoring Early learners, who in turn outscore Late learners; correlations between age of acquisition and test scores range around −.6 or −.7. The distinction between word order and other grammatical structures is in accord with results from the study of Genie (Curtiss, 1977), who after puberty mastered the basic word order of her language but did not control its morphology.

Individual morpheme scores, error patterns, and qualitative analyses of responses also show differences for early versus late learners. Native learners show highly consistent response patterns, in accord with grammatical descriptions of obligatory morphemes of ASL. In contrast, while late learners show some (well above chance) usage of the same forms, they also show several other types of usages which natives find ungrammatical in ASL. First, they show use of what we have called "*frozen*" lexical items; these are whole-word signs, without the internal morphological structure we were testing. They also show highly *variable* use of ASL morphology, with inconsistency in individual subjects' responses on items which should require the same morpheme. Occasionally, they also show omission of morphemes which are obligatory in the ASL context. These results provide strong evidence for an effect of age of acquisition on control over a primary language: The later the language is learned, the less its use is native (with crisp and grammatically consistent forms) in character.

We believe that our results are an effect of the maturational state of the learner, and not merely an artifact of variables coincidentally related to age of acquisition. For example, multiple regression analyses and an additional study of twenty-one new subjects show that the effects are not due to length of experience with the language. All of the subjects in the present studies have at least thirty years of everyday experience with ASL, and the precise number of years of use (either in this study, or comparing this study with the additional one using subjects with fewer years of experience) does not correlate with performance in our tasks. The data also do not accord with explanations on the basis of input differences, or intellectual or social deprivation differences, across the groups.

Evidence of maturational constraints in second language learning

To address a further part of the critical period hypothesis, we have also performed comparable studies on *second* language learners. Many prior investigators have studied age effects on second language learning because of the difficulty of obtaining a population for first language learning. In our view, however, the issue of age effects on second language learning versus first language learning are logically independent: In some nonlinguistic domains (though not all), maturational effects exist on *first* learning but not on *second* learning in the same domain (Scott, 1980). We therefore asked whether maturational state affects the learning of a second language, for subjects whose exposure to a first language occurred in infancy.

Surprisingly, although many prior studies had been done in the first year of second language acquisition (showing advantages for adults), few studies had been done on the competence ultimately achieved in the second language; and none of these directly examined grammatical competence in the second language (see Krashen, Long, and Scarcella, 1982, and Johnson and Newport, 1989, for a review of the literature). Our own research has examined syntactic and morphological competence in hearing subjects for whom English was a second language. One study (Johnson and Newport, 1989) tested subjects whose first language was Chinese or Korean (both languages typologically dissimilar to English). To insure homogeneous socioeconomic backgrounds and extensive exposure to English, all subjects were students or faculty at the University of Illinois who were in the US about ten years prior to testing. We ran forty-six subjects who varied in the age they first moved to the US and became immersed in English (ages of arrival were age 3 to 39), plus twenty-three native speakers of English. This wide range of ages of arrival allowed us to examine the full function relating age of acquisition to performance in the language, from early childhood to well into adulthood.

Our measures of competence in English were scores on a grammaticality judgment test, devised by us, of twelve types of rules of English morphology and syntax. Subjects listened to a recording of 276 simple, short sentences of English, spoken one at a time at a moderately slow rate of speech. Half of these sentences were grammatical sentences of English; the other half, randomly interspersed, were each exactly the same as one of the grammatical sentences, except that they contained a single violation of an obligatory grammatical pattern of colloquial English. Subjects were asked to say whether each sentence was acceptable or not. The twelve rules thus tested included rules of English morphology (e.g., verb tense, noun pluralization, verb agreement) and syntax (e.g., basic word order, permutation of word order for forming wh-questions and yes–no questions, use of the determiners *a* and *the*, use of pronouns).

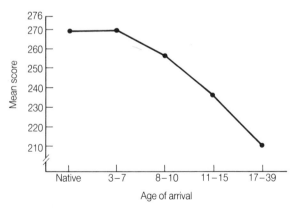

Figure 5.2.2 *Total score on a test of English grammar in relation to age of arrival in the United States (redrawn from Johnson and Newport, 1989). Reprinted with permission from Academic Press.*

Figure 5.2.2 presents total test score as a function of age of arrival in the US (i.e., age of first immersion in English). As this figure shows, there was a strong relationship between age of arrival and performance on our test, with performance declining as age of arrival increased ($r = -.77$, $p < .01$). Multiple regression analyses showed that these effects were not attributable to formal instruction in English, length of experience with English, amount of initial exposure to English, reported motivation to learn English, self-consciousness in English, or identification with the American culture.

We further hypothesized that, if our effects were truly those of maturational state of the learner, the relationship between age of arrival and ultimate performance should hold only over the period in life during which maturational changes occur (that is, during childhood). In contrast, once the organism is fully mature (that is, during adulthood), there should no longer be a systematic relationship between age of arrival and ultimate performance. Figures 5.2.3A and 5.2.3B show the scattergrams of scores in relation to age of arrival, for subjects arriving during childhood (age 15 or below) versus after maturity (age 17 or over). The correlation between age of arrival and performance for the twenty-three subjects arriving before puberty (ages 3–15) was a whopping $-.87$ ($p < .001$). In contrast, for the twenty-three subjects arriving after puberty (ages 17–39), the correlation was $-.16$, NS. These results therefore support the claim that the effects of age of acquisition are effects of the maturational state of the learner.

Finally, we examined the twelve rules individually for effects of age of arrival. Again these results were in accord with our findings for first language learning. Control over *word order* was very similar for native and late learners, as was control over the English morpheme *-ing*; both of these aspects of English were also acquired after puberty by Genie (Curtiss, 1977). In contrast, all other aspects of English morphology and syntax showed substantial differences between learners of different ages of acquisition.

We have also found effects of age of acquisition for learners with first languages other than Chinese and Korean, and for linguistic rules specific to English as well as those governed by universal syntactic principles (Johnson and Newport, 1990).

In sum, then, we have found evidence of the effects of age of acquisition on performance many years later in both a primary and a second language. In both cases the data support a maturational interpretation: Language learners who begin acquiring language at an early maturational state end up performing significantly better in that language than those who begin at a later maturational state; the effects over age are approximately linear through childhood, with a flattening of the function in adulthood. Finally, the fact that this function exists for second language learning as well as first language learning suggests that both instances of language learning are affected by maturational state; the ability to acquire language is not spared from maturational effects by exposure to another language early in life.[3]

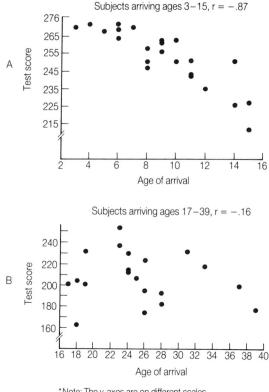

Figure 5.2.3 *Scatterplots of total score in relation to age of arrival for subjects arriving in the United States before vs. after puberty (redrawn from Johnson and Newport, 1989). Reprinted with permission from Academic Press.*

What changes over maturation: The nature of maturational constraints on language learning

Having shown evidence of the effects of maturation on language learning, I will now turn to the question of what the underlying mechanism might be. What is it that undergoes maturational change, resulting in gradually declining language abilities over age?

As I mentioned at the beginning of this article, the finding itself is somewhat paradoxical. Apparently, learners of different ages (i.e., learners in different maturational states) show differing degrees of success in inducing the internal organization of their linguistic input, with greatest success achieved by the *least* mature learners. In contrast, in most cognitive domains, children are much less capable than adults, with competence increasing over age. There are two classes of explanation one might propose for such a paradox.

First, the traditional explanation in language acquisition for findings of such discrepancies between language and other cognitive abilities (cf. Chomsky, 1965, 1981) has been to posit a special *language faculty*, which includes innate knowledge of constraints on the forms that human languages may take. Such constraints might be present from birth (the "continuity hypothesis"), or unfold during early childhood on a maturational timetable (Borer and Wexler, 1987). To account for a maturational decline in language learning within this framework, one might suppose that this language faculty is entirely intact only early in life, and then undergoes decay or deterioration as maturation continues. On such a view, later language learners show less success in acquiring their language, and more variable mastery of its rules because the constraints which permit successful acquisition are weakened.[4]

On this view, the inverse relationship between cognitive abilities and language learning (i.e., that the learner gets worse at language learning as he or she gets better at most cognitive tasks) is accidental, due to the fact that the language faculty happens to be at its peak early in life. The view would expect only that competence in language and competence in other domains are not necessarily the same, since they derive from independent faculties.

An alternative class of explanations, however, might suggest that language learning declines over maturation precisely because cognitive abilities increase. (Note that such an explanation might be agnostic on whether innate constraints particular to language also exist; it would merely hypothesize that these language-particular constraints are not the locus of maturational decline in language learning.) For example, I have proposed a view (called the "Less is More" hypothesis [Newport, 1988]) that the very limitations of the young child's information processing abilities provide the basis on which successful language acquisition occurs. Before presenting this hypothesis in more detail, I will describe some of the data on which it is based.

The hypothesis derives from the differences we have observed in the character of errors made by late learners as compared with those of native learners. As described above, the late learners' errors are predominantly of two types: First they produce "frozen" structures, in which whole-word, unanalyzed signs are produced, in contexts where morphologically constructed forms are required. Most of these frozen signs are highly frequent morpheme combinations in ASL, but are used by late learners in contexts where the particular morphemes included are not grammatical. Such responses thus suggest that the late learner has acquired them as unanalyzed wholes, failing to perform the appropriate internal morphological analysis. Second, late learners produce highly variable and inconsistently used structures. While some of the morphemes may be used correctly, others are incorrect replacements for the correct morphemes; and which morphemes are correct and which replaced may vary over the same test. Both of these types of errors suggest that late learners have experienced problems in consistently and uniquely analyzing the complex structures of the language, and have either failed to analyze, or have learned more than one analysis for the same structure.

In contrast, native learners show very different patterns of performance. When they are at asymptotic performance, they show highly consistent, cleanly analyzed, structures. A more revealing picture of how they got there, however, may emerge from examining native learners when they are at the same level of incorrect responses as the late learners described above (that is, during childhood, while they are still learning the language) (for further details, see Newport [1988]). In early stages of learning the language, native learners make very different types of errors from late learners: Theirs are predominantly componential errors, where structures are produced only in part, with whole morphemes omitted. Young signing children (like their hearing counterparts) typically produce only one or a few morphemes of a complex sign. This type of selective production and omission is characteristic of the child learner. Over time, native children add on more morphemes, while late learners either keep their holistic forms or broadly overgeneralize the patterns of a few of these forms. These differences in error types appear in the naturalistic studies of native versus late learners described above, in longitudinal studies of native versus late learners in early stages of acquiring ASL (Newport, 1981, 1988; Newport and Meier, 1985; Supalla, 1982), and in experimental studies of children versus adults in their first few minutes of exposure to ASL signs (Dufour, Newport, and Medin, 1990). We have hypothesized that these differences derive from differences between adults and children in the way linguistic input is perceived and stored, and perhaps not from differences in their knowledge of linguistic constraints or in their abilities to perform linguistic analyses once the input is stored.

In particular, the hypothesis assumes that children and adults differ in their abilities accurately to perceive and remember complex stimuli. The literature on cognitive development contains ample demonstrations, for example, that adults are capable of storing more items in short-term memory than are children, and that this ability increases regularly over maturation; on some measures the increase continues all the way up to adulthood. (See Dempster, 1981, and Kail, 1984, for reviews. As these authors discuss, there is controversy in this literature about whether the developmental change is due to maturational increases in STM capacity, or rather to changes in the ability to make more effective use of the available capacity; but the hypothesis under discussion is indifferent to this distinction.) The "Less is More" hypothesis suggests, paradoxically, that the more limited abilities of children may provide an advantage for tasks (like language learning) which involve componential analysis. If children perceive and store only component parts of the complex linguistic stimuli to which they are exposed, while adults more readily perceive and remember the whole complex stimulus, children may be in a better position to locate the components.

As an example, let us consider the way this hypothesis would work for the acquisition of morphology. The acquisition of morphology is basically a problem of analysis. The learner must find, in the linguistic input data, the particular components of word forms which map consistently onto components of meaning (these are the morphemes of the language). The learning procedure must therefore involve storing words, plus the nonlinguistic events to which they refer, and then computing for a large set of such data the consistent co-occurrences of the components of form and the components of meaning. With words that have even a small number of components of form and meaning, figuring out the right sized units of the linguistic pairing (that is, which components of form, or combination of components of form, consistently map onto which components, or combination of components, of meaning) is a surprisingly complex computational problem. Boris Goldowsky and I (Goldowsky and Newport, 1990) have been working out the mathematics of such computations, as well as a computer simulation of the procedures; the description that follows is an informal summary of our results thus far.

If the learner stores whole words, with all of their components of form, plus a reasonable number of components of meaning that might be extracted from the nonlinguistic setting, the job of figuring out the best mappings is large. (This is what the hypothesis assumes an adult learner might do.) With a single word of only three components of form (let us call them *a*, *b*, and *c*) and three components of meaning (*m*, *n*, and *o*), there are forty-nine possible pairings to examine. Form *a* by itself could mean *m*, *n*, *o*, *mn*, *no*, *mo*, or *mno*; likewise, form *b*, *c*, *ab*, *bc*, *ac*, or *abc* could have any of these meanings.

In contrast, suppose a more limited learner (that is, the child) on each exposure to a word perceives and stores only a limited number of the component pieces of form and meaning. For example, suppose on exposure 1 the child stores only *a* and *mn*, on exposure 2 the child stores *bc* and *o*, and so on. Under these circumstances at least two important advantages occur.

First, even if the selection of form and meaning components on each exposure is random, the number of possible computations to perform is greatly reduced, and is also substantially focused on morphological rather than whole-word mappings. If the system to be learned actually is morphological (that is, if the system is one with morphemes smaller than the whole word, e.g., *a-m*, *b-n*, *c-o*), it will be learned more readily with limited storage than with full storage of the whole word and its meaning. If the system to be learned actually is a whole-word system (e.g., *abc-mno*), the more limited learner will not learn it as well, but instead may interpret it (incorrectly) as a morphology. These outcomes are true despite the fact that selective storage will also sometimes eliminate relevant data; the loss of data is far outweighed by the reduction and focus in the number of computations (Goldowsky and Newport, 1990).[5] To continue with our example, exposures 1 and 2 above will each permit three (rather than forty-nine) possible pairings to be examined, one of which is the correct one; with reasonable assumptions about the form and likelihood of performing such computations over a large database, the child will learn morphology with more consistency than the adult.

Second, if the form and meaning components selected are precisely those of the morphology (e.g., if *a*, *b*, and *c* are morphemes, and these are independently stored or omitted), an even greater advantage may accrue to the learner, by perceptually highlighting the particular units which a less limited learner could only find by computational means. This second advantage may sound implausible: How could the learner know in advance the units which will turn out to be the morphemes of the language? This could occur, however, even without advance knowledge of the morphology, if the units of perceptual segmentation are (at least sometimes) the morphemes which natural languages have developed. Since human languages have presumably evolved their structural principles at least in part under the constraints of information processing and learning abilities, this advantage may not be as implausible as it sounds. Indeed, our studies of imitation of ASL signs by hearing children who have never been exposed to ASL before (Dufour, Newport, and Medin, 1990) do show that young children tend to extract and reproduce, or selectively omit, ASL morphemes. (In the ASL morphology under study, handshapes, motions, and manners of motion are independent morphemes [see above for a brief description of this morphology]; these are likewise the components into which naive young children segment their imitations.) We are currently investigating the extent to which such perceptual segmentation maps onto morphological structure in imitating foreign spoken languages, such as Turkish, where the morphology is predominantly syllabic (Goldowsky and Newport, 1990).

Note that these advantages occur for only certain aspects of language learning, particularly those that require some type of componential analysis. For these kinds of structures, adults should have more difficulty locating the right analysis (i.e., they will have more computations to perform, and will find more potential analyses which are partially supported by their input data); they should therefore produce more inconsistent and less componential forms (in accord with our research findings). On the other hand, Less is not always More: For aspects of language (or other skills) that require integration and/or complex wholes, adults should perform better than children. As described above, the hypothesis predicts that adults should excel at whole-word learning. We are still working out other similar predictions.

In short, the hypothesis suggests that, because of age differences in perceptual and memorial abilities, young children and adults exposed to similar linguistic environments may nevertheless have very different internal databases on which to perform a linguistic analysis. The young child's representation of the linguistic input will include many *pieces* of the complex forms to which she has been exposed. In contrast, the adult's representation of the linguistic input will include many more whole, complex linguistic stimuli. The limitations of perception and memory in the child will make the analysis of at least certain parts of this system easier to perform. The adult's greater capabilities, and the resulting more complete storage of complex words and sentences, may make the crucial internal components and their organization more difficult to locate and may thereby be a counterproductive skill. Furthermore, this difference alone may help to explain why language learning is different in these two groups; whether there are also differences between adults and children in other aspects of language learning (for example, in the ways in which they perform linguistic analyses on the databases they store, processes which themselves may be constrained by either nonlinguistic or inherently linguistic factors) is as yet unclear.

To repeat, this type of hypothesis suggests that the very limitations of the child in many nonlinguistic domains are the ones which insure more successful language acquisition. More generally, the hypothesis suggests that children should have the advantage in many learning tasks other than language, particularly those that involve componential analysis, at the same time that they show a disadvantage in tasks that require early integration or control over complex stimuli. Similar notions, though different in detail, have been suggested by other investigators; see, for example, a suggestion by Krashen (1982) and Rosansky (1975) that adults are worse at language learning because the emergence of formal operational abilities interferes with implicit learning strategies more suitable for language acquisition. In studies of quite different domains than that discussed here, Turkewitz and Kenney (1982) have pointed out that humans have evolved a strikingly longer period of infancy than other species, and have suggested the possibility that this period is not just a temporary state of incompetence, but may have adaptive value for the achievement of the more complex skills of the adult. The hypothesis I have suggested for language learning is one example of this type of notion.

Summary

In sum, a wide variety of studies demonstrate that language acquisition occurs successfully only under the operation of certain internal constraints or predispositions in the learner. Our own studies reviewed herein suggest that certain of these constraints undergo maturational change, such that learners who begin the task in childhood reach more systematic levels of asymptotic performance in the language than those who begin in adulthood. At least two types of mechanisms appear to be compatible with these results. One of the these suggests that the crucial constraints needed for language acquisition are those of a special language faculty, equipped in advance to expect only certain types of structures to occur in human languages. Maturational change may occur in these constraints, leading the older language learner to less success in inducing the linguistic systems to which she is exposed. A second possibility is that at least some of the constraints crucial to success in language acquisition are nonlinguistic, and that the maturational changes which lead to more difficulty in language learning occur in these nonlinguistic constraints on perception and memory. Whatever the correct account, however, it is clear from our empirical evidence that some significant internal constraints are required to account for why children, and only children, uniformly succeed in learning language.

Acknowledgments

This research was supported in part by NIH grant NS16878 to E. Newport and T. Supalla. I would like to thank Vicky Fromkin, Rochel Gelman, Jim Greeno, and Doug Medin for comments on an earlier version of this paper, and Robert Dufour for help in preparing the figures.

Notes to 5.2

1. Lenneberg also proposed a neurological mechanism to explain the critical period. While this neurological mechanism has not received support from subsequent work (Krashen, 1975) and therefore will not be discussed in this paper, the critical period hypothesis itself can be considered independently.
2. Our studies only "approximate" the ideal study for several reasons. First, as already described, even profoundly and congenitally deaf individuals have some (limited) knowledge of spoken or written English; ASL is thus the first language to which they have been fully and naturally exposed, but not always the only language they are acquainted with by the time we test them in adulthood. Second, of course, the subjects are not assigned to experimental conditions entirely at random, but are sorted into these conditions by accidents of birth and parental choice of schooling. We believe these accidents in fact produce fairly random determinations of age of acquisition, but alternative accounts of our data as due to factors correlated with age of acquisition must be considered. See below, Newport and Supalla (1990), and Newport *et al.* (1990) for further discussion.
3. It is possible, however, that early exposure to a first language has some quantitative effect on the degree to which maturational declines occur. While maturational changes occur in both first and second language learning, it is not clear whether these changes are of the same magnitude. Research is in progress to investigate this question.
4. Given our data, it would be difficult to argue that these constraints are entirely absent after maturation, since even our latest learners (including late learners without any formal instruction in the language) do succeed in acquiring grammatical rules of the language to some degree of fluency; they simply do not acquire them as well, or use them as systematically, as earlier learners.
5. There are several crucial caveats in the proposed hypothesis concerning the relationship between the character of these limitations and the nature of the system to be learned. In general, one can demonstrate that limitations in perception and memory only reduce the information on which learning must be based, and therefore will result in the possibility of more errors and the need for greater innate preprogramming to avoid learning failures (Osherson, Stob, and Weinstein, 1986; Wexler and Culicover, 1980). In order for the hypothesis to work, the limitations must be such that they more than compensate for this reduction of information.

References to 5.2

Borer, H. and Wexler, K. (1987). "The maturation of syntax." In T. Roeper and E. Williams (eds), *Parameter Setting*. Dordrecht: D. Reidel.

Chomsky, N. (1965). *Aspects of the Theory of Syntax*. Cambridge: MIT Press.

Chomsky, N. (1981). *Lectures on Government and Binding*. Dordrecht, Netherlands: Foris Publications.

Curtiss, S. (1977). *Genie: A psycholinguistic study of a modern day "wild child."* New York: Academic.

Curtiss, S. (1988). *The Case of Chelsea: A new test case of theoretical period for language acquisition*. Unpublished manuscript, University of California, Los Angeles.

Dempster, F. (1981). "Memory span: Sources of individual and developmental differences." *Psychological Bulletin*, **89**, 63–100.

Dufour, R., Newport, E., and Medin, D. (1990). "Adult–child differences in the imitation of gestures: The Less is More Hypothesis." Unpublished manuscript, University of Rochester, Rochester, NY.

Fischer, S. (1978). "Sign language and creoles." In P. Siple (ed.), *Understanding Language Through Sign Language Research*. New York: Academic.

Gold, E. (1967). "Language identification in the limit." *Information and Control*, **10**, 447–74.

Goldowsky, B. and Newport, E. (1990). "The Less is More Hypothesis: Modelling the effect of processing constraints on language learnability." Unpublished manuscript, University of Rochester, Rochester, NY.

Johnson, J. and Newport, E. (1989). "Critical period effects in second language learning: The influence of maturational state on the acquisition of English as a second language." *Cognitive Psychology*, **21**, 60–99.

Johnson, J. and Newport, E. (1990). "Critical period effects on universal properties of language: The status of subjacency in the acquisition of a second language." Unpublished manuscript, University of Virginia, Charlottesville, VA.

Kail, R. (1984). *The Development of Memory* (2nd edn). New York: W. H. Freeman & Co.

Klima, E. and Bellugi, U. (1979). *The Signs of Language*. Cambridge: Harvard University Press.

Krashen, S. (1975). "The development of cerebral dominance and language learning: More new evidence." In D. Dato (ed.), *Developmental Psycholinguistics: Theory and applications*. Washington, DC: Georgetown University.

Krashen, S. (1982). "Accounting for child–adult differences in second language rate and attainment." In S. Krashen, R. Scarcella, and M. Long (eds), *Child–Adult Differences in Second Language Acquisition*. Rowley, MA: Newbury House.

Krashen, S., Long, M., and Scarcella, R. (1982). "Age, rate, and eventual attainment in second language acquisition." In S. Krashen, R. Scarcella, and M. Long (eds), *Child–adult Differences in Second Language Acquisition*. Rowley, MA: Newbury House.

Lenneberg, E. (1967). *Biological Foundations of Language*. New York: Wiley.

Mayberry, R., Fischer, S., and Hatfield, N. (1983). "Sentence repetition in American Sign Language." In J. Kyle and B. Woll (eds), *Language in Sign: International perspectives on sign language*. London: Croom Helm.

Newport, E. (1981). "Constraints on structure: Evidence from American Sign Language and language learning." In W. A. Collins (ed.), *Aspects of the Development of Competence. Minnesota Symposia on Child Psychology, Vol. 14*. Hillsdale, NJ: Erlbaum.

Newport, E. (1988). "Constraints on learning and their role in language acquisition: Studies of the acquisition of American Sign Language." *Language Sciences*, **10**, 147–72.

Newport, E. and Meier, R. (1985). "The acquisition of American Sign Language." In D. I. Slobin (ed.), *The Cross-linguistic Study of Language Acquisition*. Hillsdale, NJ: Erlbaum.

Newport, E. and Supalla, T. (1990). *A Critical Period Effect in the Acquisition of a Primary Language*. Unpublished manuscript, University of Rochester, Rochester, NY.

Newport, E., Supalla, T., Singleton, J., Supalla, S., and Coulter, G. (1990). "Critical period effects in the acquisition of a primary language: Competence in ASL morphology and syntax as a function of age of acquisition." Unpublished manuscript, University of Rochester, Rochester, NY.

Osherson, D., Stob, M., and Weinstein, S. (1986). *Systems that Learn*. Cambridge, MA: MIT Press.

Quigley, S. and Kretschmer, R. (1982). *The Education of Deaf Children*. Baltimore: University Park Press.

Rosansky, E. (1975). "The critical period for the acquisition of language: Some cognitive developmental considerations." *Working Papers on Bilingualism*, **6**, 10–23.

Scott, J. (1980). "The domestic dog: A case of multiple identities." In M. A. Roy (ed.), *Species Identity and Attachment: A phylogenetic evaluation*. New York: Garland Press.

Supalla, T. (1982). *Structure and Acquisition of Verbs of Motion and Location in American Sign Language*. Unpublished doctoral dissertation, University of California, San Diego.

Turkewitz, G. and Kenny, P. (1982). "Limitations on input as a basis for neural organization and perceptual development: A preliminary theoretical statement." *Developmental Psychobiology*, **15**, 357–68.

Wexler, K. and Culicover, P. (1980). *Formal Principles of Language Acquisition*. Cambridge, MA: MIT Press.

Wilbur, R. (1979). *American Sign Language and Sign Systems*. Baltimore: University Park Press.

PART 6

Alternative Perspectives

Innate Constraints and Developmental Change[1]

Annette Karmiloff-Smith

Some years ago Gleitman, Gleitman, and Shipley (1972) made a simple yet thought-provoking statement, which I used as a colophon to an article published in the same journal some fourteen years later (Karmiloff-Smith, 1986). What they wrote was: "Young children know something about language that the spider does not know about web weaving." My chapter is not, of course, about spiders. Rather, my intention is to explore a number of speculations about what it is for a mind to "know" (about language, the physical environment, etc.) and what makes the human mind special in contrast to the innately specified procedures by which the spider produces its seemingly complex web. How can we account for human flexibility and creativity? My argument throughout is that developmental change, including linguistic change, can only be understood fully in terms of an epistemology that integrates both innate constraints and constructivism.[2]

Let me begin by suggesting the following: For as long as Piaget's constructivist description of the human infant held, (i.e., an assimilation/accommodation organism with no constraints from built-in knowledge), then it followed that the human mind, acquiring basic knowledge via interaction with the environment, might turn out to be cognitively flexible and creative. However, in the last decade or so, exciting new paradigms for infancy research have challenged our view of the architecture of the human mind, which is now considered to be endowed from the outset with some domain-specific predispositions.

For many psychologists, accepting a nativist viewpoint precludes constructivism completely. Yet nativism and constructivism are not necessarily incompatible.

Together with a now growing number of developmentalists, I have been grappling for some time with a paradox. On the one hand, I feel dissatisfied with Piaget's account of the human infant as a purely sensorimotor organism with nothing more to start life than a few sensory reflexes and three ill-defined processes: Assimilation, accommodation, and equilibration. The spate of infancy research now available suggests that we must invoke *some* domain-specific predispositions for the initial architecture of the infant mind. Yet, both the early plasticity of the brain, as well as the flexibility of the human mind with subsequent development, suggest that a radical nativist/maturational position must be wrong. The more general aspects of Piaget's epistemology—not his psychological theory in terms of developmental stages, but his epigenetic constructivist view of biology and knowledge (Piaget, 1967) and his vision of the cognizer as a very active participant in his or her own ontogenesis—are still a viable way of thinking about how development occurs. An attempt at reconciliation between nativism and constructivism is an important thread throughout this essay (see Karmiloff-Smith, 1992, for a full discussion of this reconciliation, as well as Feldman and Gelman's [1986] arguments in favor of a rational-constructionist view of development).

The now growing data on neonates and young infants suggest the existence of some innately-constrained, domain-specific attention biases or predispositions. The infant is not assailed by buzzing blooming confusion *à la* James (James, 1892), nor by undifferentiated and chaotically assimilated input *à la* Piaget (Piaget, 1955). Rather, from early infancy, special attention biases channel the way in which the child processes constrained classes of inputs that are numerically relevant, linguistically relevant, relevant to physical properties of objects, to cause-effect relations, and so forth (Anderson, 1992; Baillargéon, 1987a, 1987b; Butterworth, 1981; Diamond and Gilbert, 1989; Gelman, 1990; Jusczyk, 1986; Kellman, 1988; Leslie, 1984; Mehler and Fox, 1985; Rutkowska, 1987; Slater, Morison, and Rose, 1983; Spelke, 1988, 1990, 1991; Starkey, Spelke and Gelman, 1983, and many others too numerous to mention). However, as intimated above, accepting that there are *some* innate underpinnings to human development does not amount to an extreme nativist position. Whilst we need to invoke some built-in constraints, development clearly involves a more dynamic process of interaction between mind and environment than the strict nativist stance presupposes. For indeed, whatever innate component we invoke, it only becomes part of our biological potential interaction with the environment; it is only latent until it receives input (Johnson, 1988, 1990; Marler, 1991; Oyama, 1985; Thelen, 1989). And that input affects development in return. So we can endorse Piaget's constructivism but give the infant a head start by means of domain-specific predispositions.

The infancy literature abounds with examples of the domain-specific[3] knowledge available to very young infants. The details of the many different experiments needs not concern us here (see Karmiloff-Smith, 1992, and Spelke, 1985, for description and discussion). My aim is simply to point to a few examples of what we have recently discovered about infant capacities. For example, Alan Slater and his colleagues (Slater, 1990; Slater and Morison, in press; Slater, Morison, and Rose, 1983; Slater *et al.*, 1990) have demonstrated that newborns already have capacities for shape and size discriminations and constancies. Elizabeth Spelke and her collaborators (Kellman and Spelke, 1983; Baillargéon, Spelke and Wasserman, 1986; Spelke, 1988, 1990, 1991) have shown that three- to four-month-old infants are surprised when viewing an impossible event in which one solid object passes through another. However, it is not until somewhat later that infants show surprise if objects behave as if they were not subject to gravity and in need of stable support. A ball which stops in mid-air before reaching a supporting surface does not surprise three-month-olds; but it does seven-month-olds. Renée Baillargéon and her collaborators (Baillargéon, 1987a, 1987b, in press; Baillargéon and Hanko-Summers, 1990) also provide examples suggesting that young infants understand certain characteristics of gravity and support relations between objects. Seven- to nine-month-old infants show surprise at certain impossible support relations, but not others which require further learning. Thus, when a symmetrical block is placed on top of another block but the center of gravity of the top object does not lie on the surface of the supporting object, infants show surprise when it does not fall. But when the top object is asymmetrical, it is not until they are older that they show surprise when it does not fall. Baillargéon has also shown that three- to four-month-old infants understand that if one places an object behind a screen that was rotating 180 degrees, the screen can subsequently only rotate some 45 degrees; they show surprise if the screen continues to rotate 180 degrees, indicating that they expect objects to persist after they go out of view. Furthermore, four- to six-month-olds show sensitivity to object properties such as precise height and location. Yet other experiments have demonstrated young infants' capacity for cross-model matching between number of objects displayed visually and number of drumbeats (Starkey, Spelke and Gelman, 1983). All of this is a far cry from the picture Piaget depicted of early infancy.

A particularly interesting theoretical discussion of innately specified knowledge and subsequent learning is to be found in the work of Johnson, Morton and their colleagues on infant face recognition (Johnson, 1988, 1990; Johnson and Morton, 1991; Johnson *et al.*, 1991). Extending Johnson's theory of species recognition and imprinting in the domestic chick, the existence of two mechanisms was also postulated for human species recognition. The first mechanism operates from birth and is predominantly mediated by subcortical structures. Newborn infants (within the first hour of life) will track certain types of facelike patterns further than other patterns. The exact stimulus characteristics that give rise to this preferential orientating seem to involve a minimal specification of three high-contrast blobs in the appropriate locations for eyes and mouth. The actual details of the human face are filled in by the infant's experience. The second mechanism is controlled by cortical structures and gains control over behavior at around two months of age. Two months is the age which many authors have identified as the time of onset of cortical control over visually-guided behavior (Johnson, 1990). Thus the first system serves to constrain the range of inputs processed by the second system and in some sense "tutors" it before it gains subsequent control over behavior.

A further clue that the early predisposition is not a detailed template of the human face comes from work testing human infants and adults with the faces of other primates (Sargent and Nelson, 1992). Infants were habituated to a monkey face in a particular orientation. They were then shown either the same monkey face but in different orientations or other monkey faces in the same orientation. While nine-month-old infants were able to discriminate between the different monkey faces, adults could not discriminate between, on the one hand, a monkey face already seen but at a different angle and, on the other, a new monkey face. This suggests that with experience the infant's capacity *becomes* species-specific and modularized but that it starts out with a relatively underspecified but domain-specific predisposition.

The neonate and infancy data which are now accumulating serve to suggest that the nativists might have won the battle in accounting for the *initial structure* of the human mind. So, does that put the constructivists completely out of business? Not necessarily, and for two reasons. First, the infancy research suggests that development involves both some innately specified information *and* subsequent learning, and in both cases the infant is highly dependent on information from the environment which affects brain structure in return. Second, we know that human cognition manifests flexibility and creativity with development. Now, it is true that the greater the amount of primitively fixed formal properties of the infant mind, the more constrained its computational system will be (Chomsky, 1988). In other words, there is a trade-off between the efficiency and automaticity of the infant's innately specified systems, on the one hand, and the rigidity of such systems, on the other. But if systems were to remain rigid, there would be little if any room for cognitive flexibility and creativity. This is where a constructivist stance becomes essential. As we draw up a much more complex picture of the innate structure of the infant mind and its complex interaction with environmental constraints, cognitive flexibility and creativity require specific theoretical focus within a constructivist epistemology. Thus, for a comprehensive account of human development one must invoke *both* innately-specified predispositions and a constructivist view of development.

Let me now suggest some assumptions about the initial architecture of the human mind that corporate innately specified predispositions and processes which allow for a more constructivist view of development. They are as follows:

1. The human mind has some innately specified information that channel its attention to persons, objects, space, cause–effect relations, number, language, and so forth, leading to the establishment of domain-specific representations. Such innately specified predispositions do not, of course,

preclude the need for subsequent learning, but they constrain the way in which such learning takes place.

2. The human mind has a number of innately-specified processes which enable self-redescription and self-organization. Further, the mind possesses mechanisms for inferential processes, for deductive reasoning and for hypothesis testing.

3. The human mind not only tries to appropriate the external environment that it is set to begin exploring and representing from birth, but it also tries to appropriate its own *internal* representations. I shall argue for the representational redescription hypothesis, that is, that the human mind re-represents recursively its own internal representations. For a number of years, I have argued that it is the pervasiveness of this recursive capacity to represent one's own representations, that is, to construct metarepresentations, that sets us apart from other species (Karmiloff-Smith, 1979a, 1979b and, in much greater detail, in Karmiloff-Smith, 1992).

What, then, are the implications of the preceding assumptions for the question of innate constraints and developmental change, the title of this chapter? Following are two speculations I would like to explore here.

The first speculation runs as follows: None of the initial, special-purpose structures built into the human system is available to the system as a data structure. Initial, special-purpose structures are, in my view, represented as procedures that are activated as a response to external stimuli but to which other parts of the cognitive system have no access qua knowledge. This procedurally-encoded knowledge has a similar status to knowledge in nonhuman species. Subsequently, in humans, a process of representational redescription (which I outline later) enables certain aspects of knowledge to become accessible to other parts of the mind. Thus, human development crucially involves the passage from representations that constitute knowledge *in* the mind to representations that acquire the status of knowledge *to* other parts of the mind.

Fodor's dichotomy between input systems and a central processor (Fodor, 1983), although correct in essence, is too narrow. Fodor's view is that at birth, basic input analysis is modular. With development, the outputs of modules are sent to central processing, where the human belief system is built up. Whereas modules are cognitively encapsulated, central processing is not. The second speculation that I explore here endorses Fodor's basic distinction but argues that, with development, central processes end up mimicking the basic characteristics of the modular/central organization of the initial state. This leads to different degrees to which processing is ultimately modular or central. I am *not* suggesting that the modules themselves gradually open up their processes to the rest of the cognitive system (see critical discussion of Rozin, 1976, below). What I am suggesting is that, with development and in interaction with the constraints of the environment, the organism recreates its basic organization to form modular-like processes within central processing and central-like processes within specific input systems. The notion of central-like processes within input systems leads to the hypothesis that some rudimentary domain-specific metacognitive processes will be available to otherwise severely retarded children. In other words, in their particular domain of expertise (e.g., Williams syndrome children's language), retarded children may have dedicated aspects of central-like processing, although deficient in domain-neutral central processing. The notion of modular-like processes within central processing leads to the hypothesis that some late-acquired knowledge may become encapsulated and to all intents and purposes have the basic characteristics of a Fodorian module, although not innately specified nor unassembled. We take up these points shortly hereafter.

To some extent I share the views that Rozin spelled out in some detail in a now classic article published in 1976 on access to the cognitive unconscious. Rozin described evolution in terms of adaptive specializations that originate as specific solutions to specific problems in survival, as opposed to what he called calibration learning. He offered a similar account of the evolution of human intelligence. For Rozin, progress involves gaining access to the cognitive unconscious, that is, "bringing special-purpose programs to a level of consciousness, thereby making them applicable to the full realm of behavior or mental function" (Rozin, 1976: 246). Rozin argued that accessibility can be gained via two processes: " . . . establishment of a physical connection of one system to another or by duplication of one system's circuitry in another part of the brain by use of the appropriate genetic blueprint" (p. 246).

There are ways in which my views concord with Rozin's, but they differ as follows: First, it is hard to envisage how use of the same physical circuitry and genetic blueprint could lead to increased cognitive flexibility. Second, I believe that to account adequately for human development, we need to invoke more than a simple dichotomy between the cognitive unconscious and the cognitive conscious. Third, it is highly unlikely that gaining access to the cognitive unconscious results in making special-purpose programs available to the *full range* of behaviors and problems. This is where I also disagree with what is implicit in Fodor's single central processor position. It is implausible that input analyzers deliver their products immediately in a single language of thought such that the central processor has available to it *all the information* represented centrally by the organism. There must be constraints on the central encoding and access, and on interrelations between different representational codes (spatial, linguistic, kinesthetic, etc.). I return to this later. The fourth difference with Rozin's view of phylogeny and ontogeny (and with Leslie's copying mechanism [Leslie 1987] which is really about a maturationally guided structure's on-line use rather than an ontogenetic process in interaction with environmental constraints) is that I doubt that human development involves the mere "duplication"/"copy" of programs and representations. My position regarding metarepresentation has always been in terms of "redescription" of representations, rather than simple duplication (Karmiloff-Smith, 1979a, 1979b,

1984, 1986, 1992). The lower levels are left intact; copies of these are redescribed. Redescription involves a loss, at the higher level, of information that continues to be represented at the lower level. Our multiple levels of representation are not, I submit, simple duplicates of lower levels; rather, they involve increasing explicitation and accessibility at the cost of detail of information.

How does information get stored in the child's mind? I posit that there are several different ways, as follows:

1. it is innately specified as a result of evolutionary processes. Innately-specified predispositions can either be specific or non-specific (Johnson and Bolhuis, 1991). When the innate component is specified in detail, environmental input is necessary, but it is likely that in such cases the environment acts simply as a trigger for the organism to select one parameter or circuit over others (Changeux, 1985; Chomsky, 1981; Piatelli-Palmerini, 1989; see also, Johnson and Karmiloff-Smith, 1992, for discussion). By contrast, when the innate predisposition is specified merely as a bias or skeletal outline, then it is likely that the full environment acts as much more than a trigger, i.e., that it actually influences the subsequent structure of the brain via a rich epigenetic interaction between mind and physical/sociocultural environments. The skeletal outline specifies attention biases towards particular inputs and a certain number of principles constraining the computation of those inputs. Note that I am hypothesizing that the human mind has *both* a certain amount of detailed specification as well as some very skeletal domain-specific predispositions, depending on the domain.
2. it is acquired via interaction with the physical environment. When the child fails to reach a goal, s/he uses feedback information about error to modify subsequent behavior.
3. it is acquired via linguistic statements from others, which the child must learn to represent adequately, beyond the storing of a rote-learned statement.
4. it is acquired via a process that enables the mind to exploit internally the information that it has already stored, by redescribing its representations or, more precisely, by iteratively re-representing in different representational formats what its internal representations represent. This process may be triggered by external constraints but it is often self-generating, i.e., it can occur outside input/output relations.
5. it is acquired via a form of knowledge change which is more obviously solely the prerogative of the human species, i.e., explicit theory change. This involves conscious construction and exploration of analogies, thought experiments, real experiments, limiting case analyses, etc. typical of older children and adults (Carey, 1985; Inhelder and Piaget, 1958; Karmiloff-Smith, 1988; Klahr and Dunbar, 1988; Kuhn, Amsel and O'Loughlin, 1988; Piaget, Karmiloff-Smith and Bronckart, 1978). But I argue that this more obvious characteristic of human cognition is possible only on the basis of prior representational redescription, which turns *implicit* information into *explicit* knowledge.

The situations in 2 and 3 above are both provoked by external sources of change.[4] By contrast, 4 and 5, although sometimes generated exogenously, often occur endogenously. Endogenous sources of change are those which occur without external mediation. One such source might involve a process of modularization, such that input and output processing becomes progressively less influenced by other processes in the brain. This causes knowledge to become more encapsulated and less accessible to other systems. I speculate that a process of modularization, as opposed to the existence of prespecified modules (Fodor, 1983), can occur as the *product* of development (Karmiloff-Smith, 1986; see also Jusczyk and Cohen, 1985). In other words, to the extent that the mind becomes modularized, this occurs *as development proceeds*. However, while one direction of development involves a process of modularization in which information becomes *less* accessible, another essential facet of cognitive change goes in the opposite direction. It is one in which knowledge becomes progressively *more* accessible, as in 4 and 5 above.

Gaining knowledge via the representational redescription and restructuring of already stored knowledge has been the focus of almost all my work in linguistic and cognitive development. My research strategy has thus been to focus on age groups where efficient output is already present, and then to trace subsequent representational change. The process of representational redescription is posited to take place repeatedly throughout development. In other words, each level of redescription is not linked to a *stage* of development, but is part of reiterated *phases* of development within each cognitive domain.

Full details of the model of represenational redescription and empirical examples from many different cognitive domains can be found elsewhere (Karmiloff-Smith, 1992). Here I shall merely mention some of the main aspects of the process relevant to self-organization and cognitive change. The model of representational redescription (the RR model, for short) postulates that the mind stores multiple redescriptions of knowledge at different levels and in different types of representational format which are increasingly explicit and accessible.

At the initial level, I argue that the representations are in the form of procedures for responding to and analyzing stimuli in the external environment. A number of constraints are operative on the type of representations that are formed at this level:

1. information is encoded in procedural form;
2. within procedures components are sequentially specified;
3. new representations are independently stored; and
4. representations are bracketed such that no intra- or inter-domain representational links can yet be formed.

Information embedded in procedurally-encoded representations is therefore not available to other operators in the cognitive system. Thus if two procedures contain some identical component parts, this potential inter-representational commonality is not yet represented in the child's mind. A procedure *as a whole* is available to other operators; it is its component parts that are not accessible. My contention is that it takes developmental time and a process of representational redescription for component parts to become accessible to potential intra-domain links. This ultimately leads to inter-representational flexibility and creative problem-solving capacities. But at this first level, the potential representational links and the information embedded in procedures remain implicit. This allows for the computation of specific inputs in preferential ways and for effective and rapid responses to the environment. But the behavior generated from these initial representations is relatively inflexible.

The RR model posits a subsequent reiterative process of representational redescription. The redescriptions are abstractions in a higher-level language and are now open to potential intra- and inter-domain representational links, a process which enriches the system from within. At the first level of redescription (level E1), although knowledge is now available to other parts of the cognitive system, it is not available to conscious access. This requires yet further levels of redescription (levels E2 and E3) (see Karmiloff-Smith, 1992 for full details).

The process of representational redescription gives rise to a loss of some of the details of the procedurally-encoded information. A nice example of what I have in mind is mentioned in a recent article by Mandler (1992). Consider, for example, the details of the grated image delivered to the perceptual system when you see a zebra. A redescription of this into "striped animal" (either linguistic or image-like) has lost many of the perceptual details. To Mandler's example, I would add that the redescription allows the *cognitive* system to understand the analogy between the animal, zebra and, for instance, the (British) road sign for a zebra crossing (wide white and black regular stripes), even though these stimuli deliver very different derails to the *perceptual* system. A species without such representational redescriptions would not find the zebra and the zebra crossing sign analogous. The redescribed representation is, on the one hand, less special-purpose and less detailed but, on the other, more cognitively flexible because transportable to other goals and making possible inter-representational links. Unlike perceptual representations, conceptual redescriptions are productive; they make possible the invention of new terms (e.g., "zebrin," the antibody which stains certain classes of cells in striped patterns).

The passage from procedurally-encoded representations to explicit redescriptions occurs whenever a component of the child's cognitive system has reached what I call "behavioral mastery." In other words, it is representations that have reached a *stable state* that are redescribed. This success-based view of cognitive change contrasts with Piaget's view. For Piaget, a system in a state of stability would not spontaneously improve itself. Rather, the Piagetian process of equilibration takes place when the system is in a state of disequilibrium. This, I agree, may explain *some* aspects of development. The RR model also runs counter to the behaviorist view that change occurs only as the result of failure or external reinforcement. Rather, for the RR model certain types of change take place *after* the child is successful, i.e., already producing the correct linguistic output or already having consistently reached a problem-solving goal. Representational redescription is a process of "appropriating" stable states to extract the information that they contain, which can then be used more flexibly for other purposes.

I do not of course deny the role of cognitive conflict in generating other types of change through, for instance, the mismatch between input and output in language (e.g., Clark, 1987), between theory-driven expectations and actual outcomes (e.g., Carey, 1985), or competition between different internal systems (e.g., Bates and MacWhinney, 1987). What I am stressing here is the additional and, I hypothesize, crucial role of *internal system stability* as the basis for generating a special type of cognitive change pervasive in human development, i.e., representational redescription. And from the repeated process of internal representational redescription, rather than simply interaction with the external environment, cognitive flexibility and consciousness ultimately emerge. I posit that the process of representational redescription can occur without ongoing analysis of incoming data or production of output. Thus, change may take place outside normal input/output relations, i.e., simply as the product of system-internal dynamics when there are no external pressures.

Recall that the process of representational redescription does not involve the destruction or overwriting of the original representations. The human mind is not, I posit, striving for economy. Thus the original, procedurally-encoded representations remain intact in the child's mind and can continue to be called for particular cognitive goals which require speed and automaticity. The redescribed representations are used for other goals where the more explicit knowledge is required.

Once knowledge previously embedded in procedures is explicitly defined, the potential relationships between procedures can then be marked and represented internally. Moreover, once redescription has taken place and explicit representations become manipulable, the child can then introduce violations to her data-driven, veridical descriptions of the world, violations which allow for pretend play, false belief and the use of counterfactuals (see Karmiloff-Smith, 1992, for full discussion).

It is important to reiterate that although the initial redescriptions are available as data to the system, they are not necessarily available to conscious access and verbal report. There are numerous examples in the developmental literature of the formation of explicit representations which are not yet accessible to conscious reflection and verbal report, but which are clearly beyond the procedural level. In general, developmentalists have not distinguished between implicitly stored knowledge and a representational format in which knowledge *is* explicitly represented but not yet consciously accessible. Rather, a dichotomy has been used between, on the one hand, an undefined notion of "implicit" (as if information were not represented in any form) and, on the other hand, consciously accessible knowledge stateable in verbal form. The representational redescription model postulates that the human representational system is far more complex than a mere dichotomy would suggest. I argue that there are more than two kinds of representation. Levels exist between implicitly-stored procedural information and verbally-stateable declarative knowledge. The end result of these various redescriptions is the existence in the mind of multiple representations of similar knowledge at different levels of detail and explicitness.

At the highest level, knowledge is recoded into a cross-system format. It is here, as mentioned above, that my disagreement with Fodor's proposals (Fodor, 1983) is highlighted, for in my view the system does not transform *all* input immediately into a common, propositional language of thought. Rather, the translation process is constrained by the multiplicity of representational formats (spatial, linguistic, kinesthetic, etc.) available to the human mind. Only at the very highest level is there a common format. The latter is hypothesized to be close enough to natural language for easy translation into stateable, communicable form. It is possible that some knowledge learned directly in linguistic form is immediately stored at the highest level of redescription. Children learn a lot in verbal interaction with others. Nonetheless, knowledge may be stored in rote linguistic format but not yet be linked to knowledge stored in other formats.

There are thus multiple levels at which the same knowledge is re-represented. This notion of multiple encoding is important: As noted earlier, development does *not* seem to be a drive for economy. The mind may indeed turn out to be very redundant.

Before examining some empirical examples from language, let us return briefly to infancy and the issue of how the child might pass from procedurally-encoded representations to linguistically-encoded ones. Recall that Piaget granted no initial innately-specified predispositions and no initial capacity for symbolic representations. For Piaget only sensorimotor encodings of a domain-general type existed during infancy. Not until the culmination of the sensorimotor period at around eighteen months, according to Piaget, does the child represent knowledge symbolically or declaratively, and thus is able to use linguistic representations. By contrast, Mandler (1983, 1988, 1992) has made a very convincing case for the existence of symbolic representations in young infants (but perhaps not neonates) who show the capacity for both procedural and declarative (symbolic) representations of new knowledge. How, Mandler asks, could a young infant recall an action to be imitated after as long as twenty-four hours (Meltzoff, 1988, 1990), without the benefit of accessible knowledge represented in long-term memory? Likewise, how could the four- to six-month-old infant recall the exact size of an object and precisely where it was located behind a screen (Ashmead and Perlmutter, 1980; Baillargéon, in press), if it could not represent them in an accessible form?

Mandler speculates that the young infants engage in a process of perceptual analysis which goes beyond their rapid and automatic computation of perceptual input. Perceptual analysis results in the formation of perceptual primitives such as SELF-MOTION/CAUSED MOTION/PATH/SUPPORT/AGENT, etc. These primitives guide the way in which infants parse events into separate entities that are supported or contained, that move from sources to goals along specific kinds of paths according to whether movement is animate or inanimate. Mandler argues that these perceptual primitives are redescribed into accessible image-schemas, thereby providing a level of representation intermediate between perception and language. And it is these accessible image-schemas that facilitate semantic development, i.e., the mapping between language and conceptual categories. Image-schemas are nonpropositional, analog representations of spatial relations and movements, i.e., they are conceptual structures mapped from spatial structure.

Hitherto, I had applied the concept of representational redescription only to post-infancy development. However, Mandler has shown how the process of redescription can also be used to account for representational change in early infancy. In previous work, Mandler argued that procedural and declarative representations developed in parallel (Mandler, 1983, 1988). Her recent introduction of the process of redescription means that the infant's procedural representations actually constrain the content, form and timing of what is ultimately in declarative form. So, already in infancy we witness the formation of a rich system of representations ripe for further representational redescription into linguistic format.

Let us now look at some empirical examples from language acquisition with respect to infant capacities and the subsequent process of representational redescription. This will be followed by work exploring the process of redescription in older children's drawing.

Many developmental psycholinguists accept a nativist view of language acquisition (e.g., Gleitman, 1990; Hyams, 1986; Pinker, 1984; Valian, 1990), although there exist some rather compelling counter-arguments (Bates *et al.*, 1979, Bates and MacWhinney, 1987). The most thoroughly worked out nativist account of language acquisition has been offered by Chomsky (1981, 1986, 1988). Chomsky argues that what is built into the human mind is a form of universal grammar, i.e., linguistic principles that are innately specified and constrain the child's acquisition of her native tongue. Also built in are a series of parameters either with a default setting (Hyams, 1986) or with both settings available (Valian, 1990), to be fixed one way or the other in the light of the characteristics of the particular linguistic environment in which the child finds herself. Note that the postulated principles and parameters are not mere skeletal outlines, but hypothesized to be specified very precisely and then selected via interaction with the constraints of the linguistic environment.

However, as Gleitman (1990) has stressed, the Chomskyan model fails to address a prior problem. Between birth and the onset of language maturationally, how does the infant build up linguistically-relevant representations from the native tongue model on which to base subsequent acquisition? Gleitman and her colleagues argue that the child is preset biologically to represent the linguistically-relevant aspects of sound waves and differentiate these from other, non-linguistic acoustic input. Recent research suggests that infants compute a constrained class of specifically linguistic inputs such that, in their interpretation of sound waves, they make a distinction between linguistically-relevant and other, non-linguistic sounds (Mehler and Bertoncini, 1988). The normal infant attends preferentially to human language.

The development of speech perception of the particularities of the infant's mother tongue has been shown to be an innately-guided learning process (Jusczyk and Bertoncini, 1988). Results of studies have suggested that well before they can talk, young infants are already sensitive to word boundaries (Gleitman *et al.*, 1988) as well as to clause boundaries within which grammatical rules apply (Hirsh-Pasek *et al.*, 1987). Babies show distinct preference for a recording into which pauses are inserted at natural clause boundaries, as opposed to a recording in which the pauses violate such language-specific boundaries. Experiments also indicate that infants are sensitive to relative pitch which is linguistically relevant, versus absolute pitch (e.g., male versus female voice) which is socially relevant, that they are sensitive to rhythmic aspects of linguistic input, to vowel duration, to linguistic stress, to the contour of rising and falling intonation, and to subtle phonemic distinctions (DeMany, McKenzie, and Vurpillot, 1977; Eilers *et al.*, 1984; Eimas *et al.*, 1971; Fernald, 1989; Fernald and Kuhl, 1981; Fowler, Smith, and Tassinary, 1986; Kuhl, 1983; Spring and Dale, 1977; Sullivan and Horowitz, 1983). Moreover, according to Mehler and his colleagues in Paris, four-day-old infants are already sensitive to certain characteristics of their own native tongue (Mehler *et al.*, 1986). Mehler found that twelve hours after birth, babies distinguished between linguistically-relevant input and other non-linguistic acoustic input. However, they do not yet react to differences between particular languages. Thus the nine months in utero do not provide sufficient input for the child to attend preferentially to its native tongue at birth. However, already by four days of age, i.e., after exceedingly little experience, the infants studied by the Parisian team discriminated between the intonation patterns of Russian and French.

What this and other infancy work on language indicate is that by the time language production begins, there is already a large bulk of linguistically-relevant representations in the infant's mind, representations that support subsequent syntactic development. These are a result of multiple internal *and* external constraints that give rise to a discrete number of possible emergent functions (see discussion in Johnson and Karmiloff-Smith, 1992).

So, is that all there is to language acquisition? A set of constraining biases for attending to linguistically-relevant input and subsequently, with maturation, a number of parameters to be set via some inductive mechanism? Does language acquisition involve nothing more? In my view, little more is needed to provide an adequate account of language acquisition as far as the *initial* mapping operations are concerned to generate efficient language usage. Moreover, this may be all there is to the language acquisition of certain fluent-speaking retarded children. The now attested fact that semantically and syntactically fluent language can co-exist with severe cognitive retardation in children with Williams Syndrome (Bellugi, 1989; Bellugi *et al.*, 1988; Karmiloff-Smith, 1990b; Karmiloff-Smith *et al.*, 1991; Thal, Bates, and Bellugi, 1989; Udwin, Yule, and Martin, 1987) and in hydrocephalic children with associated myelomeningocele (Cromer, 1991; Tew, 1979) suggests that an explanation of language acquisition as merely part of general cognitive development with no linguistically-relevant predispositions (e.g., Sinclair, 1971, 1987) is highly challengeable. Whereas fluent language in a very retarded child is difficult to accommodate theoretically within a traditional Piagetian perspective, it is unsurprising within a perspective that allows for domain-specific predispositions. Indeed, the progressive modularization of language, on the basis of innately-specified constraints channeling the infant's attention to a class of linguistically-relevant acoustic inputs, together with innately specified linguistic principles and parameters and some form of induction and mapping mechanism, is all that the retarded child would need to carry out automatically, *without general cognitive effort*, the mapping operations between the input model and the prespecified internal constraints. With the linguistic predispositions intact, this would allow the fluent-speaking retarded child to display similar *behavior* to that of the normal child. In terms of the representational redescription model, only procedurally-encoded representations are needed to support initial fluent language usage.

However, this is *not* all there is to the language acquisition of the normally developing child. First there are some within-domain dissociations in the language of Williams Syndrome children (Karmiloff-Smith and Grant, 1993). Fluent-speaking French Williams subjects with IQs in the 50s range and for whom syntax is no problem in formal tests, scored like 3-year-olds on grammatical gender tasks, suggesting that this aspect of language involves domain-general processing which is not part of a syntactic module. Furthermore, although the fluent-speaking retarded child has relatively intact language *usage*, the normal child also has the potential to go *beyond* successful usage and to become a little grammarian. By contrast, not only do other species have no language capacity, but the constraints on spiders, ants, beavers, and the like are such that they could never become potential describers of the knowledge embedded in their procedures for interacting with the environment. In other words, they only change their representations in interaction with the external environment, they cannot exploit relations implicit in their own internally stored information. One might object that chimpanzees are much closer to humans. This is certainly true to some extent. After all, we share more than 90 percent of our genes with the chimpanzee. It used to be thought that what made us specifically human was the fact that we had language and no other species did. But in recent years, researchers have taught chimpanzees to use language-like systems (lists of lexical items from American Sign Language [Gardner and Gardner, 1969], or plastic chips standing for English words [Premack, 1986,

1990]). And we know that, like children, chimpanzees can solve problems and successfully learn from environmental constraints. So is there no qualitative difference between the human child and the chimpanzee? Of course there is. First, what.the chimpanzee learns is not a linguistic system but a list of lexical items (Premack, 1986, 1990). Second, an equally crucial difference shows up when we look at what happens *beyond successful learning*. Chimpanzees do not go beyond behavioral mastery.

The human child goes beyond successful language usage to exploit the knowledge that he or she has already stored. *External* reality serves as input to form initial representations, but it is the *internal* representations which serve to form mini-theories about the linguistic system. This necessitates the redescription of procedurally-embedded knowledge to extract the morphological components. It is pervasive in normal children's language acquisition, and leads to a flexible, creative use of language and the evolving capacity for metalinguistic reflexion.

Let us now briefly take some experimental evidence to illustrate the passage from procedurally-encoded linguistic representations to the normal child's subsequent spontaneous formation of theories about how language functions as a system.

The first example is from the acquisition of simple words like the articles and post-articles "the" and "my" (Karmiloff-Smith, 1979a). A series of experiments demonstrated that, between the ages of 2 and 5, children learn to use and interpret articles and post-articles correctly in a number of their different appropriate contexts. But at 5, they cannot give verbal explanations of the conditions of use. Yet, although their usage is correct, the knowledge of conditions of use *must* be represented (as knowledge still embedded in a procedure) to make it possible for young children to produce and understand the subtle linguistic distinctions conveyed by these words. However, the knowledge represented at that level is not available to them as consciously reportable data. A distinction must therefore be drawn between information represented explicitly in the mind and information accessible to consciousness. It is by around 9 or 10 years, for this particular aspect of language, that children have quite elaborate linguistic theories about the conditions of use of articles and post-articles and how they are related to other members of the nominal determiner system (Karmiloff-Smith, 1979a, 1986). Here is one such example from a 10-year-old. The context was two pens, one eraser, one earring and the child's own watch. The experimenter hid the child's watch and then asked: "What did I do?" The exchange was as follows:

> *Child*: You hid the watch.
> *Exp*: Why did you say "*the* watch"?
> *Child*: Well ... "*my* watch" because it belongs to me, but I said "you hid *the* watch" because there are no other watches there. If you'd put yours out, I would have had to say "you hid *my* watch," because it could have been confusing, but this way it's better for me to say "you hid the watch" so someone doesn't think yours was there too.

This is an eloquent example of how elaborate spontaneous verbal statements from children can be, once they have access to their linguistic knowledge. Note that correct usage of "the," "my" etc. occurs much earlier, around 4 to 5 years of age.

Now, if one were only to consider the difference between young children's correct usage and older children's metalinguistic statements, then one would merely postulate two levels of representation: The implicit procedurally-encoded representations sustaining correct usage, on the one hand, and the verbally stateable representations sustaining the verbal explanations, on the other. To posit the existence of a level of representational redescription between the two, one needs to find other kinds of data. Spontaneous self-repairs turned out to be one source of such data (Karmiloff-Smith, 1979a, 1986). Take the same hiding game as above. During testing children often make self-repairs. They sometimes make lexical repairs, e.g.: "you hid the pe ... no, the watch." At other times they make referential repairs, e.g.: "you hid the blue pe ... the red pen." But they also make what I call "systemic repairs," e.g.: "you hid my wat ... the watch." (Note that this is precisely the equivalent at the repair level to the metalinguistic statement above.) Such repairs are not corrections of errors; "my watch" identifies the referent unambiguously. Rather, they denote children's sensitivity to the force of different determiners, which are no longer independently stored but are part of a linguistic subsystem. Such subsystems, I argue, are built up from the extraction of common components, explicitly represented after representational redescription has taken place. Important is the fact that 4–5-year-olds do not make systemic self-repairs. But this is precisely what children of around 6 years of age display in such circumstances whereas they are still unable to provide verbal explanations of their linguistic knowledge about the relationship between "the" and "my" in referential communication. However, their self-repairs bear witness to the fact that something has changed in their internal representations beyond the period of correct usage, and that they now have linked explicitly some of the component knowledge which was previously embedded in independently-stored procedures for producing/interpreting each article or post-article.

The phenomenon of late-occurring repairs and errors, after behavioral mastery, and which are not in the child's language at earlier ages, has been explored in detail by several researchers (Bowerman, 1982; Karmiloff-Smith, 1979a, 1979b; Newport, 1981). An eloquent example comes from Elissa Newport's work on the acquisition of American Sign Language (ASL). In ASL, signs have morphological structure. Deaf parents who are non-native signers, i.e., who acquired sign language late in life, cannot analyze the signs into their morphological component parts. They produce them as unanalyzed wholes. By contrast, children acquiring ASL as a native language do analyze the morphological structure. Initially children also use signs as frozen wholes (procedurally-encoded representations). But, after they have been using the sign correctly for some time, i.e., after having reached behavioral mastery, children start to produce "errors" in their output. The errors involve separate staccato movements, isolating separate morphological components, instead of producing the normally flowing sign. It is something like the equivalent of first pronouncing "typewriter" correctly and then subsequently spelling out its morphological structure and pronouncing it as "type-write-er" which would make it potentially linkable to other words with similar component structure. The extraction of component parts in ASL from the initially frozen signs is again suggestive of representational redescription. Important, too, is the fact that nothing in Newport's data suggests that children are consciously aware of the segmented form of their new productions. In other words, the representations are not yet in a format that allows for conscious access and verbal report. Their representations are intermediate between the procedural format and the final level which allows for conscious access and verbal report. Subsequently, the overt marking of morphological structure disappears. Older children again use signs that look like the naturally flowing ones that they used when much younger. However, representational redescription model posits that the later, identical output stems from more explicit representations than the procedural ones that underlie the initial productions. (For numerous other such examples of overt marking of morphological structure in the acquisition of French, see Karmiloff-Smith, 1979a.)

Does a similar pattern of increasing access hold for the entire linguistic system? A recent series of experiments focused on metalinguistic awareness of discourse constraints[5] in contrast to the propositional content of utterances (Karmiloff-Smith *et al.*, in press). Here we looked at both adults and children. Discourse structure and propositional content are simultaneously encoded by speakers and decoded by addressees. Take the pronoun "he" as a brief example of how a linguistic marker functions both at the level of propositional content and the discourse organizational level. From the point of view of the semantics of propositional content, the pronoun "he" provides the listener with information at the sentential level about a referent being human, male, singular, etc. But in the on-line flow of discourse, the use of the pronoun *also* conveys information about the speaker's mental model of the overall discourse structure, about whether the referent can be taken by default to be the main protagonist, and so forth. Thus, in setting up a discourse model of a span of speech, speakers usually make use of pronouns (e.g., "he") to refer to the main protagonist of a story, whereas full noun phrases (e.g., "the girl") are used to refer to subsidiary characters (see Karmiloff-Smith, 1985, for full discussion of the structure of cohesive devices).

Subjects were asked to explain why a narrator had used a pronoun in some cases and a full noun phrase in others. The results of the experiment show that child and adult subjects can give elaborate explanations about, say, the pronoun "he" and how it relates to "she," "they" and "it," i.e., about its propositional content, and its relation to other pronouns stored in a subsystem in long-term memory. But neither children nor adults can say almost anything about the function of pronouns at the discourse level. In the allocation of shared computational resources, the discourse organization aspect of language turns out to be unavailable to conscious access, whereas the semantics of the propositional content can be reflected on metalinguistically (Karmiloff-Smith *et al.*, in press).

Discourse organizational structure is acquired rather late in development and unlikely to be part of the innately-specified predispositions in the same way that some aspects of sentential syntax might be. Moreover, unlike the deterministic rules of sentential syntax, discourse rules are probabilistic. The feedback from each decision regarding the choice of a discourse marker (he, the old man, Jim, etc.) becomes the input for the generation of the next choice, i.e., a closed loop control. When discourse cohesion markers first appear consistently in children's output, the propositional content of their output decreases compared to younger subjects (Karmiloff-Smith, 1985; Karmiloff-Smith *et al.*, in press). There seems to be competition in the allocation of processing resources between propositional content and discourse structure when encoding a fast-fading message in real time. Only one of these aspects, the propositional content of determiner use, is subsequently available to metalinguistic reflection. By contrast, the discourse organizational structure seems to become modularized for rapid on-line computation, and is not accessible to metalinguistic reflection, even in adults.

Development thus seems to involve two opposite processes: On the one hand, the progressive access to knowledge previously embedded in procedures and, on the other hand, the progressive modularization of parts of the system. But, if discourse organizational processes are modular-like, then how does the psycholinguist or linguist have access to that part of language inaccessible to normal adults and children? A necessary prerequisite to such access is to re-represent the language and change the spoken code to a written form, i.e., freeze the fast-fading message of spoken language into the static form of written language. It is impossible for the psycholinguist to analyze on-line the discourse organizational markers of spoken language output. Both speaker and listener have no conscious access to it. In a modular-like fashion, it runs off automatically and is cognitively impenetrable. The discourse analysis has to be carried out on a different, externalized representational format: written language.

Extensive research within both language and cognitive development has, in my view, now rendered the representational redescription model plausible. For some aspects of language progressive conscious access occurs, for others a process of modularization. But what has *not* been addressed until recently is the nature of the constraints on the first level of representational redescription. What constraints obtain when the child moves from knowledge embedded in a procedure, to redescribing that knowledge thereby making it accessible as a data structure to the system? Recent research on children's drawing has focused directly on this issue (Karmiloff-Smith, 1990a).

The same general research strategy was used as in my previous work, i.e., the selection of an age group of children who already have efficiently functioning procedures in the particular domain of interest. Children between $4\frac{1}{2}$ and 10 years of age were asked to make drawings of a house, and then to draw a house that does not exist. The same procedure was used for man and animal. The rationale for this design was as follows: By roughly $4\frac{1}{2}$ years of age, children have efficiently functioning procedures for rapidly drawing houses, for example. Asking them to draw a house that does not exist should force them into operating on the component parts of the knowledge embedded in their procedures.

My hypothesis was that there would be an initial period during which the child could merely run a procedure in its entirety, i.e., be unable to access separately its component parts and operate on them. This procedurally-encoded knowledge, I hypothesized, would be followed by a period during which the child would be able to access, via representational redescription, some of the knowledge embedded previously in the procedure, but that there would be some initial constraints on flexibility. Later development would show increasing flexibility and inter-representational relations.

Let me very briefly run through some of the data. First, the hypothesis that initially children may only be able to run through a successful procedure but be unable to access the knowledge embedded in it was borne out by the results of a few of the youngest subjects. Thus, although announcing that they were going to draw a silly/a pretend house, they proceeded to run through their normal house-drawing procedure and seemed unable to change it. In this chapter, I shall focus on those children who did achieve some flexibility. What is of particular interest in this study stems from the analysis of the constraints which obtained on the types of change children made, i.e., how much flexibility they could spontaneously display.

Figures 6.1.1–3 illustrate the types of change which children of all age groups introduced. They involved the following: shape and size of elements changed; shape of whole changed; elements deleted. In most cases, these changes do *not* involve interruption or reordering of the sequential constraints on the procedure. Although the three types of change were found in children of all ages, important differences emerged with respect to younger and older subjects

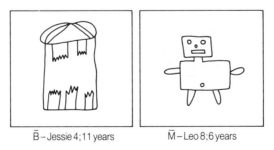

B̄ – Jessie 4;11 years   M̄ – Leo 8;6 years

Figure 6.1.1 *Shape and/or size of elements changed.*

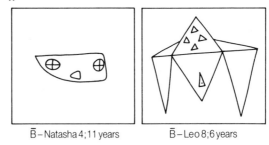

$\bar{B}$ – Natasha 4;11 years $\bar{B}$ – Leo 8;6 years

Figure 6.1.2   *Shape of whole changed.*

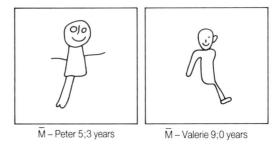

$\bar{M}$ – Peter 5;3 years $\bar{M}$ – Valerie 9;0 years

Figure 6.1.3   *Deletion of elements.*

who used deletion as a solution. We shall look at this once we have illustrated the other changes introduced.

Figures 6.1.4–6 illustrate far more flexible and creative solutions to the task. Changes here involved: insertion of new elements from same conceptual category; position and orientation changed; insertion of elements from other conceptual categories. These changes were found almost totally in older children only. They involve reordering of sequence, interruption and insertion of sub-routines, and the use of representations from other conceptual categories.

If we now reconsider Figure 6.1.3 illustrating deletions, it can be noted that although children of all ages used deletions, this category showed particularly interesting differences between younger and older subjects. It is not possible to

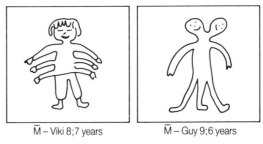

$\bar{M}$ – Viki 8;7 years $\bar{M}$ – Guy 9;6 years

Figure 6.1.4   *Insertion of new elements.*

M̄ – Jessie 9;8 years   B̄ – Justin 10;11 years

Figure 6.1.5   *Position/orientation changed.*

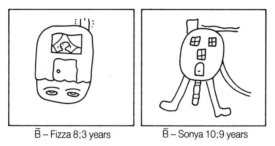

B̄ – Fizza 8;3 years   B̄ – Sonya 10;9 years

Figure 6.1.6   *Insertion of cross-category elements.*

make a formal statistical analysis of the differences in the sequence of deletions between the two age groups, because video recordings were not taken. However, written notes were made on the protocols wherever deemed necessary (e.g., "added wings at the end of the drawing," "left leg was last thing drawn," etc.). These notes, together with a systematic analysis of what can be inferred from the product of many of the drawings, made it possible to assert with some assurance that the children from the older age group frequently made their deletions in the middle of their drawing procedure. By contrast, the younger age group made deletions of elements which are drawn towards the end of a procedure and they did not continue drawing after deletions. The subjects in a follow-up study, for which sequence was carefully recorded on a copy drawn on-line during their productions by a second experimenter, confirmed this finding (see Karmiloff-Smith, 1990a for details).

The very few 4–6-year-olds who made changes classifiable in the last three categories (insertions of elements, position/orientation changes, cross-category insertions) all added elements after finishing a normal X, e.g., by adding a chimney emerging horizontally from the side wall of a house, by adding a smile on a house, etc. They did not make insertions into the middle of their drawing procedure as did older children who, for instance, drew a man with two heads which involves an insertion towards the beginning of the procedure.

The histogram in Figure 6.1.7 shows the differences between the two age groups with respect to flexibility of changes. The very striking developmental

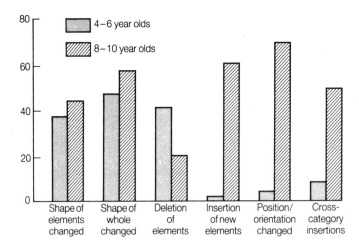

Figure 6.1.7

difference suggests that initially, when children are able to work on a redescription of the knowledge embedded in a procedure, their flexibility is relatively constrained. What form would the process take of learning to draw, say, a house, and later in development, a house that does not exist? Initially, when children build up a new procedure, like learning to draw a house, they do so laboriously, working out the different elements, watching the way others perform, and so forth. The process can be long. Next, they start to consolidate the procedure so that it runs off more or less automatically, much in the manner of skill acquisition. Ask the child to draw a house, and now she can draw it easily and quickly. She is calling on a relatively compiled procedure which is specified sequentially in the internal representations. The results of this study suggest that although at the first level of redescription, the knowledge becomes accessible, flexibility is relatively constrained. By contrast, subsequent representational redescriptions allow for greater flexibility; they are not constrained by any sequential specification. By then, the child has moved from a sequence of instructions in which order is still relatively inflexible, to a more flexibly ordered list of features in which the sequential constraint is relaxed. In computer science terms, the movement would be something like the change from a stack to an array. This makes it possible for children to be creative about insertion of new elements, change of position, orientation and so forth.

Interestingly, the interpretation in terms of sequential constraints on initial redescriptions helps to make sense of what turns out to be very similar phenomena from phonological awareness tasks done with both children and illiterate versus newly literate adults (Morais, Alegria, and Content, 1987). It is easier for subjects to delete final phonemes than to delete initial phonemes. Here, too, then, initially a sequential constraint obtains for children and for the newly-literate, which is surmounted by the fully literate adult. This is not therefore just a developmental phenomenon. The movement from the sequential constraints of procedural encoding to the flexibility of subsequent knowledge holds for new learning in adults too.

It is important to note that the sequential specification does not only act as a curtailing constraint on flexibility. The fact that initial levels of representation are sequentially specified can in fact *potentiate* development in just those areas where sequence is an essential component—language, counting, playing a musical instrument, and so forth. Whereas in each case, the child ultimately needs to surpass all sequential constraints, initially such constraints actually potentiate learning by getting the system off the ground, getting representations into the mind.

Let met conclude by summarizing the main speculations explored in this chapter on innate constraints and developmental change:

1. Innately-specified predispositions and constructivism are not necessarily incompatible.
2. Piaget's view of the initial state of the neonate mind was in some respects wrong. It is clear that at the outset *some* aspects of human knowledge are innately specified. Some structures are initially domain-specific and constrain subsequent learning in complex interaction with the environment. Language, for example, is not based solely on the outcome of domain-neutral sensorimotor action. Piaget's stress on epigenesis and constructivism must incorporate some innately specified predispositions.
3. The infant is not born with a large number of pre-specified modules. Where modules do ultimately exist, they are the result of a process of modularization as development proceeds.
4. Both innately specified knowledge and newly-acquired knowledge are initially procedurally encoded, activated as a response to external stimuli. The procedure as a whole is available to other operators, but at first its component parts are not. An exception to this is when knowledge is directly encoded in linguistic form.
5. The child is a spontaneous theory-builder (about language, physics, etc.) and exploits the knowledge that she has already stored via a process of representational redescription, in other words by representing recursively her own representations. Once redescribed, component parts of knowledge become explicitly represented and thus available as data structures to the system for theory building and ultimately, in some cases, to conscious access.
6. Dichotomies such as implicit/explicit, unconscious/conscious, automatic/controlled, etc. are insufficient to capture the complexities of representational change. One needs to invoke several different levels, namely, a level of implicit knowledge represented but embedded in procedures, a level of explicitly defined knowledge but not available to verbal report, and a level

available to verbal report. A developmental perspective is crucial to identifying these different levels of representation in the human mind.

7. Although change can occur as a result of conflict and competition, change also occurs subsequent to success, i.e., after a period of behavioral mastery.

8. Development involves two opposing but complementary processes: On the one hand, progressive access to stored information and, on the other, progressive modularization.

A question which permeates the developmental literature is whether the mind is a general-purpose, domain-neutral learning mechanism *or* whether knowledge is acquired and computed in a domain-specific fashion (see excellent discussion in Keil, 1990). I have italicized the exclusive "or" purposely, because I feel that it pinpints a developmental misconception. It is doubtful that development will turn out to be entirely domain-specific or entirely domain-general. The more interesting developmental question for the future will hinge on the relative weights of constraints imposed by innate specifications, constraints that are domain-specific and those which are domain-general, as well as constraints emanating from the structure of the environment.

Notes to 6.1

1. This chapter is an adaptation and updating of Karmiloff-Smith, A. (1991). "Beyond modularity: Innate constraints and developmental change" which appeared in S. Carey and R. Gelman (eds). *Epigenesis of the Mind: Essays in biology and knowledge.* Hillsdale, NJ: Erlbaum. Reprinted with permission of Lawrence Erlbaum Associates.
2. Fodor uses the term "constructivism" differently from Piaget, to refer to a form of empiricism: "Specifically, if mental structures can be viewed as assembled from primitive elements, then perhaps mechanisms of learning can be shown to be responsible for effecting their construction . . . real convergence between the motivations of classical associationism and those which actuate its computational reincarnation: Both doctrines find in constructivist analyses of mental structures the promise of an empiricist (i.e., non-nativist) theory of cognitive development" (Fodor, 1983: 33). Piaget argued that his constructivist genetic epistemology—the notion that new cognitive structures are emergent properties of a self-organizing system—was an *alternative* to both nativism and empiricism.
3. It is important not to confuse "domain" with "module." From the point of view of the child's mind, a "domain" is the set of representations sustaining a specific area of knowledge, e.g., language, number, physics, and so forth. A "module" is an information-processing unit that encapsulates that knowledge and computations on it. Considering development as domain-specific does not necessarily imply modularity. In other words, storing and processing of information may be domain-specific, without being encapsulated, hardwired, mandatory, and so forth, and modularization may occur as the *product* of development rather than its starting point.
4. Thelen (1989) argues that in an epigenetic system there is no formal difference between exogenous (external) and endogenous (internal) sources of change in which the action of the organism plays a crucial role.
5. By discourse constraints, I have in mind discourse organizational markers: Terms like pronouns and full noun phrases in their discourse functions of denoting the thematic structure of a discourse, and aspectual marking on verbs in its function of marking foregrounding and backgrounding in a span of discourse.

References to 6.1

Anderson, M. (1992). *Intelligence and Development: A cognitive theory.* Oxford: Blackwell.

Ashmead, D. H. and Perlmutter, M. (1980). "Infant memory in everyday life." In M. Perlmutter, (ed.), *New Directions for Child Development: Children's memory (Vol. 10).* San Francisco: Jossey-Bass.

Baillargéon, R. (1987a). "Object permanence in 3.5- and 4.5-month-old infants." *Developmental Psychology,* **23,** 655–64.

Baillargéon, R. (1987b). "Young infants' reasoning about the physical and spatial properties of a hidden object." *Cognitive Development,* **2,** 170–200.

Baillargéon, R. (in press). "Reasoning about the height and location of a hidden object in 4.5- and 6.5-month-old infants." *Cognition.*

Baillargéon, R. and Hanko-Summers, S. (1990). "Is the top object adequately supported by the bottom object? Young infants' understanding of support relations." *Cognitive Development,* **5,** 29–53.

Baillargéon, R., Spelke, E., and Wasserman, S. (1986). "Object permanence in five-month-old infants." *Cognition,* **20,** 191–208.

Bates, E., Benigni, L., Bretherton, I., Camaioni, L., and Volterra, V. (1979). *The Emergence of Symbols: Cognition and communication in infancy.* New York: Academic Press.

Bates, E. and MacWhinney, B. (1987). "Competition, variation and language learning." In B. MacWhinney, (ed.), *Mechanisms of Language Acquisition.* Hillsdale, NJ: Erlbaum, 157–93.

Bellugi, U. (1989). "Specific dissociations between language and cognitive functioning in a neurodevelopmental disorder." Paper given at the symposium on Neural Correlates underlying Dissociations of Higher Cortical Functioning. International Neuropsychology Society Meeting, Vancouver, February.

Bellugi, U., Marks, S., Bihrle, A. M., and Sabo, H. (1988). "Dissociation between language and cognitive functions in Williams Syndrome." In D. Bishop and K. Mogford, (eds), *Language Development in Exceptional Circumstances.* London: Churchill Livingstone.

Bowerman, M. (1982). "Reorganizational processes in lexical and syntactic development." In E. Wanner and R. L. Gleitman (eds), *Language Acquisition: The state of the art.* Cambridge, UK: Cambridge University Press.

Butterworth, G. (ed.) (1981). *Infancy and Epistemology: An evaluation of Piaget's theory.* Brighton: Harvester Press.

Carey, S. (1985). *Conceptual Change in Childhood.* Cambridge, MA: MIT Press/Bradford Books.

Carey, S. and Gelman, R. (1991). *Epigenesis of the Mind: Essays in biology and knowledge.* Hillsdale, NJ: Erlbaum.

Changeux, J. P. (1985). *Neuronal Man: The biology of mind.* New York: Pantheon Books.

Chomsky, N. (1981). *Lectures on Government and Binding.* Dordrecht: Foris Publications.

Chomsky, N. (1986). *Knowledge of Language: Its nature, origin and use.* New York: Praeger.

Chomsky, N. (1988). *Language and Problems of Knowledge.* Cambridge, MA: MIT Press.

Clark, E. V. (1987). "The principle of contrast: A constraint on language acquisition." In B. MacWhinney (ed.), *The 20th Annual Carnegie Symposium on Cognition.* Hillsdale, NJ: Erlbaum.

Cromer, R. (1991). *Language and Cognition in Normal and Handicapped Children.* Oxford: Blackwell.

DeMany, L., McKenzie, B., and Vurpillot, E. (1977). "Rhythm perception in early infancy." *Nature,* **266,** 718–19.

Diamond, A. and Gilbert, J. (1989). "Development as progressive inhibitory control of action: Retrieval of a contiguous object." *Cognitive Development,* **4,** 223–49.

Eilers, R. E., Bull, D. H., Oller, K., and Lewis, D. C. (1984). "The discrimination of vowel duration by infants." *Journal of the Acoustical Society of America,* **75,** 1213–18.

Eimas, P. H., Siqueland, E. R., Jusczyk, P., and Vigorito, J. (1971). "Speech perception in infants." *Science,* **171,** 303–6.

Feldman, H. and Gelman, R. (1986). "Otitis media and cognitive development." In J. F. Kavanagh (ed.), *Otitis media and child development.* Parkton M.D.: York Press, 27–41.

Fernald, A. (1989). "Four-month-old infants prefer to listen to Motherese." *Infant Behavior and Development,* **8,** 181–95.

Fernald, A. and Kuhl, P. (1981). "Fundamental frequency as an acoustic determinant of infant preference for motherese." Paper presented at the meeting of the Society for Research in Child Development, Boston.

Fodor, J. A. (1983). *The Modularity of Mind*. Cambridge, MA: MIT Press.

Fowler, C. A., Smith, M. R., and Tassinary, L. G. (1986). "Perception of syllable timing by prebabbling infants." *Journal of the Acoustical Society of America*, 79, 814–25.

Gardner, R. A. and Gardner, B. T. (1969). "Teaching sign language to a chimpanzee." *Science*, 165, 664–72.

Gelman, R. (1990). "First principles organize attention to and learning about relevant data: Number and animate-inanimate distinction as examples." *Cognitive Science*, 14, 79–106.

Gleitman, L. R. (1990). "The structural sources of verb meanings." *Language Acquisition*, 1, 3–55.

Gleitman, L. R., Gleitman, H., Landau, B., and Wanner, E. (1988). "Where learning begins: Initial representations for language learning." In F. Newmeyer, (ed.), *The Cambridge Linguistic Survey, Volume III: Language: Psychological and Biological Aspects*. New York: Cambridge University Press.

Gleitman, L. R., Gleitman, H., and Shipley, E. F. (1972). "The emergence of the child as grammarian." *Cognition*, 1, 137–64.

Hirsh-Pasek, K., Kemler-Nelson, D. G., Jusczyk, P. W., Wright Cassidy, K., Druss, B., and Kennedy, L. (1987). "Clauses are perceptual units for young infants." *Cognition*, 26, 269–86.

Hyams, N. (1986). *Language Acquisition and the Theory of Parameters*. Dordrecht: Reidel.

Inhelder, B. and Piaget, J. (1958). *The Growth of Logical Thinking from Childhood to Adolescence*. New York: Basic Books.

James, W. (1892). *Psychology*, London, Macmillan & Co.

Johnson, M. H. (1988). "Memories of mother." *New Scientist*, 18, February, 60–2.

Johnson, M. H. (1990). "Cortical maturation and the development of visual attention in early infancy." *Journal of Cognitive Neuroscience*, 2, 81–95.

Johnson, M. H. and Bolhuis, J. J. (1991). "Imprinting, predispositions and filial preference in the chick." In R. J. Andrew (ed.), *Neural and Behavioural Plasticity in the Chick*. Oxford: Oxford University Press, 133–56.

Johnson, M. H., Dziurawiec, S., Ellis, H., and Morton, J. (1991). "Newborns preferential tracking of facelike stimuli and its subsequent decline." *Cognition*, 40, 1–9.

Johnson, M. H. and Karmiloff-Smith, A. (1992). "Can neural selectionism be applied to cognitive development and its disorders?" *New Ideas in Psychology*, 10, 35–46.

Johnson, M. H. and Morton, J. (1991). *Biology and Cognitive Development: The case of face recognition*. Oxford: Blackwell.

Jusczyk, P. W. (1986). "Speech perception." In K. R. Boff, L. Kaufman, and J. P. Thomas (eds), *Handbook of Perception and Human Performance: Vol. 2. Cognitive processes and performance*. New York: Wiley.

Jusczyk, P. W. and Bertoncini, J. (1988). "Viewing the development of speech perception as an innately guided learning process." *Language and Speech*, 31, 217–38.

Jusczyk, P. W. and Cohen, A. (1985). "What constitutes a module?" *Behavioural and Brain Sciences*, 8, 20–1.

Karmiloff-Smith, A. (1979a). *A Functional Approach to Child Language*. Cambridge, UK: Cambridge University Press.

Karmiloff-Smith, A. (1979b). "Micro- and macro-developmental changes in language acquisition and other representation systems." *Cognitive Science*, 3, 91–118.

Karmiloff-Smith, A. (1984). "Children's problem solving." In M. E. Lamb, A. L. Brown, and B. Rogoff (eds), *Advances in Developmental Psychology*, Vol. 3. Hillsdale, NJ: Lawrence Erlbaum Associates, 39–90.

Karmiloff-Smith, A. (1985). "Language and cognitive processes from a developmental perspective." *Language and Cognitive Processes*, 1, 60–85.

Karmiloff-Smith, A. (1986). "From metaprocesses to conscious access: Evidence from children's metalinguistic and repair data." *Cognition*, 23, 95–147.

Karmiloff-Smith, A. (1988). "The child is a scientist, not an inductivist." *Mind and Language*, 3, 183–95.

Karmiloff-Smith, A. (1990a). "Constraints on representational change: Evidence from children's drawing." *Cognition*, 34, 57–83.

Karmiloff-Smith, A. (1990b). "Piaget and Chomsky on language acquisition: Divorce or marriage?" *First Language*, 10, 255–70.

Karmiloff-Smith, A. (1992). *Beyond Modularity: A developmental perspective on cognitive science*. Cambridge, MA: MIT Press/Bradford Books.

Karmiloff-Smith, A., Bellugi, U., Klima, E., and Grant, J. (1991). Talk prepared for the British Psychological Society's Developmental Section Annual Conference, Cambridge, September, 1991.

Karmiloff-Smith, A. and Grant, J. (1993). "Linguistic and cognitive development in Williams syndrome: A window on the normal mind." Poster presented at SRCD, New Orleans.

Karmiloff-Smith, A., Johnson, H., Grant, J., Jones, M.-C., Karmiloff, Y.-N., Bartrip, J., and Cuckle, C. (in press). "From sentential to discourse functions: Detection and explanation of speech repairs by children and adults." *Discourse Processes*.

Keil, F. C. (1990). "Constraints on constraints: Surveying the epigenetic landscape." *Cognitive Science*, **14**, 135–68.

Kellman, P. J. (1988). "Theories of perception and research in perceptual development." In A. Yonas (ed.), *Perceptual Development in Infancy: The Minnesota symposium on child psychology, (Vol. 20)*. Hillsdale, NJ: Erlbaum.

Kellman, P. J. and Spelke, E. S. (1983). "Perception of partly occluded objects in infancy." *Cognitive Psychology*, **15**, 483–524.

Klahr, D. and Dunbar, K. (1988). "Dual search space during scientific reasoning." *Cognitive Science*, **12**, 1–48.

Kuhl, P. K. (1983). "The perception of auditory equivalence classes for speech in early infancy." *Infant Behavior and Development*, **6**, 263–85.

Kuhn, D., Amsel, E. and O'Loughlin, M. (1988). *The Development of Scientific Thinking Skills*. San Diego: Academic Press.

Leslie, A. M. (1984). "Infant perception of a manual pickup event." *British Journal of Developmental Psychology*, **2**, 19–32.

Leslie, A. M. (1987). "Pretense and representation: The origins of 'theory-of-mind.'" *Psychological Review*, **94**, 412–26.

Leslie, A. M. (1988). "The necessity of illusion: Perception and thought in infancy." In L. Weiskrantz (ed.), *Thought without Language*. Oxford: Oxford University Press.

Mandler, J. M. (1983). "Representation." In J. Flavell and E. Markman, (eds), *Handbook of Child Psychology, Vol. 3*. New York: Wiley.

Mandler, J. M. (1988). "How to build a baby: On the development of an accessible representational system." *Cognitive Development*, **3**, 113–36.

Mandler, J. M. (1992). "How to build a baby II: Conceptual primitives." *Psychological Review*, **99**, 587–604.

Marler, P. (1991). "The instinct to learn." In S. Carey and R. Gelman (eds), *Epigenesis of the Mind: Essays in biology and knowledge*. Hillsdale, NJ: Erlbaum.

Mehler, J. and Bertoncini, J. (1988). "Development: A question of properties, not change?" *Cognition*, **115**, 121–33.

Mehler, J. and Fox, R. (eds) (1985). *Neonate Cognition: Beyond the blooming buzzing confusion*. Hillsdale, NJ: Erlbaum.

Mehler, J., Lambertz, G., Jusczyk, P., and Amiel-Tison, C. (1986). "Discrimination de la langue maternelle par le nouveau-né." *C.R. Académie des Sciences*, **303**, Série III, 637–40.

Meltzoff, A. N. (1988). "Infant imitation and memory: Nine-month-olds in immediate and deferred tests." *Child Development*, **59**, 217–25.

Meltzoff, A. N. (1990). "Towards a developmental cognitive science: The implications of cross-modal matching and imitation for the development of memory in infancy." In "The development and neural bases of higher cognitive functions." *Annals of the New York Academy of Sciences*, **608**, 1–37.

Morais, J., Alegria, J., and Content, A. (1987). "The relationships between segmental analysis and alphabetic literacy: An interactive view." *Cahiers de Psychologie Cognitive*, **7**, 415–38.

Newport, E. L. (1981). "Constraints on structure: Evidence from American Sign Language and language learning." In W. A. Collins (ed.), *Aspects of the Development of Competence: Minnesota Symposia on Child Psychology, Vol. 14*. Hillsdale, NJ: Erlbaum.

Oyama, S. (1985). *The Ontogeny of Information: Developmental systems and evolution*. Cambridge: Cambridge University Press.

Piaget, J. (1955). *The Child's Construction of Reality*. London: Routledge and Kegan Paul.

Piaget, J. (1967). *Biologie et Connaissance*. Paris: Gallimard.

Piaget, J., Karmiloff-Smith, A., and Bronckart, J. P. (1978). "Généralisations relatives à la pression et à la réaction." In J. Piaget (ed.), *Recherches sur la Généralisation*. Paris: Presses Universitaires de France, 169–91.

Piattelli-Palmarini, M. (1989). "Evolution, selection, and cognition: From 'learning' to parameter setting in biology and the study of language." *Cognition*, **31**, 1–44.

Pinker, S. (1984). *Language Learnability and Language Development*. Cambridge, MA: Harvard University Press.

Premack, D. (1986). *Gavagai! Or the future history of the animal language controversy*. Cambridge MA: MIT Press.

Premack, D. (1990). "Words: What are they, and do animals have them?" *Cognition*, **37**, 197–212.

Rozin, P. (1976). "The evolution of intelligence and access to the cognitive unconscious." In J. M. Sprague and A. A. Epstein (eds), *Progress in Psychobiology and Physiological Psychology (Vol. 6)*. New York: Academic Press, 245–80.

Rutkowska, J. C. (1987). "Computational models and developmental psychology." In J. C. Rutkowska and C. Cook (eds), *Computation and Development*. Chichester: Wiley.

Sargent, P. L. and Nelson, C. A. (1992). "Cross-species recognition in infant and adult humans: ERP and behavioral measures." Poster at the International Conference on Infant Studies, Miami Beach, May 1992.

Sinclair, H. (1971). "Sensorimotor action patterns as the condition for the acquisition of syntax." In R. Huxley and E. Ingrams (eds), *Language Acquisition: Models and methods*. New York: Academic Press.

Sinclair, H. (1987). "Language: A gift of nature or a homemade tool?" In S. Modgil and C. Modgil (eds), *Noam Chomsky: Consensus and controversy*. London: The Falmer Press.

Slater, A. (1990). "Size constancy and complex visual processing at birth." Poster presented at the IVth European Conference on Developmental Psychology, University of Stirling, August.

Slater, A. and Morison, V., (in press). "Visual attention and memory at birth." In M. J. Weiss and P. Zelazo, *Newborn Attention*. Norwood, NJ: Ablex.

Slater, A., Morison, V. and Rose, D. (1983). "Perception of shape by the newborn baby." *British Journal of Developmental Psychology*, **1**, 135–42.

Slater, A., Morison, V., Somers, M., Mattock, A., Brown, E., and Taylor, D. (1990). "Newborn and older infants' perception and partly occluded objects." *Infant Behaviour and Development*, **13**, 33–49.

Spelke, E. S. (1985). "Preferential-looking methods as tools for the study of cognition in infancy." In G. Gottlieb and N. A. Krasnegor (eds), *Measurement of Audition and Vision in the First Year of Postnatal Life: A methodological overview*. Norwood, NJ: Ablex.

Spelke, E. S. (1988). "Where perceiving ends and thinking begins: The apprehension of objects in infancy." In A. Yonas (ed.), *Perceptual Development in Infancy*. Hillsdale, NJ: Erlbaum.

Spelke, E. S. (1990). "Principles of object perception." *Cognitive Science*, **14**, 29–56.

Spelke, E. S. (1991). "Physical knowledge in infancy: Reflections on Piaget's theory." In S. Carey and R. Gelman (eds), *Epigenesis of the Mind: Essays in biology and knowledge*. Hillsdale, NJ: Erlbaum.

Spring, D. R. and Dale, P. S. (1977). "Discrimination of linguistic stress in early infancy." *Journal of Speech and Hearing Research*, **20**, 224–32.

Starkey, P., Spelke, E. S., and Gelman, R. (1983). "Numerican abstraction by human infants." *Cognition*, **39**, 167–70.

Sullivan, J. W. and Horowitz, F. D. (1983). "The effects of intonation on infant attention: The role of the rising intonation contour." *Journal of Child Language*, **10**, 521–34.

Tew, B. (1979). "The 'cocktail party syndrome' in children with hydrocephalus and spina bifida." *British Journal of Disorders of Communication*, **14**, 89–101.

Thal, D., Bates, E., and Bellugi, U. (1989). "Language and cognition in two children with Williams syndrome." *Journal of Speech and Hearing Research*, **32**, 489–500.

Thelen, E. (1989). "Self-organization in developmental processes: Can systems approaches work?" In M. Gunnar and E. Thelen (eds), *Systems and Development. The Minnesota Symposium in Child Psychology*, vol. 22. London: Erlbaum.

Udwin, O., Yule, W., and Martin, N. (1987). "Cognitive abilities and behavioural characteristics of children with ideopathic infantile hypercalcaemia." *Journal of Child Psychology and Psychiatry*, **28**, 297–309.

Valian, V. (1990). "Null subjects: A problem for parameter setting models of language acquisition." *Cognition*, **35**, 105–22.

The Instinct to Learn

Peter Marler

I sense from the classical debate between Piaget and Chomsky (Piattelli-Palmarini, 1980) that at least some of us are all too prone to think of learning and instinct as being virtually antithetical. According to this common view, behavior is one or the other, but it is rarely, if ever, both. Lower animals display instincts, but our own species, apart from a few very basic drives, displays instincts rarely. Instead, we are supposed to be the manifestation of what can be achieved by the emancipation from instinctive control (Gould and Marler, 1987).

It is self-evident that this antithesis is false. Just as instincts are products of interactions between genome and environment, even the most extreme case of purely arbitrary, culturally transmitted behavior must, in some sense, be the result of an instinct at work. Functions of instincts may be generalized or highly specialized, but without them learning could not occur. Thus, the question I pose is not "Do instincts to learn exist?" but rather "What is their nature, and by what behavioral and physiological mechanism do they operate?" How do they impinge on the pervasive plasticity that behavior displays at so many points in the course of its development? I suggest that concepts from the classical ethology of Konrad Lorenz (1950) and Niko Tinbergen (1951) are instructive in a search for answers to these questions.

Of the several concepts with which Lorenz and Tinbergen sought to capture the essence of instinctive behavior in animals (listed in Table 6.2.1), I concentrate especially on three. First is the notion of *sensitive periods* as phases of development with unusual potential for lability. Second and third are the

Table 6.2.1 *Concepts from classical ethology relevant to the instinct to learn*

Sensitive Periods
Imprinting
Fixed Action Patterns
Releasers
Innate Release Mechanisms
[Instincts to Learn]

complementary ideas of *releasers* (or *sign stimuli*) and *innate release mechanisms*, invoked by ethologists to explain the remarkable fact that many organisms, especially in infancy, are responsive to certain key stimuli during interactions with their social companions and with their physical environments, when they first encounter them. This responsiveness implies the possession of brain mechanisms that attune them innately to certain kinds of stimulation.

In recent years, I have come to believe that many such mechanisms have richer and more interesting functions than simply to serve as design features for animals as automata. They also provide the physiological machinery to facilitate and guide learning processes, as one set of components in what I think can be appropriately viewed as instincts to learn.

I use birdsong to make the case for instincts to learn as an approach that is productive and logical, even with behavior that is clearly and obviously learned. As a research strategy, it prepares us directly for posing the right kinds of questions in neurophysiological investigations of the underlying mechanisms. It is a position that follows naturally, once the crucial point is appreciated that instincts are not immutable and completely lacking in ontogenetic plasticity, as has so often been assumed in the past, but are themselves, by definition, susceptible to the influence of experience. I present evidence that even the most creative aspects of song development are imbued with instinctive influences, by which I refer to the aspects of the phenotype of the learning organism that are attributable to its genetic constitution (Johnston, 1988). These influences pervade all aspects of ontogeny. We cannot begin to understand how a young bird learning to sing interacts with its social and physical environments, and assimilates information from these interactions, without taking full account of innate contributions to the assimilation process. Each species accommodates most readily to those aspects of experience that are compatible with its nature.

One of the best illustrations of local dialects in birdsong is the white-crowned sparrow (Figure 6.2.1). This is a very simple case. With rare exceptions, each male has a single song type, which has about a two-second duration. Some song features conform very closely to the local dialect, and others are unique to each individual male. The dialects are so marked that someone with a cultivated ear would be able to tell where he or she was in California, blindfolded, simply by

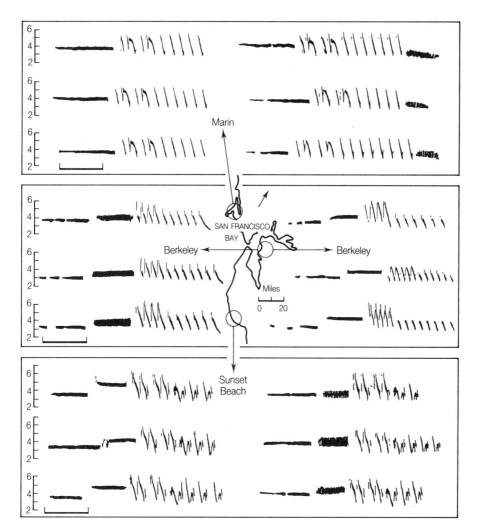

Figure 6.2.1   *An illustration of song dialects in the white-crowned sparrow in the San Francisco Bay area. Songs of eighteen males are illustrated, six from Marin County, six in the Berkeley area, and six from Sunset Beach, to the south. Each male has a single song type, for the most part. Local dialects are most evident in the second, trilled portion of the song (from Marler, 1970). These dialects have been studied in much greater detail by Baptista (1975).*

listening to their songs (Baker and Cunningham, 1985; Baptista, 1975, 1977). The fact that the dialects are learned becomes obvious when a male bird is reared without hearing the song of its own kind. A much simpler song develops, lacking all traces of the local accent (Marler, 1970; Petrinovich, 1985). What is the nature of this learning process, and what, if any, are the contributions of instinctive processes? We can detect such contributions in many aspects of the process of learning to sing.

Innate learning preferences

If we present a young bird with an array of different songs or tutors to learn from, are they equipotential as stimuli, or are some preferred over others? If there are preferences, do species differ in the songs they favor, or is a song that is a strong learning stimulus for one species, strong for others as well?

As a key feature of the research on which this report is based, a comparative approach has been taken. The underlying principle is simple. Young males of

Normal, crystallized song sparrow song

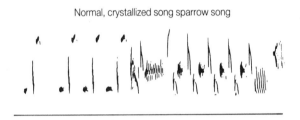

Normal, crystallized swamp sparrow song

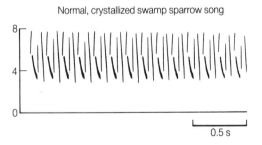

Figure 6.2.2 *Sound spectrograms of normal song and swamp sparrow songs. They differ in both syntax and phonology, and also in the size of individual song repertoires, which average about three song types in swamp sparrows and ten–twelve in song sparrows.*

two species, the swamp and the song sparrow, were brought into the laboratory and reared under identical conditions. This gave us the opportunity to observe whether they interacted similarly or differently with the experimental situations in which they were reared. Despite their close genetic relatedness, their songs are very different (Figure 6.2.2). One is simple; the other is complex. They differ in the overall "syntax" of their songs and in the "phonology" of the individual notes. They differ in repertoire size, a male song sparrow having about three times as many song types as a male swamp sparrow (three in one case, ten to twelve in the other).

How do males of these two species react if we bring them into the laboratory as nestlings, raise them by hand so that their opportunity to hear song in nature is limited, and expose them to tape-recordings with equal numbers of swamp sparrow songs and song sparrow songs? When we analyze the songs that they produce, it becomes clear that each displays a preference for songs of its own species (Figure 6.2.3).

In most of the experiments on which I report, birds were raised by hand, after being taken as nestlings from the field at an age of three–five days. We do this because it is more difficult to raise them from the egg. Might they have

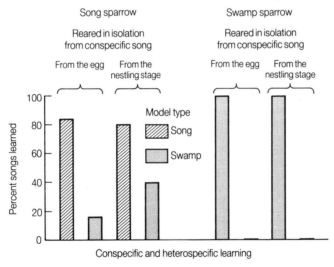

Figure 6.2.3 *Learning preferences of male song and swamp sparrows either raised in the laboratory from the egg or exposed to song in nature during the nestling phases and only then brought into the laboratory. Birds were given a choice of tape recordings to learn, some of their own species' songs and some of other species. The results show that both have an innate preference for learning songs of their own species, but the preference is stronger in swamp sparrows than in song sparrows. Song experience during the nestling phase evidently has no effect on learning preferences.*

learned something in the egg, or the first few days of life before being brought into the laboratory that has an influence on development of singing behavior, perhaps leading them to favor songs of the species heard during that period?

To check on the possibility of pre- or peri-natal experience of species-specific song on learning preferences, eggs from wild nests of the same two species were taken early in incubation, hatched in the laboratory, and raised with absolutely no opportunity to hear adult song of their species. They displayed similar learning preferences (Figure 6.2.3). The preference for conspecific song is thus innate (Marler and Peters, 1989). Interestingly, the song sparrow preference is less extreme in birds raised under both conditions. Dooling and Searcy (1980) uncovered a similar trend by looking at heart-rate changes in three-week-old song and swamp sparrows in response to song (Figure 6.2.4). It may be that, as found in some other birds (Baptista and Petrinovich, 1984, 1986; Clayton, 1988; Pepperberg, 1988), social interaction with live tutors is more important in song sparrows than in swamp sparrows, because song sparrows are not known to imitate swamp sparrows in nature, even though they live in close proximity. In swamp sparrows, learning from tape-recordings and live tutors has been shown to take place in a very similar fashion (Marler and Peters, 1988b). Social influences notwithstanding, in both species the preference *can* be sustained

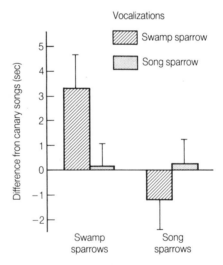

Figure 6.2.4 *Cardiac responses of young swamp and song sparrows to recorded songs of their own and of the other species. The responses are calibrated in relation to the neutral stimulus of a canary song. Each responds most strongly to songs of its own species. The swamp sparrows discriminated more strongly than the song sparrows, in which the preference was not statistically significant. The trend matches that in song learning preferences (Figure 6.2.3). These data were gathered at an age of three–four weeks, prior to any song production. (After Dooling and Searcy, 1980.)*

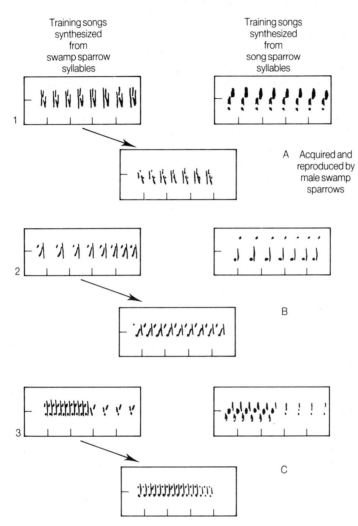

Figure 6.2.5   *A diagram of song learning preference in male swamp sparrows. Three pairs of computer-synthesized songs are illustrated with the same syntax but composed of syllables either from song sparrow or from swamp sparrow songs. In each case, male swamp sparrows preferred syllables of their own species, irrespective of the syntactical arrangement in which they were presented. In each case, the syllable chosen was produced with typical swamp sparrow syntax, regardless of the syntactical structure of the learned model.*

solely on the basis of acoustic features of song. What are the acoustic features on which these preferences are based? The answer is different in the two species.

By using computer-synthesized songs in which different acoustic features were independently varied, we found that the learning preference of male swamp sparrows is based not on syntactical features of the song but on the phonology of the syllables. As illustrated in Figure 6.2.5, male swamp sparrows presented with simplified songs consisting either of swamp sparrow syllables or song sparrow syllables unerringly favor those with conspecific syllables, irrespective of the temporal pattern in which they are presented. They then recast them in the normal syntactical pattern, whether or not this pattern has been available to them in the songs they have heard. In choosing models for learning, the song syllable is clearly the primary focus of interest for a swamp sparrow.

In contrast, song sparrows, with their more complex songs, base their learning preference not only on syllabic structure but also on a number of syntactical features, including the number of segments, their internal phrase structure—whether syllables are trilled or unrepeated, and such attributes as the tempo in which they are delivered. There is no evidence that young male swamp

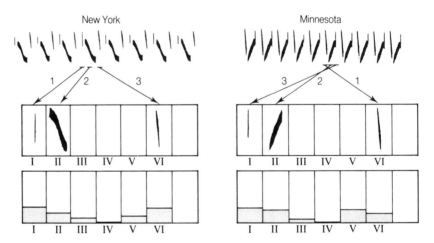

Figure 6.2.6 *Swamp sparrow songs are constructed from six basic note types (I–VI), present in similar proportions in different populations (histograms at the bottom). Two typical songs from New York and Minnesota are illustrated, with different rules for ordering note types within syllables. In New York three-note syllables, type I notes are typically in first position and type VI notes in final position, with one of the other note types between. In Minnesota three-note songs an opposite rule tends to prevail, as illustrated (Marler and Pickert, 1984). Wild males and females are both responsive to these differences in syllable construction (Balaban, 1988).*

sparrows refer to any of these syntactical features when they choose models for song learning (Marler and Peters, 1980, 1988a, 1989).

The evidence of differences in innate responsiveness to song features from species to species is thus clear and unequivocal, implying the existence of something like Lorenzian "innate-release mechanisms." This innate responsiveness is employed not to develop fixed behaviors, as we might once have thought, but as the basis for a learning process. Having focused attention on the particular set of exemplars that satisfy the innate criteria, sparrows then learn them, in specific detail, including the local dialect (if this is a species that possesses dialects). In the swamp sparrow, the dialects are defined by the patterning of notes within a syllable (Marler and Pickert, 1984), as displayed in Figure 6.2.6. Balaban (1988) has shown that both males and females acquire responsiveness to these dialect variations. Thus, the birds go far beyond the dictates of the initial ethological lock-and-key mechanism.

A further point, the importance of which cannot be overstressed, is that birds are not completely bound by these innate preferences. If conspecific songs are withheld, sparrows can be persuaded to learn nonpreferred songs (Figure 6.2.7), especially if these are accompanied by further, strong stimulation, as with a live interactive tutor of another species (Baptista and Petrinovich, 1984, 1986). Thus, the process of choosing models for song learning is probabilistically controlled, not absolutely determined. Given the normal ecology of the species, however, conspecific song tutoring will usually be available for innate preferences to be exercised, thus establishing a certain predictable trajectory to the learning process.

How might one model the mechanisms underlying such learning preferences? There is ample experimental evidence that birds can hear the songs of other species perfectly well and can discriminate between them with precision, even at the level of individual differences (Dooling, 1989). Yet they either fail to learn them in retrievable form in the normal course of song acquisition, or, if they do learn them, they forget them again. One caveat here is that we still lack a direct test of what has been memorized, and we have to rely instead on what is produced as a memorization index. Even in the earliest productions of imitations, in plastic song, copies of songs of other species are not usually in evidence. By this criterion, these sparrows behave as though any song presented as a stimulus is subjected to normal sensory processing but is then quickly lost from memory in the usual course of events, unless the exposure is massive, continuing day after day, and associated with strong arousal. There is an urgent need to develop memorization assays that are independent of song production.

When conspecific stimuli are presented, it is as though the bird suddenly becomes attentive, and a brief time window is opened during which the stimulus cluster in view becomes more salient, more likely to be memorized, and probably destined to be used later for guiding song development. One tends to think in terms of parallel processing, with certain circuits responsible for general

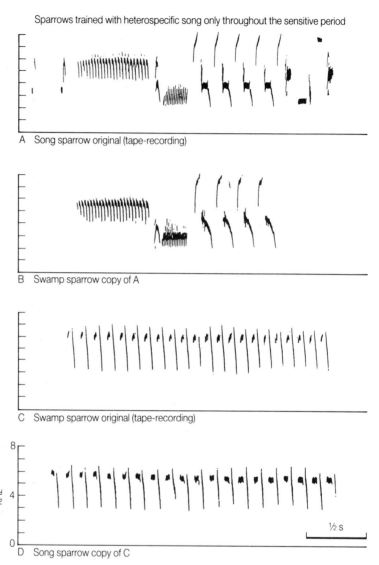

Sparrows trained with heterospecific song only throughout the sensitive period

A   Song sparrow original (tape-recording)

B   Swamp sparrow copy of A

C   Swamp sparrow original (tape-recording)

D   Song sparrow copy of C

Figure 6.2.7   *If song and swamp sparrows are raised in the laboratory and presented only with tape-recorded songs of other species, on rare occasions they will imitate them. Examples are illustrated of a swamp sparrow copy (B) of part of a song sparrow model (A) and a song sparrow copy (D) of a swamp sparrow model (C). Male swamp sparrows rarely imitate song sparrow song. Song sparrows imitate swamp sparrow song more often (cf. Figure 6.2.3), but when they do so they usually recast the swamp sparrow syllables into song sparrow-like syntax (cf. Figure 6.2.20).*

auditory processing and others committed to the identification of stimuli as worthy of the special attention of the general processing machinery, if and when they are encountered. This interaction might be thought of as a teaching process, with special mechanisms serving—especially in infancy—to instruct general mechanisms about what to pay special attention to during learning and about how the learning process can most efficiently be structured. In adulthood, once their function of establishing certain developmental trajectories has been accomplished, special mechanisms may cease to function or even cease to exist.

One may think of the sign stimuli present in conspecific songs operating not only as behavioral triggers but also as cues for learning, serving as what might be thought of as "enabling signals," their presence increasing the probability of learning other associated stimuli that might otherwise be neglected (Rauschecker and Marler, 1987). I believe that this function is served by many ethological "releasers," and it may even be the *primary* function for many of them.

Vocal learning templates

Sparrows are able to generate some aspects of normal, species-specific song syntax irrespective of the syntax of the models to which they have been exposed in the past. This potential is most clearly displayed in the songs of birds raised in isolation, completely deprived of access to adult song of their own or any other species. Figure 6.2.8 shows examples of natural song and examples of the simpler form of song that develops in males reared in isolation. There are many abnormalities in the songs of males raised in isolation, and quantitative study reveals that the variation is great. Nevertheless, by using a comparative approach, it can be clearly shown that each species is capable of generating some basic features of normal song syntax irrespective of whether these have been experienced in the form of song stimulation by others. The syntax of a swamp sparrow is rather resistant to change by experience, in comparison with the song sparrow, although stimulation by multipartite songs does result in the production of a certain proportion of bipartite song patterns (Marler and Peters, 1980). Male swamp sparrows copy syllables more readily than whole songs. This is less true of song sparrows. When they are allowed to hear conspecific song, they will sometimes imitate the entire syntax of the particular model experienced (Figure 6.2.8), even though they are innately responsive to conspecific syntax. Once more, the invocation of innate influences in no way implies a commitment to immutability.

Again, we may pose the question, "What kind of physiological mechanism underlies this ability?" Some insight is gained by studying the singing behavior of birds that are deaf. We know that the sense of hearing is important not only to permit a bird to hear the songs of others but also to enable it to hear its own voice (Konishi, 1965; Nottebohm, 1968). Male sparrows deafened early in life,

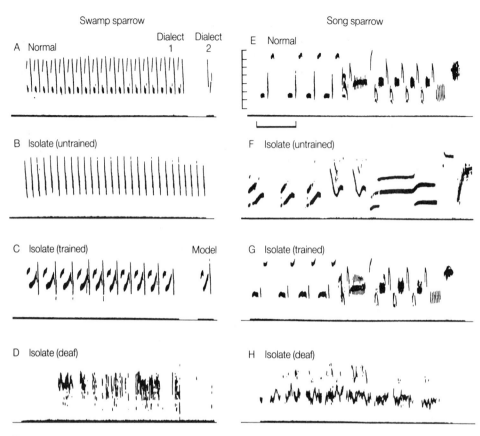

Figure 6.2.8 *Sound spectrograms illustrating typical songs of swamp and song sparrows produced under four conditions. First row: normal learning in the wild [(A) and (E), with one syllable of a second dialect also shown in (A)]. Row 2: acoustic isolation, but with intact hearing [(B) and (F)]. Row 3: isolated, but trained with tape-recordings of normal songs of their species [(C) and (G)]. Row 4: isolated and deafened [(D) and (H)]. Frequency markers indicate 1 kHz intervals and the time marker 0.5 sec.*

prior to any singing, develop songs that are highly abnormal, exceedingly variable, almost amorphous in structure (Figure 6.2.8), although certain basic species differences are sometimes still detectable (Marler and Sherman, 1983).

This highly degraded form of song results both if a male is deafened before song stimulation and also after song stimulation but before the development of singing (Konishi, 1965). Thus, there seems to be no internal brain circuitry that makes memorized songs directly available to guide motor development. To transform a memorized song into a produced song, the bird must be able to hear its own voice.

This contrast between the songs of hearing and deaf birds inspired the concept of vocal learning templates, existing in two forms: One innate and the other acquired. Acquired templates, resulting from enrichment, modification, substitution, or interaction with other mechanisms as a consequence of experience, were originally conceived of as transforms of the same basis mechanisms as innate templates (Konishi, 1965; Marler, 1976; Marler and Sherman, 1983). It now seems possible that they are functionally and neuroanatomically separate, although interconnected and interreactive, as indicated earlier. Innate auditory song templates have a potential direct influence on early learning preferences, in some circumstances, and on the later production of songs. They also serve as a vehicle for bringing innate influences to bear on the effects of intervening experience. Auditory templates for vocal learning provide one model of the kind of brain mechanisms underlying this particular instinct to learn. Many of the attributes of this model are applicable to other systems of behavioral development. Ontogeny is guided by sensory feedback from motor activity, with referral of this feedback to templates with specifications that can be supplemented, modified, or overridden by experience. The specifications incorporate innate contributions that may be unique to one species, as is the case with those stressed in this paper, or they may be more generally distributed across species, such as specifications for the tonality that characterizes many birdsongs (Nowicki and Marler, 1988).

Plans for motor development

Songs of many birds, such as sub-oscine flycatchers, develop completely normally in isolation. When such a song begins to be performed, the first efforts are clearly identifiable as immature versions of what will ultimately be the normal crystallized song. These early attempts may be noisy and fragmented,

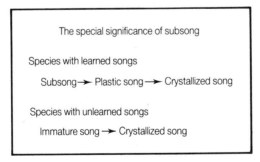

Figure 6.2.9 *The developmental sequence is different in bird species with learned and unlearned songs. Subsong is radically different from mature song in structure, and undergoes a metamorphosis in the progression through plastic song.*

but the maturational progression is clear and predictable (Kroodsma, 1984). In birds that learn their songs, the developmental progression is quite different. There is a more complex ontogenetic sequence, from subsong, through plastic song, to crystallized song (Figure 6.2.9). The general pattern of song development in sixteen male swamp sparrows in the laboratory is diagrammed in Figure 6.2.10. There is considerable individual variation, but a modal pattern can nevertheless be discerned that comprises three stages: subsong, plastic song, and crystallized song. This program unfolds similarly in males raised in isolation, suggesting that it is hormonally controlled (but see Marler *et al.*, 1988).

We still know less about subsong than any other aspect of birdsong development. Figure 6.2.11 shows examples of early subsong from male swamp and song sparrows. It illustrates the fact that the structure of subsong is quite different from that of mature song. It is typical of bird species with learned songs that a kind of metamorphosis intervenes between subsong and later stages of song development. The amorphous structure and noisy spectral organization of sparrow subsong is typical.

Despite its lack of structure, careful analysis reveals subtle species differences. Auditory templates appear to be operating even at this early stage. A difference in note duration present in normal song and in those of isolates (Marler and Sherman, 1985) also occurs in the subsong of hearing song and swamp sparrows (Figure 6.2.11) but is lacking in the early subsong of deaf birds (Figure 6.2.12). Subsong is believed to be critical for several aspects of the development of the general motor skills of singing and also for honing the ability to guide the voice

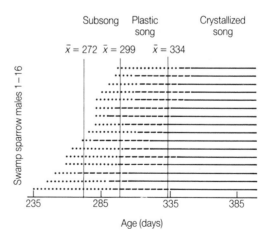

Figure 6.2.10   *Patterns of song development in sixteen male swamp sparrows, each raised in individual isolation. They are displayed with the latest developers at the top and the earliest developers at the bottom. Despite considerable individual variation, a species-typical pattern can be discerned.*

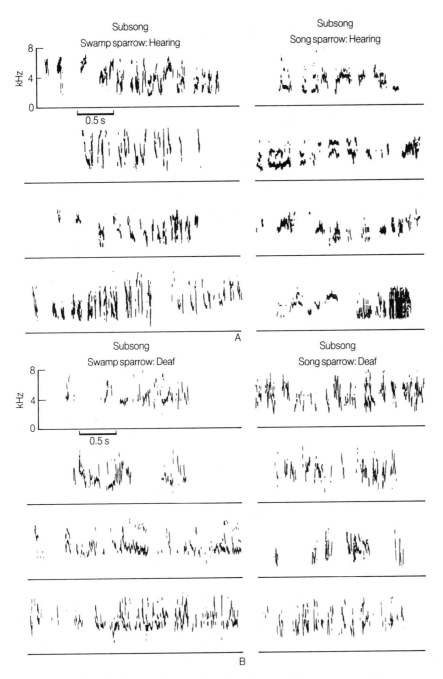

Figure 6.2.11   *Sound spectrograms of early subsong from swamp and song sparrows with hearing intact, as compared with subsong produced after early deafening. In the birds with hearing intact, note duration averages longer in the song sparrows. This difference is absent in subsong of deaf birds produced at the same age.*

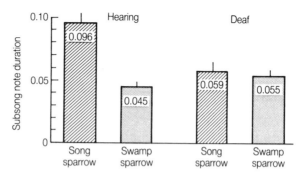

Figure 6.2.12 *Histograms of mean note durations in subsong of song and swamp sparrows with hearing intact and after deafening. It is evident that auditory song templates are already operating even at this early age, to generate species differences in subsong structure.*

by the ear, which is a prerequisite for vocal imitation (Nottebohm, 1972; Marler and Peters, 1982b); however, direct evidence has been hard to obtain.

Only in the second stage, plastic song, do the more obvious signs of mature song structure appear. Figure 6.2.13 presents samples of developing song in a single male swamp sparrow, starting with subsong and proceeding through plastic song to the stable form of crystallized song. As plastic song progresses, rehearsal of previously memorized song patterns begins. These continue to stabilize gradually until crystallization occurs. Note that normal species-specific syntax—a single trill—emerges late in swamp sparrows, irrespective of whether such patterns have been heard from others or not, suggesting that an innately specified central motor program is accessed at this stage.

Larger repertoires of songs occur during plastic song than in crystallized song (Marler and Peters, 1982a). Male swamp sparrows greatly overproduce song material at intermediate stages of development, as can be seen more clearly by summing data on numbers of songs present in an individual repertoire during the transition from plastic to crystallized song (Figure 6.2.14). A typical crystallized repertoire consists of two or three song types, but in early plastic song the repertoire may be four or five times greater. Thus, more is memorized than is manifest in the final products of motor development.

The process of discarding songs during crystallization is not a random one. For one thing, birds that have been persuaded to learn songs of other species by "hybridizing" them with conspecific song elements are more likely to reject these "hybrid" songs during the attrition process (Marler and Peters, 1982a). In addition, there are also opportunities for experience to interact with development to influence the final outcome. There is often a premium in songbirds on countersinging against rivals with similar themes if they are available. The transition from plastic song to full song takes place at a stage of

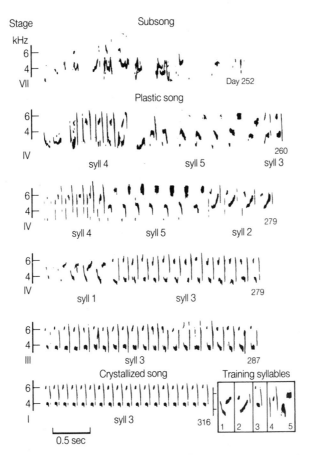

Figure 6.2.13 *Samples from the process of song development in a single male swamp sparrow, ranging from subsong to crystallized song. The age of the bird is indicated on the right ranging from 252 to 316 days of age. This bird was trained with tape-recorded songs, syllables of some of which are indicated in the boxed insert (1–5). As indicated by the labels, early efforts to reproduce imitations of these months later are imperfect in early plastic song, but they improve as progress toward crystallized song is made. The overproduction of song types during plastic song can also be seen. The two song types in the crystallized repertoire of this male consisted of syllable types 2 and 3.*

life when a young male is striving to establish his first territory, and, by a "pseudolearning" process, stimulation by the songs of rivals at this time may favor the retention of song themes that most closely match those of rivals in the attrition process. There is also a fascinating suggestion from the work of King and West (1988) on the brown-headed cowbird that females can influence the

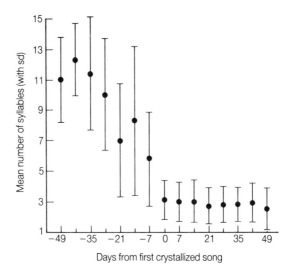

Figure 6.2.14 *A plot of mean syllable repertoires of sixteen male swamp sparrows at different stages of song development, arranged around day 0 as the time of crystallization. There is extensive overproduction of song types during plastic song, and the repertoire is drastically reduced as development proceeds toward crystallization of the mature repertoire, averaging three song types per bird (from Marler and Peters, 1982).*

choice of crystallized song by giving courtship responses to song types that they favor during the plastic song phase.

Steps in learning to sing

The diverse strategies that different birds use in learning to sing are accompanied by certain underlying consistencies. For example, there are always several phases in the process of learning to sing. Sensory and perceptual processing tends to precede production (Figure 6.2.15). Songs pass into storage during the acquisition phase, when a bird subjects songs to auditory processing, and commits some of them to memory. It seems logical that the knowledge necessary to develop patterns of action should be acquired before development of these actions commences. After acquisition, internalized representations of songs, or parts of them, may be stored for an appreciable time before the male embarks on the process of retrieving them and generating imitations. In Figure 6.2.16, time intervals are plotted between the last exposure to tape-recorded songs of sixteen male swamp sparrows, each separately housed, ending at about sixty days of age, and production of the very first hints of identifiable imitations. This storage interval was surprisingly long, on the order of eight months, an impressive achievement.

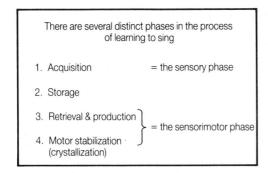

Figure 6.2.15 *Steps in the process of learning and reproducing a song.*

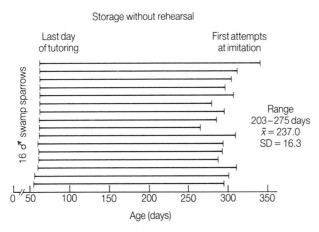

Figure 6.2.16 *The period of storage of learned songs without rehearsal in sixteen male swamp sparrows trained with tape-recorded song prior to sixty days of age. Songs were recorded and analyzed every two weeks, and the age was noted at which the first identifiable imitations were reproduced, some eight months after last exposure to the models.*

The period of storage before retrieval of stored representations from memory begins varies greatly from species to species. It is not known whether this is a phase of passive storage or whether consolidation or active reorganization of memorized material is taking place. Subsong may occur during storage, and even during acquisition, but the onset of rehearsal is the sign that plastic song has begun. Themes are rehearsed and stabilized, and eventually song crystallization occurs.

Sensitive periods for acquisition

Another aspect of instincts to learn is the timing of the acquisition phase. Is it brief, or extended? Does it occur only once, or repeatedly during life? There are striking differences between species in the timing of song acquisition (Figure 6.2.17). In some birds, acquisition is age-dependent and is restricted to a short period early in life. In other species, song remains changeable from year to year, apparently with a continuing ability to acquire new songs throughout life. Even close relatives, such as sparrows and canaries, may differ strikingly in the timing of sensitive periods, providing ideal opportunities for comparative investigation of variations in the neural and hormonal physiology that correlate with song acquisition. Such species differences can have a direct and profound impact on the potential for behavioral plasticity.

Much of the behavioral information on sensitive periods is inadequate to serve well as a springboard for comparative physiological investigation. In an effort to develop a more systematic, experimental approach to this problem, we played tape-recorded songs to male sparrows in the laboratory throughout their first year of life, changing song types every week or two (Marler and Peters, 1987, 1988b; Marler, 1987). By recording and analyzing the songs produced, we were able to extrapolate back to the time when acquisition occurred. Figure 6.2.18 shows the results for a group of male swamp sparrows, with a clear sensitive period for song acquisition beginning at about twenty days of age and then closing out about three–four months later, before the onset of plastic song. A similar picture of song acquisition was obtained with a changing roster of live tutors, brought into song by testosterone therapy (Figure 6.2.18). Differences between species in the timing of sensitive periods are sometimes gross but may also be subtle, as can be seen by comparing the timing of song acquisition from tape-recordings in male song sparrows (Figure 6.2.18). Here, the sensitive period is even more compressed into early adolescence. These birds provide ideal

Sensitive Periods	
Age-dependent learning	Age-independent learning
Zebra Finch	Canary
Chaffinch	Mockingbird
Sparrows	Starling

Figure 6.2.17   *Examples of bird species with age-dependent and age-independent song learning.*

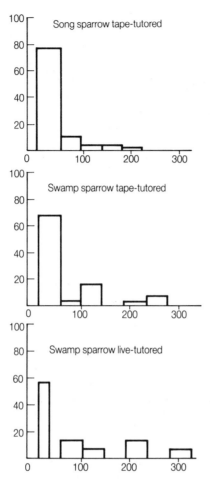

Figure 6.2.18 *The sensitive period for song acquisition peaks in male song sparrows between twenty and fifty days of age (top). The peak is attenuated somewhat in male swamp sparrows and extends to a later age, both when they are tutored with tape-recordings (middle) and when they are given live tutors (bottom). These results were obtained by training birds with a constantly changing programme of either tape-recordings or live tutors and then inferring the age at which acquisition occurred from analyses of songs produced later (from Marler and Peters, 1987, 1988b).*

opportunities for pursuing questions about the neural and hormonal changes that are correlated with these sensitive periods and perhaps bear a causal relationship with them (Marler *et al.*, 1987, 1988; Nordeen, Marler, and Nordeen, 1988).

Although sensitive periods for song acquisition are clearly significant components of instincts to learn, it is important to be aware once again that these are not fixed traits (Marler, 1987). There are degrees of lability, depending on such factors as the strength of stimulation—whether a tape recording or a live tutor is used (Baptista and Petrinovich, 1984, 1986). Physiological factors that correlate with the season are also relevant. In some species, young may be hatched so late that singing, which is a seasonal activity in most species, has ceased for the year. In such cases, it has been shown that closure of the sensitive period may be delayed until the following spring, apparently in response to the changing photoperiod (Kroodsma and Pickert, 1984). Deprivation of access to conspecific models can also delay closure of the sensitive period (Clayton, 1988). Once more, the invocation of innate influences does not mean sacrifice of the potential for behavioral flexibility; rather, instincts to learn set a species-specific context within which experience operates.

Innate inventiveness

Thus far in this account of song learning, the emphasis has been placed on the production of more-or-less precise imitations of songs heard from other birds. In fact, an element of inventiveness often intrudes. This may take several forms. One revelation from the sensitive period experiments described in the previous section is that sparrows are able to recombine components both of the same song and of songs acquired at different times. Recasting or re-editing of components of learned models into new sequences is commonly exploited as one means for generating novelty and also for producing the very large individual repertoires that some birds possess (Krebs and Kroodsma, 1980). Often, models are broken down into phrases or syllables and then reordered into several different sequences that become stable themes (Marler, 1984). Song sparrows are especially prone to indulge in such recombinations with songs acquired in later phases of the sensitive period (Marler and Peters, 1988b). This correlates with a decline in the completeness with which entire learned songs are accurately reproduced (Figure 6.2.19). This tendency to recombine segments of learned models has the effect of creating new songs from old, by reuse of the same basic raw materials.

Species differ greatly in the faithfulness with which they adhere to learned models, although imitations are rarely identical with their models, even in the best mimics. Some species imitate learned models closely, and local dialects are common in birds, but a degree of personal individuality is also virtually universal. In every case examined, this individuality has proved to provide a basis in nature for personal identification of companions and for distinguishing neighbors from strangers (reviewed in Falls, 1982).

Some degree of inventiveness is, in fact, universal, but species differ greatly in the extent to which they indulge in creative activity in song development. Figure 6.2.20 illustrates just one example of a song sparrow exposed in the laboratory to a variety of simple synthetic songs. This bird generated an

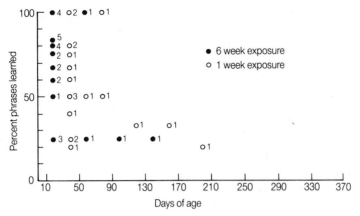

Figure 6.2.19 *When song sparrows reproduce songs acquired early in the sensitive period, they are more likely to reproduce them with the original syntax of the model than with songs acquired later in the sensitive period. For each age block, two sets of data are illustrated, from tape-recorded songs heard for a six-week period (left) and for a one-week period (right). Songs acquired later are more likely to be broken up into separate phrases that are then recombined in different ways to produce new songs (from Marler and Peters, 1987).*

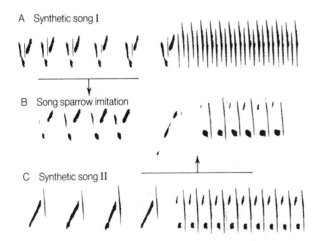

Figure 6.2.20 *Song sparrows often create new themes by breaking learned songs down into their component syllables and recombining them in various ways. Illustrated here is the song of a laboratory-reared song sparrow exposed to an array of synthetic songs. It learned two of these [(A) and (C)] and recombined parts of them, as illustrated, to create a crude approximation of normal song sparrow syntax.*

approximation of typical song sparrow syntax in highly creative fashion by drawing two components from one model and one from another model. Some species provide abundant illustrations of this kind of innovative process, both in the laboratory and in the field.

The rules for parsing acquired songs down into components and recombining them are species-specific, however. There is also species variation in the faithfulness with which a bird adheres to the structure of a given imitation. Some, like sparrows, are conservative. They recast syllables often, but they adhere to the basic syllabic structure, which makes them good subjects for studies of learning. Other species, such as the red-winged blackbird, are compulsive improvisers (Marler *et al.*, 1972), subjecting themes to continuous experimentation and embroidery during development, until the originals are barely recognizable.

Even more intriguing is the suggestion that improvisation and invention may be most consistently applied to certain segments of songs, with other segments left as pure, unadulterated imitations. A species like the white-crowned sparrow, in which birds in a given locality adhere closely to a given dialect, nevertheless has song segments or features that are more free for individual improvisation. Thus cues for personal identification may be encoded in one segment or feature, cues for the local dialect in another, and cues for species recognition in yet another set, the arrangement varying from species to species (Marler, 1960).

Conclusions

It is less illogical than it first appears to speak of instincts for inventiveness. Song development is a creative process, but the inventiveness that birds often display is governed by sets of rules. Each species has its own distinctive set of physiological mechanisms for constraining or facilitating improvisation, guiding learning preferences, directing motor development, and establishing the timing of sensitive periods. Songs are learned, and yet instinctive influences on the learning process intrude at every turn.

Instincts to learn offer priceless opportunities to pinpoint the ways in which physiological or neuroanatomical changes can affect the process of learning a new behavior. Given the striking contrasts in song development in birds that are very close genetic relatives and are otherwise very similar in structure and physiology, presumably quite limited changes in neural organization or the timing of a hormonal event can have profound effects on the course of learning. Already the proverbial bird brain has yielded many secrets about the neural biology of vocal plasticity (Konishi, 1985; Nottebohm, 1987). Yet there is a sense in which we have hardly begun to exploit the potential of comparative studies as a source of new insights into the role of innate species differences in structure and physiology in the operation of instincts to learn.

There is a need in studies of behavioral development to overcome behavioristic prejudice against the invocation of innate contributions. It is as a consequence of such prejudice against the term "innate" that most students of animal behavior have eschewed its use altogether. The result is that ethological investigations of processes of behavioral epigenetics have, for the most part, been rendered impotent. The initiative has been left to geneticists and developmental biologists, who take it for granted that the genome plays a major role in all aspects of behavioral development (Marler and Sherman, 1985).

There is nothing illogical in applying the term "innate" to *differences* between organisms. As Hinde (1970) asserted, "Evidence that a difference in behavior is to be ascribed to genetic differences must come ultimately from the rearing of animals, known to differ genetically, in similar environments" (p. 431). It is both valid and productive for students of development to address Dobzhansky's (1962) question, "To what extent are the *differences* observed between persons due to genotypic or to environmental causes?" (p. 44).

Acknowledgments

Research was conducted in collaboration with Susan Peters and supported in part by grant No. BRSG SO7 RR07065, awarded by the Biomedical Research Support Grant Program, Division of Research Resources, National Institutes of Health, and by grant number MH 14651. Esther Arruza prepared the figures and typed the manuscript. I thank Judith and Cathy Marler and Eileen McCue for rearing the birds. I am indebted to Susan Peters, Stephen Nowicki, Susan Carey, and Rochel Gelman for discussion and valuable criticism of the manuscript and to the New York Botanical Garden Institute of Ecosystem Studies at the Mary Flagler Cary Arboretum for access to study areas.

References to 6.2

Baker, M. C. and Cunningham, M. A. (1985). "The biology of birdsong dialects." *Behavioral and Brain Sciences*, **8**, 85–133.

Balaban, E. (1988). "Cultural and genetic variation in swamp sparrows (*Melospiza georgiana*). II. Behavioral salience of geographic song variants." *Behaviour*, **105**, 292–322.

Baptista, L. F. (1975). "Song dialects and demes in sedentary populations of the white-crowned sparrow (*Zonotrichia leucophrys nuttalli*)." *University of California Publications in Zoology*, **105**, 1–52.

Baptista, L. F. (1977) "Geographic variation in song and dialects of the Puget Sound white-crowned sparrow." *Condor*, **79**, 356–70.

Baptista, L. F. and Petrinovich, L. (1984). "Social interaction, sensitive phases and the song template hypothesis in the white-crowned sparrow." *Animal Behaviour*, **32**, 172–81.

Baptista, L. F. and Petrinovich, L. (1986). "Song development in the white-crowned sparrow: Social factors and sex differences." *Animal Behaviour*, **34**, 1359–71.

616   *Peter Marler*

Clayton, N. S. (1988). "Song tutor choice in zebra finches and Bengalese finches: The relative importance of visual and vocal cues." *Behaviour*, **104**, 281–99.

Dobzhansky, T. (1962). *Mankind Evolving*. New Haven, CT: Yale University Press.

Dooling, R. J. (1989). "Perception of complex, species-specific vocalizations by birds and humans." In R. J. Dooling and S. Hulse (eds), *The Comparative Psychology of Audition*. Hillsdale, NJ: Lawrence Erlbaum Associates, 423–44.

Dooling, R. J. and Searcy, M. H. (1980). "Early perceptual selectivity in the swamp sparrow." *Developmental Psychobiology*, **13**, 499–506.

Falls, J. B. (1982). "Individual recognition by sounds in birds." In D. E. Kroodsma and E. H. Miller (eds), *Acoustic Communication in Birds* (Vol. 2). New York: Academic Press, 237–78.

Gould, J. L. and Marler, P. (1987). "Learning by instinct." *Scientific American*, **256**, 74–85.

Hinde, R. A. (1970). *Animal Behaviour: A synthesis of ethology and comparative psychology* (2nd edn). New York: McGraw-Hill.

Johnston, T. D. (1988). "Developmental explanation and the ontogeny of bird song: Nature/nurture redux." *Behavioural and Brain Sciences*, **11**, 631–75.

King, A. P. and West, J. J. (1988). "Searching for the functional origins of song in eastern brown-headed cowbirds, *Molothrus ater ater*." *Animal Behaviour*, **36**, 1575–88.

Konishi, M. (1965). "The role of auditory feedback in the control of vocalization in the white-crowned sparrow." *Zeitschrift für Tierpsychologie*, **22**, 770–83.

Konishi, M. (1985). "Birdsong: From behavior to neuron." *Annual Review of Neuroscience*, **8**, 125–70.

Krebs, J. R. and Kroodsma, D. E. (1980). "Repertoires and geographical variation in bird song." In J. S. Rosenblatt, R. A. Hinde, C. Beer, and M.-C. Busnel (eds), *Advances in the Study of Behavior*. New York: Academic Press, 143–77.

Kroodsma, D. E. (1984). "Songs of the alder flycatcher (*Empidonax alnorum*) and willow flycatcher (*Empidonax traillii*) are innate." *Auk*, **101**, 13–24.

Kroodsma, D. E. and Pickert, R. (1984). "Sensitive phases for song learning: Effects of social interaction and individual variation." *Animal Behaviour*, **32**, 389–94.

Lorenz, K. Z. (1950). "The comparative method in studying innate behavior patterns." *Symposium Society Experimental Biology*, **4**, 221–68.

Marler, P. (1960). "Bird songs and mate selection." In W. N. Tavolga (ed.), *Animal Sounds and Communication*. American Institute of Biological Sciences Symposium Proceedings, 348–67.

Marler, P. (1970). "A comparative approach to vocal learning: Song development in white-crowned sparrows." *Journal of Comparative and Physiological Psychology*, **71**, 1–25.

Marler, P. (1976). "Sensory templates in species-specific behavior." In J. Fentress (ed.), *Simpler Networks and Behavior*. Sunderland, MA: Sinauer Associates, 314–29.

Marler, P. (1984). "Song learning: Innate species differences in the learning process." In P. Marler and H. S. Terrace (eds), *The Biology of Learning*. Berlin: Springer–Verlag, 289–309.

Marler, P. (1987). "Sensitive periods and the role of specific and general sensory stimulation in birdsong learning." In J. P. Rauschecker and P. Marler (eds), *Imprinting and Cortical Plasticity*. New York: John Wiley & Sons, 99–135.

Marler, P., Mundinger, P., Waser, M. S., and Lutjen, A. (1972). "Effects of acoustical stimulation and deprivation on song development in red-winged blackbirds (*Agelaius phoeniceus*)." *Animal Behaviour*, **20**, 586–606.

Marler, P. and Peters, S. (1980). "Birdsong and speech: Evidence for special processing:" In P. Eimas and J. Miller (eds), *Perspectives on the Study of Speech*. Hillsdale, NJ: Lawrence Erlbaum Associates, 75–112.

Marler, P. and Peters, S. (1982a). "Developmental overproduction and selective attrition: New processes in the epigenesis of birdsong." *Developmental Psychobiology*, **15**, 369–78.

Marler, P. and Peters, S. (1982b). "Subsong and plastic song: Their role in the vocal learning process." In D. E. Kroodsma and E. H. Miller (eds), *Acoustic Communication in Birds: Vol. 2*. New York: Academic Press, 25–50.

Marler, P. and Peters, S. (1987). "A sensitive period for song acquisition in the song sparrow, *Melospiza melodia*: A case of age-limited learning." *Ethology*, **76**, 89–100.

Marler, P. and Peters, S. (1988a). "The role of song phonology and syntax in vocal learning preferences in the song sparrow, *Melospiza melodia*." *Ethology*, **77**, 125–49.

Marler, P. and Peters, S. (1988b). "Sensitive periods for song acquisition from tape recordings and live tutors in the swamp sparrow, *Melospiza georgiana*." *Ethology*, **77**, 76–84.

Marler, P. and Peters, S. (1989). "Species differences in auditory responsiveness in early vocal learning." In S. Hulse and R. Dooling (eds), *The Comparative Psychology of Audition*. Hillsdale, NJ: Lawrence Erlbaum Associates, 243–73.

Marler, P., Peters, S., Ball, G. F., Dufty, A. M., Jr., and Wingfield, J. C. (1988). "The role of sex steroids in the acquisition of birdsong." *Nature*, **336**, 770–2.

Marler, P., Peters, S., and Wingfield, J. (1987). "Correlations between song acquisition, song production, and plasma levels of testosterone and estradiol in sparrows." *Journal of Neurobiology*, **18**, 531–48.

Marler, P., and Pickert, R. (1984). "Species-universal microstructure in the learned song of the swamp sparrow (*Melospiza georgiana*)." *Animal Behaviour*, **32**, 673–89.

Marler, P. and Sherman, V. (1983). "Song structure without auditory feedback: Emendations of the auditory template hypothesis." *Journal of Neuroscience*, **3**, 517–531.

Marler, P. and Sherman, V. (1985). "Innate differences in singing behaviour of sparrows reared in isolation from adult conspecific song." *Animal Behaviour*, **33**, 57–71.

Nordeen, K. W., Marler, P. and Nordeen, E. J. (1988). "Changes in neuron number during sensory learning in swamp sparrows." *Society of Neuroscience Abstracts*, **14**, 89.

Nottebohm, F. (1968). "Auditory experience and song development in the chaffinch (*Fringilla coelebs*)." *Ibis*, **110**, 549–68.

Nottebohm, F. (1972). "Neural lateralization of vocal control in a passerine bird. II. Subsong, calls and a theory of vocal learning." *Journal of Experimental Zoology*, **1979**, 35–49.

Nottebohm, F. (1987). "Plasticity in adult avian central nervous system: Possible relation between hormones, learning, and brain repair." In F. Plum (ed.), *Higher Functions of the Nervous System*. Washington: American Physiological Society, 85–108.

Nowicki, S. and Marler, P. (1988). "How do birds sing?" *Music Perception*, **5**, 391–426.

Pepperberg, I. M. (1988). "The importance of social interaction and observation in the acquisition of communicative competence: Possible parallels between avian and human learning." In T. R. Zentall and B. G. Galef, Jr. (eds), *Social Learning: A comparative approach*. Hillsdale, NJ: Lawrence Erlbaum Associates, 279–99.

Petrinovich, L. (1985). "Factors influencing song development in the white-crowned sparrow (*Zonotrichia leucophrys*)." *Journal of Comparative Psychology*, **99**, 15–29.

Piattelli-Palmarini, M. (ed.) (1980). *Language and Learning*. Cambridge, MA: Harvard University Press.

Rauschecker, J. P. and Marler, P. (1987). "Cortical plasticity and imprinting: Behavioral and physiological contrasts and parallels." In J. P. Rauschecker and P. Marler (eds), *Imprinting and Cortical Plasticity*. New York: John Wiley & Sons, 349–66.

Tinbergen, N. (1951). *The Study of Instinct*. Oxford: Clarendon Press.

Index

acoustic features, 59–60, 63–4, 66–8, 72–4, 76–9, 82–6
actions, 22–3, 24
    object-specific, 235–7, 240
    with objects, 101–3, 111–13, 120
active alternation, 37
adaptive functions, 52–8, 75, 81, 86–9
affectedness, 3, 285–324
agents, 253–5, 257, 260–4, 271–2, 276
agrammatic aphasia, 480
alternation, 37–9, 287, 289, 291, 315, 322–4
American Sign Language, 9, 508–10, 514, 516, 517–18, 524–8, 544–9, 553, 556, 578–9
animals, 75–83, 86–9
    instinct to learn, 591–615
aphasics, 480
approval vocalization, 62–4, 70–1, 72
arbitrariness, 38, 56–8
assertion only response, 394–5
associated objects, 229–30, 237–40, 243
associationism, 4, 36, 110, 223–4, 226, 472–8
asymmetric associates, 227, 240, 241
attachment theory, 88, 345
attention, joint, 129–30, 149
attention vocalisation, 62–3, 65

backwards anaphora constraint, 382–4
behaviorism, 5, 110, 329, 571, 577, 578
binding networks, 446, 462, 468–70
binding theory, 382–3, 385, 386–7

biologically relevant signals, 51–89
birdsong dialects, 4, 592–614
blind children, 176–80, 192–5, 245
bootstrapping hypotheses, 18, 23–5, 195–215, 316–17, 321
brain (theory of mind), 103–5
by (uses of), 251, 253–6, 261, 263–4, 266–71, 273, 275–8

causatives, 37–9, 205–6
cause, 257, 260–1, 263–4, 269–70, 276
cessation, 258–61, 277
characterising gestures, 515, 518–19, 524, 529–30, 534
children, 26–9, 321–2
    acquisition of novel verbs, 295–310
    constraints on word meanings, 154–72
    deafness in, 95–100, 106–19, 516–31
    errors with existing verbs, 293–5
    role in language acquisition, 4, 507–36
class-inclusion relations, 13, 163–4
closed-class morphology, 8
coding, 138–9, 275–8, 512–16
cognitive-general model, 104
cognitive architecture, 32–9
cognitive predispositions, 3, 329–57
cognitive system, 570–2
comfort vocalization, 62–3, 66–7, 74
communication, 61–4, 71–3, 242–3, 345
    systems, 75–83, 534–6